# Window on Humanity

## A Concise Introduction to Anthropology

### Seventh Edition

**Conrad Phillip Kottak**
*University of Michigan*

WINDOW ON HUMANITY: A CONCISE INTRODUCTION TO ANTHROPOLOGY, SEVENTH EDITION

1 2 3 4 5 6 7 8 9 0 DOC/DOC 1 0 9 8 7 6 5

ISBN 978-1-259-44271-1
MHID 1-259-44271-3

Senior Vice President, Products & Markets: *Kurt L. Strand*
Vice President, General Manager, Products & Markets: *Michael J. Ryan*
Vice President, Content Production & Technology Services: *Kimberly Meriwether David*
Managing Director: *Gina Boedeker*
Brand Manager: *Courtney Austermehle*
Lead Product Developer: *Rhona Robbin*
Brand Coordinator: *Diane Grayson*
Product Developer: *Emily Pecora*
Marketing Manager: *Philip Weaver*
Director, Product Development: *Meghan Campbell*

Director, Content Design & Delivery: *Terri Schiesl*
Program Manager: *Marianne Musni*
Content Project Managers: *Rick Hecker/Katie Klochan*
Senior Buyer: *Laura M. Fuller*
Design: *Debra Kubiak*
Cover Image: © *Michele Falzone/Getty Images*
Content Licensing Specialists: *Shawntel Schmitt/ Ann Marie Jannette*
Typeface: *10/12 Times*
Compositor: *Aptara®, Inc.*
Printer: *R. R. Donnelley*

**Library of Congress Cataloging-in-Publication Data**

Kottak, Conrad Phillip.
  Window on humanity: a concise introduction to anthropology/Conrad Phillip Kottak, University of Michigan. — Seventh edition.
    pages cm
  Includes bibliographical references and index.
  ISBN 978-1-259-44271-1 (alk. paper)—ISBN 1-259-44271-3  1. Anthropology. I. Title.
  GN25.K68 2016
  301—dc23

                                                    2015018913

mheducation.com/highered

To my wife,
Isabel Wagley Kottak

**Also available from McGraw-Hill by Conrad Phillip Kottak:**

*Mirror for Humanity: A Concise Introduction to Cultural Anthropology,* 10th ed. (2016)

*Anthropology: Appreciating Human Diversity,* 16th ed. (2015)

*Cultural Anthropology: Appreciating Cultural Diversity,* 16th ed. (2015)

*CULTURE, 2nd ed. (2014) (Lisa Gezon and Conrad Phillip Kottak)*

*On Being Different: Diversity and Multiculturalism in the North American Mainstream,* 4th ed. (2012) (with Kathryn A. Kozaitis)

*Assault on Paradise: The Globalization of a Little Community in Brazil,* 4th ed. (2006)

# Brief Contents

# Contents

# Anthropology Today Boxes

# Preface

*Window on Humanity* is intended to provide a concise, readable, introduction to general (four-field) anthropology. The shorter length increases the instructor's options for assigning additional reading—case studies, readers, and other supplements—in a semester course. *Window* also can work well in a quarter system, for which traditional texts may be too long.

This edition of *Window on Humanity* has kept pace with changes in the way students read and learn core content today through the digital program called **McGraw-Hill Connect®**. This program includes assignable and assessable quizzes, exercises, and interactive activities, organized around course-specific learning objectives. In addition, Connect includes **LearnSmart,** an adaptive testing program, and **SmartBook,** the first and only adaptive reading experience. The tools and resources provided in **Connect** are designed to engage students and enable them to improve their performance in the course.

Profound changes have affected the people and societies anthropologists traditionally have studied. In cultural anthropology, for example, it's increasingly difficult to know when to write in the present and when to write in the past tense. The field of anthropology also has experienced major changes, adding new approaches, such as molecular anthropology and new forms of spatial and historical analysis. And the fossil and archaeological records keep expanding, contributing to a deeper understanding of the past.

While any competent anthropology text must present anthropology's core, it should also demonstrate the discipline's relevance to today's globalized world. *Window on Humanity* has been written to help students make connections between what they read and their own lives.

## Content and Organization

No single or monolithic theoretical perspective orients this book. My e-mail, along with reviewers' comments, confirms that instructors with a very wide range of views and approaches have been pleased with *Window* as a teaching tool.

In Chapter 1, anthropology is introduced as an integrated four-field discipline, with academic and applied dimensions, that examines human biological and cultural diversity in time and space. Anthropology is discussed as a comparative and holistic science, featuring biological, social, cultural, linguistic, humanistic, and historical approaches. Chapter 2 examines the central anthropological concept of culture, including its symbolic and adaptive features. Chapter 3 is about doing anthropology—the methods and ethics of research in anthropology's subfields.

The chapters focusing on biological anthropology and archaeology (4–9) offer up-to-date answers to several key questions: When did humans originate, and how did we become what we are? What role do genes, the environment, society, and culture play in human variation and diversity? What can we tell about our origins and nature from the study of our nearest relatives—nonhuman primates? When and how did the primates originate? What key features of their early adaptations are still basic to our abilities, behavior, and perceptions? How did hominids develop from our primate ancestors? When, where, and how did the first hominins emerge and expand? What about the earliest real humans? How do we explain biological diversity in our own species, *Homo sapiens?* What major transitions have taken place since the emergence of *Homo sapiens?*

Chapters 8 and 9 discuss the Neolithic, especially the domestication of plants and animals, as a major adaptive change, with profound implications for human lifeways. The spread and intensification of farming and herding are tied to the appearance of the first towns, cities, and states, as well as the emergence of social stratification and major social inequalities.

The chapters on linguistic and sociocultural anthropology (10–19) are organized to place related content close together—although they are sufficiently independent to be assigned in any order the instructor might select. Thus, "Political Systems" (Chapter 12) logically follows "Making a Living" (Chapter 11). Chapters 13 and 14 ("Families, Kinship, and Marriage" and "Gender," respectively) also form a coherent unit. The chapter on religion (15) covers not just traditional religious practices but also contemporary world religions and religious movements. It is followed by four chapters (16–19) that form a natural unit exploring sociocultural transformations and expressions in today's world.

Those last four chapters address several important questions: How are race and ethnicity socially constructed and handled in different societies, and how do they generate prejudice, discrimination, and conflict? How and why did the modern world system emerge and expand? How has world capitalism affected patterns of stratification and inequality within and among nations? What were colonialism, imperialism, and Communism, and what are their legacies? What is globalization—as fact, as policy, and as ideology? How do people today actively interpret and confront the world system and the products of globalization? What factors threaten continued human diversity? How can anthropologists work to ensure the preservation of that diversity?

Let me also single out two chapters present in *Window on Humanity* but not found consistently in other anthropology texts: "Ethnicity and Race" (Chapter 16) and "Gender" (Chapter 14). I believe that systematic consideration of race, ethnicity, and gender is vital in an introductory anthropology text. Anthropology's distinctive four-field approach can shed special light on these topics. We see this not only in Chapter 16 ("Ethnicity and Race") but also in Chapter 4 ("Evolution, Genetics, and Human Variation"), in which race is discussed as a problematic concept in biology. Race and gender studies are fields in which anthropology always has taken the lead. I'm convinced that anthropology's special contributions to understanding the biological, social, cultural, and linguistic dimensions of race, ethnicity, and gender should be highlighted in any introductory text.

*Window* contains eight new "Anthropology Today" boxes. Placed consistently at the end of each chapter, "Anthropology Today" is intended to give students a chance to consider anthropology's relevance to today's world and to their own lives. Some boxes examine current events or debates. Others are more personal accounts, which add human feeling to the presentation of anthropology's subject matter. Many boxes illustrate a point with examples familiar to students from their enculturation or everyday experience.

## McGraw-Hill Connect

Connect is a premier digital teaching and learning tool that allows instructors to assign and assess course material. Connect includes assignable and assessable quizzes, exercises, and interactive activities, organized around course-specific learning objectives. In addition, Connect includes LearnSmart, an adaptive testing program, and SmartBook, the first and only adaptive reading experience.

The system is praised by users—faculty and students alike—for helping make both teaching and learning more efficient, saving time and keeping class time and independent study time focused on what is most important and only those things that still need reinforcing, and shifting the teaching/learning process away from memorization and cramming. The result is better grades, better concept retention, more students staying in class and passing, and less time spent preparing for classes or studying for tests.

**LearnSmart Advantage:** LearnSmart is one of the most effective and successful adaptive learning resources available on the market today. More than 2 million students have answered more than 1.3 billion questions in LearnSmart since 2009, making it the most widely used and intelligent adaptive study tool. Learnsmart has been proven to strengthen memory recall, keep students in class, and boost grades. Students using LearnSmart are 13% more likely to pass their classes, and 35% less likely to dropout.

**SmartBook:** SmartBook makes study time as productive and efficient as possible. It identifies and closes knowledge gaps through a continually adapting reading experience that provides personalized learning resources at the precise moment of need. This ensures that every minute spent with SmartBook is returned to the student as the most value-added minute possible. The result? More confidence, better grades, and greater success.

**Connect Insight:** Connect Insight is Connect's one-of-a-kind visual analytics dashboard—available for both instructors and students—that provides at-a-glance information regarding student performance, which is immediately actionable. By presenting assignment, assessment, and topical performance results together with a time metric that is easily visible for aggregate or individual results, Connect Insight gives the user the ability to take a just-in-time approach to teaching and learning.

## New in the Seventh Edition

All chapters of *Window on Humanity* have been updated, with charts, tables, and statistics based on the most recent information available. Of the 19 end-of-chapter boxes, eight are new to this edition. These "Anthropology Today" boxes are intended to bring home anthropology's relevance to current issues and events in today's globalized world.

## Chapter 1: What Is Anthropology?

Chapter 1 has a new "Anthropology Today" box, "Anorexia Goes Global," which illustrates the interaction of globalization and local culture in disease diagnoses.

## Chapter 2: Culture

This chapter has been updated.

## Chapter 3: Doing Anthropology

Chapter 3 adds a discussion of NAGPRA and "Kennewick Man," a new section on online ethnography, and a new "Anthropology Today" box, "Biology, Culture, and Grandparents."

## Chapter 4: Evolution, Genetics, and Human Variation

There is a new discussion of the CCR5-Δ32 allele, including the resistance it confers to HIV and AIDS.

## Chapter 5: The Primates

Chapter 5 now discusses the conservation efforts of orangutan champion Biruté Galdikas, and the recent discovery in China of *Archicebus achilles*, currently the earliest known primate. The new "Anthropology Today" box asks "Should Apes Have Human Rights?"

## Chapter 6: Early Hominins

This chapter has a new section on "Oldowan Hominins at the Kanjera Site" and a more recent "Anthropology Today" box about the important South African fossil fossil find, *Australopithecus sediba.*

## Chapter 7: The Genus Homo

This chapter has been revised substantially, with new discussions of the following:

- Recent discoveries at Blombos cave, South Africa.
- The recent discovery in Israel's Manot cave of a 55,000-year-old modern human skull suggestive of the first modern humans to colonize Europe.
- Pre-Clovis sites in the Americas.
- A new "Anthropology Today" box, titled "Being Neandertal," which discusses Neandertals' strengths and weaknesses and their ways of coping, thinking, and feeling.

## Chapter 8: The First Farmers

This chapter contains a new discussion of early pottery use by Jomon foragers in Japan.

## Chapter 9: The First Cities and States

This chapter has been updated.

## Chapter 10: Language and Communication

New to this chapter are discussions of: the language of food as an illustration of sociolinguistic variation, the origin and spread of PIE (Proto-Indo-European), and the evolution of syntax.

### Chapter 11: Making a Living

This chapter has been updated.

### Chapter 12: Political Systems

Chapter 12 contains a new "Anthropology Today" on resistance via social media, focusing on what has been called "Brazil's Facebook Revolution."

### Chapter 13: Families, Kinship, and Marriage

All charts, figures, and statistics have been updated. There is a new discussion of immigrant families, a thoroughly revised section on marriage equality, and a new section on "The Online Marriage Market."

### Chapter 14: Gender

Charts, figures, and statistics have been updated, including the "Anthropology Today" box, which discusses the latest Global Gender Gap Index.

### Chapter 15: Religion

This chapter has been updated.

### Chapter 16: Ethnicity and Race

This thoroughly updated chapter, with added information on poverty among minority groups, has a new "Anthropology Today" box titled "Why Are the Greens So White? Race and Ethnicity in Golf."

### Chapter 17: Applying Anthropology

This chapter adds a discussion of failed development efforts in Afghanistan and a new section titled "Public and Applied Anthropology."

### Chapter 18: The World System, Colonialism, and Inequality

This chapter has been updated, and its focus on inequality due to colonialism and the modern world system has been sharpened, including an expanded discussion of growing inequality in the United States.

### Chapter 19: Anthropology's Role in a Globalizing World

There is a new discussion of social media use in the Middle East, an updated and revised section on global climate change, an in-text discussion of climate change refugees, and a new "Anthropology Today" box, "The Wider World of SNS," on social media, networking, and connectivity.

## Teaching Resources

The following instructor resources can be accessed through the Library tab in **Connect:**

- Instructor's manual
- PowerPoint lecture slides
- Computerized test bank
- Word version of the test bank

# Create

Design your ideal course materials with McGraw-Hill's Create: www.mcgrawhill-create.com! Rearrange or omit chapters, combine materials from other sources, and/or upload any other content you have written to make the perfect resource for your students. You can even personalize your book's appearance by selecting the cover and adding your name, school, and course information. When you order a Create book, you receive a complimentary review copy. Get a printed copy in three to five business days or an electronic copy (eComp) via e-mail in about an hour. Register today at www.mcgrawhillcreate.com and craft your course resources to match the way you teach.

# Acknowledgments

I'm grateful to many colleagues at McGraw-Hill. Emily Pecora once again has been a wonderfully helpful and supportive developmental editor. I thank her for synthesizing and summarizing the prepublication reviews, helping me plan and implement this revision, and working with me to complete and submit the manuscript. I always benefit from Emily's careful reading of my new writing. Thanks, too, to Courtney Austermehle, Brand Manager for anthropology, to Marketing Manager Philip Weaver, and to Brand Coordinator Diane Grayson. I'm grateful as well for the support of Managing Director Gina Boedeker and Michael Ryan, Vice President and General Manager, Products & Markets.

Thanks to Rick Hecker for his work as Content Project Manager, guiding the manuscript through production and keeping everything moving on schedule. Laura Fuller, Buyer, worked with the printer to make sure everything came out right. Thanks, too, to Charlotte Goldman, freelance photo researcher, and to Scott Lukas, Lake Tahoe Community College, who created the content for the Connect products for this book. I also thank Debra DeBord for copyediting, Peter de Lissovoy for proofreading, and Debra Kubiak for executing the design.

Shawntel Schmitt also deserves thanks as content licensing specialist. I also thank Ann Marie Jannette, who has handled the literary permissions.

I'm very grateful to a long list of reviewers of this and previous editions of *Window on Humanity* and *Mirror for Humanity:*

The names and schools of the reviewers contracted by McGraw-Hill to review the 6th edition of *Window on Humanity,* in preparation for the 7th edition, or the 9th edition of *Mirror for Humanity,* in preparation for the 10th edition, are as follows:

**Jim Aimers**
*State University of New York, Geneseo*

**Jenna Andrews-Swann**
*Georgia Gwinnett College*

**Janet Lynne Altamirano**
*University of Houston, Downtown*

**Barbra Erickson**
*California State University, Fullerton*

**Shasta Gaughen**
*California State University, San Marcos*

**Nancy Gonlin**
*Bellevue College*

**Sharon Gursky**
*Texas A&M University*

**Andrew Kinkella**
*Moorpark College*

**Allan D. Meyers**
*Eckerd College*

**Tanya Mueller**
*University of New Mexico*

**Donna Rosh**
*Central New Mexico Community College*

I'm grateful to all these reviewers and professors for their enthusiasm and their suggestions for changes, additions, and deletions (sometimes in very different directions!).

Students also share their insights about Window via e-mail. Anyone—student or instructor—can reach me at the following e-mail address: ckottak@bellsouth.net.

As usual, my family provides me with understanding, support, and inspiration in my writing projects. Dr. Nicholas Kottak and Dr. Juliet Kottak Mavromatis regularly share their insights with me, as does Isabel Wagley Kottak, my long-term companion in the field and in life, to whom this book is dedicated.

During my long academic career, I've benefited from the knowledge, help, and advice of so many friends, colleagues, teaching assistants (graduate student instructors—GSIs), and students that I can no longer fit their names into a short preface. I hope they know who they are and accept my thanks. I do especially thank my co-authors of other books: Kathryn Kozaitis (*On Being Different*), Lara Descartes (*Media and Middle Class Moms*), and Lisa Gezon (*Culture*). Kathryn, Lara, and Lisa are prized former students of mine. Today they all are accomplished anthropologists in their own right, and they continue to share their wisdom with me.

I'm very grateful to my Michigan colleagues who've shared their insights and suggested ways of making my books better. Thanks especially to a 101 team that has included Tom Fricke, Stuart Kirsch, Holly Peters-Golden, and Andrew Shryock. Special thanks as well to Joyce Marcus and Kent Flannery for continuing to nurture the archaeologist in me.

Feedback from students and from my fellow anthropologists keeps me up-to-date on the interests, needs, and views of the people for whom *Window* is written, as does my ongoing participation in workshops on the teaching of anthropology. I continue to believe that effective textbooks are based in the enjoyment of teaching and respect for students. I hope this product of my experience will continue to be helpful to others.

*Conrad Phillip Kottak*

*Seabrook Island, South Carolina*

*ckottak@bellsouth.net*

# About the Author

**Conrad Phillip Kottak,**
who received his AB and PhD degrees from Columbia University, is the Julian H. Steward Collegiate Professor Emeritus of Anthropology at the University of Michigan, where he served as anthropology department chair from 1996 to 2006. He has been honored for his teaching by the university and the state of Michigan and by the American Anthropological Association. In 2005 he was elected to the American Academy of Arts and Sciences, and in 2008 to the National Academy of Sciences, where he chaired Section 51, Anthropology, from 2010 to 2013. Professor Kottak has done ethnographic fieldwork in Brazil, Madagascar, and the United States. His general interests are in the processes by which local cultures are incorporated—and resist incorporation—into larger systems. This interest links his earlier work on ecology and state formation in Africa and Madagascar to his more recent research on globalization, national and international culture, and media.

The fourth edition of Kottak's case study *Assault on Paradise: The Globalization of a Little Community in Brazil,* based on his longitudinal fieldwork in Arembepe, Bahia, Brazil, was published in 2006. In a research project during the 1980s, Kottak blended ethnography and survey research in studying "Television's Behavioral Effects in Brazil." That research is the basis of his book *Prime-Time Society: An Anthropological Analysis of Television and Culture* (updated edition, 2009).

Kottak's other books include *The Past in the Present: History, Ecology and Cultural Variation in Highland Madagascar* (1980), *Researching American Culture: A Guide for Student Anthropologists* (1982), *Madagascar: Society and History* (1986), and *Media and Middle Class Moms: Images and Realities of Work and Family* (with Lara Descartes, 2009). The most recent editions (16th) of his texts *Anthropology: Appreciating Human Diversity* and *Cultural Anthropology: Appreciating Cultural Diversity* were published by McGraw-Hill in 2015. He also is the author of *Mirror for Humanity: A Concise Introduction to Cultural Anthropology* (10th ed., McGraw-Hill, 2016) and of this book—*Window on Humanity: A Concise Introduction to Anthropology* (7th ed., McGraw-Hill, 2016).

Conrad Kottak's articles have appeared in academic journals, including *American Anthropologist, Journal of Anthropological Research, American Ethnologist, Ethnology, Human*

*Organization,* and *Luso-Brazilian Review.* He also has written for more popular journals, including *Transaction/SOCIETY, Natural History, Psychology Today,* and *General Anthropology.*

In other research projects, Professor Kottak and his colleagues have investigated ecological awareness in Brazil, biodiversity conservation in Madagascar, and media use by modern American families. Professor Kottak currently is collaborating with Professor Richard Pace and several graduate students on research investigating "The Evolution of Media Impact: A Longitudinal and Multi-Site study of Television and New Electronic/Digital Media in Brazil," a project supported by the National Science Foundation.

Conrad Kottak appreciates comments about his books from professors and students. He can be reached at the following e-mail address: **ckottak@bellsouth.net.**

# Window on
# Humanity

# 1

# What Is Anthropology?

"That's just human nature." "People are pretty much the same all over the world." Such opinions, which we hear in conversations, in the mass media, and in a dozen scenes in daily life, promote the erroneous idea that people in other countries have the same desires, feelings, values, and aspirations that we do. Such statements proclaim that because people are essentially the same, they are eager to receive the ideas, beliefs, values, institutions, practices, and products of an expansive North American culture. Often this assumption turns out to be wrong.

Anthropology offers a broader view—a distinctive comparative, cross-cultural perspective. Most people think that anthropologists study nonindustrial societies, and they do. My research has taken me to remote villages in Brazil and Madagascar, a large island off the southeast coast of Africa. In Brazil I sailed with fishers in simple sailboats on Atlantic waters. Among Madagascar's Betsileo people I worked in rice fields and took part in ceremonies in which I entered tombs to rewrap the corpses of decaying ancestors.

However, anthropology is much more than the study of nonindustrial peoples. It is a comparative science that examines all societies, ancient and modern, simple and complex. Most of the other social sciences tend to focus on a single society, usually an industrial nation such as the United States or Canada. Anthropology offers a unique cross-cultural perspective, constantly comparing the customs of one society with those of others.

To become a cultural anthropologist, one normally does *ethnography* (the first-hand, personal study of local settings). Ethnographic fieldwork usually entails spending a year or more in another society, living with the local people and learning about their way of life. No matter how much the ethnographer discovers about that society, he or she remains an alien there. That experience of alienation has a profound impact. Having learned to respect other customs and beliefs, anthropologists can never forget that there is a wider world. There are normal ways of thinking and acting other than our own.

# Human Adaptability

Anthropologists study human beings wherever and whenever they find them—in a Turkish café, a Mesopotamian tomb, or a North American shopping mall. Anthropology is the exploration of human diversity in time and space. Anthropology studies the whole of the human condition: past, present, and future; biology, society, language, and culture. Of particular interest is the diversity that comes through human adaptability.

Humans are among the world's most adaptable animals. In the Andes of South America, people wake up in villages 16,000 feet above sea level and then trek 1,500 feet higher to work in tin mines. Tribes in the Australian desert worship animals and discuss philosophy. People survive malaria in the tropics. Men have walked on the moon. The model of the *Star Trek* starship *Enterprise* in Washington's Smithsonian Institution is a symbol of the *Star Trek* mission "to seek out new life and civilizations, to boldly go where no one has gone before." Wishes to know the unknown, control the uncontrollable, and create order out of chaos find expression among all peoples. Creativity, adaptability, and flexibility are basic human attributes, and human diversity is the subject matter of anthropology.

Students often are surprised by the breadth of **anthropology,** which is the study of the human species and its immediate ancestors. Anthropology is a uniquely comparative and **holistic** science. *Holism* refers to the study of the whole of the human condition: past, present, and future; biology, society, language, and culture.

People share **society**—organized life in groups—with other animals, including baboons, wolves, mole rats, and even ants. Culture, however, is more distinctly human. **Cultures** are traditions and customs, transmitted through learning, that form and guide the beliefs and behavior of the people exposed to them. Children learn such a tradition by growing up in a particular society, through a process called *enculturation*. Cultural traditions include customs and opinions, developed over the generations, about proper and improper behavior. These traditions answer such questions as: How should we do things? How do we make sense of the world? How do we tell right from wrong? A culture produces a degree of consistency in behavior and thought among the people who live in a particular society.

The most critical element of cultural traditions is their transmission through learning rather than through biological inheritance. Culture is not itself biological, but it rests on certain features of human biology. For more than a million years, humans have had at least some of the biological capacities on which culture depends. These abilities are to learn, to think symbolically, to use language, and to employ tools and other products in organizing their lives and adapting to their environments.

Anthropology confronts and ponders major questions of human existence as it explores human biological and cultural diversity in time and space. By examining ancient bones and tools, we unravel the mysteries of human origins. When did our ancestors separate from those remote great-aunts and great-uncles whose descendants are the apes? Where and when did *Homo sapiens* originate? How has our species changed? What are we now, and where are we going? How have changes in culture and society influenced biological change? Our genus, *Homo,* has been changing for more than 2 million years. Humans continue to adapt and change both biologically and culturally.

## Adaptation, Variation, and Change

**Adaptation** refers to the processes by which organisms cope with environmental forces and stresses, such as those posed by climate and *topography* or terrains, also called landforms. How do organisms change to fit their environments, such as dry climates or high mountain altitudes? Like other animals, humans use biological means of adaptation. But humans are unique in also having cultural means of adaptation. Table 1.1 summarizes the cultural and biological means that humans use to adapt to high altitudes.

Mountainous terrains pose particular challenges, those associated with high altitude and oxygen deprivation. Consider four ways (one cultural and three biological) in which humans may cope with low oxygen pressure at high altitudes. Illustrating cultural (technological) adaptation would be a pressurized airplane cabin equipped with oxygen masks. There are three ways of adapting biologically to high altitudes: genetic adaptation, long-term physiological adaptation, and short-term physiological adaptation. First, native populations of high-altitude areas, such as the Andes of Peru and the Himalayas of Tibet and Nepal, seem to have acquired certain genetic advantages for life at very high altitudes. The Andean tendency to develop a voluminous chest and lungs probably has a genetic basis. Second, regardless of their genes, people who grow up at a high altitude become physiologically more efficient there than genetically similar people who have grown up at sea level would be. This illustrates long-term physiological adaptation during the body's growth and development. Third, humans also have the capacity for short-term or immediate physiological adaptation. Thus, when lowlanders arrive in the highlands, they immediately increase their breathing and heart rates. Hyperventilation

TABLE 1.1　**Forms of Cultural and Biological Adaptation (to High Altitude)**

| Form of Adaptation | Type of Adaptation | Example |
|---|---|---|
| Technology | Cultural | Pressurized airplane cabin with oxygen masks |
| Genetic adaptation (occurs over generations) | Biological | Larger "barrel chests" of native highlanders |
| Long-term physiological adaptation (occurs during growth and development of the individual organism) | Biological | More efficient respiratory system, to extract oxygen from "thin air" |
| Short-term physiological adaptation (occurs spontaneously when the individual organism enters a new environment) | Biological | Increased heart rate, hyperventilation |

increases the oxygen in their lungs and arteries. As the pulse also increases, blood reaches their tissues more rapidly. All these varied adaptive responses—cultural and biological—achieve a single goal: maintaining an adequate supply of oxygen to the body.

As human history has unfolded, the social and cultural means of adaptation have become increasingly important. In this process, humans have devised diverse ways of coping with a wide range of environments. The rate of cultural adaptation and change has accelerated, particularly during the past 10,000 years. For millions of years, hunting and gathering of nature's bounty—*foraging*—was the sole basis of human subsistence. However, it took only a few thousand years for **food production** (the cultivation of plants and domestication of animals), which originated some 12,000–10,000 years ago, to replace foraging in most areas. Between 6000 and 5000 B.P. (before the present), the first civilizations arose. These were large, powerful, and complex societies, such as ancient Egypt, that conquered and governed large geographic areas.

Much more recently, the spread of industrial production has profoundly affected human life. Throughout human history, major innovations have spread at the expense of earlier ones. Each economic revolution has had social and cultural repercussions. Today's global economy and communications link all contemporary people, directly or indirectly, in the modern world system. People must cope with forces generated by progressively larger systems—region, nation, and world. The study of such contemporary adaptations generates new challenges for anthropology: "The cultures of world peoples need to be constantly rediscovered as these people reinvent them in changing historical circumstances" (Marcus and Fischer 1986, p. 24).

## General Anthropology

The academic discipline of anthropology, also known as **general anthropology** or "four-field" anthropology, includes four main subdisciplines, or subfields. They are sociocultural, archaeological, biological, and linguistic anthropology. (From here on, the shorter term *cultural anthropology* will be used as a synonym for *sociocultural anthropology*.) Of the subfields, cultural anthropology has the largest membership. Most departments of anthropology teach courses in all four subfields.

There are historical reasons for the inclusion of four subfields in a single discipline. The origin of anthropology as a scientific field, and of American anthropology in particular, can be traced to the 19th century. Early American anthropologists were concerned especially with the history and cultures of the native peoples of North America. Interest in the origins and diversity of Native Americans brought together studies of customs, social life, language, and physical traits. Anthropologists still are pondering such questions as: Where did Native Americans come from? How many waves of migration brought them to the New World? What are the linguistic, cultural, and biological links among Native Americans and between them and Asia? (Note that a unified four-field anthropology did not develop in Europe, where the subfields tend to exist separately.)

There also are logical reasons for the unity of American anthropology. Each subfield considers variation in time and space (that is, in different geographic areas). Cultural and archaeological anthropologists study changes in social life and customs (among many other topics). Archaeologists use studies of living societies to imagine what life might have been like in the past. Biological anthropologists examine evolutionary changes in physical form, for example, anatomical changes that might have been associated with the origin of tool use or language. Linguistic anthropologists may reconstruct the basics of ancient languages by studying modern ones.

The subfields influence each other as anthropologists talk to each other, read books and journals, and meet in professional organizations. General anthropology explores the basics of human biology, society, and culture and considers their interrelations. Anthropologists share certain key assumptions. Perhaps the most fundamental is the idea that sound conclusions about "human nature" cannot be derived from studying a single population, nation, society, or cultural tradition. A comparative, cross-cultural approach is essential.

Early American anthropology was especially concerned with the history and cultures of Native North Americans. Ely S. Parker, or Ha-sa-no-an-da, was a Seneca Indian who made important contributions to early anthropology. Parker also served as Commissioner of Indian Affairs for the United States. Source: National Archives and Records Administration

## Cultural Forces Shape Human Biology

Anthropology's comparative, biocultural perspective recognizes that cultural forces constantly mold human biology. (**Biocultural** refers to the inclusion and combination of both biological and cultural perspectives and approaches to comment on or solve a particular issue or problem.) Culture is a key environmental force in determining how human bodies grow and develop. Cultural traditions promote certain activities and abilities, discourage others, and set standards of physical well-being and attractiveness. Physical activities, including sports, which are influenced by culture, help build the body. For example, North American girls are encouraged to pursue, and therefore do well in, competition involving figure skating, gymnastics, track and field, swimming, diving, and many other sports. Brazilian girls, although excelling in the team sports of basketball and volleyball, haven't fared nearly as well in individual sports as have their American and Canadian counterparts. Why are people encouraged to excel as athletes in some nations but not others? Why do people in some countries invest so much time and effort in competitive sports that their bodies change significantly as a result?

Cultural standards of attractiveness and propriety influence participation and achievement in sports. Americans run or swim not just to compete but to keep trim and fit. Brazil's beauty standards have traditionally accepted more fat, especially in female buttocks and hips. Brazilian men have had some international success in swimming and running, but Brazil rarely sends female swimmers or runners to the Olympics. One

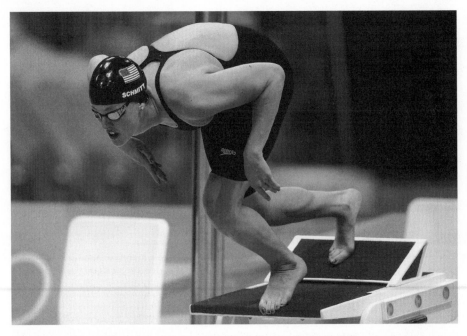

American swimmer Allison Schmitt takes off in the final of the Women's 200-meter freestyle at the 2012 London Olympics. Schmitt won the event and a gold medal, setting an Olympic record. How might years of competitive swimming affect the human body? © Al Bello/Getty Images Sport/Getty Images

reason Brazilian women avoid competitive swimming in particular may be that sport's effects on the body. Years of swimming sculpt a distinctive physique: an enlarged upper torso, a massive neck, and powerful shoulders and back. Successful female swimmers tend to be big, strong, and bulky. The countries that have produced them most consistently are the United States, Germany, Australia, the Netherlands, China, Great Britain, and the former Soviet Union, where this body type isn't as stigmatized as it is in Latin countries. Swimmers develop hard bodies, but Brazilian culture says that women should be soft, with big hips and buttocks, not big shoulders. Many young female swimmers in Brazil choose to abandon the sport rather than the "feminine" body ideal.

When you grew up, which sport did you appreciate the most—soccer, swimming, football, baseball, tennis, golf, or some other sport (or perhaps none at all)? Is this because of "who you are" or because of the opportunities you had as a child to practice and participate in this particular activity? When you were young, your parents might have told you that drinking milk and eating vegetables would help you grow up "big and strong." They probably didn't as readily recognize the role that *culture* plays in shaping bodies, personalities, and personal health. If nutrition matters in growth, so, too, do cultural guidelines. What is proper behavior for boys and girls? What kinds of work should men and women do? Where should people live? What are proper uses of their leisure time? What role should religion play? How should people relate to their family, friends, and neighbors? Although our genetic attributes provide a foundation for our growth and development, human biology is fairly plastic—that is, it is malleable. Culture is an environmental force that affects our development as much as do nutrition, heat, cold, and altitude. Culture also guides our emotional and cognitive growth and helps determine the kinds of personalities we have as adults.

# The Subdisciplines of Anthropology

## Cultural Anthropology

**Cultural anthropology** is the study of human society and culture, the subfield that describes, analyzes, interprets, and explains social and cultural similarities and differences. To study and interpret cultural diversity, cultural anthropologists engage in two kinds of activity: ethnography (based on fieldwork) and ethnology (based on cross-cultural comparison). **Ethnography** provides an account of a particular community, society, or culture. During ethnographic fieldwork, the ethnographer gathers data that he or she organizes, analyzes, and interprets to develop that account, which may be in the form of a book, an article, or a film. Traditionally, ethnographers have lived in small communities and studied local behavior, beliefs, customs, social life, economic activities, politics, and religion (see Okeley 2012; Wolcott 2008).

The anthropological perspective derived from ethnographic fieldwork often differs radically from that of economics or political science. Those fields focus on national and official organizations and policies and often on elites. However, the groups that anthropologists traditionally have studied usually have been relatively poor and powerless. Ethnographers often observe discriminatory practices directed toward such people, who experience food shortages, dietary deficiencies, and other aspects of poverty. Political scientists tend to study programs that national planners develop, while anthropologists discover how these programs work on the local level.

Cultures are not isolated. As noted by Franz Boas (1940/1966) many years ago, contact between neighboring tribes always has existed and has extended over enormous areas. "Human populations construct their cultures in interaction with one another, and not in isolation" (Wolf 1982, p. ix). Villagers increasingly participate in regional, national, and world events. Exposure to external forces comes through the mass media, migration, and modern transportation. City and nation increasingly invade local communities with the arrival of tourists, development agents, government and religious officials, and political candidates. Such linkages are prominent components of regional, national, and international systems of politics, economics, and information. These larger systems increasingly affect the people and places anthropology traditionally has studied. The study of such linkages and systems is part of the subject matter of modern anthropology.

**Ethnology** examines, compares, analyzes, and interprets the results of ethnography—the data gathered in different societies. Ethnologists use such data to compare and contrast and to make generalizations about society and culture. Looking beyond the particular to the more general, they attempt to identify and explain cultural differences and similarities, to test hypotheses, and to build theory to enhance our understanding of how social and cultural systems work. Ethnology gets its data for comparison not just

TABLE 1.2    **Ethnography and Ethnology—Two Dimensions of Cultural Anthropology**

| Ethnography | Ethnology |
|---|---|
| Requires fieldwork to collect data | Uses data collected by a series of researchers |
| Is often descriptive | Is usually synthetic |
| Is group- and community-specific | Is comparative and cross-cultural |

from ethnography but also from the other subfields, particularly from archaeological anthropology, which reconstructs social systems of the past. (Table 1.2 summarizes the main contrasts between ethnography and ethnology.)

## Archaeological Anthropology

**Archaeological anthropology** (more simply, "archaeology") reconstructs, describes, and interprets human behavior and cultural patterns through material remains (see Fagan 2012). At sites where people live or have lived, archaeologists find artifacts—material items that humans have made, used, or modified—such as tools, weapons, campsites, buildings, and garbage. Plant and animal remains and ancient garbage tell stories about consumption and activities. Wild and domesticated grains have different characteristics, which allow archaeologists to distinguish between gathering and cultivation. Examination of animal bones reveals the ages of slaughtered animals and provides other information useful in determining whether species were wild or domesticated.

Analyzing such data, archaeologists answer several questions about ancient economies: Did the group get its meat from hunting, or did it domesticate and breed animals, killing only those of a certain age and sex? Did plant food come from wild plants or from sowing, tending, and harvesting crops? Did the residents make, trade for, or buy particular items? Were raw materials available locally? If not, where did they come from? From such information, archaeologists reconstruct patterns of production, trade, and consumption.

Archaeologists have spent considerable time studying potsherds, fragments of earthenware. Potsherds are more durable than many other artifacts, such as textiles and wood. The quantity of pottery fragments allows estimates of population size and density. The discovery that potters used materials that were not available locally suggests systems of trade. Similarities in manufacture and decoration at different sites may be proof of cultural connections. Groups with similar pots may be historically related. Perhaps they shared common cultural ancestors, traded with each other, or belonged to the same political system.

Many archaeologists examine paleoecology. *Ecology* is the study of interrelations among living things in an environment. The organisms and environment together constitute an *ecosystem,* a patterned arrangement of energy flows and exchanges. Human ecology studies ecosystems that include people, focusing on the ways in which human use "of nature influences and is influenced by social organization and cultural values" (Bennett 1969, pp. 10–11). *Paleoecology* looks at the ecosystems of the past.

In addition to reconstructing ecological patterns, archaeologists may infer cultural transformations, for example, by observing changes in the size and type of sites and the distance between them. A city develops in a region where only towns, villages, and

Anthropological archaeologists from the University of Pennsylvania work to stabilize the original plaster at an Anasazi (Native American) site in Colorado's Mesa Verde National Park. © George H.H. Huey/Alamy

hamlets existed a few centuries earlier. The number of settlement levels (city, town, village, hamlet) in a society is a measure of social complexity. Buildings offer clues about political and religious features. Temples and pyramids suggest that an ancient society had an authority structure capable of marshaling the labor needed to build such monuments. The presence or absence of certain structures, like the pyramids of ancient Egypt and Mexico, reveals differences in function between settlements. For example, some towns were places where people went to attend ceremonies. Others were burial sites; still others were farming communities.

Archaeologists also reconstruct behavior patterns and lifestyles of the past by excavating. This involves digging through a succession of levels at a particular site. In a given area, through time, settlements may change in form and purpose, as may the connections between settlements. Excavation can document changes in economic, social, and political activities.

Although archaeologists are best known for studying prehistory, that is, the period before the invention of writing, they also study the cultures of historical and even living peoples (see Sabloff 2008). Studying sunken ships off the Florida coast, underwater archaeologists have been able to verify the living conditions on the vessels that brought ancestral African Americans to the New World as enslaved people. In a research project begun in 1973 in Tucson, Arizona, archaeologist William Rathje learned a great deal about contemporary life by studying modern garbage (Zimring 2012). The value of "garbology," as Rathje calls it, is that it provides "evidence of what people did, not what they think they did, what they think they should have done, or what the interviewer thinks they should have done" (Harrison, Rathje, and Hughes 1994, p. 108). What people report may contrast strongly with their real behavior as revealed by garbology. For example, the garbologists discovered that the three Tucson neighborhoods that reported the lowest beer consumption actually had the highest number of discarded beer cans per household! Rathje's garbology also has exposed misconceptions about how much of different kinds of trash are in landfills: While most people thought that fast-food containers and disposable diapers were major waste problems, in fact they were relatively insignificant compared with paper (Rathje and Murphy 2001; Zimring 2012).

## Biological, or Physical, Anthropology

The subject matter of **biological, or physical, anthropology** is human biological diversity in time and space. The focus on biological variation unites five special interests within biological anthropology:

1. Human evolution as revealed by the fossil record (paleoanthropology).
2. Human genetics.
3. Human growth and development.
4. Human biological plasticity (the body's ability to change as it copes with stresses, such as heat, cold, and altitude).
5. The biology, evolution, behavior, and social life of monkeys, apes, and other non-human primates.

These interests link biological anthropology to other fields: biology, zoology, geology, anatomy, physiology, medicine, and public health. Osteology—the study of bones—helps paleoanthropologists, who examine skulls, teeth, and bones, to identify human ancestors and to chart changes in anatomy over time. A paleontologist is a scientist who studies fossils. A paleoanthropologist is one sort of paleontologist, one who studies the fossil record of human evolution (see Wood 2011). Paleoanthropologists often collaborate with archaeologists, who study artifacts, in reconstructing biological and cultural aspects of human evolution. Fossils and tools often are found together. Different types of tools provide information about the lifestyles of the ancestral humans who used them.

More than a century ago, Charles Darwin noticed that the variety that exists within any population permits some individuals (those with the favored characteristics) to do better than others at surviving and reproducing. Genetics, which developed later, enlightens us about the causes and transmission of this variety. However, it isn't just genes that cause variety. During any individual's lifetime, the environment works along with heredity to determine biological features. For example, people with a genetic tendency to be tall will be shorter if they are poorly nourished during childhood. Thus, biological anthropology also investigates the influence of environment on the body as it grows and matures. Among the environmental factors that influence the body as it develops are nutrition, altitude, temperature, and disease, as well as cultural factors, such as standards of attractiveness.

Biological anthropology (along with zoology) also includes primatology. The primates include our closest relatives—apes and monkeys. Primatologists study their biology, evolution, behavior, and social life, often in their natural environments (see Campbell 2011).

Primatology assists paleoanthropology, because primate behavior may shed light on early human behavior and human nature.

## Linguistic Anthropology

We don't know (and probably never will) when our ancestors acquired the ability to speak, although biological anthropologists have looked to the anatomy of the face and the skull to speculate about the origin of language. And primatologists have described the communication systems of monkeys and apes. We do know that grammatically complex languages have existed for thousands of years. Linguistic anthropology offers further illustration of anthropology's interest in comparison, variation, and change. **Linguistic anthropology** studies language in its social and cultural context, across space and over time. Some linguistic anthropologists make inferences about universal features of language, linked perhaps to uniformities in the human brain. Others reconstruct ancient languages by comparing their contemporary descendants and in so doing make discoveries about history. Still others study linguistic differences to discover varied perceptions and patterns of thought in different cultures (see Bonvillain 2013).

Historical linguistics considers variation in time, such as the changes in sounds, grammar, and vocabulary between Middle English (spoken from approximately C.E. [formerly A.D.] 1050 to 1550) and modern English. **Sociolinguistics** investigates relationships between social and linguistic variation. No language is a homogeneous system in which everyone speaks just as everyone else does. How do different speakers use a given language? How do linguistic features correlate with social factors, including class and gender differences (Eckert and McConnell-Ginet 2013)? One reason for variation is geography, as in regional dialects and accents. Linguistic variation also is expressed in the bilingualism of ethnic groups. Linguistic and cultural anthropologists collaborate in studying links between language and many other aspects of culture, such as how people reckon kinship and how they perceive and classify colors.

# Anthropology and Other Academic Fields

As mentioned previously, one of the main differences between anthropology and the other fields that study people is holism, anthropology's unique blend of biological, social, cultural, linguistic, historical, and contemporary perspectives. Paradoxically, while distinguishing anthropology, this breadth is what also links it to many other disciplines. Techniques used to date fossils and artifacts have come to anthropology from physics, chemistry, and geology. Because plant and animal remains often are found with human bones and artifacts, anthropologists collaborate with botanists, zoologists, and paleontologists.

As a discipline that is both scientific and humanistic, anthropology has links with many other academic fields. Anthropology is a **science**—a "systematic field of study or body of knowledge that aims, through experiment, observation, and deduction, to produce reliable explanations of phenomena, with references to the material and physical world" (*Webster's New World Encyclopedia* 1993, p. 937). The chapters that follow present anthropology as a humanistic science devoted to discovering, describing, understanding, and explaining similarities and differences in time and space among humans and our ancestors. Clyde Kluckhohn (1944) described anthropology as "the science of human similarities and differences" (p. 9). His statement of the need for such a field still stands: "Anthropology provides a scientific basis for dealing with the crucial dilemma of the world today: how can peoples of different appearance, mutually unintelligible languages, and dissimilar ways of life get along peaceably together?" (p. 9). Anthropology has compiled an impressive body of knowledge, which this textbook attempts to encapsulate.

Besides its links to the natural sciences (e.g., geology, zoology) and social sciences (e.g., sociology, psychology), anthropology also has strong links to the humanities. The humanities include English, comparative literature, classics, folklore, philosophy, and the arts. These fields study languages, texts, philosophies, arts, music, performances, and other forms of creative expression. Ethnomusicology, which studies forms of musical expression on a worldwide basis, is especially closely related to anthropology. Also linked is folklore, the systematic study of tales, myths, and legends from a variety of cultures. One might well argue that anthropology is among the most humanistic of all academic fields because of its fundamental respect for human diversity. Anthropologists listen to, record, and represent voices from a multitude of nations and cultures. Anthropology values local knowledge, diverse worldviews, and alternative philosophies. Cultural anthropology and linguistic anthropology in particular bring a comparative and nonelitist perspective to forms of creative expression, including language, art, narratives, music, and dance, viewed in their social and cultural context.

## Applied Anthropology

Anthropology is not a science of the exotic carried on by quaint scholars in ivory towers. Rather, anthropology has a lot to tell the public. Anthropology's foremost professional organization, the American Anthropological Association (AAA), has formally acknowledged a public service role by recognizing that anthropology has two dimensions: (1) academic, or general, anthropology and (2) practicing, or **applied, anthropology.** The latter refers to the application of anthropological data, perspectives, theory, and methods to identify, assess, and solve contemporary social problems (see Bodley 2012). As Erve Chambers (1987, p. 309) states it, applied anthropology is the "field of inquiry concerned with the relationships between anthropological knowledge and the uses of that knowledge in the world beyond anthropology." More and more anthropologists from the four subfields now work in such "applied" areas as public health, family planning, business, economic development, and cultural resource management.

Applied anthropology encompasses any use of the knowledge and/or techniques of the four subfields to identify, assess, and solve practical problems. Because of anthropology's breadth, it has many applications. For example, applied medical anthropologists consider both the sociocultural and the biological contexts and implications of disease and illness. Perceptions of good and bad health, along with actual health threats and problems, differ among societies. Various ethnic groups recognize different illnesses, symptoms, and causes and have developed different health care systems and treatment strategies. (See this chapter's "Anthropology Today" feature.)

## Anthropology Today  *Anorexia Goes Global*

Both cultural and biological anthropologists contribute to *medical anthropology*, a growing field of study that examines how and why various diseases, illnesses, and health conditions affect particular populations and how illness is socially constructed, diagnosed, managed, and treated in various societies. Perceptions of good and bad health, along with actual health problems, differ among societies, and particular cultures and ethnic groups recognize different illnesses, symptoms, and causes.

Well known to anthropology are *culturally specific syndromes*—health conditions, often with a mental-psychological component, that are confined to a single culture or a group of related cultures. One example is *koro*, the East Asian term for intense anxiety arising from the fear that one's genitals will recede into one's body and cause death. A Latin American may experience a syndrome known as *susto,* characterized by extreme sadness and listlessness, often following a personal tragedy, such as the death of a loved one. A milder malady, found most typically in Mediterranean countries, is *mal de ojo* ("evil eye"), whose symptoms include fitful sleep, sickness, and fever. The influential *Diagnostic and Statistical Manual of Mental Disorders* (2013) published by the American Psychiatric Association now recognizes "culture-bound syndromes," another term for these culturally specific syndromes.

In our modern world system, as people migrate, they carry their cultural baggage, including their syndromes, with them across national boundaries. Today, diagnosticians in western Europe and the United States may encounter cases of susto, evil eye, or even koro among recent immigrants. Furthermore, certain syndromes

once confined to Western cultures are now spreading with globalization. One example is *anorexia nervosa* (food refusal or extreme dieting, resulting in self-starvation), a syndrome once specific to Western industrialized societies that has been spreading internationally.

In the early 1990s (as reported by Watters 2010), Dr. Sing Lee, a Hong Kong–based psychiatrist and researcher, documented what was, at that time, a culturally specific, and very rare, form of anorexia nervosa in Hong Kong. Unlike American anorexics, Lee's patients did not worry about getting fat. Instead, they reduced their food intake in an attempt to fend off unwanted bodily symptoms—most frequently, bloated stomachs. Just as Dr. Lee started publishing his findings, however, the understanding of anorexia in Hong Kong suddenly shifted, after a teenage anorexic girl collapsed and died on a busy downtown street. Her death was featured prominently in local newspapers, with such headlines as "Anorexia Made Her All Skin and Bones."

In interpreting the girl's symptoms, many local reporters simply copied from American diagnostic manuals, thus spreading the idea that anorexia in Hong Kong was the same disorder that existed in the United States and Europe. As Hong Kongers became more familiar with the American diagnosis of anorexia, Lee's patients started mimicking the American symptoms, and the incidence of anorexia also increased. Lee's anorexic patient load rose rapidly, from two to three per year to two to three per month. Occurring throughout Hong Kong, that increase sparked another series of media reports, such as "Children as Young as 10 Starving Themselves as Eating Ailments Rise." Eventually Lee concluded that up to 10 percent of

*continued*

## Anthropology Today *continued*

young women in Hong Kong had fallen victim to eating disorders. Unlike his earlier patients, these women—eventually 90 percent of them—now cited a fear of getting fat as the key reason for not eating (Watters 2010).

Disorders and symptoms, both physical and mental, can easily cross national borders in today's globalized and socially networked world. The *Diagnostic and Statistical Manual of Mental Disorders* serves as an increasingly transnational reference and standard. You can also imagine the role of social media, available through computers, tablets, and cell phones, in transmitting news and images of various conditions that affect, or might affect, their users. The Western form of anorexia surely would not have spread so quickly in Hong Kong without modern media. After all, it took more than half a century for Western mental health professionals to name, codify, and establish their definition of anorexia. By contrast, after a single, widely reported death on a busy downtown street, it took just hours for the people of Hong Kong to learn about anorexia and its "Western" symptoms (Watters 2010), and just months for some of them to begin suffering from the ailment. As people move about, and as new media multiply, societies and communities—both

Western and non-Western—increasingly interact with the forces of globalization, including the concepts and conditions it is spreading.

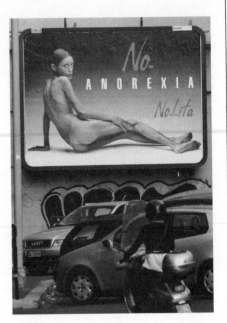

In Rome, a poster featuring an emaciated woman (in an advertisement for an Italian fashion house) bears the headline "No anorexia." How does anorexia illustrate a culturally specific syndrome? © Riccardo De Luca/MAXPPP/Newscom

Applied archaeology, usually called *public archaeology,* includes such activities as cultural resource management, contract archaeology, public educational programs, and historic preservation. An important role for public archaeology has been created by legislation requiring evaluation of sites threatened by dams, highways, and other construction activities. To decide what needs saving, and to preserve significant information about the past when sites cannot be saved, is the work of **cultural resource management (CRM).** CRM involves not only preserving sites but also allowing their destruction if they are not significant. The "management" part of the term refers to the

TABLE 1.3   **The Four Subfields and Two Dimensions of Anthropology**

| Anthropology's Subfields (General Anthropology) | Examples of Application (Applied Anthropology) |
|---|---|
| Cultural anthropology | Development anthropology |
| Archaeological anthropology | Cultural resource management (CRM) |
| Biological (physical) anthropology | Forensic anthropology |
| Linguistic anthropology | Study of linguistic diversity in classrooms |

evaluation and decision-making process. Cultural resource managers work for federal, state, and county agencies and other clients. Applied cultural anthropologists sometimes work with the public archaeologists, assessing the human problems generated by the proposed change and determining how they can be reduced. Table 1.3 relates anthropology's four subfields to its two dimensions.

## Summary

1. Anthropology is the holistic, biocultural, and comparative study of humanity. It is the systematic exploration of human biological and cultural diversity across time and space. Examining the origins of, and changes in, human biology and culture, anthropology provides explanations for similarities and differences among humans and their societies.

2. The four subfields of general anthropology are (socio)cultural, archaeological, biological, and linguistic. All consider variation in time and space. Each also examines adaptation—the process by which organisms cope with environmental stresses. Anthropology's biocultural perspective is a particularly effective way of approaching interrelations between biology and culture. Cultural forces mold human biology, including our body types and images.

3. Cultural anthropology explores the cultural diversity of the present and the recent past. Archaeology reconstructs cultural patterns, often of prehistoric populations. Biological anthropology documents diversity involving fossils, genetics, growth and development, bodily responses, and nonhuman primates. Linguistic anthropology considers diversity among languages. It also studies how speech changes in social situations and over time.

4. Concerns with biology, society, culture, and language link anthropology to many other fields—natural sciences, social sciences, and humanities.

5. Anthropology has two dimensions: general and applied. The latter uses anthropological perspectives, theory, methods, and data to identify, assess, and solve social problems. The fields in which applied anthropologists work include business, government, economic development, education, and social services, action, and outreach. Applied anthropologists come from all four subfields.

## Key Terms

adaptation, *3*
anthropology, *2*
applied
   anthropology, *12*
archaeological
   anthropology, *8*
biocultural, *5*
biological
   (physical)
   anthropology, *10*

cultural
   anthropology, *7*
cultural resource
   management
   (CRM), *14*
culture, *2*
ethnography, *7*
ethnology, *7*
food production, *4*

general
   anthropology, *4*
holistic, *2*
linguistic
   anthropology, *11*
science, *11*
society, *2*
sociolinguistics, *11*

# Chapter 2

# Culture

In Chapter 1 we saw that humans share *society,* organized life in groups, with social animals, such as apes, monkeys, wolves, and ants. Although other animals, especially apes, have rudimentary cultural abilities, only humans have fully elaborated cultures—distinctive traditions and customs transmitted over the generations through learning and through language.

The concept of culture has long been basic to anthropology. Well over a century ago, in his book *Primitive Culture,* the British anthropologist Edward Tylor proposed that cultures, systems of human behavior and thought, obey natural laws and therefore can be studied scientifically. Tylor's definition of culture still offers an overview of the subject matter of anthropology and is widely quoted.

"Culture . . . is that complex whole which includes knowledge, belief, arts, morals, law, custom, and any other capabilities and habits acquired by man as a member of society" (Tylor 1871/1958, p. 1). The crucial phrase here is "acquired . . . as a member of society." Tylor's definition focuses on attributes that people acquire not through biological inheritance but by growing up in a particular society in which they are exposed to a specific cultural tradition. **Enculturation** is the process by which a child *learns* his or her culture.

## What Is Culture?

### Culture Is Learned

The ease with which children absorb any cultural tradition rests on the uniquely elaborated human capacity to learn. Other animals may learn from experience, so that, for example, they avoid fire after discovering that it hurts. Social animals also learn from other members of their group. Wolves, for instance, learn hunting strategies from other pack members. Such social learning is particularly important among monkeys and apes, our closest biological relatives. But our own *cultural learning* depends on the uniquely developed human capacity to use **symbols,** signs that have no necessary or natural connection to the things they stand for, or signify.

Through cultural learning, people create, remember, and deal with ideas. They understand and apply specific systems of symbolic meaning. Anthropologist Clifford Geertz described cultures as sets of "control mechanisms—plans, recipes, rules, instructions" and likens them to computer programs that govern human behavior (Geertz 1973, p. 44). During enculturation, people gradually absorb and internalize their particular culture—a previously established system of meanings and symbols that helps guide their behavior and perceptions throughout their lives.

Every person begins immediately, through a process of conscious and unconscious learning and interaction with others, to internalize, or incorporate, a cultural tradition through the process of enculturation. Sometimes culture is taught directly, as when parents tell their children to say "thank you" when someone gives them something or does them a favor.

Culture also is transmitted through observation. Children pay attention to the things that go on around them. They modify their behavior not just because other people tell them to do so but as a result of their own observations and growing awareness of what their culture considers right and wrong. Culture also is absorbed unconsciously. North Americans acquire their culture's notions about how far apart people should stand when they talk, not by being told directly to maintain a certain distance but through a gradual process of observation, experience, and conscious and unconscious behavior modification. No one tells Latins to stand closer together than North Americans do; they learn to do so as part of their cultural tradition. (See this chapter's "Anthropology Today.")

### Culture Is Symbolic

Symbolic thought is unique and crucial to humans and to cultural learning. A symbol is something verbal or nonverbal, within a particular language or culture, that comes to stand for something else. There need be no obvious, natural, or necessary connection between a symbol and what it symbolizes. The familiar pet that barks is no more naturally a *dog* than it is a *chien, Hund,* or *mbwa,* the words for "dog" in French, German, and Swahili, respectively. Language is one of the distinctive possessions of *Homo sapiens.* No other animal has developed anything approaching the complexity of language, with its multitude of symbols.

Many symbols are linguistic. There also are myriad nonverbal symbols, such as flags, which stand for various countries, and the golden arches that symbolize a particular hamburger chain. Holy water is a potent symbol in Roman Catholicism. As is true of all symbols, the association between a symbol (water) and what is symbolized (holiness) is arbitrary and conventional. Water probably is not intrinsically holier than milk, blood, or other natural liquids. Nor is holy water chemically different from ordinary water. Holy water is a symbol within Roman Catholicism, which is part of an international cultural system. A natural thing has been associated arbitrarily with a particular meaning for Catholics, who share beliefs and experiences that are based on learning and transmitted across the generations.

All humans possess the abilities on which culture rests—the abilities to learn, to think symbolically, to manipulate language, and to use tools and other cultural products in organizing their lives and coping with their environments. Every contemporary human population has the ability to use symbols and thus to create and maintain culture. Our nearest relatives—chimpanzees and gorillas—have rudimentary cultural abilities. However, no other animal has elaborated cultural abilities to the extent that *Homo* has.

## Culture Is Shared

Culture is an attribute not of individuals per se but of individuals as members of *groups*. Culture is transmitted socially—in society. That is, we learn our culture by observing, listening, talking, and interacting with many other people. Shared beliefs, values, memories, and expectations link people who grow up in the same culture. Enculturation unifies people by providing us with common experiences.

People in the United States sometimes have trouble understanding the power of culture because of the value that American culture places on the idea of the individual. Americans are fond of saying that everyone is unique and special in some way. However, in American culture individualism itself is a distinctive shared value. Individualism is transmitted through hundreds of statements and settings in our daily lives. From media personalities to parents, grandparents, and teachers, our enculturative agents insist that we are all "someone special."

People become agents in the enculturation of their children, just as their parents were for them. Although a culture constantly changes, certain fundamental beliefs, values, worldviews, adages, and child-rearing practices endure. Consider a simple American example of enduring shared enculturation. As children, when we didn't finish a meal, our parents may have reminded us of starving children in some foreign country, just as our grandparents might have done a generation earlier. The specific country changes (China, India, Bangladesh, Ethiopia, Somalia, Rwanda—what was it in your home?). Still, American culture goes on transmitting the idea that by eating all our brussels sprouts or broccoli we can justify our own good fortune, compared to a hungry child in an impoverished or war-ravaged country.

## Culture and Nature

Culture takes the natural biological urges we share with other animals and teaches us how to express them in particular ways. People have to eat, but culture teaches us what, when, and how. In many cultures people have their main meal at noon, but most North Americans prefer a large dinner. English people eat fish (e.g., kippers—kippered herring) for breakfast, but North Americans prefer hot cakes and cold cereals. Brazilians put hot milk into strong coffee, whereas many North Americans pour cold milk into a weaker brew. Midwesterners dine at 5 or 6, Spaniards at 10.

Cultural habits, perceptions, and inventions mold "human nature" into many forms. People have to eliminate wastes from their bodies. But some cultures teach people to defecate standing, while others tell them to do it sitting down. Peasant women in the Andean highlands squat in the streets and urinate, getting all the privacy they need from their massive skirts. All these habits are parts of cultural traditions that have converted natural acts into cultural customs.

Culture affects how we perceive nature, human nature, and "the natural," and cultural advances have overcome many "natural" limitations. We prevent and cure diseases, such as polio and smallpox, that felled our ancestors. Viagra and Cialis are used to enhance or restore sexual potency. Through cloning, scientists have challenged the way we think about biological identity and the meaning of life itself. Culture, of course, does not always protect us from natural threats. Hurricanes, floods, earthquakes, and other natural forces regularly overthrow our wishes to modify the environment through building, development, and expansion. What are some of the other ways in which nature strikes back at culture?

## Culture Is All-Encompassing and Integrated

For anthropologists, culture includes much more than refinement, good taste, sophistication, education, and appreciation of the fine arts. Not only college graduates but all people are "cultured." The most interesting and significant cultural forces are those that affect people every day of their lives, particularly those that influence children during enculturation.

*Culture,* as defined anthropologically, encompasses features that are sometimes regarded as trivial or unworthy of serious study, such as those of "popular" culture. To understand contemporary North American culture, we must consider mass media, the Internet, fast-food restaurants, sports, and games. As a cultural manifestation, a rock star may be as interesting as a symphony conductor (or vice versa); a comic book may be as significant as a book-award winner.

Cultures are not haphazard collections of customs and beliefs. Cultures are integrated, patterned systems. If one part of the system (the overall economy, for instance) changes, other parts change as well. For example, during the 1950s most American women planned domestic careers as homemakers and mothers. Most of today's college women, by contrast, hope to get paying jobs when they graduate.

What are some of the social repercussions of this particular economic change? Attitudes and behavior regarding marriage, family, and children have changed. Late marriage, "living together," and divorce have become more common. Work competes with marriage and family responsibilities and reduces the time available to invest in child care.

Cultures are integrated not simply by their dominant economic activities and related social patterns but also by sets of values, ideas, symbols, and judgments. Cultures train their individual members to share certain personality traits. A set of characteristic **core values** (key, basic, central values) integrates each culture and helps distinguish it from others. For instance, the work ethic and individualism are core values that have integrated

Cultures are integrated systems. When one behavior pattern changes, others also change. During the 1950s, most American women expected to have careers as wives, mothers, and domestic managers. As more and more women have entered the workforce, attitudes toward work and family have changed. In the earlier photo, a 1950s mom and kids do the dishes. In the recent photo, a doctor and two nurses examine a patient's record. What do you imagine these three women do when they get home? (first): © William Gottlieb/Corbis; (second): © Tom Tracy Photography/Alamy

American culture for generations. Different sets of dominant values influence the patterns of other cultures.

## Culture Is Instrumental, Adaptive, and Maladaptive

Culture is the main reason for human adaptability and success. Other animals rely on biological means of adaptation (such as fur or blubber, which are adaptations to cold). Humans also adapt biologically—for example, by shivering when we get cold or sweating when we get hot. But in addition to biological responses, people also have cultural ways of adapting. To cope with environmental stresses we habitually use technology, or tools. We hunt cold-adapted animals and use their fur coats as our own. We turn the thermostat up in the winter and down in the summer. Or we plan action to increase our comfort. We have a cold drink, jump in a pool, or travel to someplace cooler in the summer or warmer in the winter. People use culture *instrumentally,* that is, to fulfill their basic biological needs for food, drink, shelter, comfort, and reproduction.

People also use culture to fulfill psychological and emotional needs, such as friendship, companionship, approval, and sexual desirability. People seek *informal support—* help from people who care about them—as well as *formal support* from associations and institutions. To these ends, individuals cultivate ties with others on the basis of common experiences, political interests, aesthetic sensibilities, or personal attraction.

On one level, cultural traits (e.g., air conditioning) may be called *adaptive* if they help individuals cope with environmental stresses. But on a different level, such traits can also be *maladaptive.* That is, they may threaten a group's continued existence. Thus, chlorofluorocarbons (e.g., as found in old air conditioners) have been banned in the United States because they deplete the ozone layer and, by doing so, can harm humans and other life. Many modern cultural patterns may be maladaptive in the long run. Some examples of maladaptive aspects of culture are policies that encourage overpopulation, poor food-distribution systems, overconsumption, and environmental degradation.

# Culture's Evolutionary Basis

The human capacity for culture has an evolutionary basis that extends back at least 2.6 million years to early toolmakers. Evidence for these toolmakers exists in the archaeological record. However, based on observation of tool use and manufacture by apes, scientists believe the evolutionary basis for culture may extend even further back.

Similarities between humans and apes, our closest relatives, are evident in anatomy, brain structure, genetics, and biochemistry. Most closely related to us are the African great apes: chimpanzees and gorillas. *Hominidae* is the zoological family that includes fossil and living humans, as well as chimps and gorillas. We refer to members of this family as **hominids.** The term **hominins** is used for the group that leads to humans but not to chimps and gorillas and that encompasses all the human species that ever have existed.

Many human traits reflect the fact that our primate ancestors lived in the trees. These traits include grasping ability and manual dexterity (especially opposable thumbs), depth and color vision, learning ability based on a large brain, substantial parental investment in a limited number of offspring, and tendencies toward sociality and cooperation. These traits, which offered adaptive advantages to our primate ancestors, continue as key features of human adaptation. Manual dexterity, for example, is essential to a major human adaptive capacity: tool making.

## What We Share with Other Primates

There is a substantial gap between primate *society* (organized life in groups) and fully developed human *culture,* which is based on symbolic thought. Nevertheless, studies of nonhuman primates reveal many similarities with humans, such as the ability to learn from experience and change behavior as a result. Monkeys, and especially apes, learn throughout their lives (see Choi 2011). In one group of Japanese macaques (land-dwelling monkeys), for example, a 3-year-old female started washing sweet potatoes before she ate them. First her mother, then her age peers, and finally the entire troop began washing sweet potatoes as well. The ability to benefit from experience confers a tremendous adaptive advantage, permitting the avoidance of fatal mistakes. Faced with environmental change, humans and other primates don't have to wait for a genetic or physiological response. They can modify learned behavior and social patterns instead.

Although humans employ tools much more than any other animal does, tool use also turns up among several nonhuman species, including birds, beavers, sea otters, and especially apes (see Campbell 2011). Humans are not the only animals that make tools with a specific purpose in mind. Chimpanzees living in the Tai forest of Ivory Coast make and use stone tools to break open hard, golfball-sized nuts (Mercader, Panger, and Boesch 2002; Wilford 2007*b*). Nut cracking is a learned skill, with mothers showing their young how to do it. In 1960, Jane Goodall began observing wild chimps—including their tool use and hunting behavior—at Gombe Stream National Park in Tanzania, East Africa (see Goodall 2010). The most studied form of ape tool making involves "termiting," in which chimps make tools to probe termite hills. They choose twigs, which they modify by removing leaves and peeling off bark to expose the sticky surface beneath. They carry the twigs to termite hills, dig holes with their fingers, and insert the twigs. Finally, they pull out the twigs and dine on termites that were attracted to the sticky surface. Given what is known about ape tool use and manufacture, it is almost certain that early hominins shared this ability, although the first evidence for hominin stone tool making dates back only 2.6 million years. In addition, bipedalism (moving around upright on two legs) would have permitted the carrying and use of tools and weapons against predators and competitors in an open grassland habitat.

The apes have other abilities essential to culture. Wild chimps and orangs aim and throw objects. Gorillas build nests, and they throw branches, grass, vines, and other objects. Hominins have elaborated the capacity to aim and throw, without which we never would have developed projectile technology and weaponry—or baseball.

Like tool making, hunting once was cited as a distinctive human activity not shared with the apes. Again, however, primate research shows that other primates, especially chimpanzees, are habitual hunters. For example, in Uganda's Kibale National Park chimps form large hunting parties, including an average of 26 individuals (almost always adult and adolescent males). Most hunts (78 percent) result in at least one prey item being caught—a much higher success rate than that among lions (26 percent),

Different forms of tool use by chimps. One photo shows a Liberian chimp using a hammer stone to crack palm nuts. The other shows chimps using prepared twigs to "fish" for termites from an ant hill. (first): © Clive Bromhall/Oxford Scientific/Getty Images; (second): © Stan Osolinski/Oxford Scientific/Getty Images

hyenas (34 percent), or cheetahs (30 percent). Chimps' favored prey there is the red colobus monkey (Mitani and Watts 1999).

Archaeological evidence suggests that humans have been hunting since at least 2.6 million years ago, based on stone tools found in Ethiopia and, later, at Olduvai Gorge in Tanzania. Given our current understanding of chimp hunting and tool making, we can infer that hominids may have been hunting much earlier than the first archaeological evidence attests. However, because chimps typically devour the monkeys they kill, leaving few remains, we may never find archaeological evidence for the first hominin hunt, especially if it was done without stone tools.

## How We Differ from Other Primates

Although chimps often share meat from a hunt, apes and monkeys (except for nursing infants) tend to feed themselves individually. Cooperation and sharing are much more developed among humans. Until fairly recently (12,000 to 10,000 years ago), all humans were hunter-gatherers who lived in small social groups called bands. In some world areas, the hunter-gatherer way of life persisted into recent times, permitting study by ethnographers. In such societies, men and women take resources back to the camp and share them. Everyone shares the meat from a large animal. Nourished and protected by younger band members, elders live past reproductive age and are respected for their knowledge and experience. Humans are among the most cooperative of the primates—in the food quest and other social activities. As well, the amount of information stored in a human band is far greater than that in any other primate group.

Another difference between humans and other primates involves mating. Among baboons and chimps, most mating occurs when females enter **estrus,** during which they ovulate. In estrus, the vaginal area swells and reddens, and receptive females form temporary bonds with, and mate with, males. Human females, by contrast, lack a visible estrus cycle, and their ovulation is concealed. Not knowing when ovulation is occurring, humans maximize their reproductive success by mating throughout the year. Human pair bonds for mating are more exclusive and more durable than are those of chimps. Related to our more constant sexuality, all human societies have some form of marriage. Marriage gives mating a reliable basis and grants to each spouse special, though not always exclusive, sexual rights in the other.

Marriage creates another major contrast between humans and other primates: exogamy and kinship systems. Most cultures have rules of exogamy requiring marriage outside one's kin or local group. Exogamy confers adaptive advantages because it creates ties between the spouses' different kin groups. Their children have relatives, and therefore allies, in two kin groups rather than just one. Such ties of affection and mutual support between members of different local groups tend to be absent among primates other than *Homo.* Other primates tend to disperse at adolescence. Among chimps and gorillas, females tend to migrate, seeking mates in other groups. Humans also choose mates from outside the natal group, and usually at least one spouse moves. However, *humans maintain lifelong ties with sons and daughters.* The systems of kinship and marriage that preserve these links provide a major contrast between humans and other primates (see Chapais 2008; Hill, Walker, et al. 2011). Table 2.1 lists differences in the cultural abilities of humans and chimpanzees, our nearest relatives.

TABLE 2.1    **Cultural Features of Chimpanzees (Rudimentary) and Humans (Fully Developed)**

|  | Chimpanzees | Humans |
|---|---|---|
| *Cultural learning* | Rudimentary | Fully developed |
| *Tool use* | Occasional | Habitual |
| *Tool manufacture* | Occasional: hammer stones, termiting | Habitual and sophisticated |
| *Aimed throwing* | Occasional objects, not tools | Projectile technology |
| *Hunting* | Significant, but no tools | Basic hominin subsistence strategy, with tools |
| *Food sharing* | Meat sharing after hunt | Basic to human life |
| *Cooperation* | Occasional in hunting | Basic to human life |
| *Mating and marriage* | Female estrus cycle, limited pair bonds | Year-round mating, marriage, and exogamy |
| *Kin ties* | Limited by dispersal at adolescence | Maintained through sons and daughters |

# Universality, Generality, and Particularity

Anthropologists agree that cultural learning is uniquely elaborated among humans and that all humans have culture. Anthropologists also accept a doctrine termed in the 19th century the "psychic unity" (biopsychological equality) of humankind. This means that although *individuals* differ in their emotional and intellectual tendencies and capacities, all human *populations* have equivalent capacities for culture. Regardless of their genes or their physical appearance, people can learn *any* cultural tradition.

To understand this point, consider that contemporary Americans and Canadians are the genetically mixed descendants of people from all over the world. Our ancestors were biologically varied, lived in different countries and continents, and participated in hundreds of cultural traditions. However, early colonists, later immigrants, and their descendants all have become active participants in American and Canadian life. All now share a national culture.

To recognize biopsychological equality is not to deny differences among populations. In studying human diversity in time and space, anthropologists distinguish among the universal, the generalized, and the particular. Certain biological, psychological, social, and cultural features are **universal,** found in every culture. Others are merely **generalities,** common to several but not all human groups. Still other traits are **particularities,** unique to certain cultural traditions.

## Universals and Generalities

Biologically based universals include a long period of infant dependency, year-round (rather than seasonal) sexuality, and a complex brain that enables us to use symbols, languages, and tools. Among the social universals is life in groups and in some kind of family. Generalities occur in certain times and places but not in all cultures. They may be widespread, but they are not universal. One cultural generality that is present in many but not all societies is the *nuclear family,* a kinship group consisting of parents and children. Although many middle-class Americans ethnocentrically view the nuclear family as a proper and "natural" group, it is not universal. It was absent, for example, among the Nayars, an ethnic group located on the Malabar Coast of India. Traditionally, the Nayars lived in female-headed households, and husbands and wives did not live together. In many other societies, the nuclear family is submerged in larger kin groups, such as extended families, lineages, and clans.

Societies can share beliefs and customs because of borrowing or (cultural) inheritance from a common cultural ancestor. Speaking English is a generality shared by North Americans and Australians because both countries had English settlers. Another reason for generalities is domination, as in colonial rule, when customs and procedures are imposed on one culture by another one that is more powerful. In many countries, use of the English language reflects colonial history. More recently, English has spread through **diffusion** (cultural borrowing, either direct or through intermediaries) to many other countries, as it has become the world's foremost language for business and travel.

## Particularity: Patterns of Culture

A cultural particularity is a trait or feature of culture that is not generalized or widespread; rather, it is confined to a single place, culture, or society. Yet because of cultural borrowing, which has accelerated through modern transportation and communication systems, traits that once were limited in their distribution have become more widespread. Traits that are useful, that have the capacity to please large audiences, and that don't clash with the cultural values of potential adopters are more likely to be borrowed than are others. Still, certain cultural particularities persist—for example, foods such as the pork barbecue with a mustard-based sauce available only in South Carolina and the "pasty," beef stew baked in pie dough, characteristic of Michigan's upper peninsula. Besides diffusion (which, for example, has spread McDonald's food outlets, once confined to San Bernadino, California, across the globe), there are other reasons that cultural particularities are increasingly rare. Many cultural traits are shared as cultural universals and as a result of independent invention. Facing similar problems, people in different places have come up with similar solutions. Again and again, similar cultural causes have produced similar cultural results.

At the level of the individual cultural trait or element (e.g., bow and arrow, hot dog, Netflix), particularities may be getting rarer. But at a higher level, particularity is more obvious. Different cultures emphasize different things. *Cultures are integrated and patterned differently and display tremendous variation and diversity.* When cultural traits are borrowed, they are modified to fit the culture that adopts them. They are *reintegrated*—patterned anew—to fit their new setting. Patterned beliefs, customs, and practices lend distinctiveness to particular cultural traditions.

Consider the universal life-cycle events, such as birth, puberty, marriage, parenthood, and death, that many cultures observe and celebrate. The occasions (e.g., marriage, death) may be the same and universal, but the patterns of ceremonial observance may be dramatically different. Cultures vary in just which events merit special celebration. Americans, for example, regard expensive weddings as more socially appropriate than lavish funerals. The Betsileo of Madagascar take the opposite view. The marriage ceremony is a minor event that brings together just the couple and a few close relatives. However, a funeral is a measure of the deceased person's social position and lifetime achievement, and it may attract a thousand people. Why use money on a house, the Betsileo say, when one can use it on the tomb where one will spend eternity in the company of dead relatives? Cremation, an increasingly common option in the United States, would horrify the Betsileo, for whom ancestral bones and relics are important ritual objects (see Sack 2011).

Cultures vary tremendously in their beliefs, practices, integration, and patterning. By focusing on and trying to explain alternative customs, anthropology forces us to reappraise our familiar ways of thinking. In a world full of cultural diversity, contemporary American culture is just one cultural variant, more powerful perhaps but no more natural than the others.

## Culture and the Individual: Agency and Practice

Generations of anthropologists have theorized about the relationship between the "system" on one hand and the "person" or "individual" on the other. *System* can refer to various concepts, including culture, society, social relations, or social structure. Individual human beings always make up, or constitute, the system. But living within that system, humans also are constrained (to some extent, at least) by its rules and by the actions of other individuals. Cultural rules provide guidance about what to do and how to do it, but people don't always do what the rules say should be done. People use their culture actively and creatively, rather than blindly following its dictates (see Handwerker 2009). Humans aren't passive beings doomed to follow their cultural traditions like programmed robots. Cultures are dynamic and constantly changing. People learn, interpret, and manipulate the same rule in different ways—or they emphasize different rules that better suit their interests. Culture is *contested:* Different groups in society struggle with one another over whose ideas, values, goals, and beliefs will prevail. Even common symbols may have radically different *meanings* to different individuals and groups in the same culture. Golden arches may cause one person to salivate, while another plots a vegetarian protest. The same flag may be waved to support or oppose a given war.

Even when they agree about what should be done, people don't always do as their culture directs or as other people expect. Many rules are violated, some very often (for example, automobile speed limits). Some anthropologists find it useful to distinguish between ideal and real culture. The *ideal culture* consists of what people say they should do and what they *say* they do. *Real culture* refers to their actual behavior as observed by the anthropologist.

Culture is both public and individual, both in the world and in people's minds. Anthropologists are interested not only in public and collective behavior but also in how *individuals* think, feel, and act. The individual and culture are linked because human social life is a process in which individuals internalize the meanings of *public* (i.e., cultural) messages. Then, alone and in groups, people influence culture by converting their private (and often divergent) understandings into public expressions (D'Andrade 1984).

Conventionally, culture has been seen as social glue transmitted across the generations, binding people through their common past, rather than as something being continually created and reworked in the present. The tendency to view culture as an entity rather than as a process is changing. Contemporary anthropologists now emphasize how day-to-day action, practice, or resistance can make and remake culture (Gupta and Ferguson 1997*b*). *Agency* refers to the actions that individuals take, both alone and in groups, in forming and transforming cultural identities.

The approach to culture known as *practice theory* (Ortner 1984) recognizes that individuals within a society or culture have diverse motives and intentions and different degrees of power and influence. Such contrasts may be associated with gender, age, ethnicity, class, and other social variables. Practice theory focuses on how such varied individuals—through their ordinary and extraordinary actions and practices—manage to influence, create, and transform the world they live in. Practice theory appropriately recognizes a reciprocal relation between culture (the system) and the individual. The system shapes how individuals experience and respond to external events, but individuals also play an active role in how society functions and changes. Practice theory recognizes both constraints on individuals and the flexibility and changeability of cultures and social systems.

# Popular, Civic, and Public Culture

In the contemporary world, the *systems* in which we participate as individuals are not merely local or regional; they have national and international scope. In this section, we focus on domains of national culture, which include popular, civic, and public culture. Any contemporary nation, such as the United States, Canada, Italy, Brazil, India, or Japan, has its national cultural traditions; its own media and popular culture; its own civic culture consisting of laws, institutions, and associations; and its own ways of doing things in public. To be sure, there are international spillovers. For example, the civic cultures of the United States, Canada, and India have been influenced by British law. The spillover is even greater in popular culture: American movies are watched world-wide; Rupert Murdock, owner of Fox News and *The Wall Street Journal*, is a powerful media mogul who influences public opinion in the United States, the United Kingdom, and other nations; one can take yoga or Bollywood classes in Los Angeles; Godzilla has visited New York. Despite its international spread, popular culture still varies and is patterned differently from country to country.

Today's consumption patterns both reflect and fuel *popular culture,* supplying widely shared images, information, narratives, products, events, and celebrations that have meaning for many or most people within the same national culture. American ex-amples include Thanksgiving, Halloween, homecoming dances, reality shows, dinner-and-a-movie dates, and retirement parties. Although popular culture is available to us all, we use it selectively, and its meaning varies from one person to the next. The media scholar John Fiske (1989, 2011) argues that each individual's use of popular culture is a creative act. For example, the World Cup, the Super Bowl, Taylor Swift, *The Hunger Games,* and *The Simpsons* mean something different to each of their fans. All of us creatively consume and interpret print media, music, television, films, theme parks, celebrities, politicians, and other popular culture products.

A nation's *civic culture* includes its citizens' compliance with the legal system, participation in formal elections, and membership in voluntary and faith-based asso-ciations. Fellow countrymen and -women also share a *public culture:* generally ac-cepted social behaviors, dress codes, speech, and other forms of expression that citizens enact in public spaces, including bars, parks, malls, and even grieving sites, such as Ground Zero (see Morrill, Snow, and White 2005; Shaffer 2008; and this chapter's "Anthropology Today").

# Levels of Culture

Anthropologists also recognize cultural systems—levels of culture—that are larger and smaller than nation-states. **National culture,** examined in the previous section, embodies those beliefs, learned behavior patterns, values, and institutions that are shared by citizens of the same nation. **International culture** extends beyond and across national boundaries. Because culture is transmitted through learning rather than genetics, cultural traits can spread through borrowing, or diffusion, from one group to another.

Because of diffusion, migration, colonialism, and globalization, many cultural traits and patterns have acquired international scope. The contemporary United States, Canada, Great Britain, and Australia share cultural traits they have inherited from their common linguistic and cultural ancestors in Great Britain. Roman Catholics in many countries share beliefs, symbols, experiences, and values transmitted by their church. The World Cup has become an international cultural event, as people in many countries know the rules of, play, and follow soccer.

Cultures also can be smaller than nations (see Jenks 2005). Although people who live in the same country share a national cultural tradition, all cultures also contain diversity. Individuals, families, communities, regions, classes, and other groups within a culture have different learning experiences, as well as shared ones. **Subcultures** are different symbol-based patterns and traditions associated with particular groups in the same complex society. In large or diverse nations such as the United States or Canada, a variety of subcultures originate in region, ethnicity, language, class, and religion. The religious backgrounds of Jews, Baptists, and Roman Catholics create subcultural differences among them. While sharing a national culture, U.S. northerners and southerners also differ in their beliefs, values, and customary behavior as a result of national and regional history. French-speaking Canadians sometimes pointedly contrast with English-speaking people in the same country. Italian Americans have ethnic traditions different from those of Irish, Polish, and African Americans.

Nowadays, many anthropologists are reluctant to use the term *subculture*. They feel that the prefix *sub-* is offensive because it means "below." Subcultures thus may be perceived as "less than" or somehow inferior to a dominant, elite, or national culture. In this discussion of levels of culture, I intend no such implication. My point is simply that nations may contain many different culturally defined groups. As mentioned earlier, culture is contested. Various groups may strive to promote the correctness and value of their own practices, values, and beliefs in comparison with those of other groups or the nation as a whole.

## Ethnocentrism, Cultural Relativism, and Human Rights

**Ethnocentrism** is the tendency to view one's own culture as superior and to apply one's own cultural values in judging the behavior and beliefs of people raised in other cultures. We hear ethnocentric statements all the time. Ethnocentrism contributes to social solidarity, a sense of value and community, among people who share a cultural tradition. People everywhere think that the familiar explanations, opinions, and customs are true, right, proper, and moral. They regard different behavior as strange, immoral, or savage. Often other societies are not considered fully human. Their members may be castigated as cannibals, thieves, or people who do not bury their dead.

Among several tribes in the Trans-Fly region of Papua New Guinea, sexual activity between males was valued over sex acts involving males and females (see the chapter "Gender"). Men who grew up in the Etoro tribe (Kelly 1976) favored oral sex between males, while their neighbors, the Marind-anim, encouraged men to engage in anal sex.

(In both groups heterosexual intercourse was stigmatized and allowed only for reproduction.) Etoro men considered Marind-anim anal sex to be disgusting, seeing nothing abnormal about their own oral practices.

Opposing ethnocentrism is **cultural relativism,** the viewpoint that behavior in one culture should not be judged by the standards of another culture. This position also can present problems. At its most extreme, cultural relativism argues that there is no superior, international, or universal morality, that the moral and ethical rules of all cultures deserve equal respect. In the extreme relativist view, Nazi Germany would be evaluated as nonjudgmentally as Athenian Greece.

In today's world, human rights advocates challenge many of the tenets of cultural relativism. For example, several societies in Africa and the Middle East have traditions of female genital modification (FGM). *Clitoridectomy* is the removal of a girl's clitoris. *Infibulation* involves sewing the lips (labia) of the vagina, to constrict the vaginal opening. Both procedures reduce female sexual pleasure and, it is believed in some cultures, the likelihood of adultery. Such practices have been opposed by human rights advocates, especially women's rights groups. The idea is that the tradition infringes on a basic human right—disposition over one's body and one's sexuality. Some African countries have banned or otherwise discouraged the procedures, as have Western nations that receive immigration from such cultures. Similar issues arise with circumcision and other male genital operations. Is it proper to require adolescent boys to undergo collective circumcision to fulfill cultural tradition, as has been done in parts of Africa and Australia? Is it right for a baby boy to be circumcised without his permission, as has been done routinely in the United States and as is customary among Jews and Muslims? (A 2011 initiative aimed at banning circumcision in San Francisco, California, failed to make it to the ballot.)

Some would argue that the problems with relativism can be solved by distinguishing between methodological and moral relativism (see Kellenberger 2008). In anthropology, cultural relativism is not a moral position but a methodological one. It states: To understand another culture fully, you must try to see how the people in that culture see things. What motivates them—what are they thinking—when they do those things? Such an approach does not preclude making moral judgments or taking action. When faced with Nazi atrocities, a methodological relativist would have a moral obligation to stop doing anthropology and take action to intervene. In the FGM example, one only can understand the *motivations* for the practice by looking at the situation from the point of view of those who engage in it. Having done this, one then faces the moral question of whether to intervene to stop it. We should recognize as well that different people and groups living in the same society—for example, women and men, old and young, the more and less powerful—can have widely different views about what is proper, necessary, and moral (see Hunt 2007).

The idea of **human rights** invokes a realm of justice and morality beyond and superior to the laws and customs of particular countries, cultures, and religions (see Donnelly 2013). Human rights include the rights to speak freely, to hold religious beliefs without persecution, and not to be murdered, injured, or enslaved or imprisoned without charge. Such rights are seen as *inalienable* (nations cannot abridge or terminate them) and international (larger than and superior to individual nations and cultures). Four

The notion of indigenous property rights has arisen in an attempt to conserve each society's cultural base, including its medicinal plants. The hoodia plant (shown here in Botswana) is a Kalahari Desert cactus used by the San people to stave off hunger. HoodiaThin is a commercial appetite suppressant made from imported hoodia and distributed by Los Angeles–based Prime Life Nutritionals. Hoodia is grown today on a few commercial farms in southern Africa (including the San-owned farm shown here). (first): © J.D. Dallet/age fotostock; (second): © ZUMA Press, Inc./Alamy

United Nations documents describe nearly all the human rights that have been internationally recognized. Those documents are the U.N. Charter; the Universal Declaration of Human Rights; the Covenant on Economic, Social and Cultural Rights; and the Covenant on Civil and Political Rights.

Alongside the human rights movement has arisen an awareness of the need to preserve cultural rights. Unlike human rights, **cultural rights** are vested not in individuals but in *groups,* such as religious and ethnic minorities and indigenous societies. Cultural rights include a group's ability to preserve its culture, to raise its children in the ways of its forebears, to continue its language, and not to be deprived of its economic base by the nation in which it is located. The related notion of indigenous **intellectual property rights (IPR)** has arisen in an attempt to conserve each society's cultural base—its core beliefs, knowledge, and practices. Much traditional cultural knowledge has commercial value. Examples include ethnomedicine (traditional medical knowledge and techniques), cosmetics, cultivated plants, foods, folklore, arts, crafts, songs, dances, costumes, and rituals. According to the IPR concept, a particular group may determine how indigenous knowledge and its products may be used and distributed and the level of compensation required.

The notion of cultural rights is related to the idea of cultural relativism, and the problem discussed previously arises again. What does one do about cultural rights that interfere with human rights? I believe that anthropology's main job is to present accurate accounts and explanations of cultural phenomena. The anthropologist doesn't have to approve infanticide, cannibalism, or torture to record their existence and determine their causes and the motivations behind them. However, each anthropologist has a choice about where he or she will do fieldwork. Some anthropologists choose not to study a particular culture because they discover in advance or early in fieldwork that behavior they consider morally repugnant is practiced there. Anthropologists respect human diversity. Most ethnographers try to be objective, accurate, and sensitive in their accounts of other cultures. However, objectivity, sensitivity, and a cross-cultural perspective don't mean that anthropologists have to ignore international standards of justice and morality. What do you think?

## Mechanisms of Cultural Change

Why and how do cultures change? One way is diffusion, or borrowing, of traits between cultures. Such exchange of information and products has gone on throughout human history because cultures never have been truly isolated. Contact between neighboring groups has always existed and has extended over vast areas (Boas 1940/1966). Diffusion is *direct* when two cultures trade with, intermarry among, or wage war on one another. Diffusion is *forced* when one culture subjugates another and imposes its customs on the dominated group. Diffusion is *indirect* when items or traits move from group A to group C via group B without any firsthand contact between A and C. In this case, group B might consist of traders or merchants who take products from a variety of places to new markets. Or group B might be geographically situated between A and C, so that what it gets from A eventually winds up in C, and vice versa. In today's world, much international diffusion is indirect—culture spread by the mass media and advanced information technology.

**Acculturation,** a second mechanism of cultural change, is the ongoing exchange of cultural features that results when groups have continuous firsthand contact. The cultures of either or both groups may be changed by this contact (Redfield, Linton, and Herskovits 1936). With acculturation, parts of the cultures change, but each group remains distinct. In situations of acculturation, cultures have exchanged and blended foods, recipes, music, dances, clothing, tools, languages, and technologies.

**Independent invention**—the process by which humans innovate, creatively finding solutions to problems—is a third mechanism of cultural change. Faced with comparable problems and challenges, people in different societies have innovated and changed in similar ways, which is one reason cultural generalities exist. One example is the independent invention of agriculture in the Middle East and Mexico. Often a major invention, such as agriculture, triggers a series of subsequent, interrelated changes. Thus, in both Mexico and the Middle East, agriculture led to many social, political, and legal changes, including notions of property and distinctions in wealth, class, and power.

# Globalization

The term **globalization** encompasses a series of processes that work transnationally to promote change in a world in which nations and people are increasingly interlinked and mutually dependent. The forces of globalization include international commerce and finance, travel and tourism, transnational migration, and the media—including the Internet and other high-tech information flows (see Friedman and Friedman 2008; Haugerud, Stone, and Little 2011; Kjaerulff 2010). New economic unions (which have met considerable resistance in their member nations) have been created through the World Trade Organization (WTO), the International Monetary Fund (IMF), and the European Union (EU).

The media, including the Internet, play a key role in globalization. Long-distance communication is faster and easier than ever and now covers most of the globe. I can now e-mail, call, or Skype families in Arembepe, Brazil, which lacked phones and even postal service when I first began to study the community. Information about Arembepe is now available to anyone, including potential tourists, on hundreds of websites. Anything can be Googled. The media help propel a transnational culture of consumption, as they spread information about products, services, rights, institutions, lifestyles, and the perceived costs and benefits of globalization. Emigrants transmit information and resources transnationally, as they maintain their ties with home (phoning, Skyping, texting, e-mailing, visiting, sending money). In a sense, such people live multilocally—in different places and cultures at once. They learn to play various social roles and to change behavior and identity depending on the situation.

Local people must cope increasingly with forces generated by progressively larger systems—region, nation, and world. An army of outsiders and potential change agents now intrudes on people everywhere. Tourism has become the world's number one industry. Economic development agents and the media promote the idea that work should be for cash rather than mainly for subsistence. The effects of globalization aren't always welcome. Indigenous peoples and traditional societies have devised various strategies to deal with threats to their autonomy, identity, and livelihood (Maybury-Lewis, Macdonald, and Maybury-Lewis 2009). New forms of cultural expression and political mobilization, including the rights movements discussed previously, are emerging from the interplay of local, regional, national, and international cultural forces (see Ong and Collier 2005).

Illustrating political mobilization against globalization are regular protests at meetings of the principal agencies concerned with international trade. Protesters continue to show their disapproval of policies of the WTO, the IMF, and the World Bank. Anti-globalization activists fault those organizations for policies that, they say, promote corporate wealth at the expense of farmers, workers, and others at or near the bottom of the economy. Protesters also include environmentalists seeking tougher environmental regulations and trade unionists advocating global labor standards. Related to these protests was the 2011 Occupy movement, which quickly spread from Wall Street to other American (and Canadian) cities. That movement protested growing North American inequality—between the top 1 percent and everyone else. Do you consider such protests valid and effective? What's your opinion of globalization?

## Anthropology Today *Experiencing Culture: Personal Space and Displays of Affection*

A few years ago I created and taught a course called Experiencing Culture to American college students in Italy. Students wrote biweekly journals reflecting on the cultural differences they observed between Europeans and Americans. One thing that really struck them was the greater frequency and intensity of PDAs—public displays of affection—between romantic couples in Italy, compared with the United States.

The world's nations and cultures have strikingly different notions about displays of affection and personal space. Cocktail parties in international meeting places such as the United Nations can resemble an elaborate insect mating ritual

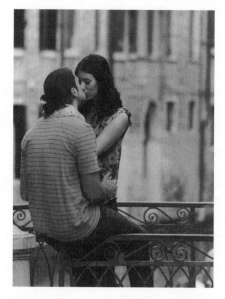

What do you think of this public display of affection by a young couple in Venice, Italy? How would such behavior be viewed in your hometown? © Alan Bailey/Getty Images RF

as diplomats from different countries advance, withdraw, and sidestep. When Americans talk, walk, and dance, they maintain a certain distance from others. Italians and Brazilians, who need less personal space, may interpret such "standoffishness" as a sign of coldness. In conversational pairs, the Italian or Brazilian typically moves in, while the American "instinctively" retreats from a "close talker." Such bodily movements illustrate not instinct, but culture—behavior programmed by years of exposure to a particular cultural tradition.

To what extent are you a product of your culture? How much does, and should, your cultural background influence your actions and decisions? Americans may not fully appreciate the power of culture because of the value their culture places on the individual. We have seen that individualism is a distinctive *shared* value, a feature of American culture, transmitted constantly in our daily lives. In the media, count how many stories focus on individuals versus groups. That we are individuals first and members of groups second is the opposite of this chapter's lesson about culture. Certainly we have distinctive features because we are individuals, but we have other distinct attributes because we belong to cultural groups.

To return to the cultural contrast that so impressed my American students in Italy, there are striking contrasts between a national culture (American) that tends to be reserved about displays of physical affection and national cultures in which the opposite is true. Brazilians approach, touch, and kiss one another much more frequently than North Americans do. Middle-class Brazilians teach their kids—both

*continued*

## Anthropology Today   *continued*

boys and girls—to kiss (on the cheek, two or three times, coming and going) every adult relative they ever see. Given the size of Brazilian extended families, this can mean hundreds of people. Women continue kissing all those people throughout their lives. Until they are adolescents, boys kiss all adult relatives. Men typically continue to kiss female relatives and friends, as well as their fathers and uncles throughout their lives.

Do you kiss your father? Your uncle? Your grandfather? How about your mother, aunt, or grandmother? The answers to these questions may differ between men and women, and for male and female relatives. Culture can help us make sense of these differences. In America, a cultural homophobia (fear of homosexuality) may prevent American men from engaging in displays of affection with other men. Similarly, American girls typically are encouraged to show affection; this is less true for boys.

However, culture is not static. Sarah Kershaw (2009) describes a surge of teenage hugging behavior in American schools. Concerned about potential sexual harassment issues, parents and school officials remain suspicious of such PDAs, even if the younger generation is more tolerant. Even American boys appear to be more likely nowadays to share nonromantic hugs, as such expressions as "bromance" and "man crush" enter our vocabulary. Hugging also has migrated online, where Facebook applications allowing friends to send hugs have tens of thousands of fans.

It's important to note that cultural traits exist because they are learned, not because they are natural or inherently right. Ethnocentrism is the error of viewing one's own culture as superior and applying one's own cultural values in judging people from other cultures. How easy is it for you to see beyond the ethnocentric blinders of your own experience? Do you have an ethnocentric position regarding displays of affection?

## Summary

1. *Culture,* which is distinctive to humanity, refers to customary behavior and beliefs that are passed on through enculturation. Culture rests on the human capacity for cultural learning. Culture encompasses rules for conduct internalized in human beings, which lead them to think and act in characteristic ways.

2. Although other animals learn, only humans have cultural learning, dependent on symbols. Humans think symbolically—arbitrarily bestowing meaning on things and events. By convention, a symbol stands for something with which it has no necessary or natural relation. Symbols have special meaning for people who share memories, values, and beliefs because of common enculturation.

3. Cultural traditions mold biologically based desires and needs in particular directions. Everyone is cultured, not just people with elite educations. Cultures may be integrated and patterned through economic and social forces, key symbols, and core values. Cultural rules don't rigidly dictate our behavior. There is room for creativity, flexibility, diversity, and disagreement within societies. Cultural means of adaptation have been crucial in human evolution. Aspects of culture also can be maladaptive.

4. The human capacity for culture has an evolutionary basis that extends back at least 2.6 million years—to early toolmakers whose products survive in the archaeological record (and most probably even further back—based on observation of tool use and manufacture by apes). Humans share with monkeys and apes such traits as manual dexterity (especially opposable thumbs), depth and color vision, learning ability based on a large brain, substantial parental investment in a limited number of offspring, and tendencies toward sociality and cooperation.

5. Many hominin traits are foreshadowed in other primates, particularly in the African apes, which, like us, belong to the hominid family. The ability to learn, basic to culture, is an adaptive advantage available to monkeys and apes. Chimpanzees make tools for several purposes. They also hunt and share meat. Sharing and cooperation are more developed among humans than among the apes, and only humans have systems of kinship and marriage that permit us to maintain lifelong ties with relatives in different local groups.

6. Using a comparative perspective, anthropology examines biological, psychological, social, and cultural universals and generalities. There also are unique and distinctive aspects of the human condition (cultural particularities). North American cultural traditions are no more natural than any others. Levels of culture can be larger or smaller than a nation. Cultural traits may be shared across national boundaries. Nations also include cultural differences associated with ethnicity, region, and social class.

7. Ethnocentrism describes judging other cultures by using one's own cultural standards. Cultural relativism, which anthropologists may use as a methodological position rather than a moral stance, is the idea of avoiding the use of outside standards to judge behavior in a given society. Human rights are those based on justice and morality beyond and superior to particular countries, cultures, and religions. Cultural rights are vested in religious and ethnic minorities and indigenous societies, and IPR, or intellectual property rights, apply to an indigenous group's collective knowledge and its applications.

8. Diffusion, migration, and colonialism have carried cultural traits and patterns to different world areas. Mechanisms of cultural change include diffusion, acculturation, and independent invention. Globalization comprises a series of processes that promote change in a world in which nations and people are interlinked and mutually dependent.

## Key Terms

| | | |
|---|---|---|
| acculturation, *33* | generality, *26* | international culture, *29* |
| core values, *20* | globalization, *34* | national culture, *29* |
| cultural relativism, *31* | hominids, *22* | particularity, *26* |
| cultural rights, *32* | hominins, *22* | subcultures, *30* |
| diffusion, *26* | human rights, *31* | symbol, *18* |
| enculturation, *18* | independent invention, *33* | universal, *26* |
| estrus, *25* | intellectual property rights (IPR), *32* | |
| ethnocentrism, *30* | | |

# Chapter

# 3

# Doing Anthropology

"Been on any digs lately?" Ask your professor how many times she or he has been asked this question. Then ask how often he or she actually has been on a dig. Remember that anthropology has four subfields, only two of which (archaeology and biological anthropology) require much digging—in the ground, at least. Even among biological anthropologists, it's mainly paleoanthropologists (those concerned with the hominin fossil record) who must dig. Students of primate behavior in the wild, such as Jane Goodall, don't do it. Nor, most of the time, is it done by forensic anthropologists, such as the title character in the TV series *Bones*.

To be sure, cultural anthropologists "dig out" information about lifestyles, as linguistic anthropologists do about the features of language. Traditionally, cultural anthropologists have done a variant on the *Star Trek* theme of seeking out, if not new, at least different "life" and "civilizations," sometimes boldly going where no scientist has gone before.

Despite globalization, the cultural diversity under anthropological scrutiny right now may be as great as ever before, because the anthropological universe has expanded to modern nations. Today's cultural anthropologists are as likely to study artists in Miami or bankers in Beirut as Polynesians in outrigger canoes. Still, we can't forget that anthropology did originate in non-Western, nonindustrial societies. Its research techniques, especially those subsumed under the label "ethnography," were developed to deal with small populations. Even when working in modern nations, anthropologists still consider ethnography with small groups to be an excellent way of learning about how people live their lives and make decisions.

Before this course, did you know the names of any anthropologists? If so, which ones—real or fictional? For the general public, biological anthropologists and archaeologists tend to be better known than cultural anthropologists because of what they study and discover—making them attractive subjects for the Discovery channel. You're more likely to have seen film of Jane Goodall with chimps or a paleoanthropologist holding a skull than a linguistic or cultural anthropologist at work. Archaeologists occasionally appear in the media to describe a new discovery or to debunk pseudo-archaeological arguments about, say, how visitors from space have left traces on Earth. One cultural anthropologist was an important public and media figure for much of the 20th century. Margaret Mead, famed for her work on teen sexuality in Samoa and gender roles in New Guinea, may well be the most famous anthropologist who ever lived. Mead, one of my own professors at Columbia University, appeared regularly on NBC's *Tonight Show*. In all her venues, including teaching, museum work, TV, anthropological films, popular books, and magazines, Mead helped Americans appreciate the relevance of anthropology to understanding their daily lives. That's a worthy goal that more contemporary anthropologists should emulate.

This chapter is about what anthropologists do. It focuses on archaeology, biological anthropology, and sociocultural anthropology. Linguistic methods are discussed in Chapter 10; applied anthropology in Chapter 17. (Given space limitations in a brief introductory textbook such as this, only some of the many methods and techniques employed by anthropologists can be covered here.)

# Research Methods in Archaeology and Biological Anthropology

Recall from Chapter 1 that archaeology and biological (physical) anthropology are two of anthropology's four subfields. Anthropological archaeology reconstructs human behavior through the analysis of material remains (and other sources, including written records, if available). Biological anthropologists study living humans (e.g., their genetics, growth, development, and physiological adaptation) and other primates, as well as ancient ones. Paleoanthropologists study human evolution through skeletal material and other material remains. Doing so, biological anthropologists share many research interests and techniques with archaeologists. Members of both subfields must collaborate with many other kinds of scientists to do their work effectively.

## Multidisciplinary Approaches

Scientists from diverse fields—e.g., soil science and **paleontology** (the study of ancient life through the fossil record)—collaborate with anthropologists in the study of sites where artifacts or fossils have been found. *Palynology,* the study of ancient plants through pollen samples, can be used to determine a site's former environment. Physicists and chemists help archaeologists and biological anthropologists with dating techniques. By examining human skeletons, *bioarchaeologists* can reconstruct their physical traits, health status, and diet (Larsen 2015; Martin 2013; Perry 2012). Evidence for social status may endure in hard materials—bones, jewels, buildings—through the ages. Chemical differences among bones at a site may help distinguish elites from less privileged commoners.

To reconstruct ancient human biological and cultural features, anthropologists and their collaborators analyze the remains of humans, plants, and animals, as well as such artifacts (manufactured items) as ceramics, casts, and metals. Visible remains found at archaeological sites include bones, charcoal from ancient fires, burials, and storage pits. Archaeologists also can draw on microscopic evidence, including fossil pollen, *phytoliths* (plant crystals), and starch grains. A phytolith is a microscopic crystal found in wheat, rice, maize, manioc (cassava), and other early domesticates. Because phytoliths are inorganic and don't decay, they can reveal which plants were present even when no other plant remains survive. Phytoliths can be recovered from teeth, tools, containers, ritual objects, and garden plots.

Starch grain analysis recovers microfossils of food plants from the stone tools used to process them. Starch grains preserve well in areas, such as the humid tropics, where other organic remains typically decay. These grains have been recovered from stone tools, pottery fragments, and basketry, as well as human coprolites (ancient feces) (Bryant 2003, 2007*a*, 2007*b*). Vaughn Bryant (2007*b*; 2013) presents a strong case for the importance of such microscopic evidence in studying the past. As one example, he cites Bonnie Williamson's analysis of Middle to Late Stone Age tools from a cave site in South Africa. Examining hundreds of stone tools, Williamson found that many still had residues stuck to their cutting edges. Previously, it had been assumed that these tools were used by men to hunt and butcher animals, but Williamson found that over 50 percent of all the residues were from plants. Williamson's analysis suggested an important role for women (in gathering and processing plant foods) in these early cultures.

Anthropologists also work with geologists, geographers, and other scientists in using satellite images to find ancient footpaths, roads, canals, and irrigation systems, which can then be investigated on the ground. Aerial photos (taken from airplanes) and satellite images are forms of *remote sensing* used in site location. Anthropologists have used satellite imagery to identify, and then investigate on the ground, regions where deforestation is especially severe and where people and bio-diversity, including nonhuman primates, may be at risk (Green and Sussman 1990; Kottak 1999).

## Studying the Past

Archaeologists and biological anthropologists share techniques that enable them to re-construct the human past. The field of **paleoanthropology** studies the fossil record of human evolution. **Fossils** are remains (e.g., bones), traces, or impressions (e.g., foot-prints) of ancient life forms. Typically, a team composed of scientists, students, and local workers participates in a paleoanthropological or archaeological study. Such teams may also include paleontologists, geologists, palynologists, paleoecologists, physicists, and chemists. Paleontologists help locate fossil beds containing remains of animals that can be dated and that are known to have coexisted with hominins at particular times. Good preservation of faunal (animal) remains may suggest that hominin fossils have survived as well. Sometimes it's impossible to date the hominin fossils and artifacts found at a given site by using the most accurate and direct (radiometric) methods. In this case, comparison of the faunal remains at that site with similar, but more securely dated, fauna at another site may suggest a date for those animal fossils and the hominins and artifacts associated with them.

## Survey and Excavation

Once potential sites have been identified, more intensive surveying begins in the search for hominin traces—bones or tools. Some early hominin sites are strewn with thousands of tools. Typically, archaeologists, paleoanthropologists, and paleontologists combine both local (excavation) and regional (systematic survey) perspectives. They recognize that sites may not be discrete and isolated, but parts of larger systems.

### Systematic Survey

**Systematic survey** provides a regional perspective by gathering information on settlement patterns over a large area. *Settlement pattern* refers to the distribution of sites within a region. Regional surveys reconstruct settlement patterns by address-ing several questions: Where were sites located? How big were they? What kinds of buildings did they have? How old are the sites? Ideally, a systematic survey in-volves walking over the entire survey area and recording the location and size of all sites. From artifacts found on the surface, the surveyor estimates when each site was occupied.

### Excavation

During an **excavation,** scientists dig through the layers of deposits that make up a site. These layers, or strata, are used to establish the time order of materials. This relative chronology is based on the principle of *superposition:* In an undisturbed sequence of strata, the oldest layer is on the bottom. Each successive layer above is younger than the one below. This relative time ordering of material lies at the heart of archaeological, paleoanthropological, and paleontological research.

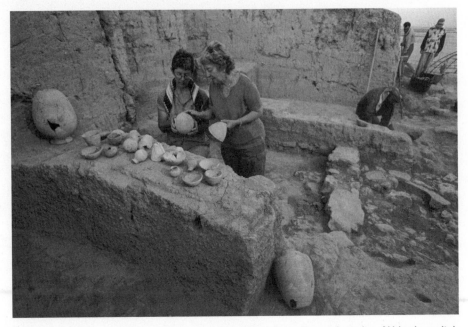

In Syria, researchers examine vessels at an archaeological site (the ancient city of Urkesh, capital of the Hurrian kingdom, dating back to 2400 B.C.E.). © Kenneth Garrett/National Geographic Stock

The archaeological and fossil records are so rich, and excavation is so labor intensive and expensive, that nobody digs a site without a good reason. Sites are excavated because they are endangered, or because they answer specific research questions (see Sabloff 2008). Cultural resource management (CRM) focuses on managing the preservation of archaeological sites that are threatened by modern development. Many countries require archaeological impact studies before construction can take place. If a site is at risk and the development cannot be stopped, CRM archaeologists are called in to salvage what information they can from the site (see King 2011).

## Kinds of Archaeology

Archaeologists pursue diverse research topics, using a wide variety of methods (see Renfrew and Bahn 2010). Experimental archaeologists try to replicate ancient techniques and processes (e.g., tool making). Historical archaeologists use written records as guides and supplements to archaeological research. Colonial archaeologists are historical archaeologists who use written records to locate postcontact sites in North and South America and to verify or question the written accounts. Classical archaeologists focus on the literate civilizations of the Old World, such as Greece, Rome, and Egypt. Underwater archaeology is a growing field that investigates submerged sites, most often shipwrecks.

# Dating the Past

The archaeological record hasn't revealed every ancient society that has existed on Earth; nor is the fossil record a representative sample of all the plants and animals that ever have lived. Some species and body parts are better represented than others are, for many reasons. Bones and teeth preserve better than do soft parts, such as flesh and skin. The chances of fossilization increase when remains are buried in silt, gravel, or sand. Good places for bone preservation include swamps, floodplains, river deltas, lakes, and caves. Species living in such areas have a better chance to be preserved than do animals in other habitats. Fossilization also is favored in areas with volcanic ash. Once remains do get buried, chemical conditions must be right for fossilization to occur. If the sediment is too acidic, even bones and teeth will dissolve. The study of the processes that affect the remains of dead animals is called **taphonomy,** from the Greek *taphos,* which means "tomb." Such processes include scattering by carnivores and scavengers, distortion by various forces, and the possible fossilization of the remains.

The conditions under which fossils are found also influence the fossil record. For example, fossils are more likely to be uncovered through erosion in arid areas than in wet areas. Sparse vegetation allows wind to scour the landscape and uncover fossils. The fossil record has been accumulating longer in Europe than in Africa because civil engineering projects and fossil hunting have been going on longer in the former than the latter. A world map showing where fossils have been found does not indicate the true range of ancient animals. Such a map tells us more about ancient geological activity, modern erosion, or recent human activity—such as paleontological research or road building. In considering the fossil record in later chapters, we'll see that certain areas provide more abundant fossil evidence for particular time periods. This doesn't necessarily mean that primates or hominins were living only in that area at that time. Nor does failure to find a fossil species in a particular place always mean the species didn't live there.

## Relative Dating

Scientists use a variety of techniques to date fossils. These methods offer different degrees of precision and are applicable to different periods of the past. Dating may be relative or absolute. **Relative dating** provides a time frame in relation to other strata or materials rather than absolute dates in numbers. Many dating methods are based on the geological study of **stratigraphy,** the science that examines the ways in which earth sediments accumulate in strata (singular, *stratum*). Soil that erodes from a hillside into a valley covers, and is younger than, the soil already deposited there. Stratigraphy permits relative dating. That is, the fossils in a given stratum are younger than those below them and older than those above them. We may not know the exact or absolute dates of the fossils, but we can place them in time relative to remains in other layers. Remains of animals and plants that lived at the same time are found in the same stratum. When fossils are found in a particular stratum, the associated geological features (such as frost patterning) and remains of particular plants and animals offer clues about the climate at the time of deposition.

## Absolute Dating

Fossils can be dated more precisely, with dates in numbers **(absolute dating),** by using several methods. For example, the $^{14}C$, or carbon-14, technique is used to date organic remains. This is a *radiometric* technique (so called because it measures radioactive decay). $^{14}C$ is an unstable radioactive isotope of normal carbon, $^{12}C$. Cosmic radiation entering the Earth's atmosphere produces $^{14}C$, and plants take in $^{14}C$ as they absorb carbon dioxide. $^{14}C$ moves up the food chain as animals eat plants and as predators eat other animals.

With death, the absorption of $^{14}C$ stops. This unstable isotope starts to break down into nitrogen ($^{14}N$). It takes 5,730 years for half the $^{14}C$ to change to nitrogen; this is the half-life of $^{14}C$. After another 5,730 years, one-quarter of the original $^{14}C$ will remain. After yet another 5,730 years, one-eighth will be left. By measuring the proportion of $^{14}C$ in organic material, scientists can determine a fossil's date of death, or the date of an ancient campfire. However, because the half-life of $^{14}C$ is short, this dating technique is less dependable for specimens older than 40,000 years than it is for more recent remains.

Fortunately, other radiometric dating techniques are available for earlier periods. One of the most widely used is the potassium-argon (K/A) technique. $^{40}K$ is a radioactive isotope of potassium that breaks down into argon-40, a gas. The half-life of $^{40}K$ is far longer than that of $^{14}C$—1.3 billion years. With this method, the older the specimen, the more reliable the dating. Furthermore, whereas $^{14}C$ dating can be done only on organic remains, K/A dating can be used only for inorganic substances: rocks and minerals. $^{40}K$ in rocks gradually breaks down into argon-40. That gas is trapped in the rock until the rock is heated intensely (as with volcanic activity), at which point it may escape. When the rock cools, the breakdown of potassium into argon resumes. Dating is done by reheating the rock and measuring the escaping gas.

In Africa's Great Rift Valley, which runs down eastern Africa and in which early hominin fossils abound, past volcanic activity permits K/A dating. In studies of strata containing fossils, scientists find out how much argon has accumulated in rocks since they were last heated. They then determine, using the standard $^{40}K$ deterioration rate (half-life), the date of that heating. Considering volcanic rocks at the top of a stratum with fossil remains, scientists establish that the fossils are older than, say, 1.8 million years. By dating the volcanic rocks below the fossil remains, they determine that the fossils are *younger than,* say, 2 million years. Thus, the age of the fossils is set at between 2.0 million and 1.8 million years. Note that absolute dating is "absolute" in name only; it may give ranges of numbers rather than exact dates.

Many fossils were discovered before the advent of modern stratigraphy. Often we can no longer determine their original stratigraphic placement. Furthermore, fossils aren't always discovered in volcanic layers. Like $^{14}C$ dating, the K/A technique applies to a limited period of the fossil record. Because the half-life of $^{40}K$ is so long, the technique cannot be used with materials less than 500,000 years old.

Other radiometric dating techniques can be used to cross-check K/A dates, again by using minerals surrounding the fossils. One such method, *uranium series dating,* measures fission tracks produced during the decay of radioactive uranium ($^{238}U$) into lead.

TABLE 3.1   **Absolute Dating Techniques**

| Technique | Abbreviation | Materials Dated | Effective Time Range |
|---|---|---|---|
| Carbon-14 | $^{14}$C | Organic materials | Up to 40,000 years |
| Potassium-argon | K/A and $^{40}$K | Volcanic rock | Older than 500,000 years |
| Uranium series | $^{238}$U | Minerals | Between 1,000 and 1,000,000 years |
| Thermoluminescence | TL | Rocks and minerals | Between 5,000 and 1,000,000 years |
| Electron spin resonance | ESR | Rocks and minerals | Between 1,000 and 1,000,000 years |

Two other radiometric techniques are especially useful for fossils that can't be dated by $^{14}$C (up to 40,000 B.P.—before the present) or $^{40}$K (more than 500,000 B.P.). These methods are *thermoluminescence (TL)* and *electron spin resonance (ESR)*. Both TL and ESR measure the electrons that are constantly being trapped in rocks and minerals. Once a date is obtained for a rock found associated with a fossil, that date also can be applied to that fossil. Table 3.1 summarizes the time spans for which the various absolute dating techniques are applicable.

## Molecular Anthropology

**Molecular anthropology** uses genetic analysis (of DNA sequences) to date, and to estimate evolutionary distance between, species. Molecular studies have been used to assess and date the origins of modern humans and to examine their relation to extinct human groups.

Molecular anthropologists examine relationships among ancient and contemporary populations and among species. It's well established, for example, that humans and chimpanzees have more than 98 percent of their DNA in common. Molecular anthropologists also reconstruct waves and patterns of migration and settlement. A *haplogroup* is a biological lineage (a large group of related people) defined by a specific cluster of genetic traits that occur together. Native Americans have three or four major haplogroups, which also are linked to East Asia. Molecular anthropologists also use "genetic clocks" to estimate divergence time (date of most recent common ancestry) among species (e.g., humans, chimps, and gorillas—7 million to 10 million years ago) and of various human groups (e.g., Neandertals and modern humans).

# Kinds of Biological Anthropology

The interests of biological anthropologists are varied and encompass recent and living as well as ancient and deceased humans and other primates. This chapter describes many, but far from all, of the topics and methods within contemporary biological anthropology.

## Bone Biology

Central to biological anthropology is **bone biology** (skeletal biology)—the study of bone as a biological tissue, including its genetics; cell structure; growth, development, and decay; and patterns of movement (biomechanics) (Katzenberg and Saunders 2007). Bone biologists study skeletal characteristics of living and deceased humans and hominins. **Paleopathology** is the study of disease and injury in skeletons from archaeological sites (see Buikstra and Roberts 2013; Cohen and Armelagos 2013). Some forms of cancer leave evidence in the bone. Breast cancer, for example, may spread (metastasize) skeletally, leaving lesions in the bones and skull. Certain infectious diseases (e.g., syphilis and tuberculosis) also mark bone, as do injuries and nutritional deficiencies (e.g., rickets, a vitamin D deficiency that deforms the bones). In *forensic anthropology,* as portrayed in the long-running TV series *Bones*, biological anthropologists work in a legal context, assisting coroners, medical examiners, and law enforcement agencies in recovering, analyzing, and identifying human remains and determining causes of death (Tersigni-Tarrant and Shirley 2012; Ubelaker 2012).

## Anthropometry

Biological anthropologists use various techniques to study nutrition, growth, and development. **Anthropometry** is the measurement of human body parts and dimensions, including skeletal parts (*osteometry*). Anthropometry is done on living people as well as on skeletal remains from sites. Body mass and composition provide measures of nutritional status in living people. *Body mass index* (kg/m$^2$) is the ratio of weight in kilograms to height in meters squared. An adult body mass above 30 is considered at risk of overweight, while one below 18 is at risk of underweight or malnutrition.

Bone affected by osteoporosis (brittle bone disease). © Eye of Science/Science Source

## Primatology

Primatology is another subfield of biological anthropology. Primate behavior has been observed in zoos and through experiments, but the most significant studies have been done in natural settings, among free-ranging apes, monkeys, and lemurs. Since the 1950s, when primatologists began their shift from zoos to natural settings, numerous studies have been done of apes (chimps, gorillas, orangutans, and gibbons), monkeys (e.g., baboons, macaques), and lemurs. Studies of primate social systems and behavior, including their mating patterns, infant care, and patterns of contact and dispersal, suggest hypotheses about behavior that humans do or do not share with our nearest relatives—as well as with our hominin ancestors.

# Research Methods in Cultural Anthropology

Early students of society, such as the French scholar Émile Durkheim, were among the founders of both sociology and anthropology. Durkheim studied the religions of Native Australians (Durkheim 1912/2001), as well as mass phenomena, such as suicide rates, in modern nations (Durkheim 1897/1951). Key differences between anthropology and sociology eventually emerged from the kinds of societies each studied. Sociologists focused on the industrial West; anthropologists, on nonindustrial societies. Different methods of data collection and analysis were developed to deal with those different kinds of societies. To study large-scale, complex nations, sociologists came to rely on questionnaires and other means of gathering masses of quantifiable data. For many years sampling and statistical techniques have been basic to sociology, whereas statistical training has been less common in anthropology (although this is changing somewhat as anthropologists increasingly work in modern nations).

Traditional ethnographers studied small, nonliterate (without writing) populations and relied on ethnographic methods appropriate to that context. "Ethnography is a research process in which the anthropologist closely observes, records, and engages in the daily life of another culture—an experience labeled as the fieldwork method—and then writes accounts of this culture, emphasizing descriptive detail" (Marcus and Fischer 1986, p. 18). One key method described in this quote is **participant observation**—taking part in the events one is observing, describing, and analyzing.

# Ethnography: Anthropology's Distinctive Strategy

Traditionally, the process of becoming a cultural anthropologist has required a field experience in another society. Early ethnographers studied small-scale, relatively isolated societies with simple technologies and economies. Ethnography thus emerged as a research strategy in societies with less social differentiation than is found in large, modern nations. Traditionally, ethnographers have tried to understand the whole of a particular culture (or, more realistically, as much as they can, given limitations of time and perception). To pursue this goal, ethnographers adopt a free-ranging strategy for gathering information. The ethnographer moves from setting to setting, person to person, and place to place to discover the totality and interconnectedness of social life. By expanding our knowledge of the range of human diversity, ethnography provides a foundation for generalizations about human behavior and social life. Ethnographers draw on varied techniques to piece together a picture of otherwise alien lifestyles. Anthropologists usually employ several (but rarely all) of the techniques discussed in the following section (see Bernard 2011; Bernard and Gravlee 2014; Wolcott 2010).

# Ethnographic Techniques

The characteristic field techniques of the ethnographer include the following:

1. Direct, firsthand observation of behavior, including participant observation.
2. Conversation with varying degrees of formality, from the daily chitchat that helps maintain rapport and provides knowledge about what is going on to prolonged interviews, which can be unstructured or structured.
3. The genealogical method.
4. Detailed work with key consultants, or informants, about particular areas of community life.
5. In-depth interviewing, often leading to the collection of life histories of particular people (narrators).
6. Discovery of local (native) beliefs and perceptions, which may be compared with the ethnographer's own observations and conclusions.
7. Problem-oriented research of many sorts.
8. Longitudinal research—the continuous, long-term study of an area or a site.
9. Team research—coordinated research by multiple ethnographers.
10. Multisited research that studies the various sites and systems in which people participate.

## Observation and Participant Observation

Ethnographers must pay attention to hundreds of details of daily life, seasonal events, and unusual happenings. They should record what they see as they see it. Things never will seem quite as strange as they do during the first few weeks in the field. The ethnographer eventually gets used to, and accepts as normal, cultural patterns that initially were alien. Staying a bit more than a year in the field allows the ethnographer to repeat the season of his or her arrival, when certain events and processes may have been missed because of initial unfamiliarity and culture shock.

Many ethnographers record their impressions in a personal diary, or notebook, which is kept separate from more formal field notes. Later, this record of early impressions will help point out some of the most basic aspects of cultural diversity. Such aspects include distinctive smells, noises people make, how they cover their mouths when they eat, and how they gaze at others. These patterns, which are so basic as to seem almost trivial, are part of what Bronislaw Malinowski called "the *imponderabilia* of native life and of typical behavior" (Malinowski 1922/1961, p. 20).

These features of culture are so fundamental that natives take them for granted. They are too basic even to talk about, but the unaccustomed eye of the fledgling ethnographer picks them up. Thereafter, becoming familiar, they fade to the edge of consciousness. Initial impressions are valuable and should be recorded. First and foremost, ethnographers should try to be accurate observers, recorders, and reporters of what they see in the field.

Ethnographers strive to establish *rapport,* a good, friendly working relationship based on personal contact, with their hosts. One of ethnography's most characteristic procedures is participant observation, which means that ethnographers take part in community life as they study it. As human beings living among others, they cannot be totally impartial and detached observers. They take part in many events and processes they are observing and trying to comprehend. By participating, ethnographers may learn why people find such events meaningful, as they see how the events are organized and conducted.

In Arembepe, Brazil, I learned about fishing by sailing on the Atlantic with local fishers. I gave Jeep rides to malnourished babies and their parents, to pregnant mothers, and once to a teenage girl possessed by a spirit. All those people needed to consult specialists outside the village. I danced on Arembepe's festive occasions, drank libations commemorating new births, and became a godfather to a village girl. Most anthropologists have similar field experiences. The common humanity of the student and the studied, the ethnographer and the research community, makes participant observation inevitable.

Bronislaw Malinowski (1884–1942), who was born in Poland but spent most of his professional life in England, did fieldwork in the Trobriand Islands from 1914 to 1918. Malinowski is generally considered to be the father of ethnography. Does this photo suggest anything about his relationship with Trobriand villagers? © Mary Evans Picture Library/The Image Works

## Conversation, Interviewing, and Interview Schedules

Participating in local life means that ethnographers constantly talk to people and ask questions. As their knowledge of the local language and culture increases, they understand more. There are several stages in learning a field language. First is the naming phase—asking name after name of the objects around them. Later they are able to pose more complex questions and understand the replies. They begin to understand simple conversations between two villagers. With improving language expertise, they eventually become able to comprehend rapid-fire public discussions and group conversations.

One data-gathering technique I have used in both Arembepe and Madagascar involves an ethnographic survey that includes an interview schedule. Soon after I began research in Arembepe, my fellow field workers and I attempted to complete an interview schedule in each of Arembepe's then 160 households. We entered almost every household (fewer than 5 percent refused to participate) to ask a set of questions on a printed form. Our results provided us with a census and basic information about the village. We wrote down the name, age, and gender of each household member. We gathered data on family type, religion, present and previous jobs, income, expenditures, diet, possessions, and many other items on our eight-page form.

Although we were doing a survey, our approach differed from the survey research design routinely used by sociologists and other social scientists working in large,

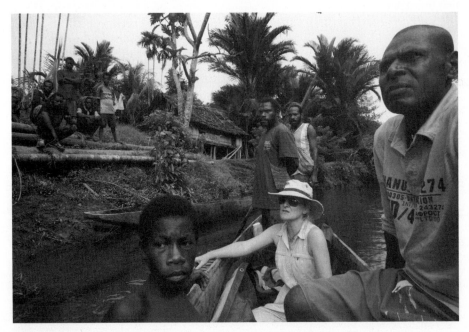

Sebastian Haraha (right), a researcher from Papua New Guinea's Office of Tourism, Arts and Culture, accompanies anthropologist Nancy Sullivan (seated) as they travel with local people up the Arafundi River on a 2009 visit to the Meakambut ethnic group. © Amy Toensing/National Geographic Stock

industrial nations. That survey research, discussed later in the chapter, involves sampling (choosing a **sample**—a small, manageable study group from a larger population). We did not select a partial sample from the total population. Instead, we tried to interview in all households in the community (that is, to have a total sample). We used an interview schedule rather than a questionnaire. With the **interview schedule,** the ethnographer talks face to face with people, asks the questions, and writes down the answers. Questionnaire procedures tend to be more impersonal; often the respondent fills in the form.

Our goal of getting a total sample allowed us to meet almost everyone in the village and helped us establish rapport. Decades later, Arembepeiros still talk warmly about how we were interested enough in them to visit their homes and ask them questions. We stood in sharp contrast to the other outsiders the villagers had known, who considered them too poor and backward to be taken seriously.

Like other survey research, however, our interview schedule did gather comparable quantifiable information. It gave us a basis for assessing patterns and exceptions in village life. Our schedules included a core set of questions that were posed to everyone. However, some interesting side issues often came up during the interview, which we pursued then or later.

We followed such leads into many dimensions of village life. One woman, for instance, a midwife, became the key cultural consultant we sought out later when we wanted detailed information about local childbirth. Another woman had done an internship in an Afro-Brazilian cult (*candomblé*) in the city. She still went there regularly to study, dance, and get possessed. She became our *candomblé* expert.

Thus, our interview schedule provided a structure that directed but did not confine us as researchers. It enabled our ethnography to be both quantitative and qualitative. The quantitative part consisted of the basic information we gathered and later analyzed statistically. The qualitative dimension came from our follow-up questions, open-ended discussions, pauses for gossip, and work with key consultants.

## The Genealogical Method

Many of us learn about our own ancestry and relatives by tracing our genealogies. Websites like ancestry.com allow us to trace our "family trees" and degrees of relationship. The **genealogical method** is a well-established ethnographic technique. Early ethnographers developed notation and symbols to deal with kinship, descent, and marriage. Genealogy is a prominent building block in the social organization of nonindustrial societies, where people live and work each day with their close kin. Anthropologists need to collect genealogical data to understand current social relations and to reconstruct history. Indeed, another term for such cultures is *kin-based societies,* because everyone is related and spends most of his or her time with relatives. (This chapter's "Anthropology Today" describes the importance of a three-generation kinship structure in human evolution.) Rules of behavior attached to particular kin relations are basic to everyday life. Marriage also is crucial in organizing nonindustrial societies, because strategic marriages between villages, tribes, and clans create political alliances.

## Key Cultural Consultants

Every community has people who by accident, experience, talent, or training can provide the most complete or useful information about particular aspects of life. These people are **key cultural consultants,** also called *key informants.* In Ivato, the Betsileo village in Madagascar where I spent most of my time, a man named Rakoto was particularly knowledgeable about village history. However, when I asked him to work with me on a genealogy of the 50 to 60 people buried in the village tomb, he called in his cousin Tuesdaysfather, who knew more about that subject. Tuesdaysfather had survived an epidemic of influenza that ravaged Madagascar, along with much of the world, around 1919. Immune to the disease himself, Tuesdaysfather had the grim job of burying his kin as they died. He kept track of everyone buried in the tomb. Tuesdaysfather helped me with the tomb genealogy. Rakoto joined him in telling me personal details about the deceased villagers.

## Life Histories

In nonindustrial societies as in our own, individual personalities, interests, and abilities vary. Some villagers prove to be more interested in the ethnographer's work and are more helpful, interesting, and pleasant than others are. Anthropologists develop likes and dislikes in the field, as they do at home. Often when they find someone unusually interesting, they collect his or her **life history.** This recollection of a lifetime of experiences provides a more intimate and personal cultural portrait than would be possible otherwise. Life histories, which may be recorded or videoed for later review and analysis, reveal how specific people perceive, react to, and contribute to changes that affect their lives. Many ethnographers include the collection of life histories as an important part of their research strategy.

## Local Beliefs and Perceptions, and the Ethnographer's

One goal of ethnography is to discover local (native) views, beliefs, and perceptions, which may be compared with the ethnographer's own observations and conclusions. In the field, ethnographers typically combine two research strategies, the emic (local-oriented) and the etic (scientist-oriented). These terms, derived from linguistics, have been applied to ethnography by various anthropologists. Marvin Harris (1968/2001) popularized the following meanings of the terms: An **emic** approach investigates how local people think. How do they perceive and categorize the world? What are their rules for behavior? What has meaning for them? How do they imagine and explain things? Operating emically, the ethnographer relies on local people to explain things and to say whether something is significant or not. The term **cultural consultant,** or informant, refers to individuals the ethnographer gets to know in the field, the people who teach him or her about their culture, who provide the emic perspective.

The **etic** (scientist-oriented) approach shifts the focus from local observations, categories, explanations, and interpretations to those of the anthropologist. The etic approach realizes that members of a culture often are too involved in what they are doing to interpret their cultures impartially. Operating etically, the ethnographer emphasizes what he or she (the observer) notices and considers important. As a trained scientist, the ethnographer should try to bring an objective and comprehensive viewpoint to the study of other cultures. Of course, the ethnographer, like any other scientist, is also a human being with cultural blinders that prevent complete objectivity. As in other sciences, proper training can reduce, but not totally eliminate, the observer's bias. But anthropologists do have special training to compare behavior between different societies.

What are some examples of emic versus etic perspectives? Consider our holidays. For North Americans, Thanksgiving Day has special significance. In our view (emically) it is a unique cultural celebration that commemorates particular historical themes. But a wider, etic, perspective sees Thanksgiving as just one more example of the postharvest festivals held in many societies. Another example: Local people give folk explanations for illnesses caused by germs and other pathogens. Emic agents that cause illness include angry or envious spirits, ancestors, witches, and sorcerers. *Illness* refers to a culture's (emic) perception and explanation of bad health, whereas *disease* refers to the scientific (etic) explanation of poor health, involving known pathogens.

Ethnographers typically combine emic and etic strategies in their fieldwork. The statements, perceptions, categories, and opinions of local people help ethnographers understand how cultures work. Local beliefs are also interesting and valuable in themselves. However, people often fail to admit, or even recognize, certain causes and consequences of their behavior. This is as true of North Americans as it is of people in other societies.

## Problem-Oriented Ethnography

Although anthropologists are interested in the whole context of human behavior, it's impossible to study everything. Most ethnographers now enter the field with a specific problem in mind, and they collect data relevant to that problem (see Sunstein and Chiseri-Strater 2012). Local people's answers to questions aren't the only data source. Anthropologists also gather information on factors such as population density, environmental quality, climate, physical geography, diet, and land use. Sometimes this involves direct measurement—of rainfall, temperature, fields, yields, dietary quantities, or time allocation. Often it means that we consult government records or archives.

The information of interest to ethnographers isn't limited to what local people can and do tell us. In an increasingly interconnected and complicated world, local people lack knowledge about many factors that affect their lives. Our local consultants may be as mystified as we are by the exercise of power from regional, national, and international centers.

## Longitudinal Studies, Team Research, and Multisited Ethnography

Geography limits anthropologists much less now than in the past, when it could take months to reach a field site and return visits were rare. Modern systems of transportation allow anthropologists to widen the scope of their research and to return repeatedly. Ethnographic reports now routinely include data from two or more field stays. We can even follow the people we study as they move from village to city, cross the border, or travel internationally. **Longitudinal research** is the long-term study of an area or a population, usually based on repeated visits.

One example is the ongoing study of Gwembe District, Zambia. This study, planned in 1956 as a longitudinal project by Elizabeth Colson and Thayer Scudder, continues with Colson, Scudder, and their associates and successors of various nationalities. As is often the case with longitudinal research, the Gwembe study also illustrates *team research*—coordinated research by multiple ethnographers (Scudder and Colson 1980). Four villages in different areas have been followed for more than half a century. Periodic censuses provide basic data on population, economy, kinship, and religious behavior. Censused people who have moved are traced and interviewed to see how their lives compare with those of people who have stayed behind. The initial focus of study was the impact of a large hydroelectric dam, which subjected the Gwembe people to forced resettlement. Thereafter, Scudder and Colson (1980) examined how education provided access to new opportunities, even as it also widened a social gap between people with different educational levels. The anthropologists next focused on a change in brewing and drinking patterns, including a rise in alcoholism, in relation to changing markets, transportation, and exposure to town values (Colson and Scudder 1988). Retired from the University of California at Berkeley, where she holds the title of Professor Emerita, Colson currently resides in Gwembe district, where the project continues.

As mentioned, longitudinal research often is team research. My own field site of Arembepe, Brazil, first entered the world of anthropology as a field-team village in the 1960s. It was one of four sites for the now defunct Columbia-Cornell-Harvard-Illinois Summer Field Studies Program in Anthropology. For at least three years, that program sent a total of about 20 undergraduates annually, the author included, to do summer research abroad. The teams were stationed in rural communities in four countries: Brazil, Ecuador, Mexico, and Peru. Since my wife, Isabel Wagley Kottak, and I began studying it in 1962, Arembepe has become a longitudinal field site. Generations of researchers have monitored various aspects of change and development. The community has changed from a village into a town and illustrates the process of globalization at the local level. Its economy, religion, and social life have been transformed (see Kottak 2006).

Brazilian and American researchers worked with us on team research projects during the 1980s (on television's impact) and the 1990s (on ecological awareness and environmental risk perception). Students from various universities have drawn on our baseline information from the 1960s in their recent studies in Arembepe. Their topics have included standards of physical attractiveness, family planning and changing female reproductive strategies, conversion to Protestantism, and changing food habits in relation to globalization. Arembepe is thus a site where various field workers have worked as members of a longitudinal, multigenerational team. The more recent researchers have built on prior contacts and findings to increase knowledge about how local people meet and manage new circumstances. As of this writing (2015), new researchers are at work in Arembepe and other Brazilian communities, updating our study of media, which began during the 1980s.

Traditional ethnographic research focused on a single community or "culture," treated as more or less isolated and unique in time and space. In recent years ethnography has shifted toward studies of change and of contemporary flows of people, technology,

Janet Dunn, one of many anthropologists who have worked in Arembepe. Where is Arembepe, and what kinds of research have been done there? © Christopher M. O'Leary

images, and information. Reflecting today's world, fieldwork must be more flexible and on a larger scale. Ethnography increasingly is *multitimed* and *multisited*. That is, it studies people through time and in multiple places. Malinowski could focus on Trobriand culture and spend most of his field time in a particular community. Nowadays we cannot afford to ignore, as Malinowski did, the outside forces that increasingly impinge on the places we study. Integral to our analyses now are the external entities (e.g., governments, corporations, nongovernmental organizations, new social movements) now laying claim to land, people, and resources throughout the world. Also important in contemporary ethnography is increased recognition of power differentials and how they affect cultures, and of the importance of diversity within cultures and societies.

Anthropologists increasingly study people in motion. Examples include people living on or near national borders, nomads, seasonal migrants, homeless and displaced people, immigrants, and refugees (see Lugo 1997). As fieldwork changes, with less and less of a spatially set field, what can we take from traditional ethnography? Gupta and Ferguson correctly cite the "characteristically anthropological emphasis on daily routine and lived experience" (1997*a*, p. 5). The treatment of communities as discrete entities may be a thing of the past. However, "anthropology's traditional attention to the close observation of particular lives in particular places" has an enduring importance (Gupta and Ferguson 1997*b*, p. 25). The method of close observation helps distinguish cultural anthropology from sociology and survey research, to which we now turn.

## Survey Research

Working increasingly in large-scale societies, anthropologists have developed innovative ways of blending ethnography and survey research (Fricke 1994). Before examining such mixed field methods, let's consider the main differences between survey research and ethnography. Sociologists have developed and refined the **survey research** design, which involves sampling, impersonal data collection, and statistical analysis. Survey research draws a sample (a manageable study group) from a much larger population. A properly selected and representative sample permits accurate inferences about the larger population.

In small communities, ethnographers can get to know almost everyone. Given the greater size and complexity of nations, survey research can't help being more impersonal. Survey researchers call the people they study *respondents*—those who respond to questions during a survey. Sometimes survey researchers interview their sample of respondents personally or by phone. Sometimes they ask them to fill out a questionnaire, often online.

Probably the most familiar example of survey research and sampling is the polling that is done to predict political races. An ever increasing number of organizations now gather information designed to estimate outcomes and to determine what kinds of people voted for which candidates. During sampling, researchers gather information about age, gender, religion, occupation, income, and political party preference. These characteristics (**variables**—attributes that vary among members of a sample or population) are known to influence political decisions.

Many more variables affect social identities, experiences, and activities in a modern nation than in the small communities where ethnography grew up. In contemporary North America, hundreds of factors influence our behavior and attitudes. These *social predictors* include our religion; the region of the country we grew up in; whether we come from a town, suburb, or city; and our parents' professions, ethnic origins, and income levels. In any large nation, many predictor variables (social indicators) influence behavior and opinions. Because we must be able to detect, measure, and compare the influence of social indicators, many contemporary anthropological studies have a statistical foundation. Even in rural fieldwork, more anthropologists now draw samples, gather quantitative data, and use statistics to interpret them (see Bernard 2011; Bernard and Gravlee 2014). Quantifiable information may permit a more precise assessment of similarities and differences among communities. Statistical analysis can support and round out an ethnographic account of local social life.

In the best studies, however, the hallmark of ethnography remains: Anthropologists enter the community and get to know the people. They participate in local activities, networks, and associations. They observe and experience social conditions and problems. They watch the effects of national policies and globalization on local life. The ethnographic method and the emphasis on personal relationships in social research are valuable gifts that cultural anthropology brings to the study of any society.

# Doing Anthropology Right and Wrong: Ethical Issues

Science exists in society and in the context of law and ethics. Anthropologists can't study things simply because they happen to be interesting or of value to science. Ethical issues must be considered as well. Anthropologists typically have worked abroad, outside their own society. In the context of international contacts and cultural diversity, different ethical codes and value systems will meet, and often compete.

Archaeologists and biological anthropologists, in particular, often work as members of international teams. These teams typically include researchers from several countries, including the host country—the place (e.g., Ethiopia) where the research takes place. Anthropologists must inform officials and colleagues in the host country about the purpose, funding, and likely results, products, and impacts of their research. They need to negotiate the matter of where the materials produced by the research will be analyzed and stored—in the host country or in the anthropologists' country—and for how long. To whom do research materials such as bones, artifacts, and blood samples belong? What kinds of restrictions will apply to their use?

Contemporary anthropologists recognize that **informed consent** (agreement to take part in the research—after having been informed about its nature, procedures, and possible impacts) should be obtained from anyone who provides information or who might be affected by the research. Although nonhuman primates can't give informed consent, primatologists still must take steps to ensure that their research doesn't endanger the animals they study. Either government agencies or nongovernmental organizations (NGOs) may be entrusted with protecting primates. If this is the case, the anthropologist will need their permission and informed consent to conduct research.

With living humans, informed consent is a necessity, not only in gathering information but especially in obtaining biological samples, such as blood or urine. The research subjects must be told how the samples will be collected, used, and identified and about the potential costs and benefits to them. Informed consent is needed from anyone providing data or information, owning materials being studied, or otherwise having an interest that might be affected by the research.

It is appropriate for North American anthropologists working in another country to (1) include host country colleagues in their research planning and requests for funding; (2) establish truly collaborative relationships with those colleagues and their institutions before, during, and after fieldwork; (3) include host country colleagues in dissemination, including publication, of the research results; and (4) ensure that something is "given back" to host country colleagues. For example, research equipment and technology are allowed to remain in the host country. Or funding is provided for host country colleagues to do research, attend international meetings, or visit foreign institutions—especially those where their international collaborators work.

Even with broad efforts to respect diverse value systems and acknowledge the contributions of the host country and its colleagues, ethical issues continue to arise. Lawsuits against museums by groups seeking the repatriation of remains and artifacts have become common. Peru, for instance, sued Yale University to recover objects removed during the exploration of Machu Picchu (an important Peruvian archaeological and touristic site) by Yale explorer Hiram Bingham in 1912. Native Australians have argued that images of native Australian fauna, such as the emu and kangaroo, belong exclusively to the Aboriginal people. Michael F. Brown (2003) describes efforts by Hopi Indians to control and restrict historic photos of secret religious ceremonies.

Many anthropologists have worked to represent or assist indigenous groups, for example, when disasters strike or when disputes arise with external agents. Sometimes, however, issues involving access to, or ownership of, physical and archaeological remains place anthropologists and indigenous people in opposed camps. The Native American Graves Protection and Repatriation Act (NAGPRA) gives ownership of Native American remains to Native Americans. The Act requires museums to return remains and artifacts to any tribe (nation) that requests them and can prove a "cultural affiliation'' between itself and the remains or artifact.

The 1996 discovery in Washington State (on federal land) of a skeleton dubbed "Kennewick Man" led to a legal case between anthropologists and five Native American tribes with homelands in the area. The anthropologists wanted to conduct a thorough scientific study of the 9,000-year-old skeleton—one of the oldest and best-preserved human remains ever discovered in North America. Believing they have always occupied the region where the remains were found, the Native American groups claimed Kennewick Man as an ancestor, whom they wanted to rebury with dignity and without contamination from testing.

U.S. Magistrate Judge John Jelderks ruled that the Kennewick remains could be studied scientifically, finding little evidence linking the find to any identifiable contemporary group or culture. He suggested that the culture to which Kennewick belonged may have ended thousands of years ago. The ruling, later backed by a federal appeals court, cleared the way for scientists to begin their ongoing study (see Burke et al. 2008; Walker and Owsley 2012).

## The Code of Ethics

To guide its members in making decisions involving ethics and values, the American Anthropological Association (AAA) offers a Code of Ethics. The most recent code, approved in 2012, points out that anthropologists have obligations to their scholarly field, to the wider society and culture, and to the human species, other species, and the environment. Like physicians who take the Hippocratic oath, the anthropologist's first concern should be to *do no harm* to the people, animals, or artifacts being studied. The stated aims of the AAA code are to offer guidelines and to promote discussion and education, rather than to investigate possible misconduct. The code addresses several contexts in which anthropologists work. Some of its main points are highlighted here.

Anthropologists should be open and honest about their research projects with all parties affected by the research. These parties should be informed about the nature, procedures, purpose(s), potential impacts, and source(s) of support for the research. Researchers should pay attention to proper relations between themselves as guests and the host nations and communities where they work. The AAA does not advise anthropologists to avoid taking stands on issues. Indeed, seeking to shape actions and policies may be as ethically justifiable as inaction. The full Code of Ethics is available at the AAA website: http://aaanet.org/coe/Code_of_Ethics.pdf.

## Anthropologists and Terrorism

Anthropologists often complain that government officials ignore anthropological find-ings that are relevant to making informed policies. The AAA has deemed it of "para-mount importance" that anthropologists study the roots of terrorism and violence. How should such studies be conducted? What ethical issues might arise?

Consider a Pentagon program, Project Minerva, initiated late in the George W. Bush administration, designed to draw on social science expertise to combat national security threats. Project Minerva sought scholars to translate original documents captured in Iraq, study China's shift to a more open political system, and explain the resurgence of the Taliban in Afghanistan (Cohen 2008). Project Minerva and related programs raised concerns that governments might use anthropological research in ethically problematic ways. Government policies and military operations have the potential to harm the people anthropologists study.

More recently, anthropologists have been especially critical of the Pentagon's Human Terrain System (HTS) program. Launched in February 2007, HTS has embedded an-thropologists and other social scientists in military teams in Iraq and Afghanistan. On October 31, 2007, the AAA Executive Board issued a statement of disapproval of HTS—outlining how HTS violates the AAA Code of Ethics (see http://www.aaanet.org/about/Policies/statements/Human-Terrain-System-Statement.cfm). The board noted that HTS places anthropologists, as contractors with the U.S. military, in war zones, where they are charged with collecting cultural and social data for use by the military. The ethical concerns raised by these activities include the following:

1. It may be impossible for anthropologists in war zones to identify themselves as anthropologists, as distinct from military personnel. This constrains their ethical responsibility as anthropologists to disclose who they are and what they are doing.

2. HTS anthropologists are asked to negotiate relations among several groups, includ-ing local populations and the military units in which they are embedded. Their re-sponsibilities to their units may conflict with their obligations to the local people they study or consult. This may interfere with the obligation, stipulated in the AAA Code of Ethics, to do no harm.

3. In an active war zone, it is difficult for local people to give "informed consent" without feeling coerced to provide information. As a result, "voluntary informed consent" (as stipulated by the AAA Code of Ethics) is compromised.

4. Information supplied by HTS anthropologists to military field commanders could help target specific groups for military action. Such use of fieldwork-derived infor-mation would violate the AAA Code of Ethics stipulation that those studied not be harmed.

5. The identification of anthropology and anthropologists with the U.S. military may indirectly (through suspicion of "guilt by association") endanger the research, and even the personal safety, of other anthropologists and their consultants throughout the world.

How should anthropologists study terrorism? What do you think about anthropolo-gists' role in war?

## Anthropology Today  *Biology, Culture, and Grandparents*

The research described here provides an excellent example of anthropology's biocultural approach. We see how a fundamental change in human biology—the lengthening of the lifespan—led to the cultural advances that marked the Upper Paleolithic period (45,000–13,000 years ago). During this period, members of our own species—Homo sapiens—first became as fully modern in their behavior as they were in their anatomy.

Language has long permitted us to share experiences with others and to preserve information across the generations. For the past 6,000 years, writing has been a key supplement to the oral transmission of information. In our 21st century, the cloud of cyberspace and a growing arsenal of audiovisual and digital media further facilitate information storage and transfer.

The extent of information transfer between generations has increased during human evolution. The increase was particularly noteworthy during the Upper Paleolithic period, when there was a significant increase in the human lifespan—probably reflecting a more productive economy based on big-game hunting.

Evidence for changes in the lifespan comes from the extent of wear on fossilized teeth: The longer the life, the more worn the teeth. Anthropologists Rachel Caspari and Sang-Hee Lee examined the teeth of 768 hominins representing fossil groups that lived at different times: from australopithecines (living some 2 million years ago), to Neandertals (130,000–28,000 years ago), to the anatomically modern humans of the Upper Paleolithic (45,000–13,000).

Caspari and Lee classified their specimens as older or younger adults based on molar eruption and degree of dental wear. Individuals with wisdom teeth (third molars) were classified as adults and capable of reproducing. The anthropologists calculated that wisdom teeth appeared at age 15, and that it would be at this age that females could become mothers. (Giving birth at age 15 is not unusual among contemporary hunter-gatherers.) A woman can become a grandmother by age 30 if she and her daughter both have their first child at 15.

Using their sample of 768 specimens, Caspari and Lee calculated a ratio of older (age 30 and older) to younger (age 15–29) adults in the different groups of hominins. That ratio has increased steadily during human evolution, with the most significant leap occurring around 30,000 years ago. With that jump, for the first time in human history, significantly more adults were dying after age 30 than before it. Among Neandertals, just 4 individuals survived past age 30 for every 10 who died before reaching that age. By contrast, the anatomically modern people of the Upper Paleolithic could benefit from a much larger group of elders: By 30,000 years ago, twice as many people were dying after age 30 as before that age.

People who lived longer had more time to share their memories orally, with more people, including their grandchildren. A cultural great leap forward occurred when humans started benefiting from the consistent association of three generations. Social groups with three generations could store, process, and transmit more information and experience than had been possible previously. The increase in the number of older people facilitated the transmission of specialized knowledge, illustrated by the sophisticated tools and art of the Upper Paleolithic, compared with what came before, when elders were much scarcer. Adults could interact with

Kinship spanning three generations was a major advance in human evolution. Shown here, three generations of women at a St. Patrick's Day parade in St Paul, Minnesota. © Steve Skjold/Alamy

Three-generation families are common cross-culturally. Shown here, a Ladakhi grandmother, mother, and child at a market in an area of India known as Little Tibet, because of its predominantly Tibetan Buddhist population. © J Marshall - Tribaleye Images/Alamy

their parents longer, and children could thrive in a larger kinship network that included grandparents.

Experience counts in child rearing. Among nonhuman primates, infant survival rates are significantly higher when the mother is experienced. One study of baboons found that infants of experienced mothers had a 63 percent survival rate, versus only 29 percent for infants of first-time mothers. There is even more experience to draw on when children have both their parents and their grandparents around.

Because of the reproductive advantage associated with living longer and in three-generation groups, a human population burst occurred during the Upper Paleolithic. This population increase likely spurred the many cultural advances known through archaeology to have occurred during the Upper Paleolithic. Among those advances were increased mobility, long-distance trade, artistic expression, and new forms of cooperation (and competition) between groups. Because of all these advantages, the extended human lifespan may well be the most important biological factor that led to the flowering of human behavioral modernity.

**Source:** Altmann et al. (1988), Caspari (2011), Caspari and Lee (2004), Diaz (2013), and McKie (2011).

## Summary

1. As they study the past, archaeologists and biological (physical) anthropologists may share research topics and methods and work together in multidisciplinary teams. Remote sensing may be used to locate ancient footpaths, roads, canals, and irrigation systems, which can then be investigated on the ground. Archaeologists combine both local (excavation) and regional (systematic survey) perspectives.

Sites are excavated because they are in danger of being destroyed or because they address specific research interests. There are many kinds of archaeology, such as historical, classical, and underwater archaeology.

2. The fossil record is not a representative sample of all the plants and animals that have ever lived. Hard parts, such as bones and teeth, preserve better than soft parts, such as flesh and skin. Stratigraphy and radiometric techniques are used to date fossils. Carbon-14 ($^{14}$C) dating is most effective with fossils less than 40,000 years old. Potassium-argon (K/A) dating can be used for fossils older than 500,000 years. Molecular anthropology uses genetic analysis (of DNA sequences) to assess and date evolutionary relationships.

3. Within biological anthropology, bone biology is the study of bone genetics; cell structure; growth, development, and decay; and patterns of movement. Paleopathology is the study of disease and injury in skeletons from archaeological sites. Anthropometry, the measurement of human body parts and dimensions, is done on living people and on skeletal remains from sites. Studies of primates suggest hypotheses about behavior that humans do or do not share with our nearest relatives—as well as with our hominid ancestors.

4. Ethnographic methods include firsthand and participant observation, rapport building, interviews, genealogies, work with key consultants or informants, the collection of life histories, the discovery of local beliefs and perceptions, problem-oriented and longitudinal research, and team research. Ethnographers work in communities and form personal relationships with local people as they study their lives.

5. An interview schedule is a form an ethnographer completes as he or she visits a series of households. Key consultants, or informants, teach us about particular areas of local life. Life histories document personal experiences with culture and culture change. Genealogical information is particularly useful in societies in which principles of kinship and marriage organize social and political life. Emic approaches focus on native perceptions and explanations. Etic approaches give priority to the ethnographer's own observations and conclusions. Longitudinal research is the systematic study of an area or a population over time. Longitudinal, team, and multisited ethnographic research are increasingly common.

6. Traditionally, anthropologists worked in small-scale societies; sociologists, in modern nations. Different techniques developed to study these different kinds of societies. Anthropologists do their fieldwork in communities and study the totality of social life. Sociologists use surveys and study samples to make inferences about a larger population. Anthropologists may employ ethnographic procedures to study cities, towns, or rural areas.

7. Because science exists in society, and in the context of law and ethics, anthropologists can't study things simply because they happen to be interesting or of scientific value. Anthropologists have obligations to their scholarly field, to the wider society and culture (including that of the host country), and to the human species, other species, and the environment. The AAA Code of Ethics offers ethical guidelines for anthropologists. Ethical problems often arise when anthropologists work for governments, especially the military.

## Key Terms

# Chapter 4

# Evolution, Genetics, and Human Variation

Humans have uniquely varied ways—cultural and biological—of evolving, of adapting to environmental stresses. Exemplifying *cultural* adaptation, we manipulate our artifacts and behavior in response to environmental conditions. We turn up thermostats or travel to Florida in the winter. We turn on fire hydrants, swim, or use air conditioning to escape the summer's heat. Although such reliance on culture has increased in the course of human evolution, people haven't stopped adapting biologically. As in other species, human populations adapt genetically in response to environmental forces, and individuals react physiologically to stresses. Thus, when we work in the sun, sweating occurs spontaneously, cooling the skin and reducing the temperature of subsurface blood vessels.

We are ready now for a more detailed look at the principles that determine human biological adaptation, variation, and change.

# The Origin of Species

During the 18th century, many scholars became interested in biological diversity, human origins, and our position within the classification of plants and animals. At that time, the commonly accepted explanation for the origin of species came from Genesis, the first book of the Bible: God created all life during six days of Creation. According to **creationism,** biological similarities and differences originated at the Creation. Characteristics of life forms were seen as immutable; they could not change. Through calculations based on genealogies in the Bible, the biblical scholars James Ussher and John Lightfoot even purported to trace the Creation to a very specific time: October 23, 4004 B.C., at 9 A.M.

Carolus Linnaeus (1707–1778) developed the first comprehensive (and still influential) classification, or taxonomy, of plants and animals, based on similarities and differences in their physical characteristics. He used traits such as the backbone to distinguish vertebrates from invertebrates and mammary glands to distinguish mammals from birds. Linnaeus viewed the differences between life forms as part of the Creator's orderly plan. He thought that biological similarities and differences had been established at the time of Creation and had not changed.

According to creationism all life originated during the six days of Creation described in the Bible. Catastrophism proposed that fires and floods, including the biblical deluge involving Noah's ark (depicted in this painting), destroyed certain species. © Philadelphia Museum of Art/Corbis

Fossil discoveries during the 18th and 19th centuries raised doubts about creationism. Fossils showed that different kinds of life once had existed. If all life had originated at the same time, why weren't ancient species still around? Why weren't contemporary plants and animals found in the fossil record? A modified explanation combining creationism with **catastrophism** arose to replace the original doctrine. In this view, fires, floods, and other catastrophes, including the biblical flood involving Noah's ark, had destroyed ancient species. After each destructive event, God had created again, leading to contemporary species. How did the catastrophists explain certain clear similarities between fossils and modern animals? They argued that some ancient species had managed to survive in isolated areas. For example, after the biblical flood, the progeny of the animals saved on Noah's ark spread throughout the world.

## Theory and Fact

The alternative to creationism and catastrophism was *transformism,* also called **evolution.** Evolutionists believe that species arise from others through a long and gradual process of transformation, or descent with modification. Charles Darwin became the best known of the evolutionists. However, he was influenced by earlier scholars, including his own grandfather. In a book called *Zoonomia,* published in 1794, Erasmus Darwin had proclaimed the common ancestry of all animal species.

Charles Darwin also was influenced by Sir Charles Lyell, the father of geology. During Darwin's famous voyage to South America aboard the *Beagle,* he read Lyell's influential book *Principles of Geology* (1837/1969), which exposed him to Lyell's principle of **uniformitarianism.** Uniformitarianism states that the present is the key to the past. Explanations for past events should be sought in the long-term action of ordinary forces that still operate today. Thus, natural forces (rainfall, soil deposition, earthquakes, and volcanic action) gradually have built and modified geological features such as mountain ranges. The Earth's structure has been transformed gradually through natural forces operating for millions of years.

Uniformitarianism was a necessary building block for evolutionary theory. It cast serious doubt on the belief that the world was only 6,000 years old. It would take much longer for such ordinary forces as rain and wind to produce major geological changes. The longer time span also allowed enough time for the biological changes that fossil discoveries were revealing. Darwin applied the ideas of uniformitarianism and long-term transformation to living things. He argued that all life forms are ultimately related and that the number of species has increased over time.

Charles Darwin provided a theoretical framework for understanding evolution. He offered natural selection as a powerful evolutionary mechanism that could explain the origin of species, biological diversity, and similarities among related life forms. Darwin proposed a *theory* of evolution in the strict sense. A **theory** is a set of ideas formulated (by reasoning based on known facts) to explain something. Theories are valuable because they suggest patterns, connections, and relationships that may be confirmed by new research. The *fact* of evolution (that evolution has occurred) was known earlier, for example, by Erasmus Darwin. The *theory* of evolution, through natural selection (*how* evolution occurred), was Darwin's major contribution. Actually, natural selection wasn't

Darwin's unique discovery. Working independently, the naturalist Alfred Russel Wallace had reached a similar conclusion (Shermer 2011; Smith and Beccaloni 2010). In a joint paper read to London's Linnaean Society in 1858, Darwin and Wallace made their discovery public. Darwin's book *On the Origin of Species* (1859/2009) offered much fuller documentation.

**Natural selection** is the process by which the forms most fit to survive and reproduce in a given environment do so in greater numbers than others in the same population. More than survival of the fittest, natural selection is differential reproductive success. Natural selection operates when there is competition for strategic resources (those necessary for life) such as food and space between members of the population. There is also the matter of finding mates. You can win the competition for food and space and have no mate and thus have no impact on the future of the species. For natural selection to work on a particular population, there must be variety within that population, as there always is.

The giraffe's neck can illustrate how natural selection works on variety within a population. In any group of giraffes, there always is variation in neck length. When food is adequate, the animals have no problem feeding themselves. But when dietary foliage is not as abundant as usual, giraffes with longer necks have an advantage. They can feed off the higher branches. If this feeding advantage permits longer-necked giraffes to survive and reproduce even slightly more effectively than shorter-necked ones, giraffes with longer necks will transmit more of their genetic material to future generations than will giraffes with shorter necks.

An incorrect alternative to this (Darwinian) explanation would be the inheritance of acquired characteristics. That is the idea that in each generation, individual giraffes strain their necks to reach just a bit higher. This straining somehow modifies their genetic material. Over generations of strain, the average neck gradually gets longer through the accumulation of small increments of neck length acquired during the lifetime of each generation of giraffes. This is *not* how evolution works. If it did work in this way, weight lifters could expect to produce especially muscular babies. Evolution works as the process of natural selection takes advantage of the variety that already is present in a population.

Evolution through natural selection continues today. For example, humans exhibit differential resistance to disease, as we will see later in the discussion of sickle-cell anemia. One classic recent example of natural selection is the peppered moth, which can be light or dark (in either case with black speckles, thus the name "peppered"). A change in this species illustrates recent natural selection (in our own industrial age) through what has been called *industrial melanism*. Great Britain's industrialization changed the environment so as to favor darker moths (those with more melanin) rather than the lighter-colored ones that had been favored previously. During the 1800s industrial pollution increased, and soot coated buildings and trees, turning them a darker color. The previously favored lighter moths now stood out against sooty backgrounds and were easily visible to their predators. Through mutations (discussed later), a new strain of moth, with a darker phenotype, was favored. Because these darker moths were fitter—that is, harder to detect—in polluted environments, they survived and reproduced in greater numbers than lighter moths did. We

A speckled (peppered) moth and a black one. Which environment would favor each of these variants? © The Natural History Museum/The Image Works

see how natural selection may favor darker moths in polluted areas and lighter ones in cleaner environments because of their variant abilities to merge with environmental colors and thus avoid predators.

The purpose of evolutionary theory is to provide explanations. The goal of science is to increase understanding through explanation: showing how and why the thing (or class of things) to be understood (e.g., the variation within species, the fossil record) depends on other things. Explanations rely on associations and theories. An association is an observed relationship between two or more variables, such as the length of a giraffe's neck and the number of its offspring, or an increase in the frequency of dark moths as industrial pollution spreads. A theory is more general, suggesting or implying associations and attempting to explain them. Something, such as the giraffe's long neck, is explained if it illustrates a general principle or association, such as the concept of adaptive advantage. The truth of a scientific statement (e.g., evolution occurs because of differential reproductive success due to variation within the population) is confirmed by repeated observations.

## Genetics

Charles Darwin recognized that for natural selection to operate, there must be variety in the population undergoing selection. Documenting and explaining such variety among humans—human biological diversity—is one of anthropology's major concerns. Genetics, a science that emerged after Darwin, helps us understand the causes of biological variation. We now know that DNA (deoxyribonucleic acid) molecules make up genes and chromosomes, which are the basic hereditary units. Biochemical changes (mutations) in DNA provide much of the variety on which natural selection operates. Through sexual reproduction, recombination of the genetic traits of mother and father in each generation leads to new arrangements of the hereditary units received from each parent. Such genetic recombination also adds variety on which natural selection may operate.

**Mendelian genetics** studies the ways in which chromosomes transmit genes across the generations. *Biochemical genetics* examines structure, function, and changes in DNA. **Population genetics** investigates natural selection and other causes of genetic variation, stability, and change in breeding populations.

## Mendel's Experiments

In 1856, in a monastery garden, the Austrian monk Gregor Mendel began a series of experiments that were to reveal the basic principles of genetics. Mendel studied the inheritance of seven contrasting traits in pea plants. For each trait there were only two forms. For example, plants were either tall (6 to 7 feet) or short (9 to 18 inches), with no intermediate forms. The ripe seeds could be either smooth and round or wrinkled. The peas could be either yellow or green, with no intermediate colors.

When Mendel began his experiments, one of the prevailing beliefs about heredity was what has been called the "paint-pot" theory. According to this theory, the traits of the two parents blended in their children, much as two pigments are blended in a can of paint. Children therefore were a unique mixture of their parents, and when these children married and reproduced, their traits would blend inextricably with those of their spouses. However, prevailing notions about heredity also recognized that occasionally the traits of one parent might swamp those of the other. If children looked far more like their mother than their father, people might say that her "blood" was stronger than his. Occasionally, too, there would be a "throwback," a child who was the image of his or her grandparent or who possessed a distinctive chin or nose characteristic of a whole line of descent.

Through his experiments with pea plants, Mendel discovered that heredity is determined by discrete particles or units. Although traits could disappear in one generation, they reemerged in their original form in later generations. For example, Mendel crossbred pure strains of tall and short plants. Their offspring were all tall. This was the first descending, or first filial, generation, designated $F_1$. Mendel then interbred the plants of the $F_1$ generation to produce a generation of grandchildren, the $F_2$ generation. In this generation, short plants reappeared. Among thousands of plants in the $F_2$ generation, there was approximately one short plant for every three tall ones.

From similar results with the other six traits, Mendel concluded that although a **dominant** form could mask the other form in *hybrid,* or mixed, individuals, the dominated trait—the **recessive**—was not destroyed; it wasn't even changed. Recessive traits would appear in unaltered form in later generations because genetic traits were inherited as discrete units.

These basic genetic units that Mendel described were factors (now called genes or alleles) located on **chromosomes.** Chromosomes are arranged in matching (homologous) pairs. Humans have 46 chromosomes, arranged in 23 pairs, 1 chromosome in each pair from the father and the other from the mother.

**FIGURE 4.1**

**Simplified Representation of a Normal Chromosome Pair**

Letters indicate genes; superscripts indicate alleles.

For simplicity, a chromosome may be pictured as a surface (see Figure 4.1) with several positions, to each of which we assign a lowercase letter. Each position is a **gene.** Each gene determines, wholly or partially, a particular biological trait, such as whether one's blood is type A, B, or O. **Alleles** (for example, $b^1$ and $b^2$ in Figure 4.1) are biochemically different forms of a given gene. In humans, A, B, AB, and O blood types reflect different combinations of alleles of a particular gene.

In Mendel's experiments, the seven contrasting traits were determined by genes located on seven different pairs of chromosomes. The gene for height occurred in one of the seven pairs. When Mendel crossbred pure tall and pure short plants to produce his $F_1$ generation, each of the offspring received an allele for tallness (T) from one parent and one for shortness (t) from the other. These offspring were mixed, or **heterozygous,** with respect to height; each had two dissimilar alleles of that gene. Their parents, in contrast, had been **homozygous,** possessing two identical alleles of that gene (see Hartl 2014).

In the next generation ($F_2$), after the mixed plants were interbred, short plants reappeared in the ratio of one short to three talls. Knowing that shorts produced only shorts, Mendel could assume that they were genetically pure. Another fourth of the $F_2$ plants produced only talls. The remaining half, like the $F_1$ generation, were heterozygous; when interbred, they produced three talls for each short (see Figure 4.2).

Dominance produces a distinction between **genotype,** or hereditary makeup, and **phenotype,** or expressed physical characteristics. Genotype is what you really are genetically; phenotype is what you appear as. Mendel's peas had three genotypes—TT, Tt, and tt—but only two phenotypes—tall and short. Because of dominance, the heterozygous plants were just as tall as the genetically pure tall ones. How do Mendel's discoveries apply to humans? Although some of our genetic traits follow Mendelian laws, with only two forms—dominant and recessive—other traits are determined differently. For instance, three alleles determine whether our blood type is A, B, AB, or O. People with two alleles for type O have that blood type. However, if they received an allele for either A or B from one parent

**FIGURE 4.2**

**Punnett Squares of a Homozygous Cross and a Heterozygous Cross**

These squares show how phenotypic ratios of the $F_1$ and $F_2$ generation are generated. Colors show genotypes.

and one for O from the other, they will have blood type A or B. In other words, A and B are both dominant over O. A and B are said to be *codominant*. If people inherit an allele for A from one parent and one for B from the other, they will have type AB blood, which is chemically different from the other varieties, A, B, and O.

These three alleles produce four phenotypes—A, B, AB, and O—and six different genotypes—OO, AO, BO, AA, BB, and AB (see Figure 4.3). There are fewer phenotypes than genotypes because O is recessive to both A and B.

**FIGURE 4.3    Determinants of Phenotypes (Blood Groups) in the ABO System**

The four phenotypes—A, B, AB, and O—are indicated in parentheses and by color.

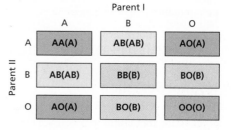

## Independent Assortment

Through additional experiments, Mendel also formulated his law of **independent assortment.** He discovered that traits are inherited independently of one another. For example, he bred pure round, yellow peas with pure wrinkled, green ones. All the $F_1$ generation peas were round and yellow, the dominant forms. But when Mendel interbred the $F_1$ generation to produce the $F_2$, four phenotypes turned up. Round greens and wrinkled yellows had been added to the original round yellows and wrinkled greens. The independent assortment and recombination of genetic traits provide one of the main ways by which variety is produced in any population.

An organism develops from a fertilized egg, or *zygote,* created by the union of two sex cells, one from each parent. The zygote grows rapidly through **mitosis,** or ordinary cell division, which continues as the organism grows. The process by which sex cells are produced is called **meiosis.** Unlike ordinary cell division, in which two cells emerge from one, in meiosis four cells are produced from one. Each has half the genetic material of the original cell. In human meiosis, four cells, each with 23 individual chromosomes, are produced from an original cell with 23 pairs.

With fertilization of egg by sperm, the father's 23 chromosomes combine with the mother's 23 to recreate the pairs in every generation. However, the chromosomes sort independently, so that a child's genotype is a random combination of the DNA of its four grandparents. It is conceivable that one grandparent will contribute very little to its grandchild's heredity. Independent assortment of chromosomes is a major source of variety because the parents' genotypes can be assorted in $2^{23}$, or more than 8 million, different ways.

# Population Genetics

Population genetics studies stable and changing populations in which most breeding normally takes place (see Gillespie 2004; Hartl and Jones 2011). The term **gene pool** refers to all the alleles, genes, chromosomes, and genotypes within a breeding population—the "pool" of genetic material available. When population geneticists use the term *evolution,* they have a more specific definition in mind than the one given earlier ("descent with modification over the generations"). Geneticists define **genetic evolution** as change in gene frequency, that is, in the frequency of alleles in a breeding population from generation to generation. Any factor that contributes to such a change can be considered a *mechanism of genetic evolution.* Those mechanisms include natural selection, mutation, random genetic drift, and gene flow (see Mayr 2001; Relethford 2012).

## Mechanisms of Genetic Evolution

### Natural Selection

The first mechanism of genetic evolution is natural selection, which remains the best explanation for evolution. Essential to understanding evolution through natural selection is the distinction between genotype and phenotype. *Genotype* refers just to hereditary factors—genes and chromosomes. Phenotype—the organism's evident biological characteristics—develops over the years as the organism is influenced by particular environmental forces. (See the photo of the identical twins.) Identical twins have exactly the same genotype, but their actual biology, their phenotypes, may differ as a result of variation in the environments in which they have been raised. Also, because of dominance, individuals with different genotypes may have identical phenotypes (like

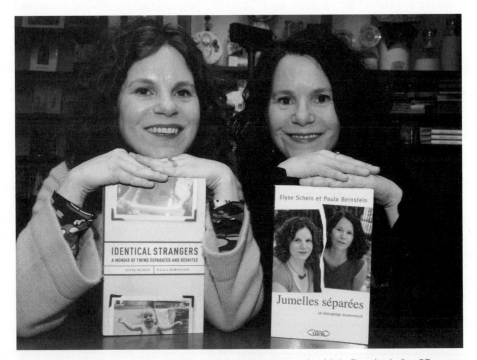

Identical twins Paula Bernstein and Elyse Schein were separated at birth. Reunited after 35 years, they co-wrote the book *Identical Strangers*. What factors other than genes influence phenotype?
© Brian Zak/SIPA/Newscom

Mendel's tall pea plants). Natural selection can operate only on phenotype—on what is exposed, not on what is hidden. For example, a harmful recessive gene can't be eliminated from the gene pool if it is masked by a favored dominant.

Phenotype includes not only outward physical appearance but also internal organs, tissues, and cells and physiological processes and systems. Many biological reactions to foods, disease, heat, cold, sunlight, and other environmental factors are not automatic, genetically programmed responses but the product of years of exposure to particular environmental stresses. Human biology is not set at birth but has considerable *plasticity*. That is, it is changeable, being affected by the environmental forces, such as diet and altitude, that we experience as we grow up.

The environment works on the genotype to build the phenotype, and certain phenotypes do better in some environments than other phenotypes do. However, remember that favored phenotypes can be produced by different genotypes. Because natural selection works only on genes that are expressed, maladaptive recessives can be removed only when they occur in homozygous form. When a heterozygote carries a maladaptive recessive, its effects are masked by the favored dominant. The process of perfecting the fit between organisms and their environment is gradual.

### Directional Selection

After several generations of selection, gene frequencies will change. Adaptation through natural selection will have occurred. Once that happens, those traits that have proved to be the most **adaptive** (favored by natural selection) in that environment will be selected again and again from generation to generation. Given such *directional selection,* or long-term selection of the same trait(s), maladaptive recessive alleles will be removed from the gene pool.

Directional selection will continue as long as environmental forces stay the same. However, if the environment changes, new selective forces start working, favoring different phenotypes. This also happens when part of the population colonizes a new environment. Selection in the changed, or new, environment continues until a new equilibrium is reached. Then there is directional selection until another environmental change or migration takes place. Over millions of years, such a process of successive adaptation to a series of environments has led to biological modification and branching. The process of natural selection has led to the tremendous array of plant and animal forms found in the world today.

Selection also operates through competition for mates in a breeding population. Males may openly compete for females, or females may choose to mate with particular males because they have desirable traits. Obviously, such traits vary from species to species. Familiar examples include color in birds; male birds, such as cardinals, tend to be more brightly colored than females are. Colorful males have a selective advantage because females like them better. Over the generations, as females have opted for colorful mates, the alleles responsible for color have built up in the species. **Sexual selection,** based on differential success in mating, is the term for this process in which certain traits of one sex are selected because of advantages they confer in winning mates.

Selection operates *only* on traits that are present in a population. A favorable mutation *may* occur, but a population doesn't normally come up with a new genotype or phenotype just because one is needed or desirable. Many species have become extinct because they weren't sufficiently varied to adapt to environmental shifts.

## Stabilizing Selection

We've seen that natural selection *reduces* variety in a population through directional selection—by favoring one trait or allele over another. Selective forces also can work to *maintain* variety through *stabilizing selection,* by favoring a **balanced polymorphism,** in which the frequencies of two or more alleles of a gene remain constant from generation to generation. This may be because the phenotypes they produce are neutral, or equally favored, or equally opposed, by selective forces. Sometimes a particular force favors (or opposes) one allele, while a different but equally effective force favors (or opposes) the other allele.

One well-studied example involves two alleles, $Hb^A$ and $Hb^S$, that affect the production of the beta strain (Hb) of human hemoglobin. Hemoglobin, which is located in our red blood cells, carries oxygen from our lungs to the rest of the body via the circulatory system. The allele that produces normal hemoglobin is $Hb^A$. Another allele, $Hb^S$, produces a different hemoglobin. Individuals who are homozygous for $Hb^S$ suffer from *sickle-cell anemia.* Such anemia, in which the red blood cells are shaped like crescents, or sickles, is associated with a disease that is usually fatal. This condition interferes with the blood's ability to store oxygen. It increases the heart's burden by clogging the small blood vessels.

Given the fatal disease associated with $Hb^S$, geneticists were surprised to discover that certain populations in Africa, India, and the Mediterranean had very high frequencies of $Hb^S$. In some West African populations, that frequency is around 20 percent. Researchers eventually discovered that both $Hb^A$ and $Hb^S$ are maintained because selective forces in certain environments favor the heterozygote over either homozygote.

Initially, scientists wondered why, if most $Hb^S$ homozygotes died before they reached reproductive age, the harmful allele hadn't been eliminated. Why was its frequency so high? The answer turned out to lie in the heterozygote's greater fitness. Only people who were homozygous for $Hb^S$ died from sickle-cell anemia. Heterozygotes suffered very mild anemia, if any. On the other hand, although people homozygous for $Hb^A$ did not suffer from anemia, they were much more susceptible to *malaria*—a killer disease that continues to plague *Homo sapiens* in the tropics.

The heterozygote, with one sickle-cell allele and one normal one, was the fittest phenotype for a malarial environment. Heterozygotes have enough abnormal hemoglobin, in which malaria parasites cannot thrive, to protect against malaria. They also have enough normal hemoglobin to fend off sickle-cell anemia. The $Hb^S$ allele has been maintained in these populations because the heterozygotes survived and reproduced in greater numbers than did people with any other phenotype.

The example of the sickle-cell allele demonstrates the relativity of evolution through natural selection: Adaptation and fitness are in relation to specific environments. Traits are not adaptive or maladaptive for all times and places. Even harmful alleles can be selected if heterozygotes have an advantage. Moreover, as the environment changes, favored phenotypes and gene frequencies can change. In malaria-free environments, normal-hemoglobin homozygotes reproduce more effectively than heterozygotes do.

With no malaria, the frequency of $Hb^S$ declines because $Hb^S$ homozygotes can't compete in survival and reproduction with the other types. This has happened in areas of West Africa where malaria has been reduced through drainage programs and insecticides. Selection against $Hb^S$ also has occurred in the United States among Americans descended from West Africans.

## Mutation

The second mechanism of genetic evolution is mutation. **Mutations** are changes in the DNA molecules of which genes and chromosomes are built. If a mutation occurs in a sex cell that combines with another as a fertilized egg, the new organism will carry the mutation in every cell. This may or may not, depending on dominance, result in a biochemical difference between the mutant child and the parent. Mutations, which occur spontaneously and regularly, provide new biochemical forms—variety—on which natural selection may operate.

## Random Genetic Drift

The third mechanism of genetic evolution is **random genetic drift.** This is a change in allele frequency that results not from natural selection but from chance. To understand why, compare the sorting of alleles to a game involving a bag of 12 marbles, 6 red and 6 blue. In step 1, you draw 6 marbles from the bag. Statistically, your chances of drawing 3 reds and 3 blues are less than those of getting 4 of one color and 2 of the other. Step 2 is to fill a new bag with 12 marbles on the basis of the ratio of marbles you drew in step 1. Assume that you drew 4 reds and 2 blues: The new bag will have 8 red marbles and 4 blue ones. Step 3 is to draw 6 marbles from the new bag. Your chances of drawing blues in step 3 are lower than they were in step 1, and the probability of drawing all reds increases. If you do draw all reds, the next bag (step 4) will have only red marbles.

Although genetic drift can operate in any population, large or small, *fixation* due to drift is more rapid in small populations. *Fixation* refers to the total replacement of blue marbles by red marbles—or, to use a human example, of blue eyes by brown eyes. The history of the human line is characterized by a series of small populations, migrations, and fixation due to genetic drift. One cannot understand human origins, human genetic variation, and a host of other important anthropological topics without recognizing the importance of genetic drift.

This game is analogous to random genetic drift operating over the generations. The blue marbles were lost purely by chance. Alleles, too, can be lost by chance rather than because of any disadvantage they confer. Lost alleles can reappear in a gene pool only through mutation.

## Gene Flow

The fourth mechanism of genetic evolution is **gene flow,** the exchange of genetic material between populations of the same species. Gene flow, like mutation, works in conjunction with natural selection by providing variety on which selection can work. Gene flow may consist of direct interbreeding between formerly separated populations of the same species (e.g., Europeans, Africans, and Native Americans in the United States), or it may be indirect.

## FIGURE 4.4    **Gene Flow between Local Populations**

$P_1$–$P_6$ are six local populations of the same species. Each interbreeds (=) only with its neighbor(s). Although members of $P_6$ never interbreed with $P_1$, $P_6$ and $P_1$ are linked through gene flow. Genetic material that originates in $P_1$ eventually will reach $P_6$, and vice versa, as it is passed from one neighboring population to the next. Because they share genetic material in this way, $P_1$–$P_6$ remain members of the same species. In many species, local populations distributed throughout a larger territory than the 250 miles depicted here are linked through gene flow.

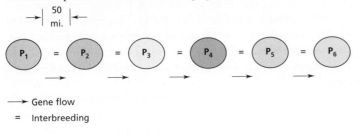

→ Gene flow

= Interbreeding

Consider the following hypothetical case (see Figure 4.4). In a certain part of the world live six local populations of a certain species. $P_1$ is the westernmost of these populations. $P_2$, which interbreeds with $P_1$, is located 50 miles to the east. $P_2$ also interbreeds with $P_3$, located 50 miles east of $P_2$. Assume that each population interbreeds with, and only with, the adjacent populations. $P_6$ is located 250 miles from $P_1$ and does not directly interbreed with $P_1$, but it is tied to $P_1$ through the chain of interbreeding that ultimately links all six populations.

Assume further that some allele exists in $P_1$ that isn't particularly advantageous in its environment. Because of gene flow, this allele may be passed on to $P_2$, by it to $P_3$, and so on until it eventually reaches $P_6$. In $P_6$ or along the way, the allele may encounter an environment in which it does have a selective advantage. If this happens, it may serve, like a new mutation, as raw material on which natural selection can operate.

Alleles are spread through gene flow even when selection is not operating on the allele. In the long run, natural selection works on the variety within a population, whatever its source: mutation, drift, or gene flow. Selection and gene flow have worked together to spread the Hb$^S$ allele in Central Africa. Frequencies of Hb$^S$ in Africa reflect not only the intensity of malaria but also the length of time gene flow has been going on.

Gene flow is important in the study of the origin of species. A **species** is a group of related organisms whose members can interbreed to produce offspring that can live and reproduce. A species has to be able to reproduce itself through time. We know that horses and donkeys belong to different species because their offspring cannot meet the test of long-term survival. A horse and a donkey may breed to produce a mule, but mules are sterile. So are the offspring of lions with tigers. Gene flow tends to prevent **speciation**— the formation of new species—unless subgroups of the same species are separated for a sufficient length of time.

When gene flow is interrupted, and isolated subgroups are maintained, new species may arise. Imagine that an environmental barrier arises between $P_3$ and $P_4$, so they no longer interbreed. If over time, as a result of isolation, $P_1$, $P_2$, and $P_3$ become incapable of interbreeding with the other three populations, speciation will have occurred.

## Race: A Discredited Concept in Biology

Historically, scientists have approached the study of human biological diversity in two main ways: (1) racial classification (now largely abandoned) versus (2) the current explanatory approach, which focuses on understanding specific differences. First we'll consider problems with **racial classification** (the attempt to assign humans to discrete categories [purportedly] based on common ancestry). Then we'll offer some explanations for specific aspects of human biological diversity. *Biological differences are real, important, and apparent to us all.* Modern scientists find it most productive to seek explanations for this diversity, rather than trying to pigeonhole people into categories called races. Certainly, human groups vary biologically—for example, in their genetic attributes. But often we observe gradual, rather than abrupt, shifts in gene frequencies between neighboring groups. Such gradual genetic shifts are called **clines,** and they are incompatible with discrete and separate races (see Edgar and Hunley 2009; Mukhopadhyay et al. 2007).

What is race, anyway? In theory, a biological race would be a geographically isolated subdivision of a species. Such a *subspecies* would be capable of interbreeding with other subspecies of the same species, but it would not actually do so because of its geographic isolation. Some biologists also use *race* to refer to *breeds,* as of dogs or roses. Thus, a pit bull and a chihuahua are different races of dogs. Such domesticated "races" have been bred by humans for generations. Humanity (*Homo sapiens*) lacks such races because human populations have not been isolated enough from one another to develop into such discrete groups. Nor have humans experienced controlled breeding like that which has created the various kinds of dogs and roses.

A race is supposed to reflect shared *genetic* material (inherited from a common ancestor), but early scholars instead used phenotypical traits (usually skin color) for racial classification. Recall that an organism's phenotype is its "manifest biology"—anatomy and physiology. Humans display hundreds of evident (detectable) physical traits. They range from skin color, hair form, eye color, and facial features (which are visible) to blood groups, color blindness, and enzyme production (which become evident through testing) (see Anemone 2011).

Racial classifications based on phenotype raise the problem of deciding which trait(s) should be primary. Should races be defined by height, weight, body shape, facial features, teeth, skull form, or skin color? Like their fellow citizens, early European and American scientists gave priority to skin color. Many schoolbooks and encyclopedias still proclaim the existence of three great races: the white, the black, and the yellow. This overly simplistic classification was compatible with the political use

The photos in this chapter illustrate only a small part of the range of human biological diversity. Shown above is a woman from Guangzhou province, People's Republic of China. © Ed George/National Geographic Stock

A young man from the Marquesas Islands in Polynesia. © Darrell Gulin/Corbis

A Native American woman from Bolivia's Altiplano highlands. © imagebroker/Alamy

A Native Australian man from Cloncurry, Queensland, Australia. © Holger Leue/Lonely Planet Images/Getty Images of race during the colonial period of the late 19th and early 20th centuries. Such a tripartite scheme kept white Europeans neatly separate from their African, Asian, and Native American subjects. Colonial empires began to break up, and scientists began to question established racial categories, after World War II (see Tattersall and DeSalle 2011).

## Races Are Not Biologically Distinct

History and politics aside, one obvious problem with "color-based" racial labels is that the terms don't accurately describe skin color. "White" people are more pink, beige, or tan than white. "Black" people are various shades of brown, and "yellow" people are tan or beige. But these terms have also been dignified by more scientific-*sounding* synonyms: Caucasoid, Negroid, and Mongoloid.

Another problem with the tripartite scheme is that many populations don't fit neatly into any one of the three "great races." For example, where would one put the Polynesians? *Polynesia* is a triangle of South Pacific islands formed by Hawaii to the north, Easter Island to the east, and New Zealand to the southwest. Does the "bronze" skin color of Polynesians connect them to the Caucasoids or to the Mongoloids? Some scientists, recognizing this problem, enlarged the original tripartite scheme to include the Polynesian "race." Native Americans presented a similar problem. Were they red or yellow? Some scientists added a fifth race—the "red," or Amerindian—to the major racial groups.

Many people in southern India have dark skin, but scientists have been reluctant to classify them with "black" Africans because of their Caucasoid facial features and hair form. Some, therefore, have created a separate race for these people. What about the Australian aborigines, hunters and gatherers native to what has been, throughout human history, the most isolated continent? By skin color, one might place some Native Australians in the same race as tropical Africans. However, similarities to Europeans in hair color (light or reddish) and facial features have led some scientists to classify them as Caucasoids. But there is no evidence that Australians are closer genetically or historically to either of these groups than they are to Asians. Recognizing this problem, scientists often regard Native Australians as a separate race.

Finally, consider the San ("Bushmen") of the Kalahari Desert in southern Africa. Scientists have perceived their skin color as varying from brown to yellow. Some who regard San skin as "yellow" have placed them in the same category as Asians. In theory, people of the same race share more recent common ancestry with each other than they do with any others. But there is no evidence for recent common ancestry between San and Asians. Somewhat more reasonably, some scholars assign the San to the Capoid race (from the Cape of Good Hope), which is seen as being different from other groups inhabiting tropical Africa.

Similar problems arise when any single trait is used as a basis for racial classification. An attempt to use facial features, height, weight, or any other phenotypical trait is fraught with difficulties. For example, consider the Nilotes, natives of the upper Nile region of Uganda and South Sudan. Nilotes tend to be tall and to have long, narrow noses. Certain Scandinavians are also tall, with similar noses. Given the distance between their homelands, to classify them as members of the same race makes little sense. There is no reason to assume that Nilotes and Scandinavians are more closely related to each other than either is to shorter and nearer populations with different kinds of noses.

Would it be better to base racial classifications on a combination of physical traits? This would avoid some of the problems mentioned earlier, but others would arise. First, skin color, stature, skull form, and facial features (nose form, eye shape, lip thickness) don't go together as a unit. For example, people with dark skin may be tall or short and have hair ranging from straight to very curly. Dark-haired populations may have light or dark skin, along with various skull forms, facial features, and body sizes and shapes. The number of combinations is very large, and the amount that heredity (versus environment) contributes to such phenotypical traits is often unclear.

## Genetic Markers Don't Correlate with Phenotype

The analysis of human DNA indicates that fully 94 percent of human genetic variation occurs within so-called races. Considering conventional geographic "racial" groupings such as Africans, Asians, and Europeans, there is only about 6 percent variation in genes from one group to the other. In other words, there is much greater variation within each of the traditional "races" than between them. Humans are much more alike genetically than are any of the living apes. This suggests a recently shared common ancestor (perhaps as recent as 70,000 to 50,000 years) for all members of modern *Homo sapiens*. Sampling the mitochondrial DNA (mtDNA) of various populations, Rebecca Cann, Mark Stoneking, and Allan C. Wilson (1987) concluded that humans are genetically uniform overall, suggesting recent common ancestry. The fact that African populations are the most diverse genetically provides evidence that Africa was where the human diaspora originated.

Contemporary work in genomics has allowed scientists to construct regional and global phylogenetic trees based on shared genetic markers. Such trees are based on mitochondrial DNA (sampling females) and the Y chromosome (sampling males). As the human genome gets better known, molecular anthropologists refine their models of actual genetic relationships among humans and how they dispersed. A **haplogroup** is a lineage, or branch, of such a genetic tree marked by one or more specific genetic mutations. For example, the global mtDNA tree includes branches known as M and N. The Y chromosome tree includes branches known as C and F. Those four branches (either M or N for mtDNA and either C or F for the Y chromosome) are known to be associated with the spread of modern humans out of Africa between 70,000 and 50,000 B.P. Because Native Australians share those four branches, they are known to be part of that diaspora.

Although such genetic trees exist, they don't correlate neatly with the distribution of human phenotypes. Because of changes in the environment that affect individuals during growth and development, the range of phenotypes characteristic of a population may change without any genetic change whatsoever. There are several examples. In the early 20th century, the anthropologist Franz Boas (1940/1966) described changes in skull form (e.g., toward rounder heads) among the children of

Europeans who had migrated to North America. The reason for this was not a change in genes, for the European immigrants tended to marry among themselves. Also, some of their children had been born in Europe and merely raised in the United States. Something in the environment, probably in the diet, was producing this change. We know now that changes in average height and weight produced by dietary differences in a few generations are common and may have nothing to do with race or genetics.

## Explaining Skin Color

Traditional racial classification assumed that biological characteristics such as skin color were determined by heredity and that they were stable (immutable) over many generations. We now know that a biological similarity doesn't necessarily indicate recent common ancestry. Dark skin color, for example, can be shared by tropical Africans, southern Indians, and indigenous Australians for reasons other than common heredity. Scientists have made considerable progress in explaining variation in human skin color, along with many other features of human biological diversity. We shift now from classification to explanation, in which natural selection plays a key role (see Anemone 2011).

The role of natural selection in producing variation in skin color will illustrate the explanatory approach to human biological diversity. Comparable explanations have been provided for many other aspects of human biological variation. Skin color is a complex biological trait—influenced by several genes. Just how many genes is not known. **Melanin,** the primary determinant of human skin color, is a chemical substance manufactured in the epidermis, or outer skin layer. The melanin cells of darker-skinned people produce more and larger granules of melanin than do those of lighter-skinned people. By screening out ultraviolet (UV) radiation from the sun, melanin offers protection against a variety of maladies, including sunburn and skin cancer.

Prior to the 16th century, most of the world's very dark-skinned peoples lived in the *tropics,* a belt extending about 23 degrees north and south of the equator, between the Tropic of Cancer and the Tropic of Capricorn. The association between dark skin color and a tropical habitat existed throughout the Old World, where humans and their ancestors have lived for hundreds of thousands of years. The darkest populations of Africa evolved in sunny, open grassland, or savanna, country.

Outside the tropics, skin color tends to be lighter. Moving north in Africa, for example, there is a gradual transition from dark brown to medium brown. Average skin color continues to lighten as one moves through the Middle East, into southern Europe, through central Europe, and to the north. South of the tropics skin color also is lighter. In the Americas, by contrast, tropical populations don't have very dark skin. This is the case because the settlement of the New World by light-skinned Asian ancestors of Native Americans was relatively recent, probably dating back no more than 20,000 years.

How, aside from migrations, can we explain the geographic distribution of human skin color? Natural selection provides an answer. In the tropics, intense UV radiation

Princess Madeleine of Sweden attends the wedding of Sweden's Crown Princess Victoria and Daniel Westling at the Stockholm Cathedral. Very light skin color, illustrated in this photo, maximizes absorption of ultraviolet radiation by those few parts of the body exposed to direct sunlight during northern winters. © Antony Jones/Julian Parker/Mark Cuthbert/UK Press via Getty Images

Before the 16th century, almost all the very dark-skinned populations of the world lived in the tropics, as does this Samburu woman from Kenya. © Jan Spieczny/Photolibrary/Getty Images

poses a series of threats, including severe sunburn, that make light skin color an adaptive disadvantage (Table 4.1 summarizes those threats). By damaging sweat glands, sunburn reduces the body's ability to perspire and thus to regulate its own temperature (thermoregulation). Sunburn also can increase susceptibility to disease. Melanin, nature's own sunscreen, confers a selective advantage (i.e., a better chance to survive and reproduce) on darker-skinned people living in the tropics. Yet another disadvantage of having light skin color in the tropics is that exposure to UV radiation can cause skin cancer.

When and why might light skin color be advantageous? Years ago, W. F. Loomis (1967) focused on the role of UV radiation in stimulating the synthesis of vitamin D by the human body. The unclothed human body can produce its own vitamin D when exposed to sufficient sunlight. However, in a cloudy environment that also is so cold that people have to wear clothing much of the year (such as northern Europe, where very light skin color evolved), clouds and clothing impede the body's manufacture of vitamin D. Vitamin D deficiency diminishes the absorption of calcium in the intestines. A nutritional disease known as *rickets,* which softens and deforms the bones, may develop. In women, deformation of the pelvic bones from rickets can interfere with childbirth. In cold northern areas, light skin color maximizes the absorption of UV radiation and the

**TABLE 4.1   Advantages and Disadvantages (Depending on Environment) of Dark and Light Skin Color**

Also shown are cultural alternatives that can make up for biological disadvantages and examples of natural selection (NS) operating today in relation to skin color.

| | | Cultural Alternatives | NS in Action Today |
|---|---|---|---|
| **DARK SKIN COLOR** Advantage | Melanin is natural sunscreen. In tropics: screens out UV Reduces susceptibility to folate destruction and thus to neural tube defects (NTDs), including spina bifida Prevents sunburn and thus enhances sweating and thermoregulation Reduces disease susceptibility Reduces risk of skin cancer | | |
| Disadvantage | Outside tropics: reduces UV absorption Increases susceptibility to rickets, osteoporosis | Foods, vitamin D supplements | East Asians in northern UK Inuit with modern diets |
| **LIGHT SKIN COLOR** Advantage | No natural sunscreen Outside tropics: admits UV Body manufactures vitamin D and thus prevents rickets and osteoporosis. | | |
| Disadvantage | Especially in tropics: increases susceptibility to folate destruction and thus to NTDs, including spina bifida Impairs spermatogenesis | Folic acid/folate supplements | Whites still have more NTDs. |
| | Increases susceptibility to sunburn and thus to impaired sweating and poor thermoregulation Increases disease susceptibility Increases susceptibility to skin cancer | Shelter, sunscreens, lotions, etc. | |

83

synthesis of vitamin D by the few parts of the body that are exposed to direct sunlight. There has been selection against dark skin color in northern areas because melanin screens out UV radiation.

This natural selection continues today: East Asians living in northern areas of the United Kingdom have a higher incidence of rickets and osteoporosis (also related to vitamin D and calcium deficiency) than the general British population. A related illustration involves Eskimos (Inuit) and other indigenous inhabitants of northern Alaska and northern Canada. According to Nina Jablonski (quoted in Iqbal 2002), "Looking at Alaska, one would think that the native people should be pale as ghosts." One reason they are not pale is that they haven't lived in this region very long in terms of geological time. Even more important, their traditional diet, which is rich in seafood, including fish oils, supplies sufficient vitamin D so as to make a reduction in pigmentation unnecessary. However, again illustrating natural selection at work today, when these people abandon their traditional diets based on fish and sea mammals, they suffer from high rates of childhood rickets and adult osteoporosis. Far from being immutable, skin color can become an evolutionary liability very quickly.

Another key factor explaining the geographic distribution of skin color involves the effects of UV on folate, an essential nutrient that the human body manufactures from folic acid (Jablonski 2012). Pregnant women require large amounts of folate to support rapid cell division in the embryo, and there is a direct connection between folate and individual reproductive success. Folate deficiency causes neural tube defects (NTDs) in human embryos. NTDs are marked by the incomplete closure of the neural tube, so the spine and spinal cord fail to develop completely. One NTD, anencephaly (with the brain an exposed mass), results in stillbirth or death soon after delivery. With spina bifida, another NTD, survival rates are higher, but babies have severe disabilities, including paralysis. NTDs are the second most common human birth defect after cardiac abnormalities. Today, women of reproductive age are advised to take folate supplements to prevent serious birth defects such as spina bifida.

Natural sunlight and UV radiation destroy folate in the human body. Because melanin, as we have seen, protects against UV hazards, such as sunburn and its consequences, dark skin coloration is adaptive in the tropics. Now we see that melanin also is adaptive because it conserves folate in the human body and thus protects against NTDs, which are much more common in light-skinned than darker-skinned populations (Jablonski 2006, 2012; Jablonski and Chaplin 2000). Africans and African Americans rarely demonstrate severe folate deficiency, even among individuals with marginal nutritional status. Folate also plays a role in another key reproductive process, spermatogenesis—the production of sperm. In mice and rats, folate deficiency can cause male sterility; it may well play a similar role in humans.

Today, of course, cultural alternatives to biological adaptation permit light-skinned people to survive in the tropics and darker-skinned people to live in the far north. People can clothe themselves and seek shelter from the sun; they can use artificial sunscreens if they lack the natural protection that melanin provides. Dark-skinned people living in the north can, indeed must, get vitamin D from their diet or take supplements. Today, pregnant women are routinely advised to take folic acid or folate supplements as a hedge against NTDs. Even so, light skin color still is correlated with a higher incidence of spina bifida.

Jablonski and Chaplin (2000) explain variation in human skin color as resulting from a balancing act between the evolutionary needs to (1) protect against all UV hazards (thus favoring dark skin in the tropics) and (2) have an adequate supply of vitamin D (thus favoring lighter skin outside the tropics). We see that common ancestry, the presumed basis of race, is not the only reason for biological similarities. Natural selection, still at work today, makes a major contribution to variations in human skin color, as well as to many other human biological differences and similarities.

# Human Biological Adaptation

This section considers additional examples of human biological diversity that reflect adaptation to environmental stresses, such as disease and diet. There is abundant evidence for human genetic adaptation and thus for evolution (change in gene frequency) through selection working in specific environments. One example is the adaptive value of the $Hb^S$ heterozygote and its spread in malarial environments, which was discussed previously.

## Genes and Disease

Microbes have been major selective agents for humans, particularly before the arrival of modern medicine. Some people are genetically more susceptible to certain diseases than others are, and the distribution of human blood types continues to change in response to natural selection.

After food production emerged around 10,000 years ago, infectious diseases posed a mounting risk and eventually became the foremost cause of human mortality. Food production favors infection for several reasons. Cultivation sustains larger, denser populations and a more sedentary lifestyle than does hunting and gathering. People live closer to each other and to their own wastes, making it easier for microbes to survive and to find hosts. Domesticated animals also transmit diseases to people.

Until 1977, when the last case of smallpox was reported, smallpox had been a major threat to humans and a determinant of blood group frequencies (Diamond 1990, 1997). Smallpox appeared in human beings after people and animals started living together. The smallpox virus is a mutation from one of the pox viruses that plague such domesticated animals as cows, sheep, goats, horses, and pigs. Smallpox epidemics have played important roles in world history, often killing one-fourth to one-half of the affected populations. Smallpox contributed to Sparta's defeat of Athens in 430 B.C.E. and to the decline of the Roman empire after 160 C.E.

The ABO blood groups have figured in human resistance to smallpox. Blood is typed according to the protein and sugar compounds on the surface of the red blood cells. Different substances (compounds) distinguish between type A and type B blood. Type A cells trigger the production of *antibodies* in B blood, so A cells clot in B blood. The different substances work like chemical passwords; they help us distinguish our own cells from invading cells, including microbes, we ought to destroy. The surfaces of some microbes have substances similar to ABO blood group substances. We don't produce antibodies to substances similar to those on our own blood cells. We can think of this as a clever evolutionary trick by the microbes to deceive their hosts, because we don't normally develop antibodies against our own biochemistry.

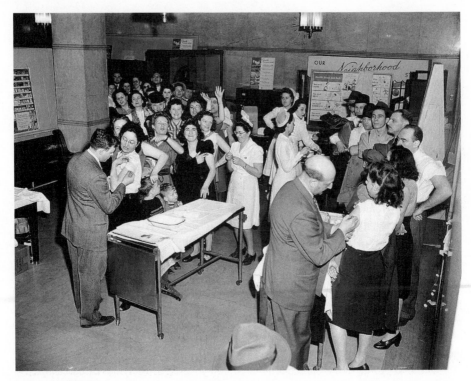

In New York City in 1947, the appearance of nine cases of smallpox, including two deaths, spurred a very successful mass vaccination program. Shown here, lines of people wait to be vaccinated at the New York Health Department on April 14, 1947. The smallpox threat made the cover of *Cosmopolitan* magazine. © Tony Camerano/AP Images; NIH History of Medicine Division, U.S. National Library of Medicine

People with A or AB blood are more susceptible to smallpox than are people with type B or type O. Presumably this is because a substance on the smallpox virus mimics the type A substance, permitting the virus to slip by the defenses of the type A individual. By contrast, type B and type O individuals produce antibodies against smallpox because they recognize it as a foreign substance.

The relation between type A blood and susceptibility to smallpox was first suggested by the low frequencies of the A allele in areas of India and Africa where smallpox had been endemic. A comparative study done in rural India in 1965–1966, during a virulent smallpox epidemic, did much to confirm this relationship. Drs. F. Vogel and M. R. Chakravartti analyzed blood samples from smallpox victims and their uninfected siblings (Diamond 1990). The researchers found 415 infected children, none ever vaccinated against smallpox. All but 8 of the infected children had an uninfected (also unvaccinated) sibling.

The results of the study were clear: Susceptibility to smallpox varied with ABO type. Of the 415 infected children, 261 had the A allele; 154 lacked it. Among their 407 uninfected siblings, the ratio was reversed. Only 80 had the A allele; 327 lacked it. The researchers calculated that a type A or type AB person had a seven times greater chance of getting smallpox than did an O or a B person.

In most human populations, the O allele is more common than A and B combined. Type A is most common in Europe; B frequencies are highest in Asia. Since smallpox was once widespread in the Old World, we might wonder why natural selection didn't eliminate the A allele entirely. The answer appears to be this: Other diseases spared the type A people and penalized those with other blood groups.

For example, type O people seem to be especially susceptible to the bubonic plague—the "Black Death" that killed a third of the population of medieval Europe. Type O people are also more likely to get cholera, which has killed as many people in India as smallpox has. On the other hand, blood group O may increase resistance to syphilis. The ravages of that sexually transmitted disease, which may have originated in the New World, may explain the very high frequency of type O blood among the native populations of Central and South America. The distribution of human blood groups appears to represent a compromise among the selective effects of many diseases.

Especially when we consider diseases for which there are no known cures, genetic resistance maintains its significance (see Hartigan 2013). As an interesting case of what might be called fortuitous preadaptation or preselection, consider the CCR5 receptor gene. This gene, which codes for a protein on the surface of white blood cells, is involved in the human immune system. The viral infection HIV, which causes AIDS, uses the CCR5 gene's receptor to invade and infect cells. But individuals who are homozygous for an allele known as CCR5-Δ32 (delta 32) are resistant to this invasion. This HIV immunity illustrates preadaptation or preselection, because the original selection for the allele had nothing to do with HIV. The allele was adaptive and spread because of the resistance it offered against other deadly epidemics, which occurred much earlier in European history.

The CCR5-Δ32 allele is found in 3 to 14 percent of Europeans, but it is absent in Africans, East Asians, and Native Americans. Among Europeans, the allele is most common in Scandinavia and Russia and least common near the Mediterranean.

Christopher Duncan and Susan Scott (2004) argue that most of the lethal epidemics that ravaged Europe between 1347 and 1660 were not bubonic plague, as is commonly thought, but rather a viral hemorrhagic fever that used the CCR5 receptor gene to invade (and usually kill) its human hosts. This hemorrhagic fever vanished from England after London's Great Plague of 1665–1666, but it persisted through 1800 in Sweden, Denmark, Russia, Poland, and Hungary, where selection for CCR5-Δ32 therefore continued, and where that gene now has its greatest frequency (see Relethford 2013). Other researchers have suggested a link between the spread of CCR5-Δ32 and resistance to smallpox. Whatever the disease that originally favored this allele, it is clear that it is merely through luck that CCR5-Δ32 also confers resistance to HIV and AIDS.

## Lactose Tolerance

Many biological traits that illustrate human adaptation are not under simple genetic control. Genetic determination of such traits may be likely but unconfirmed, or several genes may interact to influence the trait in question. Sometimes there is a genetic component but the trait also responds to stresses encountered during growth. We speak of **phenotypical adaptation** when adaptive changes occur during an individual's lifetime. Phenotypical adaptation is made possible by biological plasticity—our ability to change in response to the environments we encounter as we grow.

Genes and phenotypical adaptation work together to produce biochemical differences in adult humans' ability to digest milk—an adaptive advantage when other foods are scarce and milk is available. Milk contains a complex sugar called *lactose.* The digestion of milk depends on an enzyme called *lactase,* which works in the small intestine. Among all mammals except humans and some of their pets, lactase production ceases after weaning, so these animals can no longer digest milk.

Milk tolerance varies among human groups. About 90 percent of northern Europeans and their descendants are lactose tolerant; they can digest several glasses of milk with no difficulty. Similarly, about 80 percent of two African populations, the Tutsi of Rwanda and Burundi in East Africa and the Fulani of Nigeria in West Africa, produce lactase and digest milk easily. Both of these groups traditionally have been herders. However, such nonherders as the Yoruba and the Igbo in Nigeria, the Baganda in Uganda, the Japanese and other Asians, Eskimos, South American Indians, and many Israelis cannot digest lactose (Kretchmer 1972/1975).

Recent genetic studies have helped clarify when and how humans developed lactose tolerance. An allele known to favor adult lactose tolerance existed, but still was uncommon, in central and eastern Europe as recently as 3,800 years ago (Burger et al. 2007). Sarah Tishkoff and her associates found that the alleles behind lactose tolerance in East Africa differ from those of lactose-tolerant Europeans. Her genetic studies of 43 East African groups suggested that three different mutations favoring lactose tolerance arose in Africa between 6,800 and 2,700 years ago (Tishkoff et al. 2007). Again we see that the same phenotype—in this case, lactose tolerance—can be produced by different genotypes. Natural selection has resulted in different selective solutions to the same environmental challenge. It also should be noted that the variable human ability to digest milk seems to be a difference of degree. Some populations can tolerate very little or no milk, but others are able to metabolize much greater quantities. People who move from no-milk or low-milk diets to high-milk diets can increase their lactose tolerance; this suggests some phenotypical adaptation.

## Anthropology Today  *Devastating Encounters within the Columbian Exchange*

The Columbian exchange (named for Christopher Columbus) was a key early form of globalization, because it forever linked our globe's Western and Eastern Hemispheres. The term refers to the exchange of products, populations, and diseases between the Old World and the New World that occurred after Columbus reached the Americas in 1492.

The Columbian exchange transformed economies and lifestyles in both hemispheres as new foods became dietary staples. Among the New World crops that thrived when planted in Old World soils were potatoes, maize, and manioc. By the 1840s Ireland had become so dependent on the Andean (now "Irish") potato that a diseased crop led to the devastating Irish Potato Famine, responsible for 1 million deaths and 2 million emigrants (Nunn and Qian 2010). Two Old World crops—coffee (from Africa) and sugarcane (from Asia)—became key plantation crops in Latin America and the Caribbean. Cotton, another important cash crop grown on American plantations, was independently domesticated in the New World and the Old World. The variety of cotton that eventually was grown on plantations in the southern United States was introduced from Mexico around 1700. The Atlantic slave trade, which supplied involuntary labor for these plantations, represents the most disruptive and inhumane dimension of the early world capitalist economy.

Another devastating aspect of the Columbian exchange was the global spread of diseases previously confined to the Old World. Having lived with these pathogens for generations, Old World populations had developed various forms of immunity to many of them. Native Americans had no such resistance to Old World diseases, which included smallpox, chicken pox, measles, malaria, yellow fever, cholera, typhoid, bubonic plague, influenza, and the common cold. Only syphilis moved the other way—from the New World to the Old. By debilitating and decimating the Aztecs of Mexico and the Inca of Peru, severe smallpox epidemics helped the Spanish conquer those peoples and their territories. Up to 90 percent of the population of the New World may have perished from Old World pathogens between 1500 and 1650 (Nunn and Qian 2010).

The African slave trade emerged in the context of Native American depopulation and the demand for human labor to produce commodities on New World plantations. About 12 million human beings were involuntarily transported from Africa to the New World during the centuries of the Atlantic slave trade (the 16th through 19th centuries).

Europeans from Spain, Portugal, the Netherlands, England, and France extended their colonial empires from the Americas to Africa and Asia. Europeans had a degree of genetic resistance to many Old World pathogens, but not to malaria—the scourge of the tropics. Quinine was a New World product that, again through the Columbian exchange, eventually offered Europeans a degree of protection against malaria. Europeans might never have been able to maintain colonial empires in the tropics of Africa, Asia, and South America without quinine (Nunn and Qian 2010). This is yet another way in which western expansion, and ultimately the formation of the modern world system, depended on the Columbian exchange.

*continued*

---

## Anthropology Today    *continued*

Remember that biocultural and holistic approaches are fundamental to anthropology. One excellent example is that anthropologists view the evolution of disease not just biologically but in the context of social and political history, including the Columbian exchange. In today's world, globalization plays a key role in the spread of diseases, as anyone who has seen the movie *Contagion* knows. Syphilis, which spread through the Columbian exchange, provides an important early illustration of the globalization of disease.

A recent comprehensive genetic study investigated the origin of syphilis (see Wilford 2008; Harper et al. 2011). Known to us as a dreaded venereal, or sexually transmitted, disease (STD), syphilis apparently originated in the Americas as a nonvenereal bacterium transmitted by skin-to-skin contact, usually in children. Columbus and his men apparently carried nonvenereal syphilis back to Europe, where it mutated into venereal syphilis, which became a major killer during the Renaissance. Can you think of recent cases illustrating the globalization of disease? Do you think some people will be genetically resistant to emerging diseases? Why or why not?

---

## Summary

1. In the 18th century, Carolus Linnaeus developed biological taxonomy. He viewed differences and similarities among organisms as part of God's orderly plan rather than as evidence for evolution. In the mid-19th century, Charles Darwin and Alfred Russel Wallace proposed that natural selection could explain the origin of species, biological diversity, and similarities among related life forms. Natural selection requires variety in the population undergoing selection.

2. Through breeding experiments with peas in 1856, Gregor Mendel discovered that genetic traits pass on as units. These are now known to be chromosomes, which occur in homologous pairs. Alleles—some dominant, some recessive—are the chemically different forms that occur at a given genetic locus. Mendel also formulated the law of independent assortment. Each of the seven traits he studied in peas was inherited independently of all the others. Independent assortment of chromosomes and their recombination provide some of the variety needed for natural selection. But the major source of such variety is mutation, a chemical change in the DNA molecules of which genes are made.

3. Population genetics studies gene frequencies in stable and changing populations. Natural selection is the most important mechanism of evolutionary change. Others are mutation, random genetic drift, and gene flow. Given environmental change, nature selects traits already present in the population. If variety is insufficient to permit adaptation to the change, extinction is likely. New types don't appear just because they are needed.

4. One well-documented case of natural selection in contemporary human populations is that of the sickle-cell allele. In homozygous form, the sickle-cell allele,

Hb$^S$, produces an abnormal hemoglobin. This clogs the small blood vessels, impairing the blood's capacity to store oxygen. The result is sickle-cell anemia, which is usually fatal. Homozygotes for normal hemoglobin are susceptible to malaria and die in great numbers. Heterozygotes get only mild anemia and are resistant to malaria. In a malarial environment, the heterozygote has the advantage.

5. Other mechanisms of genetic evolution complement natural selection. Random genetic drift operates most obviously in small populations, where pure chance can easily change allele frequencies. Gene flow and interbreeding keep subgroups of the same species genetically connected and thus impede speciation.

6. How do scientists approach the study of human biological diversity? Because of a range of problems involved in classifying humans into racial categories, contemporary biologists focus on specific differences and try to explain them. Because of extensive gene flow and interbreeding, *Homo sapiens* has not evolved subspecies or distinct races. The genetic breaks that do exist among human populations have not led to the formation of discrete races. Biological similarities between groups may reflect—rather than common ancestry—similar but independent adaptations to similar natural selective forces, such as degrees of ultraviolet radiation from the sun in the case of skin color.

7. Differential resistance to infectious diseases such as smallpox has influenced the distribution of human blood groups. There are genetic antimalarials, such as the sickle-cell allele. *Phenotypical adaptation* refers to adaptive changes that occur in an individual's lifetime in response to the environment the organism encounters as it grows. Lactose tolerance is due partly to phenotypical adaptation. Biological similarities between geographically distant populations may be due to similar but independent genetic changes rather than to common ancestry. Or they may reflect similar physiological responses to common stresses during growth.

## Key Terms

adaptive, *73*
alleles, *70*
balanced
  polymorphism, *74*
catastrophism, *66*
chromosomes, *69*
cline, *77*
creationism, *65*
dominant, *69*
evolution, *66*
gene, *70*
gene flow, *75*
gene pool, *71*
genetic
  evolution, *72*
genotype, *70*

haplogroup, *80*
heterozygous, *70*
homozygous, *70*
independent
  assortment, *71*
meiosis, *71*
melanin, *81*
Mendelian
  genetics, *69*
mitosis, *71*
mutations, *75*
natural
  selection, *67*
phenotype, *70*
phenotypical
  adaptation, *88*

population
  genetics, *69*
racial
  classification, *77*
random genetic
  drift, *75*
recessive, *69*
sexual selection, *73*
speciation, *76*
species, *76*
theory, *66*
uniformitarianism,
  *66*

# Chapter 5

# The Primates

**Primatology** is the study of nonhuman **primates**—fossil and living apes, monkeys, and prosimians—including their behavior and social life. Primatology is fascinating in itself, but it also helps anthropologists make inferences about the early social organization of *hominids* (members of the zoological family that includes fossil and living humans). Of particular relevance to humans are two kinds of primates:

1. Those whose ecological adaptations are similar to our own: **terrestrial** monkeys and apes—that is, primates that live on the ground rather than in the trees.
2. Those that are most closely related to us: the great apes, specifically the chimpanzees and gorillas.

## Our Place among Primates

Similarities between humans and apes are evident in anatomy, brain structure, genetics, and biochemistry. The physical similarities between humans and apes are

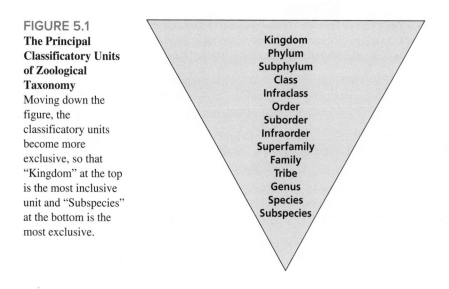

**FIGURE 5.1**

**The Principal Classificatory Units of Zoological Taxonomy**
Moving down the figure, the classificatory units become more exclusive, so that "Kingdom" at the top is the most inclusive unit and "Subspecies" at the bottom is the most exclusive.

Kingdom
Phylum
Subphylum
Class
Infraclass
Order
Suborder
Infraorder
Superfamily
Family
Tribe
Genus
Species
Subspecies

recognized in zoological **taxonomy**—the assignment of organisms to categories (*taxa;* singular, *taxon*) according to their relatedness and resemblance. Many similarities between organisms reflect their common *phylogeny*—their genetic relatedness. In other words, organisms share features they have inherited from the same ancestor. Humans and apes belong to the same taxonomic superfamily, Hominoidea (hominoids). Monkeys are placed in two others (Ceboidea and Cercopithecoidea). This means that humans and apes are more closely related to each other than either is to monkeys.

Figure 5.1 summarizes the various levels of classification used in zoological taxonomy. Each lower-level unit belongs to the one above it. Thus, toward the bottom of Figure 5.1, similar species belong to the same genus (plural, *genera*). Similar genera make up the same family, and so on through the top of Figure 5.1, where similar phyla (plural of *phylum*) are included in the same kingdom. The highest (most inclusive) taxonomic level is the *kingdom.* At that level, animals are distinguished from plants.

At the lowest level of taxonomy, a species may have subspecies. These are its more or less—but not yet totally—isolated subgroups. Subspecies can coexist in time and space. For example, the Neandertals, who lived between 130,000 and perhaps as late as 28,000 years ago, often are assigned not to a separate species but merely to a different subspecies of *Homo sapiens.* Just one subspecies of *Homo sapiens* survives today.

The similarities used to assign organisms to the same taxon are called **homologies,** similarities they have jointly inherited from a common ancestor. Table 5.1 summarizes the place of humans in zoological taxonomy. We see in Table 5.1 that we are mammals, members of the class Mammalia. This is a major subdivision of the kingdom Animalia. Mammals share certain traits, including mammary glands, that set them apart from other taxa, such as birds, reptiles, amphibians, and insects. Mammalian homologies

TABLE 5.1    **The Place of Humans (*Homo sapiens*) in Zoological Taxonomy**
*Homo sapiens* is an animal, chordate, vertebrate, mammal, eutherian, primate, anthropoid, catarrhine, hominoid, hominid, and hominin. (Table 5.2 shows the taxonomic placement of the other primates.)

| Taxon | Scientific (Latin) Name | Common (English) Name |
|---|---|---|
| Kingdom | Animalia | Animals |
| Phylum | Chordata | Chordates |
| Subphylum | Vertebrata | Vertebrates |
| Class | Mammalia | Mammals |
| Infraclass | Eutheria | Eutherians |
| Order | Primates | Primates |
| Suborder | Anthropoidea | Anthropoids |
| Infraorder | Catarrhini | Catarrhines |
| Superfamily | Hominoidea | Hominoids |
| Family | Hominidae | Hominids |
| Tribe | Hominini | Hominins |
| Genus | *Homo* | Humans |
| Species | *Homo sapiens* | Recent humans |
| Subspecies | *Homo sapiens sapiens* | Anatomically modern humans |

indicate that all mammals share more recent common ancestry with each other than they do with any bird, reptile, or insect.

Humans are mammals that, at a lower taxonomic level, belong to the *order* Primates, which also includes monkeys and apes. Another mammalian order is Carnivora—the carnivores (dogs, cats, foxes, wolves, badgers, weasels). Rodentia (rats, mice, beavers, squirrels) form yet another mammalian order. The primates share structural and biochemical homologies that distinguish them from other mammals. These resemblances were inherited from their common ancestors after those early primates became reproductively isolated from the ancestors of the other mammals.

## Homologies and Analogies

Organisms should be assigned to the same taxon on the basis of homologies. The extensive biochemical homologies between apes and humans confirm our common ancestry and support our traditional joint classification as hominoids (see Table 5.2). Humans, chimpanzees, and gorillas have more than 98 percent of their DNA in common.

However, common ancestry isn't the only reason for similarities between species. Similar traits also can arise if species experience similar selective forces and adapt to them in similar ways. We call such similarities **analogies.** The process by which analogies are produced is called **convergent evolution.** For example, fish and porpoises (dolphins) share many analogies resulting from convergent evolution to life in

TABLE 5.2   **Primate Taxonomy**

The major subdivisions of the two primate suborders are *Prosimii* and *Anthropoidea.* Humans are anthropoids who belong to the superfamily *Hominoidea,* along with the apes.

Source: R. Martin, "Classification of Primates" from *The Cambridge Encyclopedia of Human Evolution,* ed. by S. Jones, R. Martin and D. Pilbeam, pp. 20–21.

| Suborder | Infraorder | Superfamily | Family |
|---|---|---|---|
| Prosimii (prosimians) | Lemuriformes (lemurs) | Lemuroidea | Daubentoniidae (aye-ayes), indridae (indri), lemuridae (lemurs) |
| | Lorisiformes (lorises) | Lorisoidea | Lorisidae |
| | Tarsiiformes (tarsiers) | Tarsioidea | Tarsiidae |
| Anthropoidea (anthropoids) | Platyrrhini (platyrrhines—New World monkeys) | Ceboidea | Callitrichidae (tamarins and marmosets), Cebidae |
| | Catarrhini (catarrhines—Old World monkeys, apes, and humans) | Cercopithecoidea | Cercopithecidae (Old World monkeys) |
| | | Hominoidea (hominoids) | Hylobatidae (gibbons and siamangs), Pongidae (pongids—orangutans), Hominidae (hominids—gorillas, chimpanzees, and humans) |

the water. Like fish, porpoises, which are mammals, have fins. They are also hairless and streamlined for efficient locomotion. Analogies between birds and bats (wings, small size, light bones) illustrate convergent evolution to flying.

In theory, only homologies should be used in taxonomy. With reference to the hominoids, there is no doubt that humans, gorillas, and chimpanzees are more closely related to each other than any of the three is to orangutans, which are Asiatic apes. As discussed, Hominidae is the name of the zoological family that includes hominids—fossil and living humans. Because chimps and gorillas share a more recent common ancestor with humans than they do with orangutans, many scientists now also place gorillas and chimps in the hominid family. *Hominid* would then refer to the zoological family that includes fossil and living humans, chimpanzees, gorillas, and their common ancestors. This leaves the orangutan (genus *Pongo*) as the only member of the pongid family (Pongidae). If chimps and gorillas are classified as hominids, what do we call the group that leads to humans but not to chimps and gorillas? For that, some scientists insert a taxonomic level called *tribe* between family and genus. The tribe *hominini* describes all the human species that ever have existed (including the extinct ones) and excludes chimps and gorillas. Figure 5.2 illustrates our degree of relatedness to the living great apes.

FIGURE 5.2    **Humans and the Apes.**
The top drawing shows the evolutionary (phylogenetic) relationships among the living great apes and humans. Note that humans and the African apes are more closely related to each other (as hominids) than either is to the orangutan (a pongid). The bottom drawing shows the same phylogeny, along with estimated dates of divergence and last common ancestor (represented by dots). It is based on the extent of shared DNA among these groups.

From John Relethford, *The Human Species: An Introduction to Biological Anthropology,* 9th ed., (top) p. 134 and (bottom) p. 232. Copyright 2013 by McGraw-Hill Education, LLC. Reprinted with permission.

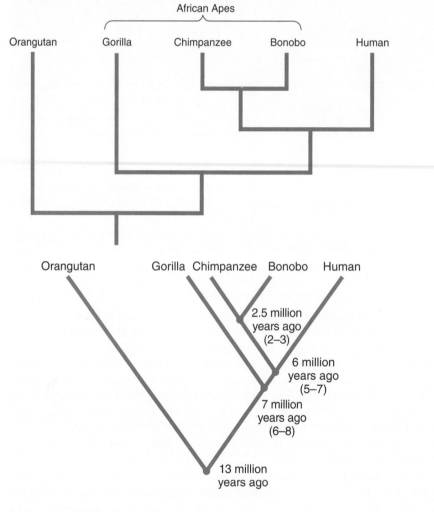

# Primate Tendencies

Primates are varied because they have adapted to diverse ecological niches. Some primates are active during the day; others, at night. Some eat insects; others, fruits; others, shoots, leaves, and bulk vegetation; and others, seeds or roots. Some primates live on the ground, others live in trees, and there are intermediate adaptations (see Campbell 2011; Nystrom and Ashmore 2008). However, because the earliest primates were tree dwellers, modern primates share homologies reflecting their common **arboreal** heritage.

Many trends in primate evolution are best exemplified by the **anthropoids:** monkeys, apes, and humans, which constitute the suborder Anthropoidea. The other primate suborder, *Prosimii,* includes lemurs, lorises, and tarsiers. These **prosimians** are more distant relatives of humans than are monkeys and apes. The primate trends—most developed in the anthropoids—can be summarized briefly. Together they constitute an anthropoid heritage that humans share with monkeys and apes.

1. *Grasping.* Primates have five-digited feet and hands that are suited for grasping. Certain features of hands and feet that originally were adaptive for arboreal life have been transmitted across the generations to contemporary primates. Flexible hands and feet that could encircle branches were important features in the early primates' tree-based existence. Thumb opposability might have been favored by the inclusion of insects in the early primate diet. Manual dexterity makes it easier to catch insects attracted to abundant arboreal flowers and fruits. Humans and many other primates have **opposable thumbs:** The thumb can touch the other fingers. Some primates also have grasping feet. However, in adapting to **bipedal** (two-footed) locomotion, humans eliminated most of the foot's grasping ability.

2. *Smell to sight.* Several anatomical changes reflect the shift from smell to sight as the primates' most important means of obtaining information. Monkeys, apes, and humans have excellent *stereoscopic* (able to see in depth) and color vision. The portion of the brain devoted to vision expanded, while the area concerned with smell shrank.

3. *Nose to hand.* The sense of touch, conveyed by *tactile organs,* also provides information. Some nonprimates, including cats and dogs, have sensitive tactile skin on their noses. Cats' facial whiskers also serve a tactile function. In primates, however, the main touch organ is the hand, specifically the sensitive pads of the "fingerprint" region.

4. *Brain complexity.* The proportion of brain tissue concerned with memory, thought, and association has increased in primates. The primate ratio of brain size to body size exceeds that of most mammals.

5. *Parental investment.* Most primates give birth to a single offspring rather than a litter. Because of this, growing primates receive more attention and have more learning opportunities than do other mammals. Learned behavior is an important part of primate adaptation.

6. *Sociality.* Primates tend to be social animals that live with others of their species. The need for longer and more attentive care of offspring places a selective value on support by a social group.

## Prosimians

The primate order has two suborders: prosimians and anthropoids. The early history of the primates is limited to prosimian-like animals known through the fossil record. The first anthropoids, ancestral to monkeys, apes, and humans, appeared more than 40 million years ago. Some prosimians managed to survive in Africa and Asia because they adapted to nocturnal life. Thus, they did not compete with anthropoids, which are active during the day. Prosimians (lemurs) in Madagascar had no anthropoid competitors until people colonized that island some 2,000 years ago.

In their behavior and biology, Madagascar's *lemurs,* with about 100 species, have adapted to an array of environments, with varied diets and times of activity. Lemurs eat fruits, other plant foods, eggs, and insects. Some are nocturnal; others are active during the day. Some are totally arboreal; others spend some time on the ground. Another kind of prosimian is the *tarsier,* today confined to Indonesia, Malaysia, and the Philippines. From the fossil record, we know that 50 million years ago, several genera of tarsier-like prosimians lived in North America and Europe. The single surviving genus of tarsier is totally nocturnal. Active at night, tarsiers don't directly compete with anthropoids, which are active during the day. Lorises are other nocturnal prosimians found in Africa and Asia.

## Monkeys

Monkeys and other anthropoids share resemblances that can be considered trends in primate evolution, because these traits are not fully developed either in the fossils of primates that lived prior to 50 million years ago or among contemporary prosimians.

The anthropoid suborder has two infraorders: *platyrrhines* (New World monkeys) and *catarrhines* (Old World monkeys, apes, and humans). The catarrhines (sharp-nosed) and platyrrhines (flat-nosed) take their names from Latin terms that describe the placement of the nostrils. Old World monkeys, apes, and humans are all catarrhines. Being placed in the same taxon (infraorder, in this case) means that Old World monkeys, apes, and humans are more closely related to each other than to New World monkeys. In other words, one kind of monkey (Old World) is more like a human than it is like another kind of monkey (New World). The New World monkeys were reproductively isolated from the catarrhines before the latter diverged into the Old World monkeys, apes, and humans. This is why New World monkeys are assigned to a different infraorder.

All New World monkeys and many Old World monkeys are arboreal. Whether in the trees or on the ground, however, monkeys move differently than apes and humans. Their arms and legs move parallel to one another, as dogs' legs do. This contrasts with the tendency toward *orthograde posture,* the straight and upright stance of apes and humans. Unlike apes, which have longer arms than legs, and humans, who have longer legs than arms, monkeys have arms and legs of about the same length. Most monkeys also have tails, which help them maintain balance in the trees. Apes and humans lack tails. The apes' tendency toward orthograde posture is most evident when they sit down. When they move about, chimps, gorillas, and orangutans habitually use all four limbs.

### New World Monkeys

New World monkeys live in the forests of Central and South America (see Strier 2011). Unlike Old World monkeys, many New World monkeys have *prehensile,* or grasping, tails. Sometimes the prehensile tail has tactile skin, which permits it to work like a hand, for instance, in conveying food to the mouth. Old World monkeys, however, have

The woolly spider monkey, or muriqui, is the largest primate native to the Americas. These New World monkeys, whose species is endangered, can be found in Brazil's depleted Atlantic rain forest. Note the grasping limbs and tail. © BrazilPhotos.com/Alamy

developed characteristic anatomical specializations. They have rough patches of skin on the buttocks, adapted to sitting on hard, rocky ground and rough branches. If a primate you see in a zoo has such patches, it's from the Old World. If it has a prehensile tail, it's a New World monkey. Among the anthropoids, there's only one nocturnal animal, a New World monkey called the night monkey or owl monkey. All other monkeys and apes, and humans, too, of course, are diurnal—active during the day.

## Old World Monkeys

The Old World monkeys include both terrestrial and arboreal species. Baboons and many macaques are terrestrial monkeys. Certain traits differentiate terrestrial from arboreal primates. Arboreal primates tend to be smaller, enabling them to reach a wider range of foods in trees and shrubs, where the most abundant foods are located at the ends of branches. Arboreal monkeys typically are lithe and agile. They escape from the few predators in their environment—snakes and monkey-eating eagles—through alertness and speed. Large size, by contrast, is advantageous for terrestrial primates in dealing with their predators, which are more numerous on the ground.

Another contrast between arboreal and terrestrial primates is in sexual dimorphism— marked differences in male and female anatomy and temperament. Sexual dimorphism tends to be more marked in terrestrial than in arboreal species. Baboon and macaque males are larger and fiercer than are females of the same species. However, it's hard to tell, without close inspection, the sex of an arboreal monkey.

A mature male mandrill—a mainly terrestrial Old World monkey—ambles through gallery forest in Lope National Park, Gabon. © Anup Shah/Corbis

Terrestrial monkeys have specializations in anatomy, psychology, and social behavior that enable them to cope with terrestrial life. Adult male baboons, for example, are fierce-looking animals that can weigh 100 pounds (45 kilograms). They display their long, projecting canines to intimidate predators and when confronting other baboons. A male baboon also can puff up his ample mane of shoulder hair, so that a would-be aggressor perceives him as larger than he actually is.

When they reach the age of puberty, baboon and macaque males typically leave their home troop for another. Because males move in and out, females form the stable core of the terrestrial monkey troop (Cheney and Seyfarth 1990). By contrast, among chimpanzees and gorillas, females are more likely to emigrate and seek mates outside their natal social groups (Chapais 2008; Wilson and Wrangham 2003). Among terrestrial monkeys, then, the core group consists of females; among apes, it is composed of males.

## Apes

The Old World monkeys have their own superfamily (Cercopithecoidea), while humans and the apes together compose the **hominoid** superfamily (Hominoidea). Among the hominoids, the so-called great apes are orangutans, gorillas, and chimpanzees. The lesser (smaller) apes are the gibbons and siamangs of Southeast Asia and Indonesia.

Several traits are shared by apes (and humans) as distinct from monkeys and other primates. Body size tends to be larger. The lifespan is longer. There is a longer interval

## FIGURE 5.3    The Limb Ratio of the Arboreal Gibbon and Terrestrial *Homo*

How does this anatomical difference fit the modes of locomotion used by gibbons and humans?

 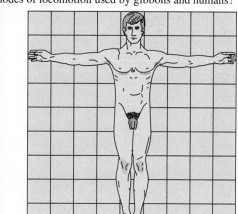

between births of infants, which depend longer on their parent(s). There is a tendency toward upright posture, although habitual upright bipedalism is only characteristic of hominins. The brain is larger, the muzzle, or face, is shorter and less projecting, and no hominoid has a tail.

Apes live in forests and woodlands. The light and agile gibbons, which are skilled brachiators, are completely arboreal. **Brachiation** is hand-over-hand movement through the trees. The heavier gorillas, chimpanzees, and adult male orangutans spend considerable time on the ground. Nevertheless, ape behavior and anatomy reveal past and present adaptation to arboreal life. For example, apes still build nests to sleep in trees. Apes have longer arms than legs, which is adaptive for brachiation (see Figure 5.3). The structure of the shoulder and clavicle (collarbone) of the apes and humans suggests that we had a brachiating ancestor. In fact, young apes still brachiate. Adult apes tend to be too heavy to brachiate safely. Their weight is more than many branches can withstand. Gorillas and chimps now use the long arms they have inherited from their more arboreal ancestors for life on the ground. The terrestrial locomotion of chimps and gorillas is called *knuckle-walking*. In it, long arms and callused knuckles support the trunk as the apes amble around, leaning forward.

## Gibbons

Gibbons are widespread in the forests of Southeast Asia, especially in Malaysia. Smallest of the apes, male and female gibbons have about the same average height (3 feet, or 1 meter) and weight (12 to 25 pounds, or 5 to 10 kilograms). Gibbons spend most of their time just below the forest canopy (treetops). For efficient brachiation, gibbons have long arms and fingers, with short thumbs. Slenderly built, gibbons are the most agile apes. They use their long arms for balance when they occasionally walk erect on the ground or along a branch. Gibbons are the preeminent arboreal specialists among the apes. They subsist on a diet mainly of fruits, with occasional insects and small animals. Gibbons and siamangs, their slightly larger relatives, tend to live in *primary groups,* which are composed of a permanently bonded male and female and their preadolescent offspring.

## Orangutans

There are two surviving species of orangutan, Asiatic great apes belonging to the genus *Pongo.* Fueled by global economic forces, deforestation has been deadly to orangutans (see Galdikas 2005, 2007). Orangutans once were found throughout Southeast Asia, but today 90 percent of them live in Indonesia. Borneo has between 20,000 and 10,000 while a mere 7,000 survive on Sumatra (Isaacson 2012).

Sexual dimorphism is marked in orangs, with the adult male weighing more than twice as much as the female. Some orang males exceed 200 pounds (90 kilograms). With only half the gorilla's bulk, male orangs can be more arboreal, although they typically climb, rather than swing through, the trees. The smaller size of females and young permits them to make fuller use of the trees. Orangutans have a varied diet of fruit, bark, leaves, and insects. Because orangutans live in jungles and feed in trees, they are especially difficult to study. However, field reports about orangutans in their natural setting have clarified their behavior and social organization (Galdikas 2005; Isaacson 2012; Schaik 2004). Researchers have found that orangs tend to be solitary

The orangutan is the most endangered ape. In this 2008 photo primatologist Dr. Biruté Mary Galdikas carries an orangutan named Isabel, soon to be released into the wild at Tanjung Puting National Park on Borneo island, Indonesia. © Irwin Fedriansyah/AP Images

animals. Their tightest social units consist of females and preadolescent young. Males forage alone.

Since 1971, Biruté Mary Galdikas has studied wild orangutans in central Borneo. She is one of three prominent primatologists who were encouraged by famed paleoanthropologist Louis B. Leakey to study and protect the great apes. The others are Jane Goodall (working with chimpanzees) and the late Dian Fossey (who worked with mountain gorillas). As Galdikas reports (2007), economic globalization has fueled worldwide demand for pulp, paper, palm oil, and precious metals, leading to the destruction of Indonesia's tropical forests and endangering the orang. About 80 percent of the orang habitat has either been depopulated or totally destroyed (Galdikas 2007). Galdikas has urged Indonesia to impose a tax on multinational companies that profit from rain forest destruction and to use the revenues for forest and orangutan conservation. Indonesia, however, is a large and populous country with millions of poor people. The temptation to exploit natural resources to feed people, and to expand the economy, is great. Is there a realistic chance that the orangutan will survive?

## Gorillas

Within just one species, *Gorilla gorilla,* there are three subspecies of gorillas. The western lowland gorilla is the one usually seen in zoos. This, the smallest subspecies of gorilla, lives mainly in forests in the Central African Republic, Congo, Cameroon, Gabon, Equatorial Guinea, and Nigeria. The eastern lowland gorilla, of which there are only four in captivity, is slightly larger and lives in eastern Congo. There are no mountain gorillas, the third subspecies, in captivity. It's estimated that no more than 900 of these animals survive in the wild. These are the largest gorillas with the longest hair (to keep them warm in their mountainous habitat). They are also the rarest gorillas, which Dian Fossey (1983) and other scientists have studied in Rwanda, Uganda, and eastern Congo.

Full-grown male gorillas may weigh 400 pounds (180 kilograms) and stand 6 feet tall (183 centimeters). Like most terrestrial primates, gorillas show marked sexual dimorphism. The average adult female weighs half as much as the male. Gorillas spend little time in the trees, where it's hard for an adult male to move his bulk. When gorillas sleep in trees, they build nests, which usually are no more than 10 feet (3 meters) off the ground. By contrast, the nests of chimps and female orangs may be 100 feet (30 meters) above the ground.

Gorillas spend most of their time moving through the jungle, eating ground plants, leaves, bark, fruits, and other vegetation (see Rothman, Raubenheimer, and Chapman 2011). Like most primates, gorillas live in social groups. The troop is a common unit of primate social organization, consisting of multiple males and females and their offspring. Although troops with up to 30 gorillas have been observed, most gorillas live in smaller groups, with 10 to 20 members. Gorilla troops tend to have fairly stable memberships, with little shifting between troops (Fossey 1983). Each troop has a silverback male, named for the strip of white hair extending down his back. This is the physical sign of full maturity among the male gorillas. The silverback is usually the only breeding male in the troop, which is why gorilla troops are sometimes called "one-male groups." However, a few younger, subordinate males may also adhere to such a one-male group.

Gorillas (and chimps) use the long arms they have inherited from their more arboreal ancestors for life on the ground. The terrestrial locomotion of these apes (such as the gorilla shown here) is called knuckle-walking. The closeup of the gorilla hand shows the knuckles. (first) © imageBROKER/Alamy; (second) © MShieldsPhotos/Alamy

## Chimpanzees

Chimpanzees belong to the genus *Pan,* which has two species: *Pan troglodytes* (the common chimpanzee) and *Pan paniscus* (the bonobo or "pygmy" chimpanzee) (Waal 2013). Like humans, chimps are closely related to gorillas, although there are some obvious differences. Like gorillas, chimps live in tropical Africa, but they span a larger area and more varied environments than gorillas do. The common chimp, *Pan troglodytes,* lives in western central Africa (Gabon, Congo, Cameroon), as well as in western Africa (Ivory Coast, Sierra Leone, Liberia, Gambia) and eastern Africa (Congo, Uganda, and Tanzania). Bonobos live in remote and densely forested areas of just one country—the Democratic Republic of Congo (DRC). Common chimps live mainly in tropical rain forests but also in woodlands and mixed forest-woodland-grassland areas, such as the Gombe Stream National Park, Tanzania, where Jane Goodall and other researchers began to study them in 1960 (see Goodall 2009, 2010).

There are dietary differences between chimps and gorillas. Gorillas eat large quantities of green bulk vegetation, but chimps, like orangutans and gibbons, prefer fruits. Chimps are actually omnivorous, adding animal protein to their diet by capturing small mammals, birds' eggs, and insects.

Chimps are lighter and more arboreal than gorillas are. The adult male's weight—between 100 and 200 pounds (45 to 90 kilograms)—is about half that of the male gorilla. There is much less sexual dimorphism among chimps than among gorillas. Females approximate 88 percent of the average male height. This is similar to the ratio of sexual dimorphism in *Homo sapiens.*

Several scientists have studied wild chimps, and we know more about the full range of their behavior and social organization than we do about the other apes (see Goodall 2009; Matsuzawa 2011; Nishida 2012). The long-term research of Jane Goodall (2010) and others at Gombe provides especially useful information. Approximately 150 chimpanzees range over Gombe's 30 square miles (80 square kilometers). Goodall has described communities of about 50 chimps, all of which know one another and interact from time to time. Communities regularly split up into smaller groups: a mother and her offspring; males, females, and young; a few males; and occasionally solitary animals. Females are more likely to migrate and mate outside their natal group than males are.

When chimps, which are very vocal, meet, they greet one another with gestures, facial expressions, and calls. They hoot to maintain contact during their daily rounds. Males habitually cooperate in hunting parties (see Hart and Sussman 2009; Mitani et al. 2012; Nishida 2012). Like baboons and macaques, chimps exhibit dominance relationships through attacks and displacement.

As with all the apes, chimp survival is threatened today, mainly by human activities. In one study, Carroll (2008) found that Ivory Coast's chimpanzee populations had fallen by 90 percent over an 18-year period. That country had been considered home to about half of all West African chimps. Scientists found just 800 to 1,200 chimps there in 2008, compared with 8,000 to 12,000 in 1990. The 1990 survey itself had confirmed a significant decline from the 1960s, when Ivory Coast was home to an estimated 100,000 chimps. Between 1990 and 2008, Ivory Coast's human population increased by 50 percent, resulting in more hunting and deforestation, threats to wildlife that remain, given continued civil unrest and political instability.

## Bonobos

Ancestral chimps, and especially humans, eventually spread out of the forests and into woodlands and more open habitats (see Choi 2011). Bonobos, which belong to

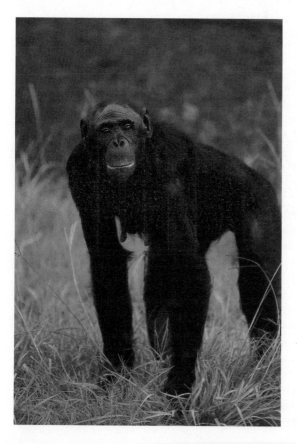

This photo was taken at a bonobo sanctuary in the Democratic Republic of Congo. Are bonobos (pygmy chimpanzees) smaller than chimps? © Purestock/Getty Images RF

the species *Pan paniscus,* apparently never left the protection of the trees. Up to 10,000 bonobos survive in the humid forests south of the Zaire River, in the Democratic Republic of Congo. Despite their common name—the *pygmy* chimpanzee—bonobos can't be distinguished from chimpanzees by size. Adult males of the smallest subspecies of chimpanzee average 95 pounds (43 kilograms), and females average 73 pounds (33 kilograms). These figures are about the same for bonobos (Waal 2013).

Although much smaller than the males, female bonobos seem to rule. Waal characterizes bonobo communities as female-centered, peace-loving, and egalitarian. The strongest social bonds are among females, although females also bond with males. The male bonobo's status reflects that of his mother, to whom he remains closely bonded for life.

The frequency with which bonobos have sex—and use it to avoid conflict—makes them exceptional among the primates. Despite frequent sex, the bonobo reproductive rate doesn't exceed that of the chimpanzee. A female bonobo gives birth every five or six years. Then, like chimps, female bonobos nurse and carry around their young for up to five years. Bonobos reach adolescence around 7 years of age. Females, which first give birth at age 13 or 14, are full grown by 15 years.

## Endangered Primates

Deforestation poses a special risk for the primates, because 90 percent of surviving primate species live in tropical forests—in Africa, Asia, South America, and Central America. As the Earth's human population swells, all nonhuman primates have become endangered, with apes in the "most endangered" category. Mountain gorillas, which once ranged widely in the forested mountains of East Africa, are limited today to a small area near the borders of Rwanda, the DRC, and Uganda. Other severely threatened species include Brazil's golden lion tamarin monkey, India's lion-tailed macaque, the woolly monkeys of Amazonia, and the orangutan of Southeast Asia.

Habitat destruction can isolate small groups of animals, leaving them vulnerable to extinction due to loss of genetic diversity. Primate populations are slow to recover from such threats. Ape species, for example, are slow reproducers, rarely having more than three or four offspring over a lifetime.

Although deforestation is the main reason primates are disappearing, it isn't the only threat. Another is human hunting for bush meat. Primates are a major food source in Amazonia and West Africa and Central Africa, where people kill thousands of monkeys annually. Hunting poses less of a threat in Asia. In India, Hindus avoid monkey meat because the monkey is sacred, while Muslims avoid it because monkeys are considered unclean and unfit for human consumption.

People also hunt primates for their skins and pelts; poachers sell their body parts as trophies and ornaments. Africans use the skins of black-and-white colobus monkeys for cloaks and headdresses, and tourists buy coats and rugs made from colobus pelts. In Amazonia, ocelot and jaguar hunters shoot monkeys to bait the traps they set for the cats. Primates also are killed when they are agricultural pests. In some areas of Africa and Asia, drills and baboons (Africa) and macaques (Asia) raid crops, resulting in drives to kill the monkeys that interfere with human subsistence.

A final threat to the primates is their capture for use in labs or as pets. Although this threat is minor compared with deforestation and hunting, it does pose a serious risk to certain endangered species in heavy demand. One of the species most hurt by this trade has been the chimpanzee, which has been widely used in biomedical research.

## Primate Evolution

The fossil record offers evidence for no more than 5 percent of extinct types of primates. Such small numbers provide the merest glimpse of the diverse bioforms—living beings—that have existed on Earth.

In considering the primate fossil record, we'll see that different world areas provide more abundant evidence for particular time periods. This doesn't necessarily mean that primates were absent elsewhere at that time. Discussions of primate and human evolution must be tentative because the fossil record is limited and spotty. Much is subject to change as knowledge increases. A key feature of science is to recognize the tentativeness and uncertainty of knowledge. Scientists, including fossil hunters, constantly seek out new evidence and devise new methods, such as DNA comparison, to improve their understanding, in this case of primate and human evolution.

## Chronology

We learned in Chapter 3 that the remains of animals and plants that lived at the same time are found in the same stratum. Based on fossils found in stratigraphic sequences, the history of vertebrate life has been divided into three main eras. The *Paleozoic* (544–245 **m.y.a.**—million years ago) was the era of ancient life—fishes, amphibians, and primitive reptiles. The *Mesozoic* (245–65 m.y.a.) was the era of middle life—reptiles, including the dinosaurs. The *Cenozoic* (65 m.y.a.–present) is the era of recent life—birds and mammals. Each era is divided into periods, and the periods are divided into epochs.

Anthropologists are concerned with the Cenozoic *era* (see Figure 5.4), which includes two *periods:* Tertiary and Quaternary. Each of these periods is subdivided into *epochs.* The Tertiary had five epochs: Paleocene, Eocene, Oligocene, Miocene, and Pliocene. The Quaternary includes just two epochs: Pleistocene and Holocene, or Recent. Figure 5.4 gives the approximate dates of these epochs. Sediments from the Paleocene epoch (65–54 m.y.a.) have yielded fossil remains of diverse small mammals, some possibly ancestral to the primates. Prosimian-like fossils abound in strata dating from the Eocene (54–34 m.y.a.). The first anthropoid fossils date to the Eocene and the early Oligocene (34–23 m.y.a.). Hominoids (apes) became widespread during the Miocene (23–5 m.y.a.). Hominins first appeared in the late Miocene, just before the Pliocene (5–2 m.y.a.).

FIGURE 5.4   **Periods and Epochs of the Cenozoic Era**
The geological time scale is based on stratigraphy. Eras are subdivided into periods, and periods into epochs. In what era, period, and epoch did *Homo* originate?

| Era | Period | Epoch | Climate and Life Forms |
|---|---|---|---|
| Cenozoic | Quaternary | Holocene 10,000 B.P. | Transition to agriculture; emergence of states |
| | | Pleistocene 2 m.y.a. | Climatic fluctuations, glaciation; *Homo, A. boisei, A. robustus* |
| | Tertiary | Pliocene 5 m.y.a. | *A. africanus, A. afarensis, A. anamensis, Ardipithecus* |
| | | Miocene 23 m.y.a. | Cooler and drier grasslands spread in middle latitudes; Africa collides with Eurasia (16 m.y.a.) |
| | | Oligocene 34 m.y.a. | Cooler and drier in the north; anthropoids in Africa (Fayum); separation of catarrhines and platyrrhines; separation of hylobatids from pongids and hominids |
| | | Eocene 54 m.y.a. | Warm tropical climates become widespread; modern orders of mammals appear; prosimianlike primates abundant; anthropoids appear |
| | | Paleocene 65 m.y.a. | First major mammal radiation |

# Early Primates

When the Mesozoic era ended, and the Cenozoic era began, some 65 million years ago, North America was connected to Europe but not to South America. (The Americas joined around 20 million years ago.) Over millions of years, the continents have "drifted" to their present locations, carried along by the gradually shifting plates of the Earth's surface (see Figure 5.5).

During the Cenozoic era, most land masses had tropical or subtropical climates. The preceding Mesozoic era had ended with a massive worldwide extinction of plants and animals, including the dinosaurs, which were reptiles. During the Cenozoic, mammals would diversify and eventually become the dominant large land animals. Trees and flowering plants also proliferated, supplying arboreal foods for the primates that eventually evolved to fill the new niches.

## Early Cenozoic Primates

A tiny, complete skeleton from China, first described in 2013, represents the earliest known primate (Ni et al. 2013; Wilford 2013). The creature was smaller than today's smallest primate—the pygmy mouse lemur of Madagascar. Named *Archicebus achilles* because of its prominent (and monkeylike) ankle and heel, the animal has been tentatively assigned to the tarsier lineage. *Archicebus,* which weighed no more than one ounce, had a 5-inch tail, which was longer than its 4-inch body. It lived 55 million years

FIGURE 5.5   **Placement of Continents at the End of the Mesozoic**
When the Mesozoic era ended, and the Cenozoic began, some 65 million years
ago, North America was connected to Europe, but not to South America.

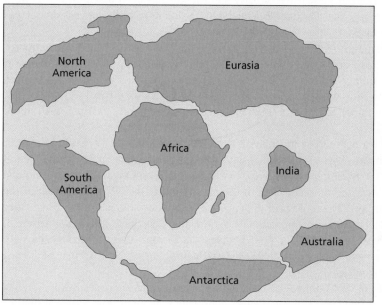

ago, when Earth was a natural greenhouse, with rain forests everywhere and palm trees growing in what is now Alaska. This finding supports the view that the first primates evolved in Asia—not too long after the dinosaurs went extinct (66 million years ago). Somehow, and sometime thereafter, primates crossed open water to reach Africa 38 million years ago. (Africa remained an island continent until 16 million years ago.) *Archicebus* lived late in the Paleocene epoch (65–54 m.y.a.), the first epoch of the Cenozoic era.

In primate evolution, the ensuing Eocene epoch (54–34 m.y.a.) was the age of the prosimians, with at least 60 genera in two main families. They lived in North America, Europe, Africa, and Asia. Sometime during the Eocene, ancestral anthropoids branched off from the prosimians by becoming more diurnal and by strengthening the trend favoring vision over smell (see Schultz, Opie, and Atkinson 2011). Eocene prosimians with bigger brains and eyes, and smaller snouts, were the ancestors of the anthropoids. Anthropoid eyes are placed more forward when compared with those of lemurs and lorises. Also, anthropoids have a fully enclosed bony eye socket, which lemurs and lorises lack.

By the end of the Eocene, many prosimian species had become extinct, reflecting competition from the first anthropoids. Ancestral lemurs reached Madagascar from Africa late in the Eocene. They must have traveled across the Mozambique Channel, which was narrower then than it is now, on thick mats of vegetation. Such naturally formed "rafts" have been observed forming in East African rivers, then floating out to sea. Isolated in Madagascar, the lemurs could live and evolve, unthreatened by other primates until the first humans arrived some 2,000 years ago.

## Oligocene Anthropoids

During the Oligocene epoch (34–23 m.y.a.), anthropoids became the most numerous primates. Most of our knowledge of early anthropoids has been based on fossils from Egypt's Fayum deposits. This area is a desert today, but 34–31 million years ago it was a tropical rain forest.

The Fayum anthropoids lived in trees and ate fruits and seeds. Compared with prosimians, they had fewer teeth, reduced snouts, larger brains, and increasingly forward-looking eyes. Among those Fayum anthropoids, one group is most primitive and perhaps ancestral to the New World monkeys. These protomonkeys were small (2 to 3 pounds, 0.9 to 1.4 kilograms), with similarities to living marmosets and tamarins, small South American monkeys.

Another Fayum group seems ancestral to the catarrhines—Old World monkeys, apes, and humans. This group shares with the later catarrhines a distinctive dental formula: 2.1.2.3, meaning two incisors, one canine, two premolars, and three molars. (The formula is based on one-fourth of the mouth, either the right or left side of the upper or lower jaw.) The more primitive primate dental formula is 2.1.3.3. Most other primates, including prosimians and New World monkeys, have the second formula, with three premolars instead of two. Besides the Fayum, Oligocene deposits with primate bones have been found in West Africa, southern Arabia, China, Southeast Asia, and the Americas.

The Oligocene was a time of major geological and climatic change: North America and Europe separated and became distinct continents; the Great Rift Valley system of East Africa formed; India drifted into Asia; and a cooling trend began, especially in the Northern Hemisphere, where primates disappeared.

# Miocene Hominoids

The earliest hominoid fossils date to the Miocene epoch (23–5 m.y.a.), which is divided into three parts: lower, middle, and upper or late. The lower, or early, Miocene (23–16 m.y.a.) was a warm and wet period, when forests covered East Africa. Recall that Hominoidea is the superfamily that includes fossil and living apes and humans. For simplicity's sake, the earliest hominoids are here called protoapes, or simply apes. Although some of these may be ancestral to living apes, none is identical, or often even very similar, to modern apes.

## Proconsul

The *Proconsul* group represents the most abundant and successful anthropoids of the early Miocene. This group lived in Africa and includes three species. These early Miocene protoapes had teeth with similarities to those of living apes. But their skeleton below the neck was more monkeylike. Some *Proconsul* species were the size of a small monkey; others, the size of a chimpanzee, usually with marked sexual dimorphism. Their dentition suggests they ate fruits and leaves. *Proconsul* probably contained the last common ancestor shared by the Old World monkeys and the apes. By the middle Miocene, *Proconsul* had been replaced by Old World monkeys and apes.

## Later Miocene Apes

During the early Miocene (23–16 m.y.a.), Africa had been cut off by water from Europe and Asia. But during the middle Miocene, Arabia drifted into Eurasia, providing a land connection between Africa, Europe, and Asia. Migrating both ways—out of and into Africa—after 16 m.y.a. were various animals, including hominoids. Protoapes were the most common primates of the middle Miocene (16–10 m.y.a.). Over 20 species have been discovered in Europe, Africa, and Asia.

Perhaps the most remarkable Miocene ape was *Gigantopithecus*—almost certainly the largest primate that ever lived. Confined to Asia, it persisted for millions of years, from the Miocene until 400,000 years ago, when it coexisted with members of our own genus, *Homo erectus*. Some people think *Gigantopithecus* is not extinct yet, and that we know it today as the yeti and bigfoot (Sasquatch).

With a fossil record consisting of nothing more than jaw bones and teeth, it is difficult to say for sure just how big *Gigantopithecus* was. Based on ratios of jaw and tooth size to body size in other apes, various reconstructions have been made. One has *Gigantopithecus* weighing 1,200 pounds (544 kilograms) and standing 10 feet (3 meters) tall (Ciochon, Olsen, and James 1990). Another puts the height at 9 feet (2.7 meters) and

Paleoanthropologist Chris Stringer is dwarfed by a reconstruction of *Gigantopithecus*. The extinct ape was reconstructed for an exhibit titled "Myths and Monsters" at London's Natural History Museum. What would be the likely environmental effects of a population of such large apes?    © Daily Mail/Rex/Alamy

## Anthropology Today　*Should Apes Have Human Rights?*

In Africa and Asia, the surviving, but dwindling, populations of great apes face extinction due to human warfare, oil exploration, deforestation, deliberate hunting, and other threats. Continents away, animal rights activists work to conserve apes, even to grant them basic legal rights.

In 2000, the U.S. Congress enacted the Great Apes Conservation Act, which authorized $5 million annually over five years to be spent protecting apes in the wild. In 2005, Congress reauthorized that act, which matched public with private funding, for another five years. The money was used to protect habitats, battle poachers, and educate local populations about the importance of the apes. In Indonesia, for example, funding has slowed the conversion of forests to commercial plantations. In Congo, one of the few countries in which the mountain gorilla survives, promotion of alternative fuels has helped reduce deforestation for charcoal production. By 2010, when it ended, the Great Apes Conservation Fund had helped fund more than 50 programs in 7 Asian and 12 African countries.

The humanlike characteristics of the great apes is evident to anyone who has seen the various *Planet of the Apes* movies, especially the most recent ones, featuring the intelligent, speaking chimpanzee named Caesar and his companions. Scientific knowledge confirms that apes are close to humans in their cognitive abilities and emotional states. Experiments teaching sign language to chimps and gorillas, described in the chapter "Language and Communication," demonstrate that apes are capable of learning hundreds of meaningful signs and of communicating with humans and other signing apes. DNA confirms the close relationship between humans, chimps, and gorillas. Scientists know that the great apes have complex mental abilities, which elevate their capability for suffering. On that basis alone, say rights advocates, apes deserve basic protections from the pain, isolation, and arbitrary imprisonment inflicted by medical experiments or captivity in zoos.

In 1993, philosophers Peter Singer and Paola Cavalieri published *The Great Ape Project,* a book that argued that chimpanzees, gorillas, bonobos, and orangutans should be granted the same basic rights as human beings. In fact, in December 2014, an Argentine court did extend legal rights to a 28-year-old orangutan named Sandra, a captive ape born in Germany and taken to the Buenos Aires zoo, where she lived for 20 years. As the world's first animal legally recognized as a "nonhuman person," Sandra's new status facilitated her transfer to a sanctuary in Brazil. A month earlier, in North America, a New York state court had denied an appeal put forth on behalf of a pet chimp named Tommy. The court argued that, regardless of their intelligence or feelings, chimpanzees cannot fulfill the social obligations expected of a person with rights.

In addition to promoting legal rights for apes, advocates have urged governments and the United Nations to ban ape captivity in zoos and circuses and their use in scientific research, especially medical testing. Several nations, including New Zealand, the United Kingdom, Sweden, Austria, Belgium, and the Netherlands have banned research on apes for ethical reasons.

In January 2013, the U.S. National Institutes of Health (NIH) accepted a committee recommendation to curtail the use of chimpanzees in research. Of the 450 chimpanzees then under NIH control, 400 would be retired and moved to sanctuaries. The remaining 50 would be retained for possible future research use, but within five years, their housing had to be upgraded to meet specific criteria. Chimps would be used for research only if not using them would significantly impede the prevention, control, or treatment of life-threatening or debilitating conditions.

NIH adopted three specific principles to assess the need for chimps in research studies:

1. *The knowledge to be gained must be necessary to advance the public's health.*

2. *There must be no other research model by which that knowledge could be gained, and the research cannot be performed ethically on human subjects.*

3. *Research chimps must be housed in appropriate physical and social environments, or in natural habitats.*

Today, the research chimps formerly used by NIH are getting their first taste of freedom in animal sanctuaries. Most of them are being moved to the federally run Chimp Haven in Shreveport, Louisiana, home to more than 120 chimps living in large social groups on 200 acres of parkland. They seem pleased with their new surroundings.

How do you feel about animal rights in general and ape rights in particular? Because the great apes are so close to humans genetically, physically, and temperamentally, do they merit special treatment among the animals?

**Source:** Becker (2013), Eldred (2013), Kahn (2011), Keim (2014), Mitani (2011), *The Week* (2013).

---

cuts the weight in half (Simons and Ettel 1970). All agree, however, that *Gigantopithecus* was the largest ape that ever lived. There have been at least two species of *Gigantopithecus:* One coexisted with *H. erectus* in China and Vietnam, and the other, much earlier (5 m.y.a.), lived in northern India.

## *Pierolapithecus catalaunicus*

In November 2004, Spanish anthropologists announced their discovery of what may be the last common ancestor of humans, chimpanzees, gorillas, and orangutans (Moyà-Solà et al. 2004). The new ape species, named *Pierolapithecus catalaunicus,* lived around 13 million years ago, during the middle Miocene. The find comes from a rich fossil site near the village of Hostalets de Pierola in Catalonia, Spain. The name *Pierolapithecus* combines part of the village's name with the Greek word for "ape" (*pithecus*), while *catalaunicus* commemorates Catalonia, the province where both the village and Barcelona are located.

The *Pierolapithecus* bones include much of the skull, hand and foot bones, three vertebrae, two complete ribs, and large pieces of a dozen others. The find appears to represent a single adult male that weighed about 75 pounds (34 kilograms). Like chimps and gorillas, *Pierolapithecus* was well adapted for tree climbing and knuckle-walking on the ground. Based on the shape of the single surviving tooth, it was probably a fruit eater. Several features distinguished *Pierolapithecus* from the lesser apes (gibbons and siamangs) and monkeys. Its rib cage, lower spine, and wrist suggest it climbed the way modern great apes do. The ape's chest, or thorax, is wider and flatter than that of monkeys and is the earliest modern apelike thorax yet found in the fossil record.

In the current timetable of primate evolution, the lineage of monkeys split off some 25 m.y.a. from the hominoid line, which led to apes and humans. The ancestors of the lesser apes separated from those of the great apes some 16–14 m.y.a. Sometime before 11 m.y.a., the orangutan (pongid) line split from that leading to the hominids. Yet another split took place thereafter when the gorilla line diverged from the line leading to chimpanzees and hominins (see Langergraber et al. 2012). By 7 m.y.a., another split in the lineage had led to the various early hominins, to be examined in the next chapter.

## Summary

1. Humans, apes, monkeys, and prosimians are primates. The primate order is subdivided into suborders, superfamilies, families, tribes, genera, species, and subspecies. Organisms in any subdivision (taxon) of a taxonomy are assumed to share more recent ancestry with each other than they do with organisms in other taxa. But it's sometimes hard to tell the difference between homologies, which reflect common ancestry, and analogies, biological similarities that develop through convergent evolution.

2. Prosimians are the older of the two primate suborders. Some 40 million years ago, anthropoids displaced prosimians from niches their ancestors once occupied. Tarsiers and lorises are prosimians that survived by adapting to nocturnal life. Lemurs survived on the island of Madagascar.

3. Anthropoids include humans, apes, and monkeys. All share fully developed primate trends, such as depth and color vision. Other anthropoid traits include a shift in tactile areas to the fingers. The New World monkeys are all arboreal. Old World monkeys include both terrestrial species (e.g., baboons and macaques) and arboreal ones. The great apes are orangutans, gorillas, chimpanzees, and bonobos. The lesser apes are gibbons and siamangs.

4. Gibbons and siamangs live in Southeast Asian forests. These apes are slight, arboreal animals whose mode of locomotion is brachiation. Sexual dimorphism, slight among gibbons, is marked among orangutans, which are confined to two Indonesian islands. Sexually dimorphic gorillas, the most terrestrial apes, are vegetarians confined to equatorial Africa. Two species of chimpanzees live in the forests and woodlands of tropical Africa. Chimps are less sexually dimorphic, more numerous, and more omnivorous than gorillas are.

5. Primates have lived during the past 65 million years, the Cenozoic era, with seven epochs: Paleocene, Eocene, Oligocene, Miocene, Pliocene, Pleistocene, and Holocene, or Recent. The arboreal theory states that primates evolved by adapting to life high up in the trees.

6. The first (prosimian-like) fossils clearly identified as primates lived during the Eocene (54–34 m.y.a.), mainly in North America and Europe. During the Oligocene (34–23 m.y.a.), anthropoids became the most numerous primates. During the Oligocene, the ancestors of the New World monkeys diverged from the line leading to the catarrhines—Old World monkeys, apes, and humans.

7. The earliest hominoid fossils are from the Miocene (23–5 m.y.a.). Africa's *Proconsul* group contained the last common ancestor shared by the Old World monkeys and the apes. Since the middle Miocene (16–10 m.y.a.), Africa, Europe, and Asia have been connected. Protoapes spread beyond Africa and became the most common primates of the middle Miocene. Asia's *Gigantopithecus,* the largest primate ever to live, persisted for millions of years, finally coexisting with *Homo erectus. Pierolapithecus catalaunicus,* which lived around 13 million years ago, could be the last common ancestor of humans, chimpanzees, gorillas, and orangutans.

## Key Terms

analogies, *94*
anthropoids, *97*
arboreal, *97*
bipedal, *97*
brachiation, *101*
convergent
  evolution, *94*

hominoid, *100*
homologies, *93*
m.y.a., *107*
opposable
  thumb, *97*
primates, *92*
primatology, *92*

prosimians, *97*
taxonomy, *93*
terrestrial, *92*

# Chapter 6

# Early Hominins

## What Makes Us Human?

In trying to determine whether a fossil is a human ancestor, should we look for traits that make us human today? Sometimes yes, sometimes no. We do look for similarities in DNA, including mutations shared by certain lineages but not others. But what about such key human attributes as bipedal locomotion, a long period of childhood dependency, big brains, and the use of tools and language? Some of these key markers of humanity are fairly recent—or have origins that are impossible to date. And ironically, some of the physical markers that have led scientists to identify certain fossils as early hominins rather than apes are features that have been lost during subsequent human evolution.

### Bipedalism

As is true of all subsequent hominins, postcranial (below the head) material from **Ardipithecus,** the earliest widely accepted hominin genus (5.8–4.4 m.y.a.), indicates a capacity—albeit an imperfect one—for upright bipedal locomotion. The *Ardipithecus* pelvis appears to be transitional between one suited for arboreal climbing and one modified for bipedalism. Reliance on bipedalism—upright, two-legged locomotion—is the key feature differentiating early hominins from the apes. This way of moving around eventually led to the distinctive hominin way of life. Based on African fossil discoveries, such as Ethiopia's *Ardipithecus,* hominin bipedalism is more than 5 million years old. Some scientists see even earlier evidence of bipedalism in two other fossil finds, described later in this chapter—one from Chad (*Sahelanthropus tchadensis*) and one from Kenya (*Orrorin tugenensis*).

Bipedalism traditionally has been viewed as an adaptation to open grassland or savanna country, although *Ardipithecus* appears to have lived in a humid woodland habitat. Perhaps bipedalism developed in the woodlands but became even more adaptive out on the savanna (see Choi 2011). Scientists have suggested several advantages of bipedalism: the ability to see over long grass and scrub, to carry items back to a home base, and to reduce the body's exposure to solar radiation (see Ferraro et al. 2013). Studies with scale models of primates suggest that quadrupedalism exposes the body to 60 percent more solar radiation than does bipedalism. The fossil and archaeological records confirm that upright bipedal locomotion preceded stone tool manufacture and the expansion of the hominin brain. However, although early hominins could move bipedally on the ground, they also preserved enough of an apelike anatomy to make them good climbers (see the description of *Ardipithecus* as well as of "Lucy's baby". They could take to the trees to sleep and to escape terrestrial predators.

Reconstruction of *Australopithecus* running bipedally with a pebble tool in hand. Along with tool use and manufacture, bipedalism is a key part of being human. © The Natural History Museum/Alamy

## Brains, Skulls, and Childhood Dependency

Compared with contemporary humans, early hominins had very small brains. *Australopithecus afarensis,* a bipedal hominin that lived more than 3 million years ago, had a cranial capacity (430 cm$^3$—cubic centimeters) that barely surpassed the chimp average (390 cm$^3$). The form of the *afarensis* skull also is like that of the chimpanzee, although the brain-to-body size ratio may have been larger. Brain size has increased during hominin evolution, especially with the advent of the genus *Homo.* But this increase had to overcome some obstacles. Compared with the young of other primates, human children have a long period of childhood dependency, during which their brains and skulls grow dramatically. Larger skulls demand larger birth canals, but the requirements of upright bipedalism impose limits on the expansion of the human pelvic opening. If the opening is too large, the pelvis doesn't provide sufficient support for the trunk. Locomotion suffers, and posture problems develop. If, by contrast, the birth canal is too narrow, mother and child (without the modern option of Caesarean section) may die. Natural selection has struck a balance between the structural demands of upright posture and the tendency toward increased brain size—the birth of immature and dependent children whose brains and skulls grow dramatically after birth.

## Tools

Given what is known about tool use and manufacture by the great apes, it is likely that early hominins shared this ability as a homology with the apes. We'll see later that the first firm evidence for hominin stone tool manufacture is dated to 2.6 m.y.a. Upright bipedalism would have permitted the use of tools and weapons against predators and competitors. Bipedal locomotion also allowed early hominins to carry things, including scavenged parts of carnivore kills, back to a home base (see Ferraro et al. 2013).

## Teeth

One example of an early hominin trait that has been lost during subsequent human evolution is big back teeth. (Indeed, a pattern of overall dental reduction has characterized human evolution.) Once they adapted to the savanna, with its gritty, tough, and fibrous vegetation, it was adaptively advantageous for early hominins to have large back teeth and thick tooth enamel. This permitted thorough chewing of tough, fibrous vegetation and mixture with salivary enzymes to permit digestion of foods that otherwise would not have been digestible. The churning, rotary motion associated with such chewing also favored reduction of the canines and first premolars (bicuspids). These front teeth are much sharper and longer in the apes than in early hominins. The apes use their sharp, self-honing teeth to pierce fruits. Males also flash their big, sharp canines to intimidate and impress others, including potential mates. Although bipedalism seems to have characterized the human lineage since it split from the line leading to the African apes, many other "human" features came later. Yet other early hominin features, such as large back teeth and thick enamel—which we don't have now—offer clues about who was a human ancestor back then.

## Chronology of Hominin Evolution

Recall that the term *hominin* is used to designate the human line after its split from ancestral chimps. *Hominid* refers to the taxonomic family that includes humans and the African apes and their immediate ancestors. In this book *hominid* is used when there is doubt about the hominin status of the fossil (e.g., with Toumai, as described later). Although recent fossil discoveries have pushed the hominin lineage back to almost 6 million years, humans actually haven't been around too long when the age of the Earth is considered. If we compare Earth's history to a 24-hour day (with one second equaling 50,000 years),

Earth originates at midnight.

The earliest fossils were deposited at 5:45 A.M.

The first vertebrates appeared at 9:02 P.M.

The earliest mammals, at 10:45 P.M.

The earliest primates, at 11:43 P.M.

The earliest hominins, at 11:57 P.M.

And *Homo sapiens* arrives 36 seconds before midnight. (Wolpoff 1999, p. 10)

Although the first hominins appeared late in the Miocene epoch, for the study of hominin evolution, the Pliocene (5–2 m.y.a.), Pleistocene (2 m.y.a.–10,000 B.P.), and Recent (10,000 B.P.–present) epochs are most important. Until the end of the Pliocene, the main hominin genus was *Australopithecus,* which lived in sub-Saharan Africa. By the start of the Pleistocene, *Australopithecus* had evolved into *Homo.*

## Who Were the Earliest Hominins?

Recent discoveries of fossils and tools have increased our knowledge of hominid and hominin evolution. The most significant recent discoveries have been made in Africa—Kenya, Tanzania, Ethiopia, Chad, and South Africa. These finds come from different sites and may be the remains of individuals that lived hundreds of thousands of years apart. Furthermore, geological processes operating over thousands or millions of years inevitably distort fossil remains. Table 6.1 summarizes the major events in hominid and hominin evolution. You should consult it throughout this chapter and the next one.

### *Sahelanthropus tchadensis*

In July 2001 anthropologists working in Central Africa—in northern Chad's Djurab Desert—unearthed the 6- to 7-million-year-old skull of the oldest possible human ancestor yet found. This discovery consists of a nearly complete skull, two lower jaw fragments, and three teeth. It dates to the time period when humans and chimps could have been diverging from a common ancestor. "It takes us into another world, of creatures that include the common ancestor, the ancestral human and the ancestral chimp," George Washington University paleobiologist Bernard Wood said (quoted in

TABLE 6.1    **Dates and Geographic Distribution of Major Hominoid, Hominid, and Hominin Fossil Groups**

| Fossil Group | Dates, m.y.a. | Known Distribution |
|---|---|---|
| Hominoid | | |
| *Pierolapithecus catalaunicus* | 13 | Spain |
| Hominid | | |
| Common ancestor of hominids | 10? | East Africa |
| *Sahelanthropus tchadensis* | 7–6 | Chad |
| *Orrorin tugenensis* | 6 | Kenya |
| Hominins | | |
| *Ardipithecus kadabba* | 5.8–5.5 | Ethiopia |
| *Ardipithecus ramidus* | 4.4 | Ethiopia |
| Australopithecines | | |
| *Au. anamensis* | 4.2–3.9 | Kenya |
| *Au. afarensis* | 3.8–3.0 | East Africa (Laetoli, Hadar) |
| *Au. garhi* | 2.5 | Ethiopia |
| Robusts | 2.6–1.2 | East and South Africa |
| *Au. robustus (Paranthropus)* | 2.0?–1.0? | South Africa |
| *Au. boisei* | 2.6?–1.2 | East Africa |
| Graciles | | |
| *Au. africanus* | 3.0?–2.0? | South Africa |
| *Au. sediba* | 1.95–1.78 | South Africa |
| Homo | | |
| *H. rudolfensis* | 2.03–1.78 | East Africa |
| *H. habilis* | 1.9–1.44 | East Africa |
| *H. erectus* | 1.9?–0.3? | Africa, Asia, Europe |
| *Homo sapiens* | 0.3–present | |
| Archaic *H. sapiens* | 0.3–0.28? (300,000–28,000?) | Africa, Asia, Europe |
| Neandertals | 0.13–0.28? (130,000–28,000?) | Europe, Middle East, North Africa |
| Anatomically modern humans (AMHs) | 0.15?–present (150,000–present) | Worldwide (after 20,000 B.P.) |

Gugliotta 2002). The discovery was made by a 40-member multinational team led by the French paleontologist Michel Brunet. The actual discoverer was the university undergraduate Ahounta Djimdoumalbaye, who spied the skull embedded in sandstone. The new fossil was dubbed *Sahelanthropus tchadensis,* referring to the northern Sahel region of Chad where it was found. The fossil also is known as Toumai, a local name meaning "hope of life."

The discovery team identified the skull as that of an adult male with a chimp-sized brain (320–380 cubic centimeters), heavy brow ridges, and a relatively flat, human-like face. Toumai's habitat included savanna, forests, rivers, and lakes—and abundant

In N'Djamena, Chad, the French paleontologist Michel Brunet holds Toumai's skull along with Ahounta Djimdoumalbaye (left), who discovered the skull. Toumai is a possible hominin ancestor. © Patrick Robert/Corbis

animal life such as elephants, antelope, horses, giraffes, hyenas, hippopotamuses, wild boars, crocodiles, fish, and rodents. The animal species enabled the team to date the site where Toumai was found (by comparison with radiometrically dated sites with similar fauna).

Toumai blends apelike and human characteristics. Although the brain was chimp-sized, the tooth enamel was thicker than a chimp's enamel, suggesting a diet that included not just fruits but also tougher vegetation of a sort typically found in the savanna. Also, Toumai's snout did not protrude as far as a chimp's, making it more humanlike, and the canine tooth was shorter than those of other apes. "The fossil is showing the first glimmerings of evolution in our direction," according to University of California at Berkeley anthropologist Tim White (quoted in Gugliotta 2002).

The *Sahelanthropus* skull is nearly complete, although distorted. The placement of its *foramen magnum* (the "big hole" through which the spinal cord joins the brain) farther forward than in apes suggests that *Sahelanthropus* moved bipedally. Its discovery in Chad indicates that early hominid (and possibly hominin) evolution was not confined to East Africa's Rift Valley. The Rift Valley's abundant early hominin fossil record may well reflect geology, preservation, and modern exposure of fossils rather than the actual geographic distribution of species in the past. The discovery of *Sahelanthropus* in Chad is the first proof of a more widespread distribution of early hominids.

## *Orrorin tugenensis*

In January 2001 Brigitte Senut, Martin Pickford, and others reported the discovery, near the village of Tugen in Kenya's Baringo district, of possible early hominin fossils they called *Orrorin tugenensis* (Aiello and Collard 2001; Senut et al. 2001). The find consisted of 13 fossils from at least five individuals. The fossils include pieces of jaw with teeth, isolated upper and lower teeth, arm bones, and a finger bone. *Orrorin* appears to have been a chimp-sized creature that climbed easily and walked on two legs when on the ground. Its date of 6 million years approaches the time of the common ancestor of humans and chimps. The fossilized left femur (thigh bone) suggests upright bipedalism, while the thick right humerus (upper arm bone) suggests tree-climbing skills. Associated animal remains indicate that *Orrorin* lived in a wooded environment.

*Orrorin*'s upper incisor, upper canine, and lower premolar are more like the teeth of a female chimpanzee than like human teeth. But other dental and skeletal features, especially bipedalism, led the discoverers to assign *Orrorin* to the hominin lineage. *Orrorin* lived after *Sahelanthropus tchadensis* but before *Ardipithecus kadabba,* discovered in Ethiopia, also in 2001, and dated to 5.8–5.5 m.y.a. The hominin status of *Ardipithecus* is more generally accepted than is that of either *Sahelanthropus tchadensis* or *Orrorin tugenensis*.

Digital representations of the *Ardipithecus ramidus* cranium and mandible released on October 1, 2009. This find, dubbed "Ardi," was heralded throughout the media.
© HO/Reuters/Corbis

## *Ardipithecus*

Early hominins assigned to *Ardipithecus kadabba* lived during the late Miocene, between 5.8 and 5.5 million years ago. *Ardipithecus* (representing *ramidus,* a later species) fossils were first discovered at Aramis in Ethiopia by Berhane Asfaw, Gen Suwa, and Tim White. Dating to 4.4 m.y.a., these *Ardipithecus ramidus* fossils consisted of the remains of some 17 individuals, with cranial, facial, dental, and upper limb bones. Subsequently, much older *Ardipithecus (kadabba)* fossils, dating back to 5.8 m.y.a., were found in Ethiopia. The *kadabba* find consists of 11 specimens, including a jawbone with teeth, plus hand and foot bones, fragments of arm bones, and a piece of collarbone. At least 5 individuals are represented. These creatures were apelike in size, anatomy, and habitat and lived in a wooded area. As of this writing, based on its probable bipedalism, *Ardipithecus kadabba* is recognized as the earliest known hominin.

In 2009, a newly reported *Ardipithecus* find—a fairly complete skeleton of *Ardipithecus ramidus,* dubbed "Ardi"—was heralded on the front page of the *New York Times* and throughout the media (Wilford 2009*b*). Ardi (4.4 m.y.a.) replaces Lucy (3.2 m.y.a.—see later in the chapter) as the earliest known hominin skeleton. Ardi's discovery site lies on what is now an arid floodplain of the Awash River, 45 miles south of Hadar, where Lucy was found. Scientists infer that Ardi was female, based on its small and lightly built (gracile) skull and its small canine teeth compared with others found at the site. At 4 feet tall and 120 pounds, Ardi stood about a foot taller and weighed twice as much as Lucy.

The *Ardipithecus* pelvis appears to be transitional between one suited for arboreal climbing and one modified for bipedal locomotion. The pelvis of later hominins such as Lucy shows nearly all the adaptations needed for full bipedalism. Although Ardi's lower pelvis remains primitive, the structure of her upper pelvis allowed her to walk on two legs with a straightened hip. Still, she probably could neither walk nor run as well as later hominins. Her feet lacked the archlike structure of later hominin feet (see Ward, Kimbel, and Johanson 2011). Ardi's apelike lower pelvis indicates retention of powerful hamstring muscles for climbing. Her hands, very long arms, and short legs all recall those of extinct apes, and her brain was no larger than that of a modern chimp.

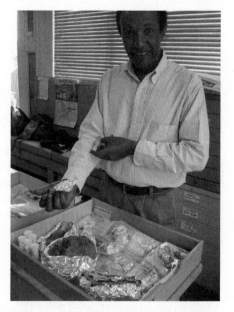

Paleoanthropologist Johannes-Haile Selassie was a key member of the multinational, multidisciplinary team responsible for the "Ardi" discovery and analysis. © AFP/Getty Images

Based on associated animal and plant remains, *Ardipithecus* lived in a humid woodland habitat. More than 145 teeth have been collected at the site. Their size, shape, and wear patterns suggest an omnivorous diet of plants, nuts, and small mammals. Although *Ardipithecus* probably fed both in trees and on the ground, the canines suggest less of a fruit diet than is characteristic of living apes. *Ardipithecus* canines resemble modern human canines more than the tusklike, piercing upper canines of chimps and gorillas. The ancestral relationship of *Ardipithecus* to *Australopithecus* has not been determined, but Ardi has been called a plausible ancestor for *Australopithecus* (see Wilford 2009*b*).

## The Varied Australopithecines

Some Miocene hominins eventually evolved into a varied group of Pliocene–Pleistocene hominins known as the **australopithecines**—for which we have an abundant fossil record. This term reflects their one-time classification as members of a distinct taxonomic subfamily, the Australopithecinae. We now know that the various species of *Australopithecus* do not form a distinct subfamily within the order Primates, but the name "australopithecine" has stuck. Today the distinction between the australopithecines and later hominins is made on the genus level. The australopithecines are assigned to the genus *Australopithecus (Au.);* later humans, to *Homo (H.).*

In the scheme followed here, *Australopithecus* had at least these seven species:

1. *Au. anamensis* (4.2 to 3.9 m.y.a.).
2. *Au. afarensis* (3.8 to 3.0 m.y.a.).
3. *Au. africanus* (3.0? to 2.0? m.y.a.).
4. *Au. garhi* (2.5 m.y.a.).
5. *Au. robustus* (2.0? to 1.0? m.y.a.).
6. *Au. boisei* (2.6? to 1.2 m.y.a.).
7. *Au. sediba* (1.95 to 1.78 m.y.a.).

The dates given for each species are approximate. The same dating techniques were not, or could not be, used for all the finds. Two South African species (*Au. africanus* and *Au. robustus*), for example, come from a nonvolcanic area where radiometric dating could not be done. Dating of those fossils has been based mainly on stratigraphy. The hominin fossils from the volcanic regions of East Africa usually have radiometric dates. (See "Anthropology Today" for the most recent *Australopithecus* find from South Africa.)

### *Australopithecus anamensis*

*Ardipithecus ramidus* may (or may not) have evolved into **Au. anamensis,** a bipedal hominin from northern Kenya, whose fossil remains were reported first by Maeve Leakey and Alan Walker in 1995 (Leakey et al. 1995). *Au. anamensis* consists of 78 fragments from two sites: Kanapoi and Allia Bay. The fossils include upper and lower jaws, cranial fragments, and the upper and lower parts of a leg bone (tibia). The Kanapoi fossils date to 4.2 m.y.a., and those at Allia Bay to 3.9 m.y.a. The molars have thick enamel, and the apelike canines are large. Based on the tibia, *anamensis* weighed about

110 pounds (50 kilograms). This would have made it larger than either the earlier *Ardipithecus* or the later *Au. afarensis*. Its anatomy implies that *anamensis* was bipedal. Because of its date and its location in the East African Rift Valley, *Au. anamensis* may be ancestral to *Au. afarensis* (3.8–3.0 m.y.a.), which usually is considered ancestral to all the later australopithecines (*garhi, africanus, robustus, boisei,* and *sediba*) as well as to *Homo* (see Figure 6.1).

FIGURE 6.1    **Phylogenetic Tree for African Apes, Hominids, and Hominins**
The presumed divergence date for ancestral chimps and hominins was 8–7 m.y.a.
Branching in later hominin evolution is also shown. For more exact dates, see the
text and Table 6.1.

## Australopithecus afarensis

The hominin species known as *Au. afarensis* includes fossils found at two sites, Laetoli in northern Tanzania and Hadar in the Afar region of Ethiopia. Laetoli is earlier (3.8–3.6 m.y.a.). The Hadar fossils probably date to between 3.3 and 3.0 m.y.a. Thus, based on the current evidence, *Au. afarensis* lived between about 3.8 and 3.0 m.y.a. Research directed by Mary Leakey was responsible for the Laetoli finds. The Hadar discoveries resulted from an international expedition directed by D. C. Johanson and M. Taieb (see Johanson and Wong 2010). The two sites have yielded significant samples of early hominin fossils. There are two dozen specimens from Laetoli, and the Hadar finds include the remains of between 35 and 65 individuals. The Laetoli remains are mainly teeth and jaw fragments, along with some very informative fossilized footprints. The Hadar sample includes skull fragments and postcranial material, most notably 40 percent of the complete skeleton of a tiny hominin female, dubbed "Lucy," who lived around 3 m.y.a.

Although the hominin remains at Laetoli and Hadar were deposited half a million years apart, their many resemblances explain their placement in the same species, *Au. afarensis*. The discovery of these fossils forced a reinterpretation of the early hominin fossil record. *Au. afarensis,* although clearly a hominin, still shared many features with the chimpanzee, suggesting very recent common ancestry—no more than 8 m.y.a. *Ardipithecus* and *Au. anamensis* are even more apelike.

Discussion of hominin fossils requires a brief review of dentition. Moving from front to back, on either side of the upper or lower jaw, humans (and apes) have two incisors, one canine, two premolars, and three molars. Our dental formula is 2.1.2.3, for a total of 8 teeth on each side, upper and lower—32 teeth in all—if we have all our "wisdom teeth" (our third molars). Now back to the australopithecines.

From the same general area of northern Ethiopia as Lucy comes another important member of *Au. afarensis* (Owen 2006). This toddler, the world's oldest fossil child, soon was dubbed "Lucy's Baby"—despite having lived a hundred thousand years before Lucy (3.3 m.y.a. for the child versus 3.2 for Lucy). The child is an amazingly complete find, with a more intact skull and much more skeletal material than exists for Lucy. Not surprisingly, given what we already know about *Au. afarensis,* the skull and upper body are apelike, while the lower body confirms bipedalism. Despite bipedalism, the skeleton's upper body includes two complete apelike shoulder blades, so it probably was better at climbing than humans are (see Owen 2012). Unearthed in 2000, the child probably was female and about 3 years old when she died. The remains include a well-preserved skull, milk teeth, tiny fingers, a torso, a foot, and a kneecap. Although Lucy doesn't have much of a head, her "baby" has a complete skull, a mandible (jaw bone), and a monkey-sized face with a smooth brow.

The *Au. afarensis* fossils show that as recently as 3.0 m.y.a., our ancestors had a mixture of apelike and hominin features. Canines, premolars, and skulls were much more apelike than most scholars had imagined would exist in such a recent ancestor. Compared with *Homo, Au. afarensis* had larger and sharper canine teeth that projected beyond the other teeth. The canines, however, were reduced compared with an ape's tusklike canines. The *afarensis* lower premolar was pointed and projecting to sharpen the upper canine. It had one long cusp and one tiny bump that hints at the bicuspid

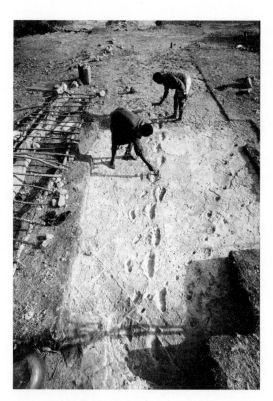

An ancient trail of hominin footprints fossilized in volcanic ash. Mary Leakey found this 230-foot (70-meter) trail at Laetoli, Tanzania, in 1979. It dates from 3.6 m.y.a. and confirms that *Au. afarensis* was a striding biped. © John Reader/ Science Photo Library/Science Source

premolar that eventually developed in hominin evolution. On the other hand, the molars, chewing apparatus, and cheekbones foreshadowed later hominin trends.

When the coarse, gritty, fibrous vegetation of grasslands and semidesert enters the diet, the back teeth change to accommodate heavy chewing stresses. Massive back teeth, jaws, and facial and cranial structures suggest a diet demanding extensive grinding and powerful crushing. *Au. afarensis* molars are large (see Figure 6.2). The lower jaw (mandible) is thick and is buttressed with a bony ridge behind the front teeth. The cheekbones are large and flare out to the side for the attachment of powerful chewing muscles.

The skull of *Au. afarensis* contrasts with those of later hominins. The cranial capacity barely surpasses the chimp average. Below the neck, however—particularly in regard to locomotion—*Au. afarensis* was unquestionably human. Early evidence of striding bipedalism comes from Laetoli, where volcanic ash, which can be dated directly by the K/A technique, covered a trail of footprints of two or three hominins walking to a water hole. These prints leave no doubt that a small, striding biped lived in Tanzania by 3.6 m.y.a. The structure of the pelvic, hip, leg, and foot bones also confirms that upright bipedalism was *Au. afarensis*'s mode of locomotion (see Choi 2012; Ward et al. 2011). As we have seen, more recent finds show that bipedalism predated *Au. afarensis*. *Au. anamensis* (4.2 m.y.a.) was bipedal, as was the even older *Ardipithecus* (5.8–4.4 m.y.a.).

FIGURE 6.2 **Comparison of Dentition in Ape, Human, and *Au. afarensis* Palates.**
Teeth of chimpanzee, *Australopithecus afarensis*, and modern human. In (a), note the
parallel tooth rows in the chimpanzee, as compared to those of the modern human. In (b),
note the sharply pointed premolar of the chimpanzee, the pointed premolar of *Au. afarensis*,
and the bicuspid premolar of the modern human.

Source: From John H. Relethford, *The Human Species: An Introduction to Biological Anthropology*, 9th ed., p. 202.
Copyright © 2013 by McGraw-Hill Education, LLC. Reprinted with permission.

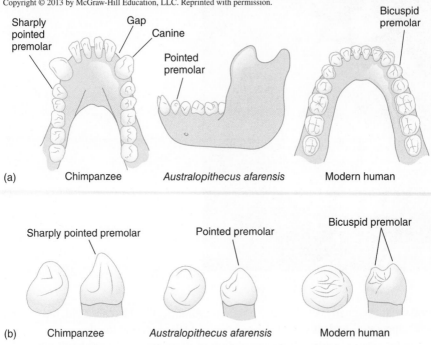

Although bidepal, *Au. afarensis* still contrasts in many ways with later hominins.
Sexual dimorphism is especially marked. The male–female contrast in jaw size in *Au.
afarensis* was more marked than in the orangutan. There was a similar contrast in body
size. *Au. afarensis* females, such as Lucy, stood between 3 and 4 feet (.9 and 1.2 meters)
tall; males might have reached 5 feet (1.5 meters). *Au. afarensis* males weighed perhaps
twice as much as the females did. Table 6.2 summarizes data on the various australopithecines, including mid-sex body weight and brain size. *Mid-sex* means midway between the male average and the female average.

Lucy and her kind were far from dainty. Lucy's muscle-engraved bones are much
more robust than ours are. With only rudimentary tools and weapons, early hominins
needed powerful and resistant bones and muscles. Lucy's arms are longer relative to
her legs than are those of later hominins. Here again her proportions are more apelike
than ours are. Although Lucy neither brachiated nor knuckle-walked, she was probably a much better climber than modern people are, and she spent some of her day in
the trees.

TABLE 6.2   **Facts about the Australopithecines Compared with Chimps and** *Homo*

| Species | Dates (m.y.a.) | Known Distribution | Important Sites | Body Weight (Mid-Sex) | Brain Size (Mid-Sex) (cm³) |
|---|---|---|---|---|---|
| Anatomically modern humans (AMHs) | 0.195 (195,000) to present | | | 132 lb/60 kg | 1,350 |
| *Pan troglodytes* (chimpanzee) | Modern | | | 93 lb/42 kg | 390 |
| *Au. sediba* | 1.98 to 1.78 | S. Africa | Malapa | Insufficient data | 420 |
| *Au. boisei* | 2.6? to 1.2 | E. Africa | Olduvai, East Turkana | 86 lb/39 kg | 490 |
| *Au. robustus* | 2.0? to 1.0? | S. Africa | Kromdraai, Swartkrans | 81 lb/37 kg | 540 |
| *Au. africanus* | 3.0? to 2.0? | S. Africa | Taung, Sterkfontein, Makapansqat | 79 lb/36 kg | 490 |
| *Au. afarensis* | 3.8 to 3.0 | E. Africa | Hadar, Laetoli | 77 lb/35 kg | 430 |
| *Au. anamensis* | 4.2 to 3.9 | Kenya | Kanapoi Allia Bay | Not enough data | No published skulls |
| *Ardipithecus* | 5.8 to 4.4 | Ethiopia | Aramis | Not enough data | Not enough data |

The pelvis, the lower spine, the hip joint, and the thigh bone change in accordance with the stresses of bipedal locomotion. With bipedalism, the pelvis forms a sort of basket that balances the weight of the trunk and supports this weight with less stress. Fossilized spinal bones (vertebrae) show that the australopithecine spine had the lower spine (lumbar) curve characteristic of *Homo*. This curvature helps transmit the weight of the upper body to the pelvis and the legs. The pelvises of the australopithecines were similar but not identical to those of *Homo*. The most significant contrast is a narrower australopithecine birth canal. Expansion of the birth canal is a trend in hominin evolution. The width of the birth canal is related to the size of the skull and brain. *Au. afarensis* had a small cranial capacity. Even in later australopithecines, brain size did not exceed 600 cubic centimeters. Undoubtedly, the australopithecine skull grew after birth to accommodate a growing brain, as it does (much more) in *Homo*. However, the brains of the australopithecines expanded less than ours do. In the australopithecines, the cranial sutures (the lines where the bones of the skull eventually come together) fused earlier in life. Young australopithecines must have depended on their parents and kin for nurturance and protection. Those years of childhood dependency would have provided time for observation, teaching, and learning. This may provide indirect evidence for a rudimentary cultural life.

## Gracile and Robust Australopithecines

The fossils of *Au. africanus* and *Au. robustus* come from South Africa. In 1924, the anatomist Raymond Dart coined the term ***Australopithecus africanus*** to describe the first fossil representative of this species, the skull of a juvenile that was found accidentally in a quarry at Taung, South Africa. Radiometric dates are lacking for this nonvolcanic region, but the fossil hominins found at the various South African sites appear (from stratigraphy) to have lived between 3 and 1 m.y.a.

There were two groups of South African australopithecines: **gracile (*Au. africanus*)** and **robust (*Au. robustus*)**. "Gracile" indicates that members of *Au. africanus* were smaller and slighter, less robust than were members of *Au. robustus*. There also were very robust—*hyperrobust*—australopithecines in East Africa. In the classification scheme used here, these have been assigned to *Au. boisei*. However, some scholars consider *Au. robustus* and *Au. boisei* to be regional variants of just one species, usually called *robustus* (sometimes given its own genus, *Paranthropus*).

Graciles and robusts probably descend from *Au. afarensis,* which itself was gracile in form, or from a South African version of *Au. afarensis*. Some scholars have argued that the graciles lived before (3.0?–2.0? m.y.a.) and were ancestral to the robusts (2.0?–1.0? m.y.a.). Others contend that the graciles and the robusts were separate species that may have overlapped in time. (Classifying them as members of different species implies they were reproductively isolated from each other in time or space.) Other paleoanthropologists view the gracile and robust australopithecines as different ends of a continuum of variation in a single *polytypic species*—one with considerable phenotypic variation.

The trend toward enlarged back teeth, chewing muscles, and facial buttressing, which already is noticeable in *Au. afarensis,* continues in the South African australopithecines. However, the canines are reduced, and the premolars are fully bicuspid. Dental form and function changed as dietary needs shifted from cutting and slashing to chewing and grinding. The mainstay of the australopithecine diet was the vegetation of the savanna grasslands. In the South African australopithecines, both deciduous

The smaller skull is an *Au. africanus* (gracile) skull (Sterkfontein 5). This cranium, discovered by Dr. Robert Broom and J. T. Robinson in April 1947, dates back to 2.9–2.4 m.y.a. The larger skull is from *Au. boisei*—Olduvai Hominid (OH) 5, originally called *Zinjanthropus boisei*. This skull of a young male, discovered by Mary Leakey in 1959 at Olduvai Gorge, Tanzania, dates back 1.8 million years. © The Natural History Museum/Alamy ("baby") and permanent molars and premolars are massive, with multiple cusps. This evolutionary trend ended with early *Homo,* which had much smaller back teeth, reflecting a dietary change that will be described later.

Contrasts with *Homo* in the front teeth are less marked. But they are still of interest because of what they tell us about sexual dimorphism. *Au. africanus*'s canines were more pointed, with larger roots, than *Homo*'s are. Still, the *Au. africanus* canines were only 75 percent the size of the canines of *Au. afarensis.* Despite this canine reduction, there was just as much canine sexual dimorphism in *Au. africanus* as there had been in *Au. afarensis* (Wolpoff 1999). Sexual dimorphism in general was much more pronounced among the early hominins than it is among *Homo sapiens. Au. africanus* females were about 4 feet (1.2 meters), and males 5 feet (1.5 meters), tall. The average female probably had no more than 60 percent the weight of the average male. (That figure contrasts with today's average female-to-male weight ratio of about 88 percent.)

Teeth, jaw, face, and skull changed to fit a diet based on tough, gritty, fibrous grasslands vegetation. A massive face housed large upper teeth and provided a base for the attachment of powerful chewing muscles. Australopithecine cheekbones were elongated, massive structures that anchored large chewing muscles running up the jaw. Another set of robust chewing muscles extended from the back of the jaw to the sides of the skull. In the more robust australopithecines (*Au. robustus* in South Africa and *Au. boisei* in East Africa), these muscles were strong enough to produce a *sagittal crest,* a bony ridge on the top of the skull. Such a crest forms as the bone grows. It develops from the pull of the chewing muscles as they meet at the midline of the skull (see Figure 6.3).

**FIGURE 6.3**
**Four Types of Early Hominins**
What are the main differences you notice?

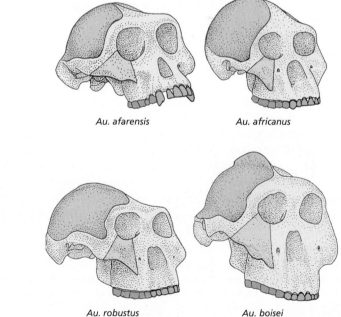

Au. afarensis        Au. africanus

Au. robustus        Au. boisei

The degree of robusticity, especially in the chewing apparatus, increased through time among the robust australopithecines. This trend was most striking in *Au. boisei,* which survived through 1.2 m.y.a in East Africa. Compared with their predecessors, the later robust australopithecines tended to have larger overall size, skulls, and back teeth. They also had thicker faces, more prominent crests, and more rugged muscle markings on the skeleton. By contrast, the front teeth stayed the same size.

Brain size (measured as cranial capacity, in cubic centimeters—$cm^3$) increased only slightly among *Au. afarensis* (430 $cm^3$), *Au. africanus* (490 $cm^3$), and *Au. robustus* (540 $cm^3$). These figures can be compared with an average cranial capacity of 1,350 $cm^3$ in *Homo sapiens.* The modern range goes from less than 1,000 $cm^3$ to more than 2,000 $cm^3$ in normal adults. The cranial capacity of chimps (*Pan troglodytes*) averages 390 $cm^3$ (see Table 6.2). Gorilla brains average around 500 $cm^3$, which is within the australopithecine range, but gorilla body size is much greater.

## The Australopithecines and Early *Homo*

By 2 m.y.a. the ancestors of *Homo* had become reproductively isolated from the later australopithecines, such as *Au. robustus* and *Au. boisei.* The fossilized hominin teeth dating to this period have two clearly different sizes. One set is huge, the largest molars and premolars in hominin evolution; those teeth belonged to the hyperrobust *Au. boisei.* The other group of (smaller) teeth belonged to early members of the genus *Homo.*

By 1.9 m.y.a., there is fossil evidence that different hominin groups occupied different ecological niches in Africa. One of them, *Homo*—by then *Homo erectus*—had a larger brain, a reproportioned skull, and a greater capacity for culture than the australopithecines had. *H. erectus* hunted and gathered, made sophisticated tools, and eventually displaced *Au. boisei.*

*Au. boisei* of East Africa, the hyperrobust australopithecines, had mammoth back teeth. The females had bigger back teeth than did earlier australopithecine males. *Au. boisei* became ever more specialized with respect to one part of the traditional australopithecine diet, concentrating on coarse vegetation with a high grit content.

We still don't know why, how, and exactly when the split between *Australopithecus* and *Homo* took place. Scholars have defended many different models, or theoretical schemes, to interpret the early hominin fossil record. Because new finds so often have forced reappraisals, most scientists are willing to modify their interpretation when given new evidence. Johanson and White (1979) proposed that *Au. afarensis* split into two groups—later australopithecines and early *Homo.* The ancestors of *Homo* became reproductively isolated from the australopithecines between 3 and 2 m.y.a. Within this group was **Homo habilis,** a term coined by L. S. B. and Mary Leakey to describe the earliest members of the genus *Homo.* Another form of early *Homo* was *H. erectus,* which appears to have lived contemporaneously with *H. habilis* between around 1.9 and 1.4 m.y.a. (Spoor et al. 2007; Wood 2011). Other members of *Au. afarensis* evolved into the various kinds of later australopithecines (*Au. africanus, Au. robustus,* and hyperrobust *Au. boisei,* the last member to become extinct).

There is good fossil evidence that *Homo* and *Au. boisei* coexisted in East Africa. *Au. boisei* seems to have lived in very arid areas, feeding on harder-to-chew vegetation than had any previous hominin. This diet would explain the hyperrobusts' huge back teeth, jaws, and associated areas of the face and skull.

"Anthropology Today" describes the most recent find, in South Africa, of a late gracile australopithecine boy, which was given the name *Au. sediba*. Its date of 1.95 to 1.78 m.y.a. and its mosaic of primitive and modern features spurred a debate among scientists about whether it should be considered *Homo* or *Australopithecus* (see Wilford 2012). We know that species of *Homo* were coexisting with australopithecines (robusts and late graciles) by this time.

## Oldowan Tools

Simple obviously manufactured stone tools were discovered in 1931 by L. S. B. and Mary Leakey at Olduvai Gorge, Tanzania. That locale gave the tools their name— **Oldowan pebble tools.** The oldest known Oldowan tools are between 2.6 and 2.0 million years old. The discovery of much earlier stone tools (3.3 m.y.a.) at the Lomekwi 3 site west of Lake Turkana in Kenya was reported in 2015.

Stone tools consist of flakes and cores. The *core* is the piece of rock, in the Oldowan case about the size of a tennis ball, from which flakes are struck. Once flakes have been removed, the core can become a tool itself. A *chopper* is a tool made by flaking the edge of such a core on one side and thus forming a cutting edge.

A modern human hand holds a rock to demonstrate how Oldowan stone tools were made. Oldowan chopper tools were rounded rocks sharpened by blows that detached a flake. The sharp flakes that were detached actually made up the bulk of the Oldowan tool industry. © Javier Trueba/MSF/Science Source

Core tools are not the most common Oldowan tools; flakes are. The purpose of flaking stone in the Oldowan tradition was not to create pebble tools or choppers but to create the sharp stone flakes that made up the mainstay of the Oldowan tool kit. Choppers were a convenient by-product of flaking and were used as well.

Oldowan choppers could have been used for food processing—by pounding, breaking, or bashing. Flakes probably were used mainly as cutters, for example, to dismember game carcasses. Crushed fossil animal bones indicate that stones were used to break open marrow cavities. Also, Oldowan deposits include pieces of bone or horn with scratch marks, suggesting they were used to dig up tubers or insects.

For decades anthropologists have debated the identity of the earliest stone toolmakers. The first *Homo habilis* find got its name (*habilis* is Latin for "able") for its presumed status as the first hominin toolmaker. The story has grown more complicated, with discoveries making it very likely that at least one kind of australopithecine also made and habitually used stone tools.

## *Au. garhi* and Early Stone Tools

In 1999 an international team reported the discovery, in Ethiopia, of a new species of hominin, along with the earliest traces of animal butchery (Asfaw, White, and Lovejoy 1999). At the same site, which dates to 2.5 m.y.a., the scientists found evidence that antelopes and horses had been butchered with early stone tools. The hominin fossils displayed a surprising combination of skeletal and dental features, which suggested their new species name, ***Australopithecus garhi.*** The word *garhi* means "surprise" in the Afar language. Evidence that large mammals were being butchered shows that early stone technologies were aimed at getting meat and marrow from big game.

In 1997 the archaeologist Sileshi Semaw announced he had found early stone tools, dating to 2.6 m.y.a., at the nearby Ethiopian site of Gona. But which hominin had made these tools, he wondered, and what were they used for? The 1999 discoveries by Asfaw, White, and their colleagues provided answers, identifying *Au. garhi* as the best candidate for toolmaker.

The association, in the same area at the same time, of *Au. garhi,* animal butchery, and early stone tools suggests that the australopithecines were toolmakers, with some capacity for culture. Nevertheless, cultural abilities developed exponentially with *Homo*'s appearance and expansion. With increasing reliance on hunting, tool making, and other cultural abilities, *Homo* eventually became the most efficient exploiter of the savanna niche. The last surviving members of *Au. boisei* may have been forced into ever-more-marginal areas. They eventually became extinct. By 1 m.y.a., a single species of hominin, *H. erectus,* not only had rendered other hominin forms extinct but also had expanded the hominin range to Asia and Europe. An essentially human strategy of adaptation, incorporating hunting as a fundamental ingredient of a generalized foraging economy, had emerged. Despite regional variation, it was to be the basic economy for our genus until about 11,000 years ago. The next chapter describes the fossils, tools, and life patterns of the various forms of *Homo.*

## Oldowan Hominins at the Kanjera Site

Comparisons with chimps and bonobos suggest that hominins always have lived in social groups composed of multiple males and females. Our closest relatives, chimps

## Anthropology Today   Au. Sediba: *Ancestor or Fascinating Sideline?*

Named by *Smithsonian* magazine as the number one hominid (and hominin) fossil discovery of 2011, *Australopithecus sediba* (actually discovered between 2008 and 2010 but described in 2011) has generated a new debate about human origins. The original find is an almost complete skull and partial skeleton of an 11- to 12-year-old boy who stood 4930 (1.3 m.) tall. Is this australopithecine a plausible human ancestor, as is claimed by its discoverer, paleoanthropologist Lee Berger? Most experts are skeptical about that claim, while appreciating the fossil for its unique blend of hominin features.

With long arms . . . and powerful fingers, the ancient creatures were built for climbing trees. But they also had long lower limbs, flat feet and a flexible lumbar spine that [allowed them to] . . . cover long distances by walking upright on two legs.

After four years of intense analysis, a team of paleoanthropologists is making its most detailed case yet that a pair of ancient skeletons discovered in a grassy South African valley could represent the direct evolutionary link between modern humans and the family of human ancestors that includes the *Australopithecus* known as Lucy.

In a series of papers published in . . . the journal *Science* [on April 12, 2013], the researchers argue that the "mosaic nature" of the *Australopithecus sediba* specimens makes them a strong candidate to be the . . . "branch of *Australopithecus* that ultimately gave rise to the genus *Homo*, which includes *Homo sapiens*."

The skeleton fossils have so many human-like features "across the whole of the body that it must be considered, at the very least, a possible ancestor," said Lee R. Berger, a paleoanthropologist at the

University of Witwatersrand in Johannesburg, South Africa, who discovered the fossils in 2008. . . . But not everyone accepts this view. Critics say the skeletons are not old enough to be the precursors to *Homo*. Others say the similarities can be chalked up to the diversity of early hominids.

At a minimum, the new details . . . are causing scientists to revise . . . some long-held assumptions about the anatomical makeup of our extended evolutionary family. For example, though it was long believed that Australopiths had six lower vertebrae, "one more than humans and at least two more than apes," it is now clear that they had the same number as humans: five. The ape-like boy and older woman who tumbled through a sinkhole and lay buried in a deep underground cave for nearly 2 million years have also given scientists a better view of how our early relatives walked. . . .

By examining bone grooves and muscle attachments in the kneecap, thigh and lower leg bones and comparing them with those in humans and apes, the scientists were able to figure out that the roughly

Lee Berger with his son, Matthew, and fossils of *Australopithecus sediba*. Matthew found one of the fossils while chasing his dog. © Alexander Joe/Agence France-Presse/Getty Images

*continued*

## Anthropology Today    *continued*

4-foot-tall [female] walked upright. But she probably did so with a peculiar gait marked by an inward rotation of the knee and hip, causing her narrow-heeled feet to twist slightly. . . . The team wrote that it would need to examine more fossils before it could say whether the entire species walked the same way. Berger said that if modern humans were to observe an *Au. sediba* walking by, their attention would probably not be drawn to its legs. "What would be a great difference would be how it swung its long upper limbs during that walk and the shrugged-shoulder appearance of its upper body," he said. The researchers speculated that the animals spent their lives both in trees and walking on the ground. In other aspects of the research, scientists reported that these specimens had jaws and teeth that are recognizably human. In earlier studies, researchers concluded too that the creature's hands were capable of precise gripping. The presence of several

human-like features has led Berger and others to suggest that *Au. sediba,* which lived an estimated 1.78 million to 1.95 million years ago, may have been the species that evolved into the earliest members of the *Homo* genus. But other paleoanthropologists have pointed out several problems with that thesis.

Donald Johanson, the Arizona State University paleoanthropologist who discovered Lucy in 1974, said the first *Homo* species appeared 2.4 million years ago in eastern Africa. Instead of giving rise to the genus *Homo, Au. sediba* would have been a contemporary. "Sediba abundantly demonstrates a unique set of anatomical features of an *Australopithecus* species that was most likely a dead-end branch on our tree," said Johanson, who was not involved in the new studies. . . .

**Source:** Monte Morin, "Evidence Points toward Solving Evolutionary 'Missing Link.'" *Los Angeles Times,* April 11, 2013. Copyright © 2013 *Los Angeles Times.* Reprinted with permission.

and bonobos, lack *pair bonding;* a chimp female in estrus will mate with multiple males, and males mate with multiple females. At some point in their evolution, hominins developed pair bonding (Lukas and Clutton-Brock 2013; Opie et al. 2013; Zimmer 2013). A male and a female would pair off, bond, and mate exclusively or mainly with each other for a significant length of time. Such a bond would increase the likelihood that the offspring of the female were also those of the male. Both parents would do all they could to ensure the child's survival and well-being. At some point, especially as hominins became dependent on hunting, a gender-based division of labor developed. Men who hunted took meat home to share with their mates, their children, and other members of their social group.

Anthropologists have found excellent evidence for hunting around 2 million years ago at a very rich site in Kenya—the Kanjera South, or KJS, site, located on the shores of Lake Victoria (Ferraro et al. 2013). The archaeologists analyzed thousands of tools and animal bones (many showing marks of cutting or cracking) from the site. Using Oldowan stone tools, the ancient hominins who occupied the site were acquiring and processing meat—from hunting and scavenging. The animal bones at the site reveal that these Oldowan hominins hunted and butchered numerous small antelopes. The archaeologists could tell this because bones of the entire animal were present at the site—indicating that carcasses had been brought back whole. Cut marks show that hominins used their simple stone tools to remove animal flesh. They also used fist-sized stones to crack open animal bones to get at the marrow. The Oldowan hominins also ate larger antelopes, which they almost certainly scavenged. These antelopes were represented by only part of the skeleton and skull, suggesting that hominins brought back remainders from the kills of other predators, which could not as easily get at the brains and bone marrow of their prey.

The Kanjera site provides the earliest, and very complete, evidence for what the anthropologists call "persistent" reliance on meat within the hominin diet. Lacking hominin fossils at the site, we don't know the genus or species of these hominins, but we do know the significance of a meat-laden diet. Meat supported population increase and territorial expansion among hominins. We hear so much today about the dangers of too much red meat that we forget that meat is an excellent and concentrated source of calories and protein. Its inclusion in the ancient hominin diet supported an increase in the size of the human body and brain, which is a very expensive organ in terms of its energy needs. Among the likely social changes associated with the new diet were pair bonding, increased parental (especially male) investment in children, and a gender-based division of labor.

## Summary

1.  A skull found in northern Chad, dated at 6–7 million years old, officially named *Sahelanthropus tchadensis,* more commonly called "Toumai," may or may not be the earliest hominin yet known, as may the somewhat less ancient *Orrorin tugenensis,* found in Kenya in 2001.

2.  Hominins lived during the late Miocene, Pliocene (5.0–2.0 m.y.a.), and Pleistocene (2.0 m.y.a.–10,000 B.P.) epochs. The australopithecines had appeared by 4.2 m.y.a. The seven species of *Australopithecus* were *Au. anamensis* (4.2–3.9 m.y.a.), *Au. afarensis* (3.8–3.0 m.y.a.), *Au. africanus* (3.0?–2.0? m.y.a.), *Au. garhi* (2.5 m.y.a.), *Au. robustus* (2.0?–1.0? m.y.a.), *Au. boisei* (2.6?–1.2 m.y.a.), and *Au. sediba* (1.95–1.78 m.y.a.). The earliest generally accepted hominin remains are classified as *Ardipithecus kadabba* (5.8–5.5 m.y.a.) and *ramidus* (4.4 m.y.a.). Next comes *Au. anamensis,* then a group of fossils from Hadar, Ethiopia, and Laetoli, Tanzania, classified as *Au. afarensis.*

3.  These earliest hominins shared many primitive features, including slashing canines; elongated premolars; a small, apelike skull; and marked sexual dimorphism. Still, *Au. afarensis* and its recently discovered predecessors were definitely hominins. In *Au. afarensis* this is confirmed by large molars and, more important, by skeletal evidence (e.g., in Lucy) for upright bipedalism.

4.  Remains of two later groups, *Au. africanus* (graciles) and *Au. robustus* (robusts), were found in South Africa. Both groups show the australopithecine trend toward a powerful chewing apparatus. They had large molars and premolars and large and

robust faces, skulls, and muscle markings. All these features are more pronounced in the robusts than they are in the graciles. The basis of the australopithecine diet was savanna vegetation.

5. By 2.0 m.y.a. there is ample evidence for two distinct hominin groups: early *Homo* and *Au. boisei,* the hyperrobust australopithecines. The latter eventually became extinct around 1.2 m.y.a. *Au. boisei* became increasingly specialized, dependent on tough, coarse, gritty, fibrous savanna vegetation. The australopithecine trend toward dental, facial, and cranial robustness continued with *Au. boisei,* but these structures were reduced in *H. habilis* (2.4?–1.4? m.y.a.) and *H. erectus* (1.9–0.37? m.y.a.).

6. Pebble tools dating to between 2.6 and 2.0 m.y.a. have been found in Ethiopia, Congo, and Malawi. Scientists have disagreed about their maker, some arguing that only early *Homo* could have made them. Evidence has been presented that *Au. garhi* made pebble tools around 2.6 m.y.a. Cultural abilities developed exponentially with *Homo*'s appearance and evolution.

**Key Terms**

*Au. afarensis, 126*
*Au. africanus, 130*
*Au. anamensis, 124*
*Au. boisei, 132*
*Au. garhi, 134*

*Au. robustus, 130*
*Ardipithecus, 116*
australopithecines,
   *124*
gracile, *130*

*Homo habilis, 132*
Oldowan pebble
   tools, *133*
robust, *130*

# Chapter 7

# The Genus *Homo*

## Early *Homo*

As we saw in Chapter 6, at 2 million years ago, there is East African evidence for two distinct hominin groups: early *Homo* and *Au. boisei,* the hyperrobust australopithecines, which became extinct around 1.2 m.y.a. *Au. boisei* became increasingly specialized, dependent on tough, coarse, gritty, fibrous savanna vegetation. The australopithecine trend toward dental, facial, and cranial robustness continued with *Au. boisei.* However, these structures were reduced as early forms of *Homo* evolved into early *H. erectus* by 1.9 m.y.a. By that date *Homo* was generalizing the subsistence quest to the hunting of large animals to supplement scavenging and the gathering of vegetation.

### H. rudolfensis and H. habilis

In 1972, in an expedition led by Richard Leakey, Bernard Ngeneo unearthed a skull designated KNM-ER 1470. The name comes from its catalog number in the Kenya National Museum (KNM) and its discovery location (East Rudolph—ER)—east of Lake Rudolph, at a site called Koobi Fora. The 1470 skull attracted immediate attention because of its unusual combination of a large brain (775 cm$^3$) and very large molars. Its brain size was more human than that of the australopithecines, but its molars recalled those of the hyperrobust australopithecines. Some paleoanthropologists attributed the large skull and teeth to a very large body, assuming that this had been one *really big* hominin. But no postcranial remains were found with 1470, nor have they been found with any later discovery of a 1470-like specimen.

How to interpret KNM-ER 1470? On the basis of its brain size, it seemed to belong in *Homo*. On the basis of its back teeth, it seemed more like *Australopithecus*. Dating estimates range from 1.8 to as far back as 2.4 m.y.a. Originally, some paleoanthropologists assigned 1470 to *H. habilis,* while others saw it as an unusual australopithecine. In 1986, it received its own species name, *Homo rudolfensis,* from the lake near which it was found. This label has stuck—although it isn't accepted by all paleoanthropologists. Those who find *H. rudolfensis* to be a valid taxon emphasize its contrasts with *H. habilis.* Note the contrasts in the two skulls in the photo below. KNM-ER 1813, on the left, is considered *H. habilis;* KNM-ER 1470, on the right, is *H. rudolfensis.* The *habilis* skull has a more marked brow ridge and a depression behind it, whereas 1470 has a less pronounced brow ridge and a longer, flatter face.

For almost 40 years after finding 1470, the Leakey family and others scoured deposits near Lake Turkana for similar fossils, and between 2007 and 2009 they found them (see Gibbons 2012; Leakey et al. 2012). In 2012 Maeve Leakey (Richard's wife) and her associates announced the discovery at Koobi Fora of a face and two jawbones, showing that 1470 was not unique. These new fossils, dating to 2.03–1.78 m.y.a., confirmed that *H. rudolfensis* lived in the same area and at the same time as at least two other species of *Homo*—*habilis* and *erectus.*

The face of the newly discovered *H. rudolfensis* skull—that of a juvenile—was well preserved and included upper teeth. It was a smaller version of the 1470 skull,

Meet two kinds of early *Homo*: on the left KNM-ER 1813, on the right KNM-ER 1470. The latter (1470) has been classified as *H. rudolfensis.* What's the classification of 1813? © Kenneth Garrett

both featuring an unusually flat face that contrasts with the more jutting upper jaw of *H. habilis*. The lower jaw bones, one of which was remarkably complete, provided new information, because the 1470 fossil had no lower jaw. The new jaw and face showed that *H. rudolfensis* had an unusual, U-shaped palate, with canines facing the front of the jaw rather than placed on the sides in a V-shaped palate, as in *H. habilis*. The new jaws also had smaller molars than expected, based on those of 1470. The new fossils were found near the 1470 discovery site, and within the same region where fossils of *H. habilis* and *H. erectus* have been discovered.

## *H. habilis* and *H. erectus*

A team headed by L. S. B. and Mary Leakey (parents of Richard) found the first representative of *Homo habilis* (OH7—Olduvai Hominid 7) at Olduvai Gorge in Tanzania in 1960. Olduvai's oldest layer, Bed I, dates to 1.8 m.y.a. This layer has yielded both small-brained *Au. boisei* (average 490 cm$^3$) fossils and *H. habilis* skulls, with cranial capacities between 600 and 700 cm$^3$.

Another important *habilis* find was made in 1986 by Tim White of the University of California, Berkeley. OH62 is the partial skeleton of a female *H. habilis* from Olduvai Bed I. This was the first find of an *H. habilis* skull with a significant amount of skeletal material. OH62, dating to 1.8 m.y.a., consists of parts of the skull, the right arm, and both legs. Because scientists had assumed that *H. habilis* would be taller than tiny Lucy (*Au. afarensis*), OH62 was surprising because of its small size and apelike limb bones. Not only was OH62 just as tiny as Lucy (3 feet, or 0.9 meter), its arms were longer and more apelike than expected. The limb proportions suggested greater tree-climbing ability than later hominins had. *H. habilis* may still have sought occasional refuge in the trees.

The small size and primitive proportions of *H. habilis* were unexpected, given what was known about early *H. erectus* in East Africa. In deposits near Lake Turkana, Kenya, Richard Leakey had uncovered two *H. erectus* skulls dating to 1.6 m.y.a. By that date, *H. erectus* (males, at least) had already attained a cranial capacity of 900 cm$^3$, along with a modern body shape and height. An amazingly complete young male *H. erectus* fossil (WT15,000) found at West Turkana in 1984 by Kimoya Kimeu, a collaborator of the Leakeys, has confirmed this. WT15,000, also known as the Nariokotome boy, was a 12-year-old male who had already reached 5 feet 5 inches (1.67 meters). He might have grown to 6 feet had he lived.

### Sister Species

Two recent hominin fossil finds from Ileret, Kenya (east of Lake Turkana), are very significant for two main reasons; they show that (1) *H. habilis* and *H. erectus* overlapped in time rather than being ancestor and descendant, as had been thought, and (2) sexual dimorphism in *H. erectus* was much greater than expected (see Spoor et al. 2007; Wilford 2007*a*).

One of these finds (KNM-ER 42703) is the upper jawbone of a 1.44-million-year-old *H. habilis*. The other (KNM-ER 42700) is the almost complete but faceless skull of a 1.55-million-year-old *H. erectus*. Their names come from their catalog numbers in the Kenya National Museum–East Rudolph, and their dates were determined from volcanic ash deposits.

This photo shows the early (1.6 m.y.a.) *Homo erectus* WT15,000, or Nariokotome boy, found in 1984 near Lake Turkana, Kenya. This is the most complete *Homo erectus* ever found. © Kenneth Garrett/ National Geographic Stock

These Ileret finds negated the conventional view (held since the Leakeys described the first *habilis* in 1960) that *habilis* and then *erectus* evolved one after the other. Instead, they apparently split from a common ancestor prior to 2 m.y.a. Then they lived side by side in eastern Africa for perhaps half a million years. According to Maeve Leakey, one of the authors of the report (Spoor et al. 2007), the fact that they remained separate species for so long "suggests that they had their own ecological niche, thus avoiding direct competition" (quoted in Wilford 2007*a*, p. A6). They coexisted in the same general area (an ancient lake basin), much as gorillas and chimpanzees do today.

Given these finds, the fossil record for early *Homo* in East Africa can be revised as follows: *H. rudolfensis* (2.03–1.78 m.y.a.), *H. habilis* (1.9–1.44 m.y.a.) and *H. erectus* (1.9–.5? m.y.a.). The oldest definite *H. habilis* (OH24) dates to 1.9 m.y.a., although some fossil fragments with *habilis* attributes have been dated as early as 2.33 m.y.a. The oldest *erectus* may date back to 1.9 m.y.a. as well.

What about sexual dimorphism in *H. erectus*? As the smallest *erectus* find ever, KNM-ER 42700 appears to be one of the rare female representatives of *erectus* found so far, most probably a young adult or late subadult. The small skull suggests that the range in overall body size among *H. erectus* was much greater than previously had been imagined, with greater sexual dimorphism than among chimps or contemporary humans. Human and chimp males are about 12 to 15 percent larger than females, but dimorphism is much greater in gorillas, and apparently also in *erectus*. Another possibility is that the (as yet undiscovered) *H. erectus* males that inhabited this lake basin along with this female at that time also were smaller than the typical *erectus* male.

## *The Significance of Hunting*

The ecological niche that separated *H. erectus* from both *H. habilis* and *Au. boisei* probably involved greater reliance on hunting, along with improved cultural means of adaptation, including better tools. Significant changes in technology occurred during the 200,000-year period between Bed I (1.8 m.y.a.) and Lower Bed II (1.6 m.y.a.) at Olduvai. Tool making got more sophisticated soon after the advent of *H. erectus*. Out of the crude tools in Bed I evolved better-made and more varied tools. Edges were straighter, for example, and differences in form suggest functional differentiation—that is, the tools were being made and used for different jobs, such as smashing bones or digging for tubers. The more sophisticated tools aided in hunting and gathering. With such tools, *Homo* could obtain meat on a more regular basis and dig and process tubers, roots, nuts, and seeds more efficiently. New tools that could batter, crush, and pulp coarse vegetation also reduced chewing demands.

With changes in the types of foods consumed, the burden on the chewing apparatus eased. Chewing muscles developed less, and supporting structures, such as jaws and cranial crests, also were reduced. With less chewing, jaws developed less, and so there was no place to put large teeth. The size of teeth, which form before they erupt, is under stricter genetic control than jaw size and bone size are. Natural selection began to operate against the genes that caused large teeth. In smaller jaws, large teeth now caused dental crowding, impaction, pain, sickness, fever, and sometimes death (there were no dentists). *H. erectus* back teeth are smaller, and the front teeth are relatively larger than australopithecine teeth. *H. erectus* used its front teeth to pull, twist, and grip objects. A massive ridge over the eyebrows (a superorbital torus) provided buttressing against the forces exerted in these activities.

As hunting became more important, encounters with large animals increased. Individuals with stronger skulls had better-protected brains and better survival rates. Given the dangers associated with larger prey, and without sophisticated spear or arrow technology, which developed later, natural selection favored the thickening of certain areas for better protection against blows and falls. The base of the skull expanded dramatically, with a ridge of spongy bone (an occipital bun) across the back, for the attachment of massive neck muscles. The frontal and parietal (side) areas of the skull also increased, indicating expansion in those areas of the brain. Finally, average cranial capacity expanded from about 500 cm$^3$ in the australopithecines to 1,000 cm$^3$ in *H. erectus,* which is within the modern range of variation.

# Out of Africa I: *H. erectus*

Hominins migrated out of Africa to the rest of the world in multiple waves. First to expand was *H. erectus*, whose spread occurred between 2 and 1 m.y.a. Did the ancestors of the Neandertals and Denisovans (see later in this chapter) branch off in, and then leave, Africa, perhaps as early as 800,000 years ago? Or did they evolve from *H. erectus* ancestors in Asia or Europe? Populations of **anatomically modern humans (AMHs)** certainly left Africa, maybe more than once, as early perhaps as 110,000 B.P., but mainly around and after 70,000 B.P. The last wave included the ancestors of all humans on Earth today.

It was *H. erectus* who first pushed the hominin range beyond Africa—to Asia and Europe. Small groups broke off from larger ones and moved a few miles away. They foraged new tracts of edible vegetation and carved out new hunting territories. Through population growth and dispersal, *H. erectus* gradually spread and changed. Hominins were following an essentially human lifestyle based on hunting and gathering. This basic pattern survived until recently in marginal areas of the world, although it is now fading rapidly. We focus in this chapter on the biological and cultural changes that led from early *Homo,* through intermediate forms, to anatomically modern humans (AMHs).

## Paleolithic Tools

The stone-tool-making techniques that evolved out of the Oldowan tradition and that lasted until about 15,000 years ago are described by the term **Paleolithic** (from Greek roots meaning "old" and "stone"). The Paleolithic, or "Old Stone Age," has three divisions: Lower (early), Middle, and Upper (late). Each part is roughly associated with a particular stage in human evolution. The Lower Paleolithic is roughly associated with *H. erectus;* the Middle Paleolithic with archaic *H. sapiens,* including the Neandertals of western Europe and the Middle East; and the Upper Paleolithic with AMHs.

The best stone tools are made from rocks such as flint that fracture sharply and in predictable ways when hammered. Quartz, quartzite, chert, and obsidian also are suitable. Each of the three main divisions of the Paleolithic had its typical *tool-making traditions*—coherent patterns of tool manufacture. The main Lower Paleolithic tool-making tradition used by *H. erectus* was the **Acheulean,** named after the French village of St. Acheul, where it was first identified. The oldest Acheulean hand axes are now dated at 1.78 m.y.a., based on recent finds at Lake Turkana, Kenya.

As we saw in Chapter 6, Oldowan flaking wasn't done to make choppers (according to a predetermined form). It was done simply to produce sharp flakes. A fundamental difference shows up in the Acheulean tool-making tradition. The Acheulean technique involved chipping the core bilaterally and symmetrically. The core was converted from a round piece of rock into a flattish, oval hand ax about 6 inches (15 centimeters) long. Its cutting edge was far superior to that of the Oldowan chopper (see Figure 7.1). The Acheulean hand ax, shaped like a teardrop, represents a predetermined shape based on a template in the mind of the toolmaker. Evidence for such a mental template in the archaeological record suggests a cognitive leap between earlier hominins and *H. erectus.*

Acheulean hand axes, routinely carried over long distances, were used in varied cutting and butchering tasks, including gutting, skinning, and dismembering animals. Analysis of their wear patterns suggests that hand axes were versatile tools used for many tasks, including wood working and vegetable preparation. Cleavers—core tools with a straight edge at one end—were used for heavy chopping and hacking at the sinews of larger animals. Stone picks, which were heavier than the hand ax, probably were used for digging. Acheulean toolmakers also used flakes, with finer edges, for light-duty tools—to make incisions and for finer work. Flakes became progressively more important in human evolution, particularly in Middle and Upper Paleolithic tool making.

FIGURE 7.1 **Evolution in Tool Making**

Finds at Olduvai Gorge and elsewhere show how pebble tools (the first tool at the left) evolved into the Acheulean hand ax of *H. erectus*. This drawing begins with an Oldowan pebble tool and moves through crude hand axes to fully developed Acheulean tools associated with *H. erectus*.

The Acheulean tradition illustrates trends in the evolution of technology: greater efficiency, manufacture of tools with predetermined forms and for specific tasks, and an increasingly complex technology. These trends became even more obvious with the advent of *H. sapiens*.

## Adaptive Strategies of *H. erectus*

Interrelated changes in biology and culture have increased human adaptability—the capacity to live in and modify an ever-wider range of environments. Improved tools helped *H. erectus* increase its range. Biological changes also increased hunting efficiency. *H. erectus* had a rugged but essentially modern skeleton that permitted long-distance stalking and endurance during the hunt. The *H. erectus* body was much larger and longer-legged than those of previous hominins, permitting longer-distance hunting of large prey. There is archaeological evidence of *H. erectus*'s success in hunting elephants, horses, rhinos, and giant baboons.

An increase in cranial capacity has been a trend in human evolution. The average *H. erectus* brain (about 1,000 cm$^3$) doubled the australopithecine average. The capacities of *H. erectus* skulls range from 800 to 1,250 cm$^3$, well above the modern minimum.

*H. erectus* had an essentially modern, though very robust, skeleton with a brain and body closer in size to *H. sapiens* than to *Australopithecus*. Still, several anatomical contrasts, particularly in the cranium, distinguish *H. erectus* from modern humans. Compared with moderns, *H. erectus* had a lower and more sloping forehead accentuated by a large brow ridge above the eyes. Skull bones were thicker, and, as

## FIGURE 7.2

**Rear Views of Three Skulls of  H. erectus and One of "Archaic" Homo sapiens (a Neandertal)**
Note the more angular shape of the *H. erectus* skulls, with the maximum breadth low down, near the base.

Source: C. J. Jolly and R. White, *Physical Anthropology and Archaeology,* 5th ed., p. 271. Copyright © 1995. Reprinted by permission of The McGraw-Hill Companies.

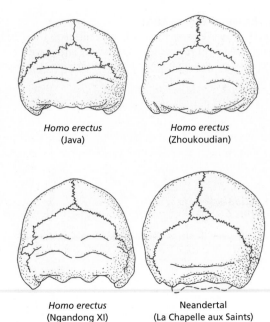

Homo erectus
(Java)

Homo erectus
(Zhoukoudian)

Homo erectus
(Ngandong XI)

Neandertal
(La Chapelle aux Saints)

noted, average cranial capacity was smaller. The brain case was lower and flatter than in *H. sapiens,* with spongy bone development at the lower rear of the skull. Seen from behind, the *H. erectus* skull has a broad-based, angular shape that has been compared to a half-inflated football and a hamburger bun (see Figure 7.2). The *H. erectus* face, teeth, and jaws were larger than those in contemporary humans but smaller than those in *Australopithecus.* The front teeth were especially large, but molar size was well below the australopithecine average. Presumably, this reduction reflected changes in diet or food processing.

Hearths at various sites confirm that fire was part of the adaptive kit controlled by *H. erectus.* Earlier evidence for human control over fire has been found in Israel, dating back to almost 800,000 years ago. The newest evidence of fire, dated at 1 m.y.a., comes from Wonderwerk Cave, South Africa, where microscopic plant ashes and burned bits of bone have been found in soil that previously yielded dozens of stone tools (Berna 2012). However, no remains of a hearth or campfire area, where fires would repeatedly have been lit, have been found in Wonderwerk Cave. The first hearths date back about 400,000 years (Rice 2012). Fire provided protection against cave bears and saber-toothed tigers. It permitted *H. erectus* to occupy cave sites, including Zhoukoudian, near Beijing, in China, which has yielded the remains of more than 40 specimens of *H. erectus.* Fire widened the range of climates open to human colonization. Its warmth enabled people to survive winter cold in temperate regions. Human control over fire offered other advantages, such as cooking, which breaks down vegetable fibers and tenderizes meat. Cooking kills parasites and makes meat more digestible, thus reducing strain on the chewing apparatus.

## The Evolution and Expansion of *H. erectus*

The archaeological record of *H. erectus* activities can be combined with the fossil evidence to provide a more complete picture of our Lower Paleolithic ancestors. We now consider some of the fossil data, whose geographic distribution is shown in Figure 7.3. Early *H. erectus* remains, found by Richard Leakey's team at East and West Turkana, Kenya, and dated to around 1.6 m.y.a., including the Nariokotome boy, were discussed previously.

One fairly complete skull, one large mandible, and two partial skulls—one of a young adult male (780 cm³) and one of an apparently adolescent female (650 cm³)— were found in the 1990s at the Dmanisi site in the former Soviet Republic of Georgia. They have been assigned a date of 1.77–1.7 m.y.a. There are notable similarities between the two partial skulls and that of the Nariokotome boy from Kenya (1.6 m.y.a.). Chopping tools of comparable age associated with the Kenyan and Georgian fossils also are similar. The most complete skull find at Dmanisi is rather primitive, with a stronger resemblance to *H. habilis* than is the case with the other Dmanisi fossils. Primitive

FIGURE 7.3   **Location of Some Major  *Homo erectus* Sites**

Source: From John Relethford, *The Human Species: An Introduction to Biological Anthropology,* 9th ed., p. 273. Copyright © 2013 by McGraw-Hill Education, LLC. Reprinted with permission.

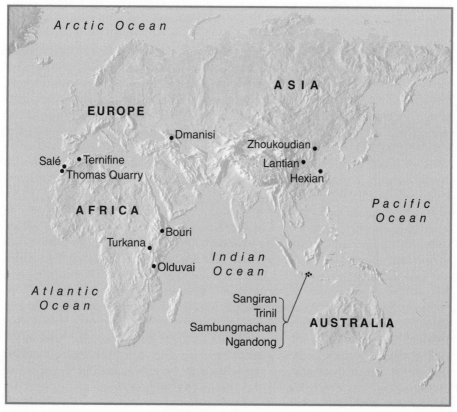

characteristics of this skull include its large canine teeth and small cranial capacity (Vekua, Lordkipanidze, and Rightmire 2002). This specimen may be that of a teenage girl whose skull had not yet reached full size but whose canines had. The simplest explanation for the anatomical diversity observed at Dmanisi is that *H. erectus* was at least as variable a species as is *H. sapiens*. The Dmanisi finds suggest a rapid spread, by 1.77 m.y.a., of early *Homo* out of Africa and into Eurasia (see Figure 7.3).

The Dmanisi fossils are the most ancient undisputed human fossils outside Africa. How did those hominins get to Georgia? The most probable answer is in pursuit of meat. As hominins became more carnivorous, they expanded their home ranges in accordance with those of the animals they hunted. Meat-rich diets provided higher-quality protein as fuel. The australopithecines, with smaller bodies and brains, could survive mainly on plants. They probably used a limited range at the edge of forests, not too deep in or too exposed far out on the savanna. Once hominins developed stronger bodies and high-protein meat diets, they could—indeed, had to—spread out. They ranged farther to find meat, and this expansion eventually led them out of Africa, into Eurasia (Georgia) and eventually Asia.

More recent skeletal finds from Dmanisi suggest how this expansion might have taken place (Wilford 2007*b*). (Previously only skulls had been found there.) Four new fossil skeletons show that the ancient Dmanisi population combined primitive skulls and upper bodies with more advanced spines and lower limbs for greater mobility. These evolved limb proportions enabled early *Homo* to expand beyond Africa.

In 1891, the Indonesian island of Java yielded the first *H. erectus* fossil find, popularly known as "Java man." Eugene Dubois, a Dutch army surgeon, had gone to Java to discover a transitional form between apes and humans. Of course, we now know that the transition to hominin had taken place much earlier than the *H. erectus* period and occurred in Africa. However, Dubois's good luck did lead him to the most ancient human fossils discovered at that time. Excavating near the village of Trinil, Dubois found parts of an *H. erectus* skull and a thigh bone. During the 1930s and 1940s, excavations in Java uncovered additional remains. The various Indonesian *H. erectus* fossils date back at least 700,000, and perhaps as much as 1.6 million, years. Fragments of a skull and a lower jaw found in northern China at Lantian may be as old as the oldest Indonesian fossils. Other *H. erectus* remains, of uncertain date, have been found in Algeria and Morocco in North Africa.

*H. erectus* remains also have been found in Upper Bed II at Olduvai, Tanzania, in association with Acheulean tools. One such find, OH9, dates back perhaps 1.4 million years. African *H. erectus* fossils also have been found in Ethiopia, Eritrea, and South Africa (in addition to Kenya and Tanzania). The time span of *H. erectus* in East Africa was long. Later *H. erectus* fossils have been found in Bed IV at Olduvai, dating to 500,000 B.P., about the same age as the Beijing fossils.

The largest group of *H. erectus* fossils was found in the Zhoukoudian Cave in China. The Zhoukoudian ("Peking"—now Beijing—"man") site, excavated from the late 1920s to the late 1930s, was a major find for the human fossil record. Zhoukoudian yielded remains of tools, hearths, animal bones, and more than 40 hominins, including five skulls. The analysis of these remains led to the conclusion that the Java and Zhoukoudian fossils were examples of the same broad stage of human evolution. Today they are commonly classified together as *H. erectus*.

Meet *Homo erectus.* On the left is a reconstruction of one of the *H. erectus* skulls from Zhoukoudian, China; on the right, an attempt to render *H. erectus* in the flesh. (first) © CM Dixon/ age fotostock; (second) © Tom McHugh/Science Source

The Zhoukoudian individuals lived more recently than did the Javanese *H. erectus,* between 670,000 and 410,000 years ago, when the climate in China was colder and moister than it is today. The inference about the climate has been made on the basis of the animal remains found with the human fossils. The people at Zhoukoudian ate venison, and seed and plant remains suggest they were both gatherers and hunters.

What about Europe? A cranial fragment found at Ceprano, Italy, in 1994 has been assigned a date of 800,000 B.P. (see Mounier, Condemi, and Manzi 2011). Other probable *H. erectus* remains have been found in Europe, but their dates are uncertain. All are later than the Ceprano skull, and they usually are classified as late *H. erectus,* or transitional between *H. erectus* and early *H. sapiens.*

## Archaic *H. sapiens*

Africa, which was center stage during the australopithecine period, is joined by Asia and Europe during the *H. erectus* and *H. sapiens* periods of hominin evolution. European fossils and tools have contributed disproportionately to our knowledge and interpretation of early (archaic) *H. sapiens.* This doesn't mean that *H. sapiens* evolved in Europe or that most early *H. sapiens* lived in Europe. Indeed, the fossil evidence confirms that *H. sapiens,* like *H. erectus* before it, originated in Africa. Anatomically modern *H. sapiens* lived in Africa for more than 100,000 years before reaching Europe around 45,000 years ago (Benazzi et al. 2011; Higham et al. 2011). There probably were many more AMHs in the tropics than in Europe during the ice ages. We merely know more about recent human evolution in Europe because archaeology and fossil hunting—not human evolution—have been going on longer there than in Africa and Asia.

Recent discoveries, along with reinterpretation of the dating and the anatomical relevance of some earlier finds, are filling in the gap between *H. erectus* and archaic *H. sapiens.* **Archaic *H. sapiens*** (300,000? to 28,000 B.P.) encompasses the earliest members of our species, along with the **Neandertals** (*H. sapiens neanderthalensis*—130,000

TABLE 7.1   **Summary of Data on *Homo* Fossil Groups**

Fossil representatives of the genus *Homo,* compared with anatomically modern humans (AMHs) and chimps *(Pan troglodytes)*

| Species | Dates | Known Distribution | Important Sites | Brain Size (in cm³) |
|---|---|---|---|---|
| Anatomically modern humans (AMHs) | 195,000 B.P. to present | Worldwide | Omo Kibish, Herto, Border Cave, Klasies River, Skhül, Qafzeh, Cro-Magnon | 1,350 |
| Neandertals | 130,000? to 28,000? B.P. | Europe, southwestern Asia | La Chapelle-aux-Saints | 1,430 |
| Archaic *H. sapiens* | 300,000 to 28,000? B.P. | Africa, Europe, Asia | Kabwe, Arago, Dali, Mount Carmel Caves | 1,135 |
| *H. erectus* | 1.9 m.y.a. to 300,000? B.P. | Africa, Asia, Europe | East/West Turkana, Olduvai, Dmanisi, Zhoukoudian, Java, Ceprano | 900 |
| *H. habilis* | 1.9 to 1.44 m.y.a. | | Olduvai, East Turkana | 650 |
| *H. rudolfensis* | 2.03 to 1.78 m.y.a. | | East Africa, East Turkana | 775 |
| Pan troglodytes | Modern | Central Africa | Gombe, Mahale | 390 |

to perhaps as late as 28,000 B.P.) of Europe and the Middle East and their Neandertal-like contemporaries in Africa and Asia. Brain size in archaic *H. sapiens* was within the modern human range. (The modern average, remember, is about 1,350 cm³.) (See Table 7.1 and Figure 7.4 for a summary of the major groups.) A rounding out of the brain case was associated with the increased brain size. As Jolly and White (1995) put it, evolution was pumping more brain into the *H. sapiens* cranium—like filling a football with air.

## Ice Ages of the Pleistocene

Traditionally and correctly, the geological epoch known as the **Pleistocene** has been considered the epoch of early human life. Its subdivisions are the Lower Pleistocene (2 to 1 m.y.a.), the Middle Pleistocene (1 m.y.a. to 130,000 B.P.), and the Upper Pleistocene (130,000 to 11,000 B.P.). These subdivisions refer to the placement of geological strata containing, respectively, older, intermediate, and younger fossils. The Lower Pleistocene extends from the start of the Pleistocene to the advent of the ice ages in the Northern Hemisphere around 1 million years ago.

Each subdivision of the Pleistocene is associated with a particular group of hominins. Late *Australopithecus* and early *Homo* lived during the Lower Pleistocene. *Homo erectus* spanned most of the Middle Pleistocene. *Homo sapiens* appeared late in the Middle Pleistocene and was the sole hominin of the Upper Pleistocene.

FIGURE 7.4 **Timeline of Species within the Genus *Homo* in Increments of 100,000 Years, from 2.5 m.y.a. through the Present**
Some scientists include *H. heidelbergensis* and the Neandertals within archaic *H. sapiens*.

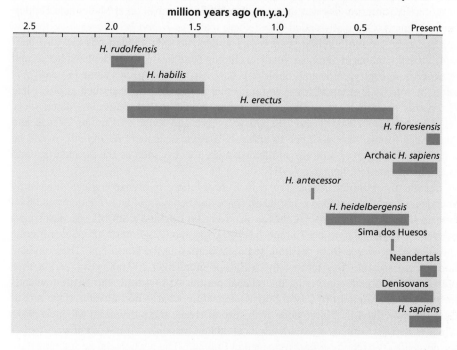

During the second million years of the Pleistocene, there were several ice ages, or **glacials,** major advances of continental ice sheets in Europe and North America. These periods were separated by **interglacials,** long warm periods between the major glacials. (Scientists used to think there were four main glacial advances, but the picture has grown more complex.) With each advance, the world climate cooled and continental ice sheets—massive glaciers—covered the northern parts of Europe and North America. Climates that are temperate today were arctic during the glacials.

During the interglacials, the climate warmed up and the *tundra*—the cold, treeless plain—retreated north with the ice sheets. Forests returned to areas, such as southwestern France, that once had tundra vegetation. The ice sheets advanced and receded several times during the last glacial, the *Würm* (75,000 to 12,000 B.P.). Brief periods of relative warmth during the Würm (and other glacials) are called *interstadials,* in contrast to the longer interglacials. Hominin fossils found in association with animals known to occur in cold or warm climates, respectively, permit us to date them to glacial or interglacial (or interstadial) periods.

## *H. antecessor* and *H. heidelbergensis*

In northern Spain's Atapuerca Mountains, the site of Gran Dolina has yielded the remains of 780,000-year-old hominins, which Spanish researchers call *H. antecessor* and see as a possible common ancestor of the Neandertals and anatomically modern humans.

At the nearby cave of Sima dos Huesos, a team led by Juan Luis Arsuaga has found thousands of fossils representing at least 33 hominins. Almost 300,000 years old, they may represent an early stage of Neandertal evolution (Lemonick and Dorfman 1999).

A massive hominin jaw was discovered in 1907 in a gravel pit at Mauer near Heidelberg, Germany. Originally called "Heidelberg man," or *Homo heidelbergensis,* the jaw appears to be around 500,000 years old. The deposits that yielded this jaw also contained fossil remains of several animals, including bear, bison, deer, elephant, horse, and rhinoceros. Recently, some anthropologists have revived the species name *H. heidelbergensis* to refer to a group of fossil hominins that in this text are described as either late *H. erectus* or archaic *H. sapiens.* This group would include hominins dated (very roughly) between 700,000 and 200,000 years ago and found in Europe, Africa, and Asia. Such fossils, here assigned to either *H. erectus* or archaic *H. sapiens,* would be transitional between *H. erectus* and later hominin forms such as the Neandertals and anatomically modern humans (AMHs).

Besides the hominin *fossils* found in Europe, there is archaeological—including abundant stone tool—evidence for the presence and behavior of late *H. erectus* and then archaic *H. sapiens* in Europe. A chance discovery on England's Suffolk seacoast shows that humans reached northern Europe 700,000 years ago (Gugliotta 2005). Several stone flakes were recovered from seashore sediment bordering the North Sea. These archaic humans crossed the Alps into northern Europe more than 200,000 years earlier than previously imagined—during an interglacial period. At that time, the fertile lowlands they inhabited were part of a land bridge connecting what is now Britain to the rest of Europe. They lived in a large delta with several rivers and a dry, mild Mediterranean climate. Various animals were among its abundant resources. It is not known whether the descendants of these settlers remained in England. The next glacial period may have been too extreme for human habitation so far back.

Archaic *H. sapiens* lived during the last part of the *Middle Pleistocene*—during the *Mindel* (second) glacial, the interglacial that followed it, and the following *Riss* (third) glacial. The distribution of the fossils and tools of archaic *H. sapiens,* which have been found in Europe, Africa, and Asia, shows that *Homo*'s tolerance of environmental diversity had increased. For example, the Neandertals and their immediate ancestors managed to survive extreme cold in Europe. Archaic *H. sapiens* occupied the Arago Cave in southeastern France at a time when Europe was bitterly cold. The only Riss glacial site with facial material, Arago, was excavated in 1971. It produced a partially intact skull, two jawbones, and teeth from a dozen individuals. With an apparent date of about 200,000 B.P., the Arago fossils have mixed features that seem transitional between *H. erectus* and the Neandertals.

## The Neandertals

Neandertals were first discovered in western Europe. The first one was found in 1856 in a German valley called Neander Valley—*tal* is the German word for a valley. Scientists had trouble interpreting the discovery. It was clearly human and similar to modern Europeans in many ways yet different enough to be considered strange and abnormal.

This was, after all, 35 years before Dubois discovered the first *H. erectus* fossils in Java and almost 70 years before the first australopithecine was found in South Africa. Darwin's *On the Origin of Species,* published in 1859, had not yet offered a theory of evolution through natural selection. There was no framework for understanding human evolution. Over time, the fossil record has filled in, with numerous subsequent discoveries of Neandertals in Europe and the Middle East.

Fossils that are not Neandertals but have similar features (such as large faces and brow ridges) have been found in Africa and Asia. The Kabwe skull from Zambia (130,000 B.P.) is an archaic *H. sapiens* with a Neandertal-like brow ridge. Archaic Chinese fossils with Neandertal-like features have been found at Maba and Dali. Neandertals have been found in central Europe and the Middle East. For example, Neandertal fossils found at the Shanidar Cave in northern Iraq and at the Israeli site of Tabun on Mount Carmel date to around 60,000 B.P., as does a Neandertal skeleton found at Israel's Kebara Cave.

## Cold-Adapted Neandertals

By 75,000 B.P., after an interglacial interlude, western Europe's hominins (Neandertals, by then) again faced extreme cold as the Würm glacial began. To deal with this environment, they wore clothes, made more elaborate tools, and hunted reindeer, mammoths, and woolly rhinos (see Conard 2011). Neandertal technology, a Middle Paleolithic tradition called **Mousterian,** improved considerably during the Würm glacial.

The Neandertals were stocky, with large trunks relative to limb length—a phenotype that minimizes surface area and thus conserves heat. Another adaptation to extreme cold was the Neandertal face, which has been likened to a *H. erectus* face that has been pulled forward by the nose. This extension increased the distance between outside air and the arteries that carry blood to the brain and was adaptive in a cold climate. The brain is sensitive to temperature changes and must be kept warm. The massive nasal cavities of Neandertal fossils suggest long, broad noses. This would expand the area for warming and moistening air.

Neandertal characteristics also include huge front teeth, broad faces, and large brow ridges, as well as ruggedness of the skeleton and musculature. What activities were associated with these anatomical traits? Neandertal teeth probably did many jobs later done by tools. The front teeth show heavy wear, suggesting that they were used for varied purposes, including chewing animal hides to make soft winter clothing out of them. The massive Neandertal face showed the stresses of constantly using the front teeth for holding and pulling. Comparison of early and later Neandertals shows a trend toward reduction of their robust features (See this chapter's "Anthropology Today" for a discussion of the Neandertal lifestyle.)

## The Neandertals and Modern People

Generations of scientists have debated whether and to what extent the Neandertals were ancestral to modern people, especially those of the Middle East and Europe, where fossils of both groups have been found. The current prevailing view proposes that *H. erectus* split into separate groups—one ancestral to the Neandertals, the other ancestral to anatomically modern humans (AMHs), who first reached Europe around 50,000 B.P.

(Early AMHs in western Europe often are referred to as **Cro-Magnon,** after the earliest fossil find of an AMH, in France's Les Eyzies region, Dordogne Valley, in 1868.) Current evidence leaves little doubt that modern humans evolved in Africa and eventually colonized Europe, displacing, or at least replacing, the Neandertals there.

Consider the contrasts between the Neandertals and AMHs. Like *H. erectus* before them, the Neandertals had heavy brow ridges and slanting foreheads. However, average Neandertal cranial capacity (more than 1,400 cm³) exceeded the modern average. Neandertal jaws were large, providing support for huge front teeth, and their faces were massive. The bones and skull were generally more rugged and had greater sexual dimorphism—particularly in the face and skull—than do those of AMHs. In some western European fossils, these contrasts between Neandertals and AMHs are accentuated—giving a stereotyped, or *classic Neandertal,* appearance (see Figure 7.5).

Those scientists who still believe that Neandertals could have contributed to the ancestry of modern Europeans cite certain fossils to support their view. For example, the

**FIGURE 7.5**    **Drawings of *H. erectus,* Archaic *H. sapiens,* Neandertal, and an Anatomically Modern Human (AMH)**
What are the main differences you notice? Is the Neandertal more like *H. erectus* or the AMH?

H. erectus

Archaic H. sapiens

Neandertal

AMH

A Neandertal skeleton (right) and a modern human skeleton (left and behind) displayed at New York's American Museum of Natural History. The Neandertal skeleton, reconstructed from casts of more than 200 fossil bones, is part of the museum's 2003 exhibit titled "The First Europeans: Treasures from the Hills of Atapuerca." © Frank Franklin II/AP Images

central European site of Mladeč (31,000 to 33,000 B.P.) has yielded remains of several hominins that combine Neandertal robustness with modern features. The fossil remains of a 4-year-old boy discovered at Largo Velho in Portugal in 1999 and dated to 24,000 B.P. also shows mixed Neandertal and modern features.

# Modern Humans

Anatomically modern humans (AMHs) evolved from an archaic *H. sapiens* African ancestor. Eventually, AMHs spread to other areas, including western Europe, where they replaced, or interbred with, the Neandertals, whose robust traits eventually disappeared.

## Out of Africa: AMH Edition
### Recent Fossil and Archaeological Evidence
Fossil and archaeological evidence has been accumulating to support the African origin of AMHs. A major find was announced in 2003: the 1997 discovery in an Ethiopian valley of three AMH skulls—two adults and a child. When found, the fossils had been fragmented so badly that their reconstruction took several years. Tim White and Berhane Asfaw were coleaders of the international team that made the find near the village of

Herto, 140 miles northeast of Addis Ababa. All three skulls were missing the lower jaw. The skulls showed evidence of cutting and handling, suggesting they had been detached from their bodies and used—perhaps ritually—after death. A few teeth, but no other bones, were found with the skulls, again suggesting their deliberate removal from the body. Layers of volcanic ash allowed geologists to date them to 160,000 to 154,000 B.P. The people represented by the skulls had lived on the shore of an ancient lake, where they hunted and fished. The skulls were found along with hippopotamus and antelope bones and some 600 tools, including blades and hand axes.

Except for a few archaic characteristics, the **Herto** skulls are anatomically modern—long with broad midfaces, featuring tall, narrow nasal bones. The cranial vaults are high, falling within modern dimensions. These finds provide additional support for the view that AMHs originated in Africa.

Omo Kibish is one of several sites along the Omo River in southwestern Ethiopia. Between 1967 and 1974 Richard Leakey and his colleagues from the Kenya National Museum recovered AMH remains originally considered to be about 125,000 years old. The specimens now appear to be much older. Indeed, with an estimated date of 195,000 B.P., they appear to be the earliest AMH fossils yet found (McDougall, Brown, and Fleagle 2005). The Omo remains include two partial skulls (Omo 1 and Omo 2), four jaws, a leg bone, and about 200 teeth. The Omo 1 site (Omo Kibish) also yielded a nearly complete skeleton of an adult male. Studies of the Omo 1 skull and skeleton indicate an overall modern human morphology with some primitive features. The Omo 2 skull is more archaic.

From sites in South Africa comes further evidence of early African AMHs. At Border Cave, a remote rock shelter in South Africa, fossil remains dating back perhaps 150,000 years are believed to be those of early AMHs. The remains of at least five AMHs have been discovered, including the nearly complete skeleton of a 4- to 6-month-old infant buried in a shallow grave. Excavations at Border Cave also have produced some 70,000 stone tools, along with the remains of several mammal species, including elephants, believed to have been hunted by the ancient people who lived there.

A complex of South African caves near the Klasies River mouth was occupied by a group of hunter-gatherers some 120,000 years ago. Fragmentary bones suggest how those people looked. A forehead fragment has a modern brow ridge. There is a thin-boned cranial fragment and a piece of jaw with a modern chin. The archaeological evidence suggests that these cave dwellers did coastal gathering.

Anatomically modern specimens, including the skull shown in Figure 7.6, have been found at Skhūl, a site on Mount Carmel in Israel. The Skhūl fossils date to 100,000 B.P. Another group of modern-looking and similarly dated (92,000 B.P.) skulls comes from the Israeli site of Qafzeh. All these skulls have a modern shape; their brain cases are higher, shorter, and rounder than Neandertal skulls. There is a more-filled-out forehead region, which rises more vertically above the brows. A marked chin is another modern feature.

## Genetic Evidence

In 1987 a group of molecular geneticists at the University of California at Berkeley offered support for the idea that AMHs arose fairly recently in Africa, then spread out and colonized the world. Rebecca Cann, Mark Stoneking, and Allan C. Wilson (1987) analyzed genetic markers in placentas donated by 147 women whose ancestors came from Africa, Europe, the Middle East, Asia, New Guinea, and Australia.

The researchers focused on mitochondrial DNA (mtDNA). This genetic material is located in the cytoplasm (the outer part of a cell—not the nucleus). Ordinary DNA, which makes up the genes that determine most physical traits, is found in the nucleus and comes from both parents. But only the mother contributes mitochondrial DNA to the fertilized egg. The father plays no part in mtDNA transmission, just as the mother has nothing to do with the transmission of the Y chromosome, which comes from the father and determines the sex of the child.

To establish a "genetic clock," the Berkeley researchers measured the variation in mtDNA in their 147 tissue samples. By estimating the number of mutations that had taken place in each sample since its common origin with the 146 others, the researchers created an evolutionary tree.

**FIGURE 7.6   Skhül V**
This AMH with some archaic features was recently redated to 100,000 B.P. This is one of several fossils found at Skhül, Israel.

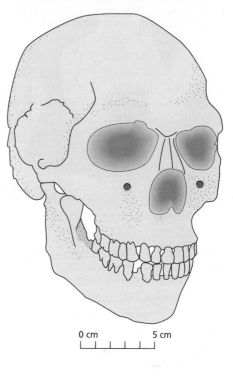

0 cm          5 cm

That tree started in Africa and then branched in two. One group remained in Africa, while the other one split off, carrying its mtDNA to the rest of the world. The variation in mtDNA was greatest among Africans. This suggests they have been evolving the longest. The Berkeley researchers concluded that everyone alive today has mtDNA that descends from a woman (dubbed Eve) who lived in sub-Saharan Africa around 200,000 years ago. Eve was not the only woman alive then; she was just the only one whose descendants have included a daughter in each generation up to the present. Because mtDNA passes exclusively through females, mtDNA lines disappear whenever a woman has no children or has only sons. The details of the Eve theory suggest that her descendants left Africa no more than 135,000, and perhaps as recently as 70,000 to 55,000, years ago. They eventually displaced the Neandertals in Europe and went on to colonize the rest of the world.

On January 28, 2015, scientists announced the discovery in Israel of a 55,000-year-old AMH skull that may be closely related to the first modern humans to colonize Europe (Hershkovitz et al. 2015). The partial skull is that of a small adult of undetermined sex. The area where the skull was found would have been a likely corridor for AMHs expanding out of Africa into Eurasia. Designated Manot 1 after Israel's Manot Cave, where it

In early 2015, scientists announced the discovery in Israel's Manot cave of a 55,000-year-old AMH (partial) skull that may be closely related to the first modern humans to colonize Europe. The skull, that of a small adult, is pictured here between a Neandertal on the left and a modern human on the right. © Jim Hollander/epa/Corbis

was found, this fossil dates to a time when AMHs are likely to have been expanding beyond Africa. Manot 1 is more similar to early European AMHs than to such earlier Middle Eastern AMHs as Skhūl and Qafzeh. Some features of Manot 1 suggest that its ancestors, although mainly African AMHs, may also have included a few Neandertals, who are known to have occupied several nearby caves between 65,000 and 50,000 B.P. During the last (Würm) glacial period, which began around 75,000 years ago, Neandertals appear to have spread from western Europe into the Middle East, as part of a general southward expansion of cold-adapted fauna (Bar-Yosef 1987). Manot 1 provides the first evidence that Neandertals and moderns were living in this area around 55,000 B.P. This suggests that whatever interbreeding did take place between Neandertals and moderns may have occurred in the Middle East, prior to the AMH colonization of Europe.

We do not know how long Neandertals and AMHs coexisted in the Middle East, or the nature of their interactions. Their overlap in Europe apparently spanned the period between 45,000 B.P. and Neandertal extinction around 28,000 B.P. The recent redatings of a piece of modern jawbone with three teeth from England, and of two baby teeth from Italy, provide the oldest known skeletal evidence for AMHs in Europe (Wilford 2011*a*). The baby teeth from Italy date to between 45,000 and 43,000 B.P. (Benazzi et al. 2011). The jawbone, from Kents Cavern in Devon, is between 44,200 and 41,500 years old (Higham et al. 2011). Prior to these dates, the earliest reliably dated European AMH had come from Romania (42,000–37,800 B.P.). The English jawbone might represent an early dispersal of AMHs through central Europe that crossed into Britain on a land bridge where the North Sea now stands. The southern Italian remains might represent an even earlier migration along the southern European coasts (Wilford 2011*a*).

## The Denisovans

In late 2010, based on ancient DNA evidence, scientists identified a hominin group known as the **Denisovans** as distant cousins to Neandertals (Callaway 2010; Zimmer 2010). The research was led by Svante Pääbo, who earlier that year had published a complete Neandertal genome. Analyzing the Neandertal genome, Pääbo and his colleagues concluded that modern humans and Neandertals descend from common ancestors that lived in Africa 600,000 years ago. They also found 2.5 percent of the Neandertal genome to be more similar to the DNA of living Europeans and Asians than to African DNA. This finding suggests that Neandertals interbred with AMHs soon after the latter emerged from Africa around 50,000 years ago.

The Denisovans get their name from Denisova, a cave in southern Siberia where their traces (so far only a finger fragment and a wisdom tooth) were found. The Denisovans apparently lived in Asia from roughly 400,000 to 50,000 years ago. Remarkably, scientists have managed to extract the entire Denisovan genome from the finger and the tooth. The common ancestors of Neandertals and Denisovans may have left Africa around half a million years ago. The DNA suggests that the split between ancestral Neandertals and Denisovans happened around 400,000 years ago. The Neandertals spread to the west, eventually reaching the Middle East and Europe. The Denisovans headed east.

Comparison of the Denisovan genome with a spectrum of modern human populations revealed a striking relationship. Melanesians, who inhabit Papua New Guinea and islands northeast of Australia, have inherited about one-twentieth of their DNA from Denisovan roots. This suggests that after the ancestors of today's Papuans split from other AMHs and migrated east, they interbred with Denisovans (see Callaway 2010). Precisely when, where, and to what extent are unclear. The oldest AMH remains in Southeast Asia, from a cave in northern Laos, date to at least 46,000 years ago (Demeter et al. 2012).

If the Denisovan range extended from Siberia to Southeast Asia, they must have been a very successful kind of hominin. The wisdom tooth resembles the teeth of neither AMHs nor Neandertals. It has bulging sides and large, flaring roots. Only when someone finds the same kind of tooth in a fossil skull, or perhaps even a complete skeleton, will we be able to see what the Denisovans really looked like.

## The Red Deer Cave People

Recently described hominin fossils from two Chinese caves are notable because of their recent date (14,300–11,500 B.P.) and their unexpected blend of primitive and modern features. The fossils, representing at least four individuals, consist of partial skulls and other bone fragments (Sample 2012). Specifically, they come from Longlin Cave (Guangxi Province) and Maludong Cave ("Red Deer Cave," in Yunnan Province), both in southwestern China. The fossils have been called the "Red Deer Cave people," based on the name of one of the caves and on evidence that they cooked giant red deer (now extinct) there. The skulls differ from modern humans in their jutting jaws, large molar teeth, prominent brows, thick skulls, broad noses, flat faces, and lack of a chin. The Longlin fossils, unearthed in 1979, lay unnoticed in the basement of a scientific institute for 30 years until their rediscovery. The Red Deer Cave fossils, discovered in 1989, also remained barely studied in a science institute. Darren Curnoe and Ji Xueping began their study and analysis in 2008 (see Curnoe, Ji et al. 2012).

The Red Deer Cave people are the most recent human remains found anywhere in the world that do not closely resemble modern humans. Scientists currently are debating their evolutionary status. Do they belong to a different and hitherto unknown species, or are they merely variable members of *H. sapiens?* Could they be late Denisovans, or maybe a product of interbreeding between Denisovans and AMHs? Confirmation awaits the eventual analysis of DNA extracted from the Red Deer Cave bones—a task that so far has been unsuccessful.

The Red Deer Cave fossils also help fill a geographic gap: Very few post–ice-age human fossils from Asia have been well described and reliably dated (Sample 2012). Our picture of recent human evolutionary history in Asia has grown more complex. We know now that multiple human populations lived in the area, perhaps representing different evolutionary lines (see, for example, the discussion of *H. floresiensis*).

## The Advent of Behavioral Modernity

Scientists agree that (1) around 6 million years ago, our hominin ancestors originated in Africa, and as apelike creatures they became habitual bipeds; (2) by 2.6 million years ago, still in Africa, hominins were making crude stone tools; (3) by 1.7 million years ago, hominins had spread from Africa to Asia and eventually Europe; and (4) sometime around 200,000 years ago, anatomically modern humans evolved from ancestors who had remained in Africa. Like earlier hominins (*Homo erectus*), AMHs spread out from Africa. Eventually they replaced nonmodern human types, such as the Neandertals in Europe and the successors of *Homo erectus* in Asia.

There is disagreement, however, about when, where, and how early AMHs achieved **behavioral modernity**—relying on symbolic thought, elaborating cultural creativity, and as a result becoming fully human in behavior as well as in anatomy. Was it as much as 165,000 or as little as 45,000 years ago? Was it in Africa, the Middle East, or Europe? What triggered the change: a genetic mutation, population increase, competition with nonmodern humans, or some other cause? The traditional view has been that modern behavior originated fairly recently, perhaps 45,000–40,000 years ago, and only after *Homo sapiens* pushed into Europe. This theory of a "creative explosion" is based on finds such as the impressive cave paintings at Lascaux, Chauvet Cave, and other sites in France, Spain, and most recently Romania (Balter 2010). However, recent discoveries outside Europe increase the possibility of a much older, more gradual evolution of modern behavior.

Discoveries made in Africa and the Middle East during the last 40 years provide substantial evidence for earlier (than in Europe) modern behavior, in the form of finely made stone and bone tools, self-ornamentation, and abstract carvings. Surveying African archaeological sites dating to between 300,000 and 30,000 years ago, Sally McBrearty and Alison Brooks (2000) conclude that what might appear to be a sudden event in Europe actually rested on a slow process of cultural accumulation within Africa,

Body ornamentation, a sign of behavioral modernity. The first photo shows a man from Mount Hagen, Western Highlands, Papua New Guinea. The second photo also features body piercing and a necklace, plus distinctive eyeglasses and body tattoos. What are the social functions of such ornamentation? (first): © John W. Banagan/Lonely Planet Images/Getty Images (second): © druvo/Vetta/Getty Images RF

where *Homo sapiens* became fully human long before 40,000 years ago. At South Africa's Blombos Cave, for example, an archaeological team led by Christopher Henshilwood found evidence that AMHs were making bone awls and weapon points more than 70,000 years ago. Three points had been shaped with a stone blade and then finely polished. Henshilwood thinks these artifacts indicate symbolic behavior and artistic creativity—people trying to make beautiful objects. Representing an even earlier occupation of Blombos Cave, Henshilwood's team has excavated a 100,000-year-old workshop, where early AMHs mixed the world's earliest known paint. Those AMHs used stones to grind colorful chunks of dirt, transported to Blombos from several miles away, into a red powder, known as ochre. They mixed the ochre with charcoal, and fat from animal bone marrow, to make it stick to the body or other surfaces. The Blombos people collected their ochre in large abalone shells, where they liquefied and stirred it, then scooped it out as paint, using a bone spatula (Wilford 2011*b*). They may have applied the mixture to their skin, perhaps as decoration for a special event. What, if anything special, did the color red mean to these ancient people? Did they associate it with blood as a sign or life or death, or with menstruation as a sign of fertility? Could they have used red ochre to inspire anger in others? The ochre makers apparently used Blombos Cave only as a work site. Archaeologists found no associated evidence of living quarters, such as hearths (Wilford 2011*b*). What they did the rest of the time remains a mystery. Surely, they hunted, gathered, and fished, most likely eating the abalone and other sea products whose shells also served as tools.

In 2007 anthropologists reported the discovery of even earlier evidence (dating back to 164,000 B.P.) for behavioral modernity in a cave site at Pinnacle Point, South Africa. The cave yielded small stone bladelets, which could be attached to wood to make spears, as well as red ochre. Also significant is the ancient diet revealed by remains from this seaside site. For the first time, we see early representatives of *H. sapiens* subsisting on a variety of shellfish and other marine resources. According to paleoanthropologist Curtis Marean, who led the discovery team, once early humans knew how to make a living from the sea, they could use coastlines as productive home ranges and move long distances (Guyot and Hughes 2007).

Cultural advances would have facilitated the spread of AMHs out of Africa. Such advances had reached the Middle East by 43,000 years ago, where, in Turkey and Lebanon, Steven Kuhn, Mary Stiner, and David Reese (2001) found evidence that coastal people made and wore beads and shell ornaments (see also Mayell 2004). Some of the shells were rare varieties, white or brightly colored. Such body ornaments could have been part of a system of communication, signaling group identity and social status and suggesting modern cognitive abilities.

The origin of behavioral modernity continues to be debated. We see, however, that archaeological work in many world areas suggests strongly that neither anatomical modernity nor behavioral modernity was a European invention. Africa's role in the origin and development of humanity has been prominent for millions of years of hominin evolution (see Stringer 2012 and Wilford 2012*b*; for a contrary view see Klein 2013).

## Advances in Technology

In Europe, Upper Paleolithic tool making is associated with AMHs. In Africa, earlier AMHs made varied tools. The terms *Lower, Middle,* and *Upper Paleolithic* are applied to stone tools from Europe. The terms *Early, Middle,* and *Late Stone Age* are applied to tools from Africa. The people who lived at the Klasies River mouth cave sites in South Africa made Middle Stone Age tools. However, some of the early tool finds at Blombos Cave and elsewhere in Africa are reminiscent of the European Upper Paleolithic. AMHs in Europe made tools in a variety of traditions, collectively known as Upper Paleolithic because of the tools' location in the upper, or more recent, layers of sedimentary deposits. Some European cave deposits have Middle Paleolithic Mousterian tools (made by Neandertals) at lower levels and increasing numbers of Upper Paleolithic tools at higher levels (see Hublin 2012).

The **Upper Paleolithic** traditions all emphasized **blade tools.** Blades were hammered off a prepared core, as in Mousterian technology, but a blade is longer than a flake—its length is more than twice its width. Blades were chipped off cores 4 to 6 inches (10 to 15 centimeters) high by hitting a punch made of bone or antler with a hammerstone (Figure 7.7). Blades were then modified to produce a variety of special-purpose implements. Some were composite tools that were made by joining reworked blades to other materials.

The blade-core method was faster than the Mousterian and produced 15 times as much cutting edge from the same amount of material. More efficient tool production might have been especially valued by people whose economy depended on cooperative hunting of mammoths, woolly rhinoceroses, bison, wild horses, bears, wild cattle, wild boars, and—principally—reindeer. It has been estimated that approximately 90 percent of the meat eaten by western Europeans between 25,000 and 15,000 B.P. came from reindeer.

Trends observable throughout the archaeological record also mark the changeover from the Mousterian to the Upper

**FIGURE 7.7    Upper Paleolithic Blade Tool Making**

Blades are flakes that are detached from a specially prepared core. A punch (usually a piece of bone or antler) and a hammerstone (not shown here) were used to knock the blade off the core.

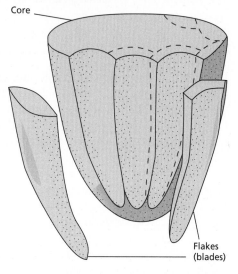

Core

Flakes (blades)

Paleolithic. First, the number of distinct tool types increased. This trend reflected functional specialization—the manufacture of special tools for particular jobs. A second trend was increasing standardization in tool manufacture. The form and inventory of tools reflect several factors: the jobs tools are intended to perform, the physical properties of the raw materials from which they are made, and distinctive cultural traditions about how to make tools.

Other trends include growth in *Homo*'s total population and geographic range and increasing local cultural diversity as people specialized in particular economic activities. Illustrating increasing economic diversity are the varied special-purpose tools made by Upper Paleolithic populations. Scrapers were used to hollow out wood and bone, scrape animal hides, and remove bark from trees. Burins, the first chisels, were used to make slots in bone and wood and to engrave designs on bone. Awls, which were drills with sharp points, were used to make holes in wood, bone, shell, and skin. Upper Paleolithic bone tools have survived: knives, pins, needles with eyes, and fishhooks. The needles suggest that clothes sewn with thread—made from the sinews of animals—were being worn. Fishhooks and harpoons confirm an increased emphasis on fishing.

Different tool types may represent culturally distinct populations that made their tools differently because of different ancestral traditions. Archaeological sites also may represent different activities carried out at different times of the year by a single population. Some sites, for example, are obviously butchering stations, where prehistoric people hunted, made their kills, and carved them up. Others are residential sites, where a wider range of activities was carried out.

With increasing technological differentiation, specialization, and efficiency, humans have become increasingly adaptable. Through heavy reliance on cultural means of adaptation, *Homo* has become (in numbers and range) the most successful primate by far. The hominin range expanded significantly in Upper Paleolithic times.

## Glacial Retreat

Consider now one regional example, western Europe, of the consequences of glacial retreat. The Würm glacial ended in Europe between 17,000 and 12,000 years ago, with the melting of the ice sheet in northern Europe (Scotland, Scandinavia, northern Germany, and Russia). As the ice retreated, the tundra and steppe vegetation grazed by reindeer and other large herbivores gradually moved north. Some people moved north, too, following their prey.

Shrubs, forests, and more solitary animals appeared in southwestern Europe. With most of the big-game animals gone, western Europeans were forced to use a greater variety of foods. To replace specialized economies based on big game, more generalized adaptations developed during the 5,000 years of glacial retreat.

As water flowed from melting glacial ice, sea levels all over the world started rising. Today, off most coasts, there is a shallow-water zone called the *continental shelf,* over which the sea gradually deepens until the abrupt fall to deep water, which is known as the *continental slope.* During the ice Ages, so much water was frozen in glaciers that most continental shelves were exposed. Dry land extended up to the slope's edge. The waters right offshore were deep, cold, and dark. Few species of marine life could thrive in this environment.

How did people adapt to the postglacial environment? As seas rose, conditions more encouraging to marine life developed in the shallower, warmer offshore waters. The quantity and variety of edible species increased tremendously in waters over the shelf. Furthermore, because rivers now flowed more gently into the oceans, fish such as salmon could ascend rivers to spawn. Flocks of birds that nested in seaside marshes migrated across Europe during the winter. Even inland Europeans could take advantage of new resources, such as migratory birds and springtime fish runs, which filled the rivers of southwestern France.

Although hunting remained important, southwestern European economies became less specialized. A wider range, or broader spectrum, of plant and animal life was being hunted, gathered, collected, caught, and fished. This was the beginning of what anthropologist Kent Flannery (1969) has called the *broad-spectrum revolution.* It was revolutionary because, in the Middle East, it led to food production—human control over the reproduction of plants and animals, a process to be examined in Chapter 8. In a mere 10,000 years—after more than a million years during which hominins had subsisted by foraging for natural resources—food production based on plant cultivation and animal domestication would replace hunting and gathering in most areas.

## Settling the Americas

Another effect of continental glaciation was to expose—during several periods of glacial advance—*Beringia,* the Bering land bridge that once connected North America and Siberia. Submerged today under the Bering Sea, Beringia was once a vast area of dry land several hundred miles wide. The original settlers of the Americas came from Northeast Asia. Living in Beringia thousands of years ago, these ancestors of Native Americans didn't realize they were embarking on the colonization of a new continent. They were merely big-game hunters who, over the generations, moved gradually eastward as they spread their camps and followed their prey—woolly mammoths and other tundra-adapted herbivores. Other ancient hunters entered North America along the shore by boat, fishing and hunting sea animals.

This was truly a "new world" to its earliest colonists, as it would be to the European voyagers who rediscovered it thousands of years later. Its natural resources, particularly its big game, never before had been exploited by humans. Early bands followed the game south. Although ice sheets covered most of what is now Canada, colonization gradually penetrated the heartland of what is now the United States. Successive generations of hunters followed game through unglaciated corridors, breaks in the continental ice sheets. Other colonists spread by boat down the Pacific coast.

On North America's rolling grasslands, early American Indians, *Paleoindians,* hunted horses, camels, bison, elephants, mammoths, and giant sloths. The **Clovis tradition**—a sophisticated stone technology based on a point that was fastened to the end of a hunting spear (see Figure 7.8)—flourished, widely but very briefly, in the Central Plains, on their western margins, and in what is now the eastern United States (Green 2006; Largent 2007*a*, 2007*b*).

Using C$^{14}$ (radiocarbon) dates, where available, for all known Clovis sites, Michael Waters and Thomas Stafford (2007) conclude that the Clovis tradition lasted no more than 450 years (13,250–12,800 B.P.) and perhaps only 200 years (13,125–12,925 B.P.). During this short time span, Clovis technology originated and spread throughout North America. Unknown is whether this spread involved the actual movement of big-game hunters or the very rapid diffusion of a superior technology from group to group (Largent 2007*b*). At least four non-Clovis sites in southern South America have C$^{14}$ dates about the same as the Clovis C$^{14}$ dates.

The archaeological record confirms that the Clovis people were not the first inhabitants of the Americas. One pre-Clovis find is a bone projectile point, embedded in a mastodon rib, at the Manis site in Washington State, dated to 13,800 B.P. (Waters et al. 2011). Sites in Wisconsin have yielded non-Clovis tools

**FIGURE 7.8**

**A Clovis Spear Point**
Such points were attached to spears used by Paleoindians of the North American plains between 12,000 and 11,000 B.P. Are there sites with comparable ages in South America?

and butchered mammoth remains dating to 13,500 B.P. and 12,500 B.P. The oldest pre-Clovis site is in South America, at the northern Patagonia settlement of Monte Verde, Chile, dating to 14,800 B.P. In Oregon's Paisley Caves, scientists have uncovered 13,200-year-old non-Clovis projectile points and human *coprolites* (fossilized feces), from which DNA has been extracted (Jenkins et al. 2012). These points date to a time during or before the Clovis tradition.

The DNA from the Paisley corprolites provides the oldest direct evidence for humans in the Americas. It represents haplogroup A, which is common in Siberia and found, along with haplogroup B, among contemporary Native Americans (see Jenkins et al. 2012). A haplogroup is a lineage marked by one or more specific genetic mutations. Analysis of DNA—bolstered, some anthropologists believe, by anatomical evidence— suggests that the Americas were settled by more than one haplogroup. The Clovis people were not the first or only early settlers of the Americas. Migration(s) of people into the Americas may date back as far as 18,000 years. Those early settlers came at different times and by different routes (see Wade 2012).

## Homo floresiensis

In 2004 news reports trumpeted the discovery of bones and tools of a group of tiny humans who inhabited Flores, an Indonesian island 370 miles east of Bali, until fairly recent times (see Roach 2007; Wade 2004). Early in hominin evolution, it wasn't unusual for different species, even genera, of hominins, to live at the same time. But until the 2003–2004 discoveries on Flores, few scientists imagined that a different human species had survived through 12,000 B.P., and possibly even later. These tiny people (fancifully dubbed "hobbits" in the popular press) lived, hunted, and gathered on Flores from about 95,000 B.P. until at least 12,000 B.P. One of their most surprising features is a very small skull, about 370 cm$^3$—slightly smaller than the chimpanzee average.

A skull and several skeletons of these miniature people were found in a limestone cave on Flores by a team of Australian and Indonesian archaeologists, who assigned them to a new human species, *H. floresiensis*. (Additional specimens have been found and described subsequently; see Gugliotta 2005; Roach 2007.) The discovery of *H. floresiensis*, described as a downsized version of *H. erectus*, shows that archaic humans survived much later than had been thought. Before modern people reached Flores, which is very isolated, the island was inhabited only by a select group of animals that had managed to reach it. These animals, including *H. floresiensis*, faced unusual evolutionary forces that pushed some toward gigantism and some toward dwarfism. The carnivorous lizards that reached Flores, perhaps on natural rafts, became giants. These Komodo dragons now are confined mainly to the nearby island of Komodo. Elephants, which are excellent swimmers, reached Flores, where they evolved to a dwarf form the size of an ox.

Previous excavations by Michael Morwood, one of the discoverers of *H. floresiensis*, estimated that *H. erectus* had reached Flores by 840,000 years ago, based on crude stone tools found there. This *H. erectus* population and its descendants are assumed to have been influenced by the same evolutionary forces that reduced the size of the elephants. The first specimen of *H. floresiensis*, an adult female, was uncovered in 2003, from

The skulls of *Homo floresiensis* (left) and modern human (right); *H. floresiensis* was a miniature hominid that inhabited Middle Earth, or at least the Indonesian island of Flores, between 95,000 and 12,000 years ago. © Sabena Jane Blackbird/Alamy

beneath 20 feet (6.1 meters) of silt coating the floor of a cave. Paleoanthropologists identified her as a very small but otherwise normal individual—a diminutive version of *H. erectus*. Because the downsizing was so extreme, smaller than that in modern human pygmies, she and her fellows were assigned to a new species. Her skeleton is estimated to date back some 18,000 years. Remains of six additional individuals found in the cave date from 95,000 to 12,000 B.P. The cave also has yielded bones of fish, birds, giant lizards, giant rats, and pygmy elephants.

*H. floresiensis* apparently controlled fire, and the stone tools found with them are more sophisticated than any known to have been made by *H. erectus*. Among the tools were small blades that might have been mounted on wooden shafts. Hunting elephants—probably cooperatively—and making complex tools, the Floresians may (or may not) have had some form of language. The suggestion of such cultural abilities is surprising for a hominin with a chimplike brain. The small cranium has raised some doubt that *H. floresiensis* actually made the tools. The ancestors of the anatomically modern people who colonized Australia more than 40,000 years ago may have traveled through this area, and it is possible that they made the stone tools. On the other hand, there is no evidence that modern humans reached Flores prior to 11,000 years ago.

The *H. floresiensis* population at the cave site appears to have been wiped out by a volcanic eruption around 12,000 B.P., but they may have survived until much later elsewhere on Flores. The Ngadha people of central Flores and the Manggarai people of West Flores still tell stories about little people who lived in caves until the arrival of the Dutch traders in the 16th century.

As reported in 2009, an analysis of the lower limbs and especially an almost complete left foot and parts of the right shows that *H. floresiensis* walked upright but possessed apelike features (Wilford 2009*a*). The big toe, for example, was stubby, like a chimp's. The feet were large, more than 7½ inches long, out of proportion to the short lower limbs. These proportions, similar to those of some African apes, have never before been seen in hominins. The feet were flat. The navicular bone, which helps form the arch in modern human feet, was more like one in the great apes. Without a strong arch *H. floresiensis* could have walked but not run like humans.

## Anthropology Today    *Being Neandertal*

In their intriguing book *How to Think Like a Neanderthal* (2011), archaeologist Thomas Wynn and psychologist Frederick L. Coolidge offer informed speculation about the Neandertals' strengths and weaknesses and their ways of coping, thinking, and feeling. Although strongly attached to their families and local communities, the Neandertals were suspicious of outsiders—whom they occasionally ate! They cared for the disabled, suggesting that they were capable of empathy and sympathy. They buried their dead, whether symbolically, as an expression of grief, or practically, to get rid of a decaying body. They used some form of language, maybe tones or whistles (see Viegas 2013), which allowed them to communicate, coordinate, and plan.

The Neandertals were very strong and had excellent mechanical skills. (If alive today, Wynn and Coolidge speculate they might work effectively as commercial fishers or mechanics.) One illustration of their mechanical skills is the Levallois spearhead, an intricately worked stone point that could kill an animal as large as a mammoth. The Neandertals learned how to fasten such points securely to a wooden shaft, perhaps using bitumen as an adhesive, or lashing the point to the spear. However, they lacked the spear thrower, an artificial extension of the hunter's arm invented by anatomically modern humans (AMHs), which kept human hunters farther from their prey. Neandertal hunting was close range, dangerous, and sometimes lethal—a pursuit that left behind few elders.

Sometimes they even hunted their own kind. Anthropologists have found Neandertal bones and stone tools dating back 50,000 years in El Sidrón Cave, a rich Neandertal site in northern Spain. These remains offer a glimpse of ancient social structure and behavior—including cannibalism.

This discovery is an excellent illustration of how anthropologists combine fossil, archaeological, and DNA evidence to reconstruct the hominin past. More than 1,800 Neandertal bone fragments have been found in the "Tunnel of the Bones" at El Sidrón. Based on the shape of the bones, scientists estimate that they came from three men, three women, three teenage boys, and three children, including one infant. The remains appear to represent a dozen members of an extended family. DNA analysis helped confirm these conclusions. El Sidrón turned out to be an excellent storehouse for ancient DNA because of its cold, dark dampness. A Y chromosome extracted from four specimens confirmed the initial assessment that these were males. DNA also gave a clue about physical appearance: Two individuals shared an allele (gene variant) that likely gave them red hair (Zimmer 2010).

How did these Neandertals die? When the discovery team closely examined the bones, they found cut marks—signs that the stone blades found with the fossils were used to slice muscle from bone. The long bones had been cracked open, presumably to get at their marrow. The scientists concluded that the El Sidrón Neandertals had been killed and eaten. Since this find almost certainly predates the arrival of modern humans in this area, these victims must have been eaten by members of their own species.

Wynn and Coolidge (2011) interpret the archaeological and fossil evidence as indicating that Neandertals were suspicious of both outsiders and change. The Neandertals moved about within a particular territory—their home range. Their contacts with those outside their territory were limited (and, as we just saw, potentially hostile).

Their unchanging tool designs suggest a limited imagination. Their tools varied little in form or function over thousands of years and miles. As far as we know, Neandertals created no art in the form of painting or carving, beyond a few pierced and pigmented shells. There is no evidence that Neandertals engaged in long-distance trade.

By contrast, we know that anatomically modern Upper Paleolithic Europeans, even those who lived far inland, used shells from the Mediterranean and Atlantic coasts. Unlike Neandertals, AMHs participated in regional social networks; they had relatives, trade partners, in-laws, and allies in other groups. These larger, re-gionally connected communities encouraged innovation, social thinking, and mental processing of complex information. The expanded, regional network and the alliances and social support it offered were key differences between AMHs and Neandertals.

Neandertals no doubt were eventually exposed to the far more effective spears and spear throwers made by their AMH contemporaries, but they borrowed none of those techniques. Their unwillingness or inability to borrow or innovate put them at a disadvantage in competing with AMHs for shrinking resources in ice age Europe. Twin deficiencies—of allies and of innovation—helped doom the Neandertals.

## Summary

1. Compared with late *Australopithecus,* dental, facial, and cranial robustness was reduced in early *Homo habilis* (1.9–1.44 m.y.a.) and *erectus* (1.9–0.3 m.y.a.). *H. erectus* extended the hominin food quest to the hunting of large animals. *H. erectus,* with a much larger body, had smaller back teeth than *Australopithecus* but larger front teeth and supporting structures, including a massive eyebrow ridge. The Lower Paleolithic Acheulean tradition provided *H. erectus* with better tools. *H. erectus*'s average cranial capacity doubled the australopithecine average. *H. erectus* extended the hominin range beyond Africa to Asia and Europe.

2. Ancient *H. erectus* skulls have been found in Kenya and Georgia (in Eurasia), dating back some 1.77–1.6 million years. At Olduvai Gorge, Tanzania, geological strata spanning more than a million years demonstrate a transition from Oldowan tools to the Acheulean implements of *H. erectus. H. erectus* persisted for more than a million years, evolving into archaic *H. sapiens* by the Middle Pleistocene epoch, some 300,000 years ago. Fire allowed *H. erectus* to expand into cooler areas, to cook, and to live in caves.

3. The classic Neandertals, who inhabited western Europe during the early part of the Würm glacial, were among the first hominin fossils found. With no examples of *Australopithecus* or *H. erectus* yet discovered, the differences between them and modern humans were accentuated. Even today, anthropologists tend to exclude the Neandertals from the ancestry of western Europeans.

4. The classic Neandertals adapted physically and culturally to bitter cold. Their front teeth were among the largest to appear in human evolution. The Neandertals manufactured Mousterian flake tools. The changeover from Neandertal to modern appears to have occurred in western Europe prior to 28,000 B.P. Denisovans were Asian cousins of the Neandertals who lived as recently as 74,000 B.P. and possibly later.

5. The ancestors of anatomically modern humans (AMHs) were archaic *H. sapiens* groups, most probably those in Africa. Early AMH fossil finds include Skhūl (100,000 B.P.), Qafzeh (92,000 B.P.), Herto (160,000–154,000 B.P.), Omo Kibish (195,000 B.P.), and various South African sites. The Neandertals (130,000–28,000 B.P.) and AMHs were contemporaries, rather than ancestor and descendant. AMHs made Upper Paleolithic blade tools in Europe and Middle and Late Stone Age flake tools in Africa.

6. As glacial ice melted, foraging patterns were generalized, adding fish, fowl, and plant foods to the diminishing big-game supply. During the major glacial phases, land bridges formed, aiding human colonization of new areas, including the Americas.

7. Humans probably entered the Americas no more than 18,000 years ago. Pursuing big game or moving by boat along the north Pacific coast, they gradually moved into North America. Adapting to different environments, Native Americans developed a variety of cultures. Some continued to rely on big game. Others became broad-spectrum foragers.

8. In 2004 and 2005 scientists reported discoveries of bones and tools of a new hominin species they called *H. floresiensis.* This population of tiny humans lived on the isolated island of Flores in Indonesia. A probable descendant of *H. erectus,* which had settled Flores by 840,000 B.P., *H. floresiensis* is marked by the unusually small size of its body and its chimp-sized skull. There is debate about whether *H. floresiensis* was smart enough to have made the stone tools found in association with the skeletal remains, though there is no evidence that AMHs reached Flores before 11,000 B.P. The *H. floresiensis* remains have been assigned dates ranging from 95,000 to 12,000 B.P.

## Key Terms

Acheulean, *144*

anatomically
   modern humans
   (AMHs), *143*

archaic
   *H. sapiens, 149*

behavioral
   modernity, *160*

blade tool, *162*

Clovis
   tradition, *165*

Cro-Magnon, *154*

Denisovans, *159*

glacials, *151*

*H. (Homo) erectus,*
   *141*

Herto, *156*

interglacials, *151*

Mousterian, *153*

Neandertals, *149*

Paleolithic, *144*

Pleistocene, *150*

Upper
   Paleolithic, *162*

# Chapter 8

# The First Farmers

In Chapter 7, we considered some of the economic implications of the end of the ice age in Europe. With glacial retreat, foragers pursued a more generalized economy, focusing less on large animals. This was the beginning of what Kent Flannery (1969) has called the **broad-spectrum revolution.** This refers to the period beginning around 15,000 B.P. in the Middle East and 12,000 B.P. in Europe, during which a wider range, or broader spectrum, of plant and animal life was hunted, gathered, collected, caught, and fished. It was revolutionary because, in the Middle East, it led to food production—human control over the reproduction of plants and animals.

## The Mesolithic

The broad-spectrum revolution in Europe includes the late Upper Paleolithic and the **Mesolithic,** which followed it. Again, because of the long history of European archaeology, our knowledge of the Mesolithic (particularly in southwestern Europe and the British Isles) is extensive. The Mesolithic had a characteristic tool type—the *microlith* (Greek for "small stone"). Of interest to anthropologists is what an abundant inventory of small and delicately shaped stone tools can tell us about the total economy and way of life of the people who made them (see Bailey and Spikins 2008).

By 10,000 B.P. the glaciers had retreated to such a point that the human range in Europe extended to the formerly glaciated British Isles and Scandinavia. The reindeer herds had gradually retreated to the far north, with some human groups following (and ultimately domesticating) them. Europe around 10,000 B.P. was forest rather than treeless steppe and tundra—as it had been during the Upper Paleolithic. Europeans were exploiting a much wider variety of resources and gearing their lives to the seasonal appearance of particular plants and animals. People still hunted, but they stalked solitary forest animals rather than herd species. The coasts and lakes of Europe, the Middle East, and Japan were fished intensively. Some important Mesolithic sites are Scandinavian shell mounds—the garbage dumps of prehistoric oyster collectors. Microliths were used as fishhooks and in harpoons. Dugout canoes were used for fishing and travel. For woodworking, Mesolithic carpenters used new kinds of axes, chisels, and gouges. The process of preserving meat and fish by smoking and salting grew increasingly important. (Meat preservation had been less of a problem previously, in a subarctic environment.) The bow and arrow became essential for hunting water fowl in swamps and marshes, and dogs were domesticated as retrievers. Recent evidence from sites in the Czech Republic (33,000 B.P.), Siberia (33,000), and Belgium (36,000) pushes domestication of the dog back much further than the old estimate of 14,000 B.P. (Rice 2012).

Such generalized, broad-spectrum economies lasted about 4,000 years longer in Europe than in the Middle East. Whereas Middle Easterners had begun to cultivate plants and breed animals by 10,000 B.P., farming and herding reached interior western Europe only around 6000 B.P. (4000 B.C.E.) and northern Europe 500 years later (see Gibson 2012; Gignoux et al. 2011).

After 15,000 B.P., throughout the inhabited world, as the big-game supply diminished, people had to pursue new resources. Human attention shifted from large-bodied, slow reproducers (such as mammoths) to such species as fish, mollusks, and rabbits, which reproduce quickly and prolifically. This happened with the European Mesolithic. It also happened at the Japanese site of Nittano (Akazawa 1980), located on an inlet near Tokyo. Nittano was occupied several times between 6000 and 5000 B.P. by members of the *Jomon* culture (16,000–2500 B.P.), for which more than 30,000 sites are known in Japan. The Jomon people made stone and bone tools, and some of the world's earliest pottery—beginning at a few sites as early as 15,500 B.P. They hunted deer, pigs, bears, and antelope, gathered plants and nuts, and ate fish and shellfish. Their sites have yielded the remains of more than 300 species of shellfish and 180 species of edible plants, including berries, nuts, and tubers (Akazawa and Aikens 1986; Habu et al. 2011).

The Jomon people used their pottery to cook and serve stews of salmon and shellfish. In burnt fragments of clay pots dating back 15,300 years, scientists have found traces of fat from fish and shellfish (Craig 2013; Subbaraman 2013). Whether in the form of a family meal, a potluck dinner, or a lavish feast, eating tends to be a social activity, just as it appears to have been in the Jomon culture. Not only did the Jomon people stew their fish, they feasted on it in groups. Their large clay pots weren't just utilitarian cooking vessels; they also brought people together to socialize (Craig 2013; Subbaraman 2013).

Even earlier than Jomon, the world's oldest known pottery has been found recently in Jiangxi Province, southern China (Wu et al. 2012). Dated to 20,000 B.P., these pots were simple vessels used for cooking. It appears that pottery making began in China 20,000 years ago and never stopped. The Chinese kitchen always has featured cooking and steaming, which ceramics facilitate. Unlike other parts of Asia and the Middle East, breads never have been prominent in Chinese cuisine. A group of mobile hunter-gatherers made these early pots; plant cultivation did not reach China for another 10,000 years.

In the Middle East, the first pottery appeared 3,000–2,000 years after, rather than before, the turn to farming. Harvard archaeologist Ofer Bar-Yosef suggests that the earliest farmers/herders in the Middle East had a diet based on barbecued meats and pita breads and didn't need pottery. In their cooking style, one simply grinds the seeds, mixes them with water, then cooks the dough right on the fire. Chinese cooking, by contrast, needed pots to cook and steam foods thousands of years earlier (*Harvard Magazine* 2012).

## The Neolithic

The term *Neolithic Revolution,* sometimes called the Agricultural Revolution, refers to the widespread transition, beginning about 12,000 years ago, of human societies from lifestyles based on foraging to lifestyles based on food production—farming and herding. The Neolithic is considered revolutionary because, in just a few thousand years, after millions of years of foraging as the sole human subsistence strategy, it would transform small, mobile groups into societies living in permanent settlements—villages, towns, and eventually cities. More productive and reliable than foraging, Neolithic economies fueled population growth, expansion, and the settlement of new environments. The many repercussions, including the costs and benefits of food production, are examined in the section "Costs and Benefits" later in this chapter.

The transition from Mesolithic to Neolithic occurs when groups become dependent on domesticated foods for more than 50 percent of their diet. Usually this happens after a very long period of experimenting with and using domesticates as supplements to

*Neolithic* was coined to refer to techniques of grinding and polishing stone tools, such as this hammer head and two polished axes found in England. Was the new tool-making style the most significant thing about the Neolithic? © CM Dixon/age fotostock

broad-spectrum foraging (see Bellwood 2005; Simmons 2007). The archaeological signature of Neolithic cultures (which are called *Formative* in the Americas) includes dependence on cultivation, sedentary (settled) life, and the use of ceramic vessels. The term **Neolithic** originally was coined to refer to new techniques of grinding and polishing stone tools (see Saville 2012). However, the primary significance of the Neolithic was the new total economy rather than just its characteristic artifacts.

## The First Farmers and Herders in the Middle East

Economies based on food production were associated with substantial changes in human lifestyles. By 12,000 B.P., the shift toward the Neolithic was under way in the Middle East (Turkey, Iraq, Iran, Syria, Jordan, and Israel). No longer simply hunting, gathering, and fishing, people started managing and modifying the characteristics of familiar plants and animals. By 10,000 B.P., domesticates were an established part of the broad spectrum of resources used by Middle Easterners. By 7500 B.P., most Middle Easterners had abandoned broad-spectrum foraging for more specialized, fully Neolithic economies based on fewer species, which were domesticates (Bar-Yosef and Valla 2013; Bellwood 2005; Simmons 2007).

They had become committed farmers and herders. Kent Flannery (1969) laid out a series of eras during which the Middle Eastern transition to farming and herding took place. The era of seminomadic hunting and gathering (12,000–11,000 B.P.) encompasses the last stages of broad-spectrum foraging. This was the period just before domesticated plants (wheat and barley) and animals (goats and sheep) were added to the diet. Next came the era of early dry farming (of wheat and barley) and caprine domestication (11,000–7500 B.P.). *Dry farming* refers to farming without irrigation; such farming depended on rainfall. *Caprine* (from *capra,* Latin for "goat") refers to goats and sheep, which were domesticated during this era.

During the era of increased specialization in food production (7500–5500 B.P.), new crops were added to the diet, along with more productive varieties of wheat and barley. Cattle and pigs were fully domesticated (Simmons 2007). By 5500 B.P., agriculture had extended to the alluvial plain of the Tigris and Euphrates Rivers (see Figure 8.1), where early Mesopotamians lived in walled towns, some of which grew into cities. Table 8.1 highlights these stages, or eras, in the transition to food production in the ancient Middle East. After more than 2 million years of stone tool making, the genus *Homo* was living in the Bronze Age, when metallurgy and the wheel were invented.

Middle Eastern food production arose in the context of four environmental zones. From highest to lowest, they are high plateau (5,000 feet, or 1,500 meters), hilly flanks, piedmont steppe (treeless plain), and alluvial desert—the area watered by the Tigris and Euphrates Rivers (100 to 500 feet, or 30 to 150 meters). The **hilly flanks** is a subtropical woodland zone that flanks those rivers to the north (see Figure 8.1). *Alluvial* describes rich, fertile soil deposited by rivers and streams.

The archaeologist Robert J. Braidwood (1975) proposed that food production began in the hilly flanks, where wheat and barley grew wild in greatest abundance (see Figure 8.1). In 1948, Braidwood's team found evidence for early food production at Jarmo, a village in the hilly flanks inhabited between 9000 and 8500 B.P. We now know, however, that there were farming villages earlier than Jarmo (see Figure 8.1) in zones adjacent to the hilly flanks. One example is Ali Kosh, a village in the foothills (piedmont steppe) of the Zagros Mountains. By 9000 B.P., the people of Ali Kosh were herding goats, collecting various wild plants, and harvesting wheat (Hole, Flannery, and Neely 1969).

FIGURE 8.1   **The Vertical Economy of the Ancient Middle East**
Geographically close but contrasting environments were linked by seasonal movements and trade patterns of broad-spectrum foragers. Traded resources included copper, obsidian, and asphalt, located in particular zones. As people traveled and traded, they removed plants from the zones, where they grew wild in the hilly flanks into adjacent zones, where humans became agents of selection.

TABLE 8.1   **The Transition to Food Production in the Middle East**

| Era | Dates (B.P.) |
| --- | --- |
| Origin of state (Sumer) | 5500 |
| Increasing specialization in food production | 7500–5500 |
| Early dry farming and caprine domestication | 11,000–7500 |
| Seminomadic hunting and gathering (e.g., Natufians) | 12,000–11,000 |

Climate change played a role in the origin of food production (Bellwood 2005). (See this chapter's "Anthropology Today" for the effects of contemporary climate change on archaeology.) The end of the ice age brought greater regional and local variation in climatic conditions. Lewis Binford (1968) proposed that in certain areas of the Middle East (such as the hilly flanks), local environments were so rich in resources that foragers could adopt **sedentism**—sedentary (settled) life in villages. Binford's prime example is the widespread Natufian culture (12,500 to 10,500 B.P.), based on broad-spectrum foraging. The **Natufians,** who collected wild cereals and hunted gazelles, had year-round villages. They were able to stay in the same place (early villages) because they could harvest nearby wild cereals for six months (see Bar-Yosef and Valla 2013; Simmons 2007).

The climate had become warmer and more humid just before the Natufian period. This expanded the altitude range of wild wheat and barley, thus enlarging the available foraging area and allowing a longer harvest season. Wheat and barley ripened in the spring at low altitudes, in the summer at middle altitudes, and in the fall at high altitudes. As locations for their villages, the Natufians chose central places where they could harvest wild cereals in all three zones.

Around 11,000 B.P., this favorable foraging pattern was threatened by a second climate change—to drier conditions. Many wild cereal habitats dried up, and the optimal zone for foraging shrank. Natufian villages were now restricted to areas with permanent water. As the population continued to grow, some Natufians attempted to maintain productivity by transferring wild cereals to well-watered areas, where they started cultivating.

In the view of many scholars, the people most likely to transition to a new subsistence strategy, such as food production, would be those having the most trouble in following their traditional subsistence strategy (Binford 1968; Flannery 1973; Wenke and Olszewski 2007). Thus, those ancient Middle Easterners living outside the area where wild foods were most abundant would be the most likely to experiment and to adopt new subsistence strategies. This would have been especially true as the climate dried up. Recent archaeological finds support this hypothesis that food production began in *marginal areas,* such as the piedmont steppe, rather than in the optimal zones, such as the hilly flanks, where traditional foods were most abundant.

People would have had no reason to invent cultivation when wild grain was ample to feed them. Wild wheat ripens rapidly and can be harvested over a three-week period. According to Flannery, over that time period a family of experienced plant collectors could harvest enough grain—2,200 pounds (1,000 kilograms)—to feed themselves for a year. But after harvesting all that wheat, they'd need a place to put it (e.g., a granary or storage pit). They could no longer maintain a nomadic lifestyle, because they'd need to stay close to their grain.

In the Middle East, sedentary village life developed before farming and herding did. The Natufians had no choice but to build villages near the densest stands of wild grains. They needed a place to keep their grain. Furthermore, sheep and goats could graze on the stubble that remained after people had harvested the grain. The fact that basic plants and animals were available in the same area also favored village life. Hilly flanks foragers built houses, dug storage pits for grain, and made ovens to roast it.

Natufian settlements, occupied year-round, show permanent architectural features and evidence for the processing and storage of wild grains. One such site is Abu Hureyra,

Syria (see Figure 8.1), which initially was occupied by Natufian foragers around 11,000 to 10,500 B.P. Then it was abandoned—to be reoccupied later by food producers, between 9500 and 8000 B.P. From the Natufian period, Abu Hureyra has yielded the remains of grinding stones, wild plants, and gazelle bones.

Prior to domestication, the favored hilly flanks zone had the densest human population. Approaching *carrying capacity* (the maximum number of people who can be supported by a given subsistence base), that population began to spill over into adjacent, more marginal areas. Colonists from the flanks tried to maintain their traditional broad-spectrum foraging in these marginal zones. But with sparser wild foods available, they had to experiment with new subsistence strategies, including food production (Binford 1968; Bouquet-Appel and Bar-Yosef 2008; Flannery 1969). *Early cultivation began as an attempt to copy, in a less favorable environment, the dense stands of wheat and barley that grew wild in the hilly flanks.*

The Middle East is a region that for thousands of years has had a *vertical economy.* (Other examples include Peru and **Mesoamerica**—Middle America, including Mexico, Guatemala, and Belize.) A vertical economy exploits environmental zones that, although close together in space, contrast with one another in altitude, rainfall, overall climate, and vegetation (see Figure 8.1). Such a close juxtaposition of varied environments allowed broad-spectrum foragers to use different resources in different seasons.

Early seminomadic foragers in the Middle East had followed game from zone to zone. In winter they hunted in the piedmont steppe region, which had winter rains rather than snow and provided winter pasture for game animals 12,000 years ago. (Indeed, it still is used for winter grazing by herders today.) When winter ended, the steppe dried up. Game moved up to the hilly flanks and high plateau country as the snow melted. Pasture land became available at higher elevations. Foragers gathered as they climbed, harvesting wild grains that ripened later at higher altitudes. Sheep and goats followed the stubble in the wheat and barley fields after people had harvested the grain.

The four Middle Eastern environmental zones shown in Figure 8.1 also were tied together through trade. Certain resources were confined to specific zones. Asphalt, used as an adhesive in the manufacture of sickles, came from the steppe. Copper and turquoise sources were located in the high plateau. Contrasting environments were therefore linked in two ways: by foragers' seasonal migration and by trade.

The movement of people, animals, and products between zones—plus population increase supported by highly productive broad-spectrum foraging—was a precondition for the emergence of food production (Bouquet-Appel and Bar-Yosef 2008). As they traveled between zones, people carried seeds into new habitats. Mutations, genetic recombinations, and human selection led to new kinds of wheat and barley. Some of the new varieties were better adapted to the steppe and, eventually, the alluvial desert than the wild forms had been.

## Genetic Changes and Domestication

What are the main differences between wild and domesticated plants? The seeds of domesticated cereals, and often the entire plant, are larger. Compared with wild plants, crops produce a higher yield per unit of area. Domesticated plants also lose their natural seed dispersal mechanisms. Cultivated beans, for example, have pods that hold together,

## FIGURE 8.2
### A Head of Wheat or Barley

In the wild, the axis comes apart as its parts fall off one by one. The connecting parts (interstices) are tough and don't come apart in domesticated grains. In wild grains, the husks are hard. In domestic plants, they are brittle, which permits easy access to the grain. How did people deal with hard husks before domestication?

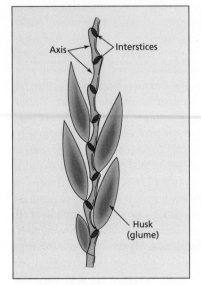

Axis  Interstices

Husk
(glume)

rather than shattering as they do in the wild. Domesticated cereals have tougher connective tissue holding the seedpods to the stem.

Grains of wheat, barley, and other cereals occur in bunches at the end of a stalk (see Figure 8.2). The grains are attached to the stalk by an *axis* (plural *axes*). In wild cereals, this axis is brittle. Sections of the axis break off one by one, and a seed attached to each section falls to the ground. This is how wild cereals spread their seeds and propagate their species. But a brittle axis is a problem for people. Imagine the annoyance experienced by broad-spectrum foragers as they tried to harvest wild wheat, only to have the grain fall off or be blown away.

In very dry weather, wild wheat and barley ripen—their axes totally disintegrating—in just three days (Flannery 1973). The brittle axis must have been even more irritating to people who planted the seeds and waited for the harvest. But fortunately, certain stalks of wild wheat and barley happened to have tough axes. These were the ones whose seeds people saved to plant the following year.

Another problem with wild cereals is that the edible portion is enclosed in a tough husk. This husk was too tough to remove with a pounding stone. Foragers had to roast the grain to make the husk brittle enough to come off. However, some wild plants happened to have genes for brittle husks. Humans chose the seeds of these plants (which would have germinated prematurely in nature) because they could be more effectively prepared for eating.

People also selected traits in animals (Diamond 1997; Miller, Zeder, and Arter 2009). Wild sheep aren't woolly; wool coats were products of domestication. Although it's hard to imagine, a wool coat offers protection against extreme heat. Skin temperatures of sheep in very hot areas are much lower than temperatures on the surface of their wool. Woolly sheep, but not their wild ancestors, could survive in hot, dry alluvial lowlands. Wool had an additional advantage: its use for clothing.

What are some of the differences between wild and domesticated animals? Plants got larger with domestication, while animals got smaller, probably because smaller animals are easier to control. Middle Eastern sites document changes in the horns of domesticated goats. Such change may have been genetically linked to some other desirable trait that has left no skeletal evidence behind.

Archaeological evidence for herd management predates anatomical evidence (e.g, in size or horns) for full animal domestication. For example, certain early sites show a focus on killing 2- to 3-year-old males, which suggests a concern with preserving female breeding stock. Those ancient herd managers realized that a steady stream of young immigrant males from surrounding territories would replace slaughtered local males. Herd management also involved moving animals (goats, sheep, cattle, and pigs) from their natural habitats to lower altitudes, where they adapted to hotter, drier climates by becoming smaller. By managing (e.g., selectively culling) wild animal populations, ancient Middle Easterners were gradually converting their prey animals into herd animals. In doing so, in a process that lasted more than a thousand years, they also were transforming themselves from hunters into herders (Zeder 2008).

## Food Production and the State

Over time, Middle Eastern economies grew more specialized, geared more exclusively toward crops and herds. The former marginal zones became centers of the new economy and of population increase and emigration. Some of the increasing population spilled back into the hilly flanks, where people eventually had to intensify production by cultivating. Domesticated crops could now provide a bigger harvest than could the grains that grew wild there. Thus, in the hilly flanks, too, farming eventually replaced foraging as the economic mainstay.

Farming colonies spread down into drier areas. By 7000 B.P., simple irrigation systems had developed, tapping springs in the foothills. By 6000 B.P., more complex irrigation techniques made agriculture possible in the arid lowlands of southern Mesopotamia. In the

Simple irrigation systems were being used in the Middle East by 7000 B.P. By 6000 B.P., complex irrigation techniques had made agriculture possible in the arid lowlands of southern Mesopotamia. Shown here, a local man performs traditional irrigation of a rice paddy in Chandbali, Orissa, India. © Lindsay Brown/Lonely Planet Images/Getty Images alluvial desert plain of the Tigris and Euphrates Rivers, a new economy based on irrigation and trade fueled the growth of an entirely new form of society. This was the *state,* a social and political unit featuring a central government, extreme contrasts of wealth, and social classes. The process of state formation is examined in the next chapter.

We now understand that the Neolithic began in marginal zones, such as the piedmont steppe, where people experimented at reproducing, artificially, the dense grain stands that grew wild in the hilly flanks. As seeds were taken to new environments, new phenotypes were favored by a combination of natural and human selection. The spread of cereal grains outside their natural habitats was part of a system of migration and trade between zones, which had developed in the Middle East during the broad-spectrum period. Food production also owed its origin to the need to intensify production to feed an increasing human population—the legacy of thousands of years of productive foraging.

## Other Old World Farmers

The path from foraging to farming was one that people followed independently in at least seven world areas. As we'll see later in this chapter, at least three were in the Americas. At least four were in the Old World. In each of these seven centers, people independently invented domestication—albeit of different sets of crops and animals.

Food production also spread out from the Middle East and other centers of domestication. This happened through trade; through diffusion of plants, animals, products, and information; and through the actual migration of farmers. The crops and livestock that first were domesticated in the Middle East spread westward to northern Africa, including Egypt's Nile Valley, and into Europe (Gibson 2012; Price, 2000: Zeder 2008). In Egypt, an agricultural economy based on Middle Eastern domesticates led to a pharaonic civilization. Trade also extended eastward from the Middle East to India and Pakistan, where another early civilization eventually arose.

Excavations in southern Egypt have uncovered very early pottery and cattle. Located in the eastern Sahara and southern Egypt, Nabta Playa is a basin that, during prehistoric summers, filled with water. Over several millennia this temporary lake attracted people who used it for social and ceremonial activities (Wendorf and Schild 2000). The earliest settlements (11,000–9300 B.P.) at Nabta were small summer camps of herders of domesticated cattle. (Note the very early domestication of cattle here.) According to Wendorf and Schild (2000), Nabta Playa provides early evidence for what anthropologists have called the "African cattle complex," in which cattle are used economically for their milk and blood, rather than killed for their meat (except on ceremonial occasions). At first, Nabta was occupied only seasonally, as people came over from the Nile, or from better-watered areas to the south. They returned to those areas in the fall.

By 9000 B.P. people were living at Nabta Playa year-round. To survive in the desert, they dug large, deep wells and lived in well-organized villages, with small huts arranged in straight lines. Plant remains show they collected sorghum, millets, legumes (peas and beans), tubers, and fruits. These were wild plants, so the economy was not fully Neolithic. By 8800 B.P., they were making their own pottery, possibly the earliest pottery in Egypt. By 8100 B.P., sheep and goats had diffused in from the Middle East (see Edwards 2004; Sadig 2010).

What about Europe? For generations, scholars have wondered how the Neolithic spread to that continent. Did Middle Eastern farmers colonize Europe, or did their ideas and techniques spread there without any actual migration? Scandinavian scientists recently have found support for the first hypothesis—the actual migration of farmers. They compared nuclear DNA from two sets of Swedish burials, both 5,000 years old. One burial represented a hunter-gatherer group; the other, a farmer group about 250 miles (400 kilometers) away. The ancient hunter-gatherer DNA linked them to living northern Europeans, especially Finns, while the farmer genome resembled that of contemporary southeastern Europeans. The researchers concluded that migrating farmers had spread their crops and technology across Europe from the Mediterranean beginning around 8,500 years ago. It took them about 3,000 years to reach northwestern Europe (Skoglund, Malmström, et al. 2012).

In the Mediterranean, new excavations on Cyprus show that the island had been colonized by 10,600 B.P.—the early Neolithic—with village life and farming of cereals well under way. This confirms that migration from the mainland began—by boat— shortly after the beginning of farming in the Middle East (Vigne, Briois, et al. 2012). Sailing just over 35 miles (60 kilometers) from the mainland to Cyprus, Neolithic colonists carried with them all four major livestock species (sheep, goats, cattle, and pigs). To Cyprus they introduced the full Neolithic package: farming and herding, technologies, and, most likely, the social networks and belief systems they had brought from their original homeland. The colonization of Cyprus can serve as a model of how the Neolithic spread across the rest of the Mediterranean basin—by boat and seafaring colonists (Zeder 2008).

The Mediterranean basin witnessed a diaspora—slow at first, then more rapid—of Neolithic people and their lifestyle westward from the Middle East and Cyprus to the shores of the Atlantic (Zeder 2008). Expansion from Cyprus to the Aegean may have taken as long as 2,000 years. Thereafter, only 500 years were needed for seafaring colonists to reach Italy, then just 500–600 years to travel the much greater distance from Italy to the Atlantic. To be more specific, by 8,000 B.P. farming villages were established in Greece and on the Italian coast, first in the southeast, then, by 7800– 7600 B.P., the northwest. Soon thereafter, seafaring migrants from Italy began to settle southern France, where a site, dated to 7700–7600 B.P., has yielded pottery, domestic sheep, and wheat. After the Neolithic reached its shores, southern France experienced a marked geographic, ecological, and cultural break between its interior Mesolithic settlements and its coastal Neolithic colonies. Rather than entirely replacing indigenous European foraging populations, the Neolithic colonists seem initially to have been confined to scattered coastal farming communities around the Mediterranean basin (Zeder 2008). By 6000 B.P., however, there were thousands of European farming villages as far west as northern France and as far east as Russia (Bogaard 2004; Gibson 2012).

In western Pakistan's Indus River Valley, ancient cities (Harappa and Mohenjodaro) emerged slightly later than did the first Mesopotamian city-states. Domestication and state formation in the Indus Valley probably were influenced by developments in, and trade with, the Middle East. Still, archaeological research confirms the early (8000 B.P.) presence of domesticated goats, sheep, cattle, wheat, and barley in Pakistan.

Rice, originally domesticated in Asia by 8400 B.P., became a key caloric staple within mixed economies, including domesticated animals. This Vietnamese woman is herding ducks near a rice paddy. © Christophe Boisvieux/Corbis

China also was one of the first world areas to develop farming, based on millet and rice. Millet is a tall, coarse cereal grass still grown in northern China. Americans use this grain, which today feeds a third of the world's population, mainly as birdseed. By ca. 10,000 B.P., two kinds of millet were supporting early farming communities in northern China, along the Yellow River. Recent studies of that area suggest that millet domestication took place gradually between 11,000 and 9000 B.P. (Yang et al. 2012; see also Lu et al. 2009). Starch grains on food processing tools show that millet seeds were being ground into flour or meal, then cooked in earthenware vessels as early as 11,000 B.P. Millet cultivation paved the way for widespread village life and eventually for Shang dynasty civilization, based on irrigated agriculture, between 3600 and 3100 B.P. The northern Chinese also had domesticated dogs, pigs, and possibly cattle, goats, and sheep by 7000 B.P. (see Jiao 2007).

Rice was domesticated in the Yangtze River corridor of southern China as early as 8400 B.P. Other early rice comes from the 7,000-year-old site Hemudu in southern China. The people of Hemudu used both wild and domesticated rice, along with domesticated water buffalo, dogs, and pigs. They also hunted wild game (Jiao 2007).

As mentioned, it appears that food production arose independently at least seven times in different world areas. Figure 8.3 highlights those seven areas: the Middle East, north China, south China, sub-Saharan Africa, central Mexico, the south central Andes, and the eastern United States. A different set of major foods was domesticated, at different times, in each area, as we see in Table 8.2. Some grains, such as millet and rice, were domesticated more than once. Millet grows wild in China and Africa, where it became an important food crop, as well as in Mexico, where it did not. Indigenous African rice, grown only in West Africa, belongs to the same genus as Asian rice. Pigs were independently domesticated in the Middle East and China. Independent domestication of the dog was virtually a worldwide phenomenon, including the Western Hemisphere. We turn now to archaeological sequences in the Americas.

FIGURE 8.3   **Seven World Areas Where Food Production Was Independently Invented**
Do any of these areas surprise you?

Source: Bruce D. Smith, "Seven World Areas Where Food Production Was Independently Invented," in *The Emergence of Agriculture,* p. 12. W. H. Freeman & Co; New Edition (February 1999).

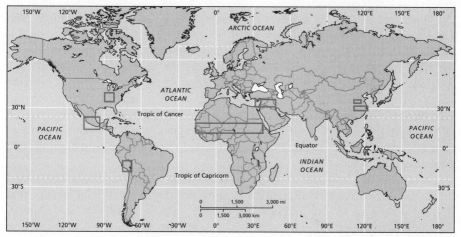

TABLE 8.2   **Seven World Areas Where Food Production Was Independently Invented**

Source: Bruce D. Smith, "Seven World Areas Where Food Production Was Independently Invented," in *The Emergence of Agriculture,* p. 12. W. H. Freeman & Co; New Ed edition (February 1999).

| World Area | Major Domesticated Plants/Animals | Earliest Date (B.P.) |
|---|---|---|
| Middle East | Wheat, barley<br>Sheep, goats, cattle, pigs | 11,000 |
| Andean region | Squash, potato, quinoa, beans<br>Camelids (llama, alpaca), guinea pigs | 11,000–5000 |
| Southern China<br>(Yangtze River corridor) | Rice<br>Water buffalo, dogs, pigs | 8500–6500 |
| Mesoamerica | Maize, beans, squash<br>Dogs, turkeys | 8000–4700 |
| Northern China<br>(Yellow River) | Millet<br>Dogs, pigs, chickens | 7500 |
| Sub-Saharan Africa | Sorghum, pearl millet, African rice | 4000 |
| Eastern United States | Goosefoot, marsh elder,<br>sunflower, squash | 4500 |

# The First American Farmers

*Homo* did not, of course, originate in the Western Hemisphere. Never have fossils of Neandertals or earlier hominins been found in North or South America. The settlement of the Americas was one of the major achievements of anatomically modern humans. This colonization continued the trends toward population increase and expansion of geographic range that have marked human evolution generally.

Spreading gradually through the Americas, early Native Americans occupied a variety of environments. Their descendants would independently invent food production, paving the way for the emergence of states based on agriculture and trade in Mexico and Peru. The most significant contrast between Old and New World food production involved animal domestication, which was much more important in the Old World than in the New World. The animals that had been hunted during the early American big-game tradition either became extinct before people could domesticate them or were not domesticable. The largest animal ever domesticated in the New World (in Peru, around 4500 B.P.) was the llama. Early Peruvians and Bolivians ate llama meat and used that animal as a beast of burden. They bred the llama's relative, the alpaca, for its wool. Peruvians also added animal protein to their diet by raising and eating guinea pigs and ducks. The turkey was domesticated in Mesoamerica and in the southwestern United States. Lowland South Americans domesticated a type of duck. The dog is the only animal that was domesticated throughout the New World.

There were no cattle, sheep, or goats in the areas of the Americas where food production arose. As a result, neither herding nor the kinds of relationships that developed between herders and farmers in many parts of the Middle East, Europe, Asia, and Africa emerged in the precolonial Americas. The New World crops were different, although staples as nutritious as those of the Old World were domesticated from native wild plants. Three key caloric staples, major sources of carbohydrates, were domesticated by Native American farmers. **Maize,** or corn, was first domesticated in the tropical lowlands of southwestern Mexico. It became the major source of calories in Mesoamerica and Central America and eventually reached coastal Peru. The two other starchy staples domesticated in the Americas were root crops (potatoes and manioc). White ("Irish") potatoes were first domesticated in the Andes. **Manioc,** or cassava, was domesticated in the South American lowlands, where other root crops such as yams and sweet potatoes also were important. Secondary crops, especially beans and squash, added variety and essential proteins, vitamins, and minerals to the diet.

Food production was independently invented in at least three areas of the Americas: Mesoamerica, the eastern United States, and the south central Andes. Food plants known as goosefoot and marsh elder, along with the sunflower and a species of squash, were domesticated in the eastern United States by 4500 B.P. Those crops supplemented a diet based mainly on hunting and gathering. They never became caloric staples like maize, wheat, rice, millet, manioc, and potatoes. Eventually, maize diffused from Mesoamerica into what is now the United States, reaching both the Southwest and the eastern area just mentioned.

Domestication of several species was under way in the south central Andes of Peru and Bolivia by 5000 B.P. They were the potato, quinoa (a cereal grain), beans, llamas, alpacas, and guinea pigs.

## The Tropical Origins of New World Domestication

On the basis of microscopic evidence from early cultivated plants, we know that New World farming began in the lowlands of South America and then spread to Central America, Mexico, and the Caribbean islands. In Chapter 3 we learned about new techniques that allow archaeologists and botanists to recover and analyze microscopic evidence from pollens, starch grains, and phytoliths (plant crystals) (Bryant 2007a, 2013). This evidence has forced the revision of old assumptions, most prominently the idea that New World farming originated in upland areas, such as the highlands of Mexico and Peru.

Dolores Piperno and Karen Stothert (2003) found that phytoliths from cultivated squashes and gourds are substantially larger than those from wild species. They then used phytolith size to confirm that domesticated squash and gourds (*Cucurbita*) were grown in coastal Ecuador between 9,000 and 10,000 years ago.

According to Piperno and Deborah Pearsall (1998), farming in the tropical lowlands of Central and South America began at about the same time as food production arose in the Middle East—around 10,000 years ago. By that time, cultural groups in Panama, Peru, Ecuador, and Colombia were cultivating plants in garden plots near their homes. Between 9000 and 8000 B.P., changes in seed form and phytolith size suggest that farmers were selecting certain characteristics in their cultivated plants. By 7,000 years ago, farmers had expanded their plots into nearby forests, which they cleared using slash-and-burn techniques. By that time also, early farming ideas and techniques were diffusing from tropical lowlands into drier regions at higher elevations (Bryant 1999, 2003; Piperno and Pearsall 1998).

What about maize (corn), a major New World crop, long thought to have been domesticated in the Mexican highlands? Recent molecular and genetic studies indicate that maize domestication actually took place in the lowlands of southwestern Mexico. The wild ancestor of maize is a species of wild grain called **teosinte** (or teocentli) that is native to the Río Balsas watershed of tropical southwestern Mexico (Holst, Moreno, and Piperno 2007). Evidence for the evolution of maize from its wild ancestor has yet to be found in that poorly studied region. Still, we can infer some of the likely steps in maize domestication.

Such a process would have included increases in the number of kernels per cob, cob size, and the number of cobs per stalk. These changes would make it increasingly profitable to collect wild teosinte and eventually to plant maize. Undoubtedly, some of the mutations necessary for domesticated maize had occurred in wild teosinte before people started growing it. However, since teosinte was well adapted to its natural niche, the mutations offered no advantage and didn't spread. But once people started harvesting wild maize intensively, they became selective agents, taking back to camp a greater proportion of plants with tough axes and cobs. These were the plants most likely to hold together during harvesting and least likely to disintegrate on the way back home. Eventually, teosinte became dependent on humans for its survival because maize lacks a natural means of dispersal—a brittle axis or cob. If humans chose plants with tough axes inadvertently, their selection of plants with soft husks must have been intentional, as was their selection of larger cobs, more kernels per cob, and more cobs per plant.

A phytolith analysis of sediments from San Andrés, in the Mexican state of Tabasco, confirms the spread of maize cultivation eastward to the tropical Mexican Gulf Coast by 7300 B.P. Data from many sites now confirm that maize spread rapidly from its domestication cradle in tropical southwestern Mexico during the eighth millennium B.P. (8000–7001) (Bryant 2007*b*; Piperno 2001; Pohl et al. 2007). For example, analysis of starch grains from stone tools in Panama's tropical lowlands confirms that maize was grown there by 7800–7000 B.P. (Dickau, Ranere, and Cooke 2007).

According to Vaughn Bryant (2003), archaeologists formerly sought evidence for early New World farming in the highlands of Mexico and Peru. These upland areas were easy to reach and had caves and rock shelters with preserved plant remains. They also were near the centers of the major civilizations that would eventually develop in the Mexican highlands (see Chapter 9). Decades ago, excavations in the Mexican valleys of Tehuacan and Oaxaca yielded well-preserved seeds and fruits, maize kernels and cobs, fibers, and rinds. Few archaeologists sought the origin of domestication in lowland and jungle regions, which were wrongly assumed to be infertile and where plants did not preserve well (Bryant 2003). Today, the microscopic evidence says otherwise and reveals the key role of tropical lowland regions in early New World farming.

## Explaining the Neolithic

Several factors had to converge to make domestication happen and to promote its spread. Most plants, and especially animals, aren't easy—or particularly valuable—to domesticate. Thus, of some 148 large animal species that seem potentially domesticable, only 14 actually have been domesticated. A mere dozen among 200,000 known plant species account for 80 percent of the world's farm production. Those 12 caloric staples are wheat, corn (maize), rice, barley, sorghum, soybeans, potatoes, cassava (manioc), sweet potatoes, sugarcane, sugar beets, and bananas.

Domestication rested on a combination of conditions and resources that had not come together previously. The development of a full-fledged Neolithic economy required settling down. Sedentism, such as that adopted by ancient Natufian hunter-gatherers, was especially attractive when several species of plants and animals were available locally for foraging and eventual domestication. The Middle East had such species, along with a Mediterranean climate favorable to the origin and spread of the Neolithic economy. Among those species were the easiest wild plants to domesticate, including wheat, which required few genetic changes for domestication. We've seen that the Natufians adopted sedentism prior to farming. They lived off abundant wild grain and the animals attracted to the stubble left after the harvest. Eventually, with climate change, population growth, and the need for people to sustain themselves in the marginal zones, hunter-gatherers started cultivating. In Mesoamerica, the shift from teosinte to maize required more genetic changes, so the domestication process took longer. The lack of domesticable animals in Mesoamerica, except for dogs and turkeys, also retarded the emergence of food production, sedentism, and a full-fledged Neolithic economy.

Compared with other world areas, the Middle East had the largest Mediterranean climate with the highest species diversity. As we saw previously, this was an area of vertical economy and closely packed microenvironments. Such diverse terrains and habitats concentrated in a limited area offered a multiplicity of plant species, as well as goats, sheep, pigs, and cattle. The first farmers eventually domesticated several crops: two kinds of wheat, barley, lentils, peas, and chickpeas (garbanzo beans). As in Mesoamerica, where corn (supplying carbohydrate) was supplemented by squash and beans (supplying protein), the Neolithic diet of the Middle East combined caloric staples such as wheat and barley with protein-rich pulses such as lentils, peas, and chickpeas.

Anthropologists once thought, erroneously, that domestication would happen almost automatically—once people gained sufficient knowledge of plants and animals and their reproductive habits to figure out how to make domestication work. Anthropologists now realize that foragers have an excellent knowledge of plants, animals, and their reproductive characteristics, and that some other trigger is needed to start and sustain the process of domestication. A full-fledged Neolithic economy requires a minimal set of nutritious domesticates. Some world areas, such as North America (north of Mesoamerica), managed independently to invent domestication, but the inventory of available plants and animals was too meager to maintain a Neolithic economy. The early domesticates— squash, sunflower, marsh elder, and goosefoot—had to be supplemented by hunting and gathering. A full Neolithic economy and sedentism did not develop in the east, southeast, and southwest of what is now the United States until maize diffused in from Mesoamerica— more than 3,000 years after the first domestication in the eastern United States.

## Geography and the Spread of Food Production

As Jared Diamond (1997, ch. 10) observes convincingly, the geography of the Old World facilitated the diffusion of plants, animals, technology (e.g., wheels and vehicles), and information (e.g., writing) (Ramachandran and Rosenberg 2011). Most crops in Eurasia were domesticated just once and spread rapidly in an east–west direction. The first domesticates spread from the Middle East to Egypt, North Africa, Europe, India, and eventually China (which, however, also had its own domesticates, as we have seen).

Figure 8.4 shows that Eurasia has a much broader east–west expanse than do Africa and the Americas, which are arranged north–south. This is important because climates are more likely to be similar moving across thousands of miles east–west than north–south. In Eurasia, plants and animals could easily spread east–west because of common day lengths and similar seasonal variations. More radical climatic contrasts have hindered north–south diffusion. In the Americas, for example, although the distance between the cool Mexican highlands and the South American highlands is just 1,200 miles, those two similar zones are separated by a low, hot, tropical region, which supports very different plant species than the highlands. Such environmental barriers to diffusion kept the Neolithic societies (of Mesoamerica and South America) more separate and independent in the Americas than they were in Eurasia. It took some 3,000 years for maize to reach what is now the United States, where productive Neolithic economies eventually did develop.

FIGURE 8.4   **Major Axes of the Continents**
Note the breadth of the east–west axis in Eurasia, compared with the much narrower east–west
spreads in Africa, North America, and South America. Those three continents have north–south
as their major axis.

Source: "Figure 10.1—Major Axes of the Continents," from *Guns, Germs and Steel: The Fates of Human Societies* by Jared
Diamond. Published by W. W. Norton & Company, Inc., and Jonathan Cape. Copyright © 1997 by Jared Diamond.

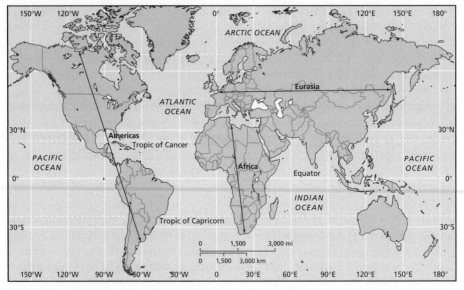

# Costs and Benefits

Neolithic economies and lifestyles had advantages and disadvantages. Among the advantages were discoveries and inventions. People eventually learned to spin and weave;
to make pottery, bricks, and arched masonry; and to smelt and cast metals. They developed trade and commerce by land and sea. By 5500 B.P., Middle Easterners were living
in vibrant cities with markets, streets, temples, and palaces. They created sculpture,
mural art, writing systems, weights, measures, mathematics, and new forms of political
and social organization.

Because it increased economic production and led to new social, scientific, and creative forms, food production often is considered an evolutionary advance. But the new
economy also brought hardships. For example, food producers typically work many
more hours than foragers do, and for a less adequate diet. Fields and irrigation systems
need care. Livestock require pens and corrals. Trade takes men, and sometimes women,
away from home, leaving burdens for those who stay behind. For several reasons, food
producers tend to have more children than foragers do. This means greater child care
demands, but child labor also tends to be more needed and valued than it is among foragers. The division of economic labor grows more complex, so that children and older
people have assigned economic roles.

# Anthropology Today  *Global Climate Change and Other Threats to Archaeology*

*Global climate change (GCC) involves not only global warming but also weather patterns that are becoming more extreme and less predictable. GCC threatens archaeological sites, and Andrew Curry (2009) highlights some of those threats, which are summarized here, in locales as diverse as the Swiss Alps, coastal Peru, Greenland, the Eurasian steppes, California's Channel Islands, and Africa's Sahara Desert.*

The Alps: Recent heat waves have melted Alpine snow and glaciers. This has been both good and bad for archaeology—good because new sites have been uncovered, bad because thawing can rot remains. In summer 2003, after a record European heat wave, a hiker high in the Alps spotted a leather quiver left there by a Neolithic hunter almost 5,000 years ago. The next summer, that hiker guided archaeologists back up the mountain, where they found a melting ice patch 260 feet long and 100 feet wide. As that ice pack shrank over two summers of fieldwork, archaeologists recovered both prehistoric and Roman remains. The finds show that people have been crossing the Alps for millennia, despite bitter cold and ice (Curry 2009).

Coastal Peru: When Spanish conquistadors arrived in Peru, they noticed a weather phenomenon that occasionally occurred around Christmas. They called it

The Peruvian village of Aguas Calientes was flooded by the Vilcanota River in January 2010. Heavy rains and mudslides that year blocked the train route to the nearby ancient Inca citadel of Machu Picchu, leaving nearly 2,000 tourists stranded. © AFP/Getty Images

*continued*

## Anthropology Today   *continued*

El Niño, or "little boy," after the Christ child. El Niño occurs every 3 to 10 years, as currents in the Pacific Ocean shift, changing global weather patterns. In Peru, El Niño brings warmer water and heavy rainfall along the coast. Peru's deserts typically get just over an inch of rain annually. In 1998, a particularly severe El Niño season, however, the region got 120 inches and serious flooding. Excess water can threaten archaeological sites, many of which are located along rivers or on easily eroded slopes (Curry 2009). Severe flooding in 2010 closed Machu Picchu, Peru's most famous ancient site, to tourism. If GCC leads to more frequent El Niño years, Peru's archaeological treasures may be further damaged.

Greenland: Violent wave action linked to GCC is destroying early coastal sites. Traditionally in summer, Greenland's coasts have been surrounded by an ice belt 30 to 40 miles wide. This drifting ice serves as a shock absorber, dampening the strength of the North Atlantic. In the past decade, however, this ice shield has virtually vanished, and Greenland's coasts are being pounded by huge waves. Most threatened are sites associated with the Thule culture, likely ancestors of the Inuit, whose members reached Greenland about 2,000 years ago. Supported by hunting and fishing, Thule villages were built close to the shore. Today, their ancient homes are disappearing, along with buried tools and artifacts (Curry 2009).

Scythian tombs: Between 3,000 and 2,200 years ago, Scythian nomads dominated the Eurasian steppes from the Black Sea in the west to China in the east. Huge Scythian burial mounds, called kurgans, have been rich resources for archaeologists. Found from Ukraine to Kazakhstan, some of the best preserved kurgans are located in the Altai Mountains, near Siberian permafrost, where the cold has protected the graves for millennia. The tombs have yielded well-preserved mummies, often with clothing, burial goods, horses, and even stomach contents intact. With GCC, as the mountains warm up and the permafrost melts, the tombs are in danger of thawing and rotting away (Curry 2009).

California's Channel Islands: Some of the early settlers of the Americas came by boat, island-hopping from Siberia down to the California coast. Some of the best evidence for this comes from the Channel Islands, which were occupied at least 13,000 years ago by settlers who hunted pygmy mammoths, elephant seals, and sea lions. Human bones found on Santa Rosa Island, radiocarbon-dated to 13,000 B.P., are the oldest human bones yet found in the Americas. At that time, the world was much colder, and the oceans much lower, than today. Rising sea levels now threaten shell middens and coastal rock shelters. As well, coastal winds, waves, storm surges, and even seals can damage coastal sites. GCC now threatens to wipe out clues about how early humans settled the Americas just as researchers have begun to focus on the likelihood of coastal migration (Curry 2009).

Sudan desertification: Encroaching desert sands increasingly threaten historic artwork at Musawwarat es-Sufra, Sudan. More than 2,000 years ago, the rulers of Meroe—a desert kingdom linked to ancient Egypt—constructed a temple complex and pilgrimage site 20 miles east of the Nile. Built of soft yellow sandstone, the walls and columns of the complex featured hieroglyphs and elaborate painted reliefs. Dominating the site was the 50-foot-long Temple of the Lion God, decorated with reliefs dedicated to the

Meroitic god of fertility. Rising temperatures and overuse have killed off the area's vegetation, and Saharan sands creep ever closer. The reliefs suffer heavily from wind erosion, because the soft sandstone abrades easily (Curry 2009).

GCC is not, of course, the only current threat to archaeological sites and research. Political events also pose risks. In 2001 in Afghanistan the Taliban destroyed a series of pre-Islamic figures, including two monumental stone Buddhas, in an attempt to stop the worship of false idols. In 2013, a group of ancient Islamic manuscripts in Mali's historic city of Timbuktu were threatened by a fire caused by fighting between Islamist militants and French troops.

Politics and regime change also can limit archaeological research. Iran and Iraq have been dangerous or off limits for decades. For on-site investigation of emerging food production and state formation in the Middle East, archaeologists turned increasingly to Syria and Turkey. The former country, too, now is off limits because of political unrest. Fortunately, previously assembled museum collections of human and animal remains outside those countries allow continuing analysis and new insights (e.g., Zeder 2008), even when national borders are closed to new fieldwork. However, archaeologists who manage museum collections increasingly must deal with nations and cultural groups who wish to repatriate remains collected, often a century ago or more, and sometimes without proper legal authorization. Can you think of other threats to archaeological sites and research?

And public health declines. Diets based on crops and dairy products tend to be less varied, less nutritious, and less healthful than foragers' diets, which usually are higher in proteins and lower in fats and carbohydrates. With the shift to food production, the physical well-being of the population often declines. Communicable diseases, protein deficiency, and dental caries increase (Cohen and Armelagos 2013).

Compared with a seminomadic foraging band, food producers tend to be sedentary. Their populations are denser, which makes it easier to transmit and maintain diseases. Malaria, sickle-cell anemia, and smallpox all spread along with food production. Population concentrations, especially cities, are breeding grounds for epidemic diseases. People live nearer other people and animals and their wastes, which also affect public health (Diamond 2005). Compared with farmers, herders, and city dwellers, foragers were relatively disease free, stress free, and well nourished.

Other hardships and stresses accompanied food production and the state. Social inequality and poverty increased. Elaborate systems of social stratification eventually replaced the egalitarianism of the past. Resources were no longer common goods, open to all, as they tend to be among foragers. Property distinctions proliferated. Slavery and other forms of human bondage eventually were invented. Crime, war, and human sacrifice became widespread.

The rate at which human beings degraded their environments also increased with food production. After food production, population increase and the need to expand farming led to deforestation in the Middle East. Many farmers and herders burn trees, brush, and pasture. Farmers burn to remove weeds and to use the ashes for fertilizer. Herders burn to promote the growth of new, tender shoots for their livestock. But such practices have environmental costs, including air pollution. Smelting and other chemical processes basic to the manufacture of metal tools also have environmental costs. Salts, chemicals, and microorganisms accumulate in irrigated fields. Pathogens and pollutants that were nonissues during the Paleolithic endanger growing human populations. To be sure, food production has benefits. But its costs are just as evident. Progress is much too optimistic a word to describe food production, the state, and many other aspects of the evolution of society.

## Summary

1. After 15,000 B.P., as the big-game supply diminished, Mesolithic foragers sought out new foods. By 11,000 B.P., domesticated plants and animals were part of a broad spectrum of resources used by Middle Easterners. By 7500 B.P., most Middle Easterners were moving away from broad-spectrum foraging toward more specialized food-producing economies. *Neolithic* refers to the period when the first signs of domestication appeared.

2. Braidwood proposed that food production started in the hilly flanks zone. Others questioned this: The wild grain supply in that zone already provided an excellent diet for the Natufians and other ancient Middle Easterners. There would have been no incentive to domesticate.

3. Ancient Middle Eastern foragers migrated seasonally in pursuit of game. They also collected wild plant foods as they ripened at different altitudes. As they moved about, these foragers took grains from the hilly flanks zone, where they grew wild, to adjacent areas. Humans became agents of selection, preferring plants with certain attributes. Population spilled over from the hilly flanks into adjacent areas like the piedmont steppe. In such marginal zones people started cultivating plants. They were trying to duplicate the dense wild grains of the hilly flanks.

4. After the harvest, sheep and goats fed off the stubble of these wild plants. Animal domestication occurred as people started selecting certain features and behavior and guiding the reproduction of goats, sheep, cattle, and pigs. Gradually, food production spread into the hilly flanks. Later, with irrigation it spread down into Mesopotamia's alluvial desert, where the first cities, states, and civilizations developed by 5500 B.P. Food production then spread west from the Middle East into North Africa and Europe and east to India and Pakistan.

5. There were at least seven independent inventions of food production: in the Middle East, sub-Saharan Africa, northern and southern China, Mesoamerica, the south central Andes, and the eastern United States.

6. In the New World, the most important domesticates were maize, potatoes, and manioc. The llama of the central Andes was the largest animal domesticated in the New World, where herding traditions analogous to those of the Old World did not develop. Economic similarities between the hemispheres must be sought in foraging and farming.

7. New World farming started in the lowlands of South America, then spread to Central America, Mexico, and the Caribbean islands. Tropical lowland cultivation in Central and South America began at about the same time as food production arose in the Middle East—around 10,000 years ago. By 7000 B.P., farming was diffusing from tropical lowlands into drier regions at higher elevations. The specific ancestor of maize, teosinte, grows wild in tropical southwestern Mexico, where maize probably was domesticated around 8000 B.P.

8. Several factors, including a diversity of useful plant and animal species and early sedentism, combined to promote early domestication in the ancient Middle East. The first domesticates spread rapidly across Eurasia, facilitated by climatic similarities across a broad territorial expanse. In the Americas, food production spread less rapidly because of north–south contrasts. Another factor that slowed the Neolithic transition in the Americas was the lack of large animals suitable for domestication.

9. Food production and the social and political system it supported brought advantages and disadvantages. The advantages included discoveries and inventions. The disadvantages included harder work, poorer health, crime, war, social inequality, and environmental degradation.

## Key Terms

broad-spectrum
  revolution, *171*
hilly flanks, *174*
maize, *184*

manioc, *184*
Mesoamerica, *177*
Mesolithic, *171*
Natufians, *176*

Neolithic, *174*
sedentism, *176*
teosinte, *185*

# Chapter 9

# The First Cities and States

## The Origin of the State

As Neolithic economies spread, diversified, and became more productive, new political entities, or *polities* (singular *polity*), developed to manage them. The major new political forms were chiefdoms and states. A **state** is a form of social and political organization that has a formal, central government and a division of society into classes. The first states had developed in Mesopotamia by 5500 B.P. and in Mesoamerica some 3,000 years later. *Chiefdoms* were precursors to states, with privileged and effective leaders—chiefs—but lacking the sharp class divisions that characterize states. By 7000 B.P. in the Middle East and 3200 B.P. in Mesoamerica, there is evidence for what archaeologists call the elite level, indicating a chiefdom or a state (see Podany 2014).

How and why did these new polities originate? Compared with foraging, Neolithic economies could support larger and denser populations. Also, the complexity of the division of social and economic labor tended to grow as food production spread and intensified. Systems of political authority and control typically develop to handle regulatory problems encountered as the population grows and the economy increases in scale and diversity.

**Primary states** are states that arose on their own, not through contact with other state societies (Wright 1994). Also called *archaic* states or *first-generation* states, primary states emerged from competition among chiefdoms, as one chiefdom managed to conquer its neighbors and to make them part of a larger political unit (Stanish and Levine 2011). Scholars have documented the process of state formation in at least six areas where first-generation states developed, including Egypt, Mesopotamia, the Indus River Valley, northern China, Mesoamerica, and the Andes (Millaire 2010; Nagle 2014; Renfrew 2014).

A systemic, regional perspective is necessary to understand any case of state formation. Primary states emerge from a regional process that requires an extended period of interaction among competing polities (Stanish and Levine 2011). Furthermore, multiple factors always contribute to state formation, with the effects of one magnifying those of the others.

## Hydraulic Systems

One factor favoring state formation has been the need to regulate *hydraulic* (water-based) agricultural economies (Wittfogel 1957). In arid areas, such as ancient Egypt and Mesopotamia, a key role of state officials was to manage systems of irrigation, drainage, and flood control. Hydraulic agriculture spurs state formation because it has certain implications. Because it can feed more people, while requiring more labor, irrigated agriculture sustains and fuels population growth, which in turn promotes expansion of the system. With larger and denser concentrations of people, the potential grows for conflict over access to water and irrigated land. Political authorities typically arise to regulate production, as well as to manage interpersonal and intergroup relations. Regulators protect the economy by mobilizing crews to maintain and repair the hydraulic system, and they settle disputes about access to water. These life-and-death functions enhance the authority of state officials. Thus, growth in hydraulic systems is often (as in Mesopotamia, Egypt, and the Valley of Mexico) but not always associated with state formation.

## Regional Trade

Charles Stanish and Abigail Levine (2011) emphasize regional trade as another key factor in primary state formation. States may arise to control and regulate key nodes in regional trade networks. Examples include crossroads of caravan routes and places (e.g., mountain passes and river narrows) situated such that they may threaten trade between centers. Long-distance trade has been important in the formation of many states, including those of Mesopotamia and Mesoamerica (Hirth and Pillsbury 2013). Systems of regional exchange develop eventually in all states, but long-distance trade sometimes follows, rather than preceding, state formation. As well, long-distance trade exists in societies where no states developed, such as in Papua New Guinea.

## Population, War, and Circumscription

Robert Carneiro (1970) proposed that three key factors work together to produce state formation. Those factors are *environmental circumscription, increasing population,* and *warfare.* Environmental circumscription may be physical or social. Physically circumscribed environments include small islands and, in arid areas, river plains, oases, and valleys with streams. Social circumscription exists when neighboring societies block expansion, emigration, or access to resources. When resources are concentrated in limited areas—even when no obstacles to migration exist—the effects are similar to those of circumscription.

Coastal Peru, usually one of the world's most arid areas, illustrates the interaction of environmental circumscription, warfare, and population increase. The earliest cultivation there was limited to valleys with springs. Each valley was circumscribed by the Andes Mountains to the east, the Pacific Ocean to the west, and desert regions to the north and south (see Millaire 2010). The advent of food production triggered population increase, leading to bigger villages in each valley. Colonists split off from the old villages and founded new ones. With more villages and people, a scarcity of land developed. Rivalries and raiding developed among villages in the same valley.

Because the valleys were circumscribed, when one village conquered another, the losers had to submit to the winners—they had nowhere else to go. Conquered villagers were allowed to keep their land only by paying tribute to their conquerors. To do this, they had to intensify production, using new techniques to produce more food. By working harder, they managed to pay tribute while meeting their own subsistence needs. Villagers brought new areas under cultivation by means of irrigation and terracing.

Those early Peruvians didn't work harder because they chose to do so. They were *forced* to pay tribute, accept political domination, and intensify production by factors beyond their control. Once established, all these trends accelerated. Population continued to grow, warfare intensified, and villages eventually were united in chiefdoms. The first states developed when one chiefdom in a valley conquered the others (Carneiro 1990). Eventually, different valleys began to fight. The winners brought the losers into growing states and empires, which eventually expanded from the coast to the highlands. By the 16th century, from their capital, Cuzco, in the high Andes, the Inca ruled one of the major empires of the tropics (see Kolata 2015).

Supporting Carneiro's theory is the fact that the association between population density, warfare, and state formation extends beyond Peru. But there are exceptions. In highland Papua New Guinea, for example, valleys that were socially or physically circumscribed had population densities close to those of many states. Warfare also was present, but no states emerged. Whether states would have formed eventually will never be known, because European conquest truncated autonomous development there.

In any case of state formation, interacting causes (often comparable ones) magnified each other's effects. Key ingredients in state formation are changes in patterns of control over resources, resulting in social stratification, and increasing regulatory concerns, fostering management by state machinery. We must remember, too, that chiefdoms and states don't inevitably arise from food production. Many societies maintained Neolithic economies without ever developing chiefdoms or states. Similarly there are chiefdoms that never developed into states, just as certain foragers never adopted food production, even when they knew about it.

# The Urban Revolution

It was V. Gordon Childe (1951), one of the most influential archaeologists of the 20th century, who coined the phrase "Neolithic Revolution" to describe the origin and impact of food production. He chose the term *revolution* deliberately, because he wanted to compare the major social transformations of prehistory (food production and the state) to the Industrial Revolution (Smith 2009). Childe used the phrase "Urban Revolution" (1950) to describe the major transformation of human life and social institutions examined in this chapter. Key features were that institutions of government, including rulers with real power, emerged for the first time, along with social stratification. As a result of the Urban Revolution, economic activity of all sorts expanded greatly, and the first cities were built. On the downside, former freedoms and independence were replaced by servitude, taxes, rules, and regulations (Smith 2009).

Childe listed 10 key attributes of early cities and states—all supported by archaeological evidence. They may be paraphrased as follows:

1. The first cities were larger and more densely populated than previous settlements.
2. Within the city were full-time specialists, including craftsmen, transport workers, merchants, officials, and priests.
3. Each primary producer (e.g., farmer) had to pay a tithe or tax to a deity or a divine king; those contributions were stored in a central place, such as a temple or treasury.
4. Monumental buildings distinguished cities from villages while symbolizing the right of rulers to draw on the treasury and to command a labor force.
5. Supported by the treasury, priests, civil officials, and military leaders made up a ruling class.
6. Writing was used for record keeping.
7. Predictive sciences developed, including arithmetic, geometry, and astronomy.
8. Sophisticated art styles developed, expressed in sculpture, painting, and architecture.
9. There was long-distance and foreign trade.
10. Society was reorganized on the basis of territorial divisions (where one lived) rather than kinship groups.

Cities and writing were key features of Childe's Urban Revolution (1950). In and after the 1960s, however, anthropologists shifted to such phrases as "the origin of the state" and "state formation" for this process. Use of such terms, which continues today, recognizes that some instances of state formation lack writing and significant urbanism (see Feder 2013; Peregrine, Ember, and Ember 2007; Spencer and Redmond 2004).

# Attributes of States

Childe's list of 10 defining attributes of the Urban Revolution aptly describes the first states in Mesopotamia and Egypt (see Lloyd 2015). Something a bit less specific, however, is needed to characterize all states, including those without writing. Most anthropologists today probably would agree that the following attributes (from Fagan 1996; some shared with Childe's list) distinguish states from earlier forms of society:

1. A state controls a specific territory, such as the Nile Valley or the Valley of Mexico. The state's large expanse contrasts with the much smaller territories controlled by kin groups and villages in prestate societies.

2. Early states had productive farming economies, supporting dense populations, often including cities. The agricultural economies of early states often depended on some form of water control or irrigation.

3. Early states used tribute and taxation to accumulate, at a central place or treasury, resources needed to support hundreds, or thousands, of specialists. These states had rulers, a military, and control over human labor.

4. States are stratified into social classes. In the first states, the non-food-producing population consisted of a tiny elite, plus artisans, officials, priests, and other specialists. Most people were commoners. Slaves and prisoners constituted the lowest rung of the social ladder. Rulers stayed in power by combining personal ability, religious authority, economic control, and force.

5. Early states had imposing public buildings and monumental architecture, including temples, palaces, and storehouses.

6. Early states developed some form of record-keeping system, frequently a written script.

Early states had hereditary rulers and a military, with the rulers often playing a military role. Rulers stayed in power by combining personal ability, religious authority, economic control, and the privileged use of force. Shown here is a detail from the painted casket of Egypt's Tutankhamun, the famous "King Tut," who ruled between 1347 and 1337 B.C.E. © Roger Wood/Corbis

# State Formation in the Middle East

In the previous chapter we saw that food production arose around 11,000 B.P. In the Middle East, in the ensuing process of change, the center of population growth shifted from the zone where wheat and barley grew wild (hilly flanks) to adjacent areas (piedmont steppe) where those grains were first domesticated. By 6000 B.P., population was increasing most rapidly in the alluvial plain of southern Mesopotamia. (**Mesopotamia** refers to the area between the Tigris and Euphrates Rivers in what is now southern Iraq and southwestern Iran.) This growing population supported itself through irrigation and intensive river valley agriculture. By 5500 B.P. towns had grown into cities (Gates 2003). The earliest city-states were Sumer (southern Iraq) and Elam (southwestern Iran), with their capitals at Uruk (Warka) and Susa, respectively.

## Urban Life

The first towns arose around 10,000 years ago in the Middle East. Over the generations houses of mud brick were built and rebuilt in the same place. Substantial *tells,* or mounds, arose from the debris of a succession of such houses (see Menez and Ur 2012). The Middle East and Asia have thousands of such mounds, only a few of which have been excavated. These sites have yielded remains of ancient community life, including streets, buildings, terraces, courtyards, wells, and other artifacts.

The earliest known town was Jericho, located in what now is Israel, below sea level at a well-watered oasis (see Figure 9.1). From the lowest (oldest) level, we know that around 11,000 years ago, Jericho was chosen as a settlement site by Natufian foragers. Occupation continued thereafter, through and beyond biblical times, when "Joshua fit the battle of Jericho, and the walls came tumbling down" (Laughlin 2006).

During the phase just after the Natufians, the earliest known town appeared. It was an unplanned, densely populated settlement with round houses and some 2,000 people. At that time, Jericho was surrounded by a sturdy wall, with a massive tower. The wall may have been built initially as a flood barrier rather than for defense. Around 9000 B.P. Jericho was destroyed, to be rebuilt later. The new occupants lived in square houses with finished plaster floors. They buried their dead beneath their homes, a pattern also seen at other sites, such as Çatal Hüyük in Turkey. Pottery reached Jericho around 8000 B.P.

Long-distance trade, especially of obsidian, a volcanic glass used to make tools and ornaments, became important in the Middle East between 9500 and 7000 B.P. One town that prospered from this trade was Çatal Hüyük in Anatolia, Turkey (Fowler 2011; Hodder 2006). A grassy mound 65 feet (20 meters) high holds the remains of this 9,000-year-old town, probably the largest settlement of the Neolithic age. Çatal Hüyük was located on a river, which deposited rich soil for crops, created a lush environment for animals, and was harnessed for irrigation by 7000 B.P. Over the mound's 32 acres (12.9 hectares), up to 10,000 people once lived in crowded mud-brick houses packed so tightly that residents entered from their roofs.

Shielded by a defensive wall, Çatal Hüyük flourished between 8000 and 7000 B.P. Its individual mud-brick dwellings had separate areas reserved for ritual and secular uses.

FIGURE 9.1    **Sites in Middle Eastern State Formation**

In a given house, the ritual images (wall paintings) were placed along the walls that faced north, east, or west, but never south. That area was reserved for cooking and other domestic tasks. People entered the dwellings at Çatal Hüyük through the roof, then had to crawl through holes from room to room.

Two or three generations of a family were buried beneath their homes. In one dwelling, archaeologists found remains of 17 individuals, mostly children. After two or three generations of family burials, the dwelling was burned. The site was then covered with fine dirt and a floor laid for a new dwelling.

Çatal Hüyük's residents, though living in a town, acted independently in family groups without any apparent control by a priestly or political elite. The town never became a full-fledged city with centralized organization. Just as it lacked priests, Çatal Hüyük never had leaders who controlled or managed trade and production. Food was stored and processed not collectively but on a smaller, domestic scale.

## The Elite Level

The first Middle Eastern pottery (ceramics) dates back a bit more than 8,000 years, when it first reached Jericho. By 7000 B.P., pottery had become widespread in the region. Archaeologists consider pottery shape, finishing, decoration, and type of clay as features used for dating. The geographic distribution of a given pottery style may indicate trade or alliance spanning a large area at a particular time.

An aerial view of, and a photo of excavation at, the 9,000 year old site of Çatal Hüyük in Anatolia, Turkey. Inhabitants of this early town lived in crowded mud-brick houses packed so tightly that residents entered from their roofs. © Images & Stories/Alamy

An early and widespread pottery style, the **Halafian,** was first found at Tell Halaf in the mountains of northern Syria. *Halafian* (7500–6000 B.P.) refers to a delicate ceramic style. It also describes the period during which the elite level and the first chiefdoms emerged. The low number of Halafian ceramics suggests they were luxury goods associated with a social hierarchy.

By 7000 B.P. chiefdoms had emerged in the Middle East. The Ubaid period (7000–6000 B.P.) is named for a southern Mesopotamian pottery type first discovered at a small site, Tell el-Ubaid, located near the major city of Ur in southern Iraq. Ubaid pottery is associated with advanced chiefdoms and perhaps the earliest states. It diffused rapidly over a large area, becoming much more widespread than the earlier Halafian style.

Archaeological research focusing on the Ubaid period in northern Syria has found evidence for emerging urbanism dating back more than 6,000 years. At a site known as Tell Zeidan, American and Syrian investigators uncovered an array of artifacts from an early town on the upper Euphrates River. People occupied this site for two millennia, until 6000 B.P. The site featured houses with mud-brick walls, floors with hearths, painted pottery, stone seals, kilns, and obsidian blades. There also is evidence suggesting the emergence of irrigated agriculture, long-distance trade, political leadership, and social differentiation (Wilford 2010).

For a time, although blocked by war and politics from Iraq and Iran (with their prime sites of Mesopotamian antiquity), archaeologists could still work in Syria. They turned their attention to the upper river valleys, across the border from Iraq in Syria and southern Turkey (see Hodder 2006; Wilford 2010). Unfortunately, recent political chaos in Syria has impeded the continuation of archaeological research there, leaving Turkey as today's prime locus for research on Neolithic transformations and the emergence of social complexity in the Middle East (see Özdogan, Başgelen, and Kuniholm 2011).

## Social Ranking and Chiefdoms

Middle Eastern state formation can be traced to the end of the Ubaid period, along with evidence for regional warfare (Stanish and Levine 2011). States are easy to identify archaeologically because they leave behind monumental architecture, central storehouses, irrigation systems, and written records. Chiefdoms also can be easy to detect archaeologically when, as in Mesoamerica, they leave behind stone works, such as temple complexes and the huge, carved Olmec heads. Ancient Mesoamericans also had a penchant for marking their elites with durable ornaments and prestige goods, including those buried with chiefs and their families (Flannery 1999).

The first Middle Eastern states developed between 6000 and 5500 B.P. The first chiefdoms emerged during the preceding 1,500 years. In the Middle East, the archaeological record of the period after 7300 B.P. reveals behavior typical of chiefdoms, including exotic goods used as markers of status, along with raiding and political instability. Early Middle Eastern chiefdoms included both the Halafian culture of northern Iraq and the Ubaid culture of southern Iraq, which eventually spread north.

As in Mesoamerica, ancient Middle Eastern chiefdoms had cemeteries where chiefly relatives were buried with distinctive items: vessels, statuettes, necklaces, and high-quality ceramics. Such goods were buried with children too young to have earned prestige on their own but who happened to be born into elite families. In the ancient village of Tell es-Sawwan, infant graves show a continuum of richness from six statuettes, to three statuettes, to one statuette, to none. Such signs of slight gradations in social status are exactly what one expects in early chiefdoms.

Based on the kinds of status distinctions that can exist in a society, Morton Fried (1960) divided societies into three types: egalitarian, ranked, and stratified. An **egalitarian society,** most typically found among foragers, lacks status distinctions except for those based on age, gender, and individual qualities, talents, and achievements. Thus, depending on the society, adult men, elder women, talented musicians, or ritual specialists might receive special respect for their activities or knowledge. In egalitarian societies, status distinctions usually are not inherited.

**Ranked societies,** in contrast, do have hereditary inequality. But they lack **stratification** (sharp social divisions—*strata*—based on unequal access to wealth and power) into noble and commoner classes. In ranked societies, individuals tend to be ranked in terms of their genealogical distance from the chief. The closer one is to the chief, the higher one's rank or social status. But there is a continuum of status, with many people ranked about equally, which can lead to competition for positions of leadership.

Not all ranked societies are chiefdoms. Carneiro (1991) has distinguished between two kinds of ranked societies, only the second of which is a chiefdom. In the first type, exemplified by certain indigenous groups in North America's Pacific Northwest, there were hereditary differences in rank among individuals, but villages were independent of one another and not ranked in relation to each other. Exemplifying the second type were the Cauca of Colombia and the Natchez of the southeastern United States. These ranked societies had become **chiefdoms,** societies in which relations among villages as well as among individuals were unequal. The smaller villages had lost their autonomy and were under the authority of leaders who lived at larger villages. According to Kent Flannery (1999), *only those ranked societies with such loss of village autonomy should be called chiefdoms.* In chiefdoms, there always is inequality—differences in rank—among both individuals and communities (see Flannery and Marcus 2012).

Archaeological evidence for social differentiation in burials convinces Flannery (1999) that hereditary status differences were present in the Middle East by 7000 B.P. But had the leaders of large villages extended their authority to the smaller villages nearby? Is there evidence for the loss of village autonomy, converting simple ranked societies into chiefdoms? One clue that villages were linked in political units is the use of a common canal to irrigate several villages. This suggests a way of resolving disputes among farmers over access to water, for example, by appeal to a strong leader. By later Halafian times in northern Mesopotamia, there is evidence for such multivillage alliances (Flannery 1999). Another clue to the loss of village autonomy is the emergence of a two-tier settlement hierarchy, with small villages clustering around a large village, especially one with public buildings. There is evidence for this pattern in northern Mesopotamia during the Halafian period.

## The Rise of the State

In southern Mesopotamia by 5700 B.P., an expanding population and increased food production from irrigation were drastically altering the social landscape. Irrigation had allowed Ubaid communities to spread along the Euphrates River. Travel and trade were expanding, with water serving as the highway system. Such raw materials as hardwood and stone, which southern Mesopotamia lacked, were imported via river routes. Population density increased as new settlements appeared. Riverine social and economic networks now linked communities in the south and in the foothills to the north. Settlements spread north into what is now Syria. Social differentials also increased. Priests and political leaders joined expert potters and other artisans. These specialists were supported by the larger population of farmers and herders (Gilmore-Lehne 2000).

Economies were being managed by central leadership. Cities had emerged, some ruled by local kings. The Uruk period (6000–5200 B.P.), which succeeded the Ubaid period, takes its name from a prominent southern city-state (see Table 9.1). The Uruk period established Mesopotamia as "the cradle of civilization."

The first writing, which originated in Sumer, southern Mesopotamia, presumably developed to handle record keeping, for example, of trade transactions. Rulers, nobles, priests, and merchants were the first to benefit from it. Writing had spread from Mesopotamia to

TABLE 9.1   **Archaeological Periods in Middle Eastern State Formation**

| Dates | Period | Age |
|---|---|---|
| 3000–2539 B.P. | Neo-Babylonian | Iron Age |
| 3600–3000 B.P. | Kassite | |
| 4000–3600 B.P. | Old Babylonian | Bronze Age |
| 4150–4000 B.P. | Third Dynasty of Ur | |
| 4350–4150 B.P. | Akkadian | |
| 4600–4350 B.P. | Early Dynastic III | |
| 4750–4600 B.P. | Early Dynastic II | |
| 5000–4750 B.P. | Early Dynastic I | |
| 5200–5000 B.P. | Jemdet Nasr | |
| 6000–5200 B.P. | Uruk | Chalcolithic |
| 7500–6000 B.P. | Ubaid (southern Mesopotamia)–Halaf (northern Mesopotamia) | |
| 10,000–7000 B.P. | | Neolithic |

Egypt by 5000 B.P. The earliest writing was pictographic, for example, with pictorial symbols of horses used to represent them. Early Mesopotamian scribes used a stylus (writing implement) to scrawl symbols on raw clay. This writing left a wedge-shaped impression on the clay, called **cuneiform** writing, from the Latin word for "wedge." Both the Sumerian (southern Mesopotamia) and Akkadian (northern Mesopotamia) languages were written in cuneiform.

Writing and temples played key roles in the Mesopotamian economy. For the historic period after 5600 B.P., when writing was invented, there are temple records of economic activities. States can exist without writing, but literacy facilitates the flow and storage of information. As the economy expanded, trade, manufacture, herding, and grain storage were centrally managed. Temples collected and distributed meat, dairy products, crops, fish, clothing, tools, and trade items. Potters, metalworkers, weavers, sculptors, and other artisans perfected their crafts.

Prior to the invention of **metallurgy** (knowledge of the properties of metals, including their extraction and processing and the manufacture of metal tools), raw copper was shaped by hammering. If copper is hammered too long, it hardens and becomes brittle, with a risk of cracking. But once heated (annealed) in a fire, copper becomes malleable again. Such annealing of copper was an early form of metallurgy. A vital step for metallurgy was the discovery of **smelting,** the high-temperature process by which pure metal is produced from an ore. Ores, including copper ore, have a much wider distribution than does native copper, which initially was traded as a luxury good because of its rarity.

When and how smelting was discovered is unknown. But after 5000 B.P., metallurgy evolved rapidly. The Bronze Age began when alloys of arsenic and copper, or tin and copper (in both cases known as **bronze**), became common and greatly extended the use of metals. Bronze flows more easily than copper does when heated to a similar temperature, so bronze was more convenient for metal casting. Early molds were carved in stone, as shaped depressions to be filled with molten metal. A copper ax cast from such a mold has been found in northern Mesopotamia and predates 5000 B.P. Thereafter, other metals came into common use. By 4500 B.P., golden objects were being placed in royal burials at Ur.

Early Mesopotamian scribes used a stylus to scrawl symbols on raw clay. This writing, called *cuneiform*, left a wedge-shaped impression on the clay. What languages were written in cuneiform?
© imageBROKER/Alamy

Iron ore is distributed more widely than is copper ore. Iron, when smelted, can be used on its own; there is no need for tin or arsenic to make a metal alloy (bronze). The Iron Age began once high-temperature iron smelting was mastered. In the Old World after 3200 B.P. iron spread rapidly. Formerly valued as highly as gold, iron crashed in value when it became plentiful.

The Mesopotamian economy, based on intensive agriculture, craft production, and trade, spurred population growth and an increase in urbanism. Sumerian cities were protected by a fortress wall and surrounded by a farming area. By 4800 B.P., Uruk, the largest early Mesopotamian city, had a population of 50,000. As irrigation and the population expanded, communities fought over water. People sought protection in the fortified cities (Adams 2008), which could defend themselves when threatened.

By 4600 B.P., secular authority had replaced temple rule. The office of military coordinator developed into kingship. This change shows up architecturally in palaces and royal tombs. The palace raised armies and supplied them with armor, chariots, and metal armaments. At Ur's royal cemetery, by 4600 B.P. monarchs were being buried with soldiers, charioteers, and ladies in waiting. These subordinates were killed at the time of royal burial to accompany the monarch to the afterworld.

Agricultural intensification made it possible for the number of people supported by a given area to increase. Population pressure on irrigated fields helped create a stratified society. Land became scarce private property that was bought and sold. Some people amassed large estates, and their wealth set them off from ordinary farmers. These landlords joined the urban elite, while sharecroppers and serfs toiled in the fields. By 4600 B.P., Mesopotamia had a well-defined class structure, with complex stratification into nobles, commoners, and slaves.

## Other Early States

In northwestern India and Pakistan, the Indus River Valley (or *Harappan*) state, with major cities at Harappa and Mohenjo-daro, takes its name from the river valley along which it extended. (Figure 9.2 maps the four great early river valley states of the Old World: Mesopotamia, Egypt, India/Pakistan, and northern China.) Trade and the spread of writing from Mesopotamia may have played a role in the emergence of the Harappan state around 4600 B.P. Located in Pakistan's Punjab Province, the ruins of Harappa were the first to be identified as part of the Indus River Valley civilization. At its peak, the Indus River Valley state incorporated 1,000 cities, towns, and villages, spanning 280,000 square miles (725,000 square kilometers). This state flourished between 4600 and 3900 B.P. It displayed such features of state organization as urban planning, social stratification, and an early writing system, which remains undeciphered. The Harappans maintained a uniform system of weights, and their cities had carefully planned residential areas with wastewater systems. An array of products from sophisticated craft industries included ceramic vessels made on potters' wheels (Meadow and Kenoyer 2000).

The Indus River Valley state collapsed, apparently through warfare, around 3900 B.P. Its cities became largely depopulated. Skeletons of massacre victims have been found in

## FIGURE 9.2   The Four Great Early River Valley States of the Old World

By approximately 4000 B.P. urban life had been established along the Tigris and Euphrates Rivers in Mesopotamia, the Nile River in Egypt, the Indus and Ganges Rivers in India/Pakistan, and the Yellow River in China.

Source: A. M. Craig, W. A. Graham, D. M. Kagan, S. Ozment, and F. M. Turner, *Heritage of World Civilizations, Volume 1 to 1650*, 4th ed., map 1-1. Copyright © 1997.

the streets of Mohenjo-daro. Harappa continued to be occupied, but on a much smaller scale than previously (Meadow and Kenoyer 2000).

The first Chinese state, dating to 3750 B.P., was that of the Shang dynasty. It arose in the Huang He (Yellow) River area of northern China, where wheat had become the dietary staple. This state was characterized by urbanism, palatial (as well as domestic) architecture, human sacrifice, and a sharp division between social classes. Burials of the aristocracy were marked by ornaments of stone, including jade. The Shang had bronze metallurgy and an elaborate writing system. In warfare they used chariots and took prisoners (Gowlett 1993; Trigger 2003).

Like Mesopotamia and China, many early civilizations came to rely on metallurgy. At Nok Nok Tha in northern Thailand, metalworking goes back 6,000 years. In Peru's Andes, metalworking appeared around 4000 B.P. The ancient inhabitants of the Andes were skilled workers of bronze, copper, and gold. They also are well known for their techniques of pottery manufacture. Their arts, crafts, and agricultural knowledge compared well with those of Mesoamerica at its height, to which we now turn. Note that both Mesoamerican and Andean state formation were truncated by Spanish conquest. The Aztecs of Mexico were conquered in 1519 C.E. (formerly A.D.); the Inca of Peru, in 1532 (see Marcus and Williams 2009; Quitter 2014).

Overlooking the Indus River Valley, where an ancient civilization flourished between 4600 and 3900 B.P., ruins of India's Lamayuru Monastery occupy the higher part of a hill, with local houses below, closer to the road. © David Samuel Robbins/Corbis

# State Formation in Mesoamerica

In the previous chapter we examined the independent inventions of farming in the Middle East and Mesoamerica. The processes of state formation that took place in these areas also were comparable, beginning with ranked societies and chiefdoms and ending with fully formed states and empires. The first monumental buildings (temple complexes) in the Western Hemisphere were constructed by Mesoamerican chiefdoms in many areas, from the Valley of Mexico to Guatemala (see Evans 2013). These chiefdoms influenced one another as they traded materials, such as obsidian, shells, jade, and pottery. (Figure 9.3 maps major sites in the emergence of Mesoamerican food production, chiefdoms, and states.)

## Early Chiefdoms and Elites

The Olmec built a series of ritual centers on Mexico's southern Gulf Coast between 3,200 and 2,500 years ago. Three of these centers, each from a different century, are known. Earthen mounds were grouped into plaza complexes, presumably for religious use. Such centers show that Olmec chiefs could marshal human labor to construct such mounds. The Olmec also were master sculptors; they carved massive stone heads, perhaps as images of their chiefs or their ancestors.

The Olmec are famous for those carved images, but other early Mexican chiefdoms also had accomplished artists and builders, who used adobes and lime plaster and

FIGURE 9.3   **Major Sites in the Emergence of Food Production and the State in Mesoamerica**

Source: C. J. Jolly and R. White, *Physical Anthropology and Archaeology*, 5th ed., p. 115. Copyright © 1995. Reprinted by permission of the McGraw-Hill Companies.

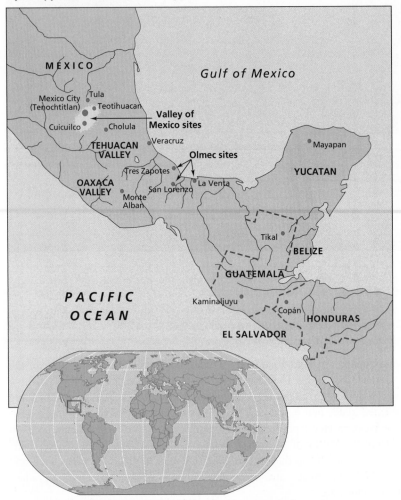

constructed stone buildings, precisely oriented 8 degrees north of east. The period between 3200 and 3000 B.P. was one of rapid social change in Mexico. Mesoamerica's chiefdoms were linked by trade and exchange. Many competing chiefly centers were intensifying agriculture, exchanging trade goods, and borrowing ideas, including art motifs and styles, from each other. Archaeologists now believe it was the *intensity of competitive interaction*—rather than the supremacy of any one chiefdom—that made social change so rapid. The social and political landscape of Mexico around 3000 B.P. was one in which 25 or so chiefly centers were (1) sufficiently separate and autonomous to adapt to local zones and conditions and (2) sufficiently interacting and competitive to borrow and incorporate new ideas and innovations as they arose in other regions (Flannery and Marcus 2000).

It used to be thought that a single chiefdom could develop into a state on its own. Archaeologists know now that state formation typically involves one chiefdom's incorporating several others into the emerging state it controls, and making changes in its own infrastructure as it acquires and retains new territories, followers, and goods. Waging warfare and attracting followers are two key elements in state formation (see Stanish and Levine 2011).

Many chiefdoms have dense populations, intensive agriculture, and settlement hierarchies that include hamlets, villages, and perhaps towns. These factors pave the way for greater social and political complexity. Political leaders emerge, and military success often solidifies their position. Such figures attract lots of followers, who are loyal to their leader. Success in warfare leads to states becoming even more densely occupied and in control of new lands and resources. States, unlike chiefdoms, can acquire labor and land and hold on to them. States have armies, warfare, developed political hierarchies, law codes, and military force, which can be used in fact or as a threat.

The Olmec area and Mexico's Oaxaca Valley (located in the highlands due west of the Olmec sites—see Figure 9.3) were two among several locales where flamboyant early Mexican chiefdoms developed. Oaxaca and other highland areas eventually came to overshadow the Olmec area and the lowlands in general (see Nichols and Pool 2012). The first Mesoamerican state, **Zapotec,** had emerged in the Oaxaca Valley by about 2100 B.P. The Zapotecs developed a distinctive art style, perfected at their capital city of Monte Alban. The Zapotec state lasted until it—along with the rest of Mexico— was conquered by Spain (see Marcus and Flannery 2003*a*). Warfare played a key role in its formation.

## Warfare and State Formation: The Zapotec Case

The city of Monte Alban served as capital of the Zapotec polity for *twelve hundred years,* between 500 B.C.E. and 700 C.E. (The Zapotec polity was a chiefdom from ca. 500 B.C.E. to 100 B.C.E., and after that a state.) Kent Flannery and Joyce Marcus (2003*b*) describe the archaeological evidence for changing warfare patterns in Oaxaca—from early raiding among sedentary villages to warfare aimed at conquest between 330 and 20 B.C.E. (formerly B.C.).

The oldest defensive palisade in the Valley of Oaxaca dates back over 3,000 years, just a few centuries after village life was established there. Over the next millennium, raiding evolved into war, with homes and temples burned, captives killed, and populations relocating to defensible hills. A monument from the site of San José Mogote, dating no later than 2500 B.P. (500 B.C.E.), is the earliest reliably dated monument with writing in Mesoamerica. It depicts a named, sacrificed captive, likely a rival chief and a probable victim of intervillage raiding. Armed conflict in Oaxaca began as raiding, with killing, burning, and captive taking but no permanent acquisition of territory. By the time the Spanish conquistadors arrived in the 16th century, however, the Zapotec state was exacting tribute from conquered territories (Flannery and Marcus 2003*b*).

The shift from raiding to warfare aimed at territorial conquest occurred prior to 300 B.C.E. This shift has been documented by hieroglyphs, surveys, and excavations. As Charles Spencer (2003) notes, the first evidence for Oaxacan conquest warfare occurs simultaneously with evidence for emerging state organization. This co-occurrence supports the idea of a causal link between conquest warfare and state formation.

Long ago, Henry Wright (1977) described the state as a society with not only a centralized but also an internally specialized administrative organization—a bureaucracy. Chiefdoms, by contrast, lack administrative specialization. States have at least four levels of decision making (Wright 1977). The center, or capital, creates subsidiary administrative centers. The result is a nested structure of secondary, tertiary, and even quaternary centers. Population size tends to follow this administrative structure: States typically have at least a four-level hierarchy of settlements according to both administrative functions and population size. Chiefdoms have no more than three levels (Spencer 2003).

To expand, a state must send delegates, such as soldiers, governors, and other officials, to subjugate and rule in distant territories. Lacking a group of bureaucrats, chiefdoms can't do this, which means that the geographic range of chiefly authority is smaller than in a state. According to Spencer (2003), the limit of a chiefdom's range is half a day's travel from its center. States, however, can transcend such limits and carry out long-distance conquests. Archaeological evidence for conquest warfare includes burned and abandoned villages, specialized forts and administrative outposts, and forced changes in the economic, social, and religious behaviors of subjugated peoples.

Expansion through conquest can play a key role in the formation of a primary state by building the administrative hierarchy. Subjugation of polities in other regions, coupled with regularized tribute exaction, can bring about a transition from chiefdom to state (Spencer 2003). For such a strategy to succeed (especially when the conquered polities lie more than a half-day's trip away), the leadership will have to dispatch agents to the conquered areas. Generals and bureaucrats are needed not only to carry out the subjugation but also to maintain long-term control and to manage tribute collection. Given its need to rely on distant representatives, the central leadership promotes internal administrative specialization and loyalty. Tribute provides new resources to support this administrative transformation. The conquest of distant polities and bureaucratic growth were integral parts of the process of Zapotec state formation.

Typically, state bureaucracies occupy a group of administrative buildings, especially at the capital. Surrounding the Main Plaza at Monte Alban were specialized buildings, including palaces, temples, and ball courts. Hieroglyphs on one building in Monte Alban's Main Plaza record how outlying areas were acquired, often by conquest. We learn that Monte Alban did not expand its rule in a concentric fashion. Although it had managed to subjugate distant regions to the north, west, and southwest by approximately 300 B.C.E., certain areas to the east and south managed to resist for centuries. For example, Monte Alban burned its chief rival, San Martín Tilcajete, a day's travel to the south, around 330 B.C.E., but its people refused to capitulate. They rebuilt their community and constructed defensive walls at a higher location. They continued to resist Monte Alban until roughly 20 B.C.E., when they finally succumbed.

Three of more than 300 carved stones depicting slain war captives at the important archaeological site of Monte Alban, Oaxaca, Mexico. Dated to 500–400 B.C.E., these images originally were set in the Prisoner Gallery of Monte Alban's Building L. This huge display of slain enemies was a form of political and military propaganda. The carved stones warned potential rivals what would happen if they defied Monte Alban. © DEA/G. Dagli Orti/Getty Images

Evidence for co-occurrence of Monte Alban's conquest strategy with the emerging Zapotec state offers strong support for an expansionist model of primary state formation (see also Stanish and Levine 2011). The Zapotec state had formed by 30–20 B.C.E., with a four-tier settlement hierarchy (see Elson 2007). After centuries of dominating the region, Monte Alban eventually lost its central role as capital. After 700 C.E., the Zapotec state fragmented into a series of smaller centers, or principalities, alternately vying for supremacy through continued warfare and peaceful alliances through marriage (Flannery and Marcus 2003*a*).

## States in the Valley of Mexico

During the first century C.E., the Valley of Mexico, located in the highlands where Mexico City now stands, came to prominence in Mesoamerican state formation. In this large valley, **Teotihuacan** flourished between 1900 and 1300 B.P. (100 and 700 C.E.).

The Valley of Mexico is a large basin surrounded by mountains. The valley has rich volcanic soils, but rainfall isn't always reliable. The northern part of the valley, where the huge city and state of Teotihuacan eventually arose, is colder and drier than the south. Frosts there limited farming until quick-growing varieties of maize were developed. Until 2500 B.P., most people lived in the warmer and wetter southern part of the valley, where rainfall made farming possible. After 2500 B.P., new maize varieties and small-scale irrigation appeared. Population increased and began to spread north.

By 1 C.E. Teotihuacan was a town of 10,000 people. It governed a territory of a few thousand square kilometers and perhaps 50,000 people (Cowgill 2015; Parsons 1974). Teotihuacan's growth reflected its agricultural potential. Perpetual springs permitted irrigation of a large alluvial plain. Rural farmers supplied food for the growing urban population. By this time, a clear **settlement hierarchy** had emerged. This is a ranked series of communities that differ in size, function, and building types. The settlements at the top of the hierarchy were political and religious centers. Those at the bottom were rural villages.

Along with state organization went large-scale irrigation, status differentiation, and complex architecture. Teotihuacan thrived between 100 and 700 C.E. It grew as a planned city built on a grid pattern, with the Pyramid of the Sun at its center. By 500 C.E., the population of Teotihuacan had reached 130,000, making it larger than imperial Rome. Farmers were one of its diverse specialized groups, along with artisans, merchants, and political, religious, and military personnel.

After 700 C.E. Teotihuacan, like the Zapotec state, declined in size and power. By 900 C.E. its population had shrunk to 30,000. Between 900 and 1200 C.E., the Toltec period, the population scattered, and small cities and towns sprang up throughout the valley. People also left the Valley of Mexico to live in larger cities—like Tula, the Toltec capital—on its edge (see Figure 9.3).

Population increase (including immigration by the ancestors of the Aztecs) and urban growth returned to the Valley of Mexico between 1200 and 1520 C.E. During the **Aztec** period (1325 to 1520 C.E.) there were several cities, the largest of which—Tenochtitlan, the capital—may have surpassed Teotihuacan at its height. A dozen Aztec towns had more than 10,000 people. Fueling this population growth was intensification of agriculture, particularly in the southern part of the valley, where the drainage of lake bottoms and swamps added new cultivable land.

Another factor in the renaissance of the Valley of Mexico was trade (see Hirth and Pillsbury 2013). Local manufacture created products for a series of markets. The major towns and markets were located on the lake shores, with easy access to canoe traffic. The Aztec capital stood on an island in the lake. In Tenochtitlan, the production of luxury goods was more prestigious and more highly organized than that of pottery, basket making, and weaving. Luxury producers, such as stone workers, feather workers, and gold- and silversmiths, occupied a special position in Aztec society. The manufacture of luxury goods for export was an important part of the economy of the Aztec capital (Kenney 2015).

# Why States Collapse

States can be fragile and decomposable, falling apart along the same cleavage lines (e.g., regional political units) that were forged together to form the state originally. Various factors might threaten their economies and political institutions. Invasion, disease, famine, or prolonged drought can upset the balance. A state's citizens might harm the environment, usually with economic costs. For example, farmers and smelters might cut down trees. Such deforestation promotes erosion and leads to a decline in the water supply. Overuse of land may deplete the soil of the nutrients needed to grow crops.

## The Decline of the Maya

Generations of scholars have puzzled over the decline of Maya civilization around 900 C.E. Classic Maya culture, featuring several competing states, flourished between 300 and 900 C.E. in parts of what are now Mexico, Honduras, El Salvador, Guatemala, and Belize. Some important Maya cities, now archaeological sites and tourist attractions, included Bonampak, Calakmul, Chichen Itzá, Copán, Palenque, Tikal, Tulum, and Uaxactún. Maya cities had marketplaces, manufacturing areas, and community gardens. The ancient Maya probably are best known for their monuments (temples and pyramids), calendars, mathematics, and hieroglyphic writing (see Coe 2011; Edwards 2015).

Important archaeological clues to the Maya decline have been found at Copán, in western Honduras. This classic Maya royal center, the largest site in the southeastern part of the Maya area, covered 29 acres. It was built on an artificial terrace overlooking the Copán River. Its rulers inscribed their monuments with accounts of their coronation, their lineage history, and reports of important battles. The Maya dated their monuments with the names of kings and when they reigned. One monument at Copán was intended to be the ruler's throne platform, but only one side was ever finished. The monument bears a date, 822 C.E., in a section of unfinished text. Copán has no monuments with later dates. The site probably had been abandoned by 830 C.E.

Environmental factors implicated in Copán's demise may have included erosion and soil exhaustion caused by overfarming. Debris at excavated hillside farms confirms erosion, probably due to unsustainable agricultural intensification beginning around 750 C.E. Eventually, most farm sites were abandoned, some buried by erosion debris. Food stress and malnutrition were clearly present at Copán, where 80 percent of the buried skeletons display signs of anemia, due to iron deficiency. One skull shows anemia severe enough to have caused death. Even the nobility were malnourished. One noble skull, identified as such by its carved teeth and cosmetic deformation, also has telltale signs of anemia: spongy areas at its rear (Annenberg/CPB Exhibits 2000).

Ruins of the Templo de los Inscripciones in the ancient Maya urban center of Palenque, now in Chiapas, Mexico. © Glow Images RF

## Anthropology Today    *The Fantastic Claims of Pseudo-Archaeology*

Interest in prehistory has spawned numerous popular-culture creations, including movies, TV programs, and books. In fictional works, the anthropologists don't bear much resemblance to their real-life counterparts. Unlike Indiana Jones, normal and reputable archaeologists don't go around fighting Nazis, lashing whips, or seizing antiquities. The archaeologist's profession isn't a matter of raiding lost arks, going on crusades, or finding crystal skulls, but of reconstructing ancient lifeways through the careful and systematic analysis of material remains.

Over the generations the media have exposed us to the pseudoscientific theories of such popular writers as Thor Heyerdahl (1971), Erich von Daniken (1971), and Graham Hancock (2011)—none of them a professional archaeologist. Heyerdahl argued that developments in one world area (e.g., Mesoamerica) were based on ideas borrowed from somewhere else (e.g., Egypt). Von Daniken carried diffusionism several steps further, proposing that major human achievements were created or assisted by extraterrestrials. These writers assume that major features of the ancient human landscape were beyond the capabilities of people actually living there.

In *The Ra Expeditions,* world traveler and adventurer Heyerdahl (1971) argued that his voyage in a papyrus boat from the Mediterranean to the Caribbean demonstrated that ancient Egyptians could have navigated to the New World. (The boat was modeled on an ancient Egyptian vessel, but Heverdahl and his crew

had with them such modern conveniences as a radio and canned goods.) Heyerdahl maintained that, given the possibility of ancient trans-Atlantic travel, Old World people could have influenced the emergence of civilization in the Americas. In *Fingerprints of the Gods* (2011) and other books aimed at popular audiences, writer-journalist Graham Hancock has advanced a series of fantastic claims, including that Africans influenced the Olmecs (because of, in his opinion, African-looking faces in Olmec sculpture).

The University of Michigan offers a popular undergraduate class titled Frauds and Fantastic Claims in Archaeology. The course examines and debunks theories that archaeologists view as fringe or pseudoscientific. Especially problematic are claims that cultural achievements by indigenous peoples result from contact with superior beings. The course textbook is Kenneth L. Feder's *Frauds, Myths, and Mysteries: Science and Pseudoscience in*

Sarajevo-born American Semir Osmanagic claims to have discovered a giant pyramid built by an ancient civilization under Visocica Hill, Bosnia. Most scientists doubt his claim.
© Fehim Demir/epa/Corbis

*Archaeology* (2014)—a must for any reader wanting to pursue this topic further.

Pseudo-archaeologists often have trouble with chronology. We've seen in this chapter that, around 2,000 years ago, states fully comparable to those of Mesopotamia and Egypt began to rise and fall in the Mexican highlands. This occurred about 1,500 years after the major period of Egyptian pyramid building. If Egypt did contribute to Mesoamerican civilization, we would expect this influence to have been exerted during Egypt's heyday as an ancient power—not 1,500 years later. There is, however, no archaeological evidence for trans-Atlantic contact at either time.

There is, on the other hand, abundant archaeological evidence for the gradual emergence of food production and the state in Mesoamerica. Fantastic claims to the contrary, changes, advances, and setbacks in ancient American social life were the products of the ideas and activities of Native Americans themselves.

Neither Mexico nor Peru has yielded a shred of accepted archaeological evidence for Old World interference prior to the European Age of Discovery, which began late in the 15th century.

The archaeological record also casts doubt on contentions that the advances of earthlings came with extraterrestrial help. Abundant, well-analyzed archaeological data from the Middle East, Mesoamerica, and Peru tell a clear story. Food production and the state were not brilliant discoveries that humans needed to learn from outsiders. They were gradual processes with down-to-earth causes and effects. They required

thousands of years of orderly change, not some chance meeting in the high Andes between an ancient Inca chief and a beneficent Johnny Appleseed from Aldebaran.

Occasionally, fantastic claims about prehistory *exaggerate,* rather than deny, the abilities of ancient humans. One example is when pseudo-archaeologists claim that Paleolithic societies could have constructed monumental structures. Writer-journalist Graham Hancock, for example, has suggested that an Upper Paleolithic civilization, rather than ancient Egyptians, built Egypt's great Sphinx, some 7,000 years earlier than its actual construction date (Hancock and Bauval 1996). Semir Osmanagic is a Bosnian amateur archaeologist who has been dubbed the Indiana Jones of the Balkans because of his favored flat-crowned Navajo hat. Osmanagic claims to have identified in Bosnia the world's largest ancient pyramid, which he thinks is "older than the last ice age" (Smith 2006). Archaeologists and geologists, however, say that his "pyramid" is actually a large, symmetrical hill formed by buckling of the Earth's crust millions of years ago.

Responding to his claims, the European Association of Archaeologists issued an official statement signed by the heads of the official archaeological organizations of seven European countries (Parzinger et al. 2006). Their statement called Osmanagic's so-called pyramid project "a cruel hoax on an unsuspecting public" that "has no place in the world of genuine science" (Parzinger et al. 2006). When and where have you heard a fantastic claim about prehistory?

Just as the causes of state formation are diverse, so are the reasons for state decline. In the long run, Maya political organization turned out to be vulnerable (see Fojas 2013). Increased warfare and political competition destabilized many of its dynasties and governments. Archaeologists now stress the role of warfare in Maya state decline.

Hieroglyphic texts document increased warfare among many Maya cities (see Houk 2015). From the period just before the collapse, there is archaeological evidence for increased concern with fortifications (moats, ditches, walls, and palisades) and relocation to defensible locations. Archaeologists have evidence of the burning of structures, the projectile points from spears, and some of the bodies of those killed. Some sites were abandoned, with the people fleeing into the forests to occupy perishable huts. (Copán, as we have seen, was depopulated soon after 822 C.E.) Archaeologists now believe that social, political, and military upheaval and competition had as much as or more to do with the Maya decline and abandonment of cities than did natural environmental factors (Marcus, personal communication).

Formerly archaeologists tended to seek explanations for state origin and decline almost exclusively in terms of natural environmental factors, such as climate change, habitat destruction, and demographic pressure (see Weiss 2005). Archaeologists now see state origins and declines more fully—in social and political terms—because we can read the texts. The Maya texts document competition and warfare between dynasties jockeying for position and power. Warfare was indeed a creator and a destroyer of ancient chiefdoms and states. What's its role in our own?

## Summary

1. States develop to handle regulatory problems as the population grows and the economy gets more complex. Multiple factors, including irrigation, regional trade, warfare, population growth, and environmental circumscription have contributed to state formation.

2. A state is a society with a formal, central government and a division of society into classes. The first cities and states, supported by irrigated farming, developed in southern Mesopotamia between 6000 and 5500 B.P. Evidence for early state organization includes monumental architecture, central storehouses, irrigation systems, and written records.

3. Towns predate pottery in the Middle East. The first towns grew up 10,000 to 9,000 years ago. The first pottery dates back just over 8,000 years. *Halafian* (7500–6000 B.P.) refers to a pottery style and to the period when the first chiefdoms emerged. Ubaid pottery (7000–6000 B.P.) is associated with advanced chiefdoms and perhaps the earliest states. Most state formation occurred during the Uruk period (6000–5200 B.P.).

4. Based on the status distinctions they include, societies may be divided into egalitarian, ranked, and stratified. In egalitarian societies, status distinctions are not usually inherited. Ranked societies have hereditary inequality, but they lack stratification. Stratified societies have sharp social divisions—social classes or strata—based on unequal access to wealth and power. Ranked societies with loss of village autonomy are chiefdoms.

5. Mesopotamia's economy was based on intensive agriculture, craft production, and trade. Writing, invented by 5600 B.P., was first used to keep accounts for trade. With the invention of smelting, the Bronze Age began just after 5000 B.P.

6. In northwestern India and Pakistan, the Indus River Valley state flourished from 4600 to 3900 B.P. The first Chinese state, dating to 3750 B.P., was that of the Shang dynasty in northern China. The major early states of the Western Hemisphere were in Mesoamerica and Peru.

7. Between 3200 and 3000 B.P., intense competitive interaction among the many chiefdoms in Mesoamerica at that time fueled rapid social change. Some chiefdoms would develop into states (e.g., Oaxaca, Valley of Mexico). Others (e.g., Olmec) would not. In the Valley of Oaxaca, changing patterns of warfare—from village raiding to conquest warfare—played a prominent role in the formation of Mesoamerica's earliest state, the Zapotec state, whose capital was Monte Alban. By 1 C.E. (2000 B.P.), the Valley of Mexico had come to prominence. In this large valley in the highlands, Teotihuacan thrived between 100 and 700 C.E. Tenochtitlan, the capital of the Aztec state (1325 to 1520 C.E.), may have surpassed Teotihuacan at its height.

8. States may collapse when they fail to keep social and economic order or to protect themselves against outsiders. The Maya state fell in the face of increased warfare among competing dynasties.

## Key Terms

Aztec, *212*
bronze, *204*
chiefdoms, *202*
cuneiform, *204*
egalitarian
 society, *202*
Halafian, *201*
Mesopotamia, *199*

metallurgy, *204*
primary states, *195*
ranked
 societies, *202*
settlement
 hierarchy, *211*
smelting, *204*
state, *194*

stratification, *202*
Teotihuacan, *211*
Zapotec, *209*

# Chapter 10

# Language and Communication

We all have stereotypes about how people in other regions talk. Some stereotypes, spread by the mass media, are more generalized than others are (see this chapter's "Anthropology Today" for stereotypes and the reality of California speech patterns). Most Americans think they can imitate a "Southern accent." We also stereotype speech in New York City (the pronunciation of *coffee,* for example), Boston ("I pahked the kah in Hahvahd Yahd"), and Canada ("oot" for "out").

It's sometimes thought that midwesterners don't have accents. This belief stems from the fact that midwestern dialects don't have many stigmatized linguistic variants—speech patterns that people in other regions recognize and look down on, such as *r*-lessness and *dem, dese,* and *dere* (instead of *them, these,* and *there*).

Far from having no accents, midwesterners, even in the same high school, exhibit linguistic diversity (see Eckert 1989, 2000). One of the best examples of variable midwestern speech, involving vowels, is pronunciation of the *e* sound (called the /e/ phoneme), in such words as *ten, rent, section, lecture, effect, best,* and *test.* In southeastern Michigan, there are four different ways of pronouncing this *e* sound. Speakers of Black

English and immigrants from Appalachia often pronounce *ten* as "tin," just as Southerners habitually do. Some Michiganders say "ten," the correct pronunciation in Standard English. However, two other pronunciations also are common. Instead of "ten," many Michiganders say "tan" or "tun" (as though they were using the word *ton,* a unit of weight).

My students often astound me with their pronunciation. One day I met one of my Michigan-raised teaching assistants in the hall. She was deliriously happy. When I asked why, she replied, "I've just had the best suction."

"What?" I said.

She finally spoke more precisely. "I've just had the best saction." She considered this a clearer pronunciation of the word *section.*

Another TA complimented me, "You luctured to great effuct today." After an exam a student lamented that she had not done her "bust on the tust" (i.e., "best on the test").

The truth is, regional patterns affect the way we all speak.

## Language

Linguistic anthropology illustrates anthropology's characteristic interests in diversity, comparison, and change—but here the focus is on language (see Ahearn 2012; Duranti 2009; Ottenheimer 2013; Salzmann 2012; Salzmann et al. 2014). Language, spoken (*speech*) and written (*writing*—which has existed for less than 6,000 years), is our primary means of communication. Like culture in general, of which language is a part, language is transmitted through learning. Language is based on arbitrary, learned associations between words and the things they stand for. Unlike the communication systems of other animals, language allows us to discuss the past and future, share our experiences with others, and benefit from their experiences.

Anthropologists study language in its social and cultural context (see Bonvillain 2012; Salzmann, Stanlaw, and Adachi 2012). Some linguistic anthropologists reconstruct ancient languages by comparing their contemporary descendants and in doing so make discoveries about history. Others study linguistic differences to discover the varied worldviews and patterns of thought in a multitude of cultures. Sociolinguists examine dialects and styles in a single language to show how speech reflects social differences, as in the preceding discussion of regional speech contrasts. Linguistic anthropologists also explore the role of language in colonization and globalization (Blommaert 2010; Trudgill 2010).

## Nonhuman Primate Communication

### Call Systems

Only humans speak. No other animal has anything approaching the complexity of language. The natural communication systems of other primates (monkeys and apes) are **call systems.** These vocal systems consist of a limited number of sounds—*calls*—that are produced only when particular environmental stimuli are encountered. Such calls may be varied in intensity and duration, but they are much less flexible than language because they are automatic and can't be combined. At some point in human evolution, however, our ancestors began to combine calls and to understand the combinations. The number of calls also expanded, eventually becoming too great to be transmitted, from generation to generation, even partly through the genes. Communication came to rely almost totally on learning.

Although wild primates use call systems, the vocal tract of apes is not suitable for speech. Until the 1960s, attempts to teach spoken language to apes suggested that they lack linguistic abilities. In the 1950s, a couple raised a chimpanzee, Viki, as a member of their family and systematically tried to teach her to speak. However, Viki learned only four words ("mama," "papa," "up," and "cup").

## Sign Language

More recent experiments have shown that apes can learn to use, if not speak, true language (Fouts 1997). Several apes have learned to converse with people through means other than speech. One such communication system is American Sign Language, or ASL, which is widely used by hearing-impaired Americans. ASL employs a limited

Apes, such as these Congo chimpanzees, use call systems to communicate in the wild. Their vocal systems consist of a limited number of sounds—calls—that are produced only when particular environmental stimuli are encountered.
© Michael Nichols/National Geographic Stock

number of basic gesture units that are analogous to sounds in spoken language. These units combine to form words and larger units of meaning.

The first chimpanzee to learn ASL was Washoe, a female, who died in 2007 at the age of 42. Captured in West Africa, Washoe was acquired by R. Allen Gardner and Beatrice Gardner, scientists at the University of Nevada in Reno, in 1966, when she was a year old. Four years later, she moved to Norman, Oklahoma, to a converted farm that had become the Institute for Primate Studies. Washoe revolutionized the discussion of the language-learning abilities of apes (Carey 2007). At first she lived in a trailer and heard no spoken language. The researchers always used ASL to communicate with each other in her presence. The chimp gradually acquired a vocabulary of more than 100 signs representing English words (Gardner, Gardner, and Van Cantfort, 1989). At the age of 2, Washoe began to combine as many as five signs into rudimentary sentences such as "you, me, go out, hurry."

The second chimp to learn ASL was Lucy, Washoe's junior by one year. Lucy died, or was murdered by poachers, in 1986, after having been introduced to "the wild" in Africa in 1979 (Carter 1988). From her second day of life until her move to Africa, Lucy lived with a family in Norman, Oklahoma. Roger Fouts, a researcher from the nearby Institute for Primate Studies, came two days a week to test and improve Lucy's knowledge of ASL. During the rest of the week, Lucy used ASL to converse with her foster parents. After acquiring language, Washoe and Lucy exhibited several human traits: swearing, joking, telling lies, and trying to teach language to others (Fouts 1997).

When irritated, Washoe called her monkey neighbors at the institute "dirty monkeys." Lucy insulted her "dirty cat." On arrival at Lucy's place, Fouts once found a pile of excrement on the floor. When he asked the chimp what it was, she replied, "dirty, dirty," her expression for feces. Asked whose "dirty, dirty" it was, Lucy named Fouts's coworker, Sue. When Fouts refused to believe her about Sue, the chimp blamed the excrement on Fouts himself.

**Cultural transmission** of a communication system through learning is a fundamental attribute of language. Washoe, Lucy, and other chimps have tried to teach ASL to other animals, including their own offspring. Washoe taught gestures to other institute chimps, including her son Sequoia, who died in infancy (Fouts, Fouts, and Van Cantfort 1989).

Because of their size and strength as adults, gorillas are less likely subjects than chimps for such experiments. Psychologist Francine Penny Patterson's work with gorillas at Stanford University therefore seems more daring than the chimp experiments. Patterson raised the now full-grown female gorilla Koko, born in 1971, in a trailer next to a Stanford museum. Koko's vocabulary surpasses that of any chimp. She has learned more than 1,000 signs, of which she regularly uses over 800. She also recognizes at least 2000 spoken words in English when she hears them (see http://www.koko.org/sign-language).

Koko and the chimps also show that apes share still another linguistic ability with humans: **productivity.** Speakers routinely use the rules of their language to produce entirely new expressions that are comprehensible to other native speakers. I can, for example, create "baboonlet" to refer to a baboon infant. I do this by analogy with English words in which the suffix -let designates the young of a species. Anyone who speaks

English immediately understands the meaning of my new word. Koko, Washoe, Lucy, and others have shown that apes also are able to use language productively. Lucy used gestures she already knew to create "drinkfruit" for "watermelon." Washoe, seeing a swan for the first time, coined "waterbird." Koko, who knew the gestures for "finger" and "bracelet," formed "finger bracelet" when she was given a ring.

Although chimps and gorillas have never invented their own meaningful gesture system in the wild, when given such a system, they show many humanlike abilities in learning and using it. They can employ it productively and creatively, although not with the sophistication of human ASL users.

Apes also have demonstrated linguistic **displacement.** Absent in call systems, displacement is our ability to talk about things that are not present. We don't have to see the objects before we say the words. We can discuss the past and future, share our experiences with others, and benefit from theirs.

Francine "Penny" Patterson has described several examples of Koko's capacity for displacement. The gorilla once expressed sorrow about having bitten Penny three days earlier. Koko has used the sign "later" to postpone doing things she doesn't want to do. Table 10.1 summarizes the contrasts between language, whether sign or spoken, and call systems.

No one denies the huge difference between human language and gorilla signs. There is surely a major gap between the ability to write a book or say a prayer and an ape's use of signs. Apes may not be people, but they aren't just animals, either. Let Koko express it: When asked by a reporter whether she was a person or an animal, Koko signed "fine animal gorilla" (Patterson 1978). For the latest on Koko, see http://www.koko.org.

## The Origin of Language

Although the capacity to remember and combine linguistic symbols may be latent in the apes, human evolution was needed for this seed to flower into language. A mutated gene known as FOXP2 helps explain why humans speak and chimps don't (Paulson 2005). The key role of FOXP2 in speech came to light in a study of a British family, identified only as KE, half of whose members had an inherited, severe deficit in speech (Trivedi 2001). The same variant form of FOXP2 that is found in chimpanzees causes this disorder.

TABLE 10.1   **Language Contrasted with Call Systems**

| Human Language | Primate Call Systems |
|---|---|
| Has the capacity to speak of things and events that are not present (displacement) | Are stimuli dependent; the food call will be made only in the presence of food; it cannot be faked |
| Has the capacity to generate new expressions by combining other expressions (productivity) | Consist of a limited number of calls that cannot be combined to produce new calls |
| Is group specific in that all humans have the capacity for language, but each linguistic community has its own language, which is culturally transmitted | Tend to be species specific, with little variation among communities of the same species for each call |

Those who have the nonspeech version of the gene cannot make the fine tongue and lip movements that are necessary for clear speech, and their speech is unintelligible—even to other members of the KE family (Trivedi 2001). Chimps have the same (genetic) sequence as the KE family members with the speech deficit. Based on genomics, it appears that the speech-friendly form of FOXP2 took hold in humans around 150,000 years ago. This mutation conferred selective advantages (linguistic and cultural abilities) that allowed those who had it to spread at the expense of those who did not (Paulson 2005).

## Nonverbal Communication

Language is our principal means of communicating, but it isn't the only one we use. We *communicate* when we transmit information about ourselves to others and receive such information from them. Our expressions, stances, gestures, and movements, even if unconscious, convey information and are part of our communication styles. Deborah Tannen (1990) discusses differences in the communication styles of American men and women, and her comments go beyond language. She notes that American girls and women tend to look directly at each other when they talk, whereas American boys and men do not. Males are more likely to look straight ahead rather than turn and make eye contact with someone, especially another man, seated beside them. Also, in conversational groups, American men tend to relax and sprawl out. American women may adopt a similar relaxed posture in all-female groups, but when they are with men, they tend to draw in their limbs and adopt a tighter stance.

**Kinesics** is the study of communication through body movements, stances, gestures, and expressions. Linguists pay attention not only to what is said but also to how it is said and to the features besides language itself that convey meaning. A speaker's enthusiasm is conveyed not only through words but also through facial expressions, gestures, and other signs of animation. We use gestures, such as a jab of the hand, for emphasis. We vary our intonation and the pitch or loudness of our voices. We communicate through strategic pauses, and even by being silent. An effective communication strategy may include altering pitch, voice level, and grammatical forms such as declaratives ("I am . . ."), imperatives ("Go forth . . ."), and questions ("Are you . . . ?"). Culture teaches us that certain manners and styles should accompany certain kinds of speech.

Much of what we communicate is nonverbal and reflects our emotional states and intentions. This can create problems when we use contemporary means of communication such as texting and online messaging. People can use emoticons (☺, ☹, :~/ [confused], :~0 ["hah!" no way!]) and abbreviations (lol—laugh out loud; lmao—laugh my a** off; wtf—what the f**; omg—oh my god) to fill in what would otherwise be communicated by tone of voice, laughter, and facial expression (see Baron 2009; Tannen and Trester 2012).

Culture always plays a role in shaping the "natural." Cross-culturally, nodding does not always mean affirmative, nor does head shaking from side to side always mean negative. Americans say "uh huh" to affirm, whereas in Madagascar a similar sound is made to deny. Americans point with their fingers; the people of Madagascar point with their lips.

Body movements communicate social differences. In Japan, bowing is a regular part of social interaction, but different bows are used depending on the social status of the people who are interacting. In Madagascar and Polynesia, people of lower status should not hold their heads above those of people of higher status. When one approaches someone older or of higher status, one bends one's knees and lowers one's head as a sign of respect. In Madagascar, one always does this, for politeness, when passing between two people. Although our gestures, facial expressions, and body stances have roots in our primate heritage, and can be seen in the monkeys and the apes, they have not escaped cultural shaping. Language, which is so highly dependent on the use of symbols, is the domain of communication in which culture plays the strongest role (see Salzmann et al. 2014).

## The Structure of Language

The scientific study of a spoken language (**descriptive linguistics**) involves several interrelated areas of analysis: phonology, morphology, lexicon, and syntax. **Phonology,** the study of speech sounds, considers which sounds are present and meaningful in a given language. **Morphology** studies how sounds combine to form *morphemes*—words and their meaningful parts. Thus, the word *cats* would be analyzed as containing two morphemes—*cat,* the name for a kind of animal, and *-s,* a morpheme indicating plurality. A language's **lexicon** is a dictionary containing all its morphemes and their meanings. **Syntax** refers to the arrangement and order of words in phrases and sentences. For example, do nouns usually come before or after verbs? Do adjectives normally precede or follow the nouns they modify?

*Syntax* refers to the arrangement and order of words in phrases and sentences. A photo of Yoda from *Star Wars* (*Revenge of the Sith*) this is. What's odd about Yoda's syntax? © Lucas Film/Topham/The Image Works

## Speech Sounds

From the movies and TV, and from meeting foreigners, we know something about foreign accents and mispronunciations. We know that someone with a marked French accent doesn't pronounce *r* as an American does. But at least someone from France can distinguish between "craw" and "claw," which someone from Japan may not be able to do. The difference between *r* and *l* makes a difference in English and in French, but it doesn't in Japanese. In linguistics we say that the difference between *r* and *l* is *phonemic* in English and French but not in Japanese. In English and French *r* and *l* are phonemes but not in Japanese. A **phoneme** is a sound contrast that makes a difference, that differentiates meaning.

We find the phonemes in a given language by comparing *minimal pairs,* words that resemble each other in all but one sound. The words have different meanings, but they differ in just one sound. The contrasting sounds therefore are phonemes in that language. An example in English is the minimal pair *pit/bit*. These two words are distinguished by a single sound contrast between /p/ and /b/ (we enclose phonemes in slashes). Thus, /p/ and /b/ are phonemes in English. Another example is the different vowel sound of *bit* and *beat* (see Figure 10.1). This contrast distinguishes these two words and the two vowel phonemes written /I/ and /i/ in English.

Standard (American) English (SE), the "region-free" dialect of TV network newscasters, has about 35 phonemes—at least 11 vowels and 24 consonants. The number of phonemes varies from language to language—from 15 to 60, averaging between 30 and 40. The number of phonemes also varies between dialects of a given language. In North American English, for example, vowel phonemes vary noticeably from dialect to dialect. Readers should pronounce the words in Figure 10.1, paying attention to (or asking someone else) whether they distinguish each of the vowel sounds. Most North Americans don't pronounce them all.

**Phonetics** is the study of speech sounds in general, what people actually say in various languages, like the differences in vowel pronunciation described in the discussion of midwestern speech at the beginning of the chapter (for California vowels, see this chapter's "Anthropology Today"). **Phonemics** studies only the *significant* sound contrasts (phonemes) of a given language. In English, like /r/ and /l/ (remember *craw* and *claw*), /b/ and /v/ also are phonemes, occurring in minimal pairs like *bat* and *vat*. In Spanish, however, the contrast between [b] and [v] doesn't distinguish meaning, and they therefore are not phonemes (we enclose sounds that are not phonemic in brackets). Spanish speakers normally use the [b] sound to pronounce words spelled with either *b* or *v*.

In any language a given phoneme extends over a phonetic range. In English the phoneme /p/ ignores the phonetic contrast between the [pʰ] in *pin* and the [p] in *spin*. Most English speakers don't even notice that there is a phonetic difference. The [pʰ] is aspirated, so that a puff of air follows the [p]. The [p] in *spin* is not. (To see the difference, light a match, hold it in front of your mouth, and watch the flame as you pronounce the two words.) The contrast between [pʰ] and [p] *is* phonemic in some languages, such as Hindi (spoken in India). That is, there are words whose meaning is distinguished only by the contrast between an aspirated and an unaspirated [p].

FIGURE 10.1   **Vowel Phonemes in Standard American English**
They are shown according to height of tongue and tongue position at front, center, or back of mouth. Phonetic symbols are identified by English words that include them; note that most are minimal pairs.

Source: Dwight Bolinger, *Aspects of Language,* 3rd ed., fig. 2.1. Copyright © 1981 Heinle/Arts & Sciences, a part of Cengage Learning, Inc.

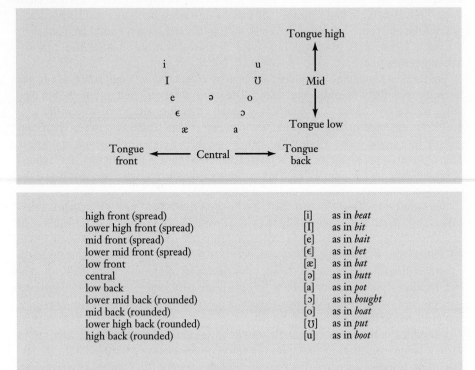

| | |
|---|---|
| high front (spread) | [i]   as in *beat* |
| lower high front (spread) | [I]   as in *bit* |
| mid front (spread) | [e]   as in *bait* |
| lower mid front (spread) | [ɛ]   as in *bet* |
| low front | [æ]   as in *bat* |
| central | [ə]   as in *butt* |
| low back | [a]   as in *pot* |
| lower mid back (rounded) | [ɔ]   as in *bought* |
| mid back (rounded) | [o]   as in *boat* |
| lower high back (rounded) | [ʊ]   as in *put* |
| high back (rounded) | [u]   as in *boot* |

Native speakers vary in their pronunciation of certain phonemes, such as the /e/ phoneme in the midwestern United States. This variation is important in the evolution of language. Without shifts in pronunciation, there could be no linguistic change. The section on sociolinguistics later in this chapter considers phonetic variation and its relationship to social divisions and the evolution of language.

## Language, Thought, and Culture

The well-known linguist Noam Chomsky (1957/2014) has argued that the human brain contains a limited set of rules for organizing language, so that all languages have a common structural basis. (Chomsky calls this set of rules *universal grammar.*) That people can learn foreign languages and that words and ideas translate from one language to another support Chomsky's position that all humans have similar linguistic abilities and thought processes. Another line of support comes from creole languages. Such languages develop from *pidgins,* which form during acculturation, when different societies come into contact and must devise a system of communication (see Gu 2012). After generations of being spoken, pidgins may develop into *creole* languages, which have fully developed grammatical rules and native speakers (people who learn the language as their primary one during enculturation).

Creoles are spoken in several Caribbean societies. Gullah, which is spoken by African Americans on coastal islands in South Carolina and Georgia, is a creole language. Supporting the idea that creoles are based on universal grammar is the fact that such languages all share certain features. Syntactically, all use particles (e.g., will, was) to form future and past tenses and multiple negation to deny or negate (e.g., he don't got none). Also, all form questions by changing inflection rather than by changing word order—for example, "You're going home for the holidays?" (with a rising tone at the end) rather than "Are you going home for the holidays?"

## The Sapir-Whorf Hypothesis

Other linguists and anthropologists take a different approach to the relation between language and thought. Rather than seeking universal linguistic structures and processes, they believe that different languages produce different ways of thinking. This position sometimes is known as the **Sapir-Whorf hypothesis** after Edward Sapir (1931) and his student Benjamin Lee Whorf (1956), its prominent early advocates. Sapir and Whorf argued that the grammatical categories of particular languages lead their speakers to think about things in different ways. For example, English divides time into past, present, and future. Hopi, a language of the Pueblo region of the Native American Southwest, does not. Rather, Hopi distinguishes between events that exist or have existed (what we use present and past to discuss) and those that don't or don't yet (our future events, along with imaginary and hypothetical events). Whorf argued that this difference leads Hopi speakers to think about time and reality in different ways than English speakers do.

A similar example comes from Portuguese, which employs a future subjunctive verb form, introducing a degree of uncertainty into discussions of the future. In English we routinely use the future tense to talk about something we think will happen. We don't hesitate to proclaim "I'll see you next year," even when we can't be absolutely sure we will. The Portuguese future subjunctive qualifies the future event, recognizing that the future can't be certain. Our way of expressing the future as certain is so ingrained that we don't even think about it, just as the Hopi don't see the need to distinguish between present and past, both of which are real, while the future remains hypothetical. It seems, however, that language does not tightly restrict thought, because cultural changes can produce changes in thought and in language, as we'll see in the next section.

## Focal Vocabulary

A lexicon (vocabulary) is a language's dictionary, its set of names for things, events, and ideas. Lexicon influences perception. Thus, Eskimos (Inuit) have several distinct words for different types of snow that in English are all called *snow.* Most English speakers

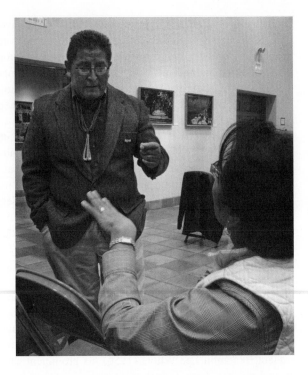

Clark Tenakhongva, who was, or is, a candidate to be Hopi Tribal Chairman, spoke (or speaks) to an audience member during a forum in Flagstaff, Arizona. The Hopi language would not distinguish between *was* and *is* or *spoke* and *speaks* in the previous sentence. For the Hopi, present and past are real and are expressed grammatically in the same way, while the future remains hypothetical and has a different grammatical expression.
© Felicia Fonseca/AP Images

never notice the differences between these types of snow and might have trouble seeing them even if someone points them out. Eskimos recognize and think about differences in snow that English speakers don't see because our language gives us just one word.

Similarly, the Nuer of South Sudan have an elaborate vocabulary to describe cattle. Eskimos have several words for snow and Nuer have dozens for cattle because of their particular histories, economies, and environments (Robson 2013). When the need arises, English speakers can also elaborate their snow and cattle vocabularies. For example, skiers name varieties of snow with words that are missing from the lexicons of Florida retirees. Similarly, the cattle vocabulary of a Texas rancher is much more ample than that of a salesperson in a New York City department store. Such specialized sets of terms and distinctions that are particularly important to certain groups (those with particular *foci* of experience or activity) are known as **focal vocabulary.**

Vocabulary is the area of language that changes most readily. New words and distinctions, when needed, appear and spread. For example, who would have "texted" someone a generation ago? Names for items get simpler as they become common and important. A television has become a *TV,* an automobile a *car,* and an application for a smartphone an *app.*

Language, culture, and thought are interrelated. Opposing the Sapir-Whorf hypothesis, however, it might be more accurate to say that changes in culture produce changes in language and thought than to say the reverse. Consider differences between female and male Americans regarding the color terms they use (Lakoff 2004). Distinctions implied by such terms as *salmon, rust, peach, beige, teal, mauve, cranberry,* and *dusky orange* aren't in the vocabularies of most American men. However, many of them weren't even in American women's lexicons 60–70 years ago. These changes reflect changes in American economy, society, and culture. Color terms and distinctions have increased with the growth of the fashion and cosmetic industries. A similar contrast (and growth) in Americans' lexicons shows up in football, baseball, basketball, and hockey vocabularies. Sports fans, more often males than females, use more terms concerning and make more elaborate distinctions involving games and sports events. Thus, cultural contrasts and changes affect lexical distinctions (for instance, *peach* versus *salmon*) within semantic domains (for instance, color terminology). **Semantics** refers to a language's meaning system.

The ways in which people divide the world—the lexical contrasts they perceive as meaningful or significant—reflect their experiences. Anthropologists have discovered that certain sets of vocabulary items evolve in a determined order. For example, after studying more than 100 languages, Berlin and Kay (1969/1992) discovered 10 basic color terms: *white, black, red, yellow, blue, green, brown, pink, orange,* and *purple* (they evolved in more or less that order). The number of terms varied with cultural complexity. Representing one extreme were Papua New Guinea cultivators and Australian hunters and gatherers, who used only 2 basic terms, which translate as *black* and *white* or *dark* and *light.* At the other end of the continuum were European and Asian languages with all the color terms. Color terminology was most developed in areas with a history of using dyes and artificial coloring.

# Sociolinguistics

## Social and Linguistic Variation

Is there anything distinctive or unusual about the way you talk? If you're from Canada, Virginia, or Savannah, you may say "oot" instead of "out." A southerner might request a "soft drink" rather than a New Yorker's "soda" or someone else's "pop." Can you imitate how a "Valley Girl" or "surfer dude" might talk? Usually when we pay attention to how we talk, it's because someone comments on our speech. It may be only when students move from one state or region to another that they realize how much of a regional accent they have. I moved as a teenager from Atlanta to New York City. Previously I hadn't realized I had a southern accent, but some guardians of linguistic correctness in my new high school did. They put me in a speech class, pointing out linguistic flaws I never knew I had. One was my "dull *s*," particularly in terminal consonant clusters, as in the words *tusks* and *breakfasts.* Apparently I didn't pronounce all three consonants at the ends of those words. Later it occurred to me that these weren't words I used very often. As far as I know, I've never had a conversation about tusks or proclaimed, "I ate seven breakfasts last week."

Unlike grammarians, linguists and anthropologists are interested in what people do say, rather than what they should say. Speech differences are associated with, and tell us a lot about, social variation, such as region, education, ethnic background, and gender. Men and women talk differently. I'm sure you can think of examples based on your own experience, although you probably never realized that women tend to peripheralize their vowels (think of the sounds in *weasel* and *whee*), whereas men tend to centralize them (think of *rough* and *ugh*). Men are more likely to speak "ungrammatically" than women are. As mentioned previously, men and women also show differences in their sports and color terminologies. Men typically know more sports terms, make more distinctions among them (e.g., *runs* versus *points*), and try to use the terms more precisely than women do. Correspondingly, women use more color terms and attempt to use them more specifically than men do. To make this point when I lecture, I bring an off-purple shirt to class. Holding it up, I first ask women to say aloud what color the shirt is. The women rarely answer with a uniform voice, as they try to distinguish the actual shade (mauve, lilac, lavender, wisteria, or some other purplish hue). I then ask the men, who consistently answer as one, "PURPLE."

No language is a uniform system in which everyone talks just like everyone else. The field of **sociolinguistics** investigates relationships between social and linguistic variation (Edwards 2013; Spencer 2010; Trudgill 2000). How do different speakers use a given language? How do linguistic features correlate with social diversity and stratification, including class, ethnic, and gender differences (Eckert and McConnell-Ginet 2013; McConnell-Ginet 2010; Tannen 1990)? How is language used to express, reinforce, or resist power (G. Lakoff 2008; Mesthrie 2011; Mooney 2011; Trudgill 2010)?

Sociolinguists focus on features that vary systematically with social position and situation. To study variation, sociolinguists must observe, define, and measure variable use of language and speakers in real-world situations.

In his book *The Language of Food*, linguist Dan Jurafsky (2014) describes a recent study based on measurement of sociolinguistic variation. Jurafsky and his colleagues analyzed the menus of 6,500 contemporary American restaurants. One of their goals was to see how the food vocabularies of upscale restaurants differed from those of cheaper establishments. One key difference they found was that upscale menus paid much more attention to the sources of the foods they served. They named specific farms, gardens, ranches, pastures, woodlands, and farmers' markets. They were careful to mention, if the season was right, that their tomatoes or peas were heirloom varieties. Very expensive restaurants mentioned the origin of food more than 15 times as often as inexpensive restaurants. Another key difference was that the cheaper restaurants offered about twice as many menu choices as the expensive ones.

Word length was another differentiator. Upscale menu words averaged half a letter longer than in the cheaper restaurants. Cheaper eateries, for instance, were more likely to use "decaf," rather than "decaffeinated," and "sides" rather than "accompaniments." Diners had to pay higher prices for those longer words: Every increase of one letter in the average length of words describing a dish meant an average increase of $.18 in the price of that dish.

Cheaper restaurants were more apt to use linguistic fillers. These included positive but vague words like "delicious," "tasty," "mouthwatering," and "flavorful," or other positive, but impossible to measure, adjectives such as "terrific," "wonderful," "delightful," and "sublime." Each positive vague word for a dish in a modest restaurant reduced its average price by 9 percent. Downscale restaurants also were more likely to assure their diners that their offerings were "fresh," as though there might be some reason to doubt that freshness. Expensive restaurants expected their patrons to assume that their offerings were fresh, without having to say it.

Jurafsy and his associates also analyzed vocabulary used in 1 million online Yelp restaurant reviews, representing seven American cities—Boston, Chicago, Los Angeles, New York, Philadelphia, San Francisco, and Washington. The researchers found that good and bad reviews differed linguistically. Reviewers used a greater variety of words, with more differentiated meanings, to express negative rather than positive opinions. This tendency, known as negative differentiation, extends to other linguistic domains in English, and even to other languages. People seem to need more varied and elaborate ways of being negative. Negative reviewers wanted to comment on the restaurant's failings as fully as possible and to present it as a shared experience. Bad reviews were much more likely than good ones to use the inclusive pronouns "we" and "us." Psychologists know that traumatized people seek comfort in groups by emphasizing their belonging, using the words "we" and "us" with high frequency when reporting about negative experiences. Next time you eat out and/or are tempted to write a review, pay attention to these findings about "the language of food."

Study these menus from two restaurants, one more upscale than the other. Note the use of names of farms (food origin) in one menu and the use of adjectives such as "delicious," "fresh," and "premium" in the other. Which menu is from the more upscale restaurant? © McGraw-Hill Education. Mark Dierker, photographer RF

## Linguistic Diversity within Nations

As an illustration of the linguistic variation encountered in all nations, consider the contemporary United States. Ethnic diversity is revealed by the fact that millions of Americans learn first languages other than English. Spanish is the most common. Many of those people eventually become bilingual, adding English as a second language. In many multilingual (including colonized) nations, people use two languages on different occasions—one in the home, for example, and the other on the job or in public.

Whether bilingual or not, we all vary our speech in different contexts; we engage in **style shifts.** In certain parts of Europe, people regularly switch dialects. This phenomenon, known as **diglossia,** applies to "high" and "low" variants of the same language, for example, in German and Flemish (spoken in Belgium). People employ the high variant at universities and in writing, professions, and the mass media. They use the low variant for ordinary conversation with family members and friends. (See Tannen [2005] and Tannen, Kendall, and Gordon [2007] for analysis of communication among American families and friends.)

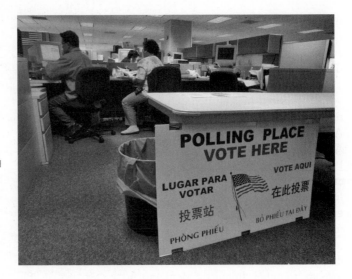

This sign at a voting place in San Jose, California is written in English, Spanish, Vietnamese, and Chinese, with the Filipino dialect of Tagalog soon to be added. The U.S. Voting Rights Act mandates that certain counties provide bilingual or multilingual ballots and voting instructions. © Paul Sakuma/AP Images

Just as social situations influence our speech, so do geographical, cultural, and socioeconomic differences. Many dialects coexist in the United States with Standard (American) English (SE). SE itself is a dialect that differs, say, from "BBC English," which is the preferred dialect in Great Britain. Different dialects are equally effective as systems of communication, which is language's main job. Our tendency to think of particular dialects as cruder or more sophisticated than others is a social rather than a linguistic judgment. We rank certain speech patterns as better or worse because we recognize that they are used by groups that we also rank. People who say *dese, dem,* and *dere* instead of *these, them,* and *there* communicate perfectly well with anyone who recognizes that the *d* sound systematically replaces the *th* sound in their speech. However, this form of speech has become an indicator of low social rank. We call it, like the use of *ain't,* "uneducated speech." The use of *dem, dese,* and *dere* is one of many phonological differences that Americans recognize and look down on (see Labov 2012).

## Gender Speech Contrasts

According to Robin Lakoff (2004), the use of certain types of words and expressions has been associated with women's traditional lesser power in American society. For example, *Oh dear, Oh fudge,* and *Goodness!* are less forceful than *Hell* and *Damn.* Watch the lips of a disgruntled athlete in a televised competition, such as a football game. What's the likelihood he's saying "Phooey on you"? Women are more likely to use such adjectives as *adorable, charming, sweet, cute, lovely,* and *divine* than men are.

Differences in the linguistic strategies and behavior of men and women are examined in several books by the well-known sociolinguist Deborah Tannen (1990; 1993). Tannen uses the terms *rapport* and *report* to contrast women's and men's overall linguistic styles. Women, says Tannen, typically use language and the body movements that accompany it to build rapport, social connections with others. Men, on the other hand, tend to make reports, reciting information to establish a place for themselves in a hierarchy, as they also attempt to determine the relative ranks of their conversation mates.

## Stratification and Symbolic Domination

We use and evaluate speech in the context of *extralinguistic* forces—social, political, and economic. Mainstream Americans evaluate the speech of low-status groups negatively, calling it "uneducated." This is not because these ways of speaking are bad in themselves but because they have come to symbolize low status. Consider variation in the pronunciation of *r*. In some parts of the United States, *r* is regularly pronounced, and in other (*r*less) areas it is not. Originally, American *r*less speech was modeled on the fashionable speech of England. Because of its prestige, *r*lessness was adopted in many areas and continues as the norm around Boston and in the South.

New Yorkers sought prestige by dropping their *r*'s in the 19th century, after having pronounced them in the 18th. However, contemporary New Yorkers are going back to the 18th-century pattern of pronouncing *r*'s. What matters, and what governs linguistic change, is not the reverberation of a strong midwestern *r* but *social* evaluation, whether *r*'s happen to be "in" or "out."

Studies of *r* pronunciation in New York City have clarified the mechanisms of phonological change. William Labov (1972*b*) focused on whether *r* was pronounced after vowels in such words as *car, floor, card,* and *fourth*. To get data on how this linguistic variation correlated with social class, he used a series of rapid encounters with employees in three New York City department stores, each of whose prices and locations attracted a different socioeconomic group. Saks Fifth Avenue (68 encounters) catered to the upper middle class, Macy's (125) attracted middle-class shoppers, and S. Klein's (71) had predominantly lower-middle-class and working-class customers. The class origins of store personnel reflected those of their customers.

Having already determined that a certain department was on the fourth floor, Labov approached ground-floor salespeople and asked where that department was. After the salesperson had answered, "Fourth floor," Labov repeated his "Where?" in order to get a second response. The second reply was more formal and emphatic, the salesperson presumably thinking that Labov hadn't heard or understood the first answer. For each salesperson, therefore, Labov had two samples of /r/ pronunciation in two words.

Labov calculated the percentages of workers who pronounced /r/ at least once during the interview. These were 62 percent at Saks, 51 percent at Macy's, but only 20 percent at S. Klein's. He also found that personnel on upper floors, where he asked, "What floor is this?" (and where more expensive items were sold), pronounced *r* more often than ground-floor salespeople did (see also Labov 2006).

In Labov's study, *r* pronunciation was clearly associated with prestige. Certainly the job interviewers who had hired the salespeople never counted *r*'s before offering employment. However, they did use speech evaluations to make judgments about how effective certain people would be in selling particular kinds of merchandise. In other words, they practiced sociolinguistic discrimination, using linguistic features in deciding who got certain jobs.

Our speech habits help determine our access to employment and other material resources. Because of this, "proper language" itself becomes a strategic resource—and a path to wealth, prestige, and power (Gal 1989; Thomas and Wareing, 2004). Illustrating this, many ethnographers have described the importance of verbal skill and oratory in politics (Geis 1987; G. Lakoff 2008; Lakoff and Wehling 2012). Ronald Reagan, known as a "great communicator," dominated American society in the 1980s as a two-term

Certain dialects are stigmatized, not because of actual linguistic deficiencies, but because of a symbolic association between a certain way of talking and low social status. In this scene from the movie *My Fair Lady,* Professor Henry Higgins (Rex Harrison) teaches Eliza Doolittle (Audrey Hepburn), formerly a Cockney flower girl, how to speak "proper English." © Warner Brothers/Album/Newscom

president. Another twice-elected president, Bill Clinton, despite his southern accent, was known for his verbal skills in certain contexts (e.g., televised debates and town-hall meetings). Communications flaws may have helped doom the presidencies of Gerald Ford, Jimmy Carter, and George Bush the elder. Does his or her use of language affect your perception of the current president of the United States?

The French anthropologist Pierre Bourdieu views linguistic practices as *symbolic capital* that properly trained people may convert into economic and social capital. The value of a dialect—its standing in a "linguistic market"—depends on the extent to which it provides access to desired positions in the labor market. In turn, this reflects its legitimation by formal institutions—educational institutions, state, church, and prestige media. Even people who don't use the prestige dialect accept its authority and correctness, its "symbolic domination" (Bourdieu 1982, 1984; Labov 2012). Thus, linguistic forms, which lack power in themselves, take on the power of the groups they symbolize. The education system, however (defending its own worth), denies linguistic relativity. It misrepresents prestige speech as being inherently better. The linguistic insecurity often felt by lower-class and minority speakers is a result of this symbolic domination.

## African American Vernacular English (AAVE)

The sociolinguist William Labov and several associates, both White and Black, have conducted detailed studies of what they call **African American Vernacular English (AAVE).** (*Vernacular* means ordinary, casual speech.) AAVE is the "relatively uniform dialect spoken by the majority of black youth in most parts of the United States today, especially in the inner city areas of New York, Boston, Detroit, Philadelphia, Washington, Cleveland, . . . and other urban centers. It is also spoken in most rural areas and used in the casual, intimate speech of many adults" (Labov 1972a, p. xiii). This does not imply that all, or even most, African Americans speak AAVE.

AAVE is a complex linguistic system with its own rules, which linguists have described. Consider some of the phonological and grammatical differences between AAVE and SE. One phonological difference is that AAVE speakers are less likely to pronounce r than SE speakers are. Actually, many SE speakers don't pronounce r's that come right before a consonant (card) or at the end of a word (car). But SE speakers usually do pronounce an r that comes right before a vowel, either at the end of a word (four o'clock) or within a word (Carol). AAVE speakers, by contrast, are much more likely to omit such intervocalic (between vowels) r's. The result is that speakers of the two dialects have different *homonyms* (words that sound the same but have different meanings). AAVE speakers who don't pronounce intervocalic r's have the following homonyms: Carol/Cal; Paris/pass.

Observing different phonological rules, AAVE speakers pronounce certain words differently than SE speakers do. Particularly in the elementary school context, the homonyms of AAVE speaking students typically differ from those of their SE-speaking teachers. To evaluate reading accuracy, teachers should determine whether students are recognizing the different meanings of such AAVE homonyms as *passed, past,* and *pass.* Teachers need to make sure students understand what they are reading, which is probably more important than whether they are pronouncing words correctly according to the SE norm.

Phonological rules may lead AAVE speakers to omit *-ed* as a past-tense marker and *-s* as a marker of plurality. However, other speech contexts demonstrate that AAVE speakers do understand the difference between past and present verbs, and between singular and plural nouns. Confirming this are irregular verbs (e.g., *tell, told*) and irregular plurals (e.g., *child, children*), in which AAVE works the same as SE.

SE is not superior to AAVE as a linguistic system, but it does happen to be the prestige dialect—the one used in the mass media, in writing, and in most public and professional contexts. SE is the dialect that has the most "symbolic capital." In areas of Germany where there is diglossia, speakers of Plattdeusch (Low German) learn the High German dialect to communicate appropriately in the national context. Similarly, upwardly mobile AAVE speaking students learn SE.

## Historical Linguistics

Sociolinguists study contemporary variation in speech, which is language change in progress. **Historical linguistics** deals with longer-term change. Historical linguists can reconstruct many features of past languages by studying contemporary **daughter languages.** These are languages that descend from the same parent language and that have been changing separately for hundreds or even thousands of years. We call the original language from which they diverge the **protolanguage.** Romance languages such as French and Spanish, for example, are daughter languages of Latin, their common protolanguage. German, English, Dutch, and the Scandinavian languages are daughter

## FIGURE 10.2    **PIE Family Tree**

Main languages and subgroups of the Indo-European language stock, showing approximate time to their divergence.

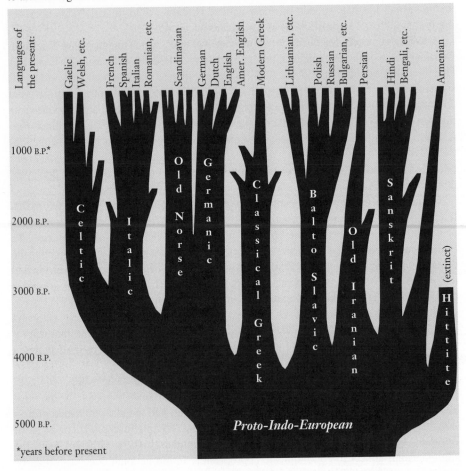

languages of proto-Germanic. The Romance languages and the Germanic languages all belong to the Indo-European (IE) language family. Their common protolanguage is called Proto-Indo-European, PIE (see Figure 10.2).

When did PIE originate and how did it spread? Decades ago, archaeologist Colin Renfrew (1987) traced the origin of PIE to a farming population living in Anatolia, now Turkey, about 9,000 years ago. Recent studies by the evolutionary biologist Quentin Atkinson and his colleagues in New Zealand support the Anatolian origin of PIE (see Bouckaert et al. 2012). Atkinson's team focused on a set of vocabulary items known to be resistant to linguistic change. These include pronouns, parts of the body, and family relations. For 103 IE languages, the researchers compared those words with the PIE ancestral word (as reconstructed by historical linguists). Words that clearly descend from the same ancestral word are known as *cognates*. For example, "mother" (English) is cognate with all these words for the same relative: "mutter" (German), "mat" (Russian), "madar" (Persian), "matka" (Polish), and "mater" (Latin). All are descendants of the PIE word "mehter."

For each language, when the word was a cognate, the researchers scored it 1; when it was not (having been replaced by an unrelated word), it was scored 0. With each language represented by a string of 1s and 0s, the researchers could establish a family tree showing the relationships among the 103 languages. Based on those relationships and the geographic areas where the daughter languages are spoken, the computer determined the likeliest routes of movement from an origin. The calculation pointed to Anatolia, southern Turkey. This is precisely the region originally proposed by Renfrew, because it was the area from which farming spread to Europe. Atkinson also ran a computer simulation on a grammar-based IE tree—once again finding Anatolia to be the most likely origin point for PIE (Wade 2012). Several lines of biological and archaeological evidence now indicate that the Neolithic economy spread more through the actual migration of farmers than through the diffusion of crops and ideas. This would seem to offer support to the Renfrew-Atkinson model of PIE origin and dispersal of Neolithic farmers.

Historically oriented linguists suspect that a very remote protolanguage, spoken perhaps 50,000 years ago in Africa, gave rise to all contemporary languages. Murray Gell-Mann and Merritt Ruhlen (2011), who co-direct the Program on the Evolution of Human Languages at the Sante Fe Institute, have reconstructed the syntax (word ordering) of this ancient protolanguage. Their study focused on how subject (S), objects (O), and verbs (V) are arranged in phrases and sentences in some 2,000 contemporary languages. There are six possible word orders: SOV, SVO, OSV, OVS, VSO, and VOS. Most common is SOV ("I you like," e.g., Latin), present in more than half of all languages. Next comes SVO ("I like you," e.g., English). Much rarer are OSV, OVS, VOS, and VSO. Gell-Mann and Ruhlen constructed a family tree of relationships among 2,000 contemporary languages. The directions of change involving the six word orders were clear. All the languages that were SVO, OVS, and OSV derived from SOV languages—never the other way around. Furthermore, any language with VSO or VOS word order always came from an SVO language (see Figure 10.3). The fact that SVO always comes from SOV confirms SOV as the original, ancestral word order.

Language changes over time. It evolves—varies, spreads, and divides into **subgroups** (languages within a taxonomy of related languages that are most closely related). Dialects of a single parent language become distinct daughter languages, especially if they are isolated from one another. Some of them split, and new "granddaughter" languages develop. If people remain in the ancestral homeland, their speech patterns also change. The evolving speech in the ancestral homeland should be considered a daughter language like the others.

**FIGURE 10.3  Evolution of Word Order from Original SVO (Subject, Object, Verb) in Ancient Ancestral Protolanguage**

A close relationship between languages doesn't necessarily mean that their speakers are closely related biologically or culturally, because people can adopt new languages. In the equatorial forests of Africa, "pygmy" hunters have discarded their ancestral languages and now speak those of the cultivators who have migrated to the area. Immigrants to the United States spoke many different languages on arrival, but their descendants now speak fluent English.

Cultural features may (or may not) correlate with the distribution of language families. Groups that speak related languages may (or may not) be more culturally similar to each other than they are to groups whose speech derives from different linguistic ancestors. Of course, cultural similarities aren't limited to speakers of related languages. Even groups whose members speak unrelated languages have contact through trade, intermarriage, and warfare. Many items of vocabulary in contemporary English, particularly food items such as "beef" and "pork," come from French. Even without written documentation of France's influence after the Norman Conquest of England in 1066, linguistic evidence in contemporary English would reveal a long period of important firsthand contact with France. Similarly, linguistic evidence may confirm cultural contact and borrowing when written history is lacking. By considering which words have been borrowed, we also can make inferences about the nature of the contact.

## Language Loss

One aspect of linguistic history is language loss. According to linguist K. David Harrison, "When we lose a language, we lose centuries of thinking about time, . . . seasons,

About 30 Native American groups are using a device known as the "phraselator" as an aid in preserving their endangered indigenous language. Shown here, Dakota tribal elder Curtis Campbell (left) and Dakota language teacher Wayne Wells work with the device at the Prairie Island Reservation in Minnesota. © Elizabeth Flores/ZUMA Press/Newscom

## Anthropology Today *I Wish They All Could Be California Vowels*

Is there a "California accent"? Popular stereotypes of how Californians talk reflect exposure to media images of White, blonde, valley girls and White, blond surfers, who say things like "dude," "gnarly," "Like, totally!" and "Gag me with a spoon!" Such stereotypes have some accuracy, as we'll see. Just as striking, however, is the linguistic diversity that also marks contemporary California.

To document this diversity, Professor Penelope Eckert, a sociolinguist at Stanford University, and her graduate students are engaged in an ongoing, multiyear research project that is called Voices of California (see http://www.stanford.edu/dept/linguistics/VoCal/). Eckert's team of 10–15 researchers visits a new site each fall, spending about 10 days interviewing residents who grew up in the area. Recently, their focus has been on inland California, which has been less studied than have the main coastal cities. In previous years, the group visited Merced and Redding; in 2012, they focused on Bakersfield. The researchers always test certain words that elicit specific pronunciations. These words include *wash*, sometimes pronounced "warsh," *greasy* ("greezy"), and *pin* and *pen*, which some people pronounce the same. Interviews in Merced and Shasta Counties have revealed ways that Depression-era migrants from Oklahoma's Dust Bowl left their mark on California speech, such as their pronunciation of *wash* and *greasy* (see King 2012).

We see, then, that one factor in determining how people speak is where their ancestors came from. Another factor is their own attitudes and feelings about the people around them and about the outside world. For example, in California's Central Valley, which is economically depressed, young people must choose whether to stay put or to move elsewhere, seeking work. When people are, and want to stay, involved in their home community, they tend to talk like locals. A desire not to be perceived as being from a particular place also affects how people talk (King 2012).

I know this feeling well, having abandoned my original southern accent when I was an adolescent. In fact, my own speech shift wasn't totally voluntary: As mentioned in the text, I was placed in a speech class when I moved from Atlanta to New York City at the age of 13. The same thing happened to my college roommate, from Baton Rouge, Louisiana, when he enrolled at Columbia University in New York City. By then, my own speech had become sufficiently accent free to avoid further speech indoctrination.

In addition to regional diversity, the speech of Californians also reflects ethnic contrasts. Non-Hispanic Whites now represent under 40 percent of the state's total population, while Latinos (Hispanics) constitute 38 percent. California also has a large and diverse Asian American population and a sizeable group of African Americans.

Representing California's largest minority, as well as its earliest nonindigenous settlers, Chicanos (Mexican Americans) display interesting speech patterns. California's Mexican-derived populations can claim the longest continuous (nonindigenous) linguistic history in the state, including Spanish/English bilingualism and the source of most important place names. So strong is the Spanish heritage that Spanish-like vowels even influence the way English is spoken by Hispanics who learn English as their first, or native, language. For example, among Chicano speakers in

*continued*

## Anthropology Today   *continued*

northern California the vowel in the second syllable of *nothing* has come to resemble the Spanish "ee" sound. Not all innovations in Chicano English come from Spanish. One widespread speech innovation in Los Angeles has been the lowering of the vowel in the first syllable of *elevator,* so that it rhymes with the first syllable of *alligator*. That shift owes nothing to Spanish (see Eckert and Mendoza-Denton 2002).

Despite the well-documented diversity in California speech, linguists have detected trends toward uniformity as well, particularly among coastal Whites. Since the 1940s, a distinctive "California accent" has been developing, and some of its features were indeed highlighted in Moon Unit Zappa's 1982 recording of "Valley Girl."

The accent is most evident in vowels, as we see in the following examples. First, the vowels in *hock* and *hawk*, or *cot* and *caught*, are pronounced the same, so that *awesome* rhymes with *possum*. Second, the vowel sound in *boot* and *dude* has

shifted and now is pronounced as in *pure* or *cute* (thus, *boot* becomes "beaut," and *dude* becomes "dewed," rather than "dood"). Third, the vowel sound in *but* and *cut* is shifting, so that those words sound more like *bet* and *ket*. Finally, *black* is being pronounced more like *block*; *bet*, like *bat* (see Eckert and Mendoza-Denton 2002).

Such coordinated phonological changes are known as chain shifts. The most extreme versions of these chain-shifted vowel sounds are found in the speech of young White Californians. Young people tend to be leaders in speech innovations, which is why linguists spend a lot of time studying them. California's communities bring together adolescents from varied backgrounds. Their linguistic styles, like their clothing and behavioral styles, influence one another. Hostility may cause people to differentiate and diversify their styles, while curiosity or admiration may cause people to copy, or adopt elements from, other styles. Whose styles, linguistic or otherwise, might you have copied—or avoided?

mathematics, landscapes, myths, music, the unknown and the everyday" (quoted in Maugh 2007). Harrison's book *When Languages Die* (2007) notes that an indigenous language goes extinct every two weeks. The world's linguistic diversity has been cut in half (measured by number of distinct languages) in the past 500 years, and half of the remaining languages are predicted to disappear during this century. Colonial languages (e.g., English, Spanish, Portuguese, French, Dutch, Russian) have expanded at the expense of indigenous ones. Of approximately 7,000 remaining languages, about 20 percent are endangered, compared with 18 percent of mammals, 8 percent of plants, and 5 percent of birds (Harrison 2010; Maugh 2007).

Harrison is director of research for the Living Tongues Institute for Endangered Languages (http://www.livingtongues.org), which works to maintain, preserve, and revitalize endangered languages. Researchers from the institute use digital audio and video equipment to record the last speakers of the most endangered languages. *National Geographic*'s Enduring Voices Project (http://travel.nationalgeographic.com/travel/enduring-voices/) strives to preserve endangered languages by identifying the geographic areas with unique, poorly understood, or threatened languages and by documenting those languages and cultures.

The website shows various language hot spots where the endangerment rate ranges from low to severe. The rate is high in an area encompassing Oklahoma, Texas, and New Mexico, where 40 Native American languages are at risk. The top hot spot is northern Australia, where 153 Aboriginal languages are endangered (Maugh 2007). Other hot spots are in central South America, the Pacific Northwest of North America, and eastern Siberia. In all these areas indigenous tongues have yielded, either voluntarily or through coercion, to a colonial language.

---

## Summary

1. Wild primates use call systems to communicate. Environmental stimuli trigger calls, which cannot be combined when multiple stimuli are present. Contrasts between language and call systems include displacement, productivity, and cultural transmission. Over time, our ancestral call systems grew too complex for genetic transmission, and hominin communication began to rely on learning. Humans still use nonverbal communication, such as facial expressions, gestures, and body stances and movements. But language is the main system humans use to communicate. Chimps and gorillas can understand and manipulate nonverbal symbols based on language.

2. No language uses all the sounds the human vocal tract can make. Phonology—the study of speech sounds—focuses on sound contrasts (phonemes) that distinguish meaning. The grammars and lexicons of particular languages can lead their speakers to perceive and think in certain ways.

3. Linguistic anthropologists share anthropology's general interest in diversity in time and space. Sociolinguistics investigates relationships between social and linguistic variation by focusing on the actual use of language. Only when features of speech acquire social meaning are they imitated. If they are valued, they will spread. People vary their speech, shifting styles, dialects, and languages.

4. As linguistic systems, all languages and dialects are equally complex, rule-governed, and effective for communication. However, speech is used, is evaluated, and changes in the context of political, economic, and social forces. Often the linguistic traits of a low-status group are negatively evaluated. This devaluation is not because of linguistic features per se. Rather, it reflects the association of such features with low social status. One dialect, supported by the dominant institutions of the state, exercises symbolic domination over the others.

5. Historical linguistics is useful for anthropologists interested in historical relationships among populations. Cultural similarities and differences often correlate with linguistic ones. Linguistic clues can suggest past contacts between cultures. Related languages—members of the same language family—descend from an original protolanguage. Relationships between languages don't necessarily mean there are biological ties between their speakers, because people can learn new languages.

6. One aspect of linguistic history is language loss. The world's linguistic diversity has been cut in half in the past 500 years, and half of the remaining 7,000 languages are predicted to disappear during this century.

**Key Terms**

African American Vernacular English (AAVE), *234*
call systems, *219*
cultural transmission, *221*
daughter languages, *235*
descriptive linguistics, *224*

diglossia, *231*
displacement, *222*
focal vocabulary, *228*
historical linguistics, *235*
kinesics, *223*
lexicon, *224*
morphology, *224*
phoneme, *225*
phonemics, *225*

phonetics, *225*
phonology, *224*
productivity, *221*
protolanguage, *235*
Sapir-Whorf hypothesis, *227*
semantics, *229*
sociolinguistics, *230*
style shifts, *231*
subgroups, *237*
syntax, *224*

# Chapter 11

# Making a Living

In today's globalizing world, communities and societies are being incorporated, at an accelerating rate, into larger systems (Caldararo 2014). The first major acceleration in the growth of human social systems can be traced back to around 12,000–10,000 years ago, when humans started intervening in the reproductive cycles of plants and animals. **Food production** refers to human control over the reproduction of plants and animals, and it contrasts with the foraging economies that preceded it and that still persist in some parts of the world. To make their living, foragers hunt, gather, and collect what nature has to offer. Foragers may harvest, but they don't plant. They may hunt animals, but (except for the dog) they don't domesticate them. Only food producers systematically select and breed for desirable traits in plants and animals. With the advent of food production, which includes plant cultivation and animal domestication, people, rather than nature, become selective agents. Human selection replaces natural selection as food collectors become food producers.

The origin and spread of food production accelerated human population growth and led to the formation of larger and more powerful social and political systems. The pace of cultural transformation increased enormously. This chapter provides a framework for understanding a variety of human adaptive strategies and economic systems.

# Adaptive Strategies

The anthropologist Yehudi Cohen (1974) used the term *adaptive strategy* to describe a society's main system of economic production. Cohen argued that the most important reason for similarities between two (or more) unrelated societies is their possession of a similar adaptive strategy. In other words, similar economic causes have similar sociocultural effects. For example, there are clear similarities among societies that have a foraging (hunting and gathering) strategy. Cohen developed a typology of societies based on correlations between their economies and their social features. His typology includes these five adaptive strategies: foraging, horticulture, agriculture, pastoralism, and industrialism. Industrialism is the focus of the last two chapters of this book. The present chapter focuses on the first four adaptive strategies, which are characteristic of nonindustrial societies.

## Foraging

Until about 12,000 years ago all humans were foragers. However, environmental differences did create substantial contrasts among the world's foragers. Some, like the people who lived in Europe during the ice ages, were big-game hunters. Today, hunters in the Arctic still focus on large animals; they have much less vegetation and variety in their diets than do tropical foragers. Moving from colder to hotter areas, the number of species increases. The tropics contain tremendous biodiversity, and tropical foragers typically hunt and gather a wide range of plant and animal species. The same may be true in temperate areas. For example, on the North Pacific Coast of North America, foragers could draw on varied sea, river, and land species, such as salmon and other fish, sea mammals, berries, and mountain goats. Despite differences caused by such environmental variation, all foraging economies have shared one essential feature: People rely on nature to make their living. They don't grow crops or breed and tend animals.

Animal domestication (initially of sheep and goats) and plant cultivation (of wheat and barley) began 12,000 to 10,000 years ago in the Middle East. Cultivation based on different crops, such as corn (maize), manioc (cassava), and potatoes, arose independently in the Americas. In both hemispheres most societies eventually turned from foraging to food production. Today most foragers have at least some dependence on food production or on food producers (Kent 2002).

The foraging way of life survived into modern times in certain forests, deserts, islands, and very cold areas—places where cultivation was not practicable with simple technology (see Lee and Daly 1999). In many areas, foragers knew about food production but never adopted it because their own economies provided a perfectly satisfactory lifestyle and an adequate and nutritious diet. In some places, people reverted to foraging after trying food production and abandoning it.

*All contemporary foragers live in nation-states and are influenced by national policies.* Typically, they are in contact with food-producing neighbors as well as with missionaries and other outsiders. We should not view contemporary foragers as isolated or pristine survivors of the Stone Age. Modern foragers are influenced by national and international policies and political and economic events in the world system.

## Geographic Distribution of Foragers

In Africa we can identify two broad belts of contemporary or recent foraging. One is the Kalahari Desert of southern Africa. This is the home of the San ("Bushmen"), who include the Ju/'hoansi (Lee 2003, 2012). The other main African foraging area is the equatorial forest of central and eastern Africa, home of the Mbuti, Efe, and other "pygmies."

People still do, or until recently did, subsistence foraging in certain remote forests in Madagascar, in South and Southeast Asia, in Malaysia, in the Philippines, and on certain islands off the Indian coast. Some of the best-known recent foragers are the aborigines of Australia. Those Native Australians lived on their island continent for perhaps 50,000 years without developing food production.

The Western Hemisphere also had recent foragers. The Eskimos, or Inuit, of Alaska and Canada are well-known hunters. These (and other) northern foragers now use modern technology, including rifles and snowmobiles, in their subsistence activities. The native populations of California, Oregon, Washington, and British Columbia all were foragers, as were those of inland subarctic Canada and the Great Lakes. For many Native Americans, fishing, hunting, and gathering remain important subsistence (and sometimes commercial) activities.

Coastal foragers also lived near the southern tip of South America, in Patagonia. On the grassy plains of Argentina, southern Brazil, Uruguay, and Paraguay, there were other hunter-gatherers. The contemporary Aché of Paraguay usually are called "hunter-gatherers," although they now get just a third of their livelihood from foraging. The Aché also grow crops, have domesticated animals, and live in or near mission posts, where they receive food from missionaries (Hawkes, O'Connell, and Hill 1982; Hill and Hurtado 1996).

Jana Fortier (2009) summarizes key attributes of foragers in South Asia, which today is home to more full- and part-time hunter-gatherers than any other world area. In India, Nepal, and Sri Lanka, about 40 societies and an estimated 150,000 people continue to derive their subsistence from full- or part-time foraging. Hill Kharias and Yanadis are the largest contemporary South Asian (SA) foraging populations, with about 20,000 members each. Several other ethnic groups are highly endangered, with fewer than 350 members still doing subsistence foraging.

Surviving SA foraging societies are those whose members, despite having lost many of their natural resources to deforestation and spreading farming populations, have been unwilling to adopt food cultivation and its cultural correlates. These hunter-gatherers share features with other foragers worldwide: small social groups, mobile settlement patterns, sharing of resources, immediate food consumption, egalitarianism, and decision making by mutual consent (Fortier 2009).

As is true elsewhere, specific foraging techniques reflect variations in environment and resource distribution. Hill and mountain SA foragers favor focused hunting of medium-sized prey (langur monkey, macaque, porcupine). Other groups pursue several small species or practice broad-spectrum foraging of bats, porcupines, and deer. Larger groups use communal hunting techniques, such as spreading nets over large fig trees to entangle sleeping bats. Some South Indian foragers focus on such wild plant resources as yams, palms, and taro, in addition to 100+ locally available plants. Harvesting honey and beeswax has been prominent in many SA foraging societies (Fortier 2009).

Their members cherish their identities as people who forage for a living in biologically rich and diverse environments. They stress their need for continued access to rich forest resources to continue their lifestyles, yet many have been evicted from their traditional habitats. Their best chances for cultural survival depend on national governments that maintain healthy forests, allow foragers access to their traditional resources, and foster cultural survival rather than assimilation (Fortier 2009).

Throughout the world, foraging survived in environments that posed major obstacles to food production. The difficulties of cultivating at the North Pole are obvious. In southern Africa the Dobe Ju/'hoansi San area studied by Richard Lee and others is surrounded by a waterless belt 43 to 124 miles (70 to 200 kilometers) in breadth (Lee 2012).

Environmental obstacles to food production aren't the only reason foragers survived. Their niches had one thing in common—their marginality. Their environments were not of immediate interest to farmers, herders, or colonialists. See Figure 11.1 for a partial distribution of recent hunter-gatherers.

As the modern world system spreads, the number of foragers continues to decline. Each year more and more foragers come under the control of nation-states and are influenced by forces of globalization. As described by Motseta (2006), for example, between 1997 and 2002, the government of Botswana in southern Africa relocated about 3,000 Basarwa San Bushmen outside their ancestral territory, which was converted into a reserve for wildlife

FIGURE 11.1    **Locations of Some Recent Hunter-Gatherers**

Source: Robert L. Kelly, *The Foraging Spectrum: Diversity in Hunter-Gatherer Lifeways*, fig. 1.1. Copyright © 2007 by Eliot Werner Publications, Inc. Reprinted by permission of the publisher.

protection. Botswana's High Court eventually ruled that the Basarwa had been wrongly evicted from the "Central Kalahari Game Reserve" and issued a court order allowing them to return, but under conditions likely to prevent most of them from doing so. Only the 189 people who had actually filed the lawsuit were granted automatic right of return with their children, compared with some 2,000 Basarwa wishing to go back. The others would have to apply for special permits. Returning Basarwa would be allowed to build only temporary structures and to use enough water for subsistence needs. Water would be a major obstacle, since the government shut the main well in 2002. Furthermore, anyone wishing to hunt would have to apply for a permit. So goes the foraging way of life in today's world.

## Correlates of Foraging

Typologies, such as Cohen's adaptive strategies, are useful because they suggest **correlations**—that is, associations or covariations between two or more variables. (Correlated variables are factors that are linked and interrelated, such as food intake and body weight, such that when one increases or decreases, the other changes as well.) Ethnographic studies in hundreds of societies have revealed many correlations between the economy and social life. Associated (correlated) with each adaptive strategy is a bundle of particular sociocultural features. Correlations, however, rarely are perfect. Some foragers lack cultural features usually associated with foraging, and some of those features are found in groups with other adaptive strategies.

What, then, are some correlates of foraging? People who subsisted by hunting and gathering often, but not always, lived in band-organized societies. Their basic social unit, the **band,** was a small group of fewer than a hundred people, all related by kinship or marriage. Among some foragers, band size stayed about the same year-round. In others, the band split up for part of the year. Families left to gather resources that were better exploited by just a few people. Later, they regrouped for cooperative work and ceremonies.

Typical characteristics of the foraging life are flexibility and mobility. In many San groups, as among the Mbuti of Congo, people shifted band membership several times in a lifetime. One could be born, for example, in a band in which one's mother had kin. Later, one's family could move to a band in which the father had relatives. Because bands were exogamous (people married outside their own band), one's parents came from two different bands, and one's grandparents could have come from four. People could join any band to which they had kin or marital links. A couple could live in, or shift between, the husband's and the wife's band.

Many foraging societies make distinctions based on age. Old people may receive respect as guardians of myths, legends, stories, and traditions. Younger people may value the elders' special knowledge of ritual and practical matters. In general, foraging societies tend to be *egalitarian*, with only minor contrasts in prestige and no significant contrasts in wealth and power.

When considering issues of "human nature," we should remember that the egalitarian society associated with the foraging strategy of adaptation was a basic form of human social life for most of our history. Food production has existed less than 1 percent of the time *Homo* has spent on Earth. However, it has created huge social differences. We now consider the main economic features of food-producing strategies.

# Adaptive Strategies Based on Food Production

In Cohen's typology, the three adaptive strategies based on food production in nonindustrial societies are horticulture, agriculture, and pastoralism. With horticulture and agriculture, plant cultivation is the mainstay of the economy, while with pastoralism, herding is key. All three strategies originated in nonindustrial societies, although they may persist as ways of making a living even after some degree of industrialization reaches the nation-states that include them. In fully industrial societies, such as the United States and Canada, most cultivation has become large-scale, commercial, mechanized, agrochemical-dependent farming. Rather than simple pastoralism, industrial societies use technologically sophisticated systems of ranch and livestock management. These industrial societies, and their global context, will be the focus of the last two chapters of this book. This chapter's focus is on nonindustrial strategies of adaptation.

Just as they do in the United States and Canada, people in nonindustrial societies carry out a variety of economic activities. In Cohen's typology, each adaptive strategy refers to the main economic activity. Pastoralists (herders), for example, consume milk, butter, blood, and meat from their animals as mainstays of their diet. However, they also add grain to their diet by doing some cultivating or by trading with neighbors.

## Horticulture

The two types of plant cultivation found in nonindustrial societies are **horticulture** (nonintensive, shifting cultivation) and **agriculture** (intensive, continuous cultivation). Both differ from the commercially oriented farming systems of industrial nations, which use large land areas and rely on machinery and petrochemicals.

Horticulturalists use simple tools such as hoes and digging sticks to grow their crops. Horticulturalists preserve their ecosystems by allowing their fields to lie fallow for varying lengths of time. Often horticulturalists employ *slash-and-burn* techniques; they clear land by cutting down (slashing) and burning forest or bush or by setting fire to the grass covering the plot. The vegetation is broken down, pests are killed, and the ashes remain to fertilize the soil. Crops then are sown, tended, and harvested. Use of the plot is not continuous. Often it is cultivated only for a year or two.

When horticulturalists abandon a plot, they clear another piece of land, and the original plot reverts to forest. After several years of fallowing, the cultivator returns to farm the original plot again. Because the relationship between people and their plots is not permanent, horticulture also is called *shifting cultivation*. Shifting cultivation does not mean that whole villages must move when plots are abandoned. Among the Kuikuru of the South American tropical forest, one village of 150 people remained in the same place for 90 years (Carneiro 1956). Kuikuru houses were large and well made. Because the work involved in building their houses was substantial, the Kuikuru preferred to walk farther to their fields than to construct a new village. They shifted their plots rather than their settlements. On the other hand, horticulturalists in the montaña (Andean foothills) of Peru lived in small villages of about 30 people (Carneiro 1961/1968). Their houses were small and simple. After a few years in one place, these people built new villages near virgin land. Because their houses were so simple, they preferred rebuilding to walking even a half mile to their fields.

In slash-and-burn cultivation, the land is cleared by cutting down (slashing) and burning trees and bush. After such clearing, digging sticks are used to plant mountain rice in Madagascar. © Frans Lanting/National Geographic Stock

## Agriculture

The greater labor demands associated with agriculture, as compared with horticulture, reflect its use of domesticated animals, irrigation, or terracing.

### Domesticated Animals

Many agriculturists use animals as means of production—for transport, as cultivating machines, and for their manure. Asian farmers typically incorporate cattle and/or water buffalo into their agricultural economies. Those rice farmers may use cattle to trample pre-tilled flooded fields, thus mixing soil and water, before transplanting. Many agriculturists attach animals to plows and harrows for field preparation before planting or transplanting. Also, agriculturists typically collect manure from their animals, using it to fertilize their plots, thus increasing yields. Animals are attached to carts for transport and to implements of cultivation.

### Irrigation

While horticulturalists must await the rainy season, agriculturists can schedule their planting in advance because they control water. Like other irrigation experts in the Philippines, the Ifugao water their fields with canals from rivers, streams, springs, and ponds. Irrigation makes it possible to cultivate a plot year after year. Irrigation enriches the soil because the irrigated field is a unique ecosystem with several species of plants and animals, many of them minute organisms, whose wastes fertilize the land.

An irrigated field is a capital investment that usually increases in value. It takes time for a field to start yielding; it reaches full productivity only after several years of cultivation. The Ifugao, like other irrigators, have farmed the same fields for generations. In some agricultural areas, including the Middle East, however, salts carried in the irrigation water can make fields unusable after 50 or 60 years.

### Terracing

Terracing is another agricultural technique the Ifugao have mastered. Their homeland has small valleys separated by steep hillsides. Because the population is dense, people

Agriculture requires longer work hours than horticulture does and uses land intensively and continuously. Labor demands associated with agriculture reflect its use of domesticated animals, irrigation, and terracing. Shown here, irrigated terraces surround the Ifugao village of Banaue on Luzon Island in the Philippines. © Michele Falzone/JAI/Corbis RF

need to farm the hills. However, if they simply planted on the steep hillsides, fertile soil and crops would be washed away during the rainy season. To prevent this, the Ifugao cut into the hillside and build stage after stage of terraced fields rising above the valley floor. Springs located above the terraces supply their irrigation water. The labor necessary to build and maintain a system of terraces is great. Terrace walls crumble each year and must be partially rebuilt. The canals that bring water down through the terraces also demand attention.

## Costs and Benefits of Agriculture

Agriculture requires human labor to build and maintain irrigation systems, terraces, and other works. People must feed, water, and care for their animals. But agricultural land can yield one or two crops annually for years, or even generations. An agricultural field does not necessarily produce a higher single-year yield than does a horticultural plot. The first crop grown by horticulturalists on long-idle land may be larger than that from an agricultural plot of the same size. Furthermore, because agriculturists have to work more hours than horticulturalists do, agriculture's yield relative to the labor time invested also is lower. Agriculture's main advantage is that the long-term yield per area is far greater and more dependable. Because a single field sustains its owners year after year, there is no need to maintain a reserve of uncultivated land as horticulturalists do. This is why agricultural societies tend to be more densely populated than horticultural ones.

## The Cultivation Continuum

Because some nonindustrial economies have features of both horticulture and agriculture, it is useful to discuss cultivators as being arranged along a cultivation continuum. Horticultural systems stand at one end—the "low-labor, shifting-plot" end. Agriculturalists are at the other—the "labor-intensive, permanent-plot" end.

We speak of a continuum because there are intermediate economies, combining horticultural and agricultural features—more intensive than annually shifting horticulture but less intensive than agriculture. Unlike horticulturalists who farm a plot just once before fallowing it, the South American Kuikuru grow two or three crops of manioc, or cassava—an edible tuber—before abandoning their plots. Cultivation is even more intense in certain densely populated areas of Papua New Guinea, where plots are planted for two or three years, allowed to rest for three to five, and then recultivated. After several of these cycles, the plots are abandoned for a longer fallow period. Such a pattern is called *sectorial fallowing* (Wolf 1966). Besides Papua New Guinea, such systems occur in places as distant as West Africa and highland Mexico. Sectorial fallowing is associated with denser populations than is simple horticulture.

The key difference between horticulture and agriculture is that horticulture always has a fallow period, whereas agriculture does not. The earliest cultivators in the Middle East and in Mexico were rainfall-dependent horticulturalists. Until recently, horticulture was the main form of cultivation in several areas, including parts of Africa, Southeast Asia, the Pacific islands, Mexico, Central America, and the South American tropical forest.

## Agricultural Intensification: People and the Environment

The range of environments available for cultivation has widened as people have increased their control over nature. Agriculturists have been able to colonize many areas that are too arid for nonirrigators or too hilly for nonterracers. Agriculture's increased labor intensity and permanent land use have major demographic, social, political, and environmental consequences.

Thus, because of their permanent fields, agriculturists tend to be sedentary. People live in larger and more permanent communities located closer to other settlements. Growth in population size and density increases contact between individuals and groups. There is more need to regulate interpersonal relations, including conflicts of interest. Economies that support more people usually require more coordination in the use of land, labor, and other resources (see the next chapter).

Intensive agriculture has significant environmental effects. Irrigation ditches and paddies (fields with irrigated rice) become repositories for organic wastes, chemicals (such as salts), and disease microorganisms. Intensive agriculture typically spreads at the expense of trees and forests, which are cut down to be replaced by fields. Accompanying such deforestation is loss of environmental diversity (see Dove and Carpenter 2008). Compared with horticulture, agricultural economies are specialized. They focus on one or a few caloric staples, such as rice, and on the animals that aid the agricultural economy. Because tropical horticulturalists typically cultivate dozens of plant species simultaneously, a horticultural plot mirrors the botanical diversity that is found in a tropical forest. Agricultural plots, by contrast, reduce ecological diversity by cutting down trees and concentrating on just a few staple foods. Such crop specialization is true of agriculturists both in the tropics (e.g., Indonesian paddy farmers) and outside the tropics (e.g., Middle Eastern irrigation farmers).

Agriculturists attempt to reduce risk in production by favoring stability in the form of a reliable annual harvest and long-term production. Tropical foragers and horticulturalists, by contrast, attempt to reduce risk by relying on multiple species and benefiting from ecological diversity. The agricultural strategy is to put all one's eggs in one big and very dependable basket. The strategy of tropical foragers and horticulturalists is to have several smaller baskets, a few of which may fail without endangering subsistence. The agricultural strategy makes sense when there are lots of children to raise and adults to be fed. Foraging and horticulture, of course, are associated with smaller, sparser, and more mobile populations.

Agricultural economies also pose a series of regulatory problems. How is water to be managed? How are disputes about access to and distribution of water to be resolved? With more people living closer together on more valuable land, agriculturists have more opportunities for interpersonal contact and conflict than foragers and horticulturalists do. The social and political implications of food production and intensification are examined more fully in the next chapter, "Political Systems."

Anthropologists know that many indigenous groups—especially foragers and nonintensive cultivators—have done a reasonable job of managing their resources and preserving their ecosystems (see Menzies 2006). Such societies had traditional ways of categorizing resources and regulating their use. Increasingly, however, these traditional management systems have been challenged by national and international incentives to exploit and degrade the environment (see Dove, Sajise, and Doolittle 2011). These challenges are the focus of the last two chapters of this book.

## Pastoralism

Herders, or **pastoralists,** are people whose activities focus on such domesticated animals as cattle, sheep, goats, camels, yak, and reindeer. They live in North and sub-Saharan Africa, the Middle East, Europe, and Asia. East African pastoralists, like many others, live in symbiosis with their herds. (*Symbiosis* is an obligatory interaction between groups—here humans and animals—that is beneficial to each.) Herders attempt to protect their animals and to ensure their reproduction in return for food (dairy products and meat) and other products, such as leather.

People use livestock in various ways. Natives of North America's Great Plains, for example, didn't eat, but only rode, their horses. (They got those horses after Europeans reintroduced them to the Western Hemisphere; the native American horse had gone extinct thousands of years earlier.) For Plains Indians, horses served as "tools of the trade," means of production used to *hunt* buffalo, the main target of their economies. So the Plains Indians were not true pastoralists but hunters who used horses—as many agriculturists use animals—as means of production.

Pastoralists, by contrast, typically use their herds for food. They consume their meat, blood, and milk, from which they make yogurt, butter, and cheese. Although some pastoralists rely on their herds more completely than others do, it is impossible to base subsistence solely on animals. Most pastoralists therefore supplement their diet by hunting, gathering, fishing, cultivating, or trading.

The Samis (also known as Lapps or Laplanders) of Norway, Sweden, and Finland domesticated the reindeer, which their ancestors had once hunted, in the 16th century. Like other herders, they follow their animals as they make an annual trek, in this case from coast to interior. Today's Samis use modern technology, such as snowmobiles and four-wheel-drive vehicles, to accompany their herds on their annual nomadic trek. Some of them probably use reindeer management software on their laptops and PDAs. Although their environment is harsher, the Samis, like other herders, live in nation-states and must deal with outsiders, including government officials, as they follow their herds and make their living through animal husbandry, trade, and sales (Hoge 2001; Paine 2009).

Unlike foraging and cultivation, which existed throughout the world before the Industrial Revolution, pastoralism was confined almost totally to the Old World. Before European conquest, the only herders in the Americas lived in the Andean region of South America. They used their llamas and alpacas for food and wool and in agriculture and transport. Much more recently, Navajo of the southwestern United States developed a pastoral economy based on sheep, which were brought to North America by Europeans. The populous Navajo became the major pastoral population in the Western Hemisphere.

Two patterns of movement occur with pastoralism: *nomadism* and *transhumance.* Both are based on the fact that herds must move to use pasture available in particular places in different seasons. In **pastoral nomadism,** the entire group—women, men, and children—moves with the animals throughout the year. The Middle East and North Africa provide numerous examples of pastoral nomads (see Salzman 2008). In Iran, for example, the Basseri and the Qashqai ethnic groups traditionally followed a nomadic route more than 300 miles (480 kilometers) long (see Salzman 2004).

With **transhumance,** part of the group moves with the herds but most people stay in the home village. There are examples from Europe and Africa. In Europe's Alps it is just the shepherds and goatherds—not the whole hamlet, village, or town—who accompany the flocks to highland meadows in summer. Among the Turkana of Uganda, men and boys take the herds to distant pastures, while much of the village stays put and does some horticultural farming. During their annual trek, pastoral nomads trade for crops and other products with more sedentary people. Transhumants don't have to trade for crops. Because only part of the population accompanies the herds, transhumants can maintain year-round villages and grow their own crops.

# Economic Systems

An **economy** is a system of production, distribution, and consumption of resources; *economics* is the study of such systems. Economists tend to focus on modern nations and capitalist systems. Anthropologists have broadened understanding of economic principles by gathering data on nonindustrial economies. Economic anthropology brings a comparative perspective to the study of economics (see Carrier 2012; Chibnik 2011; Hann and Hart 2011; Sahlins 2011; Wilk and Cliggett 2007).

A **mode of production** is a way of organizing production—"a set of social relations through which labor is deployed to wrest energy from nature by means of tools, skills, organization, and knowledge" (Wolf 1982, p. 75). In the capitalist mode of production, money buys labor power, and there is a social gap between the people (bosses and work-ers) involved in the production process. By contrast, in nonindustrial societies, labor usually is not bought but is given as a social obligation. In such a *kin-based* mode of production, mutual aid in production is one among many expressions of a larger web of social relations (see Marshall 2011).

Societies representing each of the adaptive strategies just discussed (e.g., foraging) tend to have roughly similar modes of production. Differences in the mode of produc-tion within a given strategy may reflect differences in environments, target resources, or cultural traditions. Thus, a foraging mode of production may be based on individual hunters or teams, depending on whether the game is solitary, or a herd or flocking ani-mal. Gathering usually is more individualistic than hunting, although collecting teams may assemble when abundant resources ripen and must be harvested quickly. Fishing may be done alone (as in ice or spear fishing) or in crews (as with open-sea fishing and hunting of sea mammals).

## Production in Nonindustrial Societies

Although some kind of division of economic labor related to age and gender is a cultural universal, the specific tasks assigned to each sex and to people of different ages vary (see the chapter "Gender"). Many horticultural societies assign a major productive role to women, but some make men's work primary. Similarly, among pastoralists men gen-erally tend large animals, but in some societies women do the milking. Jobs accom-plished through teamwork in some cultivating societies are done in other societies by smaller groups or by individuals working over a longer period.

The Betsileo of Madagascar have two stages of teamwork in rice cultivation: trans-planting and harvesting. Both feature a traditional division of labor by age and gender that is well known and repeated across the generations. The first job in transplanting is the trampling of a flooded, previously tilled field by young men driving cattle, in order to mix earth and water. They take cattle to the fields just before transplanting. The young men yell at and beat the cattle, striving to drive them into a frenzy, so that they will trample the fields properly. Trampling breaks up clumps of earth and mixes irrigation water with soil to form a smooth mud, into which women transplant seedlings. Once the tramplers leave the field, older men arrive. With their spades they break up the clumps the cattle missed. Meanwhile, the owner and other adults uproot rice seedlings and take them to the field. Women plant the seedlings.

At harvest time, four or five months later, young men cut the rice off the stalks. Young women carry it to the clearing above the field. Older women arrange and stack it. The oldest men and women then stand on the stack, stomping and compacting it. Three days later, young men thresh the rice, beating the stalks against a rock to remove the grain. Older men then beat the stalks with sticks to make sure all the grains have fallen off.

## Means of Production

In nonindustrial societies the relationship between the worker and the means of produc-tion is more intimate than it is in industrial nations. **Means,** or **factors, of production** include land (territory), labor, and technology.

## Land as a Means of Production

Among foragers, ties between people and land were less permanent than among food producers. Although many bands had territories, the boundaries usually were not marked, and there was no way they could be enforced. The hunter's stake in an animal was more important than where the animal finally died. A person acquired the rights to use a band's territory by being born in the band or by joining it through a tie of kinship, marriage, or fictive kinship. In Botswana in southern Africa, Ju/'hoansi San women habitually used specific tracts of berry-bearing trees. When a woman changed bands, she immediately acquired a new gathering area.

Among food producers, rights to the means of production also come through kinship and marriage. Descent groups (groups whose members claim common ancestry) are common among nonindustrial food producers. Those who descend from the founder share the group's territory and resources. If the adaptive strategy is horticulture, the estate includes gardens and fallow land for shifting cultivation. As members of a descent group, pastoralists have access to animals to start their own herds, to grazing land, to garden land, and to other means of production.

## Labor, Tools, and Specialization

Like land, labor is a means of production. In nonindustrial societies, access to both land and labor comes through social links such as kinship, marriage, and descent. Mutual aid in production is merely one aspect of ongoing social relations that are expressed on many other occasions.

Nonindustrial societies contrast with industrial nations regarding another means of production—technology. Manufacturing often is linked to age and gender. Women may weave and men may make pottery, or vice versa. Most people of a particular age and gender share the technical knowledge associated with that age and gender. If married women customarily make baskets, most married women know how to make baskets. Neither technology nor technical knowledge is very specialized.

Some tribal societies, however, do promote specialization. Among the Yanomami of Venezuela and Brazil, for instance, certain villages manufacture clay pots and others make hammocks. They don't specialize, as one might suppose, because certain raw materials happen to be available near particular villages. Clay suitable for pots is widely available. Everyone knows how to make pots, but not everybody does so. Craft specialization reflects the social and political environment rather than the natural environment. Such specialization promotes trade, which is the first step in creating an alliance with enemy villages (Chagnon 2013).

## Alienation in Industrial Economies

There are significant contrasts between nonindustrial economies and industrial ones. In the former, economic relations are just one part of a larger, multidimensional social matrix. People don't just work for and with others; they live with those same people; they pray with, feast with, and care about them. One works for and with people with whom one has long-term personal and social bonds (e.g., kin and in-laws).

In industrial societies, by contrast, workers sell their labor to bosses who can fire them. Work and the workplace are separated—*alienated*—from one's social essence. Rather than expressing an ongoing, mutual social relationship, labor becomes a thing (commodity) to be paid for, bought, and sold—and from which the boss can generate an individual profit. Furthermore, industrial workers usually don't work with their relatives and neighbors. If coworkers are friends, the personal relationship often develops out of their common employment rather than a previous social tie.

In nonindustrial societies, an individual who makes something can use or dispose of it as he or she sees fit. The maker may feel pride in such a personal product and, if it is given away, a renewed commitment to the social relationship that is reinforced by the gift. On the other hand, when factory workers produce for their employer's profit, their products as well as their labor are alienated. Their bosses have use or disposal rights. Human labor and its products belong to someone other than the individual producer. Unlike assembly-line workers, producers in nonindustrial societies typically see their work through from start to finish and feel a sense of accomplishment.

Thus, industrial workers have impersonal relations with their employers, coworkers, and products. People sell their labor for cash in a market economy, and work stands apart from family life. In nonindustrial societies, by contrast, the relations of production,

In a garment factory in Hlaing Tharyar, Myanmar, Burmese women stitch sports clothing for a Taiwanese company. Their average wage is less than one American dollar per day. Throughout Southeast Asia, hundreds of thousands of young women from peasant families now work in factories. Chances are good that you own one of their products. © Paula Bronstein/Getty Images News/Getty Images distribution, and consumption are social relations with economic aspects. Economy is not a separate entity but is *embedded* in the society.

## A Case of Industrial Alienation

For decades, the government of Malaysia has promoted export-oriented industry, allowing transnational companies to install manufacturing operations in rural Malaysia. In search of cheaper labor, corporations headquartered in Japan, Western Europe, and the United States have moved labor-intensive factories to developing countries. Malaysia has hundreds of Japanese and American subsidiaries, which produce garments, foodstuffs, and electronics components. Thousands of young Malaysian women from rural families now assemble microchips and microcomponents for transistors and capacitors. Aihwa Ong (1987, 2010) did a study of electronics assembly workers in an area where 85 percent of the workers were young, unmarried females from nearby villages.

Ong found that, unlike village women, female factory workers had to cope with a rigid work routine and constant supervision by men. The discipline that factories value was being taught in local schools, where uniforms helped prepare girls for the factory dress code. Village women wore loose, flowing tunics, sarongs, and sandals, but factory workers had to don tight overalls and heavy rubber gloves, in which they felt constrained. Assembling electronics components requires precise, concentrated labor. Labor in these factories illustrates the separation of intellectual and manual activity—the alienation that Karl Marx considered the defining feature of industrial work. One woman said about her bosses, "They exhaust us very much, as if they do not think that we too are human beings" (Ong 1987, p. 202). Nor does factory work bring women a substantial financial reward, given low wages, job uncertainty, and family claims on wages. Although young women typically work just a few years, production quotas, three daily shifts, overtime, and surveillance take their toll in mental and physical exhaustion.

One response to factory relations of production has been spirit possession (factory women are possessed by spirits). Ong interprets this phenomenon as the women's unconscious protest against labor discipline and male control of the industrial setting. Sometimes possession takes the form of mass hysteria. Spirits have simultaneously invaded as many as 120 factory workers. Weretigers (the Malay equivalent of the werewolf) arrive to avenge the construction of a factory on aboriginal burial grounds. Disturbed earth and grave spirits swarm on the shop floor. First the women see the spirits; then their bodies are invaded. The weretigers send the women into sobbing, laughing, and shrieking fits. To deal with possession, factories employ local medicine men, who sacrifice chickens and goats to fend off the spirits. This solution works only some of the time; possession still goes on. Ong argues that spirit possession expresses anguish at, and resistance to, capitalist relations of production. By engaging in this form of rebellion, however, factory women avoid a direct confrontation with the source of their distress. Ong concludes that spirit possession, while expressing repressed resentment, doesn't do much to modify factory conditions. (Other tactics, such as unionization, would do more.) Spirit possession may even help maintain the current system by operating as a safety valve for accumulated tensions.

# Economizing and Maximization

Economic anthropologists have been concerned with two main questions:

1. How are production, distribution, and consumption organized in different societies? This question focuses on *systems* of human behavior and their organization.
2. What motivates people in different societies to produce, distribute or exchange, and consume? Here the focus is not on systems of behavior but on the *individuals* who participate in those systems.

Anthropologists view economic systems and motivations in a cross-cultural perspective. Motivation is a concern of psychologists, but it also has been a concern of economists and anthropologists. American economists assume that people make decisions rationally, guided by the *profit motive*. Although anthropologists know that the profit motive is not universal, the assumption that individuals try to maximize profits is basic to capitalism and to Western economic theory. In fact, the subject matter of economics often is defined as economizing, or the rational allocation of scarce means (or resources) to alternative ends (or uses) (see Chibnik 2011).

What does that mean? Classical economic theory assumes that our wants are infinite, while our means are limited. People must make choices about how to use their scarce resources—their time, labor, money, and capital. (The "Anthropology Today" at the end of this chapter disputes the idea that people always make economic choices based on scarcity.) Western economists assume that when confronted with choices and decisions, people tend to make the one that maximizes profit. This is assumed to be the most rational choice.

The idea that individuals choose to maximize profits was a basic assumption of the classical economists of the 19th century and one held by many contemporary economists. However, certain economists now recognize that individuals may be motivated by many other goals. Depending on the society and the situation, people may try to maximize profit, wealth, prestige, pleasure, comfort, or social harmony. Individuals may want to realize their personal or family ambitions or those of another group to which they belong (see Chibnik 2011; Sahlins 2011).

## Alternative Ends

To what uses do people put their scarce resources? Throughout the world, people devote some of their time and energy to building up a *subsistence fund* (Wolf 1966). In other words, they have to work to eat, to replace the calories they use in daily activity. People also must invest in a *replacement fund*. They must maintain their technology and other items essential to production. If a hoe or plow breaks, they must repair or replace it. They also must obtain and replace items that are essential not to production but to everyday life, such as clothing and shelter.

People everywhere also have to invest in a *social fund*. They must help their friends, relatives, in-laws, and neighbors. It is useful to distinguish between a social fund and a *ceremonial fund*. The latter term refers to expenditures on ceremonies or rituals. To prepare a festival honoring one's ancestors, for example, requires time and the outlay of wealth.

Citizens of nation-states also must allocate scarce resources to a *rent fund*. We think of rent as payment for the use of property. Rent fund, however, has a wider meaning. It refers to resources that people must render to an individual or agency that is superior politically or economically. Tenant farmers and sharecroppers, for example, either pay rent or give some of their produce to their landlords, as peasants did under feudalism.

**Peasants** are small-scale agriculturists who live in nonindustrial states and have rent fund obligations. They produce to feed themselves, to sell their produce, and to pay rent. All peasants have two things in common:

1. They live in state-organized societies.
2. They produce food without the elaborate technology—chemical fertilizers, tractors, airplanes to spray crops, and so on—of modern farming or agribusiness.

Besides paying rent to landlords, peasants must satisfy government obligations, paying taxes in the form of money, produce, or labor. The rent fund is not simply an *additional* obligation for peasants. Often it becomes their foremost and unavoidable duty. Sometimes their own diets suffer as a result. The demands of social superiors may divert resources from subsistence, replacement, social, and ceremonial funds.

Motivations vary from society to society, and people often lack freedom of choice in allocating their resources. Because of obligations to pay rent, peasants may allocate their scarce means toward ends that are not their own but those of government officials. Thus, even in societies in which there is a profit motive, people often are prevented from rationally maximizing self-interest by factors beyond their control.

# Distribution, Exchange

The economist Karl Polanyi (1968) stimulated the comparative study of exchange, and several anthropologists followed his lead. Polanyi defined three principles that guide exchanges: the market principle, redistribution, and reciprocity. These principles all can be present in the same society, but in that case they govern different kinds of transactions. In any society, one of them usually dominates. The principle of exchange that dominates in a given society is the one that allocates the means of production (see Chibnik 2011; Hann and Hart 2011).

## The Market Principle

In today's world capitalist economy, the **market principle** dominates. It governs the distribution of the means of production—land, labor, natural resources, technology, knowledge, and capital. With market exchange, items are bought and sold, using money, with an eye to maximizing profit, and value is determined by the *law of supply and demand* (things cost more the scarcer they are and the more people want them). Bargaining is characteristic of market-principle exchanges. The buyer and seller strive to maximize—to get their "money's worth." Bargaining doesn't require that the buyer and seller meet. Consumers bargain whenever they shop around or use advertisements or the Internet in their decision making (see Hann and Hart 2009; Madra 2004).

## Redistribution

**Redistribution** operates when goods, services, or their equivalent move from the local level to a center. The center may be a capital, a regional collection point, or a store-house near a chief's residence. Products often move through a hierarchy of officials for storage at the center. Along the way officials and their dependents may consume some of them, but the exchange principle here is *re*distribution. The flow of goods eventually reverses direction—out from the center, down through the hierarchy, and back to the common people.

One example of a redistributive system comes from the Cherokee, the original owners of the Tennessee Valley. The Cherokee were productive cultivators of maize, beans, and squash, which they supplemented by hunting and fishing. They also had chiefs. Each of their main villages had a central plaza, where meetings of the chief's council took place and where redistributive feasts were held. According to Cherokee custom, each family farm had an area where the family could set aside part of its annual harvest for the chief. This supply of corn was used to feed the needy, as well as travelers and warriors journeying through friendly territory. This store of food was available to all who needed it, with the understanding that it "belonged" to the chief and was available through his generosity. The chief also hosted the redistributive feasts held in the main settlements.

## Reciprocity

**Reciprocity** is exchange between social equals, who normally are related by kinship, marriage, or another close personal tie. Because it occurs between social equals, it is dominant in the more egalitarian societies—among foragers, cultivators, and pastoralists. There are three degrees of reciprocity: *generalized, balanced,* and *negative* (Sahlins 2011; Service 1966). These may be imagined as areas of a continuum defined by the following questions:

1. How closely related are the parties to the exchange?
2. How quickly and unselfishly are gifts reciprocated?

Generalized reciprocity, the purest form of reciprocity, is characteristic of exchanges between closely related people. In balanced reciprocity, social distance increases, as does the need to reciprocate. In negative reciprocity, social distance is greatest and reciprocation is most calculated. This range, from generalized to negative, is called the **reciprocity continuum.**

With **generalized reciprocity,** someone gives to another person and expects nothing immediately in return. Such exchanges are not primarily economic transactions but expressions of personal relationships. Most parents don't keep accounts of every penny they spend on their children. They merely hope their children will respect their culture's customs involving obligations to parents.

Among foragers, generalized reciprocity usually has governed exchanges. People routinely have shared with other band members. So strong is the ethic of sharing that most foragers have lacked an expression for "thank you." To offer thanks would be impolite because it would imply that a particular act of sharing, which is the keystone of egalitarian society, was unusual. Among the Semai, foragers of central Malaysia (Dentan 2008), to express gratitude would suggest surprise at the hunter's success.

**Balanced reciprocity** applies to exchanges between people who are more distantly related than are members of the same band or household. In a horticultural society, for example, a man presents a gift to a distant cousin, a trading partner, or a brother's fictive kinsman. The giver expects something in return. This may not come immediately, but the social relationship will be strained if there is no reciprocation.

Exchanges in nonindustrial societies also may illustrate **negative reciprocity,** mainly in dealing with people beyond their social systems. To people who live in a world of close personal relations, exchanges with outsiders are full of ambiguity and distrust. Exchange is one way of establishing friendly relations, but when trade begins, the relationship is still tentative. Initially, people seek to get something back immediately. Just as in market economies, but without using money, they try to get the best possible immediate return for their investment (see Clark 2010; Hann and Hart 2009).

Generalized reciprocity and balanced reciprocity are based on trust and a social tie. With negative reciprocity, the goal is to get something for as little as possible, even if it means being cagey or deceitful or cheating. Among the most extreme and "negative" examples was 19th-century horse thievery by North American Plains Indians. Men would sneak into camps of neighboring tribes to steal horses. Such thefts were likely to be reciprocated. A similar pattern of livestock (cattle) raiding continues today in East Africa, among tribes such as the Kuria (Fleisher 2000). In these cases, the party that starts the raiding can expect reciprocity—a raid on their own village—or worse. The Kuria hunt down cattle thieves and kill them. It's still reciprocity, governed by "Do unto others as they have done unto you."

One way of reducing the tension in situations of potential negative reciprocity is to engage in "silent trade." One example was the silent trade of the Mbuti pygmy foragers of the African equatorial forest and their neighboring horticultural villagers. There was no personal contact during their exchanges. A Mbuti hunter left game, honey, or another forest product at a customary site. Villagers collected it and left crops in exchange. Often the parties bargained silently. If one felt the return was insufficient, he or she simply left it at the trading site. If the other party wanted to continue trade, it was increased.

## Coexistence of Exchange Principles

In today's North America, the market principle governs most exchanges, from the sale of the means of production to the sale of consumer goods. We also have redistribution. Some of our tax money goes to support the government, but some of it also comes back to us in the form of social services, education, health care, and road building. We also have reciprocal exchanges. Generalized reciprocity characterizes the relationship between parents and children. However, even here the dominant market mentality surfaces in comments about the high cost of raising children and in the stereotypical statement of the disappointed parent: "We gave you everything money could buy."

Exchanges of gifts, cards, and invitations exemplify reciprocity, usually balanced. Everyone has heard remarks like "They invited us to their daughter's wedding, so when ours gets married, we'll have to invite them" and "They've been here for dinner three times and haven't invited us yet. I don't think we should ask them back until they do."

Such precise balancing of reciprocity would be out of place in a foraging band, where resources are communal (common to all) and daily sharing based on generalized reciprocity is an essential ingredient of social life and survival.

## Potlatching

One of the most famous cultural practices studied by ethnographers is the **potlatch.** This is a festive event within a regional exchange system among tribes of the North Pacific Coast of North America, including the Salish and Kwakiutl of Washington and British Columbia. Some tribes still practice the potlatch, sometimes as a memorial to the dead. At each such event, assisted by members of their communities, potlatch sponsors traditionally gave away food, blankets, pieces of copper, or other items. In return for this, they got prestige. To give a potlatch enhanced one's reputation. Prestige increased with the lavishness of the potlatch, the value of the goods given away in it.

The fantastic Potlatch Dancers, Indian Village of Klinkwan, Alaska.
Copyright 1904 by Underwood & Underwood.

This historic (1904) photo shows potlatch dancers at the Haida village of Klinkwan, Alaska. Stereograph Cards collection, Prints & Photographs Division, Library of Congress, LC-USZ62-50908

The potlatching tribes were foragers, but atypical ones for relatively recent times. They were sedentary and had chiefs. They had access to a wide variety of land and sea resources. Among their most important foods were salmon, herring, candlefish, berries, mountain goats, seals, and porpoises.

According to classical economic theory, the profit motive is universal, with the goal of maximizing material benefits. How, then, does one explain the potlatch, in which substantial wealth is given away (and even destroyed)? Christian missionaries considered potlatching to be wasteful and antithetical to the Protestant work ethic. By 1885, both Canada and the United States had outlawed potlatching, under pressure from Indian agents, missionaries, and Indian converts to Christianity. Between 1885 and 1951 the custom went underground. By 1951, however, both countries had discreetly dropped the antipotlatching laws from the books.

Some scholars seized on this view of the potlatch as a classic case of economically wasteful behavior. The economist and social commentator Thorstein Veblen cited potlatching as an example of conspicuous consumption in his influential book *Theory of the Leisure Class* (1934), claiming that potlatching was based on an economically irrational drive for prestige. This interpretation stressed the lavishness and supposed wastefulness, especially of the Kwakiutl displays, to support the contention that in some societies people strive to maximize prestige at the expense of their material well-being. This interpretation has been challenged.

Ecological anthropology, also known as *cultural ecology,* is a theoretical school that attempts to interpret cultural practices, such as the potlatch, in terms of their long-term role in helping humans adapt to their environments. Wayne Suttles (1960) and Andrew Vayda (1961/1968) saw potlatching not in terms of its immediate wastefulness but in terms of its long-term role as a cultural adaptive mechanism. This view also helps us understand similar patterns of lavish feasting throughout the world. Here is the ecological interpretation: *Customs such as the potlatch are cultural adaptations to alternating periods of local abundance and shortage.*

How does this work? Although the natural environment of the North Pacific Coast is favorable, resources do fluctuate from year to year and place to place. Salmon and herring aren't equally abundant every year in a given locality. One village can have a good year while another is experiencing a bad one. Later, their fortunes reverse. In this context, the potlatch cycle had adaptive value; the potlatch was not a competitive display that brought no material benefit.

A village enjoying an especially good year had a surplus of subsistence items, which it could trade for more durable wealth items, such as blankets, canoes, or pieces of copper. Wealth, in turn, by being distributed, could be converted into prestige. Members of several villages were invited to any potlatch and got to take home the resources that were given away. In this way, potlatching linked villages together in a regional economy—an exchange system that distributed food and wealth from wealthy to needy communities. In return, the potlatch sponsors and their villages got prestige. The decision to potlatch was determined by the health of the local economy. If there had been subsistence surpluses, and thus a buildup of wealth over several good years, a village could afford a potlatch to convert its surplus food and wealth into prestige.

## Anthropology Today   *Scarcity and the Betsileo*

In the realm of cultural diversity, perceptions and motivations can change substantially over time. Consider some changes I've observed among the Betsileo of Madagascar during the decades I've been studying them. Initially, compared with modern consumers, the Betsileo had little perception of scarcity. Now, with population increase and the spread of a cash-oriented economy, perceived wants and needs have increased relative to means. Motivations have changed, too, as people increasingly seek profits, even if it means stealing from their neighbors or destroying ancestral farms.

In the late 1960s my wife and I first lived among the Betsileo, studying their economy and social life (Kottak 1980). Soon after our arrival we met two well-educated schoolteachers (first cousins) who were interested in our research. The woman's father was a congressional representative who became a cabinet minister during our stay. Their family came from a historically important and typical Betsileo village called Ivato, which they invited us to visit with them.

We had visited many other Betsileo villages, where often, as we drove up, children would run away screaming. Women would hurry inside, and men would retreat to doorways. This behavior expressed their fear of the *mpakafo*. Believed to cut out and devour his victim's heart and liver, the mpakafo is the Malagasy vampire. These cannibals are said to have fair skin and to be very tall. Because I have light skin and stand over 6 feet tall, I was a natural suspect. The fact that such creatures were not known to travel with their wives helped convince the Betsileo that I wasn't really a mpakafo.

When we visited Ivato, however, its people were friendly and hospitable. Our very first day there we did a brief census and found out who lived in which households. We learned people's names and their relationships to our schoolteacher friends and to each other. We met an excellent informant who knew all about the local history. In a few afternoons I learned much more than I had in the other villages in several sessions.

Ivatans were so willing to talk because we had powerful sponsors, villagers who had made it in the outside world, people the Ivatans knew would protect them. The schoolteachers vouched for us, but even more significant was the cabinet minister, who was like a grandfather and benefactor to everyone in town. The Ivatans had no reason to fear us because their more influential native son had asked them to answer our questions.

Once we moved to Ivato, the elders established a pattern of visiting us every evening. They came to talk, attracted by the inquisitive foreigners but also by the wine, tobacco, and food we offered. I asked question after question about their customs and beliefs.

As our stay neared its end, our Ivatan friends lamented, saying, "We'll miss you. When you leave, there won't be any more cigarettes, any more wine, or any more questions." They wondered what it would be like for us back in the United States. They knew we had an automobile and that we regularly purchased things, including the items we shared with them. We could afford to buy products they never would have. They commented, "When you go back to your country, you'll need a lot of money for things like cars, clothes, and food. We don't need to buy those things. We make almost everything we use. We don't need as much money as you, because we produce for ourselves."

The Betsileo weren't unusual for nonindustrial people. Strange as it may seem to an American consumer, those rice farmers actually believed *they had all they needed*.

The lesson from the Betsileo of the 1960s is that scarcity, which economists view as universal, is variable. Although shortages do arise in nonindustrial societies, the concept of scarcity (insufficient means) is much less developed in stable, subsistence-oriented economies than in industrial societies that rely on a host of consumer goods.

But with globalization over the past few decades, significant changes have affected the Betsileo—and most nonindustrial peoples. On my last visit to Ivato, in 2006, the effects of cash and of population increase were evident there—and throughout Madagascar—where the population growth rate has been about 3 percent annually. Madagascar's population has quadrupled since 1966, to about 24 million. One result of population pressure has been agricultural intensification. In Ivato, farmers who formerly grew only rice in their fields now use the same land for commercial crops, such as carrots, after the annual rice harvest. More tragically, Ivato has witnessed a breakdown of social and political order, fueled by increasing demand for cash.

Cattle rustling has become a growing threat. Cattle thieves (sometimes from neighboring villages) have terrorized peasants who previously felt secure in their villages. Some of the rustled cattle are driven to the coasts for commercial export. Prominent among the rustlers are relatively well-educated young men who have studied long enough to be comfortable negotiating with outsiders, but who have been unable to find formal work, and who are unwilling to work the rice fields as their peasant ancestors did. The formal education system has familiarized them with external institutions and norms, including the need for cash. The concepts

Women hull rice in a Betsileo village. In the village of Ivato, farmers who traditionally grew only rice in their fields now use the same land for commercial crops, such as carrots, after the annual rice harvest. © Carl D. Walsh/Aurora Photos

*continued*

## Anthropology Today  *continued*

of scarcity, commerce, and negative reciprocity now thrive among the Betsileo.

I've witnessed other striking evidence of the new addiction to cash during my most recent visits to Betsileo country. Near Ivato's county seat, people now sell precious stones—tourmalines, which were found by chance in local rice fields. We saw an amazing sight: dozens of villagers destroying an ancestral resource, digging up a large rice field, seeking tourmalines—clear evidence of the encroachment of cash on the local subsistence economy.

Throughout the Betsileo homeland, population growth and density are propelling emigration. Locally, land, jobs, and money are all scarce. One woman with ancestors from Ivato, herself now a resident of the national capital (Antananarivo), remarked that half the children of Ivato now lived in that city. Although she was exaggerating, a census of all the descendants of Ivato reveals a substantial emigrant and urban population.

Ivato's recent history is one of increasing participation in a cash economy. That history, combined with the pressure of a growing population on local resources, has made scarcity not just a concept but a reality for Ivatans and their neighbors.

The long-term adaptive value of intercommunity feasting becomes clear when a formerly prosperous village had a run of bad luck. Its people started accepting invitations to potlatches in villages that were doing better. The tables were turned as the temporarily rich became temporarily poor and vice versa. The newly needy accepted food and wealth items. They were willing to receive rather than bestow gifts and thus to relinquish some of their stored-up prestige. They hoped their luck would eventually improve, so that resources could be recouped and prestige regained.

The potlatch linked local groups along the North Pacific Coast into a regional alliance and exchange network. Potlatching and intervillage exchange had adaptive functions, regardless of the motivations of the individual participants. The anthropologists who stressed rivalry for prestige were not wrong. They were merely emphasizing *motivations* at the expense of an analysis of economic and ecological *systems*.

The use of feasts to enhance individual and community reputations and to redistribute wealth is not peculiar to populations of the North Pacific Coast. Competitive feasting is widely characteristic of nonindustrial food producers. But among most surviving foragers, who live in marginal areas, resources are too meager to support feasting on such a level. In such societies, sharing rather than competition prevails.

## Summary

1. Cohen's adaptive strategies include foraging (hunting and gathering), horticulture, agriculture, pastoralism, and industrialism. Foraging was the only human adaptive strategy until the advent of food production (farming and herding) 10,000 years ago. Food production eventually replaced foraging in most places. Almost all modern foragers have some dependence on food production or food producers.

2. Horticulture doesn't use land or labor intensively. Horticulturalists cultivate a plot for one or two years (sometimes longer) and then abandon it. There is always a fallow period. Agriculturists farm the same plot of land continuously and use labor intensively. They use one or more of the following: irrigation, terracing, domesticated animals as means of production, and manuring.

3. The pastoral strategy is mixed. Nomadic pastoralists trade with cultivators. Part of a transhumant pastoral population cultivates while another part takes the herds to pasture. Except for some Peruvians and the Navajo, who are recent herders, the New World lacks native pastoralists.

4. Economic anthropology is the cross-cultural study of systems of production, distribution, and consumption. In nonindustrial societies, a kin-based mode of production prevails. One acquires rights to resources and labor through membership in social groups, not impersonally through purchase and sale. Work is just one aspect of social relations expressed in varied contexts.

5. Economics has been defined as the science of allocating scarce means to alternative ends. Western economists assume the notion of scarcity is universal—which it isn't—and that in making choices, people strive to maximize personal profit. In nonindustrial societies, indeed as in our own, people often maximize values other than individual profit.

6. In nonindustrial societies, people invest in subsistence, replacement, social, and ceremonial funds. States add a rent fund: People must share their output with their social superiors. In states, the obligation to pay rent often becomes primary.

7. Besides studying production, economic anthropologists study and compare exchange systems. The three principles of exchange are the market principle, redistribution, and reciprocity, which may coexist in a given society. The primary exchange mode is the one that allocates the means of production.

8. Patterns of feasting and exchanges of wealth among villages are common among nonindustrial food producers, as among the potlatching societies of North America's North Pacific Coast. Such systems help even out the availability of resources over time.

## Key Terms

agriculture, *248*
balanced reciprocity, *261*
band, *247*
correlation, *247*
economy, *253*
food production, *243*
generalized reciprocity, *260*
horticulture, *248*
market principle, *259*
means (factors) of production, *254*
mode of production, *253*
negative reciprocity, *261*
pastoral nomadism, *253*
pastoralists, *252*
peasants, *259*
potlatch, *262*
reciprocity, *260*
reciprocity continuum, *260*
redistribution, *260*
transhumance, *253*

# Chapter 12

# Political Systems

Anthropologists share an interest in political systems, power, and politics with political scientists. Here again, however, the anthropological approach is global and comparative and includes nonstates, while political scientists tend to focus on contemporary nations. Anthropological studies have revealed substantial variation in power, authority, and legal systems in different societies. (**Power** is the ability to exercise one's will over others; **authority** is the formal, socially approved use of power—e.g., by government officials.)

## What Is "The Political"?

Morton Fried offered the following definition of political organization:

> Political organization comprises those portions of social organization that specifically
> relate to the individuals or groups that manage the affairs of public policy or seek
> to control the appointment or activities of those individuals or groups. (Fried 1967,
> pp. 20–21)

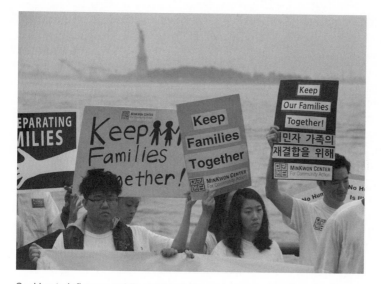

Seeking to influence public policy are these demonstrators from the New York Immigration Coalition. On July 14, 2014, they gathered in New York's Battery Park to urge President Barack Obama to take executive action on immigration reform. © Stan Honda/AFP/Getty Images

This definition certainly fits contemporary North America. Under "individuals or groups that manage the affairs of public policy" come various agencies and levels of government. Those who seek to influence public policy include political parties, unions, corporations, consumers, lobbyists, activists, political action committees (including superpacs), religious groups, and nongovernmental organizations (NGOs).

Fried's definition is less applicable to nonstates, where it's often difficult to detect any "public policy." For this reason, I prefer to speak of *socio*political organization in discussing the exercise of power and the regulation of relations among groups and their representatives. *Political regulation* includes such processes as decision making, dispute management, and conflict resolution. The study of political regulation draws our attention to those who make decisions and resolve conflicts (are there formal leaders?).

## Types and Trends

Ethnographic and archaeological studies in hundreds of places have revealed many correlations between the economy and social and political organization. Decades ago, the anthropologist Elman Service (1962) listed four types, or levels, of political organization: band, tribe, chiefdom, and state. Today, none of the first three types can be studied as a self-contained form of political organization, because all now exist within the context of nation-states and are subject to state control. There is archaeological evidence for early bands, tribes, and chiefdoms that existed before the first states appeared. However, because anthropology came into being long after the origin of the state, anthropologists never have been able to observe "in the flesh" a band, tribe, or chiefdom outside the influence of some state. There still may be local political leaders (e.g., village heads) and regional figures (e.g., chiefs) of the sort discussed in this chapter, but all now exist and function within the context of state organization.

A band is a small, kin-based group (all its members are related by kinship or marriage) found among foragers. **Tribes** typically have economies based on horticulture and pastoralism. Living in villages and organized into kin groups based on common descent, tribes have no formal government and no reliable means of enforcing political decisions. **Chiefdom** refers to a form of sociopolitical organization intermediate between the tribe and the state. In chiefdoms, social relations were based mainly on kinship, marriage, descent, age, generation, and gender—just as in bands and tribes. However, although chiefdoms were kin-based, they featured **differential access** to resources (some people had more wealth, prestige, and power than others did) and a permanent political structure. The **state** is a form of sociopolitical organization based on a formal government structure and socioeconomic stratification.

The four labels in Service's typology are much too simple to account for the full range of political diversity and complexity known to anthropologists. We'll see, for instance, that tribes have varied widely in their political systems and institutions. Nevertheless, Service's typology does highlight some significant contrasts in political organization, especially those between states and nonstates. For example, in bands and tribes—unlike states, which have clearly visible governments—political organization did not stand out as separate and distinct. In bands and tribes, it was difficult to characterize an act or event as political rather than merely social.

Service's labels "band," "tribe," "chiefdom," and "state" are categories or types within a **sociopolitical typology.** These types are correlated with the adaptive strategies (an *economic typology*) discussed in the previous chapter. Thus, foragers (an economic type) tended to have band organization (a sociopolitical type). Similarly, many horticulturalists and pastoralists lived in tribes. Although most chiefdoms had farming economies, herding was important in some Middle Eastern chiefdoms. Nonindustrial states usually had an agricultural base.

Food production led to larger, denser populations and more complex economies than was the case among foragers. Many sociopolitical trends reflect the increased regulatory demands associated with cultivation and herding. Archaeologists have studied these trends through time, and cultural anthropologists have observed them among more recent, including contemporary, groups (see Shore, Wright, and Peró 2011).

# Bands and Tribes

This chapter discusses a series of societies, as case studies, with different political systems. A common set of questions will be addressed for each one. What kinds of social groups does the society have? How do those groups represent themselves to each other?

How are their internal and external relations regulated? To answer these questions, we begin with bands and tribes and then consider chiefdoms and states.

## Foraging Bands

Modern hunter-gatherers are today's remnants of foraging band societies. The strong ties they now maintain with sociopolitical groups outside the band make them markedly different from Stone Age hunter-gatherers. Modern foragers live in nation-states and an interlinked world. The pygmies of Congo, for example, have for generations shared a social world and economic exchanges with their neighbors who are cultivators. All foragers now trade with food producers. In addition, most contemporary hunter-gatherers rely on governments and on missionaries for at least part of what they consume.

### *The San*

In the previous chapter, we saw how the Basarwa San of Botswana have been affected by government policies that relocated them after converting their ancestral lands into a wildlife reserve (Motseta 2006). More generally, San speakers ("Bushmen") of southern Africa have been influenced by Bantu speakers (farmers and herders) for 2,000 years and by Europeans for centuries. Edwin Wilmsen (1989) argues that many San descend from herders who were pushed into the desert by poverty or oppression. He sees the San today as a rural underclass in a larger political and economic system dominated by Europeans and Bantu food producers. Within this system, many San now tend cattle for wealthier Bantu rather than foraging independently. San also have their own domesticated animals, further illustrating their movement away from a foraging lifestyle.

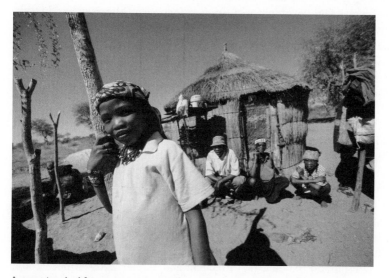

Among tropical foragers, women make an important economic contribution through gathering, as is true among the San, shown here in Namibia. What evidence do you see in this photo that contemporary foragers participate in the modern world system? © Joy Tessman/National Geographic Stock

Susan Kent (2002) noted a tendency to stereotype foragers, to treat them all as alike. They used to be stereotyped as isolated, primitive survivors of the Stone Age. A new, and more accurate, view of contemporary foragers sees them as groups forced into marginal environments by states, colonialism, and world events.

Kent (2002) focused on variation among foragers, describing considerable diversity in time and space among the San. The nature of San life has changed considerably since the 1950s and 1960s, when a series of anthropologists from Harvard University, including Richard B. Lee, embarked on a systematic study of their lives. Studying the San over time, Lee and others have documented many changes (see Lee 1979, 1984, 2003, 2012). Such longitudinal research monitors variation in time, while fieldwork in many San areas has revealed variation in space. One of the most important contrasts is between settled (sedentary) and nomadic groups (Kent and Vierich 1989). Although sedentism has increased substantially in recent years, some San groups (along rivers) have been sedentary for generations. Others, including the Dobe Ju/'hoansi San studied by Lee (1984, 2003, 2012) and the Kutse San whom Kent studied, have retained more of the hunter-gatherer lifestyle.

To the extent that foraging continues to be their subsistence base, groups like the San can illustrate links between a foraging economy and other aspects of life in bands. For example, San groups that still are mobile, or that were so until recently, emphasize social, political, and gender equality, which are traditional band characteristics. A social system based on kinship, reciprocity, and sharing is appropriate for an economy with few people and limited resources. People have to share meat when they get it; otherwise, it rots. The nomadic pursuit of wild plants and animals tends to discourage permanent settlement, wealth accumulation, and status distinctions.

In the past, foraging bands formed seasonally when component nuclear families got together. The particular families might vary from year to year. Marriage and kinship created ties between members of different bands. Trade and visiting also linked them. Band leaders were leaders in name only. In such an *egalitarian society,* they were first among equals. Sometimes they gave advice or made decisions, but they had no way to enforce those decisions. Because of the spread of states and globalization, it is increasingly difficult for ethnographers to find and observe such patterns of band organization.

## The Inuit

The aboriginal Inuit (Hoebel 1954/2006), another group of foragers, provide a classic example of methods of settling disputes—**conflict resolution**—in stateless societies. All societies have ways of settling disputes (of variable effectiveness) along with cultural rules or norms about proper and improper behavior. **Norms** are cultural standards or guidelines that enable individuals to distinguish between appropriate and inappropriate behavior in a given society (N. Kottak 2002). While rules and norms are cultural universals, only state societies, those with established governments, have formal laws that are formulated, proclaimed, and enforced (see Donovan 2007; Dresch and Skoda 2012; Freeman and Napier 2009; Moore 2005; Nader 2007; Pirie 2013).

Foragers lacked formal **law** in the sense of a legal code with trial and enforcement, but they did have methods of social control and dispute settlement. The absence of law did not mean total anarchy. As described by E. A. Hoebel (1954/2006) in a classic ethnographic study of conflict resolution, a sparse population of some 20,000 Inuit spanned 6,000 miles (9,500 kilometers) of the Arctic region. The most significant social groups were the nuclear family and the band. Some bands had headmen. There also were shamans (part-time religious specialists). However, these positions conferred little power on those who occupied them.

Hunting and fishing by men were the primary subsistence activities. The diverse and abundant plant foods available in warmer areas, where female labor in gathering is important, were absent in the Arctic. Traveling on land and sea in a bitter environment, Inuit men faced more dangers than women did. The traditional male role took its toll in lives, so that adult women outnumbered men. This permitted some men to have two or three wives. The ability to support more than one wife conferred a certain amount of prestige, but it also encouraged envy. (Prestige is social esteem, respect, or approval.) If a man seemed to be taking additional wives just to enhance his reputation, a rival was likely to steal one of them. Most Inuit disputes were between men and originated over women, caused by wife stealing or adultery.

A jilted husband had several options. He could try to kill the wife stealer. However, if he succeeded, one of his rival's kinsmen surely would try to kill him in retaliation. One dispute might escalate into several deaths as relatives avenged a succession of murders. No government existed to intervene and stop such a *blood feud* (a murderous feud between families). However, one also could challenge a rival to a song battle. In a public setting, contestants made up insulting songs about each other. At the end of the match, the audience proclaimed the winner. However, if the winner was the man whose wife had been stolen, there was no guarantee she would return. Often she stayed with her abductor.

Thefts are uncommon among foragers. Each Inuit had access to the resources he or she needed to sustain life. Every man could hunt, fish, and make the tools necessary for subsistence. Every woman could obtain the materials needed to make clothing, prepare food, and do domestic work. Inuit men could even hunt and fish in the territories of other local groups. There was no notion of private ownership of territory or animals.

## Tribal Cultivators

As is true of foraging bands, there are no totally autonomous tribes in today's world. Still, there are societies, for example, in Papua New Guinea and in South America's tropical forests, in which tribal principles continue to operate. Tribes typically have a horticultural or pastoral economy and are organized into villages and/or *descent groups* (kin groups whose members trace descent from a common ancestor). Tribes lack socioeconomic stratification (i.e., a class structure) and a formal government of their own. A few tribes still conduct small-scale warfare, in the form of intervillage raiding. Tribes have more effective regulatory mechanisms than foragers do, but tribal societies have no sure means of enforcing political decisions (see Gluckman 2012). The main regulatory officials are village heads, "big men," descent-group leaders, village councils, and leaders of pantribal associations (see later in the chapter). All these figures and groups have limited authority.

Like foragers, horticulturalists tend to be egalitarian, although some have marked *gender stratification:* an unequal distribution of resources, power, prestige, and personal freedom between men and women (see the chapter "Gender"). Horticultural villages usually are small, with low population density and open access to strategic resources. Age, gender, and personal traits determine how much respect people receive and how much support they get from others. Egalitarianism diminishes, however, as village size and population density increase. Horticultural villages usually have headmen—rarely, if ever, headwomen.

## The Village Head

The Yanomami (Chagnon 1997, 2013; Ferguson 1995; Ramos 1995) live in southern Venezuela and the adjacent part of Brazil. When anthropologists first studied them, they numbered about 26,000 people living in 200 to 250 widely scattered villages, each with a population between 40 and 250. The Yanomami are horticulturalists who also hunt and gather. Their staple crops are bananas and plantains (a banana-like crop). The Yanomami have more social groups than exist in a foraging society. They have families, villages, and descent groups. Their descent groups, which span more than one village, are *patrilineal* (ancestry is traced back through males only) and *exogamous* (people must marry outside their own descent group). However, branches of two different descent groups may live in the same village and intermarry.

Traditionally the only leadership position has been that of **village head** (always a man). His authority, like that of a foraging band's leader, is severely limited. The headman lacks the right to issue orders. He can only persuade, harangue, and try to influence public opinion. For example, if he wants people to clean up the central plaza in preparation for a feast, he must start sweeping it himself, hoping his covillagers will take the hint and relieve him.

When conflict erupts within the village, the headman may be called on as a mediator who listens to both sides. He will give an opinion and advice. If a disputant is unsatisfied, the headman has no power to back his decisions and no way to impose punishments. Like the band leader, he is first among equals.

A Yanomami village headman also must lead in generosity. Expected to be more generous than any other villager, he cultivates more land. His garden provides much of the food consumed when his village hosts a feast for another village. The headman represents the village in its dealings with outsiders, including Venezuelan and Brazilian government agents.

The way someone acts as headman depends on his personal traits and the number of supporters he can muster. Napoleon Chagnon (1983/1992, 2013) describes how one village headman, Kaobawa, guaranteed safety to a delegation from a village with which a covillager of his wanted to start a war. Kaobawa was a particularly effective headman. He had demonstrated his fierceness in battle, but he also knew how to use diplomacy to avoid offending other villagers. No one in his village had a better personality for the headmanship. Nor (because Kaobawa had many brothers) did anyone have more supporters. Among the Yanomami, when a village is dissatisfied with its headman, its members can leave and found a new village. This happens from time to time and is called *village fissioning*.

With its many villages and descent groups, Yanomami sociopolitical organization is more complicated than that of a band-organized society. The Yanomami face more problems in regulating relations between groups and individuals. Although a headman sometimes can prevent a specific violent act, intervillage raiding has been common in some areas of Yanomami territory, particularly those studied by Chagnon (1997, 2013).

It's important to recognize as well that the Yanomami are not isolated from outside events. They live in two nation-states, Venezuela and Brazil, and attacks by outsiders, especially Brazilian ranchers and miners, have plagued them (Chagnon 1997; *Cultural Survival Quarterly* 1989; Ferguson 1995). During a Brazilian gold rush between 1987 and 1991, one Yanomami died each day, on average, from such attacks. By 1991, there were some 40,000 miners in the Brazilian Yanomami homeland. Some Yanomami were killed outright. The miners introduced new diseases, and the swollen population ensured that old diseases became epidemic. In 1991, the American Anthropological Association reported on the plight of the Yanomami (*Anthropology Newsletter,* September 1991). Brazilian Yanomami were dying at a rate of 10 percent annually, and their fertility rate had dropped to zero. Since then, one Brazilian president declared a huge Yanomami territory off-limits to outsiders. Unfortunately, local politicians, miners, and ranchers have managed to evade the ban. The future of the Yanomami remains uncertain (see Romero 2008).

## The "Big Man"

Many societies of the South Pacific, particularly on the Melanesian Islands and in Papua New Guinea, had a kind of political leader that we call the big man. The **big man** (almost always a male) was an elaborate version of the village head, but with one significant difference. Unlike the village head, whose leadership is limited to one village, the big man had supporters in several villages. The big man thus was a regulator of *regional* political organization.

Consider the Kapauku Papuans, inhabitants of Irian Jaya, Indonesia (located on the island of New Guinea). Anthropologist Leopold Pospisil (1963) studied the Kapauku (then 45,000 people), who grew crops (with the sweet potato as their staple) and raised pigs. Their cultivation system was too labor-intensive to be described as simple horticulture. It required mutual aid in turning the soil before planting. The digging of long drainage ditches, which a big man often helped organize, was even more complex. Kapauku cultivation supported a larger and denser population than does the simpler horticulture of the Yanomami. The Kapauku economy required collective cultivation and political regulation of the more complex tasks. The key political figure was the big man.

Consider now the term *status,* which often is used as a synonym for *prestige.* Thus, "she's got a lot of status" means she's got a lot of prestige; people look up to her. Among social scientists, however, that's not the primary meaning of *status.* Social scientists use **status** more neutrally—for any social position, no matter what its prestige. In this sense, status encompasses all the positions that people occupy in society, such as spouse, parent, trading partner, teacher, student, salesperson, big man, and many others. People always occupy multiple statuses (e.g., son, brother, father, big man). Among the statuses we occupy, particular ones dominate in particular settings, such as son or daughter at home and student in the classroom.

The big man persuades people to organize feasts, which distribute pork and wealth. Shown here is a big man from the Huli (or Haroli) tribe of the southern highlands of Papua New Guinea. Does our society have equivalents of big men? © Edward Reeves/Alamy

Some statuses are **ascribed:** People have little or no choice about occupying them. Age is an ascribed status; we can't choose not to age. One's status as a member of the nobility, or as a male or a female, usually is ascribed; people are born members of a certain social category and remain so all their lives. **Achieved statuses,** by contrast, aren't automatic; they are based on choices, actions, efforts, or circumstances and may be positive or negative. Examples of achieved statuses include big man, healer, senator, convicted felon, terrorist, salesperson, union member, father, and college student.

The achieved status of the big man rested on certain characteristics that distinguished the big man from his fellows. Key attributes included wealth, generosity, eloquence, physical fitness, bravery, supernatural powers, and the ability to gain the support and loyalty of others. Men became big men because they had certain personalities; they did not inherit their status but created it through hard work and good judgment. Wealth resulted from successful pig breeding and trading. As a man's pig herd and prestige grew, he attracted supporters. He sponsored pig feasts in which pork (provided by the big man and his supporters) was distributed to guests, bringing him more prestige and widening his network of support.

The big man's supporters, recognizing his past favors and anticipating future rewards, recognized him as a leader and accepted his decisions as binding. The tonowi was an important regulator of regional events in Kapauku life. He helped determine the dates for feasts and markets. He initiated economic projects requiring the cooperation of a regional community.

The Kapauku big man again exemplifies a generalization about leadership in tribal societies: If someone achieves wealth and widespread respect and support, he or she must be generous. The big man worked hard not to hoard wealth but to be able to give away the fruits of his labor, to convert wealth into prestige and gratitude. A stingy big man would lose his support. Selfish and greedy big men sometimes were murdered by their fellows (Zimmer-Tamakoshi 1997).

How similar are contemporary politicians to the big man? Big men get their loyalists to produce and deliver pigs, just as modern politicians persuade their supporters to make campaign contributions. And like big men, successful American politicians try to be generous with their supporters. Payback may take the form of a night in the Lincoln bedroom, a strategic dinner invitation, an ambassadorship, or largesse to a place that was particularly supportive. Big men amass wealth, then distribute pigs and their meat. Successful American politicians also give away "pork." As with the big man, eloquence and communication skills contribute to political success (e.g., Ronald Reagan, Bill Clinton, Barack Obama), although lack of such skills isn't necessarily fatal (e.g., either President Bush). What about physical fitness? Hair, height, and health are still political advantages. Bravery, in the form of military service, also helps political careers (e.g., John McCain), but it certainly isn't required, nor does it guarantee success. Supernatural powers? Candidates who proclaim themselves atheists are even rarer than self-identified witches (or not witches). Almost all political candidates claim to belong to a mainstream religion. Some even present their candidacies as promoting God's will.

On the other hand, contemporary politics isn't just about personality, as it is in big man systems. We live in a state-organized, stratified society with inherited wealth, power, and privilege, all of which have political implications. As is typical of states, inheritance and kin connections play a role in political success. Just think of Kennedys, Bushes, Clintons, and Gandhis.

## Pantribal Sodalities

Big men could forge regional political organization, albeit temporarily, by mobilizing supporters from several villages. Other principles in tribal societies—such as a belief in common ancestry, kinship, or descent—could be used to link local groups within a region. The same descent group, for example, might span several villages, and its dispersed members might recognize the same leader.

Principles other than kinship also can link local groups, especially in modern societies. People who live in different parts of the same nation may belong to the same labor union, sorority or fraternity, political party, or religious denomination. In tribes, nonkin groups called *associations* or *sodalities* may serve a similar linking function. Often, sodalities are based on common age or gender, with all-male sodalities more common than all-female ones.

**Pantribal sodalities** are groups that extend across the whole tribe, spanning several villages. Such sodalities were especially likely to develop in situations of warfare with a neighboring tribe. Mobilizing their members from multiple villages within the same tribe, pantribal sodalities could assemble a force to attack, defend, or retaliate against another tribe.

The best examples of pantribal sodalities come from the Central Plains of North America and from tropical Africa. During the 18th and 19th centuries, Native American populations of the Great Plains of the United States and Canada experienced a rapid growth of pantribal sodalities. This development reflected an economic change that followed the spread of horses, which had been reintroduced to the Americas by the Spanish, to the area between the Rocky Mountains and the Mississippi River. Many Plains societies changed their adaptive strategies because of the horse. At first they had been foragers who hunted bison (buffalo) on foot. Later they adopted a mixed economy based on hunting, gathering, and horticulture. Finally they changed to a much more specialized economy based on horseback hunting of bison (eventually with rifles).

As the Plains tribes were undergoing these changes, other groups also adopted horse-back hunting and moved into the Plains. Attempting to occupy the same area, groups came into conflict. A pattern of warfare developed in which the members of one tribe raided another, usually for horses. The economy demanded that people follow the movement of the bison herds. During the winter, when the bison dispersed, a tribe fragmented into small bands and families. In the summer, when huge herds assembled on the Plains, the tribe reunited. They camped together for social, political, and religious activities, but mainly for communal bison hunting.

Two activities demanded strong leadership: organizing and carrying out raids on enemy camps (to capture horses) and managing the summer bison hunt. All the Plains societies developed pantribal sodalities, and leadership roles within them, to police the summer hunt. Leaders coordinated hunting efforts, making sure that people did not cause a stampede with an early shot or an ill-advised action. Leaders imposed severe penalties, including seizure of a culprit's wealth, for disobedience.

Many tribes that adopted this Plains strategy of adaptation had once been foragers for whom hunting and gathering had been individual or small-group affairs. They never had come together previously as a single social unit. Age and gender were available as social principles that could quickly and efficiently forge unrelated people into pantribal sodalities.

Raiding of one tribe by another, this time for cattle rather than horses, also was common in eastern and southeastern Africa, where pantribal sodalities also developed. Among the pastoral Masai of Kenya, men born during the same four-year period were circumcised together and belonged to the same named group, an age set, throughout their lives. The sets moved through *age grades,* the most important of which was the warrior grade. Members of a set felt a strong allegiance to one another. Masai women lacked comparable set organization, but they also passed through culturally recognized age grades: the initiate, the married woman, and the female elder.

In certain parts of western and central Africa, pantribal sodalities are secret societies, made up exclusively of men or women. Like our college fraternities and sororities, these associations have secret initiation ceremonies. Among the Mende of Sierra Leone, men's and women's secret societies were very influential. The men's group, the Poro, trained boys in social conduct, ethics, and religion and supervised political and economic activities. Leadership roles in the Poro often overshadowed village headship and played an important part in social control, dispute management, and tribal political regulation. Age, gender, and ritual can link members of different local groups into a single social collectivity in a tribe and thus create a sense of ethnic identity, of belonging to the same cultural tradition.

## Nomadic Politics

Herders have varied political systems. Unlike the Masai (just discussed) and other tribal herders, some pastoralists have chiefs and live in nation-states. The scope of political authority among pastoralists expands considerably as regulatory problems increase in densely populated regions (see Salzman 2008). Consider two Iranian pastoral nomadic tribes—the Basseri and the Qashqai (Salzman 1974). Starting each year from a plateau near the coast, these groups took their animals to grazing land 17,000 feet (5,400 meters) above sea level. The Basseri and the Qashqai shared this route with one another and with several other ethnic groups.

Use of the same pasture land at different times of year was carefully scheduled. Ethnic-group movements were tightly coordinated. Expressing this schedule is *il-rah,* a concept common to all Iranian nomads. A group's il-rah is its customary path in time and space. It is the schedule, different for each group, of when specific areas can be used in the annual trek.

Each tribe had its own leader, known as the *khan* or *il-khan.* The Basseri khan, because he dealt with a smaller population, faced fewer problems in coordinating its movements than did the leaders of the Qashqai. Correspondingly, his rights, privileges, duties, and authority were weaker. Nevertheless, his authority exceeded that of any political figure discussed so far. The khan's authority still came from his personal traits rather than from his office. That is, the Basseri followed a particular khan not because of a political position he happened to fill but because of their personal allegiance and loyalty to him as a man. The khan relied on the support of the heads of the descent groups into which Basseri society was divided.

Among the Qashqai, however, allegiance shifted from the person to the office. The Qashqai had multiple levels of authority and more powerful chiefs or khans. Managing 400,000 people required a complex hierarchy. Heading it was the il-khan, helped by a deputy, under whom were the heads of constituent tribes, under each of whom were descent-group heads.

A case illustrates just how developed the Qashqai authority structure was. A hailstorm prevented some nomads from joining the annual migration at the appointed time. Although all the nomads recognized that they were not responsible for their delay, the il-khan assigned them less favorable grazing land, for that year only, in place of their usual pasture. The tardy herders and other Qashqai considered the judgment fair and didn't question it. Thus, Qashqai authorities regulated the annual migration. They also adjudicated disputes between people, tribes, and descent groups (see Salzman 2008).

These Iranian cases illustrate the fact that pastoralism often is just one among many specialized economic activities within a nation-state. As part of a larger whole, pastoral tribes are constantly pitted against other ethnic groups. In these nations, the state becomes a final authority, a higher-level regulator that attempts to limit conflict between ethnic groups. State organization arose not just to manage agricultural economies but also to regulate the activities of ethnic groups within expanding social and economic systems (see Das and Poole, 2004; Saleh 2013).

# Chiefdoms

The first states emerged in the Old World around 5,500 years ago. The first chiefdoms developed perhaps a thousand years earlier, but few survive today. In many parts of the world, the chiefdom was a transitional form of organization that emerged during the evolution of tribes into states. State formation began in Mesopotamia (currently Iran and Iraq). It next occurred in Egypt, the Indus Valley of Pakistan and India, and northern China. A few thousand years later states arose in two parts of the Western Hemisphere—

Mesoamerica (Mexico, Guatemala, Belize) and the central Andes (Peru and Bolivia). Early states are known as *archaic,* or *nonindustrial,* states, in contrast to modern industrial nation-states. Robert Carneiro defines the state as "an autonomous political unit encompassing many communities within its territory, having a centralized government with the power to collect taxes, draft men for work or war, and decree and enforce laws" (1970, p. 733).

The chiefdom and the state, like many categories used by social scientists, are *ideal types.* That is, they are labels that make social contrasts seem sharper than they really are. In reality there is a continuum from tribe to chiefdom to state. Some societies had many attributes of chiefdoms but retained tribal features. Some advanced chiefdoms had many attributes of archaic states and thus are difficult to assign to either category. Recognizing this "continuous change" (Johnson and Earle 2000), some anthropologists speak of "complex chiefdoms" (Earle 1997), which are almost states.

## Political and Economic Systems

Geographic areas where chiefdoms existed included the circum-Caribbean (e.g., Caribbean islands, Panama, Colombia), lowland Amazonia, what is now the southeastern United States, and Polynesia. Chiefdoms created the megalithic cultures of Europe, including the one that built Stonehenge. Bear in mind that chiefdoms and states can fall (disintegrate) as well as rise. Before Rome's expansion, much of Europe was organized at the chiefdom level, to which it reverted for centuries after the fall of Rome in the 5th century C.E.

Much of our ethnographic knowledge about chiefdoms comes from Polynesia, where they were common at the time of European exploration. In chiefdoms, social relations are based mainly on kinship, marriage, descent, age, generation, and gender—just as in bands and tribes. This is a fundamental difference between chiefdoms and states. States bring nonrelatives together and oblige them all to pledge allegiance to a government.

Unlike bands and tribes, however, chiefdoms administer a clear-cut and permanent regional political system. Chiefdoms may include thousands of people living in many

Chiefdoms as widespread as Mexico's Olmecs, England's Stonehenge, and Polynesia's Easter Island (Rapanui) are famed for their major works in stone. The statues shown here are Easter Island's major tourist attraction.
© David Madison/The Image Bank/Getty Images

villages or hamlets. Regulation is carried out by the chief and his or her assistants, who occupy political offices. An **office** is a permanent position, which must be refilled when it is vacated by death or retirement. Because official vacancies are filled systematically, the political system that is the chiefdom endures across the generations, thus ensuring permanent political regulation.

Polynesian chiefs were full-time specialists whose duties included managing the economy. They regulated production by commanding or prohibiting (using religious taboos) the cultivation of certain lands and crops. Chiefs also regulated distribution and consumption. At certain seasons—often on a ritual occasion such as a first-fruit cere-mony—people would offer part of their harvest to the chief through his or her represen-tatives. Products moved up the hierarchy, eventually reaching the chief. Conversely, illustrating obligatory sharing with kin, chiefs sponsored feasts at which they gave back some of what they had received. Unlike big men, chiefs were exempt from ordinary work and had rights and privileges unavailable to the masses. Like big men, however, they still returned a portion of the wealth they took in.

Such a flow of resources to and then from a central place is known as *chiefly redis-tribution,* which offers economic advantages. If different parts of the chiefdom special-ized in particular products, chiefly redistribution made those products available to the entire society. Chiefly redistribution also helped stimulate production beyond the basic subsistence level and provided a central storehouse for goods that might become scarce in times of famine (Earle 1997).

## Status Systems

Social status in chiefdoms was based on seniority of descent. Polynesian chiefs kept extremely long genealogies. Some chiefs (without writing) managed to trace their ancestry back 50 generations. All the people in the chiefdom were thought to be related to each other. Presumably, all were descended from a group of founding ancestors.

The status of chief was ascribed, based on seniority of descent. The chief would be the oldest child (usually son) of the oldest child of the oldest child, and so on. Degrees of seniority were calculated so intricately on some islands that there were as many ranks as people. For example, the third son would rank below the second, who in turn would rank below the first. The children of an eldest brother, however, would all rank above the children of the next brother, whose children in turn would outrank those of younger brothers. However, even the lowest-ranking man or woman in a chiefdom was still the chief's relative. In such a kin-based context, everyone, even a chief, had to share with his or her relatives. Because everyone had a slightly different status, it was difficult to draw a line between elites and common people. Other chiefdoms calculated seniority differently and had shorter genealogies than did those in Polynesia. Still, the concern for seniority and the lack of sharp gaps between elites and commoners are features of all chiefdoms.

The status systems of chiefdoms, as of states, were associated with differential access to resources. Some men and women had privileged access to power, prestige, and wealth. They controlled strategic resources such as land and water. Earle characterizes chiefs as "an incipient aristocracy with advantages in wealth and lifestyle" (1987, p. 290).

Winning a lottery confers wealth, but not necessarily prestige or power. Shown here, a Bronx (New York) woman celebrates her Powerball win; she chose her numbers based on those she found in a fortune cookie. © Aaron Showalter/NY Daily News via Getty Images

Compared with chiefdoms, archaic states drew a much firmer line between elites and masses, distinguishing at least between nobles and commoners. Kinship ties did not extend from the nobles to the commoners because of *stratum endogamy*—marriage within one's own group. Commoners married commoners; elites married elites.

## The Emergence of Stratification

The status system of a chiefdom differed from that of a state because of the chiefdom's kinship basis. In the context of differential wealth and power, the chiefly type of status system didn't last very long. Chiefs would start acting like kings and try to erode the kinship basis of the chiefdom. In Madagascar they would do this by demoting their more distant relatives to commoner status and banning marriage between nobles and commoners (Kottak 1980). Such moves, if accepted by the society, created separate *social strata*—unrelated groups that differ in their access to wealth, prestige, and power. (A *stratum* is one of two or more groups that contrast in social status and access to strategic resources. Each stratum includes people of both sexes and all ages.) The creation of separate social strata is called *stratification,* and its emergence signified the transition from chiefdom to state. The presence of stratification is one of the key distinguishing features of a state.

The influential sociologist Max Weber (1922/1968) defined three related dimensions of social stratification: (1) Economic status, or **wealth,** encompasses all a person's material assets, including income, land, and other types of property. (2) Power, the ability to exercise one's will over others—to get what one wants—is the basis of political status. (3) **Prestige**—the basis of social status—refers to esteem, respect, or approval for acts, deeds, or qualities considered exemplary. Prestige, or "cultural capital" (Bourdieu 1984), gives people a sense of worth and respect, which they may often convert into economic advantage (see Table 12.1).

In archaic states—for the first time in human evolution—there were contrasts in wealth, power, and prestige between entire groups (social strata) of men and women.

| TABLE 12.1 Max Weber's Three Dimensions of Stratification | | |
|---|---|---|
| wealth | economic status | |
| power | political status | |
| prestige | social status | |

The **superordinate** (the higher, or elite) stratum had privileged access to valued resources. Access to those resources by members of the **subordinate** (lower, or underprivileged) stratum was limited by the privileged group.

# State Systems

Table 12.2 summarizes the information presented so far on bands, tribes, chiefdoms, and states. States, remember, are autonomous political units with social strata and a formal government. States tend to be large and populous, and certain statuses, systems, and subsystems with specialized functions are found in all states (see Sharma and Gupta, 2006). They include the following:

- Population control: fixing of boundaries, establishment of citizenship categories, and censusing.
- Judiciary: laws, legal procedure, and judges.
- Enforcement: permanent military and police forces.
- Fiscal support: taxation.

In archaic states, these subsystems were integrated by a ruling system or government composed of civil, military, and religious officials. Let's look at the four subsystems one by one.

## Population Control

To keep track of whom they govern, states conduct censuses. States demarcate boundaries to separate that state from other societies. Customs agents, immigration officers, navies, and coast guards patrol frontiers. States also regulate population through administrative subdivision: provinces, districts, "states," counties, subcounties, and parishes. Lower-level officials manage the populations and territories of the subdivisions.

States often promote geographic mobility and resettlement, severing longstanding ties among people, land, and kin. Population displacements have increased with globalization and as war, famine, and job seeking churn up migratory currents. People in states

**TABLE 12.2**   **Economic Basis of and Political Regulation in Bands, Tribes, Chiefdoms, and States**

| Sociopolitical Type | Economic Type | Examples | Type of Regulation |
|---|---|---|---|
| Band | Foraging | Inuit, San | Local |
| Tribe | Horticulture, pastoralism | Yanomami, Masai, Kapauku | Local, temporary, regional |
| Chiefdom | Intensive horticulture, pastoral nomadism, agriculture | Qashqai, Polynesia, Cherokee | Permanent, regional |
| State | Agriculture, industrialism | Ancient Mesopotamia, contemporary U.S., Canada | Permanent, regional |

come to identify themselves by new statuses, both ascribed and achieved—including residence, ethnicity, occupation, political party, religion, and team or club affiliation—rather than only as members of a descent group or an extended family.

States also manage their populations by granting different rights and obligations to citizens and noncitizens. Status distinctions among citizens also are common. Archaic states granted different rights to nobles, commoners, and slaves. In American history before the Emancipation Proclamation, there were different laws for enslaved and free people. In European colonies, separate courts judged cases involving only natives and cases involving Europeans. In contemporary America, a military judiciary coexists alongside the civil system.

## Judiciary

All states have laws based on precedent and legislative proclamations. Without writing, laws may be preserved in oral tradition. *Crimes* are violations of the legal code ("breaking the law"), with specified types of punishment. To handle crimes and disputes, all states have courts and judges.

A striking contrast between states and nonstates is intervention in family affairs. Governments step in to halt blood feuds and regulate previously private disputes. States attempt to curb *internal* conflict, but they aren't always successful. About 85 percent of the world's armed conflicts since the end of World War II have begun within states—in efforts to overthrow a ruling regime or as disputes over ethnic, religious, or human rights issues (see Chatterjee 2004; Nordstrom 2004; Stavenhagen 2013; Tishkov 2004).

## Enforcement

All states have agents to enforce judicial decisions, for example, to impose punishments and collect fines. Confinement requires jailers. If there is a death penalty, executioners are needed. Government officials have the power to collect fines and confiscate property. The government attempts to suppress internal disorder (with police) and to guard against external threats (with the military and border officials).

Armies help states subdue and conquer neighboring nonstates, but this isn't the only reason state organization has spread. Although states impose hardships, they also offer advantages. They have formal mechanisms designed to protect against external threats and to preserve internal order. When they are successful in promoting internal peace, states enhance production. Their economies can support massive, dense populations, which supply armies and colonists to promote expansion.

## Fiscal Support

States need financial, or **fiscal,** mechanisms (e.g., taxation) to support government officials and numerous other specialists. As in the chiefdom, the state intervenes in production, distribution, and consumption. The state may require a certain area to produce specific things or ban certain activities in particular places. Although, like chiefdoms, states have redistribution ("spreading the wealth around"), less of what comes in from the people actually goes back to the people.

Citizens also have to turn over a substantial portion of what they produce to the state. Markets and trade usually are under at least some state oversight, with officials overseeing distribution and exchange, standardizing weights and measures, and collecting taxes on goods passing into or through the state. Of the revenues the state collects, it reallocates part for the general good and keeps another part (often larger) for itself—its agents and agencies. State organization doesn't bring more freedom or leisure to the common people, who may be conscripted to build monumental public works. Some projects, such as dams and irrigation systems, may be economically necessary, but residents of archaic states also had to build temples, palaces, and tombs for the elites. Those elites reveled in the consumption of sumptuary goods—jewelry, exotic food and drink, and stylish clothing reserved for, or affordable only by, the rich. Peasants' diets suffered as they struggled to meet government demands. Commoners perished in territorial wars that had little relevance to their own needs. Are any of these observations true of contemporary states?

## Social Control

In studying political systems, anthropologists pay attention not only to the formal institutions but to other forms of social control as well. The concept of social control is broader than "the political." **Social control** refers to "those fields of the social system (beliefs, practices, and institutions) that are most actively involved in the maintenance of any norms and the regulation of any conflict" (N. Kottak 2002, p. 290). *Norms,* as defined earlier in this chapter, are cultural standards or guidelines that enable individuals to distinguish between appropriate and inappropriate behavior.

Previous sections of this chapter have focused more on formal political organization than on sociopolitical process. We've seen how the scale and strength of political systems have expanded in relation to economic changes. We've examined means of conflict resolution, or their absence, in various types of society. We've looked at political decision making, including leaders and their limits. We've also recognized that all contemporary humans have been affected by states, colonialism, and the spread of the world system (Kaplan 2014; Shore, Wright, and Peró 2011).

*Sociopolitical* was introduced as a key concept at the beginning of this chapter. So far, we've focused mainly on the *political* part of sociopolitical; now we focus on the *social* part. In this section we'll see that political systems have their informal, social, and subtle aspects along with their formal, governmental, and public dimensions.

### Hegemony and Resistance

Antonio Gramsci (1971) developed the concept of **hegemony** for a stratified social order in which subordinates comply with domination by internalizing their rulers' values and accepting the "naturalness" of domination (this is the way things were meant to be). According to Pierre Bourdieu (1977, p. 164), every social order tries to make its own arbitrariness (including its mechanisms of control and domination) seem natural and in everyone's interest. Both Bourdieu (1977) and Michel Foucault (1979) argue that it is easier and more effective to dominate people in their minds than to try to control their bodies. Nonphysical forms of social control include various techniques of persuading and managing people and of monitoring and recording their beliefs, activities, and contacts.

Hegemony, the internalization of a dominant ideology, is one way in which elites curb resistance and maintain power. Another way is to make subordinates believe they eventually will gain power—as young people usually foresee when they let their elders dominate them. Another way of curbing resistance is to separate or isolate people while supervising them closely, as is done in prisons (Foucault 1979).

Popular resistance is most likely to be expressed openly when people are allowed to assemble. (This chapter's "Anthropology Today" examines the role of social media in mobilizing protesters in today's world.) The oppressed may draw courage from their common sentiments and the anonymity of the crowd. Sensing danger, the elites often discourage public gatherings. They try to limit and control holidays, funerals, dances, festivals, and other occasions that might unite the oppressed. For example, in the American South before the Civil War, gatherings of five or more slaves were prohibited unless a White person was present.

Factors that interfere with community formation—such as geographic, linguistic, and ethnic separation—also work to curb resistance. Consequently, Southern U.S. plantation owners sought slaves with diverse cultural and linguistic backgrounds. Despite the measures used to divide them, the slaves resisted, developing their own popular culture, linguistic codes, and religious vision. The masters stressed portions of the Bible that emphasized compliance, such as the book of Job. The slaves, however, preferred the story of Moses and deliverance. The cornerstone of slave religion became the idea of a reversal in the conditions of Whites and Blacks. Slaves also resisted directly, through sabotage and flight. In many New World areas, slaves managed to establish free communities in the hills and other isolated areas.

## Weapons of the Weak

The study of sociopolitical systems also should consider the sentiments and activity that may lurk beneath the surface of evident, public behavior. In public, the oppressed may seem to accept their own domination, even as they question it in private. James Scott (1990) uses the phrase "public transcript" to describe the open, public interactions between superordinates and subordinates—the outer shell of power relations. He uses "hidden transcript" to describe the critique of power that proceeds out of sight of the power holders. In public, the elites and the oppressed may observe the etiquette of power relations. The dominants act like masters while their subordinates show humility and defer.

Scott (1985) uses Malay peasants, among whom he did fieldwork, to illustrate small-scale acts of resistance—which he calls "weapons of the weak." The Malay peasants used an indirect strategy to resist an Islamic tithe (religious tax). Peasants were expected to pay the tithe, usually in the form of rice, which was sent to the provincial capital. In theory, the tithe would come back as charity, but it never did. Peasants didn't resist the tithe by rioting, demonstrating, or protesting. Instead they used a "nibbling" strategy, based on small acts of resistance. For example, they failed to declare their land or lied about the amount they farmed. They underpaid, or they delivered rice contaminated with water, rocks, or mud, to add weight. Because of this resistance, only 15 percent of what was due actually was paid (Scott 1990, p. 89).

Hidden transcripts tend to be expressed publicly at certain times (festivals and carnavals) and in certain places (such as markets). Because of its costumed anonymity, Carnaval (Mardi Gras in New Orleans) is an excellent arena for expressing normally suppressed feelings. Carnavals celebrate freedom through immodesty, dancing, gluttony, and

"Schwellkoepp," or "Swollen Heads," caricature local characters during a Carnaval parade in Mainz, Germany. Because of its costumed anonymity, Carnaval is an excellent arena for expressing normally suppressed speech. Is there anything like Carnaval in your society?
© Daniel Roland/AP Images

sexuality (DaMatta 1991). Carnaval may begin as a playful outlet for frustrations built up during the year. Over time, it may evolve into a powerful annual critique of stratification and domination and thus a threat to the established order (Gilmore 1987).

## Shame and Gossip

Many anthropologists have cited the importance of "informal" social control, such as stigma, shame, and gossip, especially in small-scale societies (see Freilich, Raybeck, and Savishinsky 1991). Gossip, which can lead to shame, sometimes is used when a direct or formal sanction is risky or impossible. Margaret Mead (1937) and Ruth Benedict (1946) distinguished between *shame* as an external sanction (i.e., forces set in motion by others) and *guilt* as an internal sanction, psychologically generated by the individual. They regarded shame as a more prominent form of social control in non-Western societies and guilt as a more dominant emotional sanction in Western societies. Of course, to be effective as a sanction, the prospect of being shamed or of shaming oneself must be internalized by the individual. In small-scale societies, in a social environment where everyone knows everyone else, most people try to avoid behavior that might spoil their reputations and alienate them from their social network (N. Kottak 2002).

Bronislaw Malinowski (1927, 2013) described how Trobriand Islanders might climb to the top of a palm tree and dive to their deaths because they couldn't tolerate the shame associated with public knowledge of some stigmatizing action. Nicholas Kottak (2002) heard Makua villagers in northern Mozambique tell the story of a man rumored to have fathered a child with his stepdaughter. The political authorities imposed no formal sanctions (e.g., a fine or jail time) on this man, but gossip about the affair circulated widely. The gossip crystallized in the lyrics of a song that groups of young women would perform. After the man heard his name and behavior mentioned in that song, he hanged himself by the neck from a tree. (Previously we saw the role of song in the social control system of the Inuit. We'll see it again in the case of the Igbo women's war, discussed in the next section.)

Although it isn't part of any formal or official authority structure, shame can be a powerful social sanction. People aren't just citizens of governments; they are members of society, and social sanctions exist alongside governmental ones. Such sanctions exemplify other "weapons of the weak," because they often are wielded most effectively by people, such as women or young people, who have limited access to the formal authority structure.

## The Igbo Women's War

Shame and ridicule—used by women against men—played a key role in a decisive protest movement that took place in southeastern Nigeria in late 1929. This is remembered as the "Aba Women's Riots of 1929" in British colonial history and as the "Women's War" in Igbo history (see Dorward, 1983; Martin 1988; Mba 1982; Oriji 2000; Van Allen 1971). During this two-month "war," at least 25,000 Igbo women joined protests against British officials, their agents, and their colonial policies. This massive revolt touched off the most serious challenge to British rule in the history of what was then the British colony of Nigeria.

In 1914, the British had implemented a policy of indirect rule by appointing local Nigerian men as their agents—known as "warrant chiefs." These chiefs became increasingly oppressive, seizing property, imposing arbitrary regulations, and imprisoning people who criticized them. Colonial administrators further stoked local outrage when they announced plans to impose taxes on Igbo market women. These women were key suppliers of food for Nigeria's growing urban population; they feared being forced out of business by the new tax.

After hearing about the tax in November 1929, thousands of Igbo women assembled in various towns to protest both the warrant chiefs and the taxes on market women. They used a traditional practice of censoring and shaming men through all-night song and dance ridicule (often called "sitting on a man"). This process entailed constant singing and dancing around the houses and offices of the warrant chiefs. The women also followed the chiefs' every move, forcing the men to pay attention by invading their space. Disturbed by the whole process, wives of the warrant chiefs also pressured their husbands to listen to the protesters' demands.

The protests were remarkably effective. The tax was abandoned, and many of the warrant chiefs resigned, some to be replaced by women. Other women were appointed to the Native courts as judges. The position of women improved in Nigeria, where market women especially remain a powerful political force to this day. Many subsequent Nigerian political events were inspired by the Women's War, including additional tax

## Anthropology Today   *Resistance via Social Media: A Case Study*

New media, including smartphones, Face-book, and Twitter, have played a promi-nent role in recent uprisings in Turkey, Egypt, and several other countries. When Brazil underwent what was dubbed its "Facebook Revolution" between June and September of 2013, anthropologists were on site to study the ways in which these new forms of communication influenced perceptions and behaviors.

The movement started in São Paulo with small-scale demonstrations against bus fare increases. It exploded when im-ages of police brutality—many recorded by cell phone cameras—flooded first the Inter-net and then television broadcasts. These images of violence by government agents brought back memories of Brazil's repres-sive military dictatorship (1964–1985). One particularly powerful image of a young jour-nalist's eye disfigured by a riot-police rub-ber bullet, was shown repeatedly. In cities

large and small, Brazilians took to the streets (and cyberspace) to protest against government policies. Spurring the protests were concerns about Brazil's economic and political priorities. The demonstrations accelerated during the Confederation Cup soccer tournament, which Brazil was host-ing. Protesters decried lavish spending on stadiums for that competition and for the upcoming World Cup (2014) and Olympic Games (2016), rather than on public health, education, and transportation.

Facebook played a key role in planning the demonstrations and recruiting protes-tors. Television news joined in, broadcast-ing the time and location of protests and airing the ensuing encounters for nightly viewing. As this civil unrest unfolded, a team of ethnographers from American and Brazilian universities was in Brazil studying the use and impact of electronic media in several communities. The researchers

On Rio de Janeiro's Copacabana beach, protesters agitate for political reform and better public services and against PEC37, a proposed law that would have deprived independent public prosecutors of the right to probe crimes and political corruption. (The law was not passed.) © Yasuyoshi Chiba/AFP/Getty Images

*continued*

## Anthropology Today    *continued*

were able to observe how local Brazilians learned about, interpreted, and participated in the national discontent.

Local interest and participation were greatest in Ibirama, a town of about 15,000 people in southern Brazil. Overwhelmingly middle class, Ibirama has had reliable Internet access for at least a decade. Facebook has become a preferred medium of communication. People post daily, even hourly, about comings and goings; they issue invitations to local events and advertise local businesses. In that community, project researcher Cynthia Pace (University of South Florida) documented extensive use of Facebook and television to both follow and participate in the protests. For example, as the protests spread in June 2013, Cynthia Pace's housemate, Pedro, used his Facebook page to organize a protest against political and economic mismanagement by the federal government. Pace filmed the protest and Pedro posted this footage on Facebook, from which a TV station obtained it for the evening news broadcast.

Not all places in Brazil were this aware of, or interested in, the events of the "Facebook Revolution." Far from Ibirama is Gurupá, a community of 9,500 people on the Amazon River. Its inhabitants are poor by national standards, but the community has benefited from government programs for poverty alleviation and a recent boom in the export of açaí (a tropical fruit). Gurupá has a history of social activism and strongly supports President Dilma Rousseff's Workers' Party. In Gurupá proper, access to the Internet is unreliable; it is nonexistent in Gurupá's rural zone. Local people use their cell phones (available since 2011) to access Facebook when service allows. They watched the distant street protests mainly on television and tended to view them as political venting by urban residents far removed from the realities of the Amazon.

A third community studied by this research project is Turedjam, with a population of 500 Native Brazilians, located in the Kayapó Indigenous Territories. Founded in 2010, Turedjam (unlike most other Kayapó villages) has electricity, television, and cell phone service. Although the village lacks Internet access, some villagers have gone online in nearby Brazilian towns and a few even have Facebook pages. Glenn Shepard (Goeldi Museum, Belem, Brazil) documented the villagers' response to the 2013 demonstrations, which many watched on television. With limited Portuguese language proficiency, many Kayapó could not follow the details of the protests and viewed them as manifesting a general discontent among "Whites" with their own government. Opportunistically, however, the Kayapó used the national events to pursue longstanding grievances about the demarcation of Kayapó lands and a potentially destructive regional dam project. Local men, maintaining contact with other villages via short-wave radio and cell phones, made a plan to block traffic on the Transamazon Highway, aiming for concessions from the Rousseff government. Eventually they abandoned the proposed highway blockage in favor of direct talks with government officials.

These case studies show that social media can be an effective, although imperfect tool for organizing political opposition. For a few months in 2013, media-spread information about urban discontent created a partial sense of pan-Brazilian solidarity, felt most strongly by those in the urban middle class. The protests expressed general discontent with Brazil's direction, but any political goals were diffuse and poorly formulated, and there was no clear common enemy (e.g., a brutal dictator). While this political action, this form of resistance, did mobilize people, as of this writing, it has not produced significant political change.

protests. This Women's War inspired many other protests in regions all over Africa. The Igbo uprising is seen as the first major challenge to British authority in Nigeria and West Africa during the colonial period.

At the beginning of this chapter, *power* was defined as the ability to exercise one's will over others. It was contrasted with *authority*—the formal, socially approved use of power by government officials and others. The case of the Igbo Women's War shows how women effectively used their social power (through song, dance, noise, and "in-your-face" behavior) to subvert the formal authority structure and, in so doing, gained greater influence within that structure. Can you think of other, perhaps recent examples?

## Summary

1. Although no ethnographer has been able to observe a polity uninfluenced by some state, many anthropologists use a sociopolitical typology that classifies societies as bands, tribes, chiefdoms, or states. Foragers tended to live in egalitarian, band- organized societies. Personal networks linked individuals, families, and bands. Band leaders were first among equals, with no sure way to enforce decisions. Disputes rarely arose over strategic resources, which were open to all.

2. Political authority increased with growth in population size and density and in the scale of regulatory problems. More people mean more relations among individuals and groups to regulate. Increasingly complex economies pose further regulatory problems.

3. Heads of horticultural villages are local leaders with limited authority. They lead by example and persuasion. Big men have support and authority beyond a single village. They are regional regulators, but temporary ones. In organizing a feast, they mobilize labor from several villages. Sponsoring such events leaves them with little wealth but with prestige and a reputation for generosity.

4. Age and gender also can be used for regional political integration. Among North America's Plains tribes, men's associations (pantribal sodalities) organized raiding and buffalo hunting. Such sodalities provide offense and defense when there is intertribal raiding for animals. Among pastoralists, the degree of authority and political organization reflects population size and density, interethnic relations, and pressure on resources.

5. The state is an autonomous political unit that encompasses many communities. Its government collects taxes, drafts people for work and war, and decrees and enforces laws. The state is a form of sociopolitical organization based on central government and social stratification. Early states are known as archaic, or nonindustrial, states, in contrast to modern industrial nation-states.

6. Unlike tribes, but like states, chiefdoms had permanent regional regulation and differential access to resources. But chiefdoms lacked stratification. Unlike states, but like bands and tribes, chiefdoms were organized by kinship, descent, and marriage. Chiefdoms emerged in several areas, including the circum-Caribbean, lowland Amazonia, the southeastern United States, and Polynesia.

7. Weber's three dimensions of stratification are wealth, power, and prestige. In early states—for the first time in human history—contrasts in wealth, power, and prestige between entire groups of men and women came into being. A socioeconomic stratum includes people of both sexes and all ages. The superordinate—higher, or elite—stratum enjoys privileged access to resources.

8. Certain systems are found in all states: population control, judiciary, enforcement, and fiscal support. These are integrated by a ruling system or government composed of civil, military, and religious officials. States conduct censuses and demarcate boundaries. Laws are based on precedent and legislative proclamations. Courts and judges handle disputes and crimes. A police force maintains internal order, as a military defends against external threats. A financial, or fiscal, system supports rulers, officials, judges, and other specialists and government agencies.

9. *Hegemony* describes a stratified social order in which subordinates comply with domination by internalizing its values and accepting its "naturalness." Situations that appear hegemonic may have resistance that is individual and disguised rather than collective and defiant. "Public transcript" refers to the open, public interactions between the dominators and the oppressed. "Hidden transcript" describes the critique of power that goes on where the power holders can't see it. Discontent also may be expressed in public rituals such as Carnaval.

10. Broader than the political is the concept of social control—those fields of the social system most actively involved in the maintenance of norms and the regulation of conflict. Sanctions are social as well as governmental. Shame and gossip can be effective social sanctions. In the Igbo Women's War, women effectively used their social power (through song, dance, noise, and "in-your-face" behavior) to subvert the formal authority structure and, in so doing, gained greater influence within that structure.

## Key Terms

achieved status, *276*
ascribed status, *276*
authority, *268*
big man, *275*
chiefdom, *270*
conflict
   resolution, *272*
differential
   access, *270*
fiscal, *284*
hegemony, *285*

law, *272*
norms, *272*
office, *281*
pantribal
   sodality, *277*
power, *268*
prestige, *282*
social control, *285*
sociopolitical
   typology, *270*
state, *270*

status, *275*
subordinate, *283*
superordinate, *283*
tribe, *270*
village head, *274*
wealth, *282*

Chapter

# 13

# Families, Kinship, and Marriage

Although it still is something of an ideal in our culture, the nuclear family (parents and their children) now accounts for merely one-fifth of all American households. What kind of family raised you? Perhaps it was a nuclear family. Or maybe you were raised by a single parent, with or without the help of extended kin. Perhaps your extended kin acted as your parents. Or maybe you had a stepparent and/or step or half siblings in a blended family. Maybe you had two moms or two dads. Given the diversity of families in contemporary North America, your family may not have fit any of these descriptions, or perhaps it varied over time.

Although contemporary American family types are diverse, other cultures offer family alternatives that Americans might have trouble understanding. Imagine a society in which someone doesn't know for sure, and doesn't care much about, who his actual mother was. Consider Joseph Rabe, a Betsileo man who was my field assistant in Madagascar. Rabe, who had been raised by his aunt—his father's sister—told me about two sisters, one of whom was his mother and the other his mother's sister. He knew their names, but he didn't know which was which. Illustrating an adoptive pattern common among the Betsileo, Rabe was given as a toddler to his childless aunt. His mother and her sister lived far away and died in his childhood (as did his father), and so he didn't really know them. But he was very close to his father's sister, for whom he used the term for mother. Indeed, he had to call her that, because the Betsileo have only one kin term, *reny,* for mother, mother's sister, and father's sister. (They also use a single term, *ray,* for father and all uncles.) The difference between "real" (biologically based) and socially constructed kinship didn't matter to Rabe.

Contrast this Betsileo case with the common American view that kinship is, and should be, biological. It's increasingly common for adopted children to seek out their birth mothers or sperm donors (which used to be discouraged as disruptive), even after a perfectly satisfactory upbringing in an adoptive family. The American emphasis on biology for kinship is seen also in the recent proliferation of DNA testing. Viewing our beliefs through the lens of cross-cultural comparison helps us appreciate that kinship and biology don't always converge, nor do they need to.

The societies anthropologists traditionally have studied have stimulated a strong interest in families, along with larger systems of kinship and marriage. The wide web of kinship—as vital in daily life in nonindustrial societies as work outside the home is in our own—has become an essential part of anthropology because of its importance to the people we study. We are ready to take a closer look at the systems of kinship and marriage that have organized human life for much of our history.

Ethnographers quickly recognize social divisions, or groups, within any society they study. Often people live in the same village or neighborhood, or work, socialize, or celebrate together, because they are related in some way. A significant kin group might consist of descendants of the same grandfather. These people live in neighboring houses, farm adjoining fields, and help each other in daily tasks. Groups based on other kin links get together less often in that society (see Strathern and Stewart 2010).

The nuclear family is one kind of kin group that is widespread in human societies. Other kin groups include extended families (families consisting of three or more generations) and descent groups—lineages and clans. Much of kinship is *culturally constructed,* that is, based on learning and variable from culture to culture (McKinnon 2005). Different societies have different kinds of families, households, kin groups, marriage customs, and living arrangements.

## Families

Consider the term *family,* which is basic, familiar (so much so it even shares its root with *familiar*), and difficult to define in a way that applies to all cultures. A **family** is a group of people (e.g., parents, children, siblings, grandparents, grandchildren, uncles, aunts, nephews, nieces, cousins, spouses, siblings-in-law, parents-in-law, children-in-law) who are considered to be related in some way, for example, by "blood" (common ancestry or descent) or marriage. Some families, such as the nuclear family, are residentially based;

its members live together. Others are not; they live apart but come together for family reunions of various sorts from time to time.

Consider a striking contrast between the United States and Brazil in the meaning of family. American adults usually define their family as consisting of their spouse and children. However, when Brazilians talk about their family (*família*), they mean their parents, siblings, aunts, uncles, grandparents, and cousins. Later they add their children, but rarely their spouse, who has his or her own family. The children are shared by the two families. Among middle-class Americans the husband–wife relationship is supposed to take precedence over either spouse's relationship with his or her own parents. This can place a significant strain on American marriages (see this chapter's "Anthropology Today" for a study of American family life in the 21st century).

Living in a less mobile society, Brazilians stay in closer face-to-face contact with their relatives, including members of the extended family, than North Americans do. Residents of Rio de Janeiro and São Paulo, two of South America's largest cities, are reluctant to leave those urban centers to live away from family and friends. Brazilians find it hard to imagine, and unpleasant to live in, social worlds without relatives. Contrast this with a characteristic American theme: learning to live with strangers.

## Nuclear and Extended Families

A nuclear family is *impermanent;* it lasts only as long as the parents and children remain together. Most people belong to at least two nuclear families at different times in their lives. They are born into a family consisting of their parents and siblings. When they reach adulthood, they may marry and establish a nuclear family that includes the spouse and eventually children. Since most societies permit divorce, some people establish more than one family through marriage.

Anthropologists distinguish between the **family of orientation** (the family in which one is born and grows up) and the **family of procreation** (formed when one marries and has children). From the individual's point of view, the critical relationships are with parents and siblings in the family of orientation and with spouse and children in the family of procreation. In Brazil, as we just saw, the family of orientation predominates, whereas in the United States it is the family of procreation.

In most societies, relations with nuclear family members (parents, siblings, and children) take precedence over relations with other kin. Nuclear family organization is very widespread but not universal, and its significance in society differs greatly from one place to another. In a few societies, such as the classic Nayar case described later in this section, nuclear families are rare or nonexistent. In other societies, descent groups and extended families assume many of the functions otherwise associated with the nuclear family.

Consider an example from the former Yugoslavia. Traditionally, among the Muslims of western Bosnia (Lockwood 1975), nuclear families lacked autonomy. Several such families lived in an extended family household called a *zadruga*. The zadruga was headed by a male household head and his wife, the senior woman. It included married sons and their wives and children, as well as unmarried sons and daughters. Each nuclear family had a sleeping room, decorated and partly furnished from the bride's trousseau. However, possessions—even clothing and trousseau items—were shared by zadruga members. Such a residential unit is known as a *patrilocal* extended family because each couple resides in the husband's father's household after marriage.

The zadruga took precedence over its component units. There were three successive meal settings—for men, women, and children, respectively. Traditionally, all children over the age of 12 slept together in boys' or girls' rooms. When a woman wished to visit another village, she sought the permission of the male zadruga head. Although men usually felt closer to their own children than to those of their brothers, they were obliged to treat them equally. Children were disciplined by any adult in the household. When a nuclear family broke up, children under age 7 went with the mother. Older children could choose between their parents. Children were considered part of the household where they were born, even if their mother left. One widow who remarried had to leave her five children, all over the age of 7, in their father's zadruga, now headed by his brother.

Another example of an alternative to the nuclear family is provided by the Nayars (or Nair), a large and powerful caste on the Malabar Coast of southern India (Gough 1959; Shivaram 1996). Their traditional kinship system was matrilineal (descent traced only through females). Nayar lived in matrilineal extended family compounds called *tarawads*. Headed by a senior woman, assisted by her brother, the tarawad housed her siblings, sisters' children, and other matrikin—matrilineal relatives.

Traditional Nayar marriage seems to have been hardly more than a formality: a kind of coming-of-age ritual. A young woman would go through a marriage ceremony with a man, after which they might spend a few days together at her tarawad. Then the man

An extended family of cocoteros, workers on a coconut plantation in the rural town of Barigua in eastern Cuba. Try to guess the relationships among them. © James Quine/Alamy

would return to his own tarawad, where he lived with his sisters, aunts, and other matrikin. Nayar men belonged to a warrior class, who left home regularly for military expeditions, returning permanently to their tarawad on retirement. Nayar women could have multiple sexual partners. Children became members of the mother's tarawad; they were not considered to be relatives of their biological father. Indeed, many Nayar children didn't even know who their biological father (genitor) was.

## Industrialism and Family Organization

For many Americans and Canadians, the nuclear family is the only well-defined kin group. Family isolation arises from geographic mobility, which is associated with industrialism, so that a nuclear family focus is characteristic of many modern nations. Born into a family of orientation, North Americans leave home for college or work, and the break with parents is under way. Selling our labor on the market, we often move to places where jobs are available. Eventually most North Americans marry and start a family of procreation.

Many married couples live hundreds of miles from their parents. Their jobs have determined where they live. Such a postmarital residence pattern is **neolocality:** Married couples are expected to establish a new place of residence—a "home of their own." Among middle-class North Americans, neolocal residence is both a cultural preference and a statistical norm. Most middle-class Americans eventually establish households and nuclear families of their own.

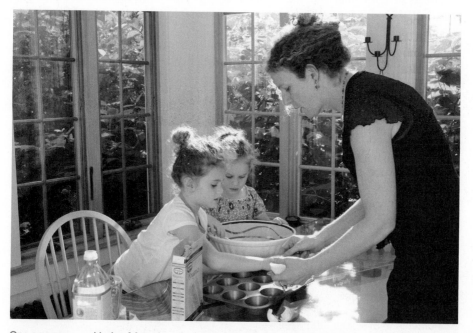

One among many kinds of American family: A single mother (by choice) bakes cupcakes with her twin daughters at their home in Brooklyn, New York. © Katja Heinemann/Aurora Photos

There are significant differences between middle-class and poorer North Americans. For example, in the lower class the incidence of *expanded family households* (those that include nonnuclear relatives) is greater than it is in the middle class. When an expanded family household includes three or more generations, it is an **extended family household**, such as the zadruga. Another type of expanded family is the *collateral household*, which includes siblings and their spouses and children.

The higher proportion of expanded family households among poorer Americans has been explained as an adaptation to poverty (Stack 1975). Unable to survive economically as nuclear family units, relatives band together and pool their resources. Adaptation to poverty causes kinship values and attitudes to diverge from middle-class norms. Thus, when North Americans raised in poverty achieve financial success, they often feel obligated to provide financial help to a wide circle of less fortunate relatives (see Willie 2003).

## Changes in North American Kinship

Although the nuclear family remains a cultural ideal for many Americans, we see in Table 13.1 that nuclear families accounted for just 20 percent of American households in 2014. Other domestic arrangements now outnumber the "traditional" American household five to one. There are several reasons for this changing household composition. Women increasingly are joining men in the cash workforce. This often removes them from their family of orientation while making it economically feasible to delay marriage. Furthermore, job demands compete with romantic attachments. The median age at first marriage for American women rose from 21 years in 1970 to 27.4 in 2013. For men the comparable ages were 23 and 29.4 (U.S. Census Bureau 2013).

Also, the U.S. divorce rate has risen substantially. Between 1970 and 2014 the number of divorced Americans increased sixfold, from 4.3 million to 25.3 million. (Note,

TABLE 13.1  **Changes in Family and Household Organization in the United States, 1970 versus 2014**

Source: From U.S. Census data located at http://www.census.gov/hhes/families/data/cps2014.html, America's Families and Living Arrangements: 2014.

|  | 1970 | 2014 |
|---|---|---|
| Numbers: |  |  |
| Total number of households | 63 million | 123 million |
| Number of people per household | 3.1 | 2.5 |
| Percentages: |  |  |
| Married couples living with children | 40% | 20% |
| Family households | 81% | 66% |
| Households with five or more people | 21% | 10% |
| People living alone | 17% | 28% |
| Percentage of single-mother families | 5% | 12% |
| Percentage of single-father families | 0% | 5% |
| Households with own children under 18 | 45% | 29% |

TABLE 13.2    **Ratio of Divorces to Marriages per 1,000 U.S. Population, Selected Years, 1950–2013**

Source: U.S. Census Bureau, American Community Study Estimates. http://factfinder.census.gov.

| 1950 | 1960 | 1970 | 1980 | 1990 | 2000 | 2013 |
|------|------|------|------|------|------|------|
| 3%   | 26%  | 35%  | 49%  | 48%  | 49%  | 52%  |

however, that each divorce creates two divorced people.) Table 13.2 shows the ratio of divorces to marriages in the United States for selected years between 1950 and 2013. A major jump in the divorce rate took place between 1960 and 1980. During that period the ratio of divorces to marriages doubled. Between 1980 and 2000, the ratio hovered around 50 percent. That is, each year there were about half as many new divorces as there were new marriages. Since 2000 the rate has drifted up a bit, to 52 percent in 2013.

The rate of growth in single-parent households also has outstripped population growth, more than tripling, from fewer than 4 million in 1970 to 14 million in 2014. (The overall American population in 2014 was 1.6 times its size in 1970.) The percentage (23.6 percent) of all American children under age 18 living in fatherless (mother-headed, no resident dad) households in 2014 was more than twice the 1970 rate, while the percentage (3.9 percent) in motherless (father-headed, no resident mom) homes also increased substantially. About 51 percent of American women and 54 percent of American men were currently married in 2014, versus 60 and 65 percent, respectively, in 1970 (Fields 2004; U.S. Census Bureau, http://www.census.gov/hhes/families/data/marital.html). However, more American women now live without a husband than with one. In 2014, 52 percent of women were living without a spouse, compared with 35 percent in 1950 (Roberts et al. 2007; U.S. Census Bureau 2014). Average household size in the United States and Canada has fallen from 2.9 in 1980 to about 2.5 today. These trends are also detectable in Western Europe and other industrial nations.

Immigrants are often shocked by what they perceive as weak kinship bonds and lack of proper respect for family in contemporary North America. In fact, most of the people whom middle-class North Americans see every day are either nonrelatives or members of the nuclear family (see Willie and Reddick 2009).

Interestingly, a recent study (Qian 2013) found that the traditional American nuclear family was best represented among recent immigrants. Sociologist Zhenchao Qian describes several differences involving marriage and the family between recent immigrants and native-born Americans. By 2010, the end point of Qian's 10-year study, immigrants constituted 13 percent of the U.S. population. They brought customs of their cultures of origin with them to the United States. One such pattern was marital stability, although brides tended to be significantly younger than their grooms. Among immigrants in their mid- to late 20s, 62 percent of women were married, compared with just 43 percent of men. At every age, however, the immigrant marriage rate was greater than that of native-born Americans, including those of their own ethnicity. Asian immigrants, for example, were twice as likely to marry as were U.S.-born Asians. Compared with native-born marriages, those of immigrants also tended to be more ethnically homogeneous and less prone to divorce. In 2010, about 30 percent of immigrant children lived in homes with a male breadwinner and a stay-at-home mother. This was 9 percentage points higher than the figure for native-born Americans, which helps explain why immigrant couples were more likely to be among the working poor than native-born families. In general, dual-income families make more than single-income ones.

## The Family among Foragers

Foraging societies are far removed from industrial nations in terms of social complexity, but they do feature geographic mobility, associated with nomadic or seminomadic hunting and gathering. Here again, the nuclear family often is the most significant kin group, although in no foraging society is it the only group based on kinship. The two basic social units of traditional foraging societies are the nuclear family and the band.

Unlike middle-class couples in industrial nations, foragers don't usually reside neolocally. Instead, they join a band in which either the husband or the wife has relatives. However, couples and families may move from one band to another several times. Although nuclear families are ultimately as impermanent among foragers as they are in any other society, they usually are more stable than bands are.

Many foraging societies lacked year-round band organization. The Native American Shoshone of Utah and Nevada provide an example. The resources available to the Shoshone were so meager that for most of the year families traveled alone through the countryside, hunting and gathering. In certain seasons families assembled to hunt cooperatively as a band, but after just a few months together they dispersed.

In neither industrial nor foraging economies are people permanently tied to the land. The mobility and the emphasis on small, economically self-sufficient family units promote the nuclear family as a basic kin group in both types of societies.

# Descent

We've seen that the nuclear family is important in industrial nations and among foragers. The analogous group among nonindustrial cultivators and herders is the descent group. A **descent group** is a *permanent* social unit whose members claim common ancestry. Descent group members believe they all descend from those common ancestors. The group endures even though its membership changes, as members are born and die, move in and move out. Often, descent-group membership is determined at birth and is life-long. In this case, it is an ascribed status.

## Descent Groups

Descent groups frequently are exogamous (members seek their mates from other descent groups). Two common rules admit certain people as descent-group members while excluding others. With a rule of **patrilineal descent,** people automatically have lifetime membership in their father's group. The children of the group's men join the group, but the children of the group's women are excluded. With **matrilineal descent,**

## FIGURE 13.1   A Patrilineage Five Generations Deep

Lineages are based on demonstrated descent from an apical ancestor. With patrilineal descent, children of the group's men (shaded) are included as descent-group members. Children of the group's women are excluded; they belong to *their* father's patrilineage.

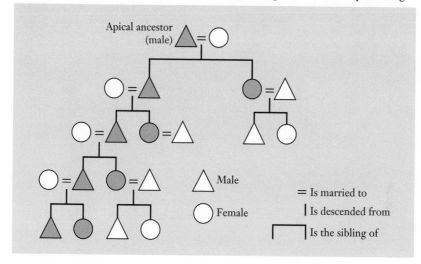

people join the mother's group automatically at birth and stay members throughout life. Matrilineal descent groups therefore include only the children of the group's women. (In Figures 13.1 and 13.2, which show patrilineal and matrilineal descent groups, respectively, the triangles stand for males and the circles for females.) Matrilineal and patrilineal descent are types of **unilineal descent.** This means the descent rule uses one line only, either the male or the female line. Patrilineal descent is much more common than matrilineal descent is. In a sample of 564 societies (Murdock 1957), about three times as many were found to be patrilineal (247 patrilineal to 84 matrilineal).

Descent groups may be **lineages** or **clans.** Common to both is the belief that members descend from the same *apical ancestor,* the person who stands at the apex, or top, of the common genealogy. For example, Adam and Eve are the apical ancestors of the biblical Jews and, according to the Bible, of all humanity. Since Eve is said to have come from Adam's rib, Adam stands as the original apical ancestor for the patrilineal genealogy laid out in the Bible.

How do lineages and clans differ? A lineage uses *demonstrated descent.* Members recite the names of their forebears from the apical ancestor through the present. (This doesn't mean their recitations are accurate, only that lineage members think they are.) In the Bible the litany of men who "begat" other men is a demonstration of genealogical descent for a large patrilineage that ultimately includes Jews and Arabs (who share Abraham as their last common apical ancestor).

Unlike lineages, clans use *stipulated descent.* Clan members merely say they descend from the apical ancestor, without trying to trace the actual genealogical links. The Betsileo of Madagascar have both clans and lineages. Descent may be demonstrated for the

FIGURE 13.2   **A Matrilineage Five Generations Deep**

Matrilineages are based on demonstrated descent from a female ancestor. Only the children of the group's women (shaded) belong to the matrilineage. The children of the group's men are excluded; they belong to *their* mother's matrilineage.

most recent 8–10 generations, then stipulated for vaguely defined ancestors in the more remote past (Kottak 1980). Like the Betsileo, many societies have both lineages and clans. In such a case, clans have more members and cover a larger geographical area than lineages do. Sometimes a clan's apical ancestor is not a human at all but an animal or a plant (called a *totem*).

The economic types that usually have descent group organization are horticulture, pastoralism, and agriculture. Such societies tend to have several descent groups. Any one of them may be confined to a single village, but usually they span more than one village. Two or more local branches of different descent groups may live in the same village. Descent groups in the same village or different villages may establish alliances through frequent intermarriage.

## Lineages, Clans, and Residence Rules

As we've seen, descent groups, unlike families, are permanent and enduring units, with new members added in every generation. Members have access to the lineage estate, where some of them must live, in order to benefit from and manage that estate across the generations. An easy way to keep members at home is to have a rule about who belongs to the descent group and where they should live after they get married. Patrilineal and matrilineal descent, and the postmarital residence rules that usually accompany them, ensure that about half the people born in each generation will spend their lives on the ancestral estate.

**Patrilocality** is the rule that when a couple marries, it moves to the husband's community, so that their children will grow up in their father's village. Patrilocality is associated with patrilineal descent. This makes sense. If the group's male members are expected to exercise their rights in the ancestral estate, it's a good idea to raise them on that estate and to keep them there after they marry. This can be done by having wives move to the husband's village, rather than vice versa.

A less common postmarital residence rule, associated with matrilineal descent, is **matrilocality:** Married couples live in the wife's community, and their children grow up in their mother's village. This rule keeps related women together (see Stone 2010). Together, patrilocality and matrilocality are known as *unilocal* rules of postmarital residence.

## Marriage

"Love and marriage," "marriage and the family": These familiar phrases show how we link the romantic love of two individuals to marriage, and how we link marriage to reproduction and family creation. But marriage is an institution with significant roles and functions in addition to reproduction. What is marriage, anyway?

No definition of marriage is broad enough to apply easily to all societies and situations. A commonly quoted definition comes from *Notes and Queries on Anthropology:*

> Marriage is a union between a man and a woman such that the children born to the woman are recognized as legitimate offspring of both partners. (Royal Anthropological Institute 1951, p. 111)

This definition isn't valid universally for several reasons. In many societies, marriages unite more than two spouses. Here we speak of *plural marriages,* as when a man weds two (or more) women (*polygyny*), or a woman weds a group of brothers—an arrangement called *fraternal polyandry* that is characteristic of certain Himalayan cultures.

This "I love you" wall is on display in an open area of Monmartre, Paris, France. It shows how to say "I love you" in various languages. Is romantic love a cultural universal? © Conrad P. Kottak

Some societies recognize various kinds of same-sex marriages. In South Sudan, a Nuer woman could marry a woman if her father had only daughters but no male heirs, who were necessary if his patrilineage was to survive. He could ask his daughter to stand as a son in order to take a bride. This daughter would become the socially recognized husband of another woman (the wife). This was a symbolic and social relationship rather than a sexual one. The "wife" had sex with a man or men until she got pregnant. The children born to the wife were accepted as the offspring of both the female husband and the wife. Although the female husband was not the actual *genitor,* the biological father, of the children, she was their *pater,* or socially recognized father. What's important in this Nuer case is *social* rather than *biological paternity.* We see again how kinship is socially constructed. The bride's children were considered the legitimate offspring of her female husband, who was biologically a woman but socially a man, and the descent line continued.

The British anthropologist Edmund Leach (1955) observed that, depending on the society, several different kinds of rights may be allocated by marriage. According to Leach, marriage can (but does not always) accomplish the following:

1. Establish legal parentage.
2. Give either or both spouses a monopoly on the sexuality of the other.
3. Give either or both spouses rights to the labor of the other.
4. Give either or both spouses rights over the other's property.
5. Establish a joint fund of property—a partnership—for the benefit of the children.
6. Establish a socially significant "relationship of affinity" between spouses and their relatives.

## Exogamy and Incest

The wider relationships of affinity are important. Indeed, marriage is one of the primary ways of converting strangers into friends, of creating and maintaining personal and political alliances. **Exogamy**—seeking a mate outside one's own group—links people into a wider social network that nurtures, helps, and protects them in times of need. Incest restrictions (prohibitions on sex with relatives) reinforce exogamy by pushing people to seek their mates outside the local group. Most societies discourage sexual contact involving close relatives, especially members of the same nuclear family.

**Incest** refers to sexual contact with a relative, but cultures define their kin, and thus incest, differently. In other words, incest, like kinship, is socially constructed. Some U.S. states, for example, permit marriage, and therefore sex, with first cousins, while others ban it. The social construction of kinship, and of incest, is far from simple.

In nonindustrial societies, when unilineal descent is very strongly developed, the parent who belongs to a different descent group than your own isn't considered a relative. Thus, with strict patrilineality, the mother is not a relative but a kind of in-law who has married a member of your own group—your father. With strict matrilineality, the father isn't a relative because he belongs to a different descent group.

The Lakher of Southeast Asia are strictly patrilineal (Leach 1961). Using the male ego (the reference point, the person in question) in Figure 13.3, let's suppose that ego's father

## FIGURE 13.3    Patrilineal Descent-Group Identity and Incest among the Lakher

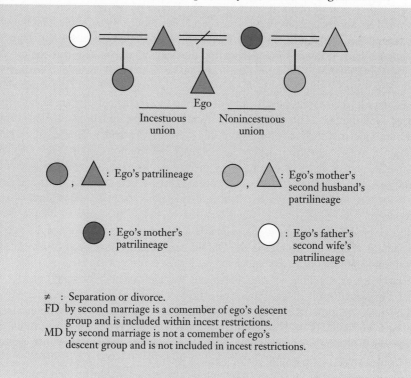

and mother get divorced. Each remarries and has a daughter by a second marriage. A Lakher always belongs to his or her father's group, all of whose members (one's *agnates,* or *patrikin*) are considered relatives, because they belong to the same descent group. Ego can't have sex with or marry his father's daughter by the second marriage, just as in contemporary North America it's illegal for half siblings to have sex and marry. However, unlike our society, where all half siblings are restricted, sex between our Lakher ego and his maternal half sister would be nonincestuous. She isn't ego's relative because she belongs to her own father's descent group rather than ego's. The Lakher illustrate very well that definitions of relatives, and therefore of incest, vary from culture to culture.

## Incest Happens

We know from primate research that adolescent males (among monkeys) or females (among apes) often move away from the group in which they were born (Rodseth et al. 1991). This emigration reduces the frequency of incestuous unions, but it doesn't eliminate them. DNA testing of wild chimps has confirmed incestuous unions between adult sons and their mothers, who reside in the same group. Human behavior with respect to mating with close relatives may express a generalized primate tendency, in which we see both urges and avoidance.

A cross-cultural study of 87 societies (Meigs and Barlow 2002) suggested that incest occurred in several of them. It's not clear, however, whether the authors of the study controlled for the social construction of incest. They report, for example, that incest occurs among the Yanomami, but they may be considering cross-cousin marriage to be incestuous, when it is not so considered by the Yanomami. Indeed, it is the preferred form of marriage, not just for the Yanomami but in many tribal societies. Another society in their sample is the Ashanti, for whom the ethnographer Meyer Fortes reports, "In the old days it [incest] was punished by death. Nowadays the culprits are heavily fined" (Fortes 1950, p. 257). This suggests that there really were violations of Ashanti incest restrictions and that such violations were, and still are, punished. More strikingly, among 24 Ojibwa individuals from whom he obtained information about incest, A. Irving Hallowell found 8 cases of parent–child incest and 10 cases of brother–sister incest (Hallowell 1955, pp. 294–95). Because reported cases of actual parent–child and sibling incest are rare in the ethnographic literature, questions about the possibility of social construction arise here, too. In many cultures, including the Ojibwa, people use the same terms for their mother and their aunt, their father and their uncle, and their cousins and siblings. Could the siblings in the Ojibwa case actually have been cousins, and the parents and children uncles and nieces?

In ancient Egypt, sibling marriage apparently was allowed both for royalty and for commoners, in some districts at least. Based on official census records from Roman Egypt (first to third centuries C.E.), 24 percent of all documented marriages in the Arsinoites district were between "brothers" and "sisters." The rates were 37 percent for the city of Arsinoe and 19 percent for the surrounding villages. These figures are much higher than any other documented levels of inbreeding among humans (Scheidel 1997). Again one wonders if the relatives involved were actually as close biologically as the kin terms would imply.

According to Anna Meigs and Kathleen Barlow (2002), for Western societies with nuclear family organization, "father–daughter incest" is much more common with stepfathers than with biological fathers. But is it really incest if they aren't biological relatives? American culture is unclear on this matter. Incest also happens with biological fathers, especially those who were absent or did little caretaking of their daughters in childhood (Williams and Finkelhor 1995). In a carefully designed study, Linda M. Williams and David Finkelhor (1995) found father–daughter incest to be least likely when there was substantial paternal parenting of daughters. This experience enhanced the father's parenting skills and his feelings of nurturance, protectiveness, and identification with his daughter, thus reducing the chance of incest.

A century ago, early anthropologists speculated that incest restrictions reflect an instinctive horror of mating with close relatives (Hobhouse 1915; Lowie 1920/1961). But why, one wonders, if humans really do have an instinctive aversion to incest would formal restrictions be necessary? No one would want to have sexual contact with a relative, yet as social workers, judges, psychiatrists, and psychologists are well aware, incest is more common than we might suppose.

## Endogamy

The practice of exogamy pushes social organization outward, establishing and preserving alliances among groups. In contrast, rules of **endogamy** dictate mating or marriage within a group to which one belongs. Endogamic rules are less common but are still familiar to anthropologists. Indeed, most cultures *are* endogamous units, although they usually do not need a formal rule requiring people to marry someone from their own society. In our society, classes and ethnic groups are quasi-endogamous groups. Members of an ethnic or religious group often want their children to marry within that group, although many of them do not do so. The outmarriage rate varies among such groups, with some more committed to endogamy than others.

### Caste

An extreme example of endogamy is India's **caste system,** which was formally abolished in 1949, although its structure and effects linger. Castes are stratified groups in which membership is ascribed at birth and is lifelong. Indian castes are grouped into five major categories, or *varna.* Each is ranked relative to the other four, and these categories extend throughout India. Each varna includes a large number of minor castes (*jati*), each of which includes people within a region who may intermarry. All the jati in a single varna in a given region are ranked, just as the varna themselves are ranked.

Occupational specialization often sets off one caste from another. A community may include castes of agricultural workers, merchants, artisans, priests, and sweepers. The untouchable varna, found throughout India, includes castes whose ancestry, ritual status, and occupations are considered so impure that higher-caste people consider even casual contact with untouchables to be defiling.

The belief that intercaste sexual unions lead to ritual impurity for the higher-caste partner has been important in maintaining endogamy. A man who has sex with a lower-caste woman can restore his purity with a bath and a prayer. However, a woman who has intercourse with a man of a lower caste has no such recourse. Her defilement cannot be undone. Because the women have the babies, these differences protect the purity of the caste line, ensuring the pure ancestry of high-caste children. Although Indian castes are endogamous groups, many of them are internally subdivided into exogamous lineages. Traditionally this meant that Indians had to marry a member of another descent group from the same caste. This shows that rules of exogamy and endogamy can coexist in the same society.

# Same-Sex Marriage

What about same-sex marriage? Such unions, of various sorts, have been recognized in many different historical and cultural settings. We saw earlier that the Nuer of South Sudan allowed a woman whose father lacked sons to take a wife and be socially recognized as her husband and as the father (pater, although not genitor) of her children. Other African cultures, including the Igbo of Nigeria and the Lovedu of South Africa, have permitted women to marry other women. In situations in which women, such as prominent market women in West Africa, are able to amass property and other forms of wealth, they may take a wife. Such marriage allows the prominent woman to strengthen her social status and the economic importance of her household (Amadiume 1987).

Sometimes, when same-sex marriage is allowed, one of the married partners is of the same biological sex as the spouse but is considered to belong to a different, socially

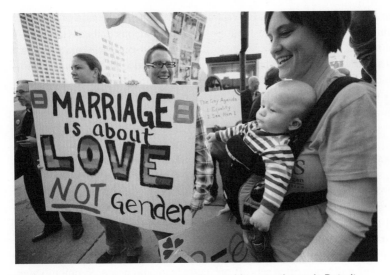

A 2013 rally in support of marriage equality outside a courthouse in Detroit, Michigan. © Bill Pugliano/Getty Images News/Getty Images

constructed gender. Several Native American groups had figures known as *berdaches,* representing a third gender (Murray and Roscoe 1998). These biological men assumed many of the mannerisms, behavior patterns, and tasks of women. Sometimes *berdaches* married men, who shared the products of their labor from hunting and filled traditional male roles, as the *berdache* fulfilled the traditional wifely role. Also, in some Native American cultures, a marriage of a "manly hearted woman" (a third or fourth gender) to another woman brought the traditional male–female division of labor to their household. The manly woman hunted and did other male tasks, while the wife played the traditional female role.

As of this writing, same-sex marriage is legal nationwide in 19 countries: Argentina, Belgium, Brazil, Canada, Denmark, France, Finland, Iceland, Luxembourg, the Netherlands, New Zealand, Norway, Portugal, South Africa, Spain, Sweden, the United Kingdom, the United States, and Uruguay. Twenty-first-century North America has witnessed a rapid and dramatic shift in public and legal opinions about same-sex marriage. In April 2000, the State of Vermont passed a bill allowing same-sex couples to unite legally in "civil unions," with virtually all the benefits of marriage. In Canada, in June 2003, a court ruling established same-sex marriages as legal in the province of Ontario. Two years later, Canada's House of Commons voted to guarantee full marriage rights to same-sex couples throughout that nation.

In May 2004, Massachusetts became the first U.S. state to allow same-sex marriage. Thereafter, legalization spread slowly at first, then rapidly in the wake of a key 2013 Supreme Court decision. The District of Columbia and 19 states—California, Connecticut, Delaware, Hawaii, Illinois, Iowa, Maine, Maryland, Massachusetts, Minnesota, New Hampshire, New Jersey, New Mexico, New York, Oregon, Pennsylvania, Rhode Island, Vermont, and Washington—allowed same-sex marriage as of July 2014. By February 2015, that number had jumped to 37. On June 26, 2015 the Supreme Court established the legality of same-sex marriage throughout the United States.

The legalization of same-sex marriage has come despite considerable opposition at the federal and state levels. In 1996 the U.S. Congress approved the Defense of Marriage Act (DOMA), which denied federal recognition and benefits to same-sex couples. Voters in at least 29 U.S. states have approved measures in their state constitutions defining marriage as an exclusively heterosexual union. In November 2008, Californians voted 52 percent to 48 percent for Proposition 8, banning same-sex marriage, which the courts had approved earlier that year. In 2012, California's 9th Circuit Court struck down that ban as unconstitutional.

On June 26, 2013, the U.S. Supreme Court struck down a key part of DOMA and granted to legally married same-sex couples the same federal rights and benefits received by any legally married couple. In August 2013, the California Supreme Court rejected an attempt to revive that state's ban on same-sex marriage. Any adult in California or, indeed, any other of the 50 United States can now marry the partner of his or her choice and receive federal benefits. Although opposition continues (often on religious grounds), public opinion has followed the judicial shift toward approval of same-sex marriage.

## Marriage across Cultures

Outside industrial societies, marriage often is more a relationship between groups than one between individuals. We think of marriage as an individual matter. Although the bride and groom usually seek their parents' approval, the final choice (to live together, to marry, to divorce) lies with the couple. The idea of romantic love symbolizes this individual relationship.

In nonindustrial societies, although there can be romantic love (Goleman 1992), marriage is a group concern. People don't just take a spouse; they assume obligations to a group of in-laws. When residence is patrilocal, for example, a woman must leave the community where she was born. She faces the prospect of spending the rest of her life in her husband's village, with his relatives.

### Gifts at Marriage

In societies with descent groups, people often enter marriage with significant help from their descent group. Often it is customary for a substantial gift to be given before, at, or after the marriage by the husband and his kin to the wife and her kin. The BaThonga of Mozambique call such a gift *lobola*, and the custom of giving something like **lobola** is very widespread in patrilineal societies (Radcliffe-Brown 1924/1952). This gift compensates the bride's group for the loss of her companionship and labor. More important, it makes the children born to the woman full members of her husband's descent group. In matrilineal societies, children are members of the mother's group, and there is no reason for a lobola-like gift.

Another kind of marital gift, **dowry,** occurs when the bride's family or kin group provides substantial gifts when their daughter marries. For rural Greece, Ernestine Friedl (1962) describes a form of dowry in which the bride gets a wealth transfer from her mother, to serve as a kind of trust fund during her marriage. Usually, however, the dowry goes to the husband's family, and the custom is correlated with low female status. In this form of dowry, best known from India, women are perceived as burdens. When a man and his family take a wife, they expect to be compensated for the added responsibility.

Lobola-like gifts exist in many more cultures than dowry does, but the nature and quantity of transferred items differ. Among the BaThonga of Mozambique, whose name—lobola—I am using for this widespread custom, the gift consists of cattle. Use of livestock (usually cattle in Africa, pigs in Papua New Guinea) for lobola is common, but the number of animals given varies from society to society. We can generalize, however, that the larger the gift, the more stable the marriage. Lobola is insurance against divorce.

Imagine a patrilineal society in which a marriage requires the transfer of about 25 cattle from the groom's descent group to the bride's. Michael, a member of descent group A, marries Sarah from group B. His relatives help him assemble the lobola. He gets the most help from his close agnates—his older brother, father, father's brother, and closest patrilineal cousins.

The distribution of the cattle once they reach Sarah's group mirrors the manner in which they were assembled. Sarah's father, or her oldest brother if the father is dead, receives her lobola. He keeps most of the cattle to use as lobola for his sons' marriages. However, a share also goes to everyone who will be expected to help when Sarah's brothers marry.

When Sarah's brother David gets married, many of the cattle go to a third group—C, which is David's wife's group. Thereafter, they may serve as lobola to still other groups. Men constantly use their sisters' lobola cattle to acquire their own wives. In a decade, the cattle given when Michael married Sarah will have been exchanged widely.

In such societies, marriage entails an agreement between descent groups. If Sarah and Michael try to make their marriage succeed but fail to do so, both groups may conclude that the marriage can't last. Here it becomes especially obvious that marriages are relationships between groups as well as between individuals. If Sarah has a younger sister or niece (her older brother's daughter, for example), the concerned parties may agree to Sarah's replacement by a kinswoman.

However, incompatibility isn't the main problem that threatens marriage in societies with lobola customs. Infertility is a more important concern. If Sarah has no children, she and her group have not fulfilled their part of the marriage agreement. If the relationship is to endure, Sarah's group must furnish another woman, perhaps her younger sister, who can have children. If this happens, Sarah may choose to stay in her husband's village. Perhaps she will someday have a child. If she does stay on, her husband will have established a plural marriage.

Most nonindustrial food-producing societies, unlike most industrial nations, allow **plural marriages,** or **polygamy.** There are two varieties; one is common and the other is very rare. The more common variant is **polygyny,** in which a man has more than one wife. The rare variant is **polyandry,** in which a woman has more than one husband. If the infertile wife remains married to her husband after he has taken a substitute wife provided by her descent group, this is polygyny.

## Durable Alliances

It is possible to exemplify the group-alliance nature of marriage by examining still another common practice—continuation of marital alliances when one spouse dies.

**FIGURE 13.4**
**Sororate and**
**Levirate**

: Sarah's descent group

: Michael's descent group

*Sororate*

What happens if Sarah dies young? Michael's group will ask Sarah's group for a substitute, often her sister. This custom is known as the **sororate** (see Figure 13.4). If Sarah has no sister, or if all her sisters already are married, another woman from her group may be available. Michael marries her, there is no need to return the lobola, and the alliance continues.

The sororate exists in both matrilineal and patrilineal societies. In a matrilineal society with matrilocal postmarital residence, a widower may remain with his wife's group by marrying her sister or another female member of her matrilineage (see Figure 13.4).

*Levirate*

What happens if the husband dies? In many societies, the widow may marry his brother. This custom is known as the **levirate** (see Figure 13.4). Like the sororate, it is a continuation marriage that maintains the alliance between descent groups, in this case by replacing the husband with another member of his group. The implications of the levirate vary with age. One study found that in African societies the levirate, although widely permitted, rarely involves cohabitation of the widow and her new husband. Furthermore, widows don't automatically marry the husband's brother just because they are allowed to. Often they prefer to make other arrangements.

# Divorce

Ease of divorce varies across cultures. What factors work for and against divorce? As we've seen, marriages that are political alliances between groups are more difficult to dissolve than are marriages that are more individual affairs. We've seen that a substantial lobola gift may reduce the divorce rate for individuals; replacement marriages (levirate and sororate) also work to preserve group alliances. Divorce tends to be more common in matrilineal than in patrilineal societies. When residence is matrilocal (in the wife's home village), the wife may simply send off a man with whom she's incompatible, or he may choose to leave.

Among the Hopi of the American Southwest, houses were owned by matrilineal clans, with matrilocal postmarital residence. The household head was the senior woman of that household, which also included her daughters and their husbands and children. A son-in-law had no important role there; he returned to his own mother's home for his clan's social and religious activities. In this matrilineal society, women were socially and economically secure and the divorce rate was high.

In a study of the marital histories of 423 Hopi women in Oraibi (Orayvi) pueblo, Mischa Titiev found 35 percent to have been divorced at least once (Titiev 1992). For comparison, of all ever-married women in the United States, only 4 percent had been divorced in 1960, 10.7 percent in 1980, and 11.3 percent in 2014 (Kreider and Ellis 2011; U.S. Census Bureau 2014). The instability of the Hopi marital bond was due, at least partially, to conflicting loyalties to matrikin versus spouse. Jerome Levy (1992) generalizes that, cross-culturally, high divorce rates are correlated with a secure female economic position. In Hopi society women were secure in their home and land ownership and in the custody of their children. In addition, there were no formal barriers to divorce.

Divorce is harder in a patrilineal society, especially when a substantial lobola gift would have to be reassembled and repaid if the marriage failed. A woman residing patrilocally (in her husband's household and community) might be reluctant to leave him. Unlike the Hopi, where the kids stay with the mother, in patrilineal, patrilocal societies the children of divorce would be expected to remain with their father, as members of his patrilineage. From the women's perspective this is a strong impediment to divorce.

In contemporary Western societies, we have the idea that romantic love is necessary for a good marriage (see Ingraham 2008). When romance fails, so may the marriage. Or it may not fail, if the other rights associated with marriage, as discussed previously in this chapter, are compelling. Economic ties and obligations to children, along with other factors, such as concern about public opinion, or simple inertia, may keep marriages intact after sex, romance, or companionship fades.

# Plural Marriages

In contemporary North America, where divorce is fairly easy and common, polygamy (marriage to more than one spouse at the same time) is against the law. North Americans are allowed, however, to practice *serial monogamy:* Individuals may have more than one spouse but never, legally, more than one at the same time. As stated earlier, the two forms of polygamy are polygyny and polyandry. Polyandry is practiced in only a few societies, notably among certain groups in Tibet, Nepal, and India. Polygyny is much more common.

## Polygyny

We must distinguish between the social approval of plural marriage and its actual frequency in a particular society. Many cultures approve of a man's having more than one wife. However, even when polygyny is encouraged, most people are monogamous, and polygyny characterizes only a fraction of the marriages. Why?

One reason is equal sex ratios. In the United States, about 105 males are born for every 100 females. In adulthood the ratio of men to women equalizes, and eventually it reverses. The average North American woman outlives the average man. In many nonindustrial societies as well, the male-biased sex ratio among children reverses in adulthood.

The custom of men marrying later than women also promotes polygyny. Among Nigeria's Kanuri people (Cohen 1967), men got married between the ages of 18 and 30; women, between 12 and 14. The age difference between spouses meant there were more widows than widowers. Most of the widows remarried, some in polygynous unions. Among the Kanuri and in other polygynous societies, such as the Tiwi of northern Australia, widows made up a large number of the women involved in plural marriages (Hart, Pilling, and Goodale 1988).

In certain societies, the first wife requests a second wife to help with household chores. The second wife's status is lower than that of the first; they are senior and junior wives. The senior wife sometimes chooses the junior one from among her close kinswomen. Among the Betsileo of Madagascar, the different wives always lived in different villages. A man's first (senior) wife, called "Big Wife," lived in the village where he cultivated his best rice field and spent most of his time. High-status men with several rice fields and multiple wives had households near each field. They spent most of their time with the senior wife but visited the others throughout the year.

Plural wives can play important political roles in nonindustrial states. The king of the Merina, a populous society in the highlands of Madagascar, had palaces for each of his 12 wives in different provinces. He stayed with them when he traveled through the kingdom. They were his local agents, overseeing and reporting on provincial matters. The king of Buganda, the major precolonial state of Uganda, took hundreds of wives,

Modern-day polygyny is illustrated by this photo (left) of South Africa's President Jacob Zuma and his three wives. In the United States as in South Africa, powerful men often have multiple wives, but legally not at the same time. The three marriages of former Speaker of the House Newt Gingrich (right) illustrate serial monogamy. (left): © Mike Hutchings/AP Images; (right): © Stan Honda/AFP/Getty Images representing all the clans in his nation. Everyone in the kingdom became the king's in-law, and all the clans had a chance to provide the next ruler. This was a way of giving the common people a stake in the government.

These examples show there is no single explanation for polygyny. Its context and function vary from society to society and even within the same society. Some men are polygynous because they have inherited a widow from a brother. Others have plural wives because they seek prestige or want to increase household productivity. Men and women with political and economic ambitions cultivate marital alliances that serve their aims. In many societies, including the Betsileo of Madagascar and the Igbo of Nigeria, women arrange the marriages.

## Polyandry

Polyandry is rare and is practiced under very specific conditions. Most of the world's polyandrous peoples live in South Asia—Tibet, Nepal, India, and Sri Lanka. In some of these areas, polyandry seems to be a cultural adaptation to mobility associated with customary male travel for trade, commerce, and military operations. Polyandry ensures there will be at least one man at home to accomplish male activities within a gender-based division of labor. Fraternal polyandry is also an effective strategy when resources are scarce. Brothers with limited resources (in land) pool their resources in expanded (polyandrous) households. They take just one wife. Polyandry restricts the number of wives and heirs. Less competition among heirs means that land can be transmitted with minimal fragmentation.

# The Online Marriage Market

People today use the Internet to shop for virtually everything, including romantic relationships, in what has been called the "online marriage market." There are huge differences in the marriage markets of industrial versus nonindustrial societies. In some of the latter, potential spouses may be limited to cross cousins or members of a specific descent group. Often, marriages are arranged by relatives. In almost all cases, however, there is some kind of preexisting social relationship between any two individuals who marry and their kin groups.

Potential mates still meet in person in modern nations. Sometimes, friends or relatives help arrange such meetings. Besides friends of friends, the marriage market also includes the workplace, bars, clubs, parties, churches, and hobby groups. Add the Internet, which has become a new place to seek out and develop "virtual" relationships, including romantic ones. As part of the "Me, My Spouse, and the Internet" project at the University of Oxford in England, Bernie Hogan, Nai Li, and William Dutton (2011) surveyed cohabiting couples in 18 countries (Table 13.3 lists those countries and the sample size for each). This study (conducted online) sampled 12,600 couples (25,200 individuals aged 18 and older), all with home Internet access. Respondents were asked about how they met their partners, their dating strategies, how they maintain their current relationships and social networks, and how they use the Internet.

**TABLE 13.3**
**Countries Sampled in the Oxford Internet Institute Project "Me, My Spouse, and the Internet"**

Source: Bernie Hogan, Nai Li, and William H. Dutton, *A Global Shift in the Social Relationships of Networked Individuals: Meeting and Dating Online Comes of Age* (February 14, 2011, Table 1.1, p. 5). Oxford Internet Institute, University of Oxford. http://ssrn.com/abstract51763884 or http://dx.doi.org/10.2139/ssrn.1763884.

| Country | Sample Size | Percentage |
|---|---|---|
| Italy | 3,515 | 13.9 |
| France | 2,970 | 11.8 |
| Spain | 2,673 | 10.6 |
| Germany | 2,638 | 10.5 |
| UK | 2,552 | 10.1 |
| Brazil | 2,438 | 9.7 |
| Japan | 2,084 | 8.3 |
| Netherlands | 1,491 | 5.9 |
| Belgium | 1,124 | 4.5 |
| Sweden | 794 | 3.1 |
| Portugal | 603 | 2.4 |
| Finland | 508 | 2.0 |
| Ireland | 368 | 1.5 |
| Norway | 317 | 1.3 |
| Austria | 309 | 1.2 |
| Greece | 297 | 1.2 |
| Switzerland | 278 | 1.1 |
| Denmark | 241 | 1.0 |
| Total | 25,200 | 100.0 |

The Oxford study found that people still seek and find partners in the old, familiar places, even as they look online as well. One-third of the respondents in the study had some experience with online dating, and about 15 percent were in a relationship that had started online. People who know someone who dates online are themselves more likely to date online and to approve of online dating. Like online banking and online shopping, Internet dating is an "experience technology" (Hogan et al. 2011): One's attitudes about that technology reflect one's experiences with it. The more one is exposed to online dating, the more one approves of it. People don't even need to have been successful at online dating to feel positive about it. Simply trying it enhances their view of the experience.

Who benefits most from the new technology? Is it young, tech-savvy people, who go online for virtually everything? Or might it be people who are socially isolated in the offline world, including divorced, older, and widowed people? Interestingly, the Oxford researchers found that older people were more likely than younger ones to use online dating to find their current partner. About 36 percent of people over 40 had done so, versus 23 percent of younger adults.

In Europe, the media-saturated nations of northern Europe were most likely to use online dating, which benefits from a critical mass of Internet connectivity (the more people online, the larger the pool of potential contacts). On the other hand, online Brazilians (who tend to be gregarious both on- and offline) were most likely to know someone who either began a relationship online or married someone first met online. Personal

## Anthropology Today    *American Family Life in the 21st Century*

*Anthropologists today increasingly study daily life in the United States, including that of middle-class families. An excellent example is* Life at Home in the Twenty-First Century: 32 Families Open Their Doors *(Arnold et al. 2012), a study of home life in 32 middle-class, dual-income families in Los Angeles, focusing on physical surroundings and material culture, the items owned and used in daily life. The book's authors are three UCLA anthropologists—Jeanne Arnold, Anthony Graesch, and Elinor Ochs—and Italian photographer Enzo Ragazzini. All did research through UCLA's Center on Everyday Lives of Families (CELF), which was founded in 2001 and is directed by Ochs.*

The families selected for, and agreeing to participate in, the study on which *Life at Home* was based were all middle-class and owned or were buying their homes. They varied in ethnicity, income level, and neighborhood. A few same-sex couples were included.

The authors took a systematic approach to their subjects. They videotaped the activities of family members, tracked their movements using positioning devices, measured their stress levels through saliva samples, and took almost 20,000 photographs (approximately 600 per family) of homes, yards, and activities. The researchers also asked family members to narrate tours of their homes and videotaped them as they did so. Over a four-year period the project generated 47 hours of family-narrated video home tours and 1,540 hours of videotaped family interactions and interviews (see Arnold et al. 2012; Feuer 2012; Sullivan 2012).

A key finding of the study was the extent of clutter in those homes, a manifestation of a high degree of consumerism among dual-income American families. Never in human history, the researchers conclude, have families accumulated so many personal possessions. Hypothesizing that dealing with so much clutter would have psychological effects, the researchers collected saliva samples from the subjects in order to measure diurnal cortisol, an indicator of stress. Mothers' saliva, it turned out, contained more diurnal cortisol than did fathers'. The researchers also noticed that, in their video tours, mothers often used words like "mess" and "chaotic" to describe their homes, while fathers rarely mentioned messiness. Author Anthony Graesch reasons that clutter bothers moms so much because it challenges deeply ingrained notions that homes should be tidy and well managed (see Feuer 2012). The role of domestic manager, of course, is traditionally a female one. For dads and kids, more than for moms, possessions appeared to be a source of pleasure, pride, and contentment rather than stress (Arnold et al. 2012; Feuer 2012).

Another finding was that children rarely went outside, despite the overall mild weather in Los Angeles. They used their possessions indoors, resulting in more clutter, including whole walls devoted to displays of dolls and toys. More than half of the 32 households had special rooms designed for work or schoolwork, but even in home offices kids' stuff tended to crowd parental items. The researchers speculate that guilt motivates dual-income parents to buy so much stuff for their kids. The parents in the study managed to spend, on an average weekday, no more than four hours with their kids, perhaps leading them to overcompensate with toys, clothes, and other possessions (Graesch quoted in Feuer 2012).

The study found that the kitchen was the center of home life. In this space, family members met, interacted, exchanged information, and socialized their children. And in the kitchen, the refrigerator played a key role. Stuck on its doors and sides were such items as pictures, displays of children's achievements, reminders, addresses, and phone lists (including many outdated ones). The typical refrigerator front panel held 52 objects. The most crowded refrigerator had 166 stick-ons. The refrigerator served as a compact representation of that family's history and activities (Feuer 2012; Sullivan 2012).

Researchers found a correlation between the number of objects on the refrigerator and the overall clutter in a home. The refrigerator thus served not only as a chronicler of family life but also as a measure of its degree of consumerism—and perhaps of stress. We might hypothesize that a high number of refrigerator stick-ons indicates that someone in the household needs to take blood pressure medication.

knowledge of an online romantic relationship was reported by 81 percent of the Brazilians in the study, versus only 40 percent of Germans.

The Internet reconfigures access to people in general. More of the respondents in the Oxford study reported making online friends or work connections than romantic liaisons. More than half (55 percent) of respondents (considering all 18 countries) had met someone new online (Hogan et al. 2011). The 2,438 Brazilians in the sample were the most likely to move from an online to a face-to-face contact. Fully 83 percent of Internet-enabled Brazilians reported meeting someone face-to-face after first meeting him or her online. Japanese respondents were least likely to meet in person after an online acquaintance. They also were least likely to engage in online dating.

With advanced Internet penetration, the online and offline worlds begin to merge. People grow less suspicious. They include more of their "real-world" contacts in their online network, and they reveal more about themselves. In countries (and regions) with less Internet access, online contacts remain more impersonal and disguised. They tend to take place on websites where icons, pseudonyms, and handles, rather than personal data and pictures, predominate. In this setting, the online world is more separate and foreign—a place where one goes to meet people who may be (and remain) otherwise inaccessible.

The Internet enhances our opportunities to meet people and to form personal relationships. But this accessibility also can be disruptive. It can spur jealousy, for example, when a partner makes new friends or reconnects to old ones—and with good reason. The Oxford researchers found that many people disclosed intimate personal details in online settings with someone other than their spouse or partner (Hogan et al. 2011; Oxford 2013). A future study might investigate whether the Internet plays a role in divorce as well as in dating and marriage.

## Summary

1. Kinship and marriage organize social and political life in nonindustrial societies. One widespread kin group is the nuclear family, consisting of a married couple and their children. Other groups, such as extended families and descent groups, may assume functions usually associated with the nuclear family. Nuclear families tend to be especially important in foraging and industrial societies.

2. In contemporary North America, the nuclear family is the characteristic kin group for the middle class. Expanded households and sharing with extended family kin occur more frequently among the poor, who may pool their resources in dealing with poverty. Today, however, even in the American middle class, nuclear family households are declining as single-person households and other domestic arrangements increase.

3. The descent group is a basic kin group among nonindustrial food producers (farmers and herders). Unlike families, descent groups have perpetuity, lasting for generations. Descent-group members share and manage an estate. Lineages are based on demonstrated descent; clans, on stipulated descent. Unilineal (patrilineal and matrilineal) descent is associated with unilocal (patrilocal and matrilocal, respectively) postmarital residence.

4. Marriage conveys various rights. It establishes the legal parents of children. It gives spouses rights to the sexuality, labor, and property of the other. And it establishes a socially significant "relationship of affinity" between spouses and each other's relatives.

5. Most societies have incest restrictions. Because kinship is socially constructed, such restrictions apply to different relatives in different societies. Human behavior with respect to mating with close relatives may express a generalized primate tendency, illustrating both urges and avoidance. But types, risks, and avoidance of incest also reflect specific kinship structures. Exogamy extends social and political ties outward; endogamy does the reverse. Endogamic rules are common in stratified societies. One extreme example is India, where castes are the endogamous units.

6. In societies with descent groups, marriages are relationships between groups as well as between spouses. With lobola, the groom and his relatives transfer wealth to the bride and her relatives. As the value of the lobola gift increases, the divorce rate declines. Lobola customs show that marriages among nonindustrial food producers create and maintain group alliances. So does the sororate, by which a man marries the sister of his deceased wife, and the levirate, by which a woman marries the brother of her deceased husband.

7. The ease and frequency of divorce vary across cultures. When marriage is a matter of intergroup alliance, as is typically true in societies with descent groups, divorce is less common. A large fund of joint property also complicates divorce.

8. Many societies permit plural marriages. The two kinds of polygamy are polygyny and polyandry. The former involves multiple wives; the latter, multiple husbands. Polygyny is much more common than polyandry.

9. The Internet, which reconfigures social relations and networks more generally, is an important addition to the marriage market in contemporary nations.

## Key Terms

caste system, *307*
clan, *301*
descent
  group, *300*
dowry, *309*
endogamy, *306*
exogamy, *304*
extended family
  household, *298*
family, *294*
family of
  orientation, *295*

family of
  procreation, *295*
incest, *304*
levirate, *311*
lineage, *301*
lobola, *309*
matrilineal
  descent, *300*
matrilocality, *303*
neolocality, *297*
patrilineal
  descent, *300*

patrilocality, *302*
plural marriages
  (polygamy), *310*
polyandry, *310*
polygyny, *310*
sororate, *311*
unilineal
  descent, *301*

# Chapter 14

# Gender

Because anthropologists study biology, society, and culture, they are in a unique position to comment on nature (biological predispositions) and nurture (environment) as determinants of human behavior. Human attitudes, values, and behavior are limited not only by our genetic predispositions—which often are difficult to identify—but also by our experiences during enculturation. Our attributes as adults are determined both by our genes and by our environment during growth and development.

## Sex and Gender

Questions about nature and nurture emerge in the discussion of human sex–gender roles and sexuality. Men and women differ genetically. Women have two X chromosomes, and men have an X and a Y. The father determines a baby's sex because only he has the Y chromosome to transmit. The mother always provides an X chromosome.

The chromosomal difference is expressed in hormonal and physiological contrasts. Humans are sexually dimorphic, more so than some primates, such as gibbons (small, tree-living Asiatic apes) and less so than others, such as gorillas and orangutans. **Sexual dimorphism** refers to differences in male and female biology besides the contrasts in breasts and genitals. Women and men differ not just in primary (genitalia and reproductive organs) and secondary (breasts, voice, hair distribution) sexual characteristics, but in average weight, height, strength, and longevity. Women tend to live longer than men and have excellent endurance capabilities. In a given population, men tend to be taller and to weigh more than women do. Of course, there is a considerable overlap between the sexes in terms of height, weight, and physical strength, and there has been a pronounced reduction in sexual dimorphism during human biological evolution.

Just how far, however, do such genetically and physiologically determined differences go? What effects do they have on the way men and women act and are treated in different societies? Anthropologists have discovered both similarities and differences in the roles of men and women in different cultures. The predominant anthropological position on sex–gender roles and biology may be stated as follows:

> The biological nature of men and women [should be seen] not as a narrow enclosure limiting the human organism, but rather as a broad base upon which a variety of structures can be built. (Friedl 1975, p. 6)

Although in most societies men tend to be somewhat more aggressive than women are, many of the behavioral and attitudinal differences between the sexes emerge from culture rather than biology. Sex differences are biological, but gender encompasses all the traits that a culture assigns to and inculcates in males and females. *Gender,* in other words, refers to the cultural construction of whether one is female, male, or something else.

Given the "rich and various constructions of gender" within the realm of cultural diversity, Susan Bourque and Kay Warren (1987) note that the same images of masculinity and femininity do not always apply. Margaret Mead did an early ethnographic study of variation in gender roles. Her book *Sex and Temperament in Three Primitive Societies* (1935/1950) was based on fieldwork in three societies in Papua New Guinea: the Arapesh, Mundugumor, and Tchambuli. The extent of personality variation in men and women in those three societies on the same island amazed Mead. She found that Arapesh men and women both acted as Americans have traditionally expected women to act: in a mild, parental, responsive way. Mundugumor men and women both, in contrast, acted as she believed we expect men to act: fiercely and aggressively. Finally, Tchambuli men were "catty," wore curls, and went shopping, but Tchambuli women were energetic and managerial and placed less emphasis on personal adornment than did the men. (Drawing on their case study of the Tchambuli, whom they call the Chambri, Errington and Gewertz [1987], while recognizing gender malleability, have disputed the specifics of Mead's account.)

There is a well-established field of feminist scholarship within anthropology (Di Leonardo 1991*a*; Rosaldo 1980*b*; Strathern 1988). Anthropologists have gathered systematic ethnographic data about similarities and differences involving gender in many cultural settings (Brettell and Sargent 2013; Burn 2011; Kimmel 2013; Mascia-Lees 2010; Ward and Edelstein 2013). Before we examine the cross-cultural data, some definitions are in order.

**Gender roles** are the tasks and activities a culture assigns by gender. Related to gender roles are **gender stereotypes,** which are oversimplified but strongly held ideas about the characteristics of males and females. **Gender stratification** describes an unequal distribution of rewards (socially valued resources, power, prestige, human rights, and personal freedom) between men and women, reflecting their different positions in a social hierarchy.

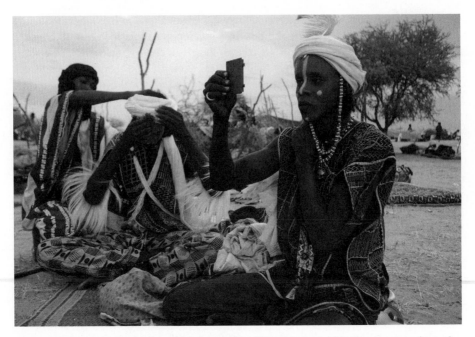

The realm of cultural diversity contains richly different social constructions and expressions of gender roles. In Niger, this Wodaabe man prepares for the Gerewol male beauty contest, an annual reunion. © Robert Harding World Imagery/Alamy

In stateless societies, gender stratification often is more obvious in regard to prestige than it is in regard to wealth. In her study of the Ilongots of northern Luzon in the Philippines, Michelle Rosaldo (1980*a*) described gender differences related to the positive cultural value placed on adventure, travel, and knowledge of the external world. More often than women, Ilongot men, as headhunters, visited distant places. They acquired knowledge of the external world, amassed experiences there, and returned to express their knowledge, adventures, and feelings in public oratory. They received acclaim as a result. Ilongot women had inferior prestige because they lacked external experiences on which to base knowledge and dramatic expression. On the basis of Rosaldo's study and findings in other stateless societies, Ong (1989) argues that we must distinguish between prestige systems and actual power in a given society. High male prestige does not necessarily entail economic or political power held by men over their families. (For more on Rosaldo's contributions to gender studies, see Lugo and Maurer 2000.)

## Recurrent Gender Patterns

You probably had chores when you were growing up. Was there any gender bias in what you were asked to do compared with your brother or sister? If you were raised by two parents, did any tension arise over your parental division of labor? Based on cross-cultural data from societies worldwide, Table 14.1 lists activities that are generally

## TABLE 14.1   Generalities in the Division of Labor by Gender, Based on Data from 185 Societies

Source: Adapted from G. P. Murdock and C. Provost, "Factors in the Division of Labor by Sex: A Cross-Cultural Analysis," *Ethnology* 12(2): 202–225.

| Generally Male Activities | Swing (Male or Female) Activities | Generally Female Activities |
|---|---|---|
| Hunting large aquatic animals (e.g., whales, walrus) | Making fire | Gathering fuel (e.g., firewood) |
| Smelting ores | Body mutilation | Making drinks |
| Metalworking | Preparing skins | Gathering wild vegetal foods |
| Lumbering | Gathering small land animals | Dairy production (e.g., churning) |
| Hunting large land animals | Planting crops | Spinning |
| Working wood | Making leather products | Doing the laundry |
| Hunting fowl | Harvesting | Fetching water |
| Making musical instruments | Tending crops | Cooking |
| Trapping | Milking | Preparing vegetal food (e.g., processing cereal grains) |
| Building boats | Making baskets | |
| Working stone | Carrying burdens | |
| Working bone, horn, and shell | Making mats | |
| Mining and quarrying | Caring for small animals | |
| Setting bones | Preserving meat and fish | |
| Butchering* | Loom weaving | |
| Collecting wild honey | Gathering small aquatic animals | |
| Clearing land | Manufacturing clothing | |
| Fishing | Making pottery | |
| Tending large herd animals | | |
| Building houses | | |
| Preparing the soil | | |
| Making nets | | |
| Making rope | | |

*All the activities above "butchering" are almost always done by men; those from "butchering" through "making rope" usually are done by men.

male, generally female, or swing (either male or female). Before you look at that table, see if you can assign the following to one gender or the other (M or F): hunting large animals ( ), gathering wild vegetable foods ( ), tending crops ( ), fishing ( ), cooking ( ), fetching water ( ), making baskets ( ), making drinks ( ). Now consult Table 14.1 and see how you did. Reflect on your results. Is what's true cross-culturally still true of the division of labor by gender in today's world, including the United States?

Even if we still think in terms of "men's work" and "women's work," ideas about gender have changed along with the employment patterns of men and women. But old beliefs, cultural expectations, and gender stereotypes linger. As of this writing, only 20 out of 100 United States senators are women. Only 4 women have ever served on the U.S. Supreme Court. Women, in general, remain less powerful than men (see this chapter's "Anthropology Today").

The lingering American expectation that proper female behavior should be polite, restrained, or meek poses a challenge for women, because American culture also values decisiveness and "standing up for your beliefs." When American men and women display certain behavior—speaking up for their ideas, for example—they are judged differently. A man's assertive behavior may be admired and rewarded, but a woman's similar behavior may be labeled "aggressive"—or worse.

Both men and women are constrained by their cultural training, stereotypes, and expectations. For example, American men are told they should "be decisive"—make decisions and stick to them. In our stereotypes, changing one's mind is more associated with women than men and may be perceived as a sign of weakness. Politicians routinely criticize their opponents for being indecisive, for "flip-flopping" on issues. What a strange idea—that people shouldn't change their positions if they've discovered there's a better way. Males, females, and humanity may be equally victimized by aspects of cultural training.

Data relevant to the cross-cultural study of gender can be drawn from the domains of economics, politics, domestic activity, kinship, and marriage. Review Table 14.1 for cross-cultural data from 185 randomly selected societies on the division of labor by gender.

Remembering the discussion in Chapter 2 of universals, generalities, and particularities, the findings in Table 14.1 about the division of labor by gender illustrate generalities rather than universals. That is, among the societies known to ethnography, there is a very strong tendency for men to build boats, but there are exceptions. One was the Hidatsa, a Native American group in which the women made the boats used to cross the Missouri River. (Traditionally, the Hidatsa were village farmers and bison hunters on the North American Plains; they now live in North Dakota.) Another exception is that Pawnee women worked wood; this is the only Native American group that assigned this activity to women. (The Pawnee, also traditionally Plains farmers and bison hunters, originally lived in what is now central Nebraska and central Kansas; they now live on a reservation in north central Oklahoma.)

Exceptions to cross-cultural generalizations may involve societies or individuals. That is, a society like the Hidatsa can contradict the cross-cultural generalization that men build boats by assigning that task to women. Or in a society where the cultural expectation is that only men build boats, a particular woman or women can contradict that expectation by doing the male activity. Table 14.1 shows that in a sample of 185 societies, certain activities ("swing activities") are assigned to either or both men and women. Among the most important of such activities are planting, tending, and harvesting crops. Some societies customarily assign more farming chores to women, whereas others make men the primary farmers. Among the tasks almost always assigned to men (see Table 14.1), some (e.g., hunting large animals on land and sea) seem clearly related to the greater average size and strength of males. Others, such as working wood and making musical instruments, seem more culturally arbitrary. And women, of course, are not exempt from arduous and time-consuming physical labor, such as gathering firewood and fetching water. In Arembepe, Bahia, Brazil, women routinely transported water in 5-gallon tins, balanced on their heads, from wells and lagoons located long distances from their homes.

The original coding of the data in Table 14.1 probably illustrates a male bias in that extradomestic activities received much more prominence than domestic activities did. Think about how female domestic activities could have been specified in greater detail in Table 14.1. One wonders whether collecting wild honey (listed in Table 14.1) is more necessary or time-consuming than nursing a baby (absent from Table 14.1). Also, notice that Table 14.1 does not mention trade and market activity, in which either or both men and women are active.

Both women and men have to fit their activities into 24-hour days. Turn now to Table 14.2, which shows that the time and effort spent in subsistence activities by men and women tend to be about equal. If anything, men do slightly less subsistence work than women do. But in domestic activities and child care, female labor clearly predominates, as we see in Tables 14.3 and 14.4. Table 14.3 shows that in about half the societies studied, men did virtually no domestic work. Even in societies where men did domestic chores, the bulk of such work was done by women. Adding together their subsistence activities and their domestic work, women tend to work more hours than men do. Has this changed in the contemporary world?

What about child care? Women tend to be the main caregivers in most societies, but men often play a role. Table 14.4 uses cross-cultural data to answer the question "Who—

TABLE 14.2    **Time and Effort Expended on Subsistence Activities by Men and Women**[*]

Source: M. F. Whyte, "Cross-Cultural Codes Dealing with the Relative Status of Women," *Ethnology* 17(2):211–239.

| | |
|---|---|
| More by men | 16 |
| Roughly equal | 61 |
| More by women | 23 |

[*]Percentage of 88 randomly selected societies for which information was available on this variable.

TABLE 14.3    **Who Does the Domestic Work?**[*]

Source: M. F. Whyte, "Cross-Cultural Codes Dealing with the Relative Status of Women," *Ethnology* 17(2):211–239.

| | |
|---|---|
| Males do virtually none | 51 |
| Males do some, but females do most | 49 |

[*]Percentage of 92 randomly selected societies for which information was available on this variable.

TABLE 14.4    **Who Has Final Authority over the Care, Handling, and Discipline of Infant Children (under 4 Years Old)?**[*]

Source: M. F. Whyte, "Cross-Cultural Codes Dealing with the Relative Status of Women," *Ethnology* 17(2):211–239.

| | |
|---|---|
| Males have more say | 18 |
| Roughly equal | 16 |
| Females have more say | 66 |

[*]Percentage of 67 randomly selected societies for which information was available on this variable.

men or women—has final authority over the care, handling, and discipline of children younger than 4 years?" Women have primary authority over infants in two-thirds of the societies. Given the critical role of breast-feeding in ensuring infant survival, it makes sense, for infants especially, for the mother to be the primary caregiver.

There are differences in male and female reproductive strategies. Women work to ensure their progeny will survive by establishing a close bond with each baby. It's also advantageous for a woman to have a reliable mate to ease the child-rearing process and ensure the survival of her children. (Again, there are exceptions, for example, the matrilineal Nayars, discussed in the previous chapter.) Women can have only so many babies during their reproductive years, which begin after menarche (the advent of first menstruation) and end with menopause (cessation of menstruation). Men, in contrast, have a longer reproductive period, which can last into the elder years. If they choose to do so, men can enhance their reproductive success by impregnating several women over a longer time period. Although men do not always have multiple mates, they do have a greater tendency to do so than women do (see Tables 14.5, 14.6, and 14.7). Among the societies known to ethnography, polygyny is much more common than polyandry (see Table 14.5).

**TABLE 14.5   Does the Society Allow Multiple Spouses?**[*]

Source: M. F. Whyte, "Cross-Cultural Codes Dealing with the Relative Status of Women," *Ethnology* 17(2):211–239.

| | |
|---|---|
| Only for males | 77 |
| For both, but more commonly for males | 4 |
| For neither | 16 |
| For both, but more commonly for females | 2 |

*Percentage of 92 randomly selected societies.

**TABLE 14.6   Is There a Double Standard with Respect to Premarital Sex?**[*]

Source: M. F. Whyte, "Cross-Cultural Codes Dealing with the Relative Status of Women," *Ethnology* 17(2):211–239.

| | |
|---|---|
| Yes—females are more restricted | 44 |
| No—equal restrictions on males and females | 56 |

*Percentage of 73 randomly selected societies for which information was available on this variable.

**TABLE 14.7   Is There a Double Standard with Respect to Extramarital Sex?**[*]

Source: M. F. Whyte, "Cross-Cultural Codes Dealing with the Relative Status of Women," Ethnology 17(2):211–239.

| | |
|---|---|
| Yes—females are more restricted | 43 |
| Equal restrictions on males and females | 55 |
| Males punished more severely for transgression | 3 |

*Percentage of 75 randomly selected societies for which information was available on this variable.

Men mate, within and outside marriage, more than women do. Table 14.6 shows cross-cultural data on premarital sex, and Table 14.7 summarizes the data on extramarital sex. In both cases, men are less restricted than women are, although the restrictions are equal in about half the societies studied. Double standards that restrict women more than men are one illustration of gender stratification, which we now examine more systematically.

# Gender Roles and Gender Stratification

Economic roles affect gender stratification. In one cross-cultural study, Sanday (1974) found that gender stratification decreased when men and women made roughly equal contributions to subsistence. She found that gender stratification was greatest when the women contributed either much more or much less than the men did.

In foraging societies, gender stratification was most marked when men contributed much *more* to the diet than women did. This was true among the Inuit and other northern hunters and fishers. Among tropical and semitropical foragers, by contrast, gathering usually supplies more food than hunting and fishing do. Gathering is generally women's work. Men usually hunt and fish, but women also do some fishing and may hunt small animals, as is true among the Agta of the Philippines (Griffin and Estioko-Griffin 1985). When gathering is prominent, gender status tends to be more equal than it is when hunting and fishing are the main subsistence activities.

Gender status also is more equal when the domestic and public spheres aren't sharply separated. (**Domestic** means within or pertaining to the home.) Strong differentiation between the home and the outside world is called the **domestic–public dichotomy,** or the *private–public contrast*. The outside world can include politics, trade, warfare, or work. Often when domestic and public spheres are clearly separated, public activities have greater prestige than domestic ones do. This can promote gender stratification, because men are more likely to be active in the public domain than women are.

## Reduced Gender Stratification—Matrilineal–Matrilocal Societies

Cross-cultural variation in gender status also is related to rules of descent and post-marital residence. With matrilineal descent and *matrilocality* (residence after marriage with the wife's relatives), female status tends to be high. Matriliny and matrilocality disperse related males, rather than consolidating them. By contrast, patriliny and *patri-locality* (residence after marriage with the husband's kin) keep male relatives together. Matrilineal–matrilocal systems tend to occur in societies where population pressure on strategic resources is minimal and warfare is infrequent.

Women tend to have high status in matrilineal–matrilocal societies for several reasons. Descent-group membership, succession to political positions, allocation of land, and over-all social identity all come through female links. Among the matrilineal Malays of Negeri Sembilan, Malaysia (Peletz 1988), matriliny gave women sole inheritance of ancestral rice fields. Matrilocality created solidary clusters of female kin. These Malay women had con-siderable influence beyond the household. In such matrilineal contexts, women are the ba-sis of the entire social structure. Although public authority nominally may be assigned to the men, much of the power and decision making actually may belong to the senior women.

## Matriarchy

Cross-culturally, anthropologists have described tremendous variation in the roles of men and women, and the power differentials between them. If a patriarchy is a political system ruled by men, is a matriarchy necessarily a political system ruled by women? Or might we apply the term *matriarchy,* as anthropologist Peggy Sanday (2002) does, to a political system in which women play a much more prominent role than men do in social and political organization? One example would be the Minangkabau of West Sumatra, Indonesia, whom Sanday (2002) has studied for decades. Sanday considers the Minangkabau a matriarchy because women are the center, origin, and foundation of the social order. Senior women are associated with the central pillar of the traditional house, the oldest one in the village. The oldest village in a cluster is called the "mother village." In ceremonies, women are addressed by the term used for their mythical Queen Mother. Women control land inheritance, and couples reside matrilocally. In the wedding ceremony, the wife collects her husband from his household and, with her female kin, escorts him to hers. If there is a divorce, the husband simply takes his things and leaves. Yet despite the special position of women, the Minangkabau matriarchy is not the equivalent of female rule, given the Minangkabau belief that all decision making should be by consensus.

A Minangkabau bride and groom in West Sumatra, Indonesia, where anthropologist Peggy Reeves Sanday has conducted several years of ethnographic fieldwork. © Lindsay Hebberd/Corbis

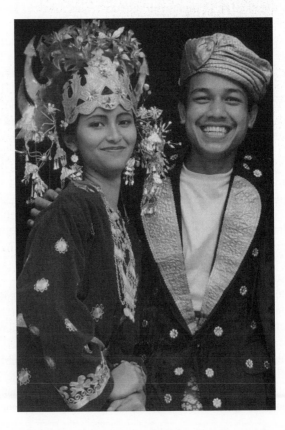

## Increased Gender Stratification—Patrilineal–Patrilocal Societies

Martin and Voorhies (1975) link the decline of matriliny and the spread of the **patrilineal–patrilocal complex** (consisting of patrilineality, patrilocality, warfare, and male supremacy) to pressure on resources. Faced with scarce resources, patrilineal–patrilocal cultivators such as the Yanomami often wage warfare against other villages. This favors patrilocality and patriliny, customs that keep related men together in the same village, where they make strong allies in battle. Such societies tend to have a sharp domestic–public dichotomy, and men tend to dominate the prestige hierarchy. Men may use their public roles in warfare and trade and their greater prestige to symbolize and reinforce the devaluation or oppression of women.

The patrilineal–patrilocal complex characterizes many societies in highland Papua New Guinea. Women work hard growing and processing subsistence crops, raising and tending pigs (the main domesticated animal and a favorite food), and doing domestic cooking, but they are isolated from the public domain, which men control. Men grow and distribute prestige crops, prepare food for feasts, and arrange marriages. The men even get to trade the pigs and control their use in ritual.

In densely populated areas of the Papua New Guinea highlands, male–female avoidance is associated with strong pressure on resources (Lindenbaum 1972). Men fear all female contact, including sexual acts. They think that sexual contact with women will weaken them. Indeed, men see everything female as dangerous and polluting. They segregate themselves in men's houses and hide their precious ritual objects from women. They delay marriage, and some never marry.

By contrast, the sparsely populated areas of Papua New Guinea, such as recently settled areas, lack taboos on male–female contacts. The image of woman as polluter fades, heterosexual intercourse is valued, men and women live together, and reproductive rates are high.

In some parts of Papua New Guinea, the patrilineal–patrilocal complex has extreme social repercussions. Regarding females as dangerous and polluting, men may segregate themselves in men's houses (such as this one, located near the Sepik River), where they hide their precious ritual objects from women. Are there places like this in your society? © George Holton/Science Source

## Patriarchy and Violence

**Patriarchy** describes a political system ruled by men in which women have inferior social and political status, including basic human rights. Barbara Miller (1997), in a study of systematic neglect of females, describes women in rural northern India as "the endangered sex." Societies that feature a full-fledged patrilineal–patrilocal complex, replete with warfare and intervillage raiding, also typify patriarchy. Such practices as dowry murders, female infanticide, and clitoridectomy exemplify patriarchy, which extends from tribal societies such as the Yanomami to state societies such as India and Pakistan.

Although more prevalent in certain social settings than in others, family violence and domestic abuse of women are worldwide problems. Domestic violence certainly occurs in nuclear family settings, such as Canada and the United States. Cities, with their impersonality and isolation from extended kin networks, are breeding grounds for domestic violence, as may be rural areas where women lead isolated lives.

When a woman resides matrilocally, she has kin nearby to look after and protect her interests. Even in patrilocal polygynous settings, women often count on the support of their cowives and sons in disputes with potentially abusive husbands. Such settings, which tend to provide a safe haven for women, are retracting rather than expanding in today's world. Isolated families and patrilineal social forms have spread at the expense of matrilineality. Many nations have declared polygyny illegal. More and more women, and men, find themselves cut off from extended kin and families of orientation.

With the spread of the women's rights movement and the human rights movement, attention to domestic violence and abuse of women has increased. Laws have been passed and mediating institutions established. Brazil's female-run police stations for

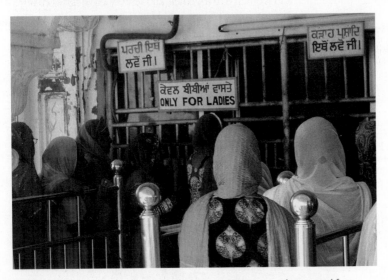

In many societies, especially patriarchal ones, women experience, and fear, intimidation as they increasingly enter the public sphere, especially in impersonal, urban settings. "Ladies Only" lines like this one at the Golden Temple in Amritsar, Punjab, India, are designed to help women move unmolested through public space. © Conrad P. Kottak battered women provide an example, as do shelters for victims of domestic abuse in the United States and Canada. But patriarchal institutions persist in what should be a more enlightened world.

## Gender in Industrial Societies

The domestic–public dichotomy also influences gender stratification in industrial societies, including Canada and the United States, where gender roles have been changing rapidly. In early industrial Europe, men, women, and children flocked to factories as wage laborers. Enslaved Americans of both sexes toiled in cotton fields. After abolition, Southern African American women continued working as field hands and domestics. Poor White women labored in the South's early cotton mills. In the 1890s more than 1 million American women held menial and repetitious unskilled factory positions.

In the early 20th century, a wave of European immigration provided a male labor force willing to work for wages lower than those of American-born men. Immigrant men were hired for factory jobs that previously would have gone to women. As machine tools and mass production further reduced the need for female labor, the notion gained ground that women were biologically unfit for factory work.

Maxine Margolis (1984, 2000) has shown how gendered work, attitudes, and beliefs have varied in response to American economic needs. For example, wartime shortages of men have promoted the idea that work outside the home is women's patriotic duty. During the world wars the notion that women were unfit for hard physical labor faded. Inflation and the culture of consumption also have spurred female employment. When prices or demand rises, multiple paychecks help maintain family living standards.

The increase in female paid employment in the United States since World War II also reflects the baby boom and industrial expansion. American culture traditionally has defined clerical work, teaching, and nursing as female occupations. With rapid population growth and business expansion after World War II, the demand for women to fill such jobs grew steadily. Employers also found they could increase their profits by paying women lower wages than they would have to pay returning male war veterans.

During the world wars the notion that women were biologically unfit for hard physical labor faded. Shown here is World War II's famous Rosie the Riveter. Is there a comparable poster woman today? What does her image say about modern gender roles? Source: National Archives and Records Administration

Economic changes paved the way for the contemporary women's movement, which also was spurred by the publication of Betty Friedan's book *The Feminine Mystique* in 1963 and the founding of NOW, the National Organization for Women, in 1966. The movement in turn promoted expanded work opportunities for women, including the as yet unrealized goal of equal pay for equal work. The female percentage of the American workforce stood at 47 percent in 2013, compared with 38 percent in 1970. In other words, almost half of all Americans who work outside the home are women. Almost 73 million women were in the labor force in 2013, compared with 82 million men. Women fill more than half (51 percent) of all management/professional jobs (U.S. Bureau of Labor Statistics 2014). Furthermore, those women working outside the home are not mainly single women, as once was the case. Table 14.8 presents figures on the workforce participation of American wives and mothers, including those with children under 6 years old, from 1970 through 2013.

Note in Table 14.8 that the workforce participation of American married men has been declining, while that of married women has been rising. (A recent overall decline in employment by mothers, married men, and married women is attributable to lingering effects of the "great recession" of 2007–2009.) There has been a dramatic shift in Americans' work-related behavior and attitudes since 1960, when 89 percent of all married men worked, compared with just 32 percent of married women. Today the comparable figures are around 74 percent for men and 59 percent for women. Among married-couple families, 53 percent had earnings from both spouses in 2012, compared with 44 percent in 1967. Working wives now provide 37 percent of their families' incomes, up from 27 percent in 1970. Furthermore, many more wives are making more money than their husbands do: 29 percent in 2012 versus 18 percent in 1987 (U.S. Bureau of Labor Statistics 2014).

Ideas about the gender roles of males and females have changed. Compare your grandparents and your parents. Chances are, you have a working mother, but your grandmother was more likely a stay-at-home mom. Your grandfather is more likely than

TABLE 14.8   **Workforce Participation Rates of American Mothers, Wives, and Husbands, 1960–2013**[*]

Source: *Proquest Statistical Abstract of the United States* 2013, Table 607, p. 396; Table 609, p. 397; U.S. Bureau of Labor Statistics 2014.

| Year | Percentage of Married Women, Husband Present with Children under 6 | Percentage of All Married Women[†] | Percentage of All Married Men[‡] |
|---|---|---|---|
| 1960 | 19 | 32 | 89 |
| 1970 | 30 | 40 | 86 |
| 1980 | 45 | 50 | 81 |
| 1990 | 59 | 58 | 79 |
| 2010 | 62 | 61 | 76 |
| 2013 | 59 | 59 | 74 |

[*]Civilian population 16 years of age and older.
[†]Husband present.
[‡]Wife present.

your father to have worked in manufacturing and to have belonged to a union. Your father is more likely than your grandfather to have shared child care and domestic responsibilities. Age at marriage has been delayed for both men and women. College educations and professional degrees have increased. What other changes do you associate with the increase in female employment outside the home?

## The Feminization of Poverty

Alongside the economic gains of many American women stands an opposite extreme: the feminization of poverty, or the increasing representation of women (and their children) among America's poorest people. Women head over half of U.S. households with incomes below the poverty line. The average income for married-couple families is more than twice that of families maintained by a single woman. The median household maintained by a single woman had an annual income of $31,408 in 2013, compared with $76,339 for a married-couple household. When both spouses were employed, that figure rose to $94,229.

The feminization of poverty is not only a North American trend. The percentage of single-parent (usually female-headed) households has been increasing worldwide. Children today are most likely to live with two parents (and extended family members) in Asia and the Middle East. The percentage of children living with single parents is especially high in the Caribbean, Central and South America, and sub-Saharan Africa. Single-parent households also have become common in North America and Western Europe. The percentage of single-parent households rose in every nation listed in Table 14.9 between 1980–1981 and 2012. Of the countries listed there, the United States had the largest percentage of single-parent households (27 percent), followed by the United Kingdom (24 percent), Canada (20 percent), France and Ireland (18 percent), and Japan (12 percent) (Sutherland 2014).

Globally, households headed by women tend to be poorer than those headed by men. In one study, the percentages of single-parent families considered poor were 18 percent in Britain, 20 percent in Italy, 25 percent in Switzerland, 40 percent in Ireland, 52 percent in Canada, and 63 percent in the United States (Buvinic 1995; see also Gunewardena and Kingsolver 2007).

It is widely believed that one way to improve the situation of poor women is to encourage them to organize. New women's groups can in some cases revive or replace traditional forms of social organization that have been disrupted. Membership in a group can help women mobilize resources, rationalize production, and reduce the risks

**TABLE 14.9**

**Percentage of Single-Parent Households, Selected Countries, 1980–1981 and 2012**

Sources: *Proquest Statistical Abstract of the United States 2013*, Table 1353, p. 869; Sutherland 2014.

| Country | 1980–1981 | 2012 |
| --- | --- | --- |
| United States | 20 | 27 |
| United Kingdom | 14 | 24 |
| Canada | 13 | 20 |
| Ireland | 7 | 18 |
| France | 10 | 18 |
| Japan | 5 | 12 |

and costs associated with credit. Organization also allows women to develop self-confidence and to decrease dependence on others. Through such organization, poor women throughout the world are working to determine their own needs and priorities and to change things so as to improve their social and economic situation (Buvinic 1995; Gunewardena and Kingsolver 2007).

## Work and Happiness

Table 14.10 shows female labor force participation in various countries—condensed from 30 countries for which data were available—in 2011. The United States, with 61.7 percent of its women employed or looking for work that year, ranked 13th, while Canada (74.4 percent) ranked 7th. Switzerland topped the list, with 82.2 percent of its women in the workforce. Turkey was lowest; only 31.8 percent of its women were employed.

In 2010, Gallup conducted a survey of the world's 132 happiest countries, based on various measures, including the percentages of people in that country who were thriving and those suffering. Respondents also rated their own lives on a scale from 0 (worst possible) to 10 (best possible). Denmark scored as the world's happiest nation; Canada came in 6th; the United States, 12th.

We see in Table 14.10 that of the 13 countries with greatest female labor force participation, 10 ranked among the world's happiest (see Levy 2010). Why, as more women work outside the home, might a country's population achieve a greater sense of well-being? Note that many of the countries listed as among the world's happiest not only have more employed women but also have a higher living standard and a more secure government safety net. Can you think of other factors that might explain a relationship between happiness and work outside the home?

**TABLE 14.10**
**Female Labor Force Participation by Country, 2011**

Source: *Proquest Statistical Abstract of the United States 2013*, Table 1383, p. 887; Huffington Post, http://www.huffingtonpost.com/2010/07/03/worlds-happiest-countries_n_633814.html#s109416title=Denmark_77.

| Country | Percentage of Women in Labor Force | Rank among World's 15 "Happiest Countries" |
|---|---|---|
| Switzerland | 82.2 | 7 |
| Iceland | 81.6 | * |
| Sweden | 79.0 | 9 |
| Norway | 77.5 | 3 |
| Denmark | 75.7 | 1 |
| New Zealand | 74.9 | 8 |
| Canada | 74.5 | 6 |
| Finland | 73.6 | 2 |
| Netherlands | 72.8 | 4 |
| Germany | 72.5 | * |
| Australia | 72.3 | 11 |
| United Kingdom | 70.8 | * |
| United States | 61.7 | 12 |
| Turkey (lowest in table) | 31.8 | |

*These countries were not among the 15 "happiest countries."

# Beyond Male and Female

Gender is socially constructed, and societies may recognize more than two genders. The contemporary United States, for example, includes individuals who self-identify using such labels as "transgender," "intersex," "third gender," and "transsexual." Such persons contradict dominant male/female gender distinctions by being part male and female, or neither male nor female. Because people who self-identify as transgender are increasingly visible, we must be careful about seeing masculine and feminine as absolute and binary categories.

Sex, we have seen, is biological, whereas gender is socially constructed. Transgender is a social category that includes individuals who *may or may not* contrast biologically with ordinary males and females. Within the transgender category, intersex people usually contrast biologically with ordinary males and females, but *transgender also includes people whose gender identity has no apparent biological roots.* The term **intersex** encompasses a group of conditions involving a discrepancy between the external genitals (penis, vagina, etc.) and the internal genitals (testes, ovaries, etc.). The older term for this condition, *hermaphroditism,* combined the names of a Greek god and goddess. Hermes was a god of male sexuality (among other things) and Aphrodite a goddess of female sexuality, love, and beauty.

The causes of intersex are varied and complex (Kaneshiro 2009): (1) An XX intersex person has the chromosomes of a woman (XX) and normal ovaries, uterus, and fallopian tubes, but the external genitals appear male. Usually this results from a female fetus having been exposed to an excess of male hormones before birth. (2) An XY intersex person has the chromosomes of a man (XY), but the external genitals are incompletely formed, ambiguous, or female. The testes may be normal, malformed, or absent. (3) A true gonadal intersex person has both ovarian and testicular tissue. The external genitals may be ambiguous or may appear to be female or male. (4) Intersex also can result from an unusual chromosome combination, such as X0 (only one X chromosome), XXY, XYY, and XXX. In the last three cases there is an extra sex chromosome, either an X or a Y. These chromosomal combinations don't typically produce a discrepancy between internal and external genitalia, but there may be problems with sex hormone levels and overall sexual development.

The XXY configuration, known as *Klinefelter syndrome,* is the most common of these combinations and the second most common condition (after Down syndrome) caused by the presence of extra chromosomes in humans. Effects of Klinefelter occur in about 1 of every 1,000 males. One in every 500 males has an extra X chromosome but lacks the main symptoms—small testicles and reduced fertility. With XXX, or *triple X syndrome,* there is an extra X chromosome in each cell of a human female. Triple X occurs in about 1 of every 1,000 female births. There usually is no physically distinguishable difference between triple X women and other women. The same is true of XYY compared with other males.

*Turner syndrome* encompasses several conditions, of which X0 (absence of one sex chromosome) is most common. In this case, all or part of one of the sex chromosomes is absent. Girls with Turner syndrome typically are sterile because of nonworking ovaries and amenorrhea (absence of a menstrual cycle).

Biology isn't destiny; people construct their identities in society. Many individuals affected by one of the biological conditions just described see themselves simply as male or female, rather than transgender. Self-identified **transgender** people tend to be individuals whose gender identity contradicts their biological sex at birth and the gender identity that society assigned to them in infancy. Feeling that their previous gender assignment was incorrect, they assert or seek to achieve a new one. The transgender category is diverse. Some transgender individuals lean toward male; some, female; some, toward neither of the dominant genders.

The anthropological record attests that gender diversity beyond male and female exists in many societies and has taken many forms across societies and cultures. Consider, for example, the eunuch, or "perfect servant" (a castrated man who served as a safe attendant to harems in Byzantium [Tougher 2008]). Hijras, who live mainly in northern India, are culturally defined as "neither men nor women," or as men who become women by undergoing castration and adopting women's dress and behavior. Hijras identify with the Indian mother goddess and are believed to channel her power. They are known for their ritualized performances at births and marriages, where they dance and sing, conferring the mother goddess's blessing on the child or the married couple. Although culturally defined as celibate, some hijras now engage in prostitution, in which their role is as women with men (Nanda 1996, 1998). Hijra social movements have campaigned for recognition as a third gender, and in 2005, Indian passport application

Neither men nor women, hijras constitute India's third gender. Many hijras get their income from performing at ceremonies, begging, or prostitution. The beauty contest shown here was organized by an AIDS prevention and relief organization that works with the local hijra community. © Maciej Dakowicz/Alamy forms were updated with three gender options: M, F, and E (for male, female, and eunuch [i.e, hijra], respectively) (Telegraph 2005).

Roscoe writes of the "Zuni man-woman," or berdache, in the 19th century. A berdache was a male who adopted social roles traditionally assigned to women and, through performance of a third gender, contributed to the social and spiritual well-being of the community (1991, 1998). Some Balkan societies included "sworn virgins," born females who assumed male gender roles and activities to meet societal needs when there was a shortage of men (Gremaux 1993).

Among the Gheg tribes of North Albania, "virginal transvestites" were biologically female, but locals considered, them "honorary men" (Shryock 1988). Some Albanian adolescent girls have chosen to become men, remain celibate, and live among men, with the support of their families and villagers (Young 2000). And consider Polynesia. In Tonga the term *fakaleitis* describes males who behave as women do, thereby contrasting with mainstream Tongan men. Similar to Tonga's *fakaleitis*, Samoan *fa'afafine* and Hawaiian *mahu* are men who adopt feminine attributes, behaviors, and visual markers.

In the contemporary West, the category transgender encompasses varied individuals whose gender performance and identity enlarge an otherwise binary gender structure. The lesbian and gay rights movement has expanded to include bisexual and transgender individuals. This Lesbian, Gay, Bisexual, and Transgender (LGBT) community works to promote government policies and social practices that protect its members' civil and human rights. In recent years, the LGBT movement and its supporters have achieved many successes, including the legalization of same-sex marriage and the repeal of the Don't Ask, Don't Tell (DADT) policy of the U.S. armed services.

## Sexual Orientation

**Gender identity** refers to whether a person feels, and is regarded as, male, female, or something else. One's gender identity does not dictate one's sexual orientation. Men who have no doubt about their masculinity can be sexually attracted to women or to other men, as can women with regard to female gender identity and variable sexual attraction. **Sexual orientation,** to which we now turn, refers to a person's sexual attraction to, and habitual sexual activities with, persons of the opposite sex (*heterosexuality*), the same sex (*homosexuality*), or both sexes (*bisexuality*). *Asexuality,* indifference toward or lack of attraction to either sex, also is a sexual orientation. All four of these forms are found throughout the world. But each type of desire and experience holds different meanings for individuals and groups. For example, male–male sexual activity may be a private affair in Mexico, rather than public, socially sanctioned, and encouraged, as it is among the Etoro and several other groups in Papua New Guinea (see also Blackwood 2010; Herdt 2006; Kottak and Kozaitis 2012; Lyons and Lyons 2011; Rathus et al. 2014).

Recently in the United States there has been a tendency to see sexual orientation as fixed and biologically based. There is not enough information at this time to determine the extent to which sexual orientation is based on biology. What we can say is that all human activities and preferences, including erotic expression, are at least partially constructed and influenced by culture.

In any society, individuals will differ in the nature, range, and intensity of their sexual interests and urges. No one knows for sure why such individual sexual differences exist. Part of the answer probably is biological, reflecting genes or hormones. Another part may have to do with experiences during growth and development. But whatever the reasons for individual variation, culture always plays a role in molding individual sexual urges toward a collective norm. And such sexual norms vary from culture to culture.

What do we know about variation in sexual norms from society to society and over time? A classic cross-cultural study of 76 societies (Ford and Beach 1951) found wide variation in attitudes about forms of sexual activity. In a single society, such as the United States, attitudes about sex differ over time and with socioeconomic status, region, and rural versus urban residence. However, even in the 1950s, prior to the "age of sexual permissiveness" (the pre-HIV period from the mid-1960s through the 1970s), research showed that almost all American men (92 percent) and more than half of American women (54 percent) admitted to masturbation. In the famous Kinsey report (Kinsey, Pomeroy, and Martin 1948), 37 percent of the men surveyed admitted having had at least one sexual experience leading to orgasm with another male. In a later study of 1,200 unmarried women, 26 percent reported same-sex sexual activities. (Because Kinsey's research relied on nonrandom samples, it should be considered merely illustrative, rather than a statistically accurate representation, of sexual behavior at the time.)

In almost two-thirds (63 percent) of the 76 societies in the Ford and Beach study, various forms of same-sex sexual activity were acceptable. Occasionally sexual relations between people of the same sex involved transvestism on the part of one of the partners (see Kulick 1998). Transvestism did not characterize male–male sex among the Sudanese Azande, who valued the warrior role (Evans-Pritchard 1970). Prospective warriors—young men aged 12 to 20—left their families and shared quarters with adult fighting men, who paid lobola for, and had sex with, them. During this apprenticeship, the young men did the domestic duties of women. Upon reaching warrior status, these young men took their own younger male brides. Later, retiring from the warrior role, Azande men married women. Flexible in their sexual expression, Azande males had no difficulty shifting from sex with older men (as male brides) to sex with younger men (as warriors) to sex with women (as husbands) (see Murray and Roscoe 1998).

Consider also the Etoro (Kelly 1976), a group of 400 people who subsisted by hunting and horticulture in the Trans-Fly region of Papua New Guinea. The Etoro illustrate the power of culture in molding human sexuality. The following account, based on ethnographic fieldwork by Raymond C. Kelly in the late 1960s, applies only to Etoro males and their beliefs. Etoro cultural norms prevented the male anthropologist who studied them from gathering comparable information about female attitudes and behavior. Note also that the activities described have been discouraged by missionaries. Because there has been no restudy of the Etoro specifically focusing on these activities, the extent to which these practices continue today is unknown. For this reason, I'll use the past tense in describing them.

Etoro opinions about sexuality were linked to their beliefs about the cycle of birth, physical growth, maturity, old age, and death. Etoro men believed that semen was necessary to give life force to a fetus, which was, they believed, implanted in a woman by an ancestral spirit. Sexual intercourse during pregnancy nourished the growing fetus. The Etoro believed that men had a limited lifetime supply of semen. Any sex act leading to ejaculation was seen as draining that supply, and as sapping a man's virility and vitality. The birth of children, nurtured by semen, symbolized a necessary sacrifice that would lead to the husband's eventual death. Male–female sexual intercourse, required only for reproduction, was discouraged. Women who wanted too much sex were viewed as witches, hazardous to their husbands' health. Etoro culture allowed male–female intercourse only about 100 days a year. The rest of the time it was tabooed. Seasonal birth clustering shows that the taboo was respected.

So objectionable was male–female sex that it was removed from community life. It could occur neither in sleeping quarters nor in the fields. Coitus could happen only in the woods, where it was risky because poisonous snakes, the Etoro believed, were attracted by the sounds and smells of male–female sex.

Although coitus was discouraged, sex acts between males were viewed as essential. Etoro believed that boys could not produce semen on their own. To grow into men and eventually give life force to their children, boys had to acquire semen orally from older men. From the age of 10 until adulthood, boys were inseminated by older men. No taboos were attached to this. This oral insemination could proceed in the sleeping area or garden. Every three years, a group of boys around the age of 20 were formally initiated into manhood. They went to a secluded mountain lodge, where they were visited and inseminated by several older men.

Male–male sex among the Etoro was governed by a code of propriety. Although sexual relations between older and younger males were considered culturally essential, those between boys of the same age were discouraged. A boy who took semen from other youths was believed to be sapping their life force and stunting their growth. A boy's rapid physical development could suggest he was getting semen from other boys. Like a sex-hungry wife, he could be shunned as a witch.

The sexual practices just described rested not on hormones or genes but on cultural beliefs and traditions. The Etoro, along with several other tribes in Papua New Guinea, especially in that country's Trans-Fly region, illustrate one extreme of a male–female avoidance pattern that is widespread in Papua New Guinea and indeed in many patrilineal–patrilocal societies.

Flexibility in sexual expression seems to be an aspect of our primate heritage. Both masturbation and same-sex sexual activity exist among chimpanzees and other primates. Male bonobos (pygmy chimps) regularly engage in a form of mutual masturbation that has been called "penis fencing." Females get sexual pleasure from rubbing their genitals against those of other females (Waal 1997). Our primate sexual potential is molded by culture, the environment, and reproductive necessity. Male–female coitus is practiced in all human societies—which, after all, must reproduce themselves—but alternatives also are widespread (Lyons and Lyons 2011; Rathus, Nevid, and Fichner-Rathus 2014). Like our gender roles, the sexual component of human personality and identity—just how we express our "natural," or biological, sexual urges—is a matter that culture and environment influence and limit.

## Anthropology Today   *A Measure of Gender Inequality*

The World Economic Forum, based in Switzerland, began publishing its annual Global Gender Gap Index in 2006. This index assesses gender inequality, and progress in reducing it, in 142 countries. For each country, the index measures the gap between males and females in four major categories: (1) economic opportunity and participation, (2) educational achievement, (3) health and survival, and (4) political empowerment.

Most of the indexed countries, representing over 90 percent of the world's population, have made progress in reducing the gap, which has favored males over females. Gains have been strongest in health and education. Worldwide, 96 percent of the gender gap in health has closed, along with 94 percent in education. Only 60 percent of the economic gap, however, and a paltry 21 percent of the political gap between men and women have closed.

Worldwide, about 25 women were serving as heads of government in 2014. In that year, *Forbes* magazine ranked Angela Merkel, Germany's chancellor, as the world's fifth most powerful person (after, in order, the heads of state of Russia, the United States, and China and the Pope). Merkel, however, was the only woman in the top 10 and was one of only two women in the top 20 most powerful people in the world (Brazil's President Dilma Rousseff was the other). In ministries, parliaments, and houses of congress, the global average has risen gradually to about 22 percent female in 2014 (see http://www.unwomen.org/en/what-we-do/leadership-and-political-participation/facts-and-figures#notes).

North America has been the world's most successful region in terms of correcting gender-based inequality. Next come Europe and Central Asia, followed by Latin

German Chancellor Angela Merkel speaks with cabinet members and economic advisors after receiving the 2014–2015 annual report of Germany's Council of Economic Experts. Is Merkel the world's most powerful woman?
© John MacDougall/AFP/Getty Images

America, Asia, and Africa. The Middle East/ North Africa places last. Four Nordic countries consistently have held the top four positions in the index: Iceland, Finland, Norway, and Sweden. Although no country has yet achieved full gender equality, those four countries have closed over 80 percent of their gender gaps, considering all criteria. The lowest-ranking country, Yemen, has closed barely 50 percent of its gap.

The United States ranked 20th overall in the Global Gender Gap Index in 2014. There was virtually no gender gap in American educational attainment. Literacy rates are high for both genders, and male and female rates of enrollment are roughly the same at all educational levels. In fact, 68 percent of American women graduating from high school in spring 2013 had enrolled in college the following fall, compared with only 64 percent of their male counterparts. The reduction in the U.S. education gap by gender has been more rapid and dramatic than most people realize. Fully one-third of American women were not high school graduates in 1970, versus a mere 6 percent today. Among women of prime working age (25 to 64), 39 percent held college degrees in 2013, compared with only 11 percent in 1970.

With respect to economics, the United States still has a pronounced, if reduced, gender gap. Among countries in the Index,

the United States ranked fourth in economic participation and opportunity, but only 65th in terms of equal pay for equal work. American women reached the peak of their labor force participation in 1999, with a rate of 60 percent (compared with 74.7 percent for men that year). By 2013, the percentage had declined for both women (to 57.2 percent in 2013) and men (to about 70 percent). American women's earnings as a proportion of men's did grow, from 62 percent of men's earnings in 1979 to 82 percent in 2013, but there is still a gap of 18 percent. In terms of politics, despite an increasing number of women in politics and elected to Congress, the United States ranked only 54th in terms of political empowerment.

Overall, what kind of progress can we see in the World Gender Gap Index between 2006 and 2014? The overall gap between men and women has narrowed in most countries, but at a slow rate. Additional and more rapid progress toward gender equality is needed. A country's overall economic development tends to reflect its degree of gender equality. Because women represent about half of any national talent base, a country's long-run competitiveness depends on the opportunities it offers to all its citizens. How might your country act to reduce its gender gap?

**Source:** Hausmann, Tyson, and Zahidi (2014); U.S. Bureau of Labor Statistics (2014).

## Summary

1. Gender roles are the tasks and activities that a culture assigns to each sex and to the genders it recognizes. Gender stereotypes are oversimplified ideas about attributes of males and females. *Gender stratification* describes an unequal distribution of rewards by gender, reflecting different positions in a social hierarchy.

2. Cross-cultural comparison reveals some recurrent patterns involving the division of labor by gender, as well as gender-based differences in reproductive strategies. Gender roles and gender stratification vary with environment, economy, adaptive

strategy, system of kinship and descent, level of social complexity, and degree of participation in the world economy.

3. When gathering is prominent, gender status is more equal than when hunting or fishing dominates a foraging economy. Gender status also is more equal when the domestic and public spheres aren't sharply separated.

4. Gender stratification also is linked to descent and residence. Women's status in matrilineal societies tends to be high because overall social identity comes through female links. Women in many societies, especially matrilineal ones, wield power and make decisions. Scarcity of resources promotes intervillage warfare, patriliny, and patrilocality. The localization of related males is adaptive for military solidarity. Men may use their warrior role to symbolize and reinforce the social devaluation and oppression of women. Patriarchy describes a political system ruled by men in which women have inferior social and political status, including basic human rights.

5. Americans' attitudes about gender roles have varied with class and region, as well as historically. A declining need for female labor promotes the idea that women are unfit for many jobs, and vice versa. Countering the economic gains of many American women is the feminization of poverty. This has become a global phenomenon as impoverished female-headed households have increased worldwide. A cross-national survey revealed a correlation between degree of happiness and women's work outside the home.

6. Societies may recognize more than two genders. The term *intersex* describes a group of conditions, including chromosomal configurations, that may produce a discrepancy between external and internal genitals. Transgender individuals may or may not contrast biologically with ordinary males and females. Self-identified transgender people tend to be individuals whose gender identity contradicts their biological sex at birth and the gender identity that society assigned to them in infancy.

7. *Gender identity* refers to whether a person feels, and is regarded as, male, female, or something else. One's gender identity does not dictate one's sexual orientation. Sexual orientation stands for a person's habitual sexual attraction to, and activities with, persons of the opposite sex (heterosexuality), the same sex (homosexuality), or both sexes (bisexuality). There has been a recent tendency to see sexual orientation as fixed and biologically based. However, anthropologists know that sexual norms vary widely from culture to culture and that, to some extent at least, erotic expression is influenced by culture.

## Key Terms

domestic, *327*
domestic–public dichotomy, *327*
gender identity, *337*
gender roles, *321*
gender stereotypes, *321*

gender stratification, *321*
intersex, *335*
patriarchy, *330*
patrilineal–patrilocal complex, *329*

sexual dimorphism, *320*
sexual orientation, *337*
transgender, *336*

# Chapter 15

# Religion

Given the worldwide and varied scope of beliefs and behavior labeled "religious," anthropologists know how difficult it is to define **religion.** In his book *Religion: An Anthropological View,* Anthony F. C. Wallace offered this definition: "belief and ritual concerned with supernatural beings, powers, and forces" (1966, p. 5). By "supernatural" he referred to a nonmaterial realm beyond (but believed to impinge on) the observable world. This realm cannot be verified or falsified empirically and is inexplicable in ordinary terms. It must be accepted "on faith." Supernatural beings—deities, ghosts, demons, souls, and spirits—make their homes outside our material world, although they may visit it from time to time. There also are supernatural or sacred forces, some of them wielded by deities and spirits, others that simply exist. In many societies, people believe they can benefit from, become imbued with, or manipulate supernatural forces (see Bielo 2015; Bowen 2014; Hicks 2010; Lambek 2008; Stein and Stein 2011; Warms, Garber, and McGee 2009).

Wallace's definition of religion focuses on presumably universal categories (beings, powers, and forces) within the supernatural realm. For Emile Durkheim (1912/2001), one of the founders of the anthropology of religion, the key distinction was between the sacred and the profane. Like the supernatural for Wallace, Durkheim's "sacred" was the domain set off from the ordinary, or the mundane (he used the word *profane*). For Durkheim, every society had its sacred, but that domain was socially constructed; it varied from society to society. Durkheim focused on Native Australian societies, which he believed had preserved the most elementary, or basic, forms of religion. He noted that their most sacred objects, including plants and animals that served as totems, were not supernatural at all. Rather, they were "real-world" entities (e.g., kangaroos, grubs) that, over the generations, had acquired special meaning for the social groups that had made them sacred and continued to "worship" them.

Many definitions of religion focus on groups of people who gather together regularly for worship (see Reese 1999). These congregants or adherents internalize common beliefs and a shared system of meaning. They accept a set of doctrines involving the relationship between the individual and divinity, the sacred, or whatever is taken to be the ultimate nature of reality. Anthropologists like Durkheim have stressed the collective, social, and shared nature of religion, the emotions it generates, and the meanings it embodies. As Michael Lambek (2008, p. 5) remarks, "good anthropology understands that religious worlds are real, vivid, and significant to those who construct and inhabit them." Durkheim (1912/2001) highlighted religious effervescence, the bubbling up of collective emotional intensity generated by worship. Victor Turner (1969/1995) updated Durkheim's notion, using the term **communitas,** an intense community spirit, a feeling of great social solidarity, equality, and togetherness.

The word *religion* derives from the Latin *religare*—"to tie, to bind"—but it is not necessary for all members of a given religion to meet together as a common body. Subgroups meet regularly at local congregation sites. They may attend occasional meetings with adherents representing a wider region. And they may form an imagined community with people of similar faith throughout the world.

Participation in a collective religious act, such as singing in this choir, can strengthen social bonds among congregants, while promoting feelings of spiritual effervescence. © Jose Luis Palaez inc./Blend Images/Getty Images RF

In studying religion cross-culturally, anthropologists pay attention to religion as a social phenomenon as well as to the meanings of religious doctrines, settings, acts, and events. Verbal manifestations of religious beliefs include prayers, chants, myths, texts, and stated rules of ethics and morality (see Hicks 2010; Moro and Meyers 2012; Stein and Stein 2011; Winzeler 2012). The anthropological study of religion also encompasses notions about purity and pollution (including taboos involving diet and physical contact), sacrifice, initiation, rites of passage, vision quests, pilgrimages, spirit possession, prophecy, study, devotion, and moral actions (Lambek 2008, p. 9).

Like ethnicity and language, religion is associated with social divisions within and between societies and nations. Religion both unites and divides. Participation in common rites may affirm, and thus maintain, the solidarity of a group of adherents. As we know from daily headlines, however, religious difference also may be associated with bitter enmity. Contacts and confrontations have increased between so-called world religions, such as Christianity and Islam, and the more localized forms of religion that missionaries typically lump together under the disparaging term "paganism." Increasingly, ethnic, regional, and class conflicts come to be framed in religious terms. Contemporary examples of religion as a social and political force include the rise of the religious right in the United States, the worldwide spread of Pentecostalism, and various Islamic movements (see Lindquist and Handelman 2013).

Long ago, Edward Sapir (1928/1956) argued for a distinction between "a religion" and "religion." The former term would apply only to a formally organized religion, such as the world religions just mentioned. The latter—"religion"—is universal; it refers to religious beliefs and behavior, which exist in all societies, even if they don't stand out as a separate and clearly demarcated sphere.

Anthropologists agree that religion exists in all human societies; it is a cultural universal. However, we'll see that it isn't always easy to distinguish the sacred from the profane and that different societies conceptualize divinity, the sacred, the supernatural, and ultimate realities very differently.

## Expressions of Religion

When did religion begin? No one knows for sure. There are suggestions of religion in Neandertal burials and on European cave walls, where painted stick figures may represent **shamans,** early religious specialists. Nevertheless, any statement about when, where, why, and how religion arose, or any description of its original nature, can only be speculative. Although such speculations are inconclusive, many have revealed important functions and effects of religious behavior. Several theories will be examined in this section.

### Spiritual Beings

Another founder of the anthropology of religion was the Englishman Sir Edward Burnett Tylor (1871/1958). Religion arose, Tylor thought, as people tried to understand phenomena they could not explain by reference to daily experience. Tylor believed that ancient humans—and contemporary nonindustrial peoples—were particularly intrigued with death, dreaming, and trance. People see images they may remember when they wake up or come out of a trance state. Tylor concluded that attempts to explain dreams and trances led early humans to believe that two entities inhabit the body. One is active during the day, and the other—a double, or soul—is active during sleep and trance states. Although they never meet, they are vital to each other. When the double permanently leaves the body, the person dies. Death is departure of the soul. From the Latin for soul, *anima,* Tylor named this belief **animism.** The soul was one sort of spiritual entity; people remembered various images from their dreams and trances—other spirits. For Tylor, animism, the earliest form of religion, was a belief in spiritual beings.

Tylor proposed that religion evolved through stages, beginning with animism. **Polytheism** (the belief in multiple gods) and then **monotheism** (the belief in a single, all-powerful deity) developed later. Because religion originated to explain things, Tylor thought it would decline as science offered better explanations. To an extent, he was right. We now have scientific explanations for many things that religion once elucidated (see Salazar and Bestard 2015). Of course, many of the "faithful" reject such secular explanations, preferring the nonscientific, religious ones. Nevertheless, because religion persists even among those who accept science, it must do something more than explain. It must, and does, have other functions and meanings.

## Powers and Forces

In addition to animism—and sometimes coexisting with it in the same society—is a view of the supernatural as a domain of impersonal power, or force, which people can control under certain conditions. (You'd be right to think of *Star Wars.*) Such a conception has been particularly prominent in Melanesia, the area of the South Pacific that includes Papua New Guinea and adjacent islands. Melanesians traditionally believed in **mana,** a sacred impersonal force existing in the universe. Mana could reside in people, animals, plants, and objects.

Melanesian mana was similar to our notion of good luck. Objects with mana could change someone's luck. For example, a charm or an amulet belonging to a successful hunter could transmit the hunter's mana to the next person who held or wore it. A woman could put a rock in her garden, see her yields improve, and attribute the change to the force contained in the rock.

Beliefs in manalike forces have been widespread, although the specifics of the religious doctrines have varied. Consider the contrast between mana in Melanesia and Polynesia (the islands included in a triangular area marked by Hawaii to the north, Easter Island to the east, and New Zealand to the southwest). In Melanesia, anyone could acquire mana by chance, or by working hard to get it. In Polynesia, however, mana wasn't potentially available to everyone but was attached to political offices. Chiefs and nobles had more mana than ordinary people did.

So charged with mana were the highest chiefs that contact with them was dangerous to commoners. The mana of chiefs flowed out of their bodies. It could infect the ground, making it dangerous for others to walk in the chief's footsteps. It could permeate the containers and utensils chiefs used in eating. Because high chiefs had so much mana, their bodies and possessions were **taboo** (set apart as sacred and off-limits to ordinary people). Because ordinary people couldn't bear as much sacred current as royalty could, when commoners were accidentally exposed, purification rites were necessary.

One function of religion is to explain. As Horton (1993) and Lambek (2008) point out, there are universals in human experience, common conditions and situations that call out for explanation. What happens in sleep and trance, and with death?—The soul leaves the body. Why do some people prosper, while others fail? Blame it on such non-material factors as luck, mana, sorcery, or being one of "God's chosen."

The beliefs in spiritual beings (e.g., animism) and supernatural forces (e.g., mana) fit within Wallace's definition of religion given at the beginning of this chapter. Most religions include both spirits and impersonal forces. Likewise, the supernatural beliefs of contemporary North Americans include beings (gods, saints, souls, demons) and forces (charms, talismans, crystals, and sacred objects).

## Magic and Religion

**Magic** refers to supernatural techniques intended to accomplish specific aims. These techniques include magical actions, offerings, spells, formulas, and incantations used with deities or with impersonal forces. Magicians employ *imitative magic* to produce a desired effect by imitating it. If magicians wish to harm someone, they may imitate that effect on an image of the victim. Sticking pins in "voodoo dolls" is an example. With *contagious magic,* whatever is done to an object is believed to affect a person who once had contact with it. Sometimes practitioners of contagious magic use body products from prospective victims—their nails or hair, for example. The spell performed on the body product is believed eventually to reach the person (see Stein and Stein 2011). Magic exists in societies with diverse religious beliefs, including animism, mana, polytheism, and monotheism.

## Uncertainty, Anxiety, Solace

Religion and magic don't just explain things. They serve emotional needs as well as cognitive (e.g., explanatory) ones. Religion helps people face death and endure life crises. Magical techniques can dispel doubts that arise when outcomes are beyond human control. According to Malinowski, when people face uncertainty and danger, they often turn to magic. The Trobriand Islanders, whom Malinowski studied, used magic during sailing—a hazardous activity in which people lacked control over wind and weather (Malinowski 1931/1978). Only in situations they could not control did Trobrianders, out of psychological stress, turn to magic.

Despite our improving technical skills, we still can't control every outcome, and magic persists in contemporary societies (see this chapter's "Anthropology Today"). Most of us still draw on magic and ritual in situations of uncertainty, such as before a test or perhaps a plane ride.

## Rituals

Several features distinguish **rituals** from other kinds of behavior (Rappaport 1974, 1999). Rituals are formal—stylized, repetitive, and stereotyped. People perform them in special (sacred) places and at set times. Rituals include liturgical orders—sequences of words and actions invented prior to the current performance of the ritual in which they occur.

These features link rituals to plays, but there are important differences. Actors merely portray something, but ritual performers—who make up congregations—are in earnest.

Rituals convey information about the participants and their traditions. Repeated year after year, generation after generation, rituals translate enduring messages, values, and sentiments into action.

Rituals are social acts. Inevitably, some participants are more committed than others are to the beliefs that lie behind the rites. However, just by taking part in a joint public act, the performers signal that they accept a common social and moral order, one that transcends their status as individuals.

## Rites of Passage

Magic and religion, as Malinowski noted, can reduce anxiety and allay fears. Ironically, beliefs and rituals also can create anxiety and a sense of insecurity and danger (Radcliffe-Brown 1962/1965). Anxiety may arise because a rite exists. Indeed, participation in a collective ritual (e.g., circumcision of early teen boys, common among East African pastoralists) can produce stress, whose common reduction, once the ritual is completed, enhances the solidarity of the participants.

**Rites of passage** can be individual or collective. The traditional vision quests of Native Americans, particularly the Plains Indians, illustrate individual rites of passage (customs associated with the transition from one place, or stage of life, to another). To move from boyhood to manhood, a youth would temporarily separate from his community. After a period of isolation in the wilderness, often featuring fasting and drug consumption, the young man would see a vision, which would become his guardian spirit. He would return then to his community as an adult.

Contemporary rites of passage include confirmations, baptisms, bar and bat mitzvahs, initiations, weddings, and application for Medicare. Passage rites involve changes in social status, such as from boyhood to manhood and from nonmember to sorority sister. More generally, a rite of passage may mark any change in place, condition, social position, or age.

All rites of passage have three phases: separation, liminality, and incorporation. In the first phase, people withdraw from ordinary society. In the third phase, they reenter society, having completed a rite that changes their status. The second, or liminal, phase is the most interesting. It is the limbo, or "time-out," during which people have left one status but haven't yet entered or joined the next (Turner 1967/1974).

**Liminality** always has certain characteristics. Liminal people exist apart from ordinary distinctions and expectations; they are living in a time out of time. A series of contrasts demarcate liminality from normal social life. For example, among the Ndembu of Zambia, a chief underwent a rite of passage before taking office. During the liminal period, his past and future positions in society were ignored, even reversed. He was subjected to a variety of insults, orders, and humiliations.

Passage rites often are collective. Several individuals—boys being circumcised, fraternity or sorority initiates, men at military boot camps, football players in summer training camps, women becoming nuns—pass through the rites together as a group. Table 15.1 summarizes the contrasts, or oppositions, between liminality and normal social life. Most notable is the social aspect of collective liminality called communitas (Turner 1967/1974), an intense community spirit, a feeling of great social solidarity, equality, and togetherness. Liminal people experience the same treatment and

## TABLE 15.1 Oppositions between Liminality and Normal Social Life

Source: Victor Turner, *The Ritual Process.* Copyright © 1969 by Victor W. Turner. Renewed 1997 by Edith Turner.

| Liminality | Normal Social Structure |
|---|---|
| transition | state |
| homogeneity | heterogeneity |
| communitas | structure |
| equality | inequality |
| anonymity | names |
| absence of property | property |
| absence of status | status |
| nakedness or uniform dress | dress distinctions |
| sexual continence or excess | sexuality |
| minimization of sex distinctions | maximization of sex distinctions |
| absence of rank | rank |
| humility | pride |
| disregard of personal appearance | care for personal appearance |
| unselfishness | selfishness |
| total obedience | obedience only to superior rank |
| sacredness | secularity |
| sacred instruction | technical knowledge |
| silence | speech |
| simplicity | complexity |
| acceptance of pain and suffering | avoidance of pain and suffering |

conditions and must act alike. Liminality may be marked ritually and symbolically by reversals of ordinary behavior. For example, sexual taboos may be intensified; conversely, sexual excess may be encouraged. Liminal symbols, such as special clothing or body paint, mark the condition as extraordinary—beyond ordinary society and everyday life.

Liminality is basic to all passage rites. Furthermore, in certain societies, including our own, liminal symbols may be used to set off one (religious) group from another and from society as a whole. Such "permanent liminal groups" (e.g., sects, brotherhoods, and cults) are found most characteristically in nation-states. Such liminal features as humility, poverty, equality, obedience, sexual abstinence, and silence (see Table 15.1) may be required for all sect or cult members. Those who join such a group agree to its rules. As if they were undergoing a passage rite—but in this case a never-ending one—they may have to abandon their previous possessions and social ties, including those with family members. Is liminality compatible with Facebook?

Members of a sect or cult often wear uniform clothing. They may adopt a common hairstyle (shaved head, short hair, or long hair). Liminal groups submerge the individual in the collective. This may be one reason Americans, whose core values include individuality and individualism, are so fearful and suspicious of "cults."

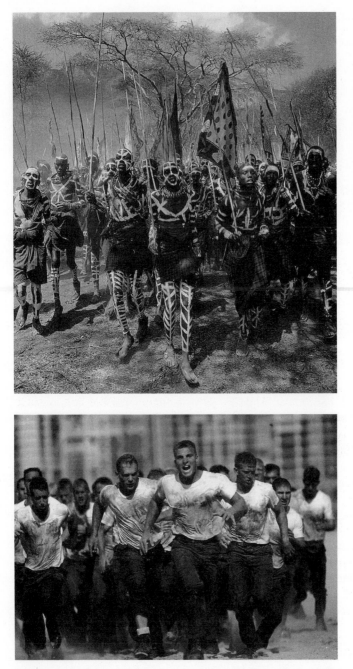

Passage rites are often collective. A group—such as these Maasai initiates in Kenya or these navy trainees in San Diego—passes through the rites as a unit. Such liminal people experience the same treatment and conditions and must act alike. They share communitas, an intense community spirit, a feeling of great social solidarity or togetherness. (first): © John Warburton-Lee Photography/Alamy; (second): © Joe McNally/Hulton Archive/Getty Images

Not all collective rites are rites of passage. Most societies observe occasions on which people come together to worship or celebrate and, in doing so, affirm and reinforce their solidarity. Rituals such as the totemic ceremonies described in the next section are *rites of intensification:* They intensify social solidarity. The ritual creates communitas and produces emotions (the collective spiritual effervescence described by Durkheim 1912/2001) that enhance social solidarity.

## Totemism

Totemism was a key ingredient in the religions of the Native Australians. **Totems** could be animals, plants, or geographical features. In each tribe, groups of people had particular totems. Members of each totemic group believed themselves to be descendants of their totem. They customarily neither killed nor ate it, but this taboo was lifted once a year, when people assembled for ceremonies dedicated to the totem. These annual rites were believed to be necessary for the totem's survival and reproduction.

Totemism uses nature as a model for society. The totems usually are animals and plants, which are part of nature. People relate to nature through their totemic association with natural species. Because each group has a different totem, social differences mirror natural contrasts. Diversity in the natural order becomes a model for diversity in the social order. However, although totemic plants and animals occupy different niches in nature, on another level they are united because they all are part of nature. The unity of the human social order is enhanced by symbolic association with and imitation of the natural order (Durkheim 1912/2001; Lévi-Strauss 1963; Radcliffe-Brown 1962/1965).

Totemic principles continue to demarcate groups, including clubs, teams, and universities, in modern societies. Think of familiar team mascots and symbols. Badgers and wolverines are animals, and buckeye nuts come from the buckeye tree. Differences between natural species (e.g., lions, tigers, and bears) distinguish sports teams and even political parties (donkeys and elephants). Although the modern context is more secular, one can still witness, in intense college football rivalries, some of the effervescence Durkheim noted in Australian totemic religion and other rites of intensification.

Totems are sacred emblems symbolizing common identity. This is true not just among Native Australians but also among Native American groups of the North Pacific Coast of North America, whose totem poles are well known. Their totemic carvings, which commemorated and told visual stories about ancestors, animals, and spirits, were also associated with ceremonies. In totemic rites, people gather together to honor their totem. In so doing, they use ritual to maintain the social oneness that the totem symbolizes.

# Social Control

Religion means a lot to people. It helps them cope with uncertainty, adversity, fear, and tragedy. It offers hope that things will get better. Lives can be transformed through spiritual healing. Sinners can repent and be saved—or they can go on sinning and be

This 19th-century woodcut depicts the trial of Anne Hutchinson, an outspoken woman who was tried as a heretic and banished from the Massachusetts Bay Colony in 1637. © North Wind Picture Archives via AP Images

damned. If the faithful truly internalize a system of religious rewards and punishments, their religion becomes a powerful influence on their attitudes and behavior, as well as what they teach their children.

Many people engage in religious activity because it works for them. Prayers get answered. Faith healers heal. Many Native American people in southwestern Oklahoma use faith healers at high monetary costs, not just because it makes them feel better but also because they think it works (Lassiter 1998). Each year legions of Brazilians visit a church, Nosso Senhor do Bomfim, in the city of Salvador, Bahia. They vow to repay "Our Lord" (Nosso Senhor) if healing happens. Showing that the vows work, and are repaid, are the thousands of *ex votos,* plastic impressions of every conceivable body part, that adorn the church, along with photos of people who have been cured.

Religion can work by getting inside people and mobilizing their emotions—their joy, their wrath, their certainty, their righteousness. People can feel a deep sense of shared joy, meaning, experience, communion, belonging, and commitment to their religion. The power of religion affects action. When religions meet, they can coexist peacefully, or their differences can be a basis for enmity and disharmony, even battle. Throughout history, political leaders have used religion to promote and justify their views and policies.

How may leaders mobilize communities and, in so doing, gain support for their own policies? One way is by persuasion; another is by hatred or fear. Consider witchcraft accusations. Witch hunts can be powerful means of social control by creating a climate of danger and insecurity that affects everyone. No one wants to seem deviant, to be accused of being a witch. Witch hunts often take aim at socially marginal people who can be accused and punished with least chance of retaliation. During the great European witch craze of the 15th, 16th, and 17th centuries (Harris 1974), most accusations and convictions were against poor women with little social support.

To ensure proper behavior, religions offer rewards (e.g., the fellowship of the religious community) and punishments (e.g., the threat of being cast out or excommunicated). Religions, especially the formal, organized ones typically found in state societies, often prescribe a code of ethics and morality to guide behavior. Moral codes are ways of maintaining order and stability that are constantly reinforced in religious sermons, catechisms, and the like. They become internalized psychologically. They guide behavior and produce regret, guilt, shame, and the need for forgiveness, expiation, and absolution when they are not followed.

# Kinds of Religion

Although religion is a cultural universal, religions exist in particular societies, and cultural differences show up systematically in religious beliefs and practices. For example, the religions of stratified, state societies differ from those of societies with less marked social contrasts—societies without kings, lords, and subjects. What can a given society afford in terms of religion? Churches, temples, and other full-time religious establishments, with their monumental structures and hierarchies of officials, must be supported in some consistent way, such as by tithes and taxes. What kinds of societies can support such hierarchies and architecture?

All societies have religious figures—those believed capable of mediating between humans and the supernatural. More generally, all societies have medico-magico-religious specialists. Modern societies can support both priesthoods and health care professionals. Lacking the resources for such specialization, foraging societies typically have only part-time specialists, who often have both religious and healing roles. *Shaman* is a general term that encompasses curers ("witch doctors"), mediums, spiritualists, astrologers, palm readers, and other independent diviners. In foraging societies, shamans are usually part-time; that is, they also hunt or gather.

Societies with productive economies (based on agriculture and trade) and large, dense populations (nation-states) can support full-time religious specialists—professional priesthoods. Like the state itself, priesthoods are hierarchically and bureaucratically organized. Anthony Wallace (1966) describes the religions of such stratified societies as "ecclesiastical" (pertaining to an established church and its hierarchy of officials) and "Olympian," after Mount Olympus, home of the classical Greek gods. In such religions, powerful anthropomorphic gods have specialized functions, for example, gods of love, war, the sea, and death. Such *pantheons* (collections of deities) were prominent in the religions of many nonindustrial nation-states, including the Aztecs of Mexico, several African and Asian kingdoms, and classical Greece and Rome. Greco-Roman religions were polytheistic, featuring many deities. In monotheism, all supernatural phenomena are believed to be manifestations of, or under the control of, a single eternal, omniscient, omnipotent, and omnipresent being. In the ecclesiastical monotheistic religion known as Christianity, a single supreme being is manifest in a trinity (see Bellah 2011).

# Protestant Values and Capitalism

Notions of salvation and the afterlife dominate Christian ideologies. However, most varieties of Protestantism lack the hierarchical structure of earlier monotheistic religions, including Roman Catholicism. With a diminished role for the priest (minister), salvation is directly available to individuals, who have unmediated access to the supernatural.

In his influential book *The Protestant Ethic and the Spirit of Capitalism* (1904/1958), the social theorist Max Weber linked the spread of capitalism to the values preached by early Protestant leaders. He saw Protestants as more successful financially than Catholics and attributed this difference to the values stressed by their religions. Weber viewed

Protestants as more ascetic, entrepreneurial, and future oriented than Catholics. Protestantism placed a premium on hard work, an ascetic life, and profit seeking. Early Protestants saw success on Earth as a sign of divine favor and probable salvation.

Weber also argued that rational business organization required the removal of production from the home. Protestantism made such a separation possible by emphasizing individualism: Individuals, not families or households, would be saved or not. Today, of course, in North America as throughout the world, people of many religions and with diverse worldviews are successful capitalists. Furthermore, traditional Protestant values often have little to do with today's economic maneuvering. Still, there is no denying that the individualistic focus of Protestantism was compatible with the severance of ties to land and kin that industrialism demanded.

## World Religions

Information on the world's major religions as of 2010 is provided in Figure 15.1, based on a comprehensive study by the Pew Research Center (2012*b*). Considering data from more than 230 countries, that study estimated that the world contains about 5.8 billion religiously affiliated people—84 percent of its population of 6.9 billion in 2010.

That study found 2.2 billion Christians (32 percent of the global population), 1.6 billion Muslims (23 percent), 1 billion Hindus (15 percent), nearly 500 million Buddhists (7 percent), and 14 million Jews (0.2 percent). In addition, more than 400 million people (6 percent) practice various folk or traditional religions. These include the traditional or folk religions of Africa and China as well as those of Native Americans and Australians. Some 58 million people, a bit less than 1 percent of the world's population, belong to

**FIGURE 15.1**
**Major World
Religions by
Percentage of World
Population, 2010**

Source: www.adherents.com.
Reprinted by permission.

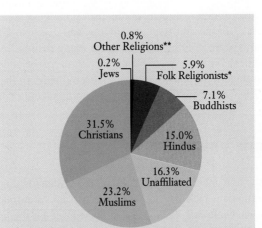

0.8%
Other Religions**

0.2%
Jews

5.9%
Folk Religionists*

7.1%
Buddhists

31.5%
Christians

15.0%
Hindus

16.3%
Unaffiliated

23.2%
Muslims

\* Includes followers of African traditional religions, Chinese folk religions, Native American religions, and Australian aboriginal religions.
\*\* Includes Baháí's, Jains, Sikhs, Shintoists, Taoists, followers of Tenrikyo, Wiccans, Zoroastrians, and many other faiths.
Percentage may not add to 100 due to rounding.

other religions, including Baháí, Jainism, Sikhism, Shintoism, Taoism, Tenrikyo, Wicca, and Zoroastrianism.

The same study found that about 1.1 billion people—16 percent of the world's population—lacked any religious affiliation. The unaffiliated therefore constitute the third-largest group worldwide with respect to religious affiliation, behind Christians and Muslims. There are about as many unaffiliated people in the world as there are Roman Catholics. Many of the unaffiliated, however, hold some religious or spiritual beliefs, even if they don't identify with a particular religion (Pew Research Center 2012*b*).

Worldwide, Islam is growing at a rate of about 2.9 percent annually, compared with 2.3 percent for Christianity. Within Christianity, the growth rate varies. There are perhaps 1 billion "born-again" Christians (e.g., Evangelicals/Pentecostals/Charismatics) in the world today, with an estimated annual worldwide growth rate well above that of Christianity overall (see Pew Research Center 2011).

## Religion and Change

Like political organization, religion helps maintain social order. And like political mobilization, religious energy can be harnessed not just for change but also for revolution. Reacting to conquest or to actual or perceived foreign domination, for instance, religious leaders may seek to alter or revitalize their society.

### Cargo Cults

**Revitalization movements** are social movements that occur in times of change, in which religious leaders emerge and undertake to alter or revitalize a society. Christianity originated as a revitalization movement. Jesus was one of several prophets who preached new religious doctrines while the Middle East was under Roman rule. It was a time of social unrest, when a foreign power ruled the land. Jesus inspired a new, enduring, and major religion. His contemporaries were not so successful.

Revitalization movements known as **cargo cults** have arisen in colonial situations in which local people have regular contact with outsiders but lack their wealth, technology, and living standards. Cargo cults attempt to explain European domination and wealth and to achieve similar success magically by mimicking European behavior and manipulating symbols of the desired lifestyle. The cargo cults of Melanesia and Papua New Guinea are hybrid creations that weave Christian doctrine with aboriginal beliefs. They take their name from their focus on cargo—European goods of the sort natives have seen unloaded from the cargo holds of ships and airplanes.

In one early cult, members believed that the spirits of the dead would arrive in a ship. These ghosts would bring manufactured goods for the natives and would kill all the Whites. Later cargo cults replaced ships with airplanes (Worsley 1959/1985). Many cults have used elements of European culture as sacred objects. The rationale is that Europeans use these objects, have wealth, and therefore must know the "secret of cargo." By mimicking how Europeans use or treat objects, natives hope also to come upon the secret knowledge needed to gain cargo.

For example, having seen Europeans' reverent treatment of flags and flagpoles, the members of one cult began to worship flagpoles. They believed the flagpoles were sacred towers that could transmit messages between the living and the dead. Other natives built airstrips to entice planes bearing canned goods, portable radios, clothing, wristwatches, and motorcycles. Some cargo cult prophets proclaimed that success would come through a reversal of European domination and native subjugation. The day was near, they preached, when natives—aided by God, Jesus, or native ancestors—would turn the tables. Native skins would turn white, and those of Europeans would turn brown; Europeans would die or be killed.

Cargo cults blend aboriginal and Christian beliefs. Melanesian myths told of ancestors shedding their skins and changing into powerful beings and of dead people returning to life. Christian missionaries also preached resurrection. The cults' preoccupation with cargo is related to traditional Melanesian big-man systems. In the chapter "Political Systems," we saw that a Melanesian big man had to be generous. People worked for the big man, helping him amass wealth, but eventually he had to give a feast and give away all that wealth.

Because of their experience with big-man systems, Melanesians believed that all wealthy people eventually had to give their wealth away. For decades they had attended Christian missions and worked on plantations. All the while they expected Europeans to return the fruits of their labor as their own big men did. When the Europeans refused to distribute the wealth or even to let natives know the secret of its production and distribution, cargo cults developed.

Like arrogant big men, Europeans would be leveled, by death if necessary. However, natives lacked the physical means of doing what their traditions said they should do.

On the island of Tanna, in Vanuatu, Melanesia, members of the John Frum cargo cult stage a military parade. The young men, who carry fake guns and have "USA" painted on their bodies, see themselves as an elite force within the American army.
© Thierry Falise/LightRocket via Getty Images

Thwarted by well-armed colonial forces, natives resorted to magical leveling. They called on supernatural beings to intercede, to kill or otherwise deflate the European big men and redistribute their wealth.

Cargo cults are religious responses to the expansion of the world capitalist economy. However, this religious mobilization had political and economic results. Cult participation gave Melanesians a basis for common interests and activities and thus helped pave the way for political parties and economic interest organizations. Previously separated by geography, language, and customs, Melanesians started forming larger groups as members of the same cults and followers of the same prophets. The cargo cults paved the way for political action through which the indigenous peoples eventually regained their autonomy.

## New and Alternative Religious Movements

The New Age movement, which emerged in the 1980s, draws on and blends cultural elements from multiple traditions. It advocates change through individual personal transformation. In the United States and Australia, respectively, some people who are not Native Americans or Native Australians have appropriated the symbols, settings, and purported religious practices of Native Americans and Native Australians for New Age religions. Native American activists decry the appropriation and commercialization of their spiritual beliefs and rituals, as when "sweat lodge" ceremonies are held on cruise ships, with wine and cheese served. They see the appropriation of their ceremonies and traditions as theft. New religious movements have varied origins. Some have been influenced by Christianity, others by Eastern (Asian) religions, still others by mysticism and spiritualism.

Many contemporary nations contain unofficial religions. One example is "Yoruba religion," a term applied to perhaps 15 million adherents in Africa as well as to millions of practitioners of *syncretic,* or blended, religions (with elements of Catholicism and spiritism) in the Western Hemisphere (see Yemoja.org). Forms of Yoruba religion include *santeria* (in the Spanish Caribbean and the United States), *candomblé* (in Brazil), and *vodoun* (in the French Caribbean). Yoruba religion, with roots in precolonial nation-states of West Africa, has spread far beyond its region of origin, as part of the African diaspora. It remains an influential, identifiable religion today, despite suppression, such as by Cuba's communist government. There are perhaps 3 million practitioners of santeria in Cuba, plus another 800,000 in the United States (see http://www.religioustolerance.org/santeri2.htm). Between 5 and 10 million Brazilians participate in candomblé, also known as macumba (Garcia-Navarro 2013). Voodoo (*vodoun*) has between 2.8 and 3.2 million practitioners (Ontario Consultants 2011), many (perhaps most) of whom would name something else, such as Catholicism, as their religion.

# Religion and Cultural Globalization

## Evangelical Protestantism and Pentecostalism

The rapid spread of Evangelical Protestantism, which originated in Europe and North America, constitutes a highly successful form of contemporary cultural globalization. A century ago, more than 90 percent of the then approximately 80 million Evangelicals in the world lived in Europe and North America (Pew Research Center 2011). Today, there are as many as 1 billion Evangelicals worldwide, with most living outside Europe and North America—in sub-Saharan Africa, the Middle East and North Africa, Latin America, and Asia.

The growth of Evangelical Protestantism has been particularly explosive in Brazil—traditionally (and still) the world's most Catholic country. In 1980, when Pope John Paul II visited the country, 89 percent of Brazil's population claimed to be Roman Catholic. Since then, Evangelical Protestantism has spread like wildfire. Having made small inroads during the first half of the 20th century, Evangelical Protestantism grew exponentially in Brazil during the second half. Protestants accounted for fewer than 5 percent of the population through the 1960s. As of 2000, Evangelical Protestants comprised more than 15 percent of Brazilians affiliated with a church. By 2010, that figure was over 22 percent and still growing. Evangelical Protestantism's penetration of Brazil has been mainly at the expense of Catholicism. Among the factors that have worked against Catholicism are these: a declining priesthood overly dependent on foreigners, sharply contrasting political agendas of many of its clerics, and its reputation as mainly a women's religion.

Evangelical Protestantism stresses conservative morality, the authority of the Bible, and a personal ("born-again") conversion experience. Most Brazilian evangelicals are Pentecostals, who additionally embrace glossolalia (speaking in tongues) and beliefs in faith healing, spirits, exorcism, and miracles. São Paulo, Brazil's largest city, has been called the Pentecostal world capital, with over 4 million adherents.

Like members of a liminal sect, converts to Pentecostalism are expected to separate themselves both from their pasts and from the secular social world that

In São Paulo, Brazil, evangelicals pray inside the Bola de Neve Church. Popular with youths, this church sponsors activities, including surfing, skating, and rock 'n' roll and reggae music with religious lyrics. © Caetano Barreira/X01990/Reuters/Corbis

surrounds them. In Arembepe, Brazil, for example, the *crentes* ("true believers," as members of the local Pentecostal community are called) set themselves apart by their beliefs, behavior, and lifestyle (Kottak 2006). They worship, chant, and pray. They dress simply and forgo such worldly temptations (seen as vices) as tobacco, alcohol, gambling, and extramarital sexuality, along with dancing, movies, and other forms of popular culture. Wherever Pentecostalism exists, the converted observe an ascetic moral code and view the surrounding social world as a realm governed by Satan (Robbins 2004).

Pentecostalism strengthens family and household through a moral code that enjoins respect for marriage and prohibits adultery, gambling, drinking, and fighting. These activities were valued mainly by men in preconversion culture. Pentecostalism has appeal for men, however, because it does not publicly question their authority and even solidifies it within the household. Although Pentecostal ideology is strongly patriarchal, with women expected to subordinate themselves to men, women tend to be more active church members than men are. Pentecostalism promotes services and prayer groups by and for women. In such settings women develop leadership skills, as they also extend their social-support network beyond family and kin.

In its focus on ecstatic and exuberant worship, Pentecostalism has been heavily influenced by—and shares features with—African American Protestantism. In Brazil it shares features with candomblé, which also features chanting and spirit possession. Pentecostalism's habitual ritual engagement with spirits distinguishes it from other forms of Christianity (Casanova 2001; Meyer 1999).

Peter Berger (2010) suggests that modern Pentecostalism may be the fastest-growing religion in human history and focuses on its social dimensions to explain why. According to Berger, Pentecostalism promotes strong communities while offering practical and psychological support to people whose circumstances are changing. My own experience in Brazil supports Berger's hypothesis; most new Pentecostals I encountered came from underprivileged, poor, and otherwise marginalized groups in areas undergoing rapid social change.

The British sociologist David Martin (1990) argues that Pentecostalism is spreading so rapidly because its adherents embody Max Weber's Protestant ethic—valuing self-discipline, hard work, and thrift. Others see Pentecostalism as a kind of cargo cult, built on the belief that magic and ritual activity can promote material success (Freston 2008; Meyer 1999). Berger (2010) suggests that today's Pentecostals probably include both types—Weberian Protestants working to produce material wealth as a sign of their salvation along with people who believe that magic and ritual will bring them good fortune.

## Homogenization, Indigenization, or Hybridization?

Any cultural form that spreads from one society to another—be it a McDonald's or a form of religion—has to fit into the country and culture it enters. We can use the rapid spread of Pentecostalism as a case study of the process of adaptation of foreign cultural forms to local settings.

Joel Robbins (2004) has examined the extent to which what he calls Pentecostal/charismatic Christianity preserves its basic form and core beliefs as it spreads and adapts to various national and local cultures. Pentecostalism is a Western invention: Its beliefs, doctrines, organizational features, and rituals originated in the United States, following the European rise and spread of Protestantism. The core doctrines of acceptance of Jesus as one's savior, baptism with the Holy Spirit, faith healing, and belief in the second coming of Jesus have spread across nations and cultures without losing their basic shape.

Scholars have argued about whether the global spread of Pentecostalism is best understood as (1) a process of Western cultural domination and homogenization (perhaps supported by a right-wing political agenda) or (2) one in which imported cultural forms respond to local needs and are differentiated and indigenized. Joel Robbins (2004) takes a middle-ground position, viewing the spread of Pentecostalism as a form of cultural hybridization. Robbins (2004) argues that global and local features appear with equal intensity within these Pentecostal cultures. Churches retain certain core Pentecostal beliefs and behaviors while responding to the local culture and being organized at the local level.

Reviewing the literature, Robbins (2004) finds little evidence that a Western political agenda is propelling the global spread of Pentecostalism. It is true that foreigners (including American pastors and televangelists) have helped introduce Pentecostalism to countries outside North America. There is little evidence, however, that overseas churches are largely funded and ideologically shaped from North America. Pentecostal churches typically are staffed from top to bottom with locals, who run them as organizations that are attentive and responsive to local situations. Conversion is typically a key feature of that agenda. Once converted, a Pentecostal is expected to be an active Evangelist, seeking to bring in new members. This Evangelization is one of the most important activities in Pentecostal culture and certainly aids its expansion.

Pentecostalism spreads as other forces of globalization displace people and disrupt local lives. To people who feel socially adrift, Pentecostal evangelists offer tightly knit communities and a weblike structure of personal connections within and between Pentecostal communities. Such networks can facilitate access to health care, job placement, educational services, and other resources.

Unlike Catholicism, which is hierarchical, Pentecostalism is egalitarian. Adherents need no special education—only spiritual inspiration—to preach or to run a church. Based on his research in Brazil, John Burdick (1993) notes that many Afro-Brazilians are drawn to the Pentecostal community because others who are socially and racially like them are in the congregation, some serving as preachers. Opportunities for participation and leadership are abundant, for example, as lay preachers, deacons, and leaders of various men's, women's, and youth groups. The churches fund outreach to the needy and other locally relevant social services.

## Antimodernism and Fundamentalism

*Antimodernism* is the rejection of the modern (including secular forces of globalization) in favor of what is perceived as an earlier, purer, and better way of life. This viewpoint arose out of disillusionment with the Industrial Revolution and with subsequent developments in science, technology, and consumption patterns. Antimodernists typically consider the use of modern technology to be misguided or think technology should have a lower priority than religious and cultural values.

Religious *fundamentalism* describes antimodernist movements in various religions, including Christianity, Islam, and Judaism. Ironically, religious fundamentalism itself is a modern phenomenon, based on its adherents' strong feelings of alienation from the perceived secularism of the surrounding (modern) culture. Fundamentalists separate from a larger religious group, whose founding principles, they believe, have been corrupted or abandoned. Fundamentalists advocate return and strict fidelity to the "true" (fundamental) religious principles of the larger religion.

Fundamentalists also seek to rescue religion from absorption into modern, Western culture, which they see as having corrupted mainstream religions. In Christianity, fundamentalists are "born-again Christians" as opposed to "mainline Protestants." In Islam they are jama'at (in Arabic, enclaves based on close fellowship) engaged in jihad (struggle) against a Western culture hostile to Islam and the God-given (shariah) way of life. In Judaism they are Haredi, "Torah-true" Jews. All such groups see a sharp divide between themselves and other religions, as well as between a "sacred" view of life and the "secular" world (see Antoun 2008).

Both Pentecostalism and Christian fundamentalism preach ascetic morality, the duty to convert others, and respect for the Bible. Fundamentalists, however, tend to cite their success in living a moral life as proof of their salvation, whereas Pentecostals find assurance of their salvation in exuberant, ecstatic experience. Fundamentalists also seek to remake the political sphere along religious lines, whereas Pentecostals tend to have less interest in politics (Robbins 2004).

## The Spread of Islam

Islam—whose 1.6 billion followers constitute over a fifth of the world's population—is another rapidly spreading global religion that can be used to illustrate cultural globalization. The globalization of Islam also illustrates cultural hybridization. Islam has adapted successfully to the many nations and cultures it has entered, adopting architectural styles, linguistic practices, and even religious beliefs from host cultures.

For example, while Mosques (Islamic houses of worship) all share certain characteristics (e.g., they face Mecca and have some common architectural features), they also incorporate architectural and decorative elements from their national setting. Although Arabic is Islam's liturgical language, used for prayer, most Muslims' discussion of their faith occurs in their local language. In China, Islamic concepts have been influenced by Confucianism. In India and Bangladesh, the Islamic idea of the prophet has blended with the Hindu notion of the avatar, a deity who takes mortal form and descends to Earth to fight evil and guide the righteous. Islam entered Indonesia by means of Muslim merchants who devised devotional exercises that fit in with preexisting religions—Hinduism and Buddhism in Java and Sumatra and animism in the eastern islands, which eventually became Christian. In Bali, Hinduism survived as the dominant religion.

Both Pentecostalism and Islam, we have learned, hybridize and become locally relevant as they spread globally. Although certain core features endure, local people always assign their own meanings to the messages and social forms they receive from outside,

Indonesian Muslims pray at the historic Sunda Kelapa port in Jakarta on August 19, 2012. Muslims around the world were celebrating the end of Ramadan, the Muslim calendar's ninth and holiest month. © Chicarito/AFP/Getty Images

including religion. Such meanings reflect their cultural backgrounds, experiences, and prior belief systems. We must consider the processes of hybridization and indigenization in examining and understanding any form of cultural diffusion or globalization.

## Secular Rituals

In concluding this chapter on religion, we may recognize some problems with the definitions of religion given at the beginning of this chapter. The first problem: If we define religion with reference to the sacred and/or supernatural beings, powers, and forces, how do we classify ritual-like behaviors that occur in secular contexts? Some anthropologists believe there are both sacred and secular rituals. Secular rituals include formal, invariant, stereotyped, earnest, repetitive behavior and rites of passage that take place in nonreligious settings.

A second problem: If the distinction between the supernatural and the natural is not consistently made in a society, how can we tell what is religion and what isn't? The Betsileo of Madagascar, for example, view witches and dead ancestors as real people who play roles in ordinary life. However, their occult powers are not empirically demonstrable.

# Anthropology Today  *Baseball Magic*

Have you ever noticed how much baseball players spit? Outside baseball—even among other male sports figures—spitting is considered impolite. Football players, with their customary headgear, don't spit, nor do basketball players, who might slip on the court. No spitting by tennis players, gymnasts, or swimmers—not even Mark Spitz (a swimmer turned dentist). But watch any baseball game for a few minutes and you'll see spitting galore. Since pitchers appear to be the spitting champions, the custom likely originated on the mound. It continues today as a carryover from the days when pitchers routinely chewed tobacco, believing that

nicotine enhanced their concentration and effectiveness. The spitting custom spread to other players, who unabashedly spew saliva from the outfield to the dugout steps.

For the student of custom, ritual, and magic, baseball is an especially interesting game, to which lessons from anthropology are easily applied. The pioneering anthropologist Bronislaw Malinowski, writing about Pacific Islanders rather than baseball players, noted they had developed all sorts of magic to use in sailing, a hazardous activity. He proposed that when people face conditions they can't control (e.g., wind and weather), they turn to magic.

Detroit Tigers slugger Miguel Cabrera kisses his maple bat before hitting his 42nd home run of 2012 at Comerica Park. Sometimes baseball magic works: Cabrera went on that year to achieve baseball's Triple Crown and win the American League's MVP award. He repeated as AL batting champion and MVP in 2013. © Stan Grossfeld/The Boston Globe via Getty Images

*continued*

## Anthropology Today   *continued*

Magic, in the form of rituals, taboos, and sacred objects, is particularly evident in baseball. Like sailing magic, baseball magic reduces psychological stress, creating an illusion of control when real control is lacking.

In several publications about baseball, the anthropologist George Gmelch makes use of Malinowski's observation that magic is most common in situations dominated by chance and uncertainty. All sorts of magical behaviors surround pitching and batting, which are full of uncertainty. There are fewer rituals for fielding, over which players have more control. (Batting averages of .350 or higher are very rare after a full season, but a fielding percentage below .900 is a disgrace.)

Especially obvious are the rituals (like the spitting) of pitchers, who may tug their cap between pitches, spit in a particular direction, magically manipulate the resin bag, talk to the ball, or wash their hands after giving up a run. Batters have their rituals, too. It isn't uncommon to see outfielder Carlos Gomez kiss his bat, which he likes to talk to, smell, threaten—and reward when he gets a hit. Another batter routinely would spit, then ritually touch his gob with his bat, to enhance his success at the plate.

Humans use tools to accomplish a lot, but technology still doesn't let us "have it all." To keep hope alive in situations of uncertainty, and for outcomes we can't control, all societies draw on magic and religion as sources of nonmaterial comfort, explanation, and control. What are your rituals?

A third problem: The behavior considered appropriate for religious occasions varies tremendously from culture to culture. One society may consider drunken frenzy the surest sign of faith, whereas another may inculcate quiet reverence. Who is to say which is "more religious"?

Apparently secular settings, things, and events can acquire intense meaning for individuals who have grown up in their presence. Identities and loyalties based on fandom can be powerful indeed. Italians, Brazilians, and several other nationalities are rarely, if ever, as nationally focused and emotionally unified as they are when their teams are playing soccer in the World Cup. The collective effervescence that Durkheim found so characteristic of religion can equally well describe what Brazilians experience when their country wins a World Cup.

In the context of comparative religion, the idea that the secular can become sacred isn't surprising. Long ago, Durkheim (1912/2001) pointed out that the distinction between sacred and profane doesn't depend on the intrinsic qualities of the sacred symbol. In Australian totemic religion, for example, sacred beings include such humble creatures as ducks, frogs, rabbits, and grubs, whose inherent qualities could hardly have given rise to the religious sentiment they inspire.

Madagascar's tomb-centered ceremonies are times when the living and the dead are joyously reunited, when people get drunk, gorge themselves, and have sexual license. Perhaps the gray, sober, ascetic, and moralistic aspects of many official religious events, in taking the fun out of religion, force some, indeed many, people to find religion (i.e., truth, beauty, meaning, passionate involvement) in fun.

# Summary

1. Given the varied and worldwide scope of beliefs and behavior labeled "religious," anthropologists recognize the difficulty of defining religion. Religion, a cultural universal, consists of beliefs and behavior concerned with supernatural beings, powers, and forces. Religion also encompasses the feelings, meanings, and congregations associated with such beliefs and behavior. Religious worlds are real, vivid, and significant to those who construct and inhabit them. Anthropological studies have revealed many forms, expressions, and functions of religion.

2. Tylor considered animism—the belief in spirits or souls—to be religion's earliest and most basic form. He focused on religion's explanatory role, arguing that religion would eventually disappear as science provided better explanations. Besides animism, another view of the supernatural also occurs in nonindustrial societies, seeing the supernatural as a domain of raw, impersonal power or force (called mana in Polynesia and Melanesia). People can manipulate and control mana under certain conditions.

3. When ordinary technical and rational means of doing things fail, people may turn to magic. Often they use magic when they lack control over outcomes. Religion offers comfort and psychological security at times of crisis. On the other hand, rites can also create anxiety. Rituals are formal, invariant, stylized, earnest acts in which people subordinate their beliefs to a social collectivity. Rites of passage have three stages: separation, liminality, and incorporation. Such rites can mark any change in social status, age, place, or social condition. Collective rites are often cemented by communitas, a feeling of intense solidarity.

4. Religion establishes and maintains social control through a series of moral and ethical beliefs and real and imagined rewards and punishments, internalized in individuals. Religion also achieves social control by mobilizing its members for collective action.

5. Religions exist in particular societies, and cultural differences show up systematically in religious beliefs and practices. The ecclesiastical and monotheistic religions of stratified, state societies, for example, differ from those of societies that lack hierarchies and specialized officials. The world's major religions vary in their growth rates, with Islam expanding more rapidly than Christianity.

6. Religion helps maintain social order, but it also can promote change. Cargo cults are revitalization movements that hybridize beliefs and that have helped people adapt to changing conditions. Among contemporary "new" religious movements, some have been influenced by Christianity, others by Eastern (Asian) religions, still others by mysticism and spiritualism or by science and technology.

7. The spread of Evangelical/Pentecostal Protestantism worldwide illustrates contemporary cultural globalization. Evangelical Protestantism stresses conservative morality, the authority of the Bible, and a personal ("born-again") conversion experience. To people who feel socially adrift, Pentecostalism offers tightly knit communities and a weblike structure of personal connections. Antimodernism is the rejection of the modern, including globalization, in favor of what is perceived

as an earlier, purer, and better way of life. Religious fundamentalism describes antimodernist movements in Christianity, Islam, and Judaism. The rapid spread of Islam also illustrates cultural globalization and hybridization. Although certain core features endure, local people always assign their own meanings to the messages and social forms they receive from outside, including religion. The processes of hybridization and indigenization are always associated with cultural diffusion and globalization.

8. There are secular as well as religious rituals. It is possible for apparently secular settings, things, and events to acquire intense meaning for individuals who have grown up in their presence.

## Key Terms

animism, *346*
cargo cults, *355*
communitas, *344*
liminality, *348*
magic, *347*
mana, *346*
monotheism, *346*
polytheism, *346*
religion, *343*
revitalization
  movements, *355*
rites of
  passage, *348*
rituals, *347*
shaman, *345*
taboo, *346*
totem, *351*

# Chapter 16

# Ethnicity and Race

Ethnicity is based on cultural similarities (with members of the same ethnic group) and differences (between that group and others) in a society or nation. Ethnic groups must deal with other such groups in the nation or region they inhabit. Interethnic relations are important in the study of any nation or region, especially because of contemporary and recent international migration (see Marger 2015; Parillo 2016). (Table 16.1 lists American ethnic groups, based on U.S. Census Bureau estimates for 2013.)

## Ethnic Groups and Ethnicity

As with any cultural identity, members of an **ethnic group** *share* certain beliefs, values, habits, customs, and norms because of their common background. They define themselves as different and special because of cultural features. This distinction may arise from language, religion, historical experience, geographic placement, kinship, or "race" (see Spickard 2012). Markers of an ethnic group may include a collective name, belief in common descent, a sense of solidarity, and an association with a specific territory, which the group may or may not hold.

TABLE 16.1   **Racial/Ethnic Identification in the United States, 2013 (as reported by the U.S. Census Bureau's American Community Survey)**

Source: http://factfinder.census.gov/faces/nav/jsf/pages/searchresults.xhtml?refresh=t.

| Claimed Identity | Number (millions) | Percentage |
|---|---|---|
| White (non-Hispanic) | 193.8 | 61.3 |
| Hispanic | 54.0 | 17.1 |
| Black | 39.9 | 12.6 |
| Asian | 16.0 | 5.1 |
| American Indian | 2.5 | 0.8 |
| Pacific Islander | 0.5 | 0.1 |
| Two or more races | 9.4 | 3.0 |
| Total population | 316.1 | 100.0 |

Ethnicity can be said to exist when people claim a certain ethnic identity for themselves and are defined by others as having that identity (Barth 1969). **Ethnicity** means identification with, and feeling part of, an ethnic group and exclusion from certain other groups because of this affiliation. Ethnic feelings and associated behavior vary in intensity within ethnic groups and countries and over time. A change in the degree of importance attached to an ethnic identity may reflect political changes (Soviet rule ends—ethnic feeling rises) or individual life-cycle changes (old people relinquish, or young people reclaim, an ethnic background).

## Shifting Status

Ethnicity is only one basis for group identity. Cultural differences also may be associated with class, region, or religion. Individuals often have more than one group identity. People may be loyal (depending on circumstances) to their neighborhood, school, town, state or province, region, nation, continent, religion, ethnic group, or interest group. People constantly negotiate their social identities. All of us "wear different hats," presenting ourselves sometimes as one thing, sometimes as another.

Sometimes our identities (social statuses) are mutually exclusive. It's hard to be both Black and White, male and female. Sometimes, assuming an identity or joining a group requires a conversion experience, acquiring a new and overwhelming primary identity, such as becoming a "born-again" Christian.

Some statuses aren't mutually exclusive but contextual. People can be both Black and Hispanic or both a mother and a senator. One identity is used in certain settings, another in different ones. We call this the *situational negotiation of social identity* Members of an ethnic group sometimes shift their ethnic identities. Hispanics, for example, may use different ethnic labels (e.g., "Cuban" or "Latino") to describe themselves depending on context. In a study reported in 2012, half (51 percent) of American Hispanics surveyed preferred to identify using their family's country of origin (as in "Mexican," "Cuban," or "Dominican") rather than "Hispanic" or "Latino." Just one-quarter (24 percent) chose one of those two pan-ethnic terms, while 21 percent said they use the term "American" most often (Taylor et al. 2012). Latinos of different national origins may mobilize to

**TABLE 16.2**
**National Origins of American Hispanics, Latinos, 2013**

Source: U.S. Census Bureau. Facts for Features: Hispanic Heritage Month 2014: Sept. 15-Oct. 15, September 8, 2014. http://www.census.gov/newsroom/facts-for-features/2014/cb14-ff22.htm.

| National Origin | Percentage |
|---|---|
| Mexican American | 64.0 |
| Puerto Rican | 9.4 |
| Salvadoran | 3.8 |
| Cuban | 3.7 |
| Dominican | 3.1 |
| Guatemalan | 2.3 |
| Other Hispanic/Latino origin | 13.7 |
| Total | 100.0 |

promote general Hispanic issues (e.g., opposition to "English-only" laws), while acting as separate interest groups in other contexts.

Among Hispanics, Cuban Americans are richer on average than Mexican Americans and Puerto Ricans, and their class interests and voting patterns differ. Cubans are more likely to vote Republican than are Puerto Ricans and Mexican Americans. Some Mexican Americans whose families have lived in the United States for generations have little in common with new Hispanic immigrants, such as those from Central America.

Hispanics represent the fastest-growing ethnic group in the United States, increasing from 35 million people in 2000 to 54 million in 2013. "Hispanic" is a category based mainly on language. It includes Whites, Blacks, and "racially" mixed Spanish speakers and their ethnically conscious descendants. (There also are Native American and even Asian Hispanics.) The label "Hispanic" lumps together people of diverse geographic origin—Mexico, Puerto Rico, Cuba, El Salvador, Guatemala, Honduras, the Dominican Republic, and other Spanish-speaking countries of Central and South America and the Caribbean. "Latino" is a broader category, which also can include Brazilians (who speak Portuguese). Table 16.2 shows the national origins of Hispanics/Latinos in the contemporary U.S. population.

## Minority Groups and Stratification

In many societies an ascribed status is associated with a position in the social-political hierarchy. Certain groups, called *minority groups,* are subordinate. They have inferior power and less secure access to resources than do *majority groups* (which are superordinate, dominant, or controlling). Often ethnic groups are minorities.

Minority groups are obvious features of stratification in the United States, and the disparity between upper and lower strata has been increasing. The 2013 *poverty rate* (14.5 percent overall) was 9.6 percent for non-Hispanic Whites, 10.5 percent for Asian Americans, 23.5 percent for Hispanics, and 27.2 percent for African Americans (DeNavas-Walt and Proctor 2014). Inequality shows up consistently in unemployment figures and in median household *income*. Median household incomes in 2013 were as follows: $67,065 for Asian Americans, $58,270 for non-Hispanic Whites, $40,963 for Hispanics, and $34,598 for African Americans (DeNavas-Walt and Proctor 2014). The median *wealth* (net worth) of White households (consisting of property, investments, and other assets) was 13 times that of Black households in 2013, compared with 8 times in 2010.

"Hispanic" and "Latino" are ethnic categories that cross-cut "racial" contrasts such as between "Black" and "White." Note the physical diversity among these children in Trinidad, Cuba. © Paul Bucknall/Alamy

Similarly, White household wealth is 10 times that of Hispanic households, compared with 9 times in 2010. The current gap between Blacks and Whites has reached its highest point since 1989, when Whites had 17 times the wealth of Black households (Kochhar and Fry 2014).

## Race and Ethnicity

When an ethnic group is assumed to have a biological basis (distinctively shared "blood" or genes), it is called a **race.** Discrimination against such a group is called **racism** (Gotkowitz 2011; Kuper 2006; Scupin 2012). Race, like ethnicity in general, is a cultural category rather than a biological reality. That is, ethnic groups, including "races," derive from contrasts perceived and perpetuated in particular societies, rather than from scientific classifications based on common genes.

It is not possible to define human races biologically. Only cultural constructions of race are possible—even though the average person conceptualizes "race" in biological terms. Most Americans, for example, believe (incorrectly) that their population includes biologically based races to which various labels can be applied. These labels include "White," "Black," "yellow," "red," "Caucasoid," "Negroid," "Mongoloid," "Amerindian," "Euro-American," "African American," "Asian American," and "Native American."

In American culture, we hear the words *ethnicity* and *race* frequently, without clear distinctions made between them. Consider a speech once delivered by Sonia Sotomayor, then an appeals court judge, now a justice of the United States Supreme Court. In a 2001 lecture titled "A Latina Judge's Voice," delivered at the University of California, Berkeley, School of Law, Sotomayor declared (as part of a much longer speech):

> I would hope that a wise Latina woman with the richness of her experiences would more often than not reach a better conclusion than a white male who hasn't lived that life. (Sotomayor 2001/2009)

Conservatives, including former House speaker Newt Gingrich and radio talk show host Rush Limbaugh, seized on this declaration as evidence that Sotomayor was a "racist" or a "reverse racist." However, "Latina" is actually an ethnic (and gendered-female) rather than a racial category. I suspect that Sotomayor also was using "white male" as an ethnic-gender category, to refer to nonminority men.

Examples like this one illustrate the difficulty in drawing a precise distinction between race and ethnicity (see Ansell 2013). It probably is better to use the term *ethnic group* rather than *race* to describe *any* such social group, for example, African Americans, Asian Americans, Anglo Americans, Hispanics, Latinos, Latinas, and even non-Hispanic Whites.

# The Social Construction of Race

The "races" we hear about every day are cultural, or social, rather than biological categories. There is no clear genetic difference between people commonly regarded as being of different races.

## Hypodescent: Race in the United States

In American culture, one acquires one's racial identity at birth, as an ascribed status, but race isn't based on biology or on simple ancestry. Take the case of the child of a "racially mixed" marriage involving one Black and one White parent. We know that 50 percent of the child's genes come from one parent and 50 percent from the other. Still, American culture overlooks heredity and classifies this child as Black. This rule is arbitrary. On the basis of genotype (genetic composition), it would be just as logical to classify the child as White.

American rules for assigning racial status can be even more arbitrary. In some states, anyone known to have any Black ancestor, no matter how remote, is classified as a member of the Black race. This is a rule of **descent** (it assigns social identity on the basis of ancestry), but of a sort that is rare outside the contemporary United States. It is called **hypodescent** (Harris and Kottak 1963), because it automatically places the children of a union between members of different groups in the minority group (*hypo* means "lower"). Hypodescent divides American society into groups that have been unequal in their access to wealth, power, and prestige.

The rule of hypodescent affects Blacks, Asians, Native Americans, and Hispanics differently (see Hunter 2005). It's easier to negotiate Native American or Hispanic identity than Black identity. The ascription rule isn't as definite, and the assumption of a biological basis isn't as strong. To be considered Native American, one ancestor out of eight (great-grandparents) or out of four (grandparents) may suffice. This depends on whether the assignment is by federal or state law or by a Native American tribal council.

An international and multiethnic American family. Joakim Noah, center, is an All-Star professional basketball player, who played in college for the Florida Gators. Also shown are his mother, a former Miss Sweden, and father, a French singer and tennis player who won the French Open in 1983. Joakim's grandfather, Zacharie Noah, was a professional soccer player from the African nation of Cameroon. What is Joakim Noah's race? © Matt Marton/AP Images

The child of a Hispanic may (or may not, depending on context) claim Hispanic identity. Many Americans with a Native American or Latino grandparent consider themselves White and lay no claim to minority group status.

## Race in the Census

The U.S. Census Bureau has gathered data by race since 1790. Figure 16.1 shows that the 2010 census asked about both race and Hispanic origin. What do you think of the racial categories included?

Attempts to add a "multiracial" category to the U.S. Census have been opposed by the National Association for the Advancement of Colored People (NAACP) and the National Council of La Raza (a Hispanic advocacy group). Racial classification is a political issue involving access to resources, including jobs, voting districts, and federal funding of programs aimed at minorities. The hypodescent rule results in all the population growth being attributed to the minority category. Minorities fear their political clout will decline if their numbers go down.

But things are changing. Choice of "some other race" in the U.S. Census tripled from 1980 (6.8 million) to 2010 (over 19 million)—suggesting imprecision in and dissatisfaction with the existing categories. In the 2000 census, 2.4 percent of Americans—almost 7 million people—chose a first-ever option of identifying themselves as belonging to two or more races. This figure rose to 2.9 percent in the 2010 census. The number of interracial marriages and children is increasing, with implications for the traditional system of American racial classification. "Interracial," "biracial," or "multiracial" children who grow up with both parents undoubtedly identify with particular qualities of either parent. It is troubling for many of them to have so important an identity as race dictated by the arbitrary rule of hypodescent. It may be especially discordant when racial identity doesn't parallel gender identity, for instance, a boy with a White father and a Black mother or a girl with a White mother and a Black father.

Rather than race, the Canadian census asks about "visible minorities." That country's Employment Equity Act defines such groups as "persons, other than Aboriginal peoples

FIGURE 16.1    **Questions on Race and Hispanic Origin from U.S. Census 2010**

Source: U.S. Census Bureau, Census 2010 questionnaire.

**5.** **Is this person of Hispanic, Latino, or Spanish origin?**

☐ No, not of Hispanic, Latino, or Spanish origin
☐ Yes, Mexican, Mexican Am., Chicano
☐ Yes, Puerto Rican
☐ Yes, Cuban
☐ Yes, another Hispanic, Latino, or Spanish origin — *Print origin, for example, Argentinean, Colombian, Dominican, Nicaraguan, Salvadoran, Spaniard, and so on.* ↗

[ ][ ][ ][ ][ ][ ][ ][ ][ ][ ][ ][ ][ ][ ][ ][ ][ ][ ][ ][ ][ ][ ][ ]

**6.** **What is this person's race?** *Mark* ☒ *one or more boxes.*

☐ White
☐ Black, African Am., or Negro
☐ American Indian or Alaska Native — *Print name of enrolled or principal tribe.* ↗

[ ][ ][ ][ ][ ][ ][ ][ ][ ][ ][ ][ ][ ][ ][ ][ ][ ][ ][ ][ ][ ][ ][ ]

☐ Asian Indian      ☐ Japanese      ☐ Native Hawaiian
☐ Chinese           ☐ Korean        ☐ Guamanian or Chamorro
☐ Filipino          ☐ Vietnamese    ☐ Samoan
☐ Other Asian — *Print race, for*           ☐ Other Pacific Islander — *Print*
   *example, Hmong, Laotian, Thai,*             *race, for example, Fijian, Tongan,*
   *Pakistani, Cambodian, and so on.* ↗          *and so on.* ↗

[ ][ ][ ][ ][ ][ ][ ][ ][ ][ ][ ][ ][ ][ ][ ][ ][ ][ ][ ][ ][ ][ ][ ]

☐ Some other race — *Print race.* ↗

[ ][ ][ ][ ][ ][ ][ ][ ][ ][ ][ ][ ][ ][ ][ ][ ][ ][ ][ ][ ][ ][ ][ ]

[First Nations in Canada], who are non-Caucasian in race or non-white in colour" (Statistics Canada 2001). "South Asian" and "Chinese" are Canada's largest visible minorities (see Figure 16.2). Canada's visible minority population of 19.1 percent in 2011 (up from 11.2 percent in 1996) contrasts with a figure of 39 percent for the United States in 2013 (up from 25 percent in 2000).

As in the United States, Canada's visible minority population has been growing much faster than the country's overall population. In 1981, visible minorities accounted for just 4.7 percent of the Canadian population, versus 19.1 percent in 2011 (the most

**FIGURE 16.2**

**Visible Minority Population of Canada, 2011 National Household Survey**

Source: From Statistics Canada, 2011 National Household Survey. http://www12.statcan. gc.ca/nhs-enm/2011/as-sa/ 99-010-x/99-010-x2011001-eng. cfm#a4.

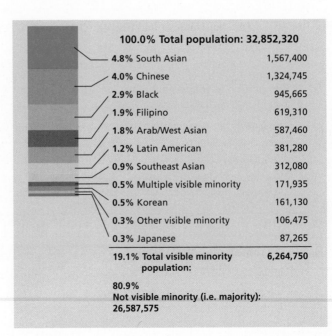

| | 100.0% Total population: 32,852,320 | |
|---|---|---|
| | 4.8% South Asian | 1,567,400 |
| | 4.0% Chinese | 1,324,745 |
| | 2.9% Black | 945,665 |
| | 1.9% Filipino | 619,310 |
| | 1.8% Arab/West Asian | 587,460 |
| | 1.2% Latin American | 381,280 |
| | 0.9% Southeast Asian | 312,080 |
| | 0.5% Multiple visible minority | 171,935 |
| | 0.5% Korean | 161,130 |
| | 0.3% Other visible minority | 106,475 |
| | 0.3% Japanese | 87,265 |
| | 19.1% Total visible minority population: | 6,264,750 |

80.9%
Not visible minority (i.e. majority):
26,587,575

recent data available as of this writing). Between 2006 and 2011, Canada's total population increased 5 percent, while visible minorities rose 24 percent. If recent immigration trends continue, by 2031 visible minorities will comprise almost one-third (31 percent) of the Canadian population (Statistics Canada 2010).

## Not Us: Race in Japan

Outsiders often see Japan as a nation that is homogeneous in race, ethnicity, language, and culture—an image the Japanese themselves cultivate. Scholars estimate, however, that 10 percent of Japan's national population are minorities of various sorts (Weiner 2009). These include aboriginal Ainu, annexed Okinawans, outcast *burakumin,* children of mixed marriages, and immigrant nationalities, especially Koreans, who number more than 700,000 (Graburn et al. 2008; Ryang and Lie 2009).

How is race culturally constructed in Japan? The (majority) Japanese define themselves by opposition to others, whether minority groups in their own nation or outsiders—anyone who is "not us." The "not us" should stay that way; assimilation generally is discouraged. Cultural mechanisms, especially residential segregation and taboos on "interracial" marriage, work to keep minorities "in their place."

In its construction of race, Japanese culture regards certain ethnic groups as having a biological basis, when there is no evidence that they do. The best example is the *burakumin,* a stigmatized group of at least 4 million outcasts, sometimes compared to India's untouchables (see Amos 2011). The burakumin are physically and genetically indistinguishable from other Japanese. Many of them "pass" as (and marry) majority Japanese, but a deceptive marriage can end in divorce if burakumin identity is discovered.

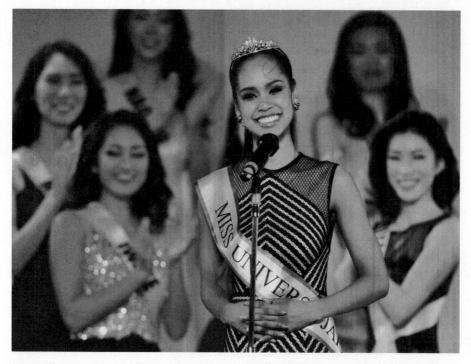

Ariana Miyamoto, the daughter of a Japanese woman and an African-American man, was crowned Miss Universe Japan in March, 2015. Soon thereafter, complaints emerged on social media that she did not look "Japanese enough" to represent Japan in an international beauty competition. Over 3 percent of new marriages in Japan each year are now international, and almost two percent of children born in Japan are biracial. © Kyodo via AP Images

Burakumin are perceived as standing apart from majority Japanese. Based on their ancestry (and thus, it is assumed, their "blood" or genetics), burakumin are considered "not us." Majority Japanese try to keep their lineage pure by discouraging mixing. The burakumin are residentially segregated in neighborhoods (rural or urban) called *buraku,* from which the racial label is derived. Compared with majority Japanese, the burakumin are less likely to attend high school and college. When burakumin attend the same schools as majority Japanese, they face discrimination. Majority children and teachers may refuse to eat with them, because burakumin are considered unclean.

In applying for university admission or a job and in dealing with the government, Japanese must list their address, which becomes part of a household or family registry. This list makes residence in a buraku, and likely burakumin social status, evident. Schools and companies use this information to discriminate. (The best way to pass is to move so often that the buraku address eventually disappears from the registry.) Majority Japanese also limit "race" mixture by hiring marriage mediators to check out the family histories of prospective spouses. They are especially careful to check for burakumin ancestry (De Vos, Wetherall, and Stearman 1983).

The origin of the burakumin lies in a historical, tiered system of stratification (from the Tokugawa period—1603–1868). The top four ranked categories were warrior-administrators (*samurai*), farmers, artisans, and merchants. The ancestors of the burakumin were below this hierarchy, an outcast group who did unclean jobs such as animal slaughter and disposal of the dead. Burakumin still do similar jobs, including work with leather and other animal products. The burakumin are more likely than majority Japanese to do manual labor (including farm work) and to belong to the national lower class. Burakumin and other Japanese minorities also are more likely to have careers in crime, prostitution, entertainment, and sports (Amos 2011).

Like Blacks in the United States, the burakumin are class-stratified. Because certain jobs are reserved for the burakumin, people who are successful in those occupations (e.g., shoe factory owners) can be wealthy. Burakumin also have found jobs as government bureaucrats. Financially successful burakumin can temporarily escape their stigmatized status by travel, including foreign travel.

Discrimination against the burakumin is strikingly like the discrimination that Blacks have experienced in the United States. The burakumin often live in villages and neighborhoods with poor housing and sanitation. They have limited access to education, jobs, amenities, and health facilities. In response to burakumin political mobilization, Japan has dismantled the legal structure of discrimination against burakumin and has worked to improve conditions in the buraku. Still Japan has yet to institute American-style affirmative action programs for education and jobs. Discrimination against nonmajority Japanese is still the rule in companies. Some employers say that hiring burakumin would give their company an unclean image and thus create a disadvantage in competing with other businesses.

## Phenotype and Fluidity: Race in Brazil

There are more flexible, less exclusionary ways of socially constructing race than those used in the United States and Japan. Along with the rest of Latin America, Brazil has less exclusionary categories, which permit individuals to change their racial classification. Brazil shares a history of slavery with the United States, but it lacks the hypodescent rule.

Brazilians use many more racial labels—over 500 were once reported (Harris 1970)—than Americans or Japanese do. In northeastern Brazil, I found 40 different racial terms in use in Arembepe, then a village of only 750 people (Kottak 2006). Through their traditional classification system Brazilians recognize and attempt to describe the physical variation that exists in their population. The system used in the United States, by recognizing only a few races, blinds Americans to an equivalent range of evident physical contrasts. The system Brazilians use to construct social race has other special features. In the United States one's race is an ascribed status; it is assigned automatically by hypodescent and usually doesn't change. In Brazil racial identity is more flexible, more of an achieved status. Brazilian racial classification pays attention to phenotype. *Phenotype* refers to an organism's evident traits, its "manifest biology"—physiology and anatomy, including skin color, hair form, facial features, and eye color. A Brazilian's phenotype and racial label may change because of environmental factors, such as the tanning rays of the sun or the effects of humidity on the hair.

A Brazilian can change his or her "race" (say from "Indian" to "mixed") by changing his or her manner of dress, language, location (e.g., rural to urban), and even attitude (e.g., by adopting urban behavior). Two racial/ethnic labels used in Brazil are *indio* (indigenous, Native American) and *cabôclo* (someone who "looks *indio*" but wears modern clothing and participates in Brazilian culture, rather than living in an indigenous community). Similar shifts in racial/ethnic classification occur in other parts of Latin America, for example, Guatemala (see Wade 2010). The perception of biological race is influenced not just by the physical phenotype but also by how one dresses and behaves.

Furthermore, racial differences in Brazil may be so insignificant in structuring community life that people may forget the terms they have applied to others. Sometimes they even forget the ones they've used for themselves. In Arembepe, I made it a habit to ask the same person on different days to tell me the races of others in the village (and my own). In the United States I am always "White" or "Euro-American," but in Arembepe I got lots of terms besides *branco* ("White"). I could be *claro* ("light"), *louro* ("blond"), *sarará* ("light-skinned redhead"), *mulato claro* ("light mulatto"), or *mulato* ("mulatto"). The racial term used to describe me or anyone else varied from person to person, week to week, even day to day. My best informant, a man with very dark skin color, changed the term he used for himself all the time—from *escuro* ("dark") to *preto* ("Black") to *moreno escuro* ("dark brunet").

For centuries the United States and Brazil have had mixed populations, with ancestors from Native America, Europe, Africa, and Asia. Although races have mixed in both countries, Brazilian and American cultures have constructed the results differently. The historical reasons for this contrast lie mainly in the different characteristics of the settlers of the two countries. The mainly English early settlers of the United States came as women, men, and families, but Brazil's Portuguese colonizers were mainly men— merchants and adventurers. Many of these Portuguese men married Native American women and recognized their racially mixed children as their heirs. Like their North American counterparts, Brazilian plantation owners had sexual relations with their slaves. But the Brazilian landlords more often freed the children that resulted—for demographic and economic reasons. (Sometimes these were their only children.) Freed offspring of master and slave became plantation overseers and foremen and filled many intermediate positions in the emerging Brazilian economy. They were not classed with the slaves, but were allowed to join a new intermediate category. No hypodescent rule developed in Brazil to ensure that Whites and Blacks remained separate (see Degler 1970; Harris 1964).

In today's world system, Brazil's system of racial classification is changing in the context of international identity politics and rights movements. Just as more and more Brazilians claim indigenous (Native Brazilian) identities, an increasing number now assert their Blackness and self-conscious membership in the African diaspora. Particularly in such northeastern Brazilian states as Bahia, where African demographic and cultural influence is strong, public universities have instituted affirmative action programs aimed at indigenous peoples and especially at Blacks. Racial identities firm up in the context of international (e.g., pan-African and pan-Indian) mobilization and access to strategic resources based on race.

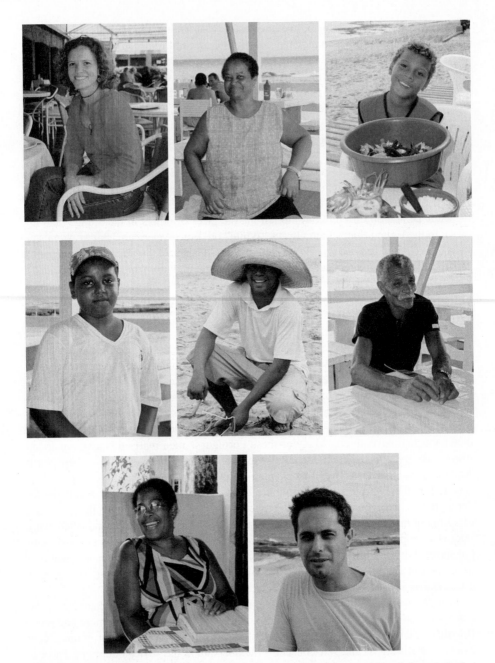

These photos, taken by the author in Brazil, give just a glimpse of the spectrum of phenotypical diversity encountered among contemporary Brazilians. © Conrad P. Kottak

# Ethnic Groups, Nations, and Nationalities

The term **nation** once was synonymous with *tribe* or *ethnic group*. All three of these terms have been used to refer to a single culture sharing a single language, religion, history, territory, ancestry, and kinship. Thus, one could speak interchangeably of the Seneca (Native American) nation, tribe, or ethnic group. Now *nation* has come to mean state—an independent, centrally organized political unit, or a government. *Nation* and *state* have become synonymous. Combined in **nation-state** they refer to an autonomous political entity, a country—like the United States, "one nation, indivisible" (see Farner, ed. 2004; Gellner 1997).

Because of migration, conquest, and colonialism, most nation-states are not ethnically homogeneous. A 2003 study by James Fearon found that about 70 percent of all countries have an ethnic group that forms an absolute majority of the population; the average population share of such groups is 65 percent. The average size of the *second* largest group, or largest ethnic minority, is 17 percent. Only 18 percent of all countries, including Brazil and Japan, have a single ethnic group that accounts for 90 percent or more of its population.

There is substantial regional variation in countries' ethnic structures. Strong states, particularly in Europe (e.g., France), have deliberately and actively worked to homogenize their diverse premodern populations to a common national identity and culture (see Beriss 2004; Gellner 1983). Although countries with no ethnic majority are fairly rare in the rest of the world, this is the norm in Africa. The average African country has a plurality group of about 22 percent, with the second largest slightly less than this. Rwanda, Burundi, Lesotho, Swaziland, and Zimbabwe are exceptions; each has a large majority group and a minority that makes up almost all the rest of the population. Botswana has a large majority (the Tswana) and a set of smaller minorities (Fearon 2003).

Most Latin American and Caribbean countries contain a majority group (speaking a European language, such as Portuguese in Brazil, Spanish in Argentina) and a single minority group—"indigenous peoples." "Indigenous peoples" is a catch-all category encompassing several small Native American tribes or remnants. Exceptions are Guatemala and the Andean countries of Bolivia, Peru, and Ecuador, with large indigenous populations (see Gotkowitz 2011; Wade 2010).

Most countries in Asia and the Middle East/North Africa have ethnic majorities. The Asian countries of Myanmar, Laos, Vietnam, and Thailand contain a large lowland majority edged by more fragmented mountain folk. Several oil-producing countries in the Middle East, including Saudi Arabia, Bahrain, United Arab Emirates, Oman, and Kuwait, contain an ethnically homogeneous group of citizens who form either a plurality or a bare majority; the rest of the population consists of ethnically diverse noncitizen workers. Several countries in the Middle East/North Africa contain two principal ethnic or ethnoreligious groups: Arabs and Berbers in Morocco, Algeria, Libya, and Tunisia; Muslims and Copts in Egypt; Turks and Kurds in Turkey; Greeks and Turks in Cyprus; and Palestinians and TransJordan Arabs in Jordan (Fearon 2003).

## Nationalities and Imagined Communities

Ethnic groups that once had, or wish to have or regain, autonomous political status (their own country) are called **nationalities.** In the words of Benedict Anderson (1991/2006), they are "imagined communities." Even when they become nation-states, they remain imagined communities because most of their members, though feeling comradeship, will never meet (Anderson 1991, pp. 6–10). They can only imagine they all participate in the same unit.

Anderson traces Western European nationalism, which arose in imperial powers such as England, France, and Spain, back to the 18th century. Over time, political upheavals, wars, and migration have divided many imagined national communities that arose in the 18th and 19th centuries. The German and Korean homelands were artificially divided after wars, according to communist and capitalist ideologies. World War I split the Kurds, who remain an imagined community, forming a majority in no state. Kurds are a minority group in Turkey, Iran, Iraq, and Syria.

In creating multitribal and multiethnic states, colonialism often erected boundaries that corresponded poorly with preexisting cultural divisions. But colonial institutions also helped create new "imagined communities" beyond nations. A good example is the idea of *négritude* ("Black identity") developed by African intellectuals in Francophone (French-speaking) West Africa. Négritude can be traced to the association and common experience in colonial times of youths from Guinea, Mali, Ivory Coast, and Senegal at the William Ponty school in Dakar, Senegal (Anderson 1991, pp. 123–124).

# Ethnic Tolerance and Accommodation

Ethnic diversity may be associated with either positive group interaction and coexistence, or with conflict (see the section "Roots of Ethnic Conflict"). There are nation-states in which multiple cultural groups live together in reasonable harmony, including some less-developed countries.

## Assimilation

**Assimilation** describes the process of change that a minority ethnic group may experience when it moves to a country where another culture dominates. By assimilating, the minority adopts the patterns and norms of its host culture. It is incorporated into the dominant culture to the point that it no longer exists as a separate cultural unit. Some countries, such as Brazil, are more assimilationist than others. Germans, Italians, Japanese, Middle Easterners, and East Europeans started migrating to Brazil late in the 19th century. These immigrants have assimilated to a common Brazilian culture, which has Portuguese, African, and Native American roots. The descendants of these immigrants speak the national language (Portuguese) and participate in the national culture. (During World War II, Brazil, which was on the Allied side, forced assimilation by banning instruction in any language other than Portuguese—especially in German.)

## The Plural Society

Assimilation isn't inevitable, and there can be ethnic harmony without it. Ethnic distinctions can persist despite generations of interethnic contact. Through a study of three ethnic groups in Swat, Pakistan, Fredrik Barth (1958/1968) challenged an old idea that interaction always leads to assimilation. He showed that ethnic groups can be in contact for generations without assimilating. Barth (1958/1968, p. 324) defines **plural society** as a society combining ethnic contrasts, ecological specialization (i.e., use of different environmental resources by each ethnic group), and the economic interdependence of those groups.

In Barth's view, ethnic boundaries are most stable and enduring when the groups occupy different ecological niches. That is, they make their living in different ways and don't compete. Ideally, they should depend on each other's activities and exchange with one another. When different ethnic groups exploit the *same* ecological niche, the militarily more powerful group will normally replace the weaker one. If they exploit more or less the same niche, but the weaker group is better able to use marginal environments, they also may coexist (Barth 1958/1968, p. 331). Given niche specialization, ethnic boundaries and interdependence can be maintained, although the specific cultural features of each group may change. By shifting the analytic focus from individual cultures or ethnic groups to *relationships* between cultures or ethnic groups, Barth (1958/1968, 1969) has made important contributions to ethnic studies (see also Kamrava 2011).

## Multiculturalism

The view of cultural diversity in a country as something good and desirable is called **multiculturalism** (see Kottak and Kozaitis 2012). The multicultural model is the opposite of the assimilationist model, in which minorities are expected to abandon their cultural traditions and values, replacing them with those of the majority population. The multicultural view encourages the practice of cultural–ethnic traditions. A multicultural society socializes individuals not only into the dominant (national) culture but also into an ethnic culture. Thus, in the United States today millions of people speak both English and another language, eat both "American" (apple pie, steak, hamburgers) and "ethnic" foods, and celebrate both national (July 4, Thanksgiving) and ethnic–religious holidays.

Multiculturalism seeks ways for people to understand and interact that don't depend on sameness but rather on respect for differences. Multiculturalism stresses the interaction of ethnic groups and their contribution to the country. It assumes that each group has something to offer to and learn from the others. Several forces have propelled North America away from the assimilationist model toward multiculturalism. First, multiculturalism reflects the fact of recent large-scale migration, particularly from the "less-developed countries" to the "developed" nations of North America and Western Europe. The global scale of modern migration introduces unparalleled ethnic variety to host nations. Multiculturalism is related to globalization: People use modern means of transportation to migrate to nations whose lifestyles they learn about through the media and from tourists who increasingly visit their own countries (see Inda and Rosaldo 2008).

Migration also is fueled by rapid population growth, coupled with insufficient jobs (both for educated and uneducated people), in the less-developed countries. As traditional rural economies decline or mechanize, displaced farmers move to cities, where they and their children often are unable to find jobs. As people in the less-developed countries get better educations, they seek more skilled employment. They hope to partake of an international culture of consumption that includes such modern amenities as refrigerators, televisions, and automobiles.

## Changing Demographics

In October 2006, the population of the United States reached 300 million people, just 39 years after reaching 200 million and 91 years after reaching the 100 million mark (in 1915). Consider how much the country's ethnic composition has changed in the past 50 or so years. The 1970 census, the first to attempt an official count of Hispanics, found they represented no more than 4.7 percent of the American population. By 2013 this figure had risen to 17.1 percent—some 54 million Hispanics. The number of African Americans grew from 11.1 percent in 1967 to 12.6 percent in 2013, while (non-Hispanic) Whites ("Anglos") declined from 83 to 61.37 percent. In 1967 fewer than 10 million people in the United States (5 percent of the population) had been born elsewhere, compared with more than 41 million foreign born today (13 percent) (all data from U.S. Census Bureau). In 2011, for the first time in American history, minorities (including Hispanics, Blacks, Asians, Native Americans, and those of mixed race) accounted for more than half (50.4 percent) of all births in the United States (Tavernise 2012).

In 1973, 78 percent of the students in American public schools were White, and 22 percent were minorities: Blacks, Hispanics, Asians, Pacific Islanders, and "others." During the 2014–2015 school year, the percentage of public school students who are White fell below 50 percent—to 49.7 percent—for the first time (Dillon 2006; Strauss 2014).

Immigration, mainly from southern and eastern Europe, had a similar effect on classroom diversity, at least in the largest American cities, a century ago. A study of American public schools in 1908–1909 found that only 42 percent of those urban students were native born, while 58 percent were immigrants. In a very different context (multicultural now versus assimilationist then), today's American classrooms have regained the ethnic diversity they demonstrated in the early 1900s, when my German-speaking Austro-Hungarian-born father and grandparents immigrated to the United States.

### The Gray and the Brown

Drawing on a 2010 Brookings Institution report titled "State of Metropolitan America: On the Front Lines of Demographic Transformation," Ronald Brownstein (2010) analyzes an intensifying confrontation between groups he describes as "the gray and the brown." Brownstein and demographer William Frey, an author of the Brookings report, focus on two key U.S. demographic trends:

1. Ethnic/racial diversity is increasing, especially among the young.
2. The country is aging, and most of the senior population is White.

Note the ethnic diversity between generations in this recent American photo. © James Marshall/Corbis

Frey (in Brookings Institution 2010, pp. 26, 63) sees these trends as creating a "cultural generation gap"—a sharp contrast in the attitudes, priorities, and political leanings of younger and older Americans. Whites now constitute 80 percent of older Americans, but less than 55 percent of children.

Politically the two groups—the gray (older) and the brown (younger)—are poles apart. The aging White population appears increasingly resistant to taxes and public spending, while younger people and minorities value government support of education, health, and social welfare. In the 2008 and 2012 elections, young people, especially minorities, strongly supported President Barack Obama. Seniors, especially White ones, voted solidly for Republicans John McCain and Mitt Romney. These differences have persisted thereafter in measures of approval for President Obama's job performance— consistently highest among non-Whites and young people.

The gray and the brown are more interdependent economically than either usually realizes. If minority children benefit disproportionately from public education today, minority workers will pay a growing share of the payroll taxes needed to sustain Social Security and Medicare in the future. These are government programs that most directly benefit old White people.

The history of U.S. national immigration policy helps us understand how the gap between the gray and the brown arose. Federal policies established in the 1920s severely curtailed immigration from areas other than northern Europe. In 1965, Congress loosened restrictions—resulting in an eventual influx of immigrants from southern Europe, Asia, Africa, the Caribbean, and Latin America (see Vigil 2012).

Non-Hispanic Whites constituted the overwhelming majority of Americans through the mid–20th century, including the post–World War II Baby Boom (1946–1964). Most baby boomers grew up and have lived much of their lives in White suburbs, residentially isolated from minorities (Brownstein 2010). As they age and retire, many older White Americans are reconstituting such communities in racially homogeneous enclaves in the Southeast and Southwest.

In such communities, except for their yard and construction workers and house cleaners, older White people live apart from multicultural America and the minorities who represent a growing share of the national population. Since 1965, expanded immigration and higher fertility rates among minorities have transformed American society. As recently as 1980, minorities made up only 20 percent of the total population (versus about 39 percent today). If recent demographic trends continue, the ethnic composition of the United States will change even more dramatically (see Figure 16.3). Similar trends are evident in western Europe and are everyday expressions of globalization.

FIGURE 16.3    **Ethnic Composition of the United States**
The proportion of the American population that is White and non-Hispanic is declining. The projection for 2050 shown here comes from a 2008 U.S. Census Bureau report. Note especially the dramatic rise in the Hispanic portion of the American population between 2013 and 2050.

Source: Based on 2013 data from http://factfinder.census.gov/faces/nav/jsf/pages/searchresults.xhtml?refresh=t and a 2008 projection by the U.S. Census Bureau, http://www.census.gov/population/www/projections/analytical-document09.pdf, Table 1, p. 17.

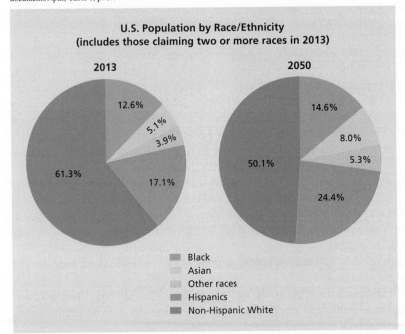

U.S. Population by Race/Ethnicity
(includes those claiming two or more races in 2013)

2013
12.6%
5.1%
3.9%
61.3%
17.1%

2050
14.6%
8.0%
5.3%
50.1%
24.4%

■ Black
■ Asian
■ Other races
■ Hispanics
■ Non-Hispanic White

# Roots of Ethnic Conflict

Ethnicity can be expressed in peaceful multiculturalism or in discrimination or violent interethnic confrontation. The roots of ethnic differentiation—and therefore, potentially, of ethnic conflict—can be political, economic, religious, linguistic, cultural, or racial (see Kuper 2006). Why do ethnic differences often lead to conflict and violence? The causes include a sense of injustice because of resource distribution, economic or political competition, and reaction to discrimination, prejudice, and other expressions of devalued identity (see Donham 2011; Friedman 2003).

In Iraq, under the dictator Saddam Hussein, there was discrimination by one Muslim group (Sunnis) against others (Shiites and Kurds). Sunnis, although a numeric minority within Iraq's population, enjoyed privileged access to power, prestige, and position. After the elections of 2005, which many Sunnis chose to boycott, Shiites gained political control. A civil war developed out of "sectarian violence" (conflicts among sects of the same religion) as Sunnis (and their foreign supporters) fueled an insurgency against the new government and its foreign supporters, including the United States. Shiites retaliated against Sunni attacks and a history of Sunni privilege and perceived discrimination against Shiites, as Shiite militias engaged in ethnic (sectarian) cleansing of their own. Sectarian conflict continues in Iraq (and Syria) as of this writing.

## Prejudice and Discrimination

Ethnic conflict often arises in reaction to prejudice (attitudes and judgments) or discrimination (action). **Prejudice** means devaluing (looking down on) a group because of its assumed behavior, values, capabilities, or attributes. People are prejudiced when they hold stereotypes about groups and apply them to individuals. (**Stereotypes** are fixed ideas—often unfavorable—about what the members of a group are like.) Prejudiced people assume that members of the group will act as they are "supposed to act" (according to the stereotype) and interpret a wide range of individual behaviors as evidence of the stereotype. They use this behavior to confirm their stereotype (and low opinion) of the group.

**Discrimination** refers to policies and practices that harm a group and its members. Discrimination may be *de facto* (practiced, but not legally sanctioned) or *de jure* (part of the law). An example of de facto discrimination is the harsher treatment that American minorities (compared with other Americans) tend to get from the police and the judicial system. This unequal treatment isn't legal, but it happens, anyway. Segregation in the southern United States and *apartheid* in South Africa provide two examples of de jure discrimination, which no longer are in existence. In both systems, by law, Blacks and Whites had different rights and privileges. Their social interaction ("mixing") was legally curtailed.

## Chips in the Mosaic

Although the multicultural model is increasingly prominent in North America, ethnic competition and conflict also are evident. There is conflict between newer arrivals, for instance, Central Americans and Koreans, and longer-established ethnic groups, such as African Americans. Ethnic antagonism flared in South-Central Los Angeles in spring

1992 in rioting that followed the acquittal of four White police officers who were tried for the videotaped beating of Rodney King (see Abelmann and Lie 1995).

Angry Blacks attacked Whites, Koreans, and Latinos. This violence expressed frustration by African Americans about their prospects in an increasingly multicultural society. A *New York Times* CBS News poll conducted just after the Los Angeles riots found that Blacks had a bleaker outlook than Whites about the effects of immigration on their lives. Only 23 percent of the Blacks felt they had more opportunities than recent immigrants, compared with twice that many Whites (Toner 1992).

## Aftermaths of Oppression

Expressing and further fueling ethnic conflict are such severe forms of discrimination as genocide, forced assimilation, ethnocide, and cultural colonialism. The most extreme form of ethnic discrimination is **genocide,** the deliberate elimination of a group (such as Jews in Nazi Germany, Muslims in Bosnia, or Tutsi in Rwanda) through mass murder (see Hinton and O'Neill 2011). A dominant group may try to destroy the cultures of certain ethnic groups **(ethnocide)** or force them to adopt the dominant culture *(forced assimilation)*. Many countries have penalized or banned the language and customs of an ethnic group (including its religious observances). One example of forced assimilation is the anti-Basque campaign that the dictator Francisco Franco (who ruled between 1939 and 1975) waged in Spain. Franco banned Basque books, journals, newspapers, signs, sermons, and tombstones and imposed fines for using the Basque language in schools (Ryan 1990). His policies led to the formation of a Basque terrorist group and spurred strong nationalist sentiment in the Basque region.

A policy of *ethnic expulsion* aims at removing groups who are culturally different from a country. There are many examples, including Bosnia-Herzegovina in the 1990s. Uganda expelled 74,000 Asians in 1972. The Far Right parties of contemporary Western Europe advocate repatriation (expulsion) of immigrant workers (West Indians in England, Algerians in France, and Turks in Germany) (see Friedman 2003). A policy of expulsion may create **refugees**—people who have been forced (involuntary refugees) or who have chosen (voluntary refugees) to flee a country, to escape persecution or war.

In many countries, colonial nation-building left ethnic strife in its wake. Thus, over a million Hindus and Muslims were killed in the violence that accompanied the division of the Indian subcontinent into India and Pakistan. Problems between Arabs and Jews in Palestine began during the British mandate period (see Kamrava 2011).

Multiculturalism may be growing in the United States and Canada, but the opposite is happening in the former Soviet Union, where ethnic groups (nationalities) want their own nation-states. The flowering of ethnic feeling and conflict as the Soviet empire disintegrated illustrates that years of political repression and ideology provide insufficient common ground for lasting unity. **Cultural colonialism** refers to internal domination—by one group and its culture or ideology over others. One example is the domination over the former Soviet empire by Russian people, language, and culture and by communist ideology. The dominant culture makes itself the official culture. This is reflected in schools, the media, and public interaction. Under Soviet rule, ethnic minorities had very limited self-rule in republics and regions controlled by Moscow. All the republics and their

## Anthropology Today   *Why Are the Greens So White?*
### *Race and Ethnicity in Golf*

How do race and ethnicity figure in the world of golf, a sport whose popularity has been growing not only in the United States but also in Europe, Asia, and Australia? More than 20 million Americans play golf, an industry that also supports about 400,000 workers. For decades, golf has been the preferred sport of business tycoons and politicians—mainly White. President Dwight D. Eisenhower (1953–1960), whose love for golf was well known, etched a lasting (and accurate) image of golf as a Republican sport (despite the fact that Presidents Bill Clinton and Barack Obama also play the game). A recent survey found that only 2 of the top 125 PGA touring pros identified as Democrats.

A glance at golfers in any televised game reveals a remarkable lack of variation in skin color. American golf was the nation's last major sport to desegregate, and minorities traditionally have been relegated to supporting roles. Latinos maintain golf's greens and physical infrastructure. Until the motorized golf cart replaced them, African Americans had significant opportunities to observe and learn the game by caddying. Indeed, there once was a tradition of African American caddies becoming excellent golfers.

The best example of this trajectory is Dr. Charlie Sifford (1922–2015), who, in 1961, broke the color barrier in American professional golf. Sifford's golf career began as a caddie for White golfers. He went on to dominate the all-Black United Golfers Association, winning five straight national titles, but he wanted to play with the world's best golfers. At the age of 39, Sifford successfully challenged—and ended—the White-only policy of the PGA Professional Golfers' Association (PGA), becoming its first African American member.

Sifford, who had to endure phone threats, racial slurs, and other indignities at the beginning of his PGA career, went on to win the greater Hartford open in 1967, the Los Angeles open in 1969, and the 1975 senior PGA championship. In 2004 he became the first African American inducted into the World Golf Hall of Fame. His major regret was that he never got to play in a Masters Tournament. That event, held annually in Augusta, Georgia, did not invite its first Black player until Lee Elder in 1975. Sifford's bitterness about his own exclusion from the Masters was tempered somewhat by his pleasure when Tiger Woods, another African American golfer, won the first of his four green Masters jackets in 1997.

In terms of diversity, golf has actually regressed since the 1970s, when 11 African Americans played on the PGA tour. If we consider multiracial players to be African American, there currently is only 1 African American (Tiger Woods) among the 125 top players on the PGA tour. In Britain, only 2 percent of an estimated 850,000 regular golfers are non-White. Economic factors continue to limit minority access to golf. Prospective golfers need money for instruction, equipment, access to top-notch courses, and travel to tournaments. Asian Americans, who enjoy a relatively high socioeconomic status, are the only minority group in the United States with a growing representation in golf, for both men and women.

Tiger Woods is currently the single exceptional non-White individual in this mainly White, affluent, Republican sport. Woods became one of America's most celebrated and popular athletes by combining golfing

*continued*

## Anthropology Today   *continued*

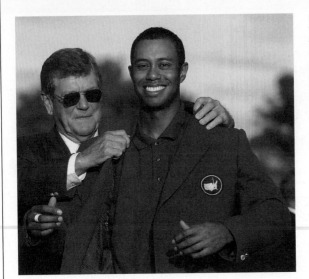

In Augusta, Georgia, Tiger Woods receives the traditional green jacket from tournament chair Hootie Johnson, after winning his second (of four) Masters Tournaments. © Roberto Schmidt/AFP/Getty Images

success with a carefully cultivated reputation as a family man. He presented himself as the hard-working and achievement-oriented son of an Asian mother and an African American father, and as the devoted husband and father of his Scandinavian wife and two photogenic children. Woods's fall from grace began late in 2009, as a flood of media reports converted his image from family man into serial philanderer. Although his marriage did not survive his transgressions, his golfing career did. Woods gradually reintegrated into the world of golf, even receiving the 2013 PGA Tour Player of the Year Award. He had won 5 of the 16 tournaments he played that year and placed in the top 10 in 3 others. Tiger Woods remains the world's most prominent and celebrated African American golfer. No longer, however, is he the untarnished hero of yesteryear. What role, if any, do you think race, ethnicity, racism, and racial stereotyping have played in the rise, fall, and reintegration of Tiger Woods?

**Source:** Ferguson (2015); Riach (2013); Orin Starn, *The Passion of Tiger Woods: An Anthropologist Reports on Golf, Race, and Celebrity Scandal* (2011).

peoples were to be united by the oneness of "socialist internationalism." One common technique in cultural colonialism is to flood ethnic areas with members of the dominant ethnic group. Thus, in the former Soviet Union, ethnic Russian colonists were sent to many areas, to diminish the cohesion and clout of the local people.

The Commonwealth of Independent States (CIS), founded in 1991 and headquartered in Minsk, Belarus, is what remains of the once-powerful Soviet Union (see Yurchak 2005). In Russia and other formerly Soviet nations, ethnic groups (nationalities) have

In the Darfur region of western Sudan (shown here), government-supported Arab militias, called the Janjaweed, have forced Black Africans off their land. The militias are accused of genocide, of killing up to 30,000 darker-skinned Africans. In this photo, a group of new refugees arrives by truck at a camp. © Sarah El Deeb/AP Images

sought to forge separate and viable nation-states based on cultural boundaries. This celebration of ethnic autonomy is part of an ethnic florescence that—as surely as globalization and transnationalism—is a trend of the late 20th and early 21st centuries.

## Summary

1. An ethnic group consists of members of a particular culture in a nation or region that contains others. Ethnicity is based on actual, perceived, or assumed cultural similarities (among members of the same ethnic group) and differences (between that group and others). Ethnic distinctions can be based on language, religion, history, geography, kinship, or race. A race is an ethnic group assumed to have a biological basis. Usually, race and ethnicity are ascribed statuses; people are born members of a group and remain so all their lives.

2. Human races are cultural rather than biological categories. Such races derive from contrasts perceived in particular societies, rather than from scientific classifications based on common genes. In the United States, racial labels such as "White" and "Black" designate socially constructed categories defined by American culture. American racial classification, governed by the rule of hypodescent, is based neither on phenotype nor on genes. Children of mixed unions, no matter what their appearance, are classified with the minority group parent.

3. Racial attitudes in Japan illustrate intrinsic racism—the belief that a perceived racial difference is a sufficient reason to value one person less than another. The valued group is majority (pure) Japanese, who are believed to share the same blood. Majority Japanese define themselves by opposition to others, such as Koreans and burakumin. These may be minority groups in Japan or outsiders—anyone who is "not us."

4. Such exclusionary racial systems are not inevitable. Although Brazil shares a history of slavery with the United States, it lacks the hypodescent rule. Brazilian racial identity is more of an achieved status. It can change during someone's lifetime, reflecting phenotypical changes.

5. The term *nation* once was synonymous with *ethnic group*. Now *nation* has come to mean a state—a centrally organized political unit. Because of migration, conquest, and colonialism, most nation-states are not ethnically homogeneous. Ethnic groups that seek autonomous political status (their own country) are nationalities. Political upheavals, wars, and migrations have divided many imagined national communities.

6. Assimilation is the process of change an ethnic group may experience when it moves to a country where another culture dominates. By assimilating, the minority adopts the patterns and norms of its host culture. Assimilation isn't inevitable, and there can be ethnic harmony without it. A plural society combines ethnic contrasts and economic interdependence between ethnic groups. The view of cultural diversity in a nation-state as good and desirable is multiculturalism. A multicultural society socializes individuals not only into the dominant (national) culture but also into an ethnic one.

7. In the United States, ethnic/racial diversity is increasing, especially among the young. Simultaneously, the country is aging, and most of the senior population is White. These trends are associated with contrasting attitudes, priorities, and political leanings of younger and older Americans. Minorities constitute a growing percentage of the total U.S. population, especially among children under 18.

8. Ethnicity can be expressed either in peaceful multiculturalism or in discrimination or violent confrontation. Ethnic conflict often arises in reaction to prejudice (attitudes and judgments) or discrimination (action). The most extreme form of ethnic discrimination is genocide, the deliberate elimination of a group through mass murder. A dominant group may try to destroy certain ethnic practices (ethnocide) or to force ethnic group members to adopt the dominant culture (forced assimilation). A policy of ethnic expulsion may create refugees. Cultural colonialism is internal domination—by one group and its culture or ideology over others.

| Key Terms | | | |
|---|---|---|---|
| | assimilation, *380* | ethnocide, *386* | plural society, *381* |
| | cultural | genocide, *386* | prejudice, *385* |
| |    colonialism, *386* | hypodescent, *371* | race, *370* |
| | descent, *371* | multiculturalism, *381* | racism, *370* |
| | discrimination, *385* | nation, *379* | refugees, *386* |
| | ethnic group, *367* | nation-state, *379* | stereotypes, *385* |
| | ethnicity, *368* | nationalities, *380* | |

# Chapter 17

# Applying Anthropology

Applied anthropology is the use of anthropological data, perspectives, theory, and methods to identify, assess, and solve contemporary problems (see Ervin 2005; Wasson, Butler, and Copeland-Carson 2012; Nolan 2013). Applied anthropologists help make anthropology relevant and useful to the world beyond anthropology. Medical anthropologists, for instance, have worked as cultural interpreters in public health programs, helping such programs fit into local culture. Development anthropologists work for or with international development agencies, such as the World Bank and the U.S. Agency for International Development (USAID). The findings of garbology, the archaeological study of waste, are relevant to the Environmental Protection Agency, the paper industry, and packaging and trade associations. Archaeology also is applied in cultural resource management and historic preservation. Biological anthropologists apply their expertise in programs aimed at public health, nutrition, genetic counseling, aging, substance abuse, and mental health. Forensic anthropologists work with the police, medical examiners, the courts, and international organizations to identify victims of crimes, accidents, wars, and terrorism. Linguistic anthropologists study physician–patient communication and show how speech differences influence classroom learning. Most applied anthropologists seek humane and effective ways of helping people.

The ethnographic method is a particularly valuable tool in applying anthropology. Remember that ethnographers study societies firsthand, living with, observing, and learning from ordinary people. Nonanthropologists working in social-change programs often are content to converse with officials, read reports, and copy statistics. However, the applied anthropologist's likely early request is some variant of "take me to the local people." Anthropologists know that people must play an active role in the changes that affect them and that "the people" have information that "the experts" lack (see Field and Fox 2009).

Anthropological *theory,* the body of findings and generalizations of the four subfields, also guides applied anthropology. Just as theory aids practice, application fuels theory (see Nolan 2013; Rylko-Bauer, Singer, and Van Willigen 2006). As we compare social-change programs, our understanding of cause and effect increases. We add new generalizations about culture change to those discovered in traditional and ancient cultures.

# The Role of the Applied Anthropologist

## Early Applications

Application was a central concern of early anthropology in Great Britain (in the context of colonialism) and the United States (in the context of Native American policy). Before turning to the new, we should consider some problems with the old. For the British empire, specifically its African colonies, Bronislaw Malinowski (1929) proposed that "practical anthropology" (his term for colonial applied anthropology) should focus on Westernization, the diffusion of European culture into tribal societies. Malinowski did not question the legitimacy of colonialism or the anthropologist's role in making it work. He saw nothing wrong with aiding colonial regimes by studying land tenure and land use, to recommend how much of their land local people should be allowed to keep and how much Europeans should be permitted to take. Malinowski's views exemplify a historical association between early anthropology, particularly in Europe (especially England, France, and Portugal), and colonialism (see also Duffield and Hewitt 2009; Lange 2009; Rylko-Bauer, Singer, and Van Willigen 2006).

Margaret Mead (1977) estimated that during the 1940s, 95 percent of American anthropologists were engaged in some way in the war effort (World War II). For example, American anthropologists studied Japanese and German "culture at a distance" in an attempt to predict the behavior of the enemies of the United States. After that war, applied anthropologists worked on Pacific islands to promote local-level cooperation with American policies in various trust territories. The American Anthropological Association (AAA) has raised strong ethical objections to applying anthropology in war zones and for military intelligence (see Lucas 2009). Such concerns were voiced during the Vietnam War. More recently they have emerged in criticisms of anthropologists' participation in the Human Terrains System (HTS) project in Iraq and Afghanistan, as discussed in the chapter "Doing Anthropology." Anthropological research should not harm the people anthropologists study.

## Academic and Applied Anthropology

After World War II, the baby boom, which began in 1946 and peaked in 1957, fueled a tremendous expansion of the American educational system. New junior, community, and four-year colleges opened, and anthropology became a standard part of the college curriculum. During the 1950s and 1960s, most American anthropologists were college professors, although some still worked in agencies and museums.

The growth of academic anthropology continued through the early 1970s. Especially during the Vietnam War, undergraduates flocked to anthropology classes to learn about other cultures. Students were especially interested in Southeast Asia, whose indigenous societies were being disrupted by war. Many anthropologists protested the superpowers' apparent disregard for non-Western lives, values, customs, and social systems.

Most anthropologists still worked in colleges and museums during the 1970s and 1980s. However, an increasing number of anthropologists were employed by international organizations, governments, businesses, hospitals, and schools. The AAA estimates that nowadays more than half of anthropology PhDs seek nonacademic employment. This shift toward application has benefited the profession. It has forced anthropologists to consider the wider social value and implications of their research.

## Applied Anthropology Today

Most contemporary applied anthropologists see their work as radically removed from the colonial enterprise. Modern applied anthropology usually is seen as a helping profession, devoted to assisting local people, as anthropologists speak up for the disenfranchised. However, applied anthropologists also have clients that are neither poor nor powerless. An applied anthropologist working as a market researcher for a business may be concerned with designing a more effective product, increasing market share, and, ultimately, expanding profits for an employer or a client. Such goals can pose ethical dilemmas, as can work in cultural resource management (CRM). The CRM anthropologist helps decide how to preserve significant remains when sites are threatened by development or public works. A CRM firm typically is hired by someone seeking to build a road or a factory. That client may have a strong interest in an outcome in which no sites are found that need protecting. Even if they don't work for colonial powers or the military, applied anthropologists still face ethical questions: To whom does the researcher owe loyalty? How does one criticize programs in which one has participated? Anthropology's professional organizations have addressed such questions by establishing codes of ethics and ethics committees. As Karen Tice (1997) notes, attention to ethical issues has become paramount in the teaching of applied anthropology.

Anthropologists are experts on human problems and social change, who study, understand, and respect diverse cultural values. Given this background, anthropologists are highly qualified to suggest, plan, and implement social policy affecting people. Proper roles for applied anthropologists include (1) identifying needs for change that local people perceive, (2) working with those people to design culturally appropriate and socially sensitive change, and (3) protecting local people from harmful policies and projects that may threaten them.

# Development Anthropology

**Development anthropology** is the branch of applied anthropology that focuses on social issues in, and the cultural dimension of, economic development (see Crewe and Axelby 2013). Development anthropologists don't just carry out development policies planned by others; they also plan and guide policy. (For more detailed discussions of issues in development anthropology, see Edelman and Haugerud 2005; Escobar 2012; Nolan 2002.)

Still, ethical dilemmas often confront development anthropologists (Escobar 1991, 2012). Foreign aid, including funds for economic development, usually doesn't go where need and suffering are greatest. Rather, such funds are spent on political, economic, and strategic priorities as international donors, political leaders, and powerful interest groups perceive them. Planners' interests don't always coincide with the best interests of the local people. Although the stated aim of most development projects is to enhance the quality of life, living standards often decline in the affected area.

## Equity

A commonly stated goal of recent development policy is to promote equity. **Increased equity** means reduced poverty and a more even distribution of wealth. However, if projects are to increase equity, they must have the support of reform-minded governments. Wealthy and powerful people typically resist projects that threaten their vested interests.

Some development projects actually widen wealth disparities; that is, they have a negative equity impact. An initial uneven distribution of resources often becomes the basis for even greater inequality after the project. In Bahia, Brazil, for example, sailboat owners (but not nonowners) got loans to buy motors for their boats (Kottak 2006). To repay the loans, the owners increased the percentage of the catch they took from the men who fished in their boats. Over the years, they used their rising profits to buy larger and more expensive boats. The result was stratification—the creation of a group of wealthy

A mix of boats harbored in Pucasana, a fishing village in Peru. A boat owner gets a loan to buy a motor. To repay it, he increases the share of the catch he takes from his crew. Later, he uses his rising profits to buy a more expensive boat and takes even more from his crew. Can a more equitable solution be found? © Sean Sprague/ The Image Works people within a formerly more egalitarian community. New boats became so expensive that ambitious young men, who once would have sought careers in fishing, no longer could afford to buy a boat of their own. They sought wage labor on land instead. To avoid such results, credit-granting agencies must seek out and invest in enterprising young fishers, rather than giving loans only to owners and established businesspeople.

# Strategies for Innovation

Development anthropologists should work closely with local people to assess, and help them realize, their own wishes and needs for change. Funding development projects in area A that are inappropriate there but needed in area B, or that are unnecessary anywhere, is a waste of money when so many true local needs cry out for a solution. Development anthropology can help sort out the needs of the As and Bs and fit projects accordingly. Projects that put people first by consulting with them and responding to their expressed needs must be identified (Cernea 1991). Thereafter, development anthropologists can work to ensure socially compatible ways of implementing a good project.

In a comparative study of 68 rural development projects from around the world, I found the culturally compatible economic development projects to be twice as successful financially as the incompatible ones (Kottak 1990*b*, 1991). This finding suggests that using anthropological expertise in planning, to ensure cultural compatibility, is cost effective. To maximize social and economic benefits, projects must (1) be culturally compatible, (2) respond to locally perceived needs, (3) involve men and women in planning and carrying out the changes that affect them, (4) harness traditional organizations, and (5) be flexible.

Consider a recent example of a development initiative that failed because it ignored local culture. Working in Afghanistan after the fall of the Taliban, ethnographer Noah Coburn (2011) studied Istalif, a village of potters. During his fieldwork there, Coburn discovered that an NGO had spent $20,000 on an electric kiln that could have greatly enhanced the productivity of local potters. The only problem was that the kiln was donated to a women's center that men could not enter. The misguided donors ignored the fact that Istalif's men did the work—pot-making and firing—that a kiln could facilitate. Women's role in pottery came later—in glazing and decorating.

## Overinnovation

In my comparative study, the compatible and successful projects avoided the fallacy of **overinnovation** (too much change). People usually are willing to change just enough to maintain, or slightly improve on, what they already have. Motives for modifying behavior come from the traditional culture and the small concerns of ordinary life. Peasants' values are not such abstract ones as "learning a better way," "progressing," "increasing technical know-how," "improving efficiency," or "adopting modern techniques." Their objectives are down-to-earth and specific—e.g., to enhance the productivity of their crops, amass resources for a ceremony, get a child through school, or have enough cash to pay the tax bill. The goals and values of subsistence producers differ from those of people who work for cash, just as they differ from those of development planners. Different value systems must be considered during planning.

Development projects that fail usually are either (or both) economically and cultur-ally incompatible. For example, one South Asian project promoted the cultivation of onions and peppers, expecting this practice to fit into a preexisting labor-intensive sys-tem of rice-growing. Cultivation of these cash crops wasn't traditional in the area, and the labor peaks for pepper and onion production coincided with those for rice, to which the farmers gave priority.

Another naive and incompatible project was an overinnovative scheme in Ethiopia. Its major fallacy was to try to convert free-ranging nomadic herders into farm workers. Outsiders—commercial farmers—were to get much of the herders' territory, to convert to commercial farmland—plantations. The pastoralists were expected to settle down and start working on those plantations. The planners naively expected the herders to give up a generations-old way of life to work three times harder growing rice and picking cotton for bosses.

Reporting on social-change efforts in Afghanistan after the fall of the Taliban, an-thropologists Noah Coburn (2011) and Thomas Barfield (2010) have criticized various top-down initiatives that proved incompatible with local culture and community organi-zation. Destined for failure, according to Coburn, are modernizing plans aimed at creat-ing impersonal, merit-oriented bureaucracies. Also doomed at the village level are attempts to impose liberal beliefs about gender and religion. Echoing findings of applied anthropology, Coburn suggests that the best strategy to maintain peace in the Afghan countryside is to work with existing resources (including local beliefs and social organi-zation). To be avoided are overinnovative plans from outside, whether from the national government or foreign donors.

Barfield faults Western powers for trying to impose an autocratic system (the Karzai regime, which ended in 2014) on a country where autocracy is politically unsustainable. Barfield also cites the futility of direct attempts to change rural Afghans' beliefs about such entrenched matters as religion and gender equality. A better strategy, he suggests, is for change agents to work first in urban areas, where innovation is more welcome, then let those changes spread gradually to the countryside.

In 2014, Afghanistan elected an anthropologist as its president. President Ashraf Ghani, who received his doctorate in anthropology from Columbia University in New York, has worked for the World Bank as a development anthropologist. Let us hope that Ghani's background in anthropology and development will encourage more culturally appropriate development strategies in the nation he now leads.

## Underdifferentiation

The fallacy of **underdifferentiation** is planners' tendency to view "the less-developed countries" as more alike than they are. Often development agencies have ignored huge cultural contrasts (e.g., between Brazil and Burundi) and adopted a uniform approach to deal with very different sets of people. Planners also have tried to impose incompatible property concepts and social units.

Ethnocentrically, planners often assume that the individual and the nuclear family are key social units among the intended beneficiaries. This was true of one project in West Africa, where the extended family was the basic social unit. The project succeeded de-spite a faulty social design that assumed that nuclear families would be the primary beneficiaries. The actual project participants used their traditional extended family networks to attract additional settlers. Eventually, twice as many people as planned benefited as extended family members flocked to the project area. Here, settlers used the principles of their traditional society to modify the project design that had been imposed on them.

Another dubious social model that has been common in development planning is the cooperative. In the comparative study of rural development projects, new cooperatives fared badly. Cooperatives succeeded only when they harnessed preexisting local-level communal institutions. This is a corollary of a more general rule: *Participants' groups are most effective when they are based on traditional social organization or on a socioeconomic similarity among members.*

An alternative to such foreign models is needed: greater use of indigenous social models in economic development (see Bodley 2013). These are traditional social units, such as the clans, lineages, and other extended kin groups of Africa, Oceania, and many other nations, with their communally held estates and resources. *The most humane and productive strategy for change is to base the social design for innovation on traditional social forms in each target area.*

## Indigenous Models

Many governments are not genuinely, or realistically, committed to improving the lives of their citizens. Interference by major powers also has kept governments from enacting needed reforms. Occasionally, however, a government does act as an agent of and for its people. One historic example is Madagascar, whose people, the Malagasy, were organized into descent groups prior to indigenous state formation in the 18th century. The Merina, creators of the major precolonial state of Madagascar, wove descent groups into its structure, making members of important groups advisers to rulers—thus giving them authority in government. The Merina state collected taxes and organized labor for public works projects. In return, it redistributed resources to peasants in need. It also granted them some protection against war and slave raids and allowed them to cultivate their rice fields in peace. The government maintained the water works for rice cultivation. It opened to ambitious peasant boys the chance of becoming state bureaucrats, through hard work and study.

Throughout the history of the Merina state—and continuing to some extent in postcolonial Madagascar—there have been strong relationships between the individual, the descent group, and the state. Local Malagasy communities, where residence is based on descent, are more cohesive and homogeneous than are communities in Latin America or North America. Madagascar gained political independence from France in 1960. Its new government had an economic development policy aimed at increasing the ability of the Malagasy to feed themselves. Government policy emphasized increased production of rice, a subsistence crop, rather than cash crops. Furthermore, local communities, with their traditional cooperative patterns and solidarity based on kinship and descent, were treated as partners in, not obstacles to, the development process.

In a sense, the descent group is preadapted to equitable national development. In Madagascar, descent groups pooled their resources to educate their most ambitious members. Once educated, those men and women gained economically secure positions in the nation. They then shared the advantages of their new positions with their kin. For example, they gave room and board to rural cousins attending school and helped them find jobs.

This Madagascar example suggests that when government officials are of "the people" (rather than the elites) and have strong personal ties to common folk, they are more likely to promote democratic reform. In Latin America, by contrast, leaders and followers too often have been from different social classes, with no connections based on kinship, descent, marriage, or common background. When elites rule, elites usually prosper. Recently, however, Latin America has elected some nonelite leaders. Brazil's lower class (indeed the entire nation) benefited socioeconomically when one of its own was elected president. Luis Inácio da Silva, or Lula, a former factory worker with only a fourth-grade education, served two terms (ending in 2011) as one of the Western Hemisphere's most popular leaders.

## Anthropology and Education

Attention to culture also is fundamental to **anthropology and education,** a field whose research extends from classrooms into homes, neighborhoods, and communities (see Anderson-Levitt 2012; Levinson and Pollock 2011; Spindler and Hammond 2006). In classrooms, anthropologists have observed interactions among teachers, students, parents, and visitors. Anthropologists view children as total, cultural creatures whose enculturation and attitudes toward education belong to a context that includes family and peers (see also Kontopodis et al. 2011; Reyhner et al. 2013).

Sociolinguists and cultural anthropologists have worked side by side in education research. In one classic study of Puerto Rican seventh-graders in the urban Midwest,

Afghan girls attend a lesson at the secondary school in Sarkani village, Kunar Province, eastern Afghanistan. What do you see here that differs from classrooms in your country? © Oleg Popov/Reuters/Corbis

anthropologists uncovered some key misconceptions held by teachers (Hill-Burnett 1978). The teachers mistakenly had assumed that Puerto Rican parents valued education less than did non-Hispanics, but in-depth interviews revealed that the Puerto Rican parents valued it more. The anthropologists also identified certain practices that were preventing Hispanics from being adequately educated. For example, the teachers' union and the board of education had agreed to teach "English as a foreign language." However, they had provided no bilingual teachers to work with Spanish-speaking students. The school was assigning all students (including non-Hispanics) with low reading scores and behavior problems to the English-as-a-foreign-language classroom. This educational disaster brought together in the classroom a teacher who spoke no Spanish, children who barely spoke English, and a group of English-speaking students with reading and behavior problems. The Spanish speakers were falling behind not just in reading but in all subjects. They could at least have kept up in the other subjects if a Spanish speaker had been teaching them science, social studies, and math until they were ready for English-language instruction in those areas.

# Urban Anthropology

For centuries, cities have been influenced by global forces, including world capitalism and colonialism (Zukin et al. 2015). However, the roles of cities in the world system have changed recently because of the time–space compression made possible by modern transportation and communication systems. That is, everything appears closer today because contact and movement are so much easier.

In the context of globalization, the mass media have joined local factors in guiding people's routines, dreams, and aspirations. Although people live in particular places, their imaginations are not locally confined (Appadurai 1996). Media-transmitted images and information help draw people to cities. People migrate partly for economic reasons, but also to be where the action is. Rural Brazilians routinely cite *movimento*, urban activity and excitement, as something to be valued. International migrants tend to settle in large cities, where a lot is going on and where they can feel at home in ethnic enclaves. Consider Canada, which, after Australia, is the country with the highest percentage of foreign-born population. Three-quarters of immigrants to Canada settle in Toronto, Vancouver, or Montreal. It is estimated that, by 2031, nearly one-half (46%) of Canadians aged 15 and over will be foreign born or will have at least one foreign-born parent, up from 39% in 2006 (Statistics Canada 2010).

Urban living has increased steadily since the Industrial Revolution. The world's urban population was 3 percent in 1800 and 13 percent in 1900. By 1960, over a third (34 percent) of the world's population lived in cities, rising to over half (54 percent) in 2014. Urban population growth is greatest in the less-developed countries (LDCs), where by 2017 a majority of people will be urban dwellers (WHO 2014).

More than a billion people now live in urban slums, mostly without reliable water, sanitation, and public services (Handwerk 2008). If current trends continue, urban population increase and the concentration of people in slums will be accompanied by rising rates of crime, along with water, air, and noise pollution. These problems will be most severe in the LDCs.

One-sixth of the Earth's population lives in urban slums. Roçinha (shown here) is a populous shantytown city within the city of Rio de Janeiro, Brazil. How might anthropologists study slums?
© Caio Leal/AFP/Getty Images

As industrialization and urbanization spread globally, anthropologists increasingly study these processes and the social problems they create. **Urban anthropology,** which has theoretical (basic research) and applied dimensions, is the cross-cultural and ethnographic study of urbanization and life in cities (see Gmelch, Kemper, and Zenner 2010; Nononi 2014; Pardo and Prato 2012). The United States and Canada have become popular arenas for urban anthropological research on topics such as immigration, ethnicity, poverty, class, and urban violence (Vigil 2010).

## Urban versus Rural

An early student of urbanization, the anthropologist Robert Redfield, contrasted rural communities, whose social relations are on a face-to-face basis, with cities, where impersonality reigns. Redfield (1941) proposed that urbanization be studied along a rural–urban continuum. He described differences in values and social relations in four sites that spanned such a continuum. In Mexico's Yucatán peninsula, Redfield compared an isolated Mayan-speaking Indian community, a rural peasant village, a small provincial city, and a large capital. Several studies in Africa (Little 1971) and Asia were influenced by Redfield's view that cities are centers through which cultural innovations spread to rural and tribal areas.

In any nation, urban and rural represent different social systems. However, cultural diffusion or borrowing occurs as people, products, images, and messages move from one to the other. Migrants take rural practices and beliefs to cities and take urban patterns back home. The experiences and social forms of the rural area affect adaptation to city life. City folk also develop new institutions to meet specific urban needs.

An applied anthropology approach to urban planning starts by identifying key social groups in specific urban contexts. After identifying those groups, the anthropologist might elicit their wishes for change, convey those needs to funding agencies, and work with agencies and local people to realize those goals. In Africa relevant groups might include ethnic associations, occupational groups, social clubs, religious groups, and burial societies. The groups provide cash support and lodging for their rural relatives. Sometimes such groups think of themselves as a gigantic kin group that includes urban and rural members. Members may call one another "brother" and "sister." As in an extended family, richer members help their poorer relatives. A member's improper behavior, however, can lead to expulsion—an unhappy fate for a migrant in a large, ethnically heterogeneous city.

## Medical Anthropology

**Medical anthropology** is a biocultural field that studies variation in health care systems, including disease, illness, health standards, and disease theories. All societies have **health care systems** consisting of beliefs, customs, specialists, and techniques aimed at ensuring health and diagnosing and curing illness. Medical anthropology is both academic and applied and includes anthropologists from all four subfields (see Brown and Barrett 2010; Joralemon 2010; Singer 2012; Trevathan, Smith, and McKenna 2008; Wiley and Allen 2012). Medical anthropologists examine such questions as which diseases and health conditions affect particular populations (and why) and how illness is socially constructed, diagnosed, managed, and treated in various societies.

**Disease** refers to a scientifically identified health threat caused by genetics or a bacterium, virus, fungus, parasite, or other pathogen. **Illness** is a condition of poor health perceived or felt by an individual (Inhorn and Brown 1990). Perceptions of good and bad health are culturally constructed. Various cultures and ethnic groups recognize different illnesses, symptoms, and causes and have developed different health care systems and treatment strategies (Womack 2010).

The incidence and severity of *disease* vary as well (see Baer, Singer, and Susser 2013). Group differences are evident in the United States. One study examined health status indicators for groups named in the U.S. census: non-Hispanic Whites, African Americans, Hispanics, American Indians, and Asians or Pacific Islanders (Keppel, Pearch, and Wagener 2002). African Americans' rates for six measures (total mortality, heart disease, lung cancer, breast cancer, stroke, and homicide) exceeded those of the other groups by a factor ranging from 2.5 to almost 10. Whites had the highest suicide rates and Native Americans the highest rates for motor vehicle accidents. Asian Americans lived longest (see Dressler, Oths, and Gravlee 2005).

Magdalena Hurtado and colleagues (2005) note that the life expectancy at birth for indigenous South Americans is at least 20 years shorter than that of other South Americans. What can applied anthropologists do to help improve health conditions among indigenous peoples? Hurtado and colleagues (2005) suggest three steps: (1) Identify the most pressing health problems; (2) gather information on possible solutions; and (3) implement solutions in partnership with the agencies that are in charge of public health programs for indigenous populations.

In many areas, the world system and colonialism worsened the health of indigenous peoples by spreading diseases, warfare, servitude, and other stressors. Traditionally and in ancient times, hunter-gatherers, because of their small numbers, mobility, and relative isolation from other groups, lacked most of the epidemic infectious diseases that affect agrarian and urban societies (Cohen and Armelagos 2013; Singer 2015). Epidemic diseases such as cholera, typhoid, and bubonic plague thrive in dense populations, and thus among farmers and city dwellers. The spread of malaria has been linked to population growth and deforestation associated with food production.

Certain diseases, and physical conditions such as obesity, have spread with economic development and globalization (Baer, Singer, and Susser 2013; Inhorn and Wentzell 2012; Ulijaszek and Lofink 2006). Schistosomiasis, or bilharzia (liver flukes), is probably the fastest-spreading and most dangerous parasitic infection now known. It is propagated by snails that live in ponds, lakes, and waterways, usually ones created by irrigation projects. The applied anthropology approach to reducing such diseases is to see if local people perceive a connection between the vector (e.g., snails in the water) and the disease. If not, such information may be provided by enlisting active local groups, schools, and the media.

The highest global rates of HIV infection and AIDS-related deaths are in Africa, especially southern Africa. As it kills productive adults, AIDS leaves behind dependent children and seniors (Baro and Deubel 2006). In southern and eastern Africa, AIDS and other sexually transmitted diseases (STDs) have spread along highways, via encounters between truckers and prostitutes. STDs also are spread through prostitution as young men from rural areas seek wage work in cities, labor camps, and mines. When the men return home, they infect their wives. Cities also are prime sites of STD transmission in Europe, Asia, and North and South America. Cultural factors also affect the spread of HIV, which is less likely to be transmitted when men are circumcised.

The kinds of and incidence of disease vary among societies, and cultures perceive and treat illness differently. Still, all societies have what George Foster and Barbara Anderson call "disease-theory systems" to identify, classify, and explain illness. Foster and Anderson (1978) identified three basic theories about the causes of illness: personalistic, naturalistic, and emotionalistic. *Personalistic* disease theories blame illness on agents, such as sorcerers, witches, ghosts, or ancestral spirits.

*Naturalistic* disease theories explain illness in impersonal terms. One example is Western medicine, or biomedicine, which aims to link illness to scientifically demonstrated agents that bear no personal malice toward their victims (see Lupton 2012). Thus, Western medicine attributes illness to organisms (e.g., bacteria, viruses, fungi, or parasites), accidents, toxic materials, or genes. Other naturalistic systems blame poor health on unbalanced body fluids. Many Latin cultures classify food, drink, and environmental conditions as "hot" or "cold." People believe their health suffers when

A curer at work: At a market in Yangshuo, China, a woman undergoes a moxibustion treatment, in which mugwort, a small, spongy herb, is burned to facilitate healing. © age fotostock/Alamy

they eat or drink hot or cold substances together or under inappropriate conditions. For example, one shouldn't drink something cold after a hot bath or eat a pineapple (a "cold" fruit) when one is menstruating (a "hot" condition).

*Emotionalistic* disease theories assume that emotional experiences cause illness. For example, Latin Americans may develop *susto,* an illness caused by anxiety or fright (see the "Anthropology Today" in Chapter 1). Its symptoms (lethargy, vagueness, distraction) are similar to those of "soul loss," a diagnosis of similar symptoms made by people in Madagascar. Modern psychoanalysis also focuses on the role of the emotions in physical and psychological well-being.

A society's illness-causation theory is important for treatment. When illness has a personalistic cause, shamans may be effective curers. They draw on varied techniques (occult and practical) that are part of their special expertise. A shaman may cure soul loss by enticing the spirit back into the body. Shamans may ease difficult childbirths by asking spirits to travel up the birth canal to guide the baby out (Lévi-Strauss 1967). A shaman may cure a cough by counteracting a curse or removing a substance introduced by a sorcerer.

If there is a "world's oldest profession" besides hunter and gatherer, it is curer, often a shaman. The curer's role has some universal features (Foster and Anderson 1978). Thus, a **curer** emerges through a culturally defined process of selection (e.g., parental prodding, inheritance of the role, visions, dream instructions) and training (apprentice shamanship, medical school). Eventually, the curer is certified by older practitioners and acquires a professional image. Patients believe in the skills of the curer, whom they consult and compensate.

We should not lose sight, ethnocentrically, of the difference between **scientific medicine** and Western medicine per se. To be sure, there have been scientific advances in technology, genomics, molecular biology, pathology, surgery, diagnostics, and applications. However, many Western medical procedures have little justification in science, logic, or fact. Overprescription of drugs, unnecessary surgery, and the impersonality and inequality of the physician–patient relationship are questionable features of Western medical systems (see Briggs 2005 for linguistic aspects of this inequality). Also, overuse of antibiotics seems to be triggering an explosion of resistant microorganisms, which may pose a long-term global public health hazard.

Still, biomedicine surpasses tribal treatment in many ways. Although medicines such as quinine, coca, opium, ephedrine, and rauwolfia were discovered in nonindustrial societies, thousands of effective drugs are available today to treat myriad diseases. Today's surgical procedures are much safer and more effective than those of traditional societies.

But industrialization and globalization have spawned their own health problems. Modern stressors include uneven nutrition, dangerous machinery, impersonal work, isolation, poverty, homelessness, substance abuse, and noise, air, and water pollution (see McElroy and Townsend 2009). Health problems in industrial nations are caused as much by economic, social, political, and cultural factors as by pathogens. In modern North America, for example, poverty contributes to many illnesses, including arthritis, heart conditions, back problems, and hearing and vision impairment. Poverty also is a factor in the differential spread of infectious diseases (see Singer 2015).

In the United States and other developed countries, good health has become something of an ethical imperative (Foucault 1990). Individuals are expected to shape themselves in accordance with new medical knowledge. Those who do so acquire the status of *sanitary citizens*—people with proper, modern understanding of the body, health, and illness. Such citizens practice hygiene and look to health care professionals when they are sick. People who act differently (e.g., smokers, overeaters, those who avoid doctors) are blamed for their own health problems (Briggs 2005; Foucault 1990).

Even getting an epidemic disease such as cholera may be interpreted today as a moral failure. It's assumed that people who act rationally can avoid "preventable" diseases. Individuals are expected to follow scientifically based imperatives (e.g., "boil water," "wash your hands," "don't smoke"). People can become objects of avoidance and discrimination simply by belonging to a group seen as having a greater risk of disease or poor health (e.g., gay men, smokers, veterans) (Briggs 2005).

Health interventions always have to fit into local cultures and be accepted by local people. When Western medicine is introduced, people usually retain many of their old methods while accepting new ones. Native curers may continue to treat certain conditions (spirit possession), while physicians deal with others. When patients get better, the native curer and the physician share the credit.

A more personal treatment of illness that emulates the non-Western curer–patient–community relationship might benefit Western systems. Western medicine tends to draw a rigid line between biomedical and psychological causation. Non-Western theories usually lack this sharp distinction, recognizing that poor health has intertwined physical, emotional, and social causes. The mind–body opposition is part of Western folk taxonomy, not of science (see also Brown and Barrett 2010; Helman 2007; Joralemon 2010; Strathern and Stewart 2010).

Medical anthropology also considers the impact of new scientific and medical techniques on ideas about life, death, and *personhood* (what it means to be a person). For decades, disagreements about personhood—such as when life begins and ends—have been part of political and religious discussions of contraception, abortion, assisted suicide, and euthanasia (mercy killing). More recent additions to such discussions include stem cells, "harvested" embryos, assisted reproduction, genetic screening, cloning, and life-prolonging medical treatments. How long should a human body be kept alive if there is no hope of recovery?

# Anthropology and Business

For decades anthropologists have used ethnography to understand business settings (Jordan, A., 2013; Jordan, B., 2013). Ethnographic research in an auto factory, for example, may view workers, managers, and executives as different social categories participating in a common system. Each group has characteristic attitudes and behavior patterns. These are transmitted through *microenculturation,* the process by which people learn particular roles within a limited social system. The free-ranging nature of ethnography takes the anthropologist back and forth from worker to executive. Each employee is both an individual with a personal viewpoint and a cultural creature whose perspective is, to some extent, shared with other members of his or her group. Applied anthropologists have acted as "cultural brokers," translating managers' goals or workers' concerns to the other group (see Ferraro and Briody 2013).

Carol Taylor (1987) has stressed the value of an "anthropologist-in-residence" in a large, complex organization, such as a hospital or corporation (see also Briody and Trotter 2008; Cefkin 2009; Jordan 2013). A free-ranging ethnographer can be a perceptive oddball when information and decisions typically move through a rigid hierarchy. If allowed to observe and converse freely with all types and levels of personnel, the anthropologist may acquire a unique perspective on organizational conditions and problems. Such high-tech companies as Xerox, IBM, and Apple have employed anthropologists in

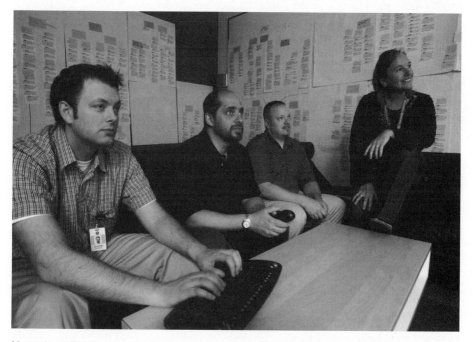

Motorola staff anthropologist Crysta Metcalf (right) and her team sample a new technology at Motorola in Schaumburg, Illinois. This innovation allows people to communicate easily with others while watching the same televised show or event from different locations. © Charles Cherney/MCT/Newscom

various roles. Closely observing how people actually use computer products, anthropologists have worked with engineers to design products that are more user-friendly.

Key features of anthropology that are of value to business include (1) ethnography and observation as ways of gathering data in real-world settings, (2) a focus on diversity, and (3) cross-cultural expertise. Hallmark Cards has hired anthropologists to observe parties, holidays, and celebrations of ethnic groups to improve its ability to design cards for targeted audiences. Applied anthropologists routinely go into people's homes to see how they actually use products (see Denny and Sunderland 2014 and the "Anthropology Today" at the end of this chapter).

## Public and Applied Anthropology

Many academic anthropologists, myself included, occasionally work as applied anthropologists. Most typically, we advise and consult about the direction of change in nations, regions, and communities where we originally did "academic" research. In my case, this has meant policy-relevant work on environmental preservation in Madagascar and poverty reduction in northeastern Brazil.

Other academics, while not doing applied anthropology per se, have urged anthropologists to engage more in what they call **public anthropology** (Borofsky 2000) or *public interest anthropology* (Sanday 2003). Suggested ways of making anthropology more visible and relevant to the public include nonacademic publishing, testifying at government hearings, consulting, acting as an expert witness, and engaging in citizen activism, electoral campaigns, and political administrations. Public anthropologists work to oppose policies that promote injustice and to reframe discussions of key social issues in the media and by public officials. As Barbara Rylko-Bauer and her colleagues (2006) point out, there is also a long tradition of work guided by such goals in applied anthropology (see also Beck and Maida 2013).

New media are helping to disseminate anthropological knowledge to a wider public. The world of cyberspace, including the blogosphere, constantly grows richer in the resources and communication opportunities available to anthropologists. Some of the most widely read anthropological blogs include Savage Minds, a group blog (http://savageminds.org); Living Anthropologically, by Jason Antrosio (http://www.livinganthropologically.com); and Neuroanthropology, by Greg Downey and Daniel Lende (http://blogs.plos.org/neuroanthropology/). Also see this detailed list of anthropology blogs, as updated for 2015: http://anthropologyreport.com/anthropology-blogs-2015/. Anthropologists participate as well in various listservs and networking groups (e.g., on LinkedIn and Research Gate). A bit of googling on your part will take you to anthropologists' personal websites, as well as research project websites.

## Careers and Anthropology

Many college students find anthropology interesting and consider majoring in it. However, their parents or friends may discourage them by asking, "What kind of job are you going to get with an anthropology degree?" The first step in answering that question is to consider the more general question "What do you do with any college major?" The answer is "Not much, without a good bit of effort, thought, and planning." A survey of graduates of the University of Michigan's literary college showed that few had jobs that were clearly linked to their majors. Most professions, including medicine and law, require advanced degrees. Although many colleges offer bachelor's degrees in engineering, business, accounting, and social work, master's degrees often are needed to get the best jobs in those fields. Anthropologists, too, need an advanced degree, almost always a PhD, to find gainful employment in academic, museum, or applied anthropology.

A broad college education, and even a major in anthropology, can be an excellent foundation for success in many fields. One survey of women executives showed that most had not majored in business but in the social sciences or humanities. Only after graduating from college did they study business, leading to a master's degree in business administration (MBA). Those executives felt that the breadth of their college educations had contributed to their business careers. Anthropology majors go on to medical, law, and business schools and find success in many professions that often have little explicit connection to anthropology.

Anthropology's breadth provides knowledge and an outlook on the world that are useful in many kinds of work. For example, an anthropology major combined with a master's degree in business is excellent preparation for work in international business. Breadth is anthropology's hallmark. Anthropologists study people biologically, culturally, socially, and linguistically, across time and space, in various countries, in simple and complex settings. Most colleges offer anthropology courses that compare cultures, along with others that focus on particular world areas, such as Latin America, Asia, Africa, the Middle East, and Eastern Europe. The knowledge of foreign areas acquired in such courses can be useful in many jobs. Anthropology's comparative outlook and its focus on diverse lifestyles combine to provide an excellent foundation for overseas employment (see Ellick and Watkins 2011; Omohundro 2001).

For work in contemporary North America as well, anthropology's focus on culture is increasingly relevant. Every day we hear about cultural differences and about problems whose solutions require a multicultural viewpoint—an ability to recognize and reconcile ethnic differences (see Kottak and Kozaitis 2012). Government, schools, hospitals, and businesses constantly deal with people from different social classes, ethnic groups, and cultural backgrounds. Physicians, attorneys, social workers, police officers, judges, teachers, and students can all do a better job if they understand cultural differences in a nation that is one of the most ethnically diverse in history.

Knowledge of the traditions and beliefs of the groups that make up a modern nation is important in planning and carrying out programs that affect those groups. Experience in planned social change—whether community organization in North America or economic development overseas—shows that a proper social study should be done before a project or policy is implemented. When local people want the change and it fits their lifestyle and traditions, it has a better chance of being successful, beneficial, and cost effective.

People with anthropology backgrounds do well in many fields. Even if one's job has little or nothing to do with anthropology in a formal or obvious sense, a background in anthropology provides a useful orientation when we work with our fellow human beings. For most of us, this means every day of our lives.

## Anthropology Today   *Culturally Appropriate Marketing*

Innovation succeeds best when it is culturally appropriate. This axiom of applied anthropology could guide the international spread not only of development projects but also of businesses, such as fast food. Each time McDonald's or Burger King expands to a new nation, it must devise a culturally appropriate strategy for fitting into the new setting.

McDonald's has been very successful internationally. Almost 70 percent of its current annual revenue comes from sales outside the United States. As the world's most successful restaurant chain, McDonald's has more than 36,000 restaurants in some 120 countries. One place where McDonald's has expanded successfully is Brazil, where 100 million middle-class people, most living in densely packed cities, provide a concentrated market for a fast-food chain. Still, it took McDonald's some time to find the right marketing strategy for Brazil.

In 1980 when I visited Brazil after a seven-year absence, I first noticed, as a manifestation of Brazil's growing participation in the world economy, the appearance of two McDonald's restaurants in Rio de Janeiro. There wasn't much difference between the Brazilian and an American McDonald's. The restaurants looked alike. The menus were more or less the same, as was the taste of the quarter-pounders. I

picked up an artifact, a white paper bag with yellow lettering, exactly like the takeout bags then used in American McDonald's. An advertising device, it carried several messages about how Brazilians could bring McDonald's into their lives. However, it seemed to me that McDonald's Brazilian ad campaign was missing some important points about how fast food should be marketed in a culture that valued large, leisurely lunches.

The bag proclaimed, "You're going to enjoy the [McDonald's] difference," and listed several "favorite places where you can enjoy McDonald's products." This list confirmed that the marketing people were trying to adapt to Brazilian middle-class culture, but they were making some mistakes. "When you go out in the car with the kids" transferred the uniquely developed North American cultural combination of highways, affordable cars, and suburban living to the very different context of urban Brazil. A similar suggestion was "traveling to the country place." Even Brazilians who owned country places could not find McDonald's, still confined to the cities then, on the road. The ad creator had apparently never attempted to drive up to a fast-food restaurant in a neighborhood with no parking spaces.

Several other suggestions pointed customers toward the beach, where *cariocas*

McDonald's adapting to local culture: Coconut water is available to wash down a Brazilian Big Mac, and the Indian McDonald's has no beef or pork products on its menu.
(first): © Paulo Fridman/Bloomberg/Getty Images; (second): © David Pearson/Alamy

(Rio natives) do spend much of their leisure time. One could eat McDonald's products "after a dip in the ocean," "at a picnic at the beach," or "watching the surfers." These suggestions ignored the Brazilian custom of consuming cold things, such as beer, soft drinks, ice cream, and ham and cheese sandwiches, on the beach. Brazilians don't consider a hot, greasy hamburger proper beach food. They view the sea as "cold" and hamburgers as "hot"; they avoid "hot" foods at the beach.

Also culturally dubious was the suggestion to eat McDonald's hamburgers "lunching at the office." Brazilians prefer their main meal at midday, often eating at a leisurely pace with business associates. Many firms serve ample lunches to their employees. Other workers take advantage of a two-hour lunch break to go home to eat with the spouse and children. Nor did it make sense to suggest that children should eat hamburgers for lunch, since most kids attend school for half-day sessions and have lunch at home. Two other suggestions—"waiting for the bus" and "in the beauty parlor"—did describe common aspects of daily life in a Brazilian city. However, these settings have not proved especially inviting to hamburgers or fish filets.

The homes of Brazilians who can afford McDonald's products often have cooks and maids to do many of the things that fast-food restaurants do in the United States. The suggestion that McDonald's products be eaten "while watching your favorite television program" is culturally

appropriate, because Brazilians watch TV a lot. However, Brazil's consuming classes can ask the cook to make a snack when hunger strikes. Indeed, much televiewing occurs during the light dinner served when the husband gets home from the office.

Most appropriate to the Brazilian lifestyle was the suggestion to enjoy McDonald's "on the cook's day off." Throughout Brazil, Sunday is that day. The Sunday pattern for middle-class families who live on the coast is a trip to the beach, liters of beer, a full midday meal around 3:00 P.M., and a light evening snack. McDonald's found its niche in the Sunday evening meal, when families flock to the fast-food restaurant.

McDonald's has expanded rapidly in Brazil, where, as in North America, young appetites have fueled the fast-food explosion. McDonald's outlets now dot urban neighborhoods throughout Brazil, and the cost of hiring in-home help has skyrocketed. Given these changes, Brazilian teenagers increasingly use McDonald's for after-school snacks, and whole families have evening meals there. As an anthropologist could have predicted, the fast-food industry has not revolutionized Brazilian food and meal customs. Rather, McDonald's is succeeding because it has adapted to preexisting Brazilian cultural patterns.

Once McDonald's realized that more money could be made by fitting in with, rather than trying to Americanize, Brazilian meal habits, it started aiming its advertising at that goal. By 2014, McDonald's had more than 800 outlets in Brazil.

## Summary

1. Applied anthropology uses anthropological perspectives, theory, methods, and data to identify, assess, and solve problems. Applied anthropologists have a range of employers. Examples are government agencies; development organizations; NGOs; tribal, ethnic, and interest groups; businesses; hospitals; social services;

and educational agencies. Applied anthropologists come from all four subfields. Ethnography is one of applied anthropology's most valuable research tools.

2. Development anthropology focuses on social issues in, and the cultural dimension of, economic development. Not all governments seek to increase equality and end poverty. Resistance by elites to reform is typical. At the same time, local people rarely cooperate with projects requiring major and risky changes in their daily lives. Many projects seek to impose inappropriate property notions and incompatible social units on their intended beneficiaries. The best strategy for change is to base the social design for innovation on traditional social forms in each target area.

3. Anthropology and education researchers work in classrooms, homes, and other settings relevant to education and make policy recommendations based on their findings. Both academic and applied anthropologists study migration from rural areas to cities and across national boundaries. North America has become a popular arena for urban anthropological research on migration, ethnicity, poverty, and related topics. Although rural and urban are different social systems, there is cultural diffusion from one to the other.

4. Medical anthropology is a biocultural field that studies variation in health care systems, including disease, illness, health standards, and disease theories. In a given setting, the characteristic diseases reflect diet, population density, economy, and social complexity. Native theories of illness may be personalistic, naturalistic, or emotionalistic. In applying anthropology to business, the key features are (1) ethnography and observation as ways of gathering data, (2) a focus on diversity, and (3) cross-cultural expertise. Public anthropology attempts to extend anthropological knowledge of social problems and issues to a wider and more influential audience.

5. A broad college education, including anthropology and foreign-area courses, offers an excellent background for many fields. Anthropology's comparative, cross-cultural outlook provides an excellent basis for overseas employment. Even for work in North America, a focus on culture and cultural diversity is valuable. Anthropology majors attend medical, law, and business schools and succeed in many fields, some of which have little explicit connection with anthropology.

## Key Terms

anthropology and education, *398*
curer, *403*
development anthropology, *393*
disease, *401*
health care systems, *401*
illness, *401*
increased equity, *394*
medical anthropology, *401*
overinnovation, *395*
public anthropology, *406*
scientific medicine, *403*
underdifferentiation, *396*
urban anthropology, *400*

# Chapter 18

# The World System, Colonialism, and Inequality

Although fieldwork in small communities has been anthropology's hallmark, isolated groups are impossible to find today. Truly isolated human societies probably never have existed. For thousands of years, human groups have been in contact with one another. Local societies always have participated in a larger system, which today has global dimensions. We call it the *modern world system,* by which we mean a world in which nations are economically and politically interdependent.

## The World System

A huge increase in international trade during and after the 15th century led to the **capitalist world economy** (Wallerstein 1982, 2004*b*), a single world system committed to production for sale or exchange, with the object of maximizing profits rather than supplying domestic needs. The world system and the relations among the countries within it are shaped by the capitalist world economy. **Capital** refers to wealth or resources invested in business, with the intent of generating further wealth—making a profit.

Illustrating the contemporary global spread of capitalism is this scene from central Shanghai, China. Pedestrians walk near an upscale shopping mall. What evidence of globalization do you see in this photo? © Iain Masterton/Alamy

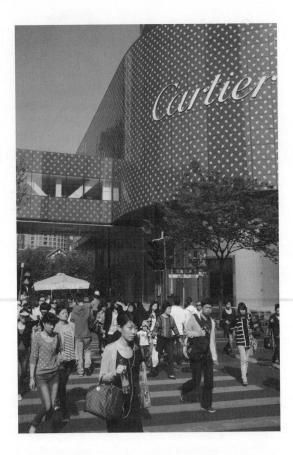

World-system theory can be traced to the French social historian Fernand Braudel. In his three-volume work *Civilization and Capitalism, 15th–18th Century* (1981, 1982, 1992), Braudel argues that society consists of interrelated parts assembled into a system. Societies are subsystems of larger systems, with the world system the largest. The key claim of **world-system theory** is that an identifiable social system, featuring wealth and power differentials, extends beyond individual countries. That system has been formed by a set of economic and political relations that has characterized much of the globe since the 16th century, when the Old World established regular contact with the Americas (see Bodley 2014).

According to Wallerstein (1982, 2004*b*), countries within the world system occupy three different positions of economic and political power: core, periphery, and semiperiphery. The **core,** the dominant position, includes the strongest, most powerful, and technically most advanced industrial nations. In core nations, "the complexity of economic activities and the level of capital accumulation is the greatest" (Thompson 1983, p. 12). According to Arrighi (2010), the core monopolizes the most profitable activities, especially the control of world finance.

The **semiperiphery** is intermediate between the core and the periphery. Contemporary nations of the semiperiphery are industrialized. Like core nations, they export both industrial goods and commodities, but they lack the power and economic dominance of

Jobs continue to migrate from core nations to places in the semiperiphery, such as this call center in India. © Fredrik Renander/Alamy

core nations. Thus Brazil, a semiperiphery nation, exports automobiles to Nigeria (a periphery nation) and auto engines, orange juice extract, coffee, and shrimp to the United States (a core nation). The **periphery** includes the world's least privileged and powerful countries. Economic activities there are less mechanized than are those in the core and semiperiphery, although some degree of industrialization has reached even peripheral nations. The periphery produces raw materials, agricultural commodities, and, increasingly, human labor for export to the core and the semiperiphery (Shannon 1996).

In the United States and Western Europe today, immigration—documented and undocumented—from the periphery and semiperiphery supplies cheap labor, especially for agriculture, construction, and paid domestic labor. U.S. states as distant as California, Michigan, and South Carolina make significant use of farm labor from Mexico. The availability of relatively cheap workers from noncore nations such as Mexico (in the United States) and Turkey (in Germany) benefits farmers and business owners in core countries while supplying remittances to families in the semiperiphery and periphery. As a result of 21st-century telecommunications technology, cheap labor doesn't even need to migrate to the United States. Thousands of families in India are being supported as American companies outsource jobs—from telephone assistance to software engineering—to nations outside the core (see Nadeem 2011).

## The Emergence of the World System

By the 15th century, Europeans were profiting from a transoceanic trade-oriented economy, and people worldwide entered Europe's sphere of influence. What was new was the transatlantic component of a long history of Old World sailing and commerce. As early as 600 B.C.E., the Phoenicians/Carthaginians sailed around Britain on regular trade routes and circumnavigated Africa. Likewise, Indonesia and Africa have been linked in Indian Ocean trade for at least 2,000 years. In the 15th century, Europe established regular contact with Asia, Africa, and eventually the New World (the Caribbean and the Americas). Christopher Columbus's first voyage from Spain to the Bahamas and the Caribbean in 1492 was soon followed by additional voyages. These journeys opened the way for a major exchange of people, resources, products, ideas, and diseases, as the Old and New Worlds were forever linked (Crosby 2003; Mann 2011; Nunn and Qian 2010). Led by Spain and Portugal, Europeans extracted silver and gold, conquered indigenous peoples (taking some as slaves), and colonized their lands.

Previously in Europe as throughout the world, rural people had produced mainly for their own needs, growing their own food and making clothing, furniture, and tools from local products. People produced beyond their immediate needs in order to pay taxes and to purchase trade items such as salt and iron. As late as 1650 the English diet was based on locally grown starches. In the 200 years that followed, however, the English became extraordinary consumers of imported goods. One of the earliest and most popular of those goods was sugar (Mintz 1985).

Sugarcane, originally domesticated in Papua New Guinea, was first processed in India. Reaching Europe via the eastern Mediterranean, it was carried to the Americas by Columbus (Mintz 1985). The climate of Brazil and the Caribbean proved ideal for growing sugarcane, and Europeans built plantations there to supply the growing demand for sugar. This led to the development in the 17th century of a plantation economy based on a single cash crop—a system known as *monocrop* production.

The demand for sugar in a growing international market spurred the development of the transatlantic slave trade and New World plantation economies based on slave labor. By the 18th century, an increased English demand for raw cotton led to rapid settlement of what is now the southeastern United States and the emergence there of another slave-based monocrop production system. Like sugar, cotton was a key trade item that fueled the growth of the world system.

## Industrialization

By the 18th century the stage had been set for the **Industrial Revolution**—the historical transformation (in Europe, after 1750) of "traditional" into "modern" societies through industrialization. The seeds of industrial society were planted well before the 18th century (Gimpel 1988). For example, a knitting machine invented in England in 1589 was so far ahead of its time that it played a profitable role in factories two and three centuries later. The appearance of cloth mills late in the Middle Ages foreshadowed the search for new sources of wind and water power that characterized the Industrial Revolution. Industrialization required capital for investment. The established system of transoceanic commerce supplied this capital from the profits it generated. As wealthy people invested in machines and engines to drive machines, capital and scientific innovation fueled invention. Industrialization increased production in both farming and manufacturing.

*The Art of* STOCKING-FRAME-WORK-KNITTING.

*Engrav'd for the Universal Magazine 1750, for J. Hinton at the Kings Arms in S.t Pauls Church Yard* LONDON.

In the home-handicraft, or domestic, system of production, an organizer supplied raw materials to workers in their homes and collected their products. Family life and work were intertwined, as in this English scene. Is there a modern equivalent to the domestic system of production?
© ARPL/Topham/The Image Works

European industrialization developed from and eventually replaced the *domestic system* of manufacture (the home-handicraft system). In this system, an organizer–entrepreneur supplied the raw materials to workers in their homes and collected the finished products from them. The entrepreneur, whose sphere of operations might span several villages, owned the materials, paid for the work, and arranged the marketing.

## Causes of the Industrial Revolution

The Industrial Revolution began with cotton products, iron, and pottery. These were widely used items whose manufacture could be broken down into simple routine motions that machines could perform. When manufacturing moved from homes to factories, where machinery replaced handwork, agrarian societies evolved into industrial ones. As factories produced cheap staple goods, the Industrial Revolution led to a dramatic increase in production. Industrialization fueled urban growth and created a new kind of city, with factories crowded together in places where coal and labor were cheap.

The Industrial Revolution began in England, and, as its industrialization proceeded, Britain's population began to increase dramatically. It doubled during the 18th century (especially after 1750) and did so again between 1800 and 1850. This demographic explosion fueled consumption, but British entrepreneurs couldn't meet the increased demand with the traditional production methods. This spurred further experimentation, innovation, and rapid technological change.

English industrialization drew on national advantages in natural resources. Britain was rich in coal and iron ore and had navigable coasts and waterways. It was a seafaring island-nation located at the crossroads of international trade. These features gave Britain a favored position for importing raw materials and exporting manufactured goods. Another factor in England's industrial growth was the fact that much of its 18th-century colonial empire was occupied by English settler families who looked to the mother country as they tried to replicate European civilization abroad. These colonies bought large quantities of English staples.

It also has been argued that particular cultural values and religion contributed to industrialization. Many members of the emerging English middle class were Protestant nonconformists. Their beliefs and values encouraged industry, thrift, the dissemination of new knowledge, inventiveness, and willingness to accept change (Weber 1904/1958).

# Socioeconomic Effects of Industrialization

The socioeconomic effects of industrialization were mixed. English national income tripled between 1700 and 1815 and increased 30 times more by 1939. Standards of comfort rose, but prosperity was uneven. At first, factory workers got wages higher than those available in the domestic system. Later, however, owners started recruiting labor in places where living standards were low and labor (including that of women and children) was cheap. Filth and smoke polluted 19th-century cities. Housing was crowded and unsanitary. People experienced rampant disease and rising death rates. This was the world of Ebenezer Scrooge, Bob Cratchit, Tiny Tim—and Karl Marx.

## Industrial Stratification

The social theorists Karl Marx and Max Weber focused on the stratification systems associated with industrialization. From his observations in England and his analysis of 19th-century industrial capitalism, Marx (Marx and Engels 1848/1976) saw socioeconomic stratification as a sharp and simple division between two opposed classes: the bourgeoisie (capitalists) and the proletariat (propertyless workers). The bourgeoisie traced its origins to overseas ventures and the world capitalist economy, which had created a wealthy commercial class (White 2009).

Industrialization shifted production from farms and cottages to mills and factories, where mechanical power was available and where workers could be assembled to operate heavy machinery. The **bourgeoisie** owned the factories, mines, estates, and other means of production. Members of the **working class,** or **proletariat,** had to sell their labor to survive.

Industrialization, and the rural to urban migration it fueled, hastened the process of *proletarianization*—the separation of workers from the means of production. Bourgeoisie domination extended to the means of communication, the schools, and other key institutions. *Class consciousness* (recognition of collective interests and personal identification with one's economic group) was a vital part of Marx's view of class. He saw bourgeoisie and proletariat as socioeconomic divisions with radically opposed interests. Marx viewed classes as powerful collective forces that could mobilize human energies to influence the course of history. On the basis of their common experience, workers, he thought, would develop class consciousness, which could lead to revolutionary change. Although no proletarian revolution was to occur in England, workers did develop organizations to protect their interests and increase their share of industrial profits. During the 19th century, trade unions and socialist parties emerged to express a rising anticapitalist spirit. The concerns of the English labor movement were to remove young children from factories and limit the hours during which women and children could work. The profile of stratification in industrial core nations gradually took shape. Capitalists controlled production, but labor was organizing for better wages and working conditions. By 1900 many governments had factory legislation and social-welfare programs. Mass living standards in core nations improved as population grew.

Today, the existence of publicly traded companies complicates the division between capitalists and workers. Through pension plans and personal investments, some workers have become part-owners rather than propertyless workers. Today's key capitalist isn't the factory owner, who may have been replaced by stockholders, but the CEO or the chair of the board of directors, neither of whom may actually own the corporation.

Modern stratification systems aren't simple and dichotomous. They include (particularly in core and semiperiphery nations) a middle class of skilled and professional workers. Gerhard Lenski (1966) argued that social equality tends to increase in advanced industrial societies. The masses improve their access to economic benefits and political power. In Lenski's scheme, the shift of political power to the masses reflects the growth of the middle class, which reduces the polarization between owning and working classes. The proliferation of middle-class occupations creates opportunities for social mobility and a more complex stratification system (Giddens 1973; Kerbo 2012).

In the United States the complexity of this system goes largely unnoticed by many Americans. Most contemporary Americans claim to belong to the middle class, which they tend to perceive as a vast, undifferentiated group. There are, however, significant, and growing, socioeconomic contrasts within the middle class, and especially between the richest and the poorest Americans. Table 18.1 shows how income varied from the top to the bottom fifth (quintile) of American earners in 2013. In that table, we see that the top fifth earned almost half (48.8 percent) of all income generated in the United States, 13 times the share of the bottom fifth. The top 5 percent of earners got 21.3 percent of U.S. national aggregate income. Until about 1980, incomes of all Americans grew at about the same rate. Since 1980, however, income has increased most for the top earners. For the poorest 20 percent (lowest quintile) of households, median income actually has been declining.

Incomes for the top 1 percent of American earners soared 31 percent from 2009 (when the Great Recession officially ended) through 2012. For everyone else, income growth averaged less than 1 percent (Rugaber and Boak 2014). Higher stock

TABLE 18.1

**U.S. National Income by Quintile, 2013**

Source: Carmen DeNavas-Walt and Bernadette D. Proctor, "Income and Poverty in the United States: 2013." U.S. Census Bureau, Current Population Report, P60-249, September 2014. http://www.census.gov/content/dam/Census/library/publications/2014/demo/p60-249.pdf

| Segment of Population | % Share of National Income | Mean Household Income |
|---|---|---|
| Top 20 percent | 51.0 | $185,206 |
| Second 20 percent | 23.0 | 83,519 |
| Third 20 percent | 14.4 | 53,322 |
| Fourth 20 percent | 8.4 | 30,509 |
| Bottom 20 percent | 3.2 | 11,651 |
| Top 5 percent | 22.2 | 322,343 |

prices, home values, and corporate profits have propelled the recovery among affluent Americans, while blue- and white-collar workers still feel the effects of high unemployment and stagnant wages (Lowrey 2013). When we consider wealth (investments, property, possessions, etc.) rather than income, the contrast is even more striking. Between 2000 and 2011, the median net worth of the richest 40 percent of Americans (the top two quintiles) increased, while it was dropping for everyone else (U.S. Census Bureau 2014). The richest 1 percent of Americans now own more wealth than the bottom 90 percent combined. Those ultra-wealthy households hold over one-third (35 percent) of the nation's wealth (Allegretto 2011; Economic Policy Institute 2012). Their net worth is 288 times greater than the median, or typical, household's net worth. This is the highest ratio on record. Recognition of such disparities, and that the rich have been getting richer and the poor poorer, led to the Occupy movement of 2011. That movement began on Wall Street in New York City and quickly spread to many other cities in an attempt to draw attention to the lack of economic recovery for 99 percent of Americans.

Max Weber faulted Karl Marx for an overly simple and exclusively economic view of stratification. As we saw in the chapter "Political Systems," Weber (1922/1968) defined three dimensions of social stratification: wealth, power, and prestige. Although, as Weber showed, wealth, power, and prestige are separate components of social ranking, they tend to be correlated. Weber also believed that social identities based on ethnicity, religion, race, nationality, and other attributes could take priority over class (social identity based on economic status). In addition to class contrasts, the modern world system *is* cross-cut by collective identities based on ethnicity, religion, and nationality (Shannon 1996). Class conflicts tend to occur within nations, and nationalism has impeded global class solidarity, particularly of proletarians.

Although the capitalist class dominates politically in most countries, growing wealth made it easier for core nations to grant higher wages (Hopkins and Wallerstein 1982). However, the improvement in core workers' living standards wouldn't have occurred without the world system. Without the periphery, core capitalists would have trouble maintaining their profits and satisfying the demands of core workers. In the periphery, wages and living standards are much lower. The current *world stratification system* features a substantial contrast between both capitalists and workers in the core nations and workers on the periphery (see Kerbo 2012).

# Colonialism

The major forces influencing global cultural interactions during the past 500 years have been commercial expansion, industrial capitalism, and the dominance of colonial and core nations (Wallerstein 1982, 2004b; Wolf 1982). As state formation had done previously, industrialization accelerated local participation in larger networks. According to Bodley (2014), the goal of perpetual expansion is a distinguishing feature of industrial economic systems.

During the 19th century, European business interests initiated a concerted search for markets. This process led to European imperialism in Africa, Asia, and Oceania. **Imperialism** refers to a policy of extending the rule of a country or an empire over foreign nations and of taking and holding foreign colonies. Imperialism goes back to early states, including Egypt in the Old World and the Incas in the New. A Greek empire was forged by Alexander the Great, and Julius Caesar and his successors spread the Roman empire. More recent examples include the British, French, and Soviet empires.

After 1850, European imperial expansion was aided by improved transportation, which facilitated the colonization of vast areas of sparsely settled lands in Australia and the interior of North and South America. The new colonies purchased goods from the industrial centers and shipped back wheat, cotton, wool, mutton, beef, and leather. The first phase of European colonialism had been the exploration and exploitation of the Americas and the Caribbean after Columbus. A second phase began as European nations competed for colonies between 1875 and 1914.

**Colonialism** is the political, social, economic, and cultural domination of a territory and its people by a foreign power for an extended time (see Bremen and Shimizu 1999; Stoler, McGranahan, and Perdue 2007). If imperialism is almost as old as the state, colonialism can be traced back to the Phoenicians, who established colonies along the eastern Mediterranean 3,000 years ago. The ancient Greeks and Romans were avid colonizers, as well as empire builders.

The first phase of modern colonialism began with the European "Age of Discovery"— of the Americas and of a sea route to the Far East. After 1492, the Spanish, the original conquerors of the Aztecs and the Incas, explored and colonized widely in the Caribbean, Mexico, the southern portions of what was to become the United States, and Central and South America. In South America, Portugal ruled over Brazil. Rebellions and wars aimed at independence ended the first phase of European colonialism by the early 19th century. Brazil declared independence from Portugal in 1822. By 1825 most of Spain's colonies were politically independent. Spain held on to Cuba and the Philippines until 1898 but otherwise withdrew from the colonial field. During the first phase of colonialism, Spain and Portugal, along with Britain and France, were major colonizing nations. The last two (Britain and France) dominated the second phase.

## British Colonialism

At its peak about 1914, the British empire covered a fifth of the world's land surface and ruled a fourth of its population (see Figure 18.1). Like several other European nations, Britain had two stages of colonialism (see Darwin 2013). The first began with the

FIGURE 18.1   **Map of the British Empire in 1765 and 1914**

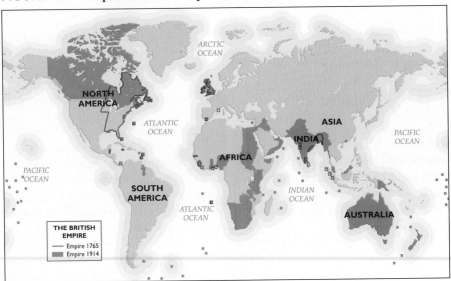

Elizabethan voyages of the 16th century. During the 17th century, Britain acquired most of the eastern coast of North America, Canada's St. Lawrence basin, islands in the Caribbean, slave stations in Africa, and interests in India.

The British shared the exploration of the New World with the Spanish, Portuguese, French, and Dutch. The British by and large left Mexico, along with Central and South America, to the Spanish and the Portuguese. The end of the Seven Years' War in 1763 forced a French retreat from most of Canada and India, where France previously had competed with Britain.

The American revolution ended the first stage of British colonialism. A second colonial empire, on which the "sun never set," rose from the ashes of the first. Beginning in 1788, but intensifying after 1815, the British settled Australia. Britain had acquired Dutch South Africa by 1815. The establishment of Singapore in 1819 provided a base for a British trade network that extended to much of South Asia and along the coast of China. By this time, the empires of Britain's traditional rivals, particularly Spain, had been severely diminished in scope. Britain's position as imperial power and the world's leading industrial nation was unchallenged.

During the Victorian Era (1837–1901), as Britain's colonial expansion continued, Prime Minister Benjamin Disraeli implemented a foreign policy justified by a view of imperialism as shouldering "the white man's burden"—a phrase coined by the poet Rudyard Kipling. People in the empire were seen as unable to govern themselves, so that British guidance was needed to civilize and Christianize them. This paternalistic and racist doctrine was used to legitimize Britain's acquisition and control of parts of central Africa and Asia.

After World War II, the British empire began to fall apart, with nationalist movements for independence. India became independent in 1947, as did Ireland in 1949.

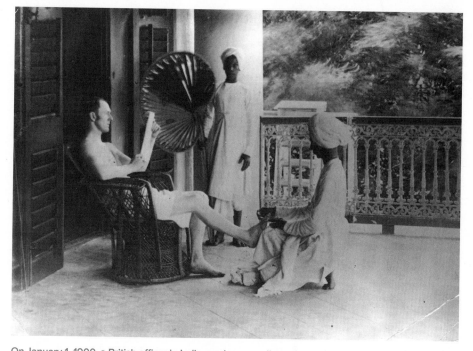

On January 1, 1900, a British officer in India receives a pedicure from a servant. What does this photo say to you about colonialism? Who gives pedicures in your society? © Hulton Archive/Getty Images

Decolonization in Africa and Asia accelerated during the late 1950s (see Thomas, Butler, and Moore 2015; Thompson 2012; White 2014). Today, the ties that remain between Britain and its former colonies are mainly linguistic or cultural rather than political (Thompson 2012; White 2014).

## French Colonialism

French colonialism also had two phases. The first began with the explorations of the early 1600s. Prior to the French revolution in 1789, missionaries, explorers, and traders carved out niches for France in Canada, the Louisiana territory, several Caribbean islands, and parts of India, which were lost along with Canada to Great Britain in 1763 (Harvey 1980).

The foundations of the second French empire were established between 1830 and 1870. In Great Britain the drive for profit led expansion, but French colonialism was spurred more by the state, church, and armed forces than by pure business interests. France acquired Algeria and part of what eventually became Indochina (Cambodia, Laos, and Vietnam). By 1914 the French empire covered 4 million square miles and included some 60 million people (see Figure 18.2). By 1893 French rule had been fully established in Indochina. Tunisia and Morocco became French protectorates in 1883 and 1912, respectively (see Conklin, Fishman, and Zaretsky 2015).

To be sure, the French, like the British, had substantial business interests in their colonies, but they also sought, again like the British, international glory and prestige. The

**FIGURE 18.2    Map of the French Empire at Its Height around 1914**

French promulgated a *mission civilisatrice,* their equivalent of Britain's "white man's burden." The goal was to implant French culture and language throughout the colonies.

The French used two forms of colonial rule: *indirect rule,* governing through native leaders and established political structures, in areas with long histories of state organization, such as Morocco and Tunisia; and *direct rule* by French officials in many areas of Africa, where the French imposed new government structures to control diverse societies, many of them previously stateless. Like the British empire, the French empire began to disintegrate after World War II. France fought long—and ultimately futile—wars to keep its empire intact in Indochina and Algeria.

## Colonialism and Identity

Many geopolitical labels in the news today had no equivalent meaning before colonialism. Whole countries, along with social groups and divisions within them, were colonial inventions. In West Africa, for example, by geographic logic, several adjacent countries could be one (Togo, Ghana, Ivory Coast, Guinea, Guinea-Bissau, Sierra Leone, Liberia). Instead, they are separated by linguistic, political, and economic contrasts promoted under colonialism.

Hundreds of ethnic groups and "tribes" are colonial constructions (see Ranger 1996). The Sukuma of Tanzania, for instance, were first registered as a single tribe by the colonial administration. Then missionaries standardized a series of dialects into a single Sukuma language, into which they translated the Bible and other religious texts. Thereafter, those texts were taught in missionary schools and to European foreigners and other non-Sukuma speakers. Over time this standardized the Sukuma language and ethnicity (Finnstrom 1997).

In the East African countries of Rwanda and Burundi, farmers and herders live in the same areas and speak the same language. Historically they have shared the same social world, although their social organization is "extremely hierarchical," almost "castelike" (Malkki 1995, p. 24). There has been a tendency to see the pastoral Tutsis as superior to the agricultural Hutus. Tutsis have been presented as nobles, Hutus as commoners. Yet when distributing identity cards in Rwanda, the Belgian colonizers simply identified all people with more than 10 head of cattle as Tutsi. Owners of fewer cattle were registered as Hutus (Bjuremalm 1997). Years later, these arbitrary colonial registers were used systematically for "ethnic" identification during the mass killings (genocide) that took place in Rwanda in 1994 (see Totten and Ubaldo 2011).

## Postcolonial Studies

In anthropology, history, and literature, the field of postcolonial studies has gained prominence since the 1970s (see Chakrabarty 2007; Stoler 2013). **Postcolonial** refers to the study of the interactions between European nations and the societies they colonized (mainly after 1800). In 1914, European empires, which broke up after World War II, ruled more than 85 percent of the world. The term *postcolonial* also has been used to describe the second half of the 20th century in general, the period succeeding colonialism. Even more generically, *postcolonial* may be used to signify a position against imperialism and Eurocentrism (see Miles 2014).

The former colonies (*postcolonies*) can be divided into settler, nonsettler, and mixed (Petraglia-Bahri 1996). The settler countries, with large numbers of European colonists and sparser native populations, include Australia and Canada. Examples of nonsettler countries include India, Pakistan, Bangladesh, Sri Lanka, Malaysia, Indonesia, Nigeria, Senegal, Madagascar, and Jamaica. All these had substantial native populations and relatively few European settlers. Mixed countries include South Africa, Zimbabwe, Kenya, and Algeria. Such countries had significant European settlement despite having sizable native populations.

Given the varied experiences of such countries, *postcolonial* has to be a loose term. The United States, for instance, was colonized by Europeans and fought a war for independence from Britain. Is the United States a postcolony? It usually isn't perceived as such, given its current world power position, its treatment of Native Americans (sometimes called internal colonization), and its annexation of other parts of the world. Research in postcolonial studies is growing, permitting a wide-ranging investigation of power relations in varied contexts. Broad topics in the field include the formation of an empire, the impact of colonization, and the state of the postcolony today.

# Development

During the Industrial Revolution, a strong current of thought viewed industrialization as a beneficial process of organic development and progress. Many economists still assume that industrialization increases production and income. They seek to create in Third World ("developing") countries a process like the one that first occurred spontaneously in 18th-century Great Britain.

We have seen that Britain used the notion "a white man's burden" to justify its imperialist expansion and that France claimed to be engaged in a *mission civilisatrice,* a civilizing mission, in its colonies. Both these ideas illustrate an **intervention philosophy,** an ideological justification for outsiders to guide native peoples in specific directions. Economic development plans also have intervention philosophies. John Bodley (2012) argues that the basic belief behind interventions—whether by colonialists, missionaries, governments, or development planners—has been the same for more than one hundred years. This belief is that industrialization, modernization, Westernization, and individualism are desirable evolutionary advances that will bring long-term benefits to local people.

## Neoliberalism

One currently influential intervention philosophy is neoliberalism. This term encompasses a set of assumptions that have become widespread during the last 30 years. Neoliberal policies are being implemented in developing nations, including postsocialist societies (e.g., those of the former Soviet Union). **Neoliberalism** is the current form of the classic economic liberalism laid out in Adam Smith's famous capitalist manifesto, *The Wealth of Nations,* published in 1776, soon after the Industrial Revolution. Smith advocated laissez-faire (hands-off) economics as the basis of capitalism: The government should stay out of its nation's economic affairs. Free, unregulated trade, Smith argued, is the best way for a nation's economy to develop. There should be no restrictions on manufacturing, no barriers to commerce, and no tariffs. This philosophy is called "liberalism" because it aims at liberating, or freeing, the economy from government controls. Economic liberalism encouraged "free" enterprise and competition, with the goal of generating profits. (Ironically, Adam Smith's liberalism is today's capitalist "conservatism.")

Economic liberalism prevailed in the United States until President Franklin Roosevelt's New Deal during the 1930s. The Great Depression produced a turn to Keynesian economics, which challenged liberalism. John Maynard Keynes (1927, 1936) insisted that full employment was necessary for capitalism to grow, that governments and central banks should intervene to increase employment, and that government should promote the common good.

Especially since the fall of Communism (1989–1991), there has been a revival of neoliberalism, which has been spreading globally. Around the world, neoliberal policies have been imposed by powerful financial institutions such as the International Monetary Fund (IMF), the World Bank, and the Inter-American Development Bank (see Edelman and Haugerud 2005). Neoliberalism entails open (tariff- and barrier-free) international trade and investment. Profits are sought through the lowering of costs, whether through improving productivity, laying off workers, or seeking workers who accept lower wages. In exchange for loans, the governments of postsocialist and developing nations have been required to accept the neoliberal premise that deregulation leads to economic growth, which will eventually benefit everyone through a process sometimes called "trickle down." Accompanying the belief in free markets and the idea of cutting costs is a tendency to impose austerity measures that cut government expenses. This can entail reduced public spending on education, health care, and other social services.

# The Second World

The labels "First World," "Second World," and "Third World" represent a common, although ethnocentric, way of categorizing nations. The *First World* refers to the "democratic West"—traditionally conceived in opposition to a "Second World" ruled by "Communism." The *Second World* refers to the former Soviet Union and the socialist and once-socialist countries of Eastern Europe and Asia. Proceeding with this classification, the "less-developed countries," or "developing nations," make up the *Third World*.

## Communism

The two meanings of communism involve how it is written, whether with a lowercase (small) or an uppercase (large) *c*. Small-*c* **communism** describes a social system in which property is owned by the community and in which people work for the common good. Large-*C* **Communism** was a political movement and doctrine seeking to overthrow capitalism and to establish a form of communism such as that which prevailed in the Soviet Union (USSR) from 1917 to 1991. The heyday of Communism was a 40-year period from 1949 to 1989, when more Communist regimes existed than at any time before or after. Today only 5 Communist states remain—China, Cuba, Laos, North Korea, and Vietnam, compared with 23 in 1985.

Communism, which originated with Russia's Bolshevik Revolution in 1917 and took its inspiration from Karl Marx and Friedrich Engels, was not uniform over time or among countries. All Communist systems were *authoritarian* (promoting obedience to authority rather than individual freedom). Many were *totalitarian* (banning rival parties and demanding total submission of the individual to the state). The Communist Party monopolized power in every Communist state, and relations within the party were highly centralized and strictly disciplined. Communist nations had state ownership, rather than private ownership, of the means of production. Finally, all Communist regimes, with the goal of advancing communism, cultivated a sense of belonging to an international movement (Brown 2001).

## Postsocialist Transitions

Social scientists have tended to refer to "Second World" societies as socialist rather than Communist. Today research by anthropologists is thriving in *postsocialist* societies—those that once emphasized bureaucratic redistribution of wealth according to a central plan (Giordano, Ruegg, and Boscoboinik 2014; Grudzinska-Gross and Tymowski 2014; Verdery 2001). In the postsocialist period, states that once had planned economies have been following the neoliberal agenda, by divesting themselves of state-owned resources in favor of privatization. Some of them have moved toward formal liberal democracy, with political parties, elections, and a balance of powers.

Neoliberal economists assumed that dismantling the Soviet Union's planned economy would raise gross domestic product (GDP) and living standards. The goal was to enhance production by substituting a free market system and providing incentives through privatization. In October 1991, Boris Yeltsin, who had been elected president of Russia that June, announced a program of radical market-oriented reform, pursuing a changeover to capitalism. Yeltsin's program of "shock therapy" cut subsidies to farms and industries and ended price controls. Since then, postsocialist Russia has faced many problems. After the fall of the Soviet Union, Russia's GDP fell by half. Life expectancy and the birth rate declined, and poverty increased.

## The World System Today

The spread of industrialization continues today, although nations have shifted their positions within the world system. By 1900, the United States had become a core nation, having overtaken Great Britain in iron, coal, and cotton production. In a few decades (1868–1900), Japan changed from a medieval handicraft economy to an industrial one, joining the semiperiphery by 1900 and moving to the core between 1945 and 1970. India and China have joined Brazil as leaders of the semiperiphery. The map in Figure 18.3 shows the world system today.

Twentieth-century industrialization added hundreds of new industries and millions of new jobs. Production increased, often beyond immediate demand, spurring strategies, such as advertising, to sell everything industry could churn out. Mass production gave rise to a culture of consumption, which valued acquisitiveness and conspicuous consumption.

How do things stand today? Worldwide, young people are abandoning traditional subsistence pursuits and seeking cash. A popular song once queried "How're you gonna keep 'em down on the farm after they've seen Paree?" Nowadays most people *have* seen

FIGURE 18.3   **The World System Today**
Conrad Kottak, *Anthropology*, 10th ed., fig 23.5, p. 660. Used with permission of McGraw-Hill Education, LLC.

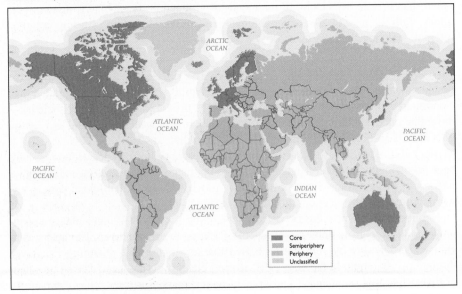

Paree—Paris, that is—along with other world capitals, maybe not in person but in print or on-screen. Young people today are better educated and wiser in the ways of the world than ever before. Increasingly they are exposed to the material and cultural promises of a better life away from the farm. They seek paying jobs, but work is scarce, spurring migration within and across national boundaries. If they can't get cash legally, they seek it illegally.

Recently work has been scarce as well in the industrial world, including the United States and Western Europe. As the United States struggled to emerge from the recession of 2007–2009, its stock market had almost tripled, from a low of 6,443 on March 6, 2009, to over 18,000 as of this writing. In what many saw as a "jobless recovery," corporations held on to their profits, rather than using them to hire new workers. In a global economy, profitability doesn't necessarily come from hiring workers who are fellow citizens. Jobs continue to be outsourced. Machines and information technology continue to replace people. Corporations, from airlines to banks, offer their customers incentives to bypass humans. Even outside the industrial world, but especially within it, the Internet allows an increasing number of people to buy plane tickets, print boarding passes, rent cars, reserve hotel rooms, move money, or pay bills online. Amazon has become a virtual department store that threatens to send not only "mom and pop" shops but even national chains such as Barnes and Noble, Office Depot, Radio Shack, and Sears into oblivion. Nowadays, when one does manage to speak by phone to a human, that person is as likely to be in Mumbai or Manila as Minneapolis or Miami.

Companies claim, with some justification, that labor unions limit their flexibility, adaptability, and profitability. American corporations (and the politicians who represent them) have become more ideologically opposed to unions and more aggressive in discouraging unionization. Unions still bring benefits to their workers. Median weekly earnings for union members—$970 in 2014—remain higher than those of nonunion workers—$763 (U.S. Bureau of Labor Statistics 2014). Still, union membership in the United States has fallen to its lowest point in more than 70 years. The unionized percentage of the American workforce fell to 11.1 percent in 2014, compared with 20.1 percent in 1983 and a high of 35 percent during the mid-1950s. The number of unionized private sector workers increased from 7.1 million in 2010 to 7.4 million in 2014, while the number of public sector union members declined from 7.6 to 7.2 million. This mainly reflected growth in private sector jobs, while jobs in the public sector were being reduced (U.S. Bureau of Labor Statistics 2014). What jobs do you know that are unionized? How likely is it that you will join a union?

## Neoliberalism and NAFTA's Economic Refugees

In recent decades, many of the migrants seeking work in the United States have come from Mexico. Most Americans are aware of recent large-scale Mexican immigration, often of undocumented workers. Most Americans are unaware, however, of the extent to which international forces, including new technologies and the neoliberal North American Free Trade Agreement (NAFTA), are responsible for this migration. Ana Aurelia López (2011) shows how such forces have destroyed traditional Mexican farming systems, degraded agricultural land, and displaced Mexican farmers and small-business people—thereby fueling the migration of millions of undocumented Mexicans to the United States. The following account is a synopsis of her findings.

To understand what is happening in North America today, we need to be aware of an agricultural tradition that began at least 7,000 years ago. For thousands of years, Mexican farmers have grown corn (maize) in a sustainable manner. For all those millennia, Mexican farmers planted corn, beans, and squash (known as "the three sisters") together. This polyculture (cultivation of multiple crops) results in corn yields higher than those obtained when corn is cultivated by itself (monoculture). To preserve the fertility of the soil, a "three sisters" plot was allowed to "rest" for five years after being cultivated for two.

Over the generations Mexican farmers selected diverse strains of corn well adapted to a huge variety of specific microclimates. Mexico became a repository of corn genetic diversity for the world. When corn grown elsewhere developed disease or pest susceptibility or was of poor quality, Mexico could provide other countries with genetically superior plants.

Prior to NAFTA, Mexico supported its farmers by buying a portion of their harvest each year at an elevated cost through price supports. This corn went to a countrywide chain of successful CONASUPO (Compañía Nacional de Subsistencias Populares) stores, which sold corn and other staple foodstuffs below market price to the urban and rural poor. Border tariffs protected Mexican farmers from the entrance of foreign corn, such as that grown in the United States.

The first assault on Mexico's sustainable farming culture began in the 1940s when "Green Revolution" technologies were introduced, including seeds that require chemical inputs (e.g., fertilizer). The Mexican government encouraged farmers to replace their traditional, genetically diverse *maíz crillo* ("creole corn") with the genetically homogenized *maíz mejorado* ("improved corn"), a hybrid from the United States. Agrochemical companies initially supplied the required chemical inputs free of charge.

Company representatives visited rural villages and offered free samples of seeds and agrochemicals to a few farmers. As news of unusually large first-year crops spread, other farmers abandoned their traditional corn strains for the "improved," chemically dependent corn. As the transition accelerated, the price of both the new seeds and associated inputs rose gradually. Eventually farmers no longer could afford either the seeds or the required agrochemicals. When cash-strapped farmers tried to return to planting their former *maíz criollo* seeds, the plants would grow but corn would not appear. Only the hybrid seeds from the United States would produce corn on the chemically altered soils. Today over 60 percent of Mexico's farmland is degraded due to the spread of agrochemicals—chemical fertilizers and pesticides. (This chapter's "Anthropology Today" describes another case of environmental degradation due to chemical pollution, with mining as the culprit.)

The second major assault on traditional Mexican farming came when NAFTA went into effect in 1994. The World Bank granted Mexico a loan to restructure its economy to fit the neoliberal "free trade" agreement. The loan required Mexico to end corn price supports for its small-scale corn farmers. Also ended were Mexico's CONASUPO food stores, which had benefited the rural and urban poor.

While small-scale Mexican farmers have suffered, American agricultural industries have profited from NAFTA. The U.S. government continues to subsidize its own corn farmers. Prior to NAFTA, Mexico's border tariffs made the sale of U.S. corn in Mexico unprofitable. Under NAFTA, Mexican corn tariffs were supposed to be phased out over

Demonstrators in Mexico City protest NAFTA's removal of import tariffs on farm goods entering Mexico from the United States and Canada. © Eduardo Verdugo/AP Images

15 years, providing time for small farmers to adjust to the NAFTA economy. In fact, the Mexican corn tariffs mysteriously disappeared after only 30 months. Corn from the United States began flooding the Mexican markets.

The NAFTA economy offers Mexico's small-scale corn farmers few options: (1) stay in rural Mexico and suffer, (2) look for work in a Mexican city, or (3) migrate to the United States in search of work. NAFTA did not create a common labor market (i.e., the ability of Mexicans, Americans, and Canadians to move freely across each country's borders and work legally anywhere in North America). Nor did NAFTA make provisions for the predicted 15 million Mexican corn farmers who would be forced off the land as a result of the trade agreement. As could have been expected (and planned for), millions of Mexicans migrated to the United States.

Because of NAFTA and neoliberalism, Mexico's 7,000-year-old traditional farming culture is disappearing. Corn farmers have fled the countryside, and U.S.-subsidized corn has flooded the Mexican market. A declining number of traditional farmers remain to plant and conserve Mexico's unique corn varieties. Between one-third and one-half of Mexico's corn now is imported from the United States, much of it by U.S.-based Archer-Daniels-Midland, the world's largest corporate corn exporter. NAFTA also has facilitated the entrance of other giant U.S. corporations into Mexico: Walmart, Dow Agribusiness, Monsanto, Marlboro cigarettes, and Coca-Cola. These multinationals, in turn, have displaced many small Mexican businesses, creating yet another wave of immigrants—former shopkeepers and their employees—to the United States.

## Anthropology Today   *Mining Giant Compatible with Sustainability Institute?*

*The spread of industrialization has contributed to the destruction of indigenous economies, ecologies, and populations. Discharges from the Ok Tedi mine, described here, have severely harmed about 50,000 people living in more than 100 villages downstream. Today, multinational corporations, along with the governments of nations such as Papua New Guinea (PNG), are accelerating the process of resource depletion that began with the Industrial Revolution. Fortunately, however, today's world also contains environmental watchdogs, including concerned anthropologists, lawyers, and NGOs. Described here is a conundrum confronting a major university. Are multinational corporations whose operations have destroyed the landscapes and livelihoods of indigenous peoples proper advisers for an institute devoted to ecological sustainability?*

In the 1990s, the giant mining company now known as BHP Billiton drew worldwide condemnation for the environmental damage caused by its copper and gold mine in Papua New Guinea. Its mining practices destroyed the way of life of thousands of farming and fishing families who lived along and subsisted on the rivers polluted by the mine, and it was only after being sued in a landmark class-action case that the company agreed to compensate them.

Today several activists and academics who work on behalf of indigenous people around the world say the company continues to dodge responsibility for the problems its mines create. . . .

Yet at the University of Michigan at Ann Arbor, BHP Billiton . . . is one of 14 corporate members of an External Advisory Board for the university's new Graham Environmental Sustainability Institute.

Critics at and outside the university contend that Michigan's decision to enlist BHP Billiton as an adviser to an institute devoted to sustainability reflects badly on the institution and allows the company to claim [an undeserved] mantle of environmental and social responsibility. . . .

The arguments echo the discussions about corporate "greenwashing" that have arisen at Stanford University and the University of California at Berkeley over major research grants from ExxonMobil and BP, respectively. . . .

For one BHP Billiton critic at Michigan, the issue is personal. Stuart Kirsch, a professor of anthropology, has spent most of his academic career documenting the damage caused by BHP Billiton's Ok Tedi mine in Papua New Guinea. . . .

Mr. Kirsch, who first visited some of the affected communities as a young ethnographer in 1987, became involved in the class-action lawsuit brought against the company and helped villagers participate in the 1996 legal settlement. "I put my career on hold while being an activist," he says.

He subsequently published several papers related to his work with the Yonggom people as they fought for recognition and compensation from mine operators—scholarship that helped him win tenure. . . . He remains involved with the network of activists and academics who follow mining and its impact on undeveloped communities around the world. . . .

The company's practices polluted the Ok Tedi and Fly Rivers and caused thousands of people to leave their homes because the mining-induced flooding made it impossible for them to grow food to feed themselves, says Mr. Kirsch.

BHP Billiton, based in Australia, later acknowledged that the mine was "not compatible with our environmental values," and spun it off to an independent company that pays all of its mining royalties to the government of Papua New Guinea.

But Mr. Kirsch says that in doing so, the company skirted responsibility for ameliorating the damage it caused. BHP Billiton says it would have preferred to close the mine, but the Papua New Guinea government, in need of the mine revenues, pressed to keep it open. The deal freed BHP Billiton from any future liabilities for environmental damage. . . .

Illtud Harri, a BHP Billiton spokesman, says the company regrets its past with Ok Tedi but considers its pullout from the mine "a responsible exit" that left in place a system that supports educational, agricultural, and social programs for the people of the community. . . .

BHP Billiton, a company formed from the 2001 merger of the Australian mining enterprise Broken Hill Proprietary Company with London-based Billiton, is now the world's largest mining company, with more than 100 operations in 25 countries. . . .

The BHP Billiton charter includes a statement that the company has "an overriding commitment to health, safety, environmental responsibility, and sustainable development." But its critics say the company continues to play a key role in mining projects with questionable records on environmental and human rights, even though in many of those cases, it is not directly responsible. . . .

BHP Billiton has the resources to present itself as the "golden boy," but, says Mr. Kirsch, "it's much harder to see the people on the Ok Tedi and Fly rivers."

A forum could help to right that imbalance, he says. "Let the students and faculty decide whether this is an appropriate company to advise the University of Michigan," says Mr. Kirsch. "It would be an educational process for everyone involved."

*Update: As of this writing (2015) BHP Billiton no longer is listed as a member of the advisory board of Michigan's Graham Institute. And in PNG, after BHP Billiton transferred its ownership of the mine to Ok Tedi Mining Limited, that independent company has spent more than a billion dollars on environmental remediation. The 1996 settlement decreed that BHP would be spared future legal claims in return for giving all its shares to the people of Papua New Guinea. Those shares are now held in trust (valued at over $1 billion, and growing) in a Singapore-based entity, PNG Sustainable Development Program Limited. The mission of that trust is to promote development in PNG's Western Province, where the mine is located, and across PNG. Today, the provincial and national governments of PNG and the PNG Sustainable Development Program are the only shareholders of Ok Tedi Mining Limited, which pays all its royalties to the PNG government. For hundreds of miles down the Fly River, fishers and farmers still complain about the destruction of their habitat, even as the Ok Tedi mine supplies 16 percent of PNG's national revenue.*

**Sources:** Goldie Blumenstyk, "Mining Company Involved in Environmental Disaster Now Advises Sustainability Institute at U. of Michigan," *Chronicle of Higher Education,* December 7, 2007. Copyright © 2007, The Chronicle of Higher Education. Reprinted with permission; http://www.radioaustralia.net.au/pacific/radio/program/pacific-beat/documentary-special-ok-tedi/1069558; Stuart Kirsch (personal communication).

In this summary of Ana Aurelia López's (2011) insightful analysis, we see how farmers and small-business men and women have been forced, by decisions beyond their control, to leave Mexico for the United States. In migrating, these millions of economic refugees continue to face daunting challenges, including separation from their families and homeland, dangerous border crossings, and the ever-present possibility of deportation from the United States.

Within today's world system, comparable effects of neoliberal policies extend well beyond Mexico. As forces of globalization transform rural landscapes throughout the world, rural–urban and transnational migration have become global phenomena. Over and over again, Green Revolution technologies have transformed subsistence into cash economies, fueling a need for money to acquire foreign inputs, while hooking the land on chemicals, reducing genetic diversity and sustainability, and forcing the poorest farmers off the land. Few Americans are aware, specifically, of NAFTA's role in ending a 7,000-year-old sustainable farming culture and displacing millions of Mexicans, and, more generally, that comparable developments are happening all over the world. The next chapter considers several other forces of globalization and anthropology's role in a globalizing world.

## Summary

1. Local societies increasingly participate in wider systems—regional, national, and global. The capitalist world economy depends on production for sale, with the goal of maximizing profits. The key claim of world-system theory is that an identifiable social system, based on wealth and power differentials, extends beyond individual countries. That system is formed by a set of economic and political relations that has characterized much of the globe since the 16th century. World capitalism has political and economic specialization at the core, semiperiphery, and periphery.

2. Columbus's voyages opened the way for a major exchange between the Old and New Worlds. Seventeenth-century plantation economies in the Caribbean and Brazil were based on sugar. In the 18th century, plantation economies based on cotton arose in the southeastern United States.

3. The Industrial Revolution began in England around 1760. Transoceanic commerce supplied capital for industrial investment. Industrialization hastened the separation of workers from the means of production. Marx saw a sharp division between the bourgeoisie and the proletariat. Class consciousness was a key feature of Marx's view of this stratification. Weber believed that social solidarity based on ethnicity, religion, race, or nationality could take priority over class. Today's capitalist world economy maintains the contrast between those who own the means of production and those who don't, but the division is now worldwide. There is a substantial contrast between not only capitalists but workers in the core nations and workers on the periphery.

4. Imperialism is the policy of extending the rule of a nation or an empire over other nations and of taking and holding foreign colonies. Colonialism is the domination of a territory and its people by a foreign power for an extended time. European colonialism had two main phases. The first started in 1492 and lasted through 1825.

For Britain this phase ended with the American Revolution. For France it ended when Britain won the Seven Years' War, forcing the French to abandon Canada and India. For Spain, it ended with Latin American independence. The second phase of European colonialism extended approximately from 1850 to 1950. The British and French empires were at their height around 1914, when European empires controlled 85 percent of the world. Britain and France had colonies in Africa, Asia, Oceania, and the New World.

5. Many geopolitical labels and identities were created under colonialism that had little or nothing to do with existing social demarcations. The new ethnic or national divisions were colonial inventions, sometimes aggravating conflicts.

6. Like colonialism, economic development has an intervention philosophy that provides a justification for outsiders to guide native peoples toward particular goals. Development usually is justified by the idea that industrialization and modernization are desirable evolutionary advances. Neoliberalism revives and extends classic economic liberalism: the idea that governments should not regulate private enterprise and that free market forces should rule. This intervention philosophy currently dominates aid agreements with postsocialist and developing nations.

7. Spelled with a lowercase *c*, *communism* describes a social system in which property is owned by the community and in which people work for the common good. Spelled with an uppercase *C*, *Communism* indicates a political movement and doctrine seeking to overthrow capitalism and to establish a form of communism such as that which prevailed in the Soviet Union from 1917 to 1991. The heyday of Communism was between 1949 and 1989. The fall of Communism can be traced to 1989–1990 in Eastern Europe and 1991 in the Soviet Union. Postsocialist states have followed the neoliberal agenda, through privatization, deregulation, and democratization.

8. By 1900 the United States had become a core nation. Mass production gave rise to a culture that valued acquisitiveness and conspicuous consumption. As subsistence economies yield increasingly to cash, job seeking and unemployment have become global problems. One effect of industrialization has been an accelerated rate of resource depletion.

## Key Terms

bourgeoisie, *416*
capital, *411*
capitalist world
   economy, *411*
colonialism, *419*
communism, *425*
Communism, *425*

core, *412*
imperialism, *419*
Industrial
   Revolution, *414*
intervention
   philosophy, *424*
neoliberalism, *424*

periphery, *413*
postcolonial, *423*
semiperiphery, *412*
working class, or
   proletariat, *416*
world-system
   theory, *412*

# Chapter 19

# Anthropology's Role in a Globalizing World

This chapter applies an anthropological perspective to contemporary global issues. We begin by considering different meanings of the term *globalization*. The fact that certain risks now have global implications leads to a discussion of energy consumption and environmental degradation, including climate change, or global warming. Also considered are the threats that deforestation and emerging diseases pose to global biodiversity and human life. The second half of this chapter turns from ecology to the contemporary flows of people, technology, finance, media, information, images, and ideology that contribute to a global culture of consumption. Globalization promotes intercultural communication, through the media, travel, and migration, which bring people from different societies into direct contact. Finally, we'll consider how such contacts and external linkages affect indigenous peoples and how those groups have organized to confront and deal with national and global issues.

It would be impossible in a single chapter to discuss all or even most of the global issues that are salient today and that anthropologists have studied. Some such issues (e.g., war, displacement, terrorism, NGOs) have been considered in previous chapters.

For timely anthropological analysis of a range of global issues, see recent books by John H. Bodley (2012; 2014) and Richard H. Robbins (2014).

# Globalization: Its Meanings and Its Nature

Chapter 2 characterized globalization as a series of processes that promote change in a world in which nations and people are increasingly interlinked. Forces of globalization include international manufacture, commerce, and finance; travel and tourism; transnational migration; and the media, the Internet, and other high-tech information flows.

Mark Smith and Michele Doyle (2002) distinguish between two meanings of globalization:

1. *Globalization as fact:* the spread and connectedness of production, communication, and technologies across the world. This meaning is like the one described in the previous paragraph and in Chapter 2.

2. *Globalization as ideology and policy:* efforts by the International Monetary Fund (IMF), the World Bank, and other international financial powers to create a global free market for goods and services.

In the second sense, for neoliberal economists, globalization is the way the world should go. For their opponents—anti-neoliberals—it is the way the world should *not* go (Kotz 2015; Lewellen 2010). It is this neoliberal view of globalization that has generated the protests described in Chapter 2.

The first meaning is more neutral. Globalization as *systemic connectedness* reflects the relentless and ongoing growth of the world system. In its current form, that system has some radical new aspects. Especially noteworthy are the *speed* of global communication, the *scale* (size and complexity) of global networks, and the *volume* of international transactions.

The fall of the Soviet empire (in 1989–1991) allowed a truly global economy to emerge (Lewellen 2010). Consider three key features of this new economy: (1) It is based on knowledge and information; (2) its networks are transnational; and (3) its core activities, no matter where they take place, can proceed as a unit in real time (Castells 2001).

The Internet makes possible the very rapid global transmission of information and resources. Activities that once involved face-to-face contact are now conducted impersonally and coordinated across vast distances. The computers that take and process your order from Amazon can be on different continents, and the products you order can come from a warehouse anywhere in the world. The average food product now travels 1,300 miles and changes hands a dozen times before it reaches an American consumer (Lewellen 2010). When you order something from the Internet, the only human being you might speak to is the delivery driver (Smith and Doyle 2002).

People increasingly live their lives across borders, maintaining social, financial, cultural, and political connections with more than one nation-state (see Lugo 1997). Examples of such "multiplaced" people include business and intellectual leaders, development workers, and members of multinational corporations, as well as migratory domestic, agricultural, and construction workers (see Lewellen 2010).

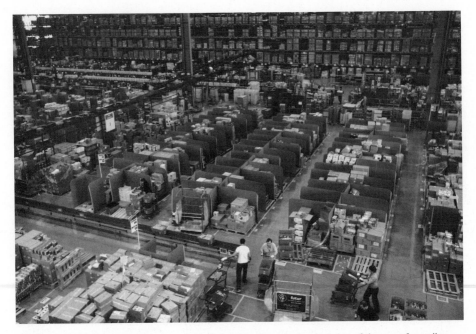

A scene from an Amazon warehouse on a Cyber Monday, the busiest day of the year for online shoppers. This warehouse could be in a lot of places, but it happens to be in Great Britain.
© Geoffrey Robinson/Alamy

By the year 2000, multinational corporations accounted for a third of global output and two-thirds of world trade (Gray 1999, p. 62). Profit-seeking multinationals move their operations to places where labor and materials are cheap. This globalization of labor creates unemployment "back home" as industries relocate and outsource abroad.

Multinationals seek out new markets and strive to create new needs among specific target groups. Young people, for example, increasingly construct their identities around consumption, especially of brand-name products. Successful multinationals, including Nike, Apple, Coca-Cola, and McDonald's, invest huge sums in promoting their brands. The goal is to make a particular brand an integral part of the way people see themselves (Smith and Doyle 2002; Sukarieh and Tannock 2015).

Multinational companies attempt to forge beneficial alliances with politicians and government officials, especially those who are most concerned with world trade. The influence of multinationals extends to key transnational players, such as the European Union and the World Bank. With the globalization of financial markets, nations have less control over their own economies. Such institutions as the World Bank, the International Monetary Fund, the European Union, and the European Central Bank routinely constrain and dictate national economic policies.

As capitalism has spread globally, the gap between rich and poor has widened both within and between nations (see Hirai 2015). The widening gap in the United States was discussed in the chapter "The World System, Colonialism, and Inequality." According to the International Monetary Fund, the difference in per capita income between the world's richest nation (Qatar) and the poorest nation (Central African Republic) was 241 to 1 in

2013, versus around 5 to 1 when the Industrial Revolution began. The key role of knowledge in today's global economy has accelerated this gap, because knowledge tends to be concentrated in core countries and certain regions within them. Knowledge has commercial value as new ideas are converted into products and services that consumers want.

## Energy Consumption and Industrial Degradation

Industrialization entailed a shift from reliance on renewable resources to the use of fossil fuels. Oil, gas, and coal are being depleted rapidly to support a previously unknown level of consumption. For the world's top 10 energy-consuming countries, Table 19.1 shows total and per capita energy use. The United States accounts for 18.6 percent of the world's annual energy consumption, compared with China's 21.5 percent. However, the average American consumes almost 4 times the energy used by the average Chinese, and 16 times the energy used by the average person in India. Consumption has been rising in China and India, while declining a bit in the United States and Canada and more dramatically in Europe.

Industrialization and factory labor have spread to Asia, Latin America, Africa, and the Pacific. One result of industrial expansion has been the destruction of indigenous economies, ecologies, and populations. At the end of the 18th century, as industrialization was developing, 50 million people still lived in politically independent bands, tribes, and chiefdoms. Occupying vast areas, those nonstate societies, although not totally isolated, were only marginally affected by nation-states and the world capitalist economy. In 1800, bands, tribes, and chiefdoms controlled half the globe and 20 percent of its population (Bodley 2014). Industrialization tipped the balance in favor of states (see Hornborg and Crumley, 2007).

Globally many contemporary nations are repeating—at an accelerated rate—the process of resource depletion that started in Europe and, later, in the United States during the Industrial Revolution. Fortunately, however, today's world has some environmental watchdogs that did not exist during the first centuries of the Industrial Revolution.

**TABLE 19.1**
**Total Energy Consumption, 2012, by Country, Top 10 Countries (in quadrillion BTUs)**

Source: U.S. Energy Information Administration, International Energy Statistics (2015). http://www.eia.gov/countries/country-data.cfm?fips=US

| | Total | Per Capita |
|---|---|---|
| World | 520.0* | 74.4[†] |
| China | 110.6 | 82.0 |
| United States | 95.1 | 312.8 |
| Russia | 31.5 | 229.9 |
| India | 23.9 | 19.9 |
| Japan | 20.3 | 163.6 |
| Germany | 13.5 | 160.6 |
| Canada | 13.4 | 396.6 |
| Brazil | 12.1 | 59.0 |
| South Korea | 11.5 | 228.9 |
| France | 10.7 | 165.1 |

*520.0 quadrillion (520,000,000,000,000,000) BTUs.
[†]74.4 million BTUs.

Given national and international cooperation and sanctions, the modern world may benefit from the lessons of the past (see Hornborg, McNeill, and Martinez-Alier, 2007).

A key component of globalization is the globalization of risk (Smith and Doyle 2002). Hazards linked to industrial production, emerging diseases, or a cyber attack can spread quickly beyond their point of origin. Climate risks clearly have become globalized, as each consumer of fossil fuels makes his or her individual contribution (the consumer's "carbon footprint") to global climate change, to which we now turn.

# Global Climate Change

Fourteen of the 15 hottest years on record have occurred since 2000, according to the UN World Meteorological Organization, as rising carbon emissions continue to trap heat and drive climate change. The average temperatures over land and oceans were higher in 2014 than any year since 1880, when recordkeeping began (Botelho and Martinez 2015). Scientific measurements confirm that global warming is not due to increased solar radiation. As most scientists recognize, the causes are mainly *anthropogenic*—caused by humans and their activities. Who can reasonably deny that 7 billion people, along with their animals, crops, machines, and increasing use of fossil fuels, have a greater environmental impact than the 5 million or so pre-Neolithic hunter-gatherers who lived on our planet 12,000 years ago?

The **greenhouse effect** is a natural phenomenon that keeps the Earth's surface warm. Greenhouse gases include water vapor ($H_2O$), carbon dioxide ($CO_2$), methane ($CH_4$), nitrous oxide ($N_2O$), halocarbons, and ozone ($O_3$). Without them, life as we know it would not exist. Like a greenhouse window, those gases allow sunlight to enter and then trap heat from escaping the atmosphere. The atmospheric concentration of greenhouse gases has grown significantly since the Industrial Revolution and is today at its highest level in 400,000 years. It will continue to rise—as will global temperatures—without actions to slow it down (National Research Council 2011).

Scientists prefer the term **climate change** to *global warming*. The former term points out that, beyond rising temperatures, there have been changes in sea levels, precipitation, storms, and ecosystem effects. The precise effects of climate change on regional weather patterns have yet to be fully determined (see DiMento and Doughman 2014). Land areas are predicted to warm more than oceans, with the greatest warming in higher latitudes, such as Canada, the northern United States, and northern Europe. Climate change may benefit these areas, offering milder winters and extended growing seasons. However, many more people worldwide probably will be harmed (see Cribb 2010). Already we know that, in the Arctic, temperatures have risen almost twice as much as the global average. Arctic landscapes and ecosystems are changing rapidly and perceptibly, creating hundreds of "climate refugees" in areas of Alaska where the permafrost is melting and indigenous villages are sinking below sea level (see Yardley 2007). Coastal communities worldwide can anticipate increased flooding and more severe storms and surges. At risk are people, animals, plants, freshwater supplies, and such industries as tourism and farming.

Meeting global energy demand is the single greatest obstacle to slowing climate change. Worldwide, energy use continues to grow with economic and population expansion. China

In the global economy, India and China (shown here) in particular have increased their use of fossil fuels, and consequently their emissions of $CO_2$. This scene, near Beijing, shows the Shougang steel plant, a major source of air pollution. What's the most polluted place you've ever been to? © Fritz Hoffman/The Image Works

and India, in particular, are rapidly increasing their use of energy, mainly from fossil fuels, and consequently their emissions. Among the alternatives to fossil fuels are nuclear power and such renewable energy technologies as solar, wind, and biomass generators.

In 2015 the American Anthropological Association (AAA) issued a "Statement on Humanity and Climate Change," which can be found at this website: http://www.aaanet. org/cmtes/commissions/CCTF/upload/AAA-Statement-on-Humanity-and-Climate-Change.pdf. That statement makes several key points, including the following:

- Human cultures and actions are the most important causes of the dramatic environmental changes that have taken place during the last 100 years. Two key factors influencing climate change are (1) reliance on fossil fuels as the primary energy source, and (2) an ever-expanding culture of consumerism.

- Climate change will accelerate migration, destabilize communities, and exacerbate the spread of infectious diseases.

- Most affected will be people living on coasts, in island nations, and in high-latitude (e.g., far north) and high-altitude (e.g., very mountainous) areas.

- The tendency has been to address climate change at the international and national levels. We also need planning at the regional and local levels, because the impacts of climate change vary in specific locales. Affected communities, perhaps working with anthropologists, must be active participants in planning how to adapt to climate change—and in implementing those plans.

# Environmental Anthropology

Anthropology always has been concerned with how environmental forces influence humans and how human activities affect the environment. The 1950s–1970s witnessed the emergence of an area of study known as cultural ecology, or **ecological anthropology** (see Haenn and Wilk 2006). That field focused on how cultural beliefs and practices helped human populations adapt to their environments, as well as how people used elements of their culture to maintain their ecosystems. Ecological anthropologists showed that many indigenous groups did a reasonable job of managing their resources and preserving their ecosystems. Such groups had traditional ways of categorizing resources and using them sustainably (see Dagne 2015). The term **ethnoecology** describes a society's set of environmental perceptions and practices (see Vinyeta and Lynn 2013).

Outside forces increasingly challenge indigenous ethnoecologies. Given national and international incentives to exploit and degrade, ethnoecological systems that once preserved local and regional environments increasingly are ineffective or irrelevant (see Dove, Sajise, and Doolittle 2011). Anthropologists routinely witness threats to the people they study and their environments. Among such threats are commercial logging, industrial pollution, and the imposition of external management systems on local ecosystems (see Johnston 2009). Today's ecological anthropology, *environmental anthropology,* attempts not only to understand but also to find solutions to environmental problems. As aspects of the globalization of risk, such problems must be tackled at the national and international levels (e.g., global warming).

Local people and their landscapes, ideas, values, and traditional management systems face attacks from all sides (see Hornborg, Clark, and Hermele 2011). Outsiders attempt to remake native landscapes and cultures in their own image. The aim of many agricultural development projects, for example, seems to be to make the world as much like a midwestern American agricultural state as possible. Often there is an attempt to impose mechanized farming and nuclear family ownership, even though these institutions may be inappropriate in areas far removed from the midwestern United States. Anthropologists know that development projects usually fail when they try to replace indigenous institutions with culturally alien concepts.

## Global Assaults on Local Autonomy

A clash of cultures related to environmental change may occur when development threatens indigenous peoples and their environments. A second clash of cultures related to environmental change may occur when external regulation aimed at conservation confronts indigenous peoples and their ethnoecologies. Like development projects, conservation schemes may ask people to change their ways in order to satisfy planners' goals rather than local goals. In places as different as Madagascar, Brazil, and the Pacific Northwest of the United States, people have been asked, told, or forced to abandon basic economic activities because to do so is good for "nature" or "the globe." "Good for the globe" doesn't play very well in Brazil, whose Amazon region has been a focus of international environmentalist attention. Brazilians complain that outsiders (e.g., Europeans and North Americans) promote "global needs" and "saving the Amazon" after having destroyed their own forests for economic growth. Well-intentioned conservation plans can be as insensitive as development schemes that promote radical changes without involving local people in planning and carrying out the policies that affect them. When people are asked to give up the basis of their livelihood, they usually resist.

The spread of environmentalism may reveal radically different notions about the "rights" and value of plants and animals versus humans. In Madagascar, many intellectuals and officials complain that foreigners seem more concerned about lemurs and other endangered species than about the people of Madagascar (the Malagasy). As a geographer there remarked to me, "The next time you come to Madagascar, there'll be no more Malagasy. All the people will have starved to death, and a lemur will have to meet you at the airport." Most Malagasy perceive human poverty as a more pressing problem than animal and plant survival.

On the other hand, who can doubt that conservation, including the preservation of biodiversity, is a worthy goal? The challenge for applied ecological anthropology is to devise culturally appropriate strategies for achieving biodiversity conservation in the face of unrelenting population growth and commercial expansion. How does one get people to support conservation measures that may, in the short run at least, diminish their access to resources? Like development plans in general, the most effective conservation strategies pay attention to the needs and wishes of the local people.

## Deforestation

Generations of anthropologists have studied how human economic activities (ancient and modern) affect the environment. Anthropologists know that food producers (farmers and herders) typically do more to degrade the environment than foragers do. Population increase and the need to expand farming caused deforestation in many parts of the ancient Middle East and Mesoamerica (see Cairns 2015; Hornborg and Crumley, 2007). Even today, many farmers think of trees as giant weeds to be removed and replaced with productive fields.

Often, deforestation is demographically driven—caused by population pressure. For example, Madagascar's population is growing at a rate of 3 percent annually, doubling every generation. Population pressure leads to migration, including rural–urban migration. Madagascar's capital, Antananarivo, had just 100,000 people in 1967. Its population today is over 2 million. Urban growth promotes deforestation if city dwellers rely on fuelwood from the countryside, as is true in Madagascar. As forested watersheds disappear, crop productivity declines. Madagascar is known as the "great red island," after the color of its soil. On that island, the effects of soil erosion and water runoff are visible to the naked eye. From the look of its rivers, Madagascar appears to be bleeding to death. Increasing runoff of water no longer trapped by trees causes erosion of low-lying rice fields near swollen rivers as well as siltation in irrigation canals (Kottak 2007).

Causes of deforestation include demographic pressure (from births or immigration) on subsistence economies, commercial logging, road building, cash cropping, fuelwood needs associated with urban expansion, and clearing and burning associated with livestock and grazing. The fact that forest loss has several causes has a policy implication: Different deforestation scenarios require different conservation strategies.

Applied anthropology uses anthropological perspectives to identify and solve contemporary problems that affect humans. Deforestation is one such problem. Here, women take part in a reforestation project in coastal Tanzania near Dar es Salaam. © Ed Parker/Alamy

What can be done? On this question applied anthropology weighs in, spurring policy makers to think about new conservation strategies. The traditional approach has been to restrict access to forested areas designated as parks, then employ park guards and punish violators. Modern strategies are more likely to consider the needs, wishes, and abilities of the people (often impoverished) living in and near the forest. Since effective conservation depends on the cooperation of the local people, their concerns must be addressed in devising conservation strategies.

Reasons to change behavior must make sense to local people (see Sillitoe 2007). In Madagascar, the economic value of the forest for agriculture (as an antierosion mechanism and reservoir of potential irrigation water) provides a much more powerful incentive against forest degradation than do such global goals as "preserving biodiversity." Most Malagasy have no idea that lemurs and other endemic species exist only in Madagascar. Nor would such knowledge provide much of an incentive for them to conserve the forests if doing so jeopardized their livelihoods.

To curb the global deforestation threat, we need conservation strategies that work. Laws and enforcement may help reduce commercially driven deforestation caused by burning and clear-cutting. But local people also use and abuse forested lands. A challenge for the environmentally oriented applied anthropologist is to find ways to make forest preservation attractive to local people and ensure their cooperation. Applied anthropologists must work to make "good for the globe" good for the people.

## Emerging Diseases

When humans modify or destroy environments and ecosystems, nature has a way of striking back. Most or all infectious diseases that have emerged in the last few decades are due to human encroachment on wild lands, particularly forests, and to changes in demography (human population increase and changing settlement patterns). In the Amazon, one study showed that an increase in deforestation of just 4 percent produced a 50 percent increase in the incidence of malaria. This is because mosquitoes, which transmit malaria, thrive in the right mix of sunlight and water in recently deforested areas (Robbins 2012). The recent emergence and spread of infectious diseases like HIV/AIDS, Ebola, West Nile, SARS (severe acute respiratory syndrome), and Lyme disease are all the result of things people have done to their environments.

The spread of disease from wild to domesticated animals and then to humans has been going on since the Neolithic, when animals were first domesticated. Diseases that spread from animals to humans are known as *zoonotic* diseases, and they pose a huge threat today because of human population increase and forces of globalization. Emerging diseases kill more than 2 million people annually, and 60 percent of those diseases originate in animals (Robbins 2012).

Especially since the Neolithic, infectious diseases, including malaria and plague, have moved from woods and wildlife to humans, often through their domesticated animals. One such disease, the Nipah virus, began its migration from fruit bats to humans in South Asia. Because fruit bats have co-evolved with the Nipah virus for millions of years, it does little damage to their health. When the virus moves from bats into other species, however, it can be lethal. Fruit bats eat the pulp of fruit and spit out the residue. In rural Malaysia in 1999, an infected bat appears to have dropped a piece of chewed fruit into the food supply of a swine herd (a scenario depicted in the movie *Contagion*). The virus then spread from those pigs to humans. Of 276 people infected in Malaysia, 106 died. Eleven more people died in Singapore, when the virus was exported there via live pigs. South Asia has experienced a dozen smaller Nipah outbreaks in recent years. A bat also may be the source of the Ebola epidemic that ravaged Liberia and Sierra Leone and sparked near panic in the United States in the fall of 2014.

Spillovers from wildlife to humans have quadrupled in the last half-century, reflecting increasing human encroachment on disease hotspots, especially in the tropics (Robbins 2012). Wildlife trafficking and modern air travel contribute to the potential for a serious outbreak or pandemic among humans. (A *pandemic* is an epidemic with global scope.) The zero patient for the HIV/AIDS pandemic (in North America, at least) is reputed to have been a flight attendant who flew internationally. HIV/AIDS originally jumped from chimpanzees to humans through bush-meat hunters in Africa, who kill and butcher chimps.

The threat posed by zoonotic diseases has been recognized by biologists and physicians. One international project, called PREDICT, funds teams of veterinarians, conservation biologists, medical doctors, and epidemiologists to identify disease-causing organisms in wildlife before they spread to humans (see http://www.vetmed.ucdavis.edu/ohi/predict/index.cfm). PREDICT, which is financed by the United States Agency for International Development (USAID), attempts to "predict," spot, and prevent the spread of zoonotic diseases in global geographic hotspots with high potential for disease transmission. At least 24 countries in Africa, Latin America, and Asia participate in the program. PREDICT scientists monitor areas where deadly viruses are known to exist and where humans are encroaching. One such locale is a new highway being built to link the Atlantic and Pacific Oceans in South America, traversing Brazil and the Peruvian Andes.

PREDICT scientists also gather blood, saliva, and other samples from high-risk wildlife species to create a "library" of viruses, in order to facilitate identification when a threat is imminent. This library focuses on the animals most likely to carry diseases that affect people, such as primates, rats, and bats. PREDICT scientists also study ways of preventing disease spillovers and the pandemics that might follow. Sometimes solutions can be remarkably simple. In Bangladesh, for example, outbreaks of the Nipah virus were contained by placing bamboo screens (which cost 8 cents each) over the containers used to collect date palm sap (Robbins 2012). Because human groups create the conditions that allow zoonotic pathogens to jump species and to spread, anthropologists have a key role to play in studying the cultural (including economic) causes of environmental encroachment and in suggesting culturally appropriate and workable solutions.

# Interethnic Contact

Since at least the 1920s anthropologists have studied the changes that arise from contact between industrial and nonindustrial societies. *Acculturation* refers to changes that result when groups come into continuous firsthand contact—changes in the cultural patterns of either or both groups (Redfield, Linton, and Herskovits 1936, p. 149). Acculturation differs from *diffusion,* or cultural borrowing, which can occur without firsthand contact. For example, most North Americans who eat hot dogs ("frankfurters") have never been to Frankfurt, Germany, nor have most North American Toyota owners or sushi eaters ever visited Japan. Although *acculturation* can be applied to any case of sustained cultural contact and change, the term most often has described **Westernization**—the influence of Western expansion on indigenous peoples and their cultures. Thus, local people who wear store-bought clothes, learn Indo-European languages, and otherwise adopt Western customs are called acculturated. Acculturation may be voluntary or forced, and there may be considerable resistance to the process.

Often, when powerful outsiders (e.g., colonialists) threaten, conquer, or annex an indigenous group, a "shock phase" follows (Bodley 2014). Foreign contact may increase mortality, disrupt subsistence, fragment kin groups, and damage social support systems. In the most extreme cases, contact may lead to the group's cultural collapse (ethnocide) or physical extinction (genocide).

## Cultural Imperialism and Indigenization

**Cultural imperialism** refers to the spread or advance of one culture at the expense of others, or its imposition on other cultures, which it modifies, replaces, or destroys—usually because of differential economic or political influence. Thus, children in the French colonial empire learned French history, language, and culture from standard

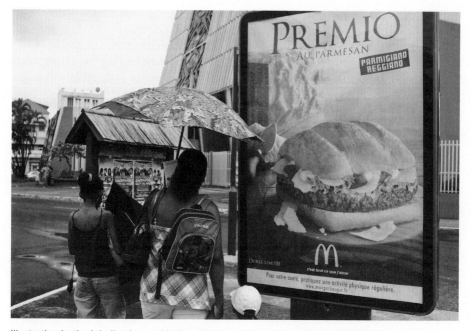

Illustrating both globalization and indigenization, McDonalds's now routinely tries to tailor its offerings to specific cultural appetites. Shown here in downtown Fort de France, Martinique (French West Indies), is a billboard advertising a hamburger topped with Italian cheese (Parmigiano-Reggiano). © Guiziou Franck/hemis.fr/Getty Images

textbooks also used in France. Tahitians, Malagasy, Vietnamese, and Senegalese learned the French language by reciting from books about "our ancestors the Gauls."

To what extent do contemporary global forces promote cultural imperialism? Some commentators see the spread of modern technology, the media, and global brands as erasing cultural differences, as homogeneous products reach more people worldwide. Others note that certain innovations have allowed social groups (local cultures) to express themselves and to survive (Marcus and Fischer 1999). For example, modern radio, TV, film, digital media, and increasingly the Internet (e.g., YouTube) constantly bring local happenings to the attention of a larger public (see Fuchs and Sandoval 2014). Contemporary media play a role in stimulating and organizing local and community activities of many sorts. Think of ways in which this is done by YouTube, Facebook, and Twitter—global networks all (see this chapter's "Anthropology Today").

In Brazil, local practices, celebrations, and performances have changed in the context of outside forces, including the mass media and tourism. In the town of Arembepe (Kottak 2006), TV coverage stimulated increased participation in a traditional annual performance, the Chegança. This is a danceplay that reenacts the Portuguese discovery of Brazil. Arembepeiros have traveled to the state capital to perform the Chegança before television cameras, for a nationally televised program featuring traditional performances from many rural communities, and cameras have gone to Arembepe to record it.

In San Gimignano, Italy, boys and young men don medieval costumes and beat drums in a parade through the streets during one of the town's many pageants. Increasingly, local communities perform "traditional" ceremonies for TV and tourists. © Paul Seheult/Eye Ubiquitous/Corbis

In several towns along the Amazon River, annual folk ceremonies now are staged more lavishly for TV and video cameras. In the Amazon town of Parantíns, for example, boatloads of tourists arriving any time of year are shown a video recording of the town's annual Bumba Meu Boi festival. This is a costumed performance mimicking bullfighting, parts of which have been shown on national TV. This pattern, in which local communities preserve, revive, and intensify the scale of traditional ceremonies to perform for the media and tourists, is expanding. To see whether I could, I just managed to watch snippets of these annual events in Arembepe and Parantíns on YouTube!

In the process of globalization, people constantly make and remake culture as they assign their own meanings to the information, images, and products they receive from outside. One example of such a process of **indigenization**—how a globally spreading Evangelical Protestantism adapts to local circumstances—was discussed in the chapter "Religion." Indigenization occurs in cultural domains as different as fast food, music, housing styles, science, religion, terrorism, celebrations, and political ideas and institutions (Ellen et al. 2013; Fiske 2011; Wilk 2006).

## A Global System of Images

With globalization more people in many more places imagine "a wider set of 'possible' lives than they ever did before. One important source of this change is the mass media . . ." (Appadurai 1991, p. 197). The United States as a global media center has been joined by Canada, Japan, Western Europe, Brazil, Mexico, Nigeria, Egypt, India, and Hong Kong.

Like print, the electronic mass media can diffuse the cultures of different countries within (and often beyond) their own boundaries, thus enhancing national cultural identity. For example, millions of Brazilians who once were cut off (by geographic isolation or illiteracy) from urban, national, and international events and information now participate in a larger "mediascape" (Appadurai 1991) through mass media and the Internet (Kottak 2009).

Brazil's most popular network (Rede Globo) relies heavily on its own productions, especially *telenovelas* (nightly serial programs often compared to American soap operas). Globo plays each night to the world's largest and most devoted audience (perhaps 80 million viewers throughout the nation and beyond—via satellite TV). The programs that attract this horde are made by Brazilians, for Brazilians.

The mass media and the Internet also play a prominent role in maintaining ethnic and national identities among people who lead transnational lives. Arabic-speaking Muslims, including migrants in several countries, follow the TV network Al Jazeera, based in Qatar, which helps reinforce ethnic and religious identities. As groups move, they can stay linked to each other and to their homeland through global media. **Diasporas** (people who have spread out from an original, ancestral homeland) have enlarged the markets for media, communication, brands, and travel services targeted at specific ethnic, national, or religious groups who now live in various parts of the world.

## A Global Culture of Consumption

Besides the electronic media, other key global forces are production, commerce, and finance. As Arjun Appadurai (1991, p. 194) puts it, "money, commodities, and persons unendingly chase each other around the world." Residents of many Latin American communities now depend on outside cash, remitted from international labor migration. The American economy is increasingly influenced by foreign investment and dependent on foreign labor—whether through the immigration of laborers or the export of jobs.

Business, technology, and the media have increased the craving for commodities and images throughout the world. This has forced nation-states to open to a global culture of consumption. In the Middle East, for example, social media use exploded during the Arab Spring of 2011. In cyberspace Middle Easterners found something missing from their ordinary, offline worlds: platforms permitting social connectivity and the collective airing of grievances. Since then, social media have entered the region commercially, promoting and selling digital advertising (Hamdan 2013). In 2012 the number of Twitter users tripled in the Arab world, growing fastest in Saudi Arabia, Egypt, Kuwait, and the United Arab Emirates. Arabic has become Twitter's fastest-growing language. Facebook's Middle Eastern user base grew from 16 million in 2010 to 45 million in 2012. LinkedIn (a professional social networking and job search site) has 5 million Middle Eastern users. (This region has one of the highest youth unemployment rates in the world.) This rapidly rising Middle Eastern Internet presence is occurring in an area where 40 percent of the population (of 380 million) is younger than 30 years. The smartphone is another key element in the Middle Eastern marketing mediascape. A global survey by Google found that 93 percent of smartphone users notice mobile ads, and 39 percent of those follow up with an online purchase. Saudi Arabia's mobile phone penetration rate is 190 percent, meaning that everyone has almost two cell phones (Hamdan 2013). Media and marketing are the new It couple.

Almost everyone today participates in the global consumers' culture. Few people have never seen a T-shirt advertising a Western product. American and English rock stars' recordings blast through the streets of Rio de Janeiro, while taxi drivers from Toronto to Madagascar play Brazilian music. Peasants and tribal people participate in the global economy, not only because they have been hooked on cash but also because their products and images are appropriated by world capitalism. They are commercialized by others (like the Quileute nation in the *Twilight* series). Furthermore, indigenous peoples also market their own images and products, through outlets like Cultural Survival.

## People in Motion

Globalization has both enlarged and erased old boundaries and distinctions. Arjun Appadurai (1990, p. 1) characterizes today's world as a "translocal" "interactive system" that is "strikingly new." Whether as refugees, migrants, tourists, pilgrims, proselytizers, laborers, businesspeople, development workers, politicians, terrorists, soldiers, sports figures, or media-borne images, people travel more than ever.

The scale of human movement has expanded dramatically. Most emigrants maintain their ties with their native land, however—by phoning, Skyping, Facetiming, texting, e-mailing, visiting, sending money, or watching home videos or "ethnic TV." In a sense, they live multilocally—in different places at once. With so many people "in motion," the unit of anthropological study expands from the local community to the diaspora. Anthropologists increasingly follow descendants of the villages they have studied as they move from rural to urban areas and across national boundaries.

**Postmodernity** describes our time and situation: today's world in flux, these people on the move who have learned to manage multiple identities depending on place and context. In its most general sense, **postmodern** refers to the blurring and breakdown of established canons (rules or standards), categories, distinctions, and boundaries. The word is taken from **postmodernism**—a style and movement in architecture that succeeded modernism, beginning in the 1970s. Postmodern architecture rejected the rules, geometric order, and austerity of modernism. Modernist buildings were expected to have a clear and functional design. Postmodern design is "messier" and more playful. It draws on a diversity of styles from different times and places—including popular, ethnic, and non-Western cultures. Postmodernism extends "value" globally—well beyond classic, elite, and Western cultural forms. *Postmodern* now is used to describe comparable developments beyond architecture—in music, literature, and visual art. From this origin, postmodernity describes a world in which traditional standards, contrasts, groups, boundaries, and identities are opening up, reaching out, and breaking down.

New kinds of political and ethnic units have emerged along with globalization. In some cases, cultures and ethnic groups have banded together in larger associations. There is a growing pan-Native-American identity as well as an international pantribal movement. Thus, in June 1992, the World Conference of Indigenous Peoples met in Rio de Janeiro concurrently with UNCED (the United Nations Conference on the Environment and Development). Along with diplomats, journalists, and environmentalists came

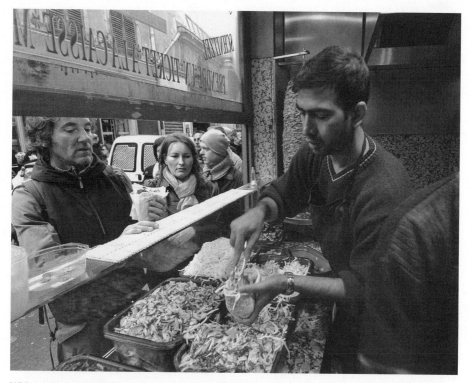

With so many people on the move, the unit of anthropological study has expanded from the local community to the diaspora. This refers to the offspring of an area who have spread to many lands, such as the owners of this falafel shop in Paris, France. © Lionel Derimais/VISUM/ The Image Works

300 representatives of the tribal diversity that survives under globalization—from Lapland to Mali (Brooke 1992; see also Maybury-Lewis, Macdonald, and Maybury-Lewis 2009). In May 2012, the United Nations sponsored a high-level commemoration of the fifth anniversary of the adoption of the UN Declaration on the Rights of Indigenous Peoples (see Doyle 2015; Drahos 2014). The most recent World Conference on Indigenous Peoples (WCIP) was held at the United Nations in New York in September 2014 (see http://wcip2014.org).

## Indigenous Peoples

All too often, conquest, annexation, and development have been associated with genocide—the deliberate extermination of a specific ethnic group. Examples include the Holocaust, Rwanda in 1994, and Bosnia in the early 1990s. Bodley (2014) estimates that an average of 250,000 indigenous people perished annually between 1800 and 1950. The causes included warfare, outright murder, introduced diseases, slavery, land grabbing, and other forms of dispossession and impoverishment.

The indigenous groups that have survived now live within nation-states. Often they maintain a distinct ethnic identity, despite having lost their ancestral cultures to varying degrees. Many such groups aspire to autonomy. As the original inhabitants of their territories, they are called indigenous peoples.

The term *indigenous people* entered international law in 1982 with the creation of the United Nations Working Group on Indigenous Populations (WGIP). This group meets annually and has members from six continents. The UN General Assembly adopted its Declaration of Indigenous Rights in 2007. Convention 169, a document supporting cultural diversity and indigenous empowerment, was approved by the International Labor Organization (ILO) in 1989. Such documents, along with the global work of the WGIP, have influenced governments, NGOs, and international agencies to adopt policies favorable to indigenous peoples. Social movements worldwide now use *indigenous people* as a self-identifying label in their quests for social, cultural, and political rights (Brower and Johnston 2007).

In Spanish-speaking Latin America, social scientists and politicians now favor the term *indígena* (indigenous person) over *indio* (Indian), the colonial term that European

Mary Simat, with the Maasai Women for Education and Economic Development from Kenya, testifies at the Indigenous Peoples' Global Summit on Climate Change in Anchorage, Alaska, in April 2009. The five-day United Nations—affiliated conference attracted about 400 people from 80 nations. © Al Grillo/AP Images conquerors used for Native Americans (de la Peña 2005). Until the mid- to late 1980s, Latin American public policy emphasized assimilation. During the past 30 years, the emphasis has shifted from assimilation—*mestizaje*—to cultural difference. In Ecuador, groups seen previously as Quichua-speaking peasants are classified now as indigenous communities with their own territories. Brazil has recognized 30 new indigenous communities in the northeast, a region previously seen as having lost its native population. Guatemala, Nicaragua, Brazil, Colombia, Mexico, Paraguay, Ecuador, Argentina, Bolivia, Peru, and Venezuela now are officially multicultural (Jackson and Warren 2005). Several national constitutions recognize the rights of indigenous peoples to cultural distinctiveness and political representation (de la Peña 2005).

Ceuppens and Geschiere (2005) explore a recent upsurge, in multiple world areas, of the notion of *autochthony* (being native to, or formed in, the place where found), with an implicit call for excluding strangers. The terms *autochthony* and *indigenous* both go back to classical Greek history, with similar implications. *Autochthony* refers to self and soil. *Indigenous* literally means born inside, with the connotation in classical Greek of being born "inside the house." Both notions stress the rights of first-comers to privileged status and protection versus later immigrants—legal or illegal (Ceuppens and Geschiere 2005; Hornborg, Clark, and Hermele 2011).

During the 1990s, autochthony became an issue in many parts of Africa, inspiring violent efforts to exclude (European and Asian) "strangers." Simultaneously, autochthony became a key notion in debates about immigration and multiculturalism in Europe. European majority groups have claimed the label *autochthon*. This term highlights the prominence that the exclusion of strangers has assumed in day-to-day politics worldwide (Ceuppens and Geschiere 2005). One familiar example is the United States, as represented in debates over undocumented immigration.

### Identity in Indigenous Politics

**Essentialism** describes the process of viewing an identity as established, real, and frozen, thus ignoring the historical processes within which that identity was forged. Identities, however, are not fixed. We saw in the chapter "Ethnicity and Race" that identities can be fluid and multiple. People draw on particular, sometimes competing, self-labels and identities. Some Peruvian groups, for instance, self-identify as *mestizos* but still see themselves as indigenous. Identity is a fluid, dynamic process, and there are multiple ways of being indigenous. Neither speaking an indigenous language nor wearing "native" clothing is required (Jackson and Warren 2005).

## Anthropology's Lessons

Anthropology teaches us that the adaptive responses of humans can be more flexible than those of other species because our main adaptive means are sociocultural. However, in the face of globalization, the cultural institutions of the past always influence subsequent adaptation, producing continued diversity in the actions and reactions of different groups as they indigenize global inputs. In our globalizing world, anthropology offers a people-centered vision of social change. The existence of anthropology is itself a tribute to the

## Anthropology Today    *The Wider World of SNS*

For generations, anthropologists have stressed the linking functions of such ages-old institutions as marriage and trade. Our globalized world offers some radically new, and rapidly spreading, ways of connecting socially. Aaron Sorkin chose *The Social Network* as the title for his movie about the founding of Facebook, which is precisely that—a social networking site (SNS)—which people visit to get linked in cyberspace. Increasingly, modern media connect local people to a wider, external world, which includes people, information, entertainment, and potential social validation.

Consider Brazil, which is rapidly increasing its Internet access and its use of social media. During the last decade, Internet access has spread across the country, although it remains unreliable in rural areas. About 40 percent of Brazilians are now online (compared with about 80 percent of Americans). Most of those online Brazilians (68 million of about 78 million) use Facebook, which has been free on cell phones since 2010. Brazil is now second in the world in number of Facebook, Twitter, and YouTube users (Holmes 2013). At least 35 percent of all Brazilians are on Facebook, compared with 51 percent of Americans. Facebook's growth rate in Brazil has been phenomenal, with 30 million new users added between 2012 and 2013. Offline, Brazilians tend to be social people, and they seem to be transferring this sociability to the online world. As in the United States, SNS reinforce family connections while establishing and maintaining contacts in a wider world of nonrelatives.

Research in the United States also confirms the role of SNS in enhancing social connectivity, rather than (as some have feared) isolating people and truncating their social relationships. The Pew Research Center's ongoing Internet & American Life Project has investigated how the use of SNS is related to various connectivity factors, including trust and political engagement (see Hampton et al. 2011). In a 2010–2011 Pew study, 79 percent of American adults said they used the Internet, and 59 percent of those users participated in at least one SNS, usually Facebook. Slightly more than half the Facebook users were daily users.

In the Pew study, as SNS use increased, so did measures of trust and political engagement. Internet users overall were twice as likely as nonusers to say people can be trusted. Facebookers tended to be more trusting that other Internet users were. The most frequent Facebook participants (visiting the site multiple times daily) were 43 percent more likely than other Internet users (and three times as likely as non-Internet users) to say most people can be trusted. Given that Facebookers routinely reveal details about their personal and family lives, it's not surprising they would be more trusting.

Facebook users also were much more politically engaged than most Americans. The Pew study spanned the November 2010 mid-term elections, when Internet users turned out to be significantly more likely than offliners to attend political meetings, to vote, and to try to influence someone else's vote. Here again, heavy Facebook users stood out as even more likely than the average Internet user to do those things.

In another Pew Internet study, Kate Purcell (2013) describes how Americans increasingly are sharing action images of their lives and social connections. The percentage (31 percent) of American adult Internet users posting video doubled between 2009 and 2013. Of American adults who use SNS, 71 percent have displayed a video. As is true of Internet use generally, online video use is greatest among younger, better-educated, and higher-earning Americans.

While Internet and SNS use thrives among the young, educated, and affluent (in the United States and worldwide), a significant chunk (15–20 percent) of Americans remain cut off from this connectivity (Zickuhr 2013). In a few (mainly rural) areas of the United States, access remains unavailable or limited. Cost (e.g., of computer and broadband) is another limitation. Forty-four percent of Americans aged 65 and older lack connectivity, versus only 2 percent of those aged 18–29. Of Americans who never finished high school, 41 percent lack Internet access, compared with only 4 percent of college graduates (Ortutay 2013). Millions of Americans, therefore, remain isolated offline because of their advanced age or limited education. One-third of those offliners claim to be uninterested in the Internet, to be unwilling to try it, or not to need it. The remainder cite various obstacles, including affordability and availability (Zickuhr 2013). In an increasingly interconnected world, these obstacles and excuses will surely diminish, as a growing percentage of humanity finds its way online.

(Author thanks Professor Richard Pace for providing some of the information cited about the Internet in Brazil.).

continuing need to understand similarities and differences among human beings throughout the world.

Anthropology offers relevant, indeed powerful, ways of understanding how the world actually works. Lessons of the past can and should be applied to the present and future, hopefully to benefit humanity. Anthropologists know that civilizations and world powers rise and fall, and that social transformations typically follow major innovations, such as the Neolithic and the Industrial Revolution. There is no guarantee that the current world system and the power relations within it will last forever. What will happen if humans do survive and find themselves living in entirely new systems? Try to answer this question using your new knowledge of anthropology.

## Summary

1. Fueling global climate change are human population growth and use of fossil fuels, which produce greenhouse gases. The atmospheric concentration of those gases has increased since the Industrial Revolution, and especially since 1978. Climate change encompasses global warming along with changing sea levels, precipitation, storms, and ecosystem effects. Coastal communities can anticipate increased flooding and more severe storms and surges.

2. Anthropology always has been concerned with how environmental forces influence humans and how human activities affect the biosphere. Many indigenous groups did a reasonable job of preserving their ecosystems. An ethnoecology is

any society's set of environmental practices and perceptions. Indigenous ethno-ecologies increasingly are being challenged by global forces that work to exploit and degrade—and that sometimes aim to protect—the environment. The challenge for applied ecological anthropology is to devise culturally appropriate strategies for conservation in the face of unrelenting population growth and commercial expansion.

3. Deforestation is a major factor in the loss of global biodiversity. Causes of deforestation include demographic pressure (from births or immigration) on subsistence economies; commercial logging; road building; cash cropping; fuelwood needs associated with urban expansion; and clearing and burning associated with livestock and grazing. The fact that forest loss has several causes has a policy implication: Different deforestation scenarios require different conservation strategies. Applied anthropologists must work to make "good for the globe" good for the people.

4. The recent emergence and spread of infectious diseases like HIV/AIDS, Ebola, West Nile, SARS, and Lyme disease are the result of things people have done to their environments. The spread of zoonotic diseases from wild to domesticated animals and then to humans has been going on since the Neolithic. Because human groups create the conditions that allow zoonotic pathogens to jump species and to spread, anthropologists have a key role to play in studying the causes of environmental encroachment and in suggesting culturally appropriate solutions.

5. Cultural imperialism is the spread of one culture and its imposition on other cultures, which it modifies, replaces, or destroys—usually because of differential economic and political power. Some worry that modern technology, including the mass media, is destroying traditional cultures. But others see an important role for new technology in allowing local cultures to express themselves. As the forces of globalization spread, they are modified (indigenized) to fit local cultures. The mass media can help diffuse a national culture within and beyond its own boundaries. The media, including the Internet, also play a role in preserving ethnic and national identities among people who lead transnational lives.

6. People travel more than ever. But migrants also maintain ties with home, so they live multilocally. With so many people "in motion," the unit of anthropological study expands from the local community to the diaspora. *Postmodernity* describes this world in flux, such people on the move who manage multiple social identities depending on place and context. With globalization, new kinds of political and ethnic units are emerging as others break down or disappear.

7. The term and concept *indigenous people* has gained legitimacy within international law. Governments, NGOs, and international agencies have adopted policies designed to recognize and benefit indigenous peoples. Social movements worldwide have adopted this term as a self-identifying and political label based on past oppression but now signaling a search for social, cultural, and political rights.

8. In Latin America, emphasis has shifted from assimilation to identities that value difference. Transnational organizations have helped indigenous peoples influence

national legislative agendas. Recent use of the notion of autochthony (being native to, or formed in, the place where found) includes a call to exclude strangers, such as recent and illegal immigrants. Identity is a fluid, dynamic process, and there are multiple ways of being indigenous. No social movement exists apart from the nation and world that include it.

## Key Terms

climate change, *438*
cultural imperialism, *444*
diaspora, *447*
ecological anthropology, *440*

essentialism, *451*
ethnoecology, *440*
greenhouse effect, *438*
indigenization, *446*
postmodern, *448*

postmodernism, *448*
postmodernity, *448*
Westernization, *444*

# Glossary

## A

***Au. (Australopithecus) afarensis*** Early form of *Australopithecus,* found in Ethiopia at Hadar ("Lucy") and in Tanzania at Laetoli; dating to the period between 3.8 and 3.0 m.y.a. (126)

***Au. africanus*** First *Australopithecus* discovered, in South Africa; dating to 3.0–2.5 m.y.a. (130)

***Au. anamensis*** Earliest form of *Australopithecus* yet discovered; found in Kenya and dating to 4.2 m.y.a. (124)

***Au. boisei*** Late, hyperrobust form of *Australopithecus,* found in East Africa and dating to the period between 2.6 and 1.2 m.y.a. (132)

***Au. garhi*** Found in Ethiopia in association with tools and dating to 2.5 m.y.a. (134)

***Au. robustus*** Robust form of *Australopithecus,* found in South Africa and dating to the period between 2.6 and 2.0 m.y.a., aka Paranthropus. (130)

**absolute dating** Dating techniques that establish dates in numbers or ranges of numbers; examples include the radiometric methods of $^{14}$C, K/A, $^{238}$U, TL, and ESR dating. (44)

**acculturation** The exchange of cultural features that results when groups come into continuous firsthand contact; the original cultural patterns of either or both groups may be altered, but the groups remain distinct. (33)

**Acheulean** Derived from the French village of St. Acheul, where these tools were first identified; Lower Paleolithic tool tradition associated with *H. erectus*. (144)

**achieved status** Social status that comes through talents, actions, efforts, activities, and accomplishments, rather than ascription. (276)

**adaptation** The process by which organisms cope with environmental stresses. (3)

**adaptive** Favored by natural selection in a particular environment. (73)

**African American Vernacular English (AAVE)** A rule-governed dialect of American English spoken by some African Americans in their casual, intimate speech. (234)

**agriculture** Nonindustrial system of plant cultivation characterized by continuous and intensive use of land and labor. (248)

**allele** A biochemical difference involving a particular gene. (70)

**analogies** Similarities arising as a result of similar selective forces; traits produced by convergent evolution. (94)

**anatomically modern humans (AMHs)** Including the Cro-Magnons of Europe (31,000 B.P.) and the older fossils from Skhūl (100,000) and Qafzeh (92,000); continue through the present. (143)

**animism** Belief in souls or doubles. (346)

**anthropoids** Members of Anthropoidea, one of the two suborders of primates; monkeys, apes, and humans are anthropoids. (97)

**anthropology** The study of the human species and its immediate ancestors. (2)

**anthropology and education** Anthropological research in classrooms, homes, and neighborhoods, viewing students as total cultural creatures whose enculturation and attitudes toward education belong to a larger context that includes family, peers, and society. (398)

**anthropometry** The measurement of human body parts and dimensions, including skeletal parts (*osteometry*). (46)

**applied anthropology** The application of anthropological data, perspectives, theory, and methods to identify, assess, and solve contemporary social problems. (12)

**arboreal** Tree-dwelling. (97)

**archaeological anthropology** The branch of anthropology that reconstructs, describes, and interprets human behavior and cultural patterns through material remains; best known for the study of prehistory. Also known as *archaeology*. (8)

**archaic *H. sapiens*** Early *H. sapiens,* consisting of the Neandertals of Europe and the Middle East, the Neandertal-like hominins of Africa and Asia, and the immediate ancestors of all these hominins; lived from about 300,000 to 30,000 B.P. (149)

***Ardipithecus*** The earliest widely accepted hominin genus (5.8–4.4 m.y.a.); includes species *kadabba* (earlier) and *ramidus* (later). (116)

**ascribed status** Social status (e.g., race or gender) that people have little or no choice about occupying. (276)

**assimilation** The process of change that a minority group may experience when it moves to a country where another culture dominates; the minority is incorporated into the dominant culture to the point that it no longer exists as a separate cultural unit. (380)

**australopithecines** Varied group of Pliocene–Pleistocene hominins. The term is derived from their former classification as members of a distinct subfamily, the Australopithecinae; now they are distinguished from *Homo* only at the genus level. (124)

**authority** The formal, socially approved use of power, e.g., by government officials. (268)

**Aztec** Last independent state in the Valley of Mexico; capital was Tenochtitlan. It thrived between 1325 C.E. and the Spanish conquest in 1520. (212)

# B

**balanced polymorphism** Two or more forms, such as alleles of the same gene, that maintain a constant frequency in a population from generation to generation. (74)

**balanced reciprocity** See *generalized reciprocity.* (261)

**band** Basic unit of social organization among foragers. A band includes fewer than one hundred people; it often splits up seasonally. (247)

**behavioral modernity** The advent of modern human behavioral capabilities based on symbolic thought and language, in addition to modern anatomy. (160)

**big man** Figure often found among tribal horticulturalists and pastoralists. The big man occupies no office but creates his reputation through entrepreneurship and generosity to others. Neither his wealth nor his position passes to his heirs. (275)

**biocultural** Referring to the inclusion and combination (to solve a common problem) of both biological and cultural approaches—one of anthropology's hallmarks. (5)

**biological anthropology** The branch of anthropology that studies human biological diversity in time and space—for instance, hominid evolution, human genetics, human biological adaptation; also includes primatology (behavior and evolution of monkeys and apes). Also called *physical anthropology.* (10)

**bipedal** Upright two-legged locomotion, the key feature differentiating early hominins from the apes. (97)

**blade tool** The basic Upper Paleolithic tool type, hammered off a prepared core. (163)

**bone biology** The study of bone as a biological tissue, including its genetics; cell structure; growth, development, and decay; and patterns of movement (biomechanics). (46)

**bourgeoisie** One of Karl Marx's opposed classes; owners of the means of production (factories, mines, large farms, and other sources of subsistence). (416)

**brachiation** Swinging, hand-over-hand movement through trees, characteristic of arboreal apes and some New World monkeys. (101)

**broad-spectrum revolution** Period beginning around 20,000 B.P. in the Middle East and 12,000 B.P. in Europe, during which a wider range, or broader spectrum, of plant and animal life was hunted, gathered, collected, caught, and fished; revolutionary because it led to food production. (171)

**bronze** An alloy of arsenic and copper or of tin and copper. (204)

# C

**call systems**   Systems of communication among nonhuman primates, composed of a limited number of sounds that vary in intensity and duration; tied to environmental stimuli. (219)

**capital**   Wealth or resources invested in business, with the intent of producing a profit. (411)

**capitalist world economy**   The single world system, which emerged in the 16th century, committed to production for sale, with the object of maximizing profits rather than supplying domestic needs. (411)

**cargo cults**   Postcolonial, acculturative, religious movements common in Melanesia that attempt to explain European domination and wealth and to achieve similar success magically by mimicking European behavior. (355)

**caste system**   Closed, hereditary system of stratification, often dictated by religion; hierarchical social status is ascribed at birth, so that people are locked into their parents' social position. (307)

**catastrophism**   View that extinct species were destroyed by fires, floods, and other catastrophes. After each destructive event, God created again, leading to contemporary species. (66)

**chiefdom**   Form of sociopolitical organization intermediate between the tribe and the state; kin-based with differential access to resources and a permanent political structure. A ranked society in which relations among villages as well as among individuals are unequal, with smaller villages under the authority of leaders in larger villages; has a two-level settlement hierarchy. (202, 270)

**chromosomes**   Basic genetic units, occurring in matching (homologous) pairs; lengths of DNA made up of multiple genes. (69)

**clan**   Unilineal descent group based on stipulated descent. (301)

**climate change**   Global warming, plus changing sea levels, precipitation, storms, and ecosystem effects. (438)

**cline**   Gradual shift in gene (allele) frequencies between neighboring populations. (77)

**Clovis tradition**   Stone technology based on a projectile point that was fastened to the end of a hunting spear; it flourished between 12,000 and 11,000 B.P. in North America. (165)

**colonialism**   The political, social, economic, and cultural domination of a territory and its people by a foreign power for an extended time. (419)

**communism**   Spelled with a lowercase *c*, describes a social system in which property is owned by the community and in which people work for the common good. (425)

**Communism**   Spelled with a capital *C*, a political movement and doctrine seeking to overthrow capitalism and to establish a form of communism such as that which prevailed in the Soviet Union (USSR) from 1917 to 1991. (425)

**communitas**   Intense community spirit, a feeling of great social solidarity, equality, and togetherness; characteristic of people experiencing liminality together. (344)

**conflict resolution**   The means by which disputes are socially regulated and settled; found in all societies, but the resolution methods tend to be more formal and effective in states than in nonstates. (272)

**convergent evolution**   Independent operation of similar selective forces; process by which analogies are produced. (94)

**core**   Dominant structural position in the world system; consists of the strongest and most powerful states with advanced systems of production. (412)

**core values**   Key, basic, or central values that integrate a culture and help distinguish it from others. (20)

**correlation**   An association between two or more variables such that when one changes (varies), the other(s) also change(s) (covaries)— for example, temperature and sweating. (247)

**creationism**   Explanation for the origin of species given in Genesis: God created the species during the original six days of Creation. (65)

**Cro-Magnon**   The first fossil find (1868) of an AMH, from France's Dordogne Valley. (154)

**cultural anthropology** The study of human society and culture; describes, analyzes, interprets, and explains social and cultural similarities and differences. (7)

**cultural colonialism** Within a nation or an empire, domination by one ethnic group or nationality and its culture/ideology over others—e.g., the dominance of Russian people, language, and culture in the former Soviet Union. (386)

**cultural consultant** Someone the ethnographer gets to know in the field, who teaches him or her about the consultant's society and culture; also called an *informant*. (52)

**cultural imperialism** The rapid spread or advance of one culture at the expense of others, or its imposition on other cultures, which it modifies, replaces, or destroys—usually because of differential economic or political influence. (444)

**cultural relativism** The position that the values and standards of cultures differ and deserve respect. Anthropology is characterized by methodological rather than moral relativism: In order to understand another culture fully, anthropologists try to understand its members' beliefs and motivations. Methodological relativism does not preclude making moral judgments or taking action. (31)

**cultural resource management (CRM)** The branch of applied archaeology aimed at preserving sites threatened by dams, highways, and other projects. (14)

**cultural rights** Doctrine that certain rights are vested not in individuals but in identifiable groups, such as religious and ethnic minorities and indigenous societies. (32)

**cultural transmission** A basic feature of language; transmission through learning. (221)

**culture** Traditions and customs that govern behavior and beliefs; distinctly human; transmitted through learning. (2)

**cuneiform** Early Mesopotamian writing that used a stylus (writing implement) to write wedge-shaped impressions on raw clay; from the Latin word for "wedge." (204)

**curer** Specialized role acquired through a culturally appropriate process of selection, training, certification, and acquisition of a professional image; the curer is consulted by patients, who believe in his or her special powers, and receives some form of special consideration; a cultural universal. (403)

# D

**daughter languages** Languages developing out of the same parent language; for example, French and Spanish are daughter languages of Latin. (235)

**Denisovans** Cousins of the Neandertals who lived in Asia from roughly 400,000 to 50,000 B.P. (159)

**descent** Rule assigning social identity on the basis of some aspect of one's ancestry. (371)

**descent group** A permanent social unit whose members claim common ancestry; fundamental to tribal society. (300)

**descriptive linguistics** The scientific study of a spoken language, including its phonology, morphology, lexicon, and syntax. (224)

**development anthropology** The branch of applied anthropology that focuses on social issues in, and the cultural dimension of, economic development. (393)

**diaspora** The offspring of an area who have spread to many lands. (447)

**differential access** Unequal access to resources; basic attribute of chiefdoms and states. Superordinates have favored access to such resources, while the access of subordinates is limited by superordinates. (270)

**diffusion** Borrowing between cultures either directly or through intermediaries. (26)

**diglossia** The existence of "high" (formal) and "low" (familial) dialects of a single language, such as German. (231)

**discrimination** Policies and practices that harm a group and its members. (385)

**disease** A scientifically identified health threat caused by a bacterium, virus, fungus, parasite, or other pathogen. (401)

**displacement**   A linguistic capacity that allows humans to speak of things and events that are not present. (222)

**domestic**   Within or pertaining to the home. (327)

**domestic–public dichotomy**   Contrast between women's role in the home and men's role in public life, with a corresponding social devaluation of women's work and worth. (327)

**dominant**   Allele that masks another allele in a heterozygote. (69)

**dowry**   A marital exchange in which the wife's group provides substantial gifts to the husband's family. (309)

# E

**ecological anthropology**   Study of cultural adaptations to environments. (440)

**economy**   A population's system of production, distribution, and consumption of resources. (253)

**egalitarian society**   A type of society, most typically found among foragers, that lacks status distinctions except for those based on age, gender, and individual qualities, talents, and achievements. (202)

**emic**   The research strategy that focuses on native explanations and criteria of significance. (52)

**enculturation**   The social process by which culture is learned and transmitted across the generations. (18)

**endogamy**   Marriage between people of the same social group. (306)

**equity, increased**   A reduction in absolute poverty and a fairer (more even) distribution of wealth. (394)

**essentialism**   The process of viewing an identity as established, real, and frozen, so as to hide the historical processes and politics within which that identity developed. (451)

**estrus**   Period of maximum sexual receptivity in female baboons, chimpanzees, and other primates, signaled by vaginal area swelling and coloration. (25)

**ethnic group**   Group distinguished by cultural similarities (shared among members of that group) and differences (between that group and others); ethnic group members share beliefs, values, habits, customs, norms, and a common language, religion, history, geography, kinship, and/or race. (367)

**ethnicity**   Identification with, and feeling part of, an ethnic group and exclusion from certain other groups because of this affiliation. (368)

**ethnocentrism**   The tendency to view one's own culture as best and to judge the behavior and beliefs of culturally different people by one's own standards. (30)

**ethnocide**   Destruction by a dominant group of the culture of an ethnic group. (386)

**ethnoecology**   A culture's set of environmental practices and perceptions. (440)

**ethnography**   Fieldwork in a particular culture. (7)

**ethnology**   The theoretical, comparative study of society and culture; compares cultures in time and space. (7)

**etic**   The research strategy that emphasizes the observer's rather than the natives' explanations, categories, and criteria of significance. (52)

**evolution**   Descent with modification; change in form over generations. (66)

**excavation**   Digging through the layers of deposits that make up an archaeological site. (41)

**exogamy**   Mating or marriage outside one's kin group; a cultural universal. (304)

**extended family household**   Expanded household including three or more generations. (298)

# F

**family**   A group of people (e.g., parents, children, siblings, grandparents, grandchildren, uncles, aunts, nephews, nieces, cousins, spouses, siblings-in-law, parents-in-law, children-in-law) who are considered to be related in some way, for example, by "blood" (common ancestry or descent) or marriage. (294)

**family of orientation**    Nuclear family in which one is born and grows up. (295)

**family of procreation**    Nuclear family established when one marries and has children. (295)

**fiscal**    Pertaining to finances and taxation. (284)

**focal vocabulary**    A set of words and distinctions that are particularly important to certain groups (those with particular foci of experience or activity), such as types of snow to Eskimos or skiers. (228)

**food production**    Cultivation of plants and domestication (stockbreeding) of animals; first developed in the Middle East 10,000 to 12,000 years ago. (4, 243)

**fossils**    Remains (e.g., bones), traces, or impressions (e.g., footprints) of ancient life. (41)

# G

**gender identity**    Identity based on whether a person feels, and is regarded as, male, female, or something else. (337)

**gender roles**    The tasks and activities that a culture assigns to each sex. (321)

**gender stereotypes**    Oversimplified but strongly held ideas about the characteristics of males and females. (321)

**gender stratification**    Unequal distribution of rewards (socially valued resources, power, prestige, and personal freedom) between men and women, reflecting their different positions in a social hierarchy. (321)

**gene**    Area in a chromosome pair that determines, wholly or partially, a particular biological trait, such as whether one's blood type is A, B, AB, or O. (70)

**gene flow**    Exchange of genetic material between populations of the same species through direct or indirect interbreeding. (75)

**gene pool**    All the alleles and genotypes within a breeding population—the "pool" of genetic material available. (71)

**genealogical method**    Procedures by which ethnographers discover and record connections of kinship, descent, and marriage, using diagrams and symbols. (51)

**general anthropology**    The field of anthropology as a whole, consisting of cultural, archaeological, biological, and linguistic anthropology. (4)

**generality**    Culture pattern or trait that exists in some but not all societies. (26)

**generalized reciprocity**    Principle that characterizes exchanges between closely related individuals: As social distance increases, reciprocity becomes balanced and finally negative. (260)

**genetic evolution**    Change in gene frequency within a breeding population. (72)

**genocide**    Policies aimed at, and/or resulting in, the physical extinction (through mass murder) of a people perceived as a racial group, that is, as sharing defining physical, genetic, or other biological characteristics. (386)

**genotype**    An organism's hereditary makeup. (70)

**glacials**    The four or five major advances of continental ice sheets in northern Europe and North America. (151)

**globalization**    The accelerating interdependence of nations in a world system linked economically and through mass media and modern transportation systems. (34)

**gracile**    Small, slight; opposite of *robust*. (130)

**greenhouse effect**    Warming from trapped atmospheric gases. (438)

# H

**H. (Homo) erectus**    Hominin type that lived from approximately 1.9 to 300,000 m.y.a.; widely distributed throughout the Old World; immediate predecessor of *Homo sapiens*. (141)

**Halafian**    An early (7500–6500 B.P.) and widespread pottery style, first found in northern Syria; refers to a delicate ceramic style and to the period when the first chiefdoms emerged. (201)

**haplogroup**    Lineage or branch of a genetic tree marked by one or more specific genetic mutations. (80)

**head, village**    See *village head*. (274)

**health care systems**   Beliefs, customs, and specialists concerned with ensuring health and preventing and curing illness; a cultural universal. (401)

**hegemony**   The internalization of a dominant ideology. (285)

**Herto**   Very early (151,000 m.y.a.) AMH fossils, found in Ethiopia. (156)

**heterozygous**   Having dissimilar alleles of a given gene. (70)

**hilly flanks**   Woodland zone that flanks the Tigris and Euphrates Rivers to the north; zone of wild wheat and barley and of sedentism (settled, nonmigratory life) preceding food production. (174)

**historical linguistics**   Subdivision of linguistics that studies languages over time. (235)

**holistic**   Interested in the whole of the human condition: past, present, and future; biology, society, language, and culture. (2)

**hominid**   A member of the taxonomic family that includes humans and the African apes and their immediate ancestors. (22)

**hominin**   A member of the human lineage after its split from ancestral chimps; used to describe all the human species that ever have existed, including the extinct ones, but excluding chimps and gorillas. (22)

**hominoid**   Zoological superfamily that includes all fossil and living apes and hominins. (100)

*Homo erectus*   See *H. (Homo) erectus.* (141)

*Homo habilis*   Term coined by L. S. B. and Mary Leakey; ancestor or contemporary of *H. erectus;* lived from about 1.9 to 1.44 m.y.a. (132)

**homologies**   Traits that organisms have jointly inherited from their common ancestor. (93)

**homozygous**   Possessing identical alleles of a particular gene. (70)

**horticulture**   Nonindustrial system of plant cultivation in which plots lie fallow for varying lengths of time. (248)

**human rights**   Doctrine that invokes a realm of justice and morality beyond and superior to particular countries, cultures, and religions. Human rights, usually seen as vested in individuals, include the right to speak freely, to hold religious beliefs without persecution, and not to be enslaved. (31)

**hypodescent**   Rule that automatically places the children of a union or mating between members of different socioeconomic groups in the less privileged group. (371)

# I

**illness**   A condition of poor health perceived or felt by an individual. (401)

**imperialism**   A policy of extending the rule of a nation or an empire over foreign nations and of taking and holding foreign colonies. (419)

**incest**   Sexual relations with a close relative. (304)

**increased equity**   See *equity, increased.* (394)

**independent assortment (Mendel's law of)**   Chromosomes are inherited independently of one another. (71)

**independent invention**   Development of the same culture trait or pattern in separate cultures as a result of comparable needs and circumstances. (33)

**indigenization**   Process by which cultural items introduced from outside are modified to fit the local culture. (446)

**Industrial Revolution**   The historical transformation (in Europe, after 1750) of "traditional" into "modern" societies through industrialization of the economy. (414)

**informed consent**   Agreement to take part in research, after the people being studied have been told about that research's purpose, nature, procedures, and potential impact on them. (57)

**intellectual property rights (IPR)**   Each society's cultural base—its core beliefs and principles. IPR is claimed as a group right—a cultural right, allowing indigenous groups to control who may know and use their collective knowledge and its applications. (32)

**interglacials**   Extended warm periods between such major glacials as Riss and Würm. (151)

**international culture**   Cultural traditions that extend beyond national boundaries. (29)

**intersex**    Pertaining to a group of conditions reflecting a discrepancy between the external genitals (penis, vagina, etc.) and the internal genitals (testes, ovaries, etc.). (335)

**intervention philosophy**    Guiding principle of colonialism, conquest, missionization, or development; an ideological justification for outsiders to guide native peoples in specific directions. (424)

**interview schedule**    Ethnographic tool for structuring a formal interview. A prepared form (usually printed) that guides interviews with households or individuals being compared systematically. Contrasts with a questionnaire because the researcher has personal contact and records people's answers. (51)

## K

**key cultural consultant**    An expert on a particular aspect of local life who helps the ethnographer understand that aspect. Also called *key informant*. (52)

**kinesics**    The study of communication through body movements, stances, gestures, and facial expressions. (223)

## L

**law**    A legal code, including trial and enforcement; characteristic of state-organized societies. (272)

**levirate**    Custom by which a widow marries the brother of her deceased husband. (311)

**lexicon**    Vocabulary; a dictionary containing all the morphemes in a language and their meaning. (224)

**life history**    Of a cultural consultant; provides a personal cultural portrait of existence or change in a culture. (52)

**liminality**    The critically important marginal or in-between phase of a rite of passage. (348)

**lineage**    Unilineal descent group based on demonstrated descent. (301)

**linguistic anthropology**    The branch of anthropology that studies linguistic variation in time and space, including interrelations between language and culture; includes *historical linguistics* and *sociolinguistics*. (11)

**lobola**    A customary gift before, at, or after marriage from the husband and his kin to the wife and her kin. (309)

**longitudinal research**    Long-term study of a community, society, culture, or other unit, usually based on repeated visits. (53)

## M

**magic**    Use of supernatural techniques to accomplish specific aims. (347)

**maize**    Corn; domesticated in highland Mexico. (184)

**mana**    Sacred impersonal force in Melanesian and Polynesian religions. (346)

**manioc**    Cassava; a tuber domesticated in the South American lowlands. (184)

**market principle**    Profit-oriented principle of exchange that dominates in states, particularly industrial states. Goods and services are bought and sold, and values are determined by supply and demand. (259)

**matrilineal descent**    Unilineal descent rule in which people join the mother's group automatically at birth and stay members throughout life. (300)

**matrilocality**    Customary residence with the wife's relatives after marriage, so that children grow up in their mother's community. (303)

**means (or factors) of production**    Land, labor, technology, and capital—major productive resources. (254)

**medical anthropology**    Unites biological and cultural anthropologists in the study of disease, health problems, health care systems, and theories about illness in different cultures and ethnic groups. (401)

**meiosis**    Special process by which sex cells are produced; four cells are produced from one, each with half the genetic material of the original cell. (71)

**melanin**    Substance manufactured in specialized cells in the lower layers of the epidermis (outer skin layer); melanin cells in dark skin produce more melanin than do those in light skin. (81)

**Mendelian genetics**   Studies ways in which chromosomes transmit genes across the generations. (69)

**Mesoamerica**   "Middle America," including Mexico, Guatemala, and Belize. (177)

**Mesolithic**   Tool-making tradition between Upper Paleolithic and Neolithic, based on very small stone tools—*microliths*. (171)

**Mesopotamia**   The area between the Tigris and Euphrates Rivers in what is now southern Iraq and southwestern Iran; location of the first cities and states. (199)

**metallurgy**   Knowledge of the properties of metals, including their extraction and processing and the manufacture of metal tools. (204)

**mitosis**   Ordinary cell division; DNA molecules copy themselves, creating two identical cells out of one. (71)

**mode of production**   Way of organizing production—a set of social relations through which labor is deployed to wrest energy from nature by means of tools, skills, and knowledge. (253)

**molecular anthropology**   Genetic analysis, involving comparison of DNA sequences, to determine evolutionary links and distances among species and among ancient and modern populations. (45)

**monotheism**   Worship of an eternal, omniscient, omnipotent, and omnipresent supreme being. (346)

**morphology**   The study of form; used in linguistics (the study of morphemes and word construction) and for form in general—for example, biomorphology relates to physical form. (224)

**Mousterian**   Middle Paleolithic tool-making tradition associated with Neandertals. (153)

**multiculturalism**   The view of cultural diversity in a country as something good and desirable; a multicultural society socializes individuals not only into the dominant (national) culture but also into an ethnic culture. (381)

**mutation**   Change in the DNA molecules of which genes and chromosomes are built. (75)

**m.y.a.**   Million years ago. (107)

# N

**nation**   Once a synonym for *ethnic group,* designating a single culture sharing a language, religion, history, territory, ancestry, and kinship; now usually a synonym for *state* or *nation-state*. (379)

**nation-state**   An autonomous political entity; a country like the United States or Canada. (379)

**national culture**   Cultural experiences, beliefs, learned behavior patterns, and values shared by citizens of the same nation. (29)

**nationalities**   Ethnic groups that once had, or wish to have or regain, autonomous political status (their own country). (380)

**Natufians**   Widespread Middle Eastern culture, dated to between 12,500 and 10,500 B.P.; subsisted on intensive wild cereal collecting and gazelle hunting and had year-round villages. (176)

**natural selection**   Originally formulated by Charles Darwin and Alfred Russel Wallace; the process by which nature selects the forms most fit to survive and reproduce in a given environment, such as the tropics. (67)

**Neandertals**   *H. sapiens neanderthalensis,* representing an archaic *H. sapiens* subspecies; lived in Europe and the Middle East between 130,000 and 30,000 B.P. (149)

**negative reciprocity**   See *generalized reciprocity*. (261)

**neoliberalism**   Revival of Adam Smith's classic economic liberalism, the idea that governments should not regulate private enterprise and that free market forces should rule; a currently dominant intervention philosophy. (424)

**Neolithic**   "New Stone Age," coined to describe techniques of grinding and polishing stone tools; the first cultural period in a region in which the first signs of domestication are present. (174)

**neolocality**   Postmarital residence pattern in which a couple establishes a new place of residence rather than living with or near either set of parents. (297)

**norms**   Cultural standards or guidelines that enable individuals to distinguish between appropriate and inappropriate behavior in a given society. (272)

# O

**office**   Permanent political position. (281)

**Oldowan pebble tools**   Earliest (1.8–2.6 m.y.a.) stone tools; first discovered in 1931 by L. S. B. and Mary Leakey at Olduvai Gorge. (133)

**opposable thumb**   A thumb that can touch all the other fingers. (97)

**overinnovation**   Characteristic of development projects that require major changes in people's daily lives, especially ones that interfere with customary subsistence pursuits. (395)

# P

**paleoanthropology**   The study of hominin evolution and human life as revealed by the fossil record. (41)

**Paleolithic**   Old Stone Age (from Greek roots meaning "old" and "stone"); divided into Lower (early), Middle, and Upper (late). (144)

**paleontology**   Study of ancient life through the fossil record. (40)

**paleopathology**   Study of disease and injury in skeletons from archaeological sites. (46)

**pantribal sodality**   A non-kin-based group that exists throughout a tribe, spanning several villages. (277)

**participant observation**   A characteristic ethnographic technique; taking part in the events one is observing, describing, and analyzing. (47)

**particularity**   Distinctive or unique culture trait, pattern, or integration. (26)

**pastoral nomadism**   Movement throughout the year by the whole pastoral group (men, women, and children) with their animals; more generally, such constant movement in pursuit of strategic resources. (253)

**pastoralists**   People who use a food-producing strategy of adaptation based on care of herds of domesticated animals. (252)

**patriarchy**   Political system ruled by men in which women have inferior social and political status, including basic human rights. (330)

**patrilineal descent**   Unilineal descent rule in which people join the father's group automatically at birth and stay members throughout life. (300)

**patrilineal–patrilocal complex**   An interrelated constellation of patrilineality, patrilocality, warfare, and male supremacy. (329)

**patrilocality**   Customary residence with the husband's relatives after marriage, so that children grow up in their father's community. (302)

**peasant**   Small-scale agriculturist living in a state, with rent fund obligations. (259)

**periphery**   Weakest structural position in the world system. (413)

**phenotype**   An organism's evident traits; its "manifest biology"—anatomy and physiology. (70)

**phenotypical adaptation**   Adaptive biological changes that occur during the individual's lifetime, made possible by biological plasticity. (88)

**phoneme**   Significant sound contrast in a language that serves to distinguish meaning, as in minimal pairs. (225)

**phonemics**   The study of the sound contrasts (phonemes) of a particular language. (225)

**phonetics**   The study of speech sounds in general; what people actually say in various languages. (225)

**phonology**   The study of sounds used in speech. (224)

**physical anthropology**   See *biological anthropology*. (10)

**Pleistocene**   Epoch of *Homo*'s appearance and evolution; began 2 million years ago; divided into Lower, Middle, and Upper. (150)

**plural marriage**   Marriage of a man to two or more women (polygyny) or marriage of a woman to two or more men (polyandry) at the same time; see also *polygamy*. (310)

**plural society**   A society that combines ethnic contrasts, ecological specialization (i.e., use of different environmental resources by each ethnic group), and the economic interdependence of those groups. (381)

**polyandry**   Variety of plural marriage in which a woman has more than one husband. (310)

**polygamy**   Marriage with three or more spouses, at the same time; see also *plural marriage*. (310)

**polygyny**   Variety of plural marriage in which a man has more than one wife. (310)

**polytheism**   Belief in several deities who control aspects of nature. (346)

**population genetics**   Field that studies causes of genetic variation, maintenance, and change in breeding populations. (69)

**postcolonial**   Referring to interactions between European nations and the societies they colonized (mainly after 1800); more generally, *postcolonial* may be used to signify a position against imperialism and Eurocentrism. (423)

**postmodern**   In its most general sense, describes the blurring and breakdown of established canons (rules, standards), categories, distinctions, and boundaries. (448)

**postmodernism**   A style and movement in architecture that succeeded modernism. Compared with modernism, postmodernism is less geometric, less functional, less austere, more playful, and more willing to include elements from diverse times and cultures; *postmodern* now describes comparable developments in music, literature, and visual art. (448)

**postmodernity**   Condition of a world in flux, with people on-the-move, in which established groups, boundaries, identities, contrasts, and standards are reaching out and breaking down. (448)

**potlatch**   Competitive feast among Indians on the North Pacific Coast of North America. (262)

**power**   The ability to exercise one's will over others—to do what one wants; the basis of political status. (268)

**prejudice**   Devaluing (looking down on) a group because of its assumed behavior, values, capabilities, or attributes. (385)

**prestige**   Esteem, respect, or approval for acts, deeds, or qualities considered exemplary. (282)

**primary states**   States that arise on their own (through competition among chiefdoms), and not through contact with other state societies. (195)

**primates**   Monkeys, apes, and prosimians; members of the zoological order that includes humans. (92)

**primatology**   The study of the biology, behavior, social life, and evolution of monkeys, apes, and other nonhuman primates. (92)

**productivity**   The ability to use the rules of one's language to create new expressions comprehensible to other speakers; a basic feature of language. (221)

**prosimians**   The primate suborder that includes lemurs, lorises, and tarsiers. (97)

**protolanguage**   Language ancestral to several daughter languages. (235)

**public anthropology**   Efforts to extend anthropology's visibility beyond academia and to demonstrate its public policy relevance. (406)

# R

**race**   An ethnic group assumed to have a biological basis. (370)

**racial classification**   The attempt to assign humans to discrete categories (purportedly) based on common ancestry. (77)

**racism**   Discrimination against an ethnic group assumed to have a biological basis. (370)

**random genetic drift**   Change in gene frequency that results not from natural selection but from chance; most common in small populations. (75)

**ranked society**   A type of society with hereditary inequality but not social stratification; individuals are ranked in terms of their genealogical closeness to the chief, but there is a continuum of status, with many individuals and kin groups ranked about equally. (202)

**recessive**   Genetic trait masked by a dominant trait. (69)

**reciprocity**   One of the three principles of exchange; governs exchange between social equals; major exchange mode in band and tribal societies. (260)

**reciprocity continuum**   Regarding exchanges, a range running from generalized reciprocity (closely related/deferred return) through balanced reciprocity to negative reciprocity (strangers/immediate return). (260)

**redistribution**   Major exchange mode of chiefdoms, many archaic states, and some states with managed economies. (260)

**refugees**   People who have been forced (involuntary refugees) or who have chosen (voluntary refugees) to flee a country, to escape persecution or war. (386)

**relative dating**   Dating technique (e.g., stratigraphy) that establishes a time frame in relation to other strata or materials, rather than absolute dates in numbers. (43)

**religion**   Beliefs and rituals concerned with supernatural beings, powers, and forces. (343)

**revitalization movements**   Movements that occur in times of change, in which religious leaders emerge and undertake to alter or revitalize a society. (355)

**rites of passage**   Culturally defined activities associated with the transition from one place or stage of life to another. (348)

**ritual**   Behavior that is formal, stylized, repetitive, and stereotyped, performed earnestly as a social act; rituals are held at set times and places and have liturgical orders. (347)

**robust**   Large, strong, sturdy; said of skull, skeleton, muscle, and teeth; opposite of *gracile*. (130)

# S

**sample**   A smaller study group chosen to represent a larger population. (51)

**Sapir-Whorf hypothesis**   Theory that different languages produce different ways of thinking. (227)

**science**   A systematic field of study or body of knowledge that aims, through experiment, observation, and deduction, to produce reliable explanations of phenomena,

with reference to the material and physical world. (11)

**scientific medicine**   As distinguished from Western medicine, a health care system based on scientific knowledge and procedures, encompassing such fields as pathology, microbiology, biochemistry, surgery, diagnostic technology, and applications. (403)

**sedentism**   Settled (sedentary) life; preceded food production in the Old World and followed it in the New World. (176)

**semantics**   A language's meaning system. (229)

**semiperiphery**   Structural position in the world system intermediate between core and periphery. (412)

**settlement hierarchy**   A ranked series of communities differing in size, function, and type of building; a three-level settlement hierarchy indicates state organization. (211)

**sexual dimorphism**   Marked differences in male and female biology, besides the contrasts in breasts and genitals, and temperament. (320)

**sexual orientation**   A person's habitual sexual attraction to and activities with persons of the opposite sex (*heterosexuality*), the same sex (*homosexuality*), or both sexes (*bisexuality*). (337)

**sexual selection**   Based on differential success in mating, the process in which certain traits of one sex (e.g., color in male birds) are selected because of advantages they confer in winning mates. (73)

**shaman**   A part-time religious practitioner who mediates between ordinary people and supernatural beings and forces. (345)

**smelting**   The high-temperature process by which pure metal is produced from an ore. (204)

**social control**   Those fields of the social system (beliefs, practices, and institutions) that are most actively involved in the maintenance of any norms and the regulation of any conflict. (285)

**society**   Organized life in groups; typical of humans and other animals. (2)

**sociolinguistics**   Study of relationships between social and linguistic variation; study of language in its social context. (11, 230)

**sociopolitical typology**   Classification scheme based on the scale and complexity of social organization and the effectiveness of political regulation; includes band, tribe, chiefdom, and state. (270)

**sodality**   See *pantribal sodality*. (277)

**sororate**   Custom by which a widower marries the sister of the deceased wife. (311)

**speciation**   Formation of new species; occurs when subgroups of the same species are separated for a sufficient length of time. (76)

**species**   Population whose members can interbreed to produce offspring that can live and reproduce. (76)

**state**   Complex sociopolitical system that administers a territory and populace with substantial contrasts in occupation, wealth, prestige, and power. An independent, centrally organized political unit; a government. A form of social and political organization with a formal, central government and a division of society into classes. (194, 270)

**status**   Any position that determines where someone fits in society; may be ascribed or achieved. (275)

**stereotypes**   Fixed ideas—often unfavorable—about what members of a group are like. (385)

**stratification**   Characteristic of a system with socioeconomic strata. (202)

**stratigraphy**   Science that examines the ways in which earth sediments are deposited in demarcated layers known as strata (singular, stratum). (43)

**style shifts**   Variations in speech in different contexts. (231)

**subcultures**   Different cultural symbol-based traditions associated with subgroups in the same complex society. (30)

**subgroups**   Languages within a taxonomy of related languages that are most closely related. (237)

**subordinate**   The lower, or underprivileged, group in a stratified system. (283)

**superordinate**   The upper, or privileged, group in a stratified system. (283)

**survey research**   Characteristic research procedure among social scientists other than anthropologists. Studies society through sampling, statistical analysis, and impersonal data collection. (56)

**symbol**   Something, verbal or nonverbal, that arbitrarily and by convention stands for something else, with which it has no necessary or natural connection. (18)

**syntax**   The arrangement and order of words in phrases and sentences. (224)

**systematic survey**   Information gathered on patterns of settlement over a large area; provides a regional perspective on the archaeological record. (41)

# T

**taboo**   Prohibition backed by supernatural sanctions. (346)

**taphonomy**   The study of the processes—biological and geological—by which dead animals become fossils; from the Greek *taphos,* which means "tomb." (43)

**taxonomy**   Classification scheme; assignment to categories (*taxa;* singular, *taxon*). (93)

**teosinte**   Wild grass; apparent ancestor of maize; also called *teocentli.* (185)

**Teotihuacan**   First state in the Valley of Mexico and earliest major Mesoamerican empire, 100 to 700 C.E. (211)

**terrestrial**   Ground-dwelling. (92)

**theory**   An explanatory framework, containing a series of statements, that helps us understand why (something exists); theories suggest patterns, connections, and relationships that may be confirmed by new research. (66)

**totem**   An animal, plant, or geographic feature associated with a specific social group, to which that totem is sacred or symbolically important. (351)

**transgender**   A category of varied individuals whose gender identity contradicts their biological sex at birth and the gender identity that society assigned to them in infancy. (336)

**transhumance**   One of two variants of pastoralism; part of the population moves seasonally with the herds while the other part remains in home villages. (253)

**tribe**    Form of sociopolitical organization usually based on horticulture or pastoralism. Socioeconomic stratification and centralized rule are absent in tribes, and there is no means of enforcing political decisions. (270)

**typology, sociopolitical**    See *sociopolitical typology*. (270)

# U

**underdifferentiation**    Planning fallacy of viewing less-developed countries as an undifferentiated group; ignoring cultural diversity and adopting a uniform approach (often ethnocentric) for very different types of project beneficiaries. (396)

**uniformitarianism**    Belief that explanations for past events should be sought in ordinary forces that continue to work today. (66)

**unilineal descent**    Matrilineal or patrilineal descent. (301)

**universal**    Something that exists in every culture. (26)

**Upper Paleolithic**    Blade tool-making traditions associated with AMHs; named from their location in upper, or more recent, layers of sedimentary deposits. (163)

**urban anthropology**    The anthropological study of life in and around world cities, including urban social problems, differences between urban and other environments, and adaptation to city life. (400)

# V

**variables**    Attributes (e.g., age, occupation, income) that differ from one person or case to the next. (56)

**village head**    Leadership position in a village (as among the Yanomami, where the head is always a man); has limited authority; and leads by example and persuasion. (274)

# W

**wealth**    All a person's material assets, including income, land, and other types of property; the basis of economic status. (282)

**Westernization**    The acculturative influence of Western expansion on other cultures. (444)

**working class (or proletariat)**    Those who must sell their labor to survive; the antithesis of the bourgeoisie in Marx's class analysis. (416)

**world-system theory**    Argument for the historic and contemporary social, political, and economic significance of an identifiable global system, based on wealth and power differentials, that extends beyond individual countries. (412)

# Z

**Zapotec state**    Mesoamerica's earliest state, which developed in Mexico's Valley of Oaxaca from a chiefdom by about 100 B.C.E. and lasted until its overthrow by Spain in the 1500s. (209)

# Bibliography

Abelmann, N., and J. Lie 1995. *Blue Dreams: Korean Americans and the Los Angeles Riots.* Cambridge, MA: Harvard University Press.

Adams, R. M. 1981. *Heartland of Cities.* Chicago: Aldine.

———. 2008. An Interdisciplinary Overview of a Mesopotamian City and its Hinterlands, *Cuneiform Digital Library Journal.*

Ahearn, L. M. 2012. *Living Language: An Introduction to Linguistic Anthropology.* Malden, MA: Wiley-Blackwell.

Ahmed, A. S. 2004. *Postmodernism and Islam: Predicament and Promise,* rev. ed. New York: Routledge.

Aiello, L., and M. Collard 2001. Our Newest Oldest Ancestor? *Nature* 410 (March 29): 526–527.

Akazawa, T. 1980. *The Japanese Paleolithic: A Techno-Typological Study.* Tokyo: Rippo Shobo.

Akazawa, T., and C. M. Aikens, eds. 1986. *Prehistoric Hunter-Gatherers in Japan: New Research Methods.* Tokyo: University of Tokyo Press.

Allegretto, S. A. 2011. The State of Working America's Wealth, Briefing Paper no. 292, Economic Policy Institute, March 23. http://www.epi.org/page/-/BriefingPaper292.pdf.

Amadiume, I. 1987. *Male Daughters, Female Husbands.* Atlantic Highlands, NJ: Zed.

American Psychiatric Association 2013. *Diagnostic and Statistical Manual of Mental Disorders: DSM-5,* 5th ed. Washington: American Psychiatric Association.

Amos, T. D. 2011. *Embodying Difference: The Making of the Burakumin in Modern Japan.* Honolulu: University of Hawaii Press.

Anderson, B. 1991. *Imagined Communities: Reflections on the Origin and Spread of Nationalism,* rev. ed. London: Verso.

———. 2006. *Imagined Communities: Reflections on the Origin and Spread of Nationalism,* rev. ed. New York: Verso.

Anderson, R. 1996. *Magic, Science, and Health: The Aims and Achievements of Medical Anthropology.* Fort Worth, TX: Harcourt Brace.

Anderson-Levitt, K. M. 2012. *Anthropologies of Education: A Global Guide to Ethnographic Studies of Learning and Schooling.* New York: Berghahn Books.

Anemone, R. L. 2011. *Race and Human Diversity: A Biocultural Approach.* Upper Saddle River, NJ: Prentice Hall/Pearson.

Annenberg/CPB Exhibits 2000. Collapse, Why Do Civilizations Fall? http://www.learner.org/exhibits/collapse/.

*Anthropology Newsletter.* Published 9 times annually by the American Anthropological Association, Washington, DC.

Antoun, R. T. 2008. *Understanding Fundamentalism: Christian, Islamic, and Jewish Movements,* 2nd ed. Lanham, MD: AltaMira.

Ansell, A. E. 2013. *Race and Ethnicity: The Key Concepts.* New York: Routledge.

Aoki, M. Y., and M. B. Dardess, eds. 1981. *As the Japanese See It: Past and Present.* Honolulu: University Press of Hawaii.

Appadurai, A. 1990. Disjuncture and Difference in the Global Cultural Economy. *Public Culture* 2(2):1–24.

———. 1991. Global Ethnoscapes: Notes and Queries for a Transnational Anthropology. In *Recapturing Anthropology: Working in the Present,* R. G. Fox, ed., pp. 191–210. Santa Fe, NM: School of American Research Advanced Seminar Series.

———. 1996. *Modernity at Large. Cultural Dimensions of Globalization.* Minneapolis: University of Minnesota Press.

Appadurai, A., ed. 2001. *Globalization.* Durham, NC: Duke University Press.

Arnold, J. E., et al. 2012. *Life at Home in the Twenty-first Century: 32 Families Open Their Doors.* Los Angeles: Cotsen Institute of Archaeology Press.

Arrighi, G. 2010. *The Long Twentieth Century: Money, Power, and the Origins of Our Times*, new and updated ed. New York: Verso.

Asad, T. 2008 (orig. 1983). The Construction of Religion as an Anthropological Category. In *A Reader in the Anthropology of Religion*, M. Lambek, ed., pp. 110–132. Malden, MA: Blackwood.

Asfaw, B., T. White, and O. Lovejoy 1999. *Australopithecus garhi:* A New Species of Early Hominid from Ethiopia. *Science* 284 (April 23):629.

Ashcroft, B., G. Griffiths, and H. Tiffin 1989. *The Empire Writes Back: Theory and Practice in Post-colonial Literatures*. New York: Routledge.

Baer, H. A., M. Singer, and I. Susser 2013. *Medical Anthropology and the World System*, 3rd ed. Santa Barbara, CA: Praeger.

Bailey, G., and P. Spikins, eds. 2008. *Mesolithic Europe*. New York: Cambridge University Press.

Bailey, R. C. 1990. *The Behavioral Ecology of Efe Pygmy Men in the Ituri Forest, Zaire*. Ann Arbor: Anthropological Papers, Museum of Anthropology, University of Michigan, no. 86.

Bailey, R. C., G. Head, M. Jenike, B. Owen, R. Rechtman, and E. Zechenter 1989. Hunting and Gathering in Tropical Rain Forests: Is It Possible? *American Anthropologist* 91:59–82.

Balter, M. 2010. Romanian Cave Art May Boast Central Europe's Oldest Cave Art. *Science Now,* June 21. http://news.sciencemag.org/sciencenow/2010/06/romanian-cave-may-boast-central.html.

Bar-Yosef, O., and F. R. Valla, eds. 2013. *Natufian Foragers in the Levant: Terminal Pleistocene Social Changes in Western Asia*. Ann Arbor, MI: International Monographs in Prehistory.

Barfield, T. J. 2010. *Afghanistan: A Cultural and Political History*. Princeton, NJ: Princeton University Press.

Barnaby, F., ed. 1984. *Future War: Armed Conflict in the Next Decade*. London: M. Joseph.

Barnard, A., ed. 2004. *Hunter-Gatherers in History, Archaeology and Anthropology*. New York: Oxford University Press.

Baro, M., and T. F. Deubel 2006. Persistent Hunger: Perspectives on Vulnerability, Famine, and Food Security in Sub-Saharan Africa. *Annual Review of Anthropology* 35:521–538.

Baron, D. E. 2009. *A Better Pencil: Readers, Writers, and the Digital Revolution*. New York: Oxford University Press.

Barringer, F. 1992. New Census Data Show More Children Living in Poverty. *New York Times,* May 29, pp. A1, A12–A13.

Barth, F. 1968. (orig. 1958). Ecologic Relations of Ethnic Groups in Swat, North Pakistan. In *Man in Adaptation: The Cultural Present,* Yehudi Cohen, ed., pp. 324–331. Chicago: Aldine.

Bar-Yosef, O. 1987. Pleistocene Connections between Africa and Southwest Asia: An Archaeological Perspective. *African Archaeological Review* 5:29–38.

Beeman, W. 1986. *Language, Status, and Power in Iran*. Bloomington: Indiana University Press.

Beck, S., and C. A. Maida, eds. 2013. *Toward Engaged Anthropology*. New York: Berghahn Books.

Becker, K. 2013. 400 Research Chimpanzees to Be Retired. Healthy Pets, March 18. http://healthypets.mercola.com/sites/healthypets/archive/2013/03/18/research-chimpanzees.aspx

Behar, R. 1993. *Translated Woman: Crossing the Border with Esperanza's Study*. Boston: Beacon Press.

Bellah, R. N. 2011. *Religion in Human Evolution: From the Paleolithic to the Axial Age*. Cambridge, MA: Belknap Press of Harvard University Press.

Bellwood, P. S. 2005. *The First Farmers: Origins of Agricultural Societies*. Malden, MA: Blackwell.

Benazzi, S., et al. 2011. Early Dispersal of Modern Humans in Europe and Implications for Neanderthal Behaviour. *Nature* 479 (November 24): 525–528. doi:10.1038/nature10617.

Benedict, R. F. 1946. *The Chrysanthemum and the Sword*. Boston: Houghton Mifflin.

Berger, P. 2010. Pentecostalism—Protestant Ethic or Cargo Cult? *Peter Berger's blog,* July 29. http://blogs.the-american-interest.com/berger/2010/07/29/pentecostalism-%E2%80%93-protestant-ethic-or-cargo-cult/.

Beriss, D. 2004. *Black Skins, French Voices: Caribbean Ethnicity and Activism in Urban France.* Boulder, CO: Westview.

*Berkeleyan* 1999. Berkeley Researchers Head Team That Discovers New Species of Human Ancestor: Earliest Evidence of Meat-Eating, Early Beings Has Been Unearthed in Ethiopia. April 28–May 4, 1999 (27,32). http://www.berkeley.edu/news/berkeleyan/1999/0428/species.html.

Berlin, B., and P. Kay 1992 (orig. 1969). *Basic Color Terms: Their Universality and Evolution,* 2nd ed. Berkeley: University of California Press.

Berna, F. et al. 2012. Microstratigraphic evidence of in situ fire in the Acheulean strata of Wonderwerk Cave, Northern Cape province, South Africa. *Proceedings of the National Academy of Sciences.* doi:10.1073/pnas.1117620109.

Bernard, H. R. 2011. *Research Methods in Anthropology: Qualitative and Quantitative Approaches.* 5th ed. Lanham, MD: AltaMira.

Bernard, H. R., ed. 1998. *Handbook of Methods in Cultural Anthropology,* Walnut Creek, CA: AltaMira.

Bernard, H. R., and C. C. Gravlee, eds. 2014. *Handbook of Methods in Cultural Anthropology,* 2nd ed. Lanham: Rowman & Littlefield.

Bicker, A., P. Sillitoe, and J. Pottier, eds. 2004. *Investigating Local Knowledge: New Directions, New Approaches.* Burlington, VT: Ashgate.

Bielo, J. S. 2015. *Anthropology of Religion: The Basics.* New York: Routledge.

Binford, L. R. 1968. Post-Pleistocene Adaptations. In *New Perspectives in Archeology,* S. R. Binford and L. R. Binford, eds., pp. 313–341. Chicago: Aldine.

Bird-David, N. 1992. Beyond "The Original Affluent Society": A Culturalist Reformulation. *Current Anthropology* 33(1):25–47.

Bjuremalm, H. 1997. Rattvisa kan skippas i Rwanda: Folkmordet 1994 gar attt forklara och analysera pa samma satt som forintelsen av judarna. *Dagens Nyheter* [06-03-1977, p. B3].

Blackwood, E. 2010. *Falling into the Lesbi World: Desire and Difference in Indonesia.* Honolulu: University of Hawaii Press.

Blau, S., and D. Ubelaker, eds. 2009. *Handbook of Forensic Anthropology and Archaeology.* Walnut Creek, CA: Left Coast Press.

Blommaert, J. 2010. *Sociolinguistics of Globalization.* New York: Cambridge University Press.

Blum, H. F. 1961. Does the Melanin Pigment of Human Skin Have Adaptive Value? *Quarterly Review of Biology* 36:50–63.

Boas, F. 1966 (orig. 1940). *Race, Language, and Culture.* New York: Free Press.

Boaz, N. T. 1997. *Eco Homo: How the Human Being Emerged from the Cataclysmic History of the Earth.* New York: Basic Books.

Bodley, J. H. 2008. *Victims of Progress,* 5th ed. Lanham, MD: AltaMira.

———. 2012. *Anthropology and Contemporary Human Problems,* 6th ed. Lanham, MD: AltaMira.

———. 2013. *The Small Nation Solution: How the World's Smallest Nations Can Solve the World's Biggest Problems.* Lanham, MD: Altamira.

———. 2014. *Victims of Progress,* 6th ed. Lanham, MD: Rowman & Littlefield.

Boellstorff, T. 2007. Queer Studies in the House of Anthropology. *Annual Review of Anthropology* 36:375–389.

Bogaard, A. 2004. *Neolithic Farming in Central Europe: An Archaeobotanical Study of Crop Husbandry Practices.* New York: Routledge.

Bogin, B. 2001. *The Growth of Humanity.* New York: Wiley.

Bolton, R. 1981. Susto, Hostility, and Hypoglycemia. *Ethnology* 20(4):227–258.

Bonvillain, N. 2007. *Women and Men: Cultural Constructs of Gender,* 4th ed. Upper Saddle River, NJ: Prentice Hall.

———. 2012. *Language, Culture, and Communication: The Meaning of Messages,* 7th ed. Boston: Pearson Prentice Hall.

Botelho, G., and M. Martinez 2015. 2014 Was Earth's Hottest Year on Record. CNN, Jan. 16. http://www.cnn.com/2015/01/16/world/earth-hottest-year/.

Bouquet-Appel, J-P., and O. Bar-Yosef, eds. 2008. *The Neolithic Demographic Transition and Its Consequences.* New York; Springer.

Bourdieu, P. 1977. *Outline of a Theory of Practice.* R. Nice (trans.). Cambridge: Cambridge University Press.

_____. 1982. *Ce Que Parler Veut Dire.* Paris: Fayard.

_____. 1984. *Distinction: A Social Critique of the Judgment of Taste.* R. Nice (trans.). Cambridge, MA: Harvard University Press.

Bourque, S. C., and K. B. Warren 1987. Technology, Gender and Development. *Daedalus* 116(4):173–197.

Bowen, J. R. 2011. *Religion in Practice: An Approach to Anthropology of Religion,* 5th ed. Boston: Pearson/Allyn and Bacon.

_____. 2014. *Religions in Practice: An Approach to the Anthropology of Religion,* 6th ed. Boston: Pearson.

Bowie, F. 2006. *The Anthropology of Religion: An Introduction.* Malden, MA: Blackwell.

Brace, C. L. 1995. *The Stages of Human Evolution,* 5th ed. Upper Saddle River, NJ: Prentice Hall.

Boyd, R., and J. B. Silk 2015. *How Humans Evolved.* New York: W.W. Norton.

Bradley, B., D. M. Doran-Sheehy, D. Lukas, C. Boesch, and L. Vigilant 2004. Dispersed Male Networks in Western Gorillas. *Current Biology* 14 (March):510–513.

Braudel, F. 1981. *Civilization and Capitalism, 15th–18th Century,* Volume I, *The Structure of Everyday Life: The Limits.* S. Reynolds (trans.). New York: Harper and Row.

_____. 1982. *Civilization and Capitalism, 15th–18th Century,* Volume II, *The Wheels of Commerce.* New York: Harper and Row.

_____. 1992. *Civilization and Capitalism, 15th–18th Century,* Volume III, *The Perspective of the World.* Berkeley: University of California Press.

Bremen, J., and A. Shimizu, eds. 1999. *Anthropology and Colonialism in Asia and Oceania.* London: Curzon.

Brenneis, D. 1988. Language and Disputing. *Annual Review of Anthropology* 17:221–237.

Brettell, C. B., and C. F. Sargent, eds. 2009. *Gender in Cross-Cultural Perspective,* 5th ed. Upper Saddle River, NJ: Pearson/Prentice Hall.

Brettell, C. B., and C. F. Sargent, eds. 2012. *Gender in Cross-Cultural Perspective,* 6th ed. Upper Saddle River, NJ: Pearson/Prentice Hall.

Briggs, C. L. 2005. Communicability, Racial Discourse, and Disease. *Annual Review of Anthropology* 34:269–291.

Briody, E. K., and R. T. Trotter II 2008. *Partnering for Organizational Performance; Collaboration and Culture in the Global Workplace.* Lanham, MD: Rowman & Littlefield.

Brooke, J. 1992. Rio's New Day in Sun Leaves Laplander Limp. *New York Times,* June 1, p. A7.

Brookings Institution 2010. *State of Metropolitan America: On the Front Lines of Demographic Transition.* The Brookings Institution Metropolitan Policy Program. http://www.brookings.edu/~/media/Files/Programs/Metro/state_of_metro_america/metro_america_report1.pdf.

Brower, B., and B. R. Johnston 2007. *Disappearing Peoples? Indigenous Groups and Ethnic Minorities in South and Central Asia.* Walnut Creek, CA: Left Coast Press.

Brown, A. 2001. Communism. *International Encyclopedia of the Social & Behavioral Sciences,* pp. 2323–2326. New York: Elsevier.

Brown, D. 1991. *Human Universals.* New York: McGraw-Hill.

Brown, M. F. 2003. *Who Owns Native Culture?* Cambridge, MA: Harvard University Press.

Brown, P. J., and R. L. Barrett 2010. *Understanding and Applying Medical Anthropology,* 2nd ed. New York: McGraw-Hill.

Brownstein, R. 2010. The Gray and the Brown: The Generational Mismatch. *National Journal,* July 24. http://www.nationaljournal.com/njmagazines/cs_20100724_3946php.

Bryant, V. M. 1999. Review of Piperno, D. R., and D. M. Pearsall, *The Origins of Agriculture in the Lowland Neotropics* (1998), *North American Archaeologist* (26):245–246.

———. 2003. Invisible Clues to New World Domestication. *Science* 299 (February 14) 1029–1030.

———. 2007a. Artifact: Maize Pollen. *Archaeology* 60(4). www.archaeology. org/0707/etc/artifact.html.

———. 2007b. Little Things Mean a Lot: The Search for Starch Grains at Archaeological Sites. *Mammoth Trumpet* 22(4):3–4, 16.

———. 2013. Please Don't Wash the Artifacts. *General Anthropology* 20(2):1–7.

Buikstra, J. E., and C. A. Roberts, eds. 2012. *The Global History of Paleopathology: Pioneers and Prospects*. Oxford, NY: Oxford University Press.

Burdick, J. 1993. *Looking for God in Brazil: The Progressive Catholic Church in Urban Brazil's Religious Arena*. Berkeley: University of California Press.

Burger, J., M. Kirchner, B. Bramanti, W. Haak, and M. G. Thomas 2007. Absence of the Lactase-Persistence Associated Allele in Early Neolithic Europeans. *Proceedings of the National Academy of Sciences* 104(10):3736–3741.

Burke, H., et al. 2008. *Kennewick Man: Perspectives on the Ancient One*. Walnut Creek, CA: Left Coast Press.

Burn, S. M. 2011. *Women Across Cultures,* 3rd ed. New York: McGraw-Hill.

Butler, R. 2005. World's Largest Cities: [Ranked by City Population]. http://www. mongabay.com/cities_pop_01.htm.

Buvinic, M. 1995. The Feminization of Poverty? Research and Policy Needs. In *Reducing Poverty through Labour Market Policies*. Geneva: International Institute for Labour Studies.

Cachel, S. 2006. *Primate and Human Evolution*. New York: Cambridge University Press.

Caldararo, N. L. 2014. *The Anthropology of Complex Economic Systems: Inequality,* *Stability, and Cycles of Crisis*. Lanham, MD: Lexington Books.

Callaway, E. 2010. Fossil Genome Reveals Ancestral Link: A Distant Cousin Raises Questions about Human Origins. *Nature* 468, 1012. doi:10.1038/4681012a, published online December 22, 2010.

Campbell, C. J., ed. 2011. *Primates in Perspective,* 2nd ed. New York: Oxford University Press.

Cann, R. L., M. Stoneking, and A. C. Wilson 1987. Mitochondrial DNA and Human Evolution. *Nature* 325:31–36.

Carey, B. 2007. Washoe, a Chimp of Many Words Dies at 42. *New York Times,* November 1. http://www.nytimes.com.

Carneiro, R. L. 1956. Slash-and-Burn Agriculture: A Closer Look at Its Implications for Settlement Patterns. In *Men and Cultures.* Selected Papers of the Fifth International Congress of Anthropological and Ethnological Sciences, pp. 229–234. Philadelphia: University of Pennsylvania Press.

———. 1968 (orig. 1961). Slash-and-Burn Cultivation among the Kuikuru and Its Implications for Cultural Development in the Amazon Basin. In *Man in Adaptation: The Cultural Present,* Y. A. Cohen, ed., pp. 131–145. Chicago: Aldine.

———. 1970. A Theory of the Origin of the State. *Science* 69:733–738.

———. 1990. Chiefdom-Level Warfare as Exemplified in Fiji and the Cauca Valley. In *The Anthropology of War,* J. Haas, ed., pp. 190–211. Cambridge: Cambridge University Press.

———. 1991. The Nature of the Chiefdom as Revealed by Evidence from the Cauca Valley of Colombia. In *Profiles in Cultural Evolution,* A. T. Rambo and K. Gillogly, eds. Anthropological Papers 85, pp. 167–190. Ann Arbor: University of Michigan Museum of Anthropology.

Carrier, J. G. 2012. *A Handbook of Economic Anthropology.* Cheltenham, UK: Edward Edgar.

Carroll, R. 2008. Chimps 90 Percent Gone in a "Final Stronghold." *National Geographic News,* October 13, 2008. http://news.national-geographic.com/news/pf/69848470.html.

Carsten, J. 2004. *After Kinship*. New York: Cambridge University Press.

Carter, J. 1988. Freed from Keepers and Cages, Chimps Come of Age on Baboon Island. *Smithsonian,* June, pp. 36–48.

Casanova, J. 2001. Religion, the New Millennium, and Globalization. *Sociology of Religion* 62:415–441.

Caspari, R. 2011 The Evolution of Grandparents, Senior Citizens May Have Been the Secret of our Species's Success. *Scientific American,* August. http://www.scientificamerican.com/magazine/sa/2011/08-01/.

Castells, M. 2001. Information Technology and Global Capitalism. In *On the Edge: Living with Global Capitalism,* W. Hutton and A. Giddens, eds. London: Vintage.

Cefkin, M., ed. 2009. *Ethnography and th Corporate Encounter: Reflections on Research in and of Corporations*. New York: Berghahn Books.

Cernea, M., ed. 1991. *Putting People First: Sociological Variables in Rural Development,* 2nd ed. New York: Oxford University Press (published for the World Bank).

Ceuppens, B., and P. Geschiere 2005. Autochthony: Local or Global? New Modes in the Struggle over Citizenship and Belonging in Africa and Europe. *Annual Review of Anthropology* 34:385–407.

Chagnon, N. A. 1992 (orig. 1983). *Yanomamo: The Fierce People,* 4th ed. New York: Harcourt Brace.

———. 1997. *Yanomamo,* 5th ed. Fort Worth, TX: Harcourt Brace.

———. 2013 *Noble Savages: My Life among Two Dangerous Tribes—the Yanomamo and the Anthropologists.* New York: Simon and Schuster.

Chakrabarty, D. 2007. *Provincializing Europe: Postcolonial Thought and Historical Difference.* Princeton, NJ: Princeton University Press.

Chambers, E. 1987. Applied Anthropology in the Post-Vietnam Era: Anticipations and Ironies. *Annual Review of Anthropology* 16:309–337.

Champion, T., and C. Gamble, eds. 1984. *Prehistoric Europe.* New York: Academic Press.

Chapais, B. 2008. *Primeval Kinship: How Pair Bonding Gave Birth to Human Society.* Cambridge, MA: Harvard University Press.

Chatterjee, P. 2004. *The Politics of the Governed: Reflections on Popular Politics in Most of the World.* New York: Columbia University Press.

Cheney, D. L., and R. M. Seyfarth 1990. In the Minds of Monkeys: What Do They Know and How Do They Know It? *Natural History,* September, pp. 38–46.

Chibnik, M. 2011. *Anthropology, Economics, and Choice.* Austin: University of Texas Press.

Childe, V. G. 1950. The Urban Revolution, *Town Planning Review* 21:3–17.

Choi, C. Q. 2011. Savanna, Not Forest, Was Human Ancestors' Proving Ground. *Live Science,* August 3. http://www.livescience.com/15377-savannas-human-ancestors-evolution.html.

———. 2012 Ancient Foot Suggests How Man Gave Up Treehouses. *Live Science,* March 28. http://www.livescience.com/19333-hominin-foot-humanity-bipedalism.html.

Chomsky, N. 1957. *Syntactic Structures.* The Hague: Mouton.

Chomsky, N. 2014. *Aspects of the Theory of Syntax,* 50th Anniversary ed. Cambridge, MA: MIT Press.

Ciochon, R. L., J. Olsen, and J. James 1990. *Other Origins: The Search for the Giant Ape in Human Prehistory.* New York: Bantam Books.

Clark, G. 2010. *African Market Women: Seven Life Stories from Ghana.* Indianapolis: Indiana University Press.

Clifford, J. 1982. *Person and Myth: Maurice Leenhardt in the Melanesian World.* Berkeley: University of California Press.

———. 1988. *The Predicament of Culture: Twentieth-Century Ethnography, Literature and Art.* Cambridge, MA: Harvard University Press.

Coburn, N. 2011. *Bazaar Politics: Power and Pottery in an Afghan Market Town*. Stanford, CA: Stanford University Press.

Cody, D. 1998. British Empire, May 18.

Coe, M. D. 2011. *The Maya*, 8th ed. New York: Thames and Hudson.

Cohen, M. N., and G. J. Armelagos, eds. 1984. *Paleopathology at the Origins of Agriculture*. New York: Academic Press.

Cohen, P. 2008. The Pentagon Enlists Social Scientists to Study Security Issues. *New York Times,* June 18.

Cohen, R. 1967. *The Kanuri of Bornu*. New York: Holt, Rinehart & Winston.

Cohen, Y. 1974. Culture as Adaptation. In *Man in Adaptation: The Cultural Present,* 2nd ed., Y. A. Cohen, ed., pp. 45–68. Chicago: Aldine.

Cohen, M. N., and G. J. Armelagos, eds. 2013. *Paleopathology at the Origins of Agriculture*, 2nd ed. Gainesville: University of Florida Press.

Colson, E., and T. Scudder 1975. New Economic Relationships between the Gwembe Valley and the Line of Rail. In *Town and Country in Central and Eastern Africa,* David Parkin, ed., pp. 190–210. London: Oxford University Press.

———. 1988. *For Prayer and Profit: The Ritual, Economic, and Social Importance of Beer in Gwembe District, Zambia, 1950–1982*. Stanford, CA: Stanford University Press.

Conard, N. J. 2011 *Neanderthal Lifeways, Subsistence, and Technology*. New York: Springer.

Conklin, A. L., S. Fishman, and R. Zaretsky 2015. *France and its Empire since 1870*. New York: Oxford University Press.

Cooper, F., and A. L. Stoler, eds. 1997. *Tensions of Empire: Colonial Cultures in a Bourgeois World*. Berkeley: University of California Press.

Cowgill, G. L. 2015. *Ancient Teotihuacan: Early Urbanism in Central Mexico*. New York: Cambridge University Press.

Crapo, R. H. 2003. *Anthropology of Religion: The Unity and Diversity of Religions*. Boston: McGraw-Hill.

Crate, S. A., and M. Nuttall 2008. *Anthropology and Climate Change: From Encounters to Actions*. Walnut Creek, CA: Left Coast Press.

Crewe, E., and R. Axelby 2013. *Anthropology and Development: Culture, Morality, and Politics in a Globalised World*. Cambridge, UK: Cambridge University Press

Cribb, J. 2010. *The Coming Famine: The Global Food Crisis and What We Can Do to Avoid It*. Berkeley: University of California Press.

Crosby, A. W., Jr. 2003. *The Columbian Exchange: Biological and Cultural Consequences of 1492*. Westport, CT: Praeger.

*Cultural Survival Quarterly*. Quarterly journal. Cambridge, MA: Cultural Survival, Inc.

Curnoe, D., Ji Xueping, et al. 2012. Human Remains from the Pleistocene-Holocene Transition of Southwest China Suggest a Complex Evolutionary History for East Asians. *Plos One Online*, March 14. http://www.plosone.org/article/info%3Adoi%2F10.1371%2Fjournal.pone.0031918.

Curry, A. 2009. Climate Change: Sites in Peril. *Archaeology* 62(2). http://archive.archaeology.org/0903/etc/climate_change.html.

Dalton, R. 2006. Ethiopia: Awash with Fossils. http://www.nature.com/news/2006/060102/full/439014a.html.

DaMatta, R. 1991. *Carnivals, Rogues, and Heroes: An Interpretation of the Brazilian Dilemma*. Translated from the Portuguese by John Drury. Notre Dame, IN: University of Notre Dame Press.

D'Andrade, R. 1984. Cultural Meaning Systems. In *Culture Theory: Essays on Mind, Self, and Emotion,* R. A. Shweder and R. A. Levine, eds., pp. 88–119. Cambridge: Cambridge University Press.

Dagne, T. W. 2015 *Intellectual Property and Traditional Knowledge in the Global Economy: Translating Geographical Indications for Development*. New York: Routledge.

Darwin, C. 2009 (orig. 1859). *On the Origin of Species*, ed. J. Endersby. New York: Cambridge University Press.

Darwin, J. 2013. *Unfinished Empire: The Global Expansion of Britain*. New York: Bloomsbury Press.

Das, V., and D. Poole, eds. 2004. *Anthropology in the Margins of the State*. Santa Fe, NM: School of American Research Press.

Degler, C. 1970. *Neither Black nor White: Slavery and Race Relations in Brazil and the United States*. New York: Macmillan.

de la Peña, G. 2005. Social and Cultural Policies toward Indigenous Peoples: Perspectives from Latin America. *Annual Review of Anthropology* 34:717–739.

Demeter, F. et al. 2012. Anatomically Modern Humans in Southeast Asia (Laos) by 46 ka. *Proceedings of the National Academy of Sciences*, 109(36):14375–14380, September 4.

DeNavas-Walt, C., B. D. Proctor, and J. C. Smith 2010. *Income, Poverty, and Health Insurance Coverage in the United States: 2009*. U.S. Census Bureau, Current Population Reports, P60-238. Washington, DC: U.S. Government Printing Office. http://www.census.gov/prod/2010pubs/p60-238.pdf.

DeNavas-Walt, C., and B. D. Proctor 2014 *Income and Poverty in the United States: 2013*. U.S. Census Bureau, Current Population Reports, P60-249. Washington, DC: U.S. Government Printing Office. http://www.census.gov/prod/2010pubs/p60-249.pdf.

Denny, R. M., and P. L. Sunderland, eds. 2014 *Handbook of Anthropology in Business*. Walnut Creek, CA: Left Coast Presss.

Dentan, R. K. 1979. *The Semai: A Nonviolent People of Malaya*, Fieldwork edn. New York: Harcourt Brace.

———. 2008. *Overwhelming Terror: Love, Fear, Peace and Violence among the Semai of Malaysia*. Lanham, MD: Rowman & Littlefield.

De Vos, G. A., W. O. Wetherall, and K. Stearman 1983. *Japan's Minorities: Burakumin, Koreans, Ainu and Okinawans*. Report no. 3. London: Minority Rights Group.

De Waal, F. B. M. 1995. Bonobo Sex and Society: The Behavior of a Close Relative Challenges Assumptions about Male Supremacy in Human Evolution. *Scientific American*, March, pp. 82–88.

———. 1997. *Bonobo: The Forgotten Ape*. Berkeley: University of California Press.

———. 1998. *Chimpanzee Politics: Power and Sex among Apes*, rev. ed. Baltimore: Johns Hopkins University Press.

———. F. B. M. 2013. *The Bonobo and the Atheist: In Search of Humanism among the Primates*. New York: W.W. Norton.

Diamond, J. M. 1990. A Pox upon Our Genes. *Natural History*, February, pp. 26–30.

———. 1997. *Guns, Germs, and Steel: The Fates of Human Societies*. New York: Norton.

———. 2005 (orig. 1997). *Guns, Germs, and Steel: The Fates of Human Societies*. New York: W. W. Norton.

Diaz, R. 2013. Rachel Caspari, Paleoanthropologist, Science Communication Program, University of California, Santa Cruz. April 2. http://scicom.ucsc.edu/publications/QandA/2013/caspari.html

Dickau, R., A. J. Ranere, and R. G. Cooke 2007. Starch Grain Evidence for the Preceramic Dispersals of Maize and Root Crops into Tropical Dry and Humid Forests of Panama. *Proceedings of the National Academy of Sciences of the United States of America* 104(9):3651–3656. http://www.pnas.org/cgi/content/full/104/9/3651.

Di Leonardo, M., ed., 1991. *Gender at the Crossroads of Knowledge: Feminist Anthropology in the Postmodern Era*. Berkeley: University of California Press.

Dillon, S. 2006. In School across U.S., the Melting Pot Overflows. *New York Times*, August 27. http://www.nytimes.com.

DiMento, J. F. C., and P. Doughman 2014. *Climate Change: What It Means for Us, Our Children, and Our Grandchildren*. Cambridge, MA: MIT Press.

Divale, W. T., and M. Harris 1976. Population, Warfare, and the Male Supremacist Complex. *American Anthropologist* 78:521–538.

Donham, D. L. 2011. *Violence in a Time of Liberation: Murder and Ethnicity at a South African Gold Mine, 1994*. Durham, NC: Duke University Press.

Donnelly, J. 2013. *Universal Human Rights in Theory and Practice*, 3rd ed. Ithaca, NY: Cornell University Press.

Donovan, J. M. 2007. *Legal Anthropology*. Lanham, MD: Altamira.

Dorward, D. C., ed. 1983. *The Igbo "Women's War" of 1929: Documents Relating to the Aba Riots in Eastern Nigeria*. Wakefield, England: East Ardsley.

Dove, M. R., and C. Carpenter, eds. 2008. *Environmental Anthropology: A Historical Reader*. Malden, MA: Blackwell.

Dove, M. R., P. E. Sajise, and A. A. Doolittle, eds. 2011. *Beyond the Sacred Forest: Complicating Conservation in Southeast Asia*. Durham, NC: Duke University Press.

Doyle, C. M. 2015. *Indigenous Peoples, Title to Territory, Rights, and Resources: The Transformative Role of Free Prior and Informed Consent*. New York: Routledge.

Drahos, P. 2014. *Intellectual Property, Indigenous People, and Their Knowledge*. Cambridge, UK: Cambridge University Press.

Dresch, P., and H. Skoda, eds. 2012. *Legalism: Anthropology and History*. New York: Oxford University Press.

Dressler, W. W., K. S. Oths, and C. C. Gravlee 2005. Race and Ethnicity in Public Health Research. *Annual Review of Anthropology* 34:231–252.

Duffield, M., and V. Hewitt, eds. 2009. *Empire, Development, and Colonialism: The Past in the Present*. Rochester, NY: James Currey.

Duranti, A., ed. 2009. *Linguistic Anthropology: A Reader*. Malden, MA: Wiley Blackwell.

Durkheim, E. 1951 (orig. 1897). *Suicide: A Study in Sociology*. Glencoe, IL: Free Press.

———. 2001 (orig. 1912). *The Elementary Forms of the Religious Life*. Translated by Carol Cosman. Abridged with an introduction and notes by Mark S. Cladis. New York: Oxford University Press.

Dwyer, K. 1982. *Moroccan Dialogues: Anthropology in Question*. Baltimore: Johns Hopkins University Press.

Earle, T. K. 1987. Chiefdoms in Archaeological and Ethnohistorical Perspective. *Annual Review of Anthropology* 16:279–308.

———. 1997. *How Chiefs Come to Power: The Political Economy in Prehistory*. Stanford, CA: Stanford University Press.

Eckert, P. 1989. *Jocks and Burnouts: Social Categories and Identity in the High School*. New York: Teachers College Press, Columbia University.

———. 2000. *Linguistic Variation as Social Practice: The Linguistic Construction of Identity in Belten High*. Malden, MA: Blackwell.

Eckert, P., and S. McConnell-Ginet 2013. *Language and Gender*, 2nd ed. Cambridge, UK: Cambridge University Press.

Eckert, P., and N. Mendoza-Denton 2002. Getting Real in the Golden State. *Language*, March 29.

Edelman, M., and A. Haugerud 2005. *The Anthropology of Development and Globalization: From Classical Political Economy to Contemporary Neoliberalism*. Malden, MA: Blackwell.

Edwards, D. N. 2004. *The Nubian Past: An Archaeology of Sudan*. New York: Routledge.

Edwards, J. 2013. *Sociolinguistics: A Very Short Introduction*. New York: Oxford Universiry Press.

Edwards, S. B. 2015. *Ancient Maya*. Minneapolis, MN: Abdo.

Eldred, S. M. 2013. Chimp Research Curtailed: Will Science Suffer? *Discovery News*, January 23. http://news.discovery.com/animals/zoo-animals/chimp-research-curtailed-will-science-suffer-130123.htm.

Ellen, R., S. J. Lycett, and S. E. Johns, eds. 2013. *Understanding Cultural Transmission in Anthropology: A Critical Synthesis*. New York: Berghahn.

Ellick, C. J., and J. E. Watkins 2011. *The Anthropology Graduate's Guide: From Student to a Career*. Walnut Creek, CA: Left Coast Press.

Elson, C. 2007. *Excavations at Cerro Tilcajete: A Monte Alban II Administrative Center in the Valley of Oaxaca*. Memoir 42 of the Museum of Anthropology, University of Michigan, Ann Arbor.

Enfield, N. J., Kochelman, P., and Sidnell, J., eds. 2014. *The Cambridge Handbook of Linguistic Anthropology*. Cambridge, UK: Cambridge University Press.

Eriksen, T. H. 2014. *Globalization: The Key Concepts*, 2nd ed. New York: Bloomsbury Academic.

Errington, F., and D. Gewertz 1987. *Cultural Alternatives and a Feminist Anthropology: An Analysis of Culturally Constructed Gender Interests in Papua New Guinea*. New York: Cambridge University Press.

Ervin, A. M. 2005. *Applied Anthropology: Tools and Perspectives for Contemporary Practice,* 2nd ed. Boston: Pearson/Allyn & Bacon.

———. 2014. *Cultural Transformation and Globalization: Theory, Development and Social Change*. Boulder, CO: Paradigm.

Escobar, A. 1991. Anthropology and the Development Encounter: The Making and Marketing of Development Anthropology. *American Ethnologist* 18:658–682.

———. 1994. Welcome to Cyberia: Notes on the Anthropology of Cyberculture. *Current Anthropology* 35(3):211–231.

———. 2012. *Encountering Development: The Making and Unmaking of the Third World*. Princeton, NJ: Princeton University Press.

Eskridge, W. N., Jr. 1996. *The Case for Same-Sex Marriage: From Sexual Liberty to Civilized Commitment*. New York: Free Press.

Evans, S. T., 2013 *Ancient Mexico and Central America: Archaeology and Culture History*, 3rd ed. New York: Thames and Hudson.

Evans-Pritchard, E. E. 1970. Sexual Inversion among the Azande. *American Anthropologist* 72:1428–1433.

Fagan, B. M. 1996. *World Prehistory: A Brief Introduction,* 3rd ed. New York: HarperCollins.

———. 1998. *World Prehistory: A Brief Introduction,* 4th ed. New York: Longman.

———. 2012. *Archeology: A Brief Introduction*, 11th ed. Upper Saddle River, NJ: Prentice Hall.

Farner, R. F., ed. 2004. *Nationalism, Ethnicity, and Identity: Cross-National and Comparative Perspectives*. New Brunswick, NJ: Transaction.

Farr, D. M. L. 1980. British Empire. *Academic American Encyclopedia*. Princeton, NJ: Arete, volume 3, pp. 495–496.

Fasold, R. W., and J. Connor-Linton 2006. *An Introduction to Language and Linguistics*. New York: Cambridge University Press.

Fearon, James D. 2003. Ethnic and Cultural Diversity by Country. *Journal of Economic Growth* 8:2 (June):195–222.

Feder, K. 2011. *Frauds, Myths, and Mysteries: Science and Pseudoscience in Archaeology*. New York: McGraw-Hill.

Feder, K. L. 2013. *The Past in Perspective: An Introduction to Human Prehistory*. New York: Oxford University Press.

Fedorak, S. 2014. *Global Issues: A Cross-Cultural Perspective*. Toronto: University of Toronto Press.

Ferguson, R. B. 1995. *Yanomami Warfare: A Political History*. Santa Fe, NM: School of American Research Press.

———. 2002. *The State, Identity, and Violence: Political Disintegration in the Post-Cold War Era*. New York: Routledge.

Ferguson, D. 2015. First Black Player on PGA Tour Dies. *Associated Press, Post and Courier*. Charleston, SC, Feb. 5.

Ferraro, G., and E. Briody 2013. *The Cultural Dimension of Global Business,* 7th ed. Boston: Pearson.

Ferraro, J. V., et al. 2013. Earliest Archaeological Evidence of Persistent Hominin Carnivory. *Plos One Online,* April 5, 2013. http://www.plosone.org/article/info%3Adoi%2F10.1371%2Fjournal.pone.0062174.

Feuer, J. 2012. The Clutter Culture, *UCLA Magazine Online*, July 1, 2012. http://magazine.ucla.edu/features/the-clutter-culture/.

Fields, J. M. 2004. America's Families and Living Arrangements: 2003. U.S. Census Bureau. *Current Population Reports,* P20–553, November. http://www.census.gov.

Field, L. W., and R. G. Fox 2007. *Anthropology Put to Work*. New York: Berg.

Finkler, K. 1985. *Spiritualist Healers in Mexico: Successes and Failures of Alternative Therapeutics*. South Hadley, MA: Bergin and Garvey.

Finnstrom, S. 1997. Postcoloniality and the Postcolony: Theories of the Global and the Local.

Fiske, J. 1989. *Understanding Popular Culture*. Boston: Unwin Hyman.

———. 2011. *Reading the Popular,* 2nd ed. New York: Routledge.

Flannery, K. V. 1969. Origins and Ecological Effects of Early Domestication in Iran and the Near East. In *The Domestication and Exploitation of Plants and Animals,* P. J. Ucko and G. W. Dimbleby, eds., pp. 73–100. Chicago: Aldine.

———. 1973. The Origins of Agriculture. *Annual Review of Anthropology* 2:271–310.

———. 1999. Chiefdoms in the Early Near East: Why It's So Hard to Identify Them. In *The Iranian World: Essays on Iranian Art and Archaeology,* A. Alizadeh, Y. Majidzadeh, and S. M. Shahmirzadi, eds. Tehran: Iran University Press.

Flannery, K. V., and J. Marcus 2000. Formative Mexican Chiefdoms and the Myth of the "Mother Culture." *Journal of Anthropological Archaeology* 19:1–37.

———. 2003a. *The Cloud People: Divergent Evolution of the Zapotec and Mixtec Civilizations*. Clinton Corners, NY: Percheron Press.

———. 2003b. The Origin of War: New $^{14}$C Dates from Ancient Mexico. *Proceedings of the National Academy of Sciences of the United States of America* 100(20): 11801–11805.

———. 2012. *The Creation of Inequality: How Our Prehistoric Ancestors Set the Stage for Monarchy, Slavery, and Empire*. Cambridge: Harvard University Press.

Flannery, K. V., J. Marcus, and R. G. Reynolds 1989. *The Flocks of the Wamani: A Study of Llama Herders on the Punas of Ayacucho, Peru*. San Diego: Academic Press.

Flannery, M. A. 2011. *Alfred Russell Wallace: A Rediscovered Life*. Seattle: Discovery Institute Press.

Fleisher, M. L. 2000. *Kuria Cattle Raiders: Violence and Vigilantism on the Tanzania/Kenya Frontier*. Ann Arbor: University of Michigan Press.

Fojas, A. E. 2013. *Ancient Maya Political Dynamics*. Gainesville: University Press of Florida.

Ford, C. S., and F. A. Beach 1951. *Patterns of Sexual Behavior*. New York: Harper Torchbooks.

Fortes, M. 1950. Kinship and Marriage among the Ashanti. In *African Systems of Kinship and Marriage,* A. R. Radcliffe-Brown and D. Forde, eds., pp. 252–284. London: Oxford University Press.

Fortier, J. 2009. The Ethnography of South Asian Foragers. *Annual Review of Anthropology* 39:99–114.

Fossey, D. 1983. *Gorillas in the Mist*. Boston: Houghton Mifflin.

Foster, G. M., and B. G. Anderson 1978. *Medical Anthropology*. New York: McGraw-Hill.

Foucault, M. 1979. *Discipline and Punish: The Birth of the Prison*. A. Sheridan (trans.). New York: Vintage Books.

———. 1990. *The History of Sexuality,* Volume 2, *The Use of Pleasure*. R. Hurley (trans.). New York: Vintage.

Fouts, R. S. 1997. *Next of Kin: What Chimpanzees Have Taught Me about Who We Are*. New York: William Morrow.

Fouts, R. S., D. H. Fouts, and T. E. Van Cantfort 1989. The Infant Loulis Learns Signs from Cross-Fostered Chimpanzees. In *Teaching Sign Language to Chimpanzees,* R. A. Gardner, B. T. Gardner, and T. E. Van Cantfort, eds., pp. 280–292. Albany: State University of New York Press.

Fowler 2011. Into the Stone Age with a Scalpel: A Dig with Clues on Early Urban Life. *New York Times*, September 7. http://www.nytimes.com/2011/09/08/world/europe/08iht-M08C-TURKEY-DIG.html?pagewanted=all.

Freilich, M., D. Raybeck, and J. Savishinsky 1991. *Deviance: Anthropological Perspectives.* Westport, CT: Bergin and Garvey.

Freeman, M., and D. Napier, eds. 2009. *Law and Anthropology.* New York: Oxford University Press.

Freston, P., ed. 2008. *Evangelical Christianity and Democracy in Latin America.* New York: Oxford University Press.

Fricke, T. 1994. *Himalayan Households: Tamang Demography and Domestic Processes,* 2nd ed. New York: Columbia University Press.

Fried, M. H. 1960. On the Evolution of Social Stratification and the State. In *Culture in History,* S. Diamond, ed., pp. 713–731. New York: Columbia University Press.

_____. 1967. *The Evolution of Political Society: An Essay in Political Anthropology.* New York: McGraw-Hill.

Friedl, E. 1962. *Vasilika: A Village in Modern Greece.* New York: Holt, Rinehart, and Winston.

_____. 1975. *Women and Men: An Anthropologist's View.* New York: Holt, Rinehart & Winston.

Friedman, J., ed. 2003. *Globalization, the State, and Violence.* Walnut Creek, CA: AltaMira.

Friedman, K. E., and J. Friedman 2008. *The Anthropology of Global Systems.* Lanham, MD: AltaMira.

Fuchs, C., and M. Sandoval, eds. 2014. *Critique, Social Media, and the Information Society.* New York: Routledge/Taylor and Francis.

Gal, S. 1989. Language and Political Economy. *Annual Review of Anthropology* 18: 345–367.

Galdikas, B. M. 2005. *Great Ape Odyssey.* New York: Harry N. Abrams.

_____. 2007. The Vanishing Man of the Forest. *International Herald Tribune,* January 7. http://www.nytimes.com/2007/01/07/opinion/07iht-edgald.4127210.html?_r=1&scp=1&sq=orangutan%20endangered&st=cse.

Garcia-Navarro, L. 2013 Brazilian Believers of Hidden Religion Step out of Shadows, September 16. National Public Radio. http://www.npr.org/blogs/parallels/2013/09/16/216890587/brazilian-believers-of-hidden-religion-step-out-of-shadows.

Gardner, R. A., B. T. Gardner, and T. E. Van Cantfort, eds. 1989. *Teaching Sign Language to Chimpanzees.* Albany: State University of New York Press.

Gates, C. 2003. *Ancient Cities: The Archaeology of Urban Life in the Ancient Near East, Egypt, Greece, and Rome.* New York: Routledge.

Geertz, C. 1973. *The Interpretation of Cultures.* New York: Basic Books.

Geis, M. L. 1987. *The Language of Politics.* New York: Springer-Verlag.

Gellner, E. 1983. *Nations and Nationalism.* Ithaca, NY: Cornell University Press.

_____. 1997. *Nationalism.* New York: New York University Press.

Gibbons, A. 2012. A New Face Reveals Multiple Lineages Alive at the Dawn of Our Genus *Homo. Science* 337:635.

Gibson, A. 2012. *Enclosing the Neolithic: Recent Studies in Britain and Europe.* Oxford: Archaeopress.

Giddens, A. 1973. *The Class Structure of the Advanced Societies.* New York: Cambridge University Press.

Gignoux, C. R., et al. 2011. Rapid, Global Demographic Expansions after the Origins of Agriculture. *Proceedings of the National Academy of Sciences* 108(15):6044–6049.

Gillespie, J. H. 2004. *Population Genetics: A Concise Guide,* 2nd ed. Baltimore: Johns Hopkins University Press.

Gillis, J. 2013. It's Official: 2012 Was Hottest Year Ever in U.S. *New York Times,* January 8. http://www.nytimes.com/2013/01/09/science/earth/2012-was-hottest-year-ever-in-us.html?hp&_r=0.

Gilmore, D. D. 1987. *Aggression and Community: Paradoxes of Andalusian Culture.* New Haven, CT: Yale University Press.

Gilmore-Lehne, W. J. 2000. Pre-Sumerian Cultures: Natufian through Ubaid Eras:

10,500–3500 B.C.E. http://www.stockton.
edu/~gilbmorew/consorti/1bnear.htm.

Gimpel, J. 1988. *The Medieval Machine:
The Industrial Revolution of the Middle
Ages,* 2nd ed. Aldershot, Hants, England:
Wildwood House.

Giordano, C., F. Ruegg, and A. Boscoboinik,
eds. 2014. *Does East Go West?: Anthropological Pathways through Postsocialism.* Zurich:
Lit Verlag.

Gluckman, M. 2012. *Politics, Law, and Ritual in
Tribal Society.* New Brunswick, NJ: Transaction.

Gmelch, G., R. V. Kemper, and W. P. Zenner,
eds. 2010. *Urban Life: Readings in the Anthropology of the City,* 5th ed. Long Grove,
IL: Waveland.

Goldberg, D. T. 2002. *The Racial State.* Malden,
MA: Blackwell.

Goleman, D. 1992. Anthropology Goes Looking for Love in All the Old Places. *New York
Times,* November 24, p. B1.

Goodall, J. 1996. *My Life with the Chimpanzees.* New York: Pocket Books.

———. 2009. *Jane Goodall: 50 Years at
Gombe, a Tribute to Five Decades of Wildlife
Research, Education, and Conservation.* New
York: Stewart, Tabori, and Chang.

———. 2010. *In the Shadow of Man,* new ed.
Boston: Mariner Books.

Gotkowitz, L., ed. 2011. *Histories of Race and
Racism: The Andes and Mesoamerica from
Colonial Times to the Present.* Durham, NC:
Duke University Press.

Gottdiener, M., ed. 2000. *New Forms of Consumption: Consumers, Culture, and Commodification.* Lanham, MD: Rowman &
Littlefield.

Gough, E. K. 1959. The Nayars and the Definition of Marriage. *Journal of the Royal Anthropological Institute* 89:23–34.

Gould, S. J. 1999. *Rock of Ages: Science and
Religion in the Fullness of Life.* New York:
Ballantine Books.

Gowlett, J. A. J. 1993. *Ascent to Civilization:
The Archaeology of Early Humans.* New
York: McGraw-Hill.

Graburn, N. H. H., et al., eds. 2008. *Multicul-
turalism in the New Japan: Crossing the
Boundaries Within.* New York: Berghahn
Books.

Gramsci, A. 1971. *Selections from the Prison
Notebooks.* Q. Hoare and G. N. Smith, ed. and
trans. London: Wishart.

Gray, J. 1999. *False Dawn. The Delusions of
Global Capitalism.* London: Granta.

Greaves, T. C. 1995. Problems Facing Anthropologists: Cultural Rights and Ethnography.
*General Anthropology* 1(2):1, 3–6.

Green, G. M., and R. W. Sussman 1990.
Deforestation History of the Eastern Rain
Forests of Madagascar from Satellite Images.
*Science* 248 (April 13):212–215.

Green, T. 2006. Archaeologist Makes the Case
for Burying Dominant Theory of First Americans. Austin: University of Texas Research.
http://www.utexas.edu/research/features/story.
php?item/2006/01/collins16.xml.

Greenhouse, S. 2011. Union Membership in
U.S. Fell to a 70-Year Low Last Year. *New York
Times,* January 21.

Greiner, T. M. 2003. What Is the Difference
between Hominin and Hominid When Classifying Humans? *MadSci Network:* Evolution.
http://www.madsci.org/posts/archives/
Apr2003/1050350684.Ev.r.html.

Grekova, M. 2001. Postsocialist Societies.
*International Encyclopedia of the Social &
Behavioral Sciences,* pp. 11877–11881. New
York: Elsevier.

Gremaux, R. 1993. Woman Becomes Man in the
Balkans. In *Third Sex, Third Gender: Beyond
Sexual Dimorphism in Culture and History,*
G. Herdt, ed. Cambridge, MA: MIT Press.

Griffin, P. B., and A. Estioko-Griffin, eds.
1985. *The Agta of Northern Luzon: Recent
Studies.* Cebu City, Philippines: University of
San Carlos.

Grudzinska-Gross, and A. W. Tymowski, eds.
2014. *Eastern Europe: Continuity and Change
(1987–1995).* New York: Peter Lang.

Gu, S. 2012. *Language and Culture in the
Growth of Imperialism.* Jefferson, NC:
McFarland.

Gudeman, S., ed. 1999. *Economic Anthropology*. Northhampton, MA: E. Elgar.

Gugliotta, G. 2002. Earliest Human Ancestor? Skull Dates to When Apes, Humans Split. *Washington Post,* July 11, p. A01.

———. 2005. Tools Found in Britain Show Much Earlier Human Existence. *Washington Post,* December 15, p. A24.

Gumperz, J. J., and S. C. Levinson, eds. 1996. *Rethinking Linguistic Relativity.* New York: Cambridge University Press.

Gunewardena, N., and A. Kingsolver, eds. 2007. *The Gender of Globalization: Women Navigating Cultural and Economic Marginalities.* Santa Fe, NM: School for Advanced Research Press.

Gupta, A., and J. Ferguson 1997a. Culture, Power, Place: Ethnography at the End of an Era. In *Culture, Power, Place: Explorations in Critical Anthropology,* A. Gupta and J. Ferguson, eds., pp. 1–29. Durham, NC: Duke University Press.

———. 1997b. Beyond "Culture": Space, Identity, and the Politics of Difference. In *Culture, Power, Place,* A. Gupta and J. Ferguson, eds., pp. 33–51. Durham, NC: Duke University Press.

Guyot, J., and C. Hughes 2007. Researchers Find Earliest Evidence for Modern Human Behavior. *Arizona State University Research Magazine.* http://researchmag.asu.edu/2008/02researchers_find_earliest_evid.html.

Habu, J., A. Matsui, N. Yamamoto, and T. Kanno T. 2011. Shell Midden Archaeology in Japan: Aquatic Food Acquisition and Long-Term Change in the Jomon Culture. *Quaternary International* 239(1-2):19-27.

Haenn, N., and R. R. Wilk, eds. 2006. *The Environment in Anthropology: A Reader in Ecology, Culture, and Sustainable Living.* New York: New York University Press.

Hallowell, A. I. 1955. *Culture and Experience.* Philadelphia: University of Pennsylvania Press.

Hamdan, S. 2013. Social Media Firms Move to Capitalize on Popularity in Middle East. *New York Times,* February 6. http://www.nytimes.com/2013/02/07/world/middleeast/social-media-firms-move-to-capitalize-on-popularity-in-middle-east.html?pagewanted=print.

Hancock, G. 2011. *Fingerprints of the Gods.* New York: MJF Books.

Handwerk, B. 2008. Half of Humanity Will Live in Cities by Year's End. *National Geographic News,* March 13. www.nationalgeographic.com/news/pf30472163.html.

Handwerker, W. P. 2009. *The Origins of Cultures: How Individual Choices Make Cultures Change.* Walnut Creek, CA: Left Coast Press.

Hann, C., and K. Hart 2011. *Economic Anthropology: History, Ethnography, Critique.* Malden, MA: Polity Press.

Hann, C., and K. Hart, eds. 2009. *Market and Society: The Great Transformation Today.* New York: Cambridge University Press.

Harcourt, A. H., D. Fossey, and J. Sabater-Pi 1981. Demography of *Gorilla gorilla. Journal of Zoology* 195:215–233.

Harlow, H. F. 1971. *Learning to Love.* San Francisco: Albion.

Harper, K.N., M. K. Zuckerman, M. L. Harper, J. D. Kingston, and G. J. Armelagos 2011. The Origin and Antiquity of Syphilis Revisited: An Appraisal of Old World Pre-Columbian Evidence for Treponemal Infection. *American Journal of Physical Anthropology* 146(53):99–133.

Harris, M. 1964. *Patterns of Race in the Americas.* New York: Walker.

———. 1970. Referential Ambiguity in the Calculus of Brazilian Racial Identity. *Southwestern Journal of Anthropology* 26(1):1–14.

———. 1974. *Cows, Pigs, Wars, and Witches: The Riddles of Culture.* New York: Random House.

———. 1978. *Cannibals and Kings.* New York: Vintage Books.

———. 2001 (orig. 1968). *The Rise of Anthropological Theory.* Walnut Creek, CA: AltaMira.

Harris, M., and C. P. Kottak 1963. The Structural Significance of Brazilian Racial Categories. *Sociologia* 25:203–209.

Harrison, G. G., W. L. Rathje, and W. W. Hughes 1994. Food Waste Behavior in an Urban Population. In *Applying Anthropology: An Introductory Reader,* 3rd ed., A. Podolefsky and P. J. Brown, eds., pp. 107–112. Mountain View, CA: Mayfield.

Harrison, K. D. 2007. *When Languages Die: The Extinction of the World's Languages and the Erosion of Human Knowledge.* New York: Oxford University Press.

———. 2010. *The Last Speakers: The Quest to Save the World's Most Endangered Languages.* Washington: National Geographic.

Hart, C. W. M., A. R. Pilling, and J. C. Goodale 1988. *The Tiwi of North Australia,* 3rd ed. Fort Worth, TX: Harcourt Brace.

Hart, D., and R. W. Sussman 2009. *Man the Hunted: Primates, Predators, and Human Evolution,* expanded ed. Boulder, CO: Westview.

Hartl, D. L., and E. W. Jones 2011. *Essential Genetics: A Genomics Perspective*, 5th ed. Boston: Jones and Bartlett.

*Harvard Magazine* 2012. Pottery Predates Agriculture. *Harvard Magazine,* June 19. http://harvardmagazine.com/2012/06/pottery-20000-years-old.

Harvey, D. J. 1980. French Empire. *Academic American Encyclopedia.* Princeton, NJ: Arete, volume 8, pp. 309–310.

Hassig, R. 1985. *Trade, Tribute, and Transportation: The Sixteenth-Century Political Economy of the Valley of Mexico.* Norman: University of Oklahoma Press.

Haugerud, A., M. P. Stone, and P. D. Little, eds. 2011. *Commodities and Globalization: Anthropological Perspectives.* Lanham, MD: Rowman & Littlefield.

Hausmann, R., L. D. Tyson, and S. Zahidi 2012. *The Global Gender Gap Report.* World Economic Forum. http://www3. weforum.org/docs/WEF_GenderGap_Report_2012.pdf.

Hawkes, K., J. O'Connell, and K. Hill 1982. Why Hunters Gather: Optimal Foraging and the Aché of Eastern Paraguay. *American Ethnologist* 9:379–398.

Helman, C. 2007. *Culture, Health, and Illness* 5th ed. New York: Oxford University Press.

Henry, D. O. 1995. *Prehistoric Cultural Ecology and Evolution: Insights from Southern Jordan.* New York: Plenum Press.

Henry, J. 1955. Docility, or Giving Teacher What She Wants. *Journal of Social Issues* 2:33–41.

Herdt, G. H. 2006. *The Sambia: Ritual, Sexuality, and Change in Papua New Guinea.* Belmont, CA: Thomson/Wadsworth.

Hershkovitz, I., et al. 2015. Levantine Cranium from Manot Cave (Israel) Foreshadows the First European Modern Humans. *Nature,* January 28. http://www.nature.com/nature/journal/vaop/ncurrent/full/nature14134.html.

Herskovits, M. 1937. *Life in a Haitian Valley.* New York: Knopf.

Hess, E. 2008. *Nim Chimpsky: The Chimp Who Would Be Human.* New York: Bantam Books.

Heyerdahl, T. 1971. *The Ra Expeditions.* P. Crampton (trans.). Garden City, NY: Doubleday.

Hicks, D., ed. 2010. *Ritual and Belief: Readings in the Anthropology of Religion,* 3rd ed. Lanham, MD: AltaMira.

Higham, T., et al. 2011. The Earliest Evidence for Anatomically Modern Humans in Northwestern Europe. *Nature* 479 (November 24): 521–524. doi:10.1038/nature10484.

Hill, J. H. 1978. Apes and Language. *Annual Review of Anthropology* 7:89–112.

Hill, K., and A. M. Hurtado 1996. *Ache Life History: The Ecology and Demography of a Foraging People.* New York: Aldine de Gruyter.

Hill, K., H. Kaplan, K. Hawkes, and A. Hurtado 1987. Foraging Decisions among Ache Hunter-Gatherers: New Data and Implications for Optimal Foraging Models. *Ethology and Sociobiology* 8:1–36.

Hill, K. R., R. S. Walker, et al. 2011. Co-residence Patterns in Hunter-Gatherer Societies Show Unique Human Social Structure. *Science* (March 11):1286–1289.

Hill-Burnett, J. 1978. Developing Anthropological Knowledge through Application. In *Applied Anthropology in America,* E. M. Eddy and W. L. Partridge, eds., pp. 112–128. New York: Columbia University Press.

Hinton, A. L., and K. L. O'Neill, eds. 2011. *Genocide: Truth, Memory, and Representation.* Durham, NC: Duke University Press.

Hirai, T., ed. 2015. *Capitalism and the World Economy: The Light and Shadow of Globalization.* New York: Routledge.

Hirth, K. G., and J. Pillsbury, eds. 2013. *Merchants, Markets, and Exchange in the Pre-Columbian World.* Washington, DC: Dumbarton Oaks Research Library and Collection.

Hobhouse, L. T. 1915. *Morals in Evolution,* rev. ed. New York: Holt.

Hodder, I. 2006. *The Leopard's Tale: Revealing the Mysteries of Çatalhöyük.* New York: Thames & Hudson.

Hoebel, E. A. 1954. *The Law of Primitive Man.* Cambridge, MA: Harvard University Press.

———. 1968 (orig. 1954). The Eskimo: Rudimentary Law in a Primitive Anarchy. In *Studies in Social and Cultural Anthropology,* J. Middleton, ed., pp. 93–127. New York: Crowell.

———. 2006. *The Law of Primitive Man: A Study in Comparative Legal Dynamics.* Cambridge, MA: Harvard University Press.

Hogan, B., N. Li, and W. H. Dutton 2011. *A Global Shift in the Social Relationships of Networked Individuals: Meeting and Dating Online Comes of Age* (February 14). Oxford Internet Institute, University of Oxford. http://ssrn.com/abstract=1763884 or http://dx.doi.org/10.2139/ssrn.1763884.

Hoge, W. 2001. Kautokeino Journal; Reindeer Herders, at Home on a (Very Cold) Range. *New York Times,* March 26, late ed.—final, sec. A, p. 4.

Holden, A. 2005. *Tourism Studies and the Social Sciences.* New York: Routledge.

Hole, F., K. V. Flannery, and J. A. Neely 1969. *The Prehistory and Human Ecology of the Deh Luran Plain.* Memoir no. 1. Ann Arbor: University of Michigan Museum of Anthropology.

Holst, I., J. E. Moreno, and D. R. Piperno 2007. The Identification of Teosinte, Maize, and *Tripsacum* in Mesoamerica by Using Pollen, Starch Grains, and Phytoliths. *Proceedings of the National Academy of Sciences USA* 104:17608–17613.

Hornborg, A., B. Clark, and K. Hermele, eds. 2011. *Ecology and Power: Struggles over Land and Material Resources in the Past, Present and Future.* New York: Routledge.

Hornborg, A., and C. L. Crumley, eds. 2007. *The World System and the Earth System: Global Socioenvironmental Change and Sustainability since the Neolithic.* Walnut Creek, CA: Left Coast Press.

Hornborg, A., J. R. McNeill, and J. Martinez-Alier, eds. 2007. *Rethinking Environmental History: World-System History and Global Environmental Change.* Lanham, MD: AltaMira.

Horton, R. 1993. *Patterns of Thought in Africa and the West: Essays on Magic, Religion, and Science.* Cambridge: Cambridge University Press.

Houk, B. A. 2015 *Ancient Maya Cities of the Eastern Lowlands.* Gainesville: University Press of Florida.

Hublin, J.-J. 2012. The Earliest Modern Human Colonization of Europe. *Proceedings of the National Academy of Sciences.* PNAS 109 (34): 13471–13472. http://www.pnas.org/content/109/34/13471.full.

Hunt, R. C. 2007. *Beyond Relativism: Comparability in Cultural Anthropology.* Lanham, MD: AltaMira.

Hunter, M. L. 2005. *Race, Gender, and the Politics of Skin Tone.* New York: Routledge.

Hurtado, A. M., C. A. Lambourne, P. James, K. Hill, K. Cheman, and K. Baca 2005. Human Rights, Biomedical Science, and Infectious Diseases among South American Indigenous Groups. *Annual Review of Anthropology* 34:639–665.

Inda, J. X., and R. Rosaldo, eds. 2008. *The Anthropology of Globalization: A Reader.* Malden, MA: Blackwell.

Ingraham, C. 2008. *White Weddings: Romancing Heterosexuality in Popular Culture,* 2nd ed. New York: Routledge.

Inhorn, M. C., and P. J. Brown 1990. The Anthropology of Infectious Disease. *Annual Review of Anthropology* 19:89–117.

Inhorn, M. C., and E. A. Wentzell, eds. 2012. *Medical Anthropology at the Intersections: Histories, Activisms, and Futures.* Durham, NC: Duke University Press.

Iqbal, S. 2002. A New Light on Skin Color. *National Geographic Online Extra.* http://magma.nationalgeographic.com/ngm/0211/feature2/online_extra.html.

Isaac, G. L. 1972. Early Phases of Human Behavior: Models in Lower Paleolithic Archaeology. In *Models in Archaeology,* ed. D. L. Clarke, pp. 167–199. London: Methuen.

Isaacson, A. 2012. A Mini-Eden for Endangered Orangutans. *New York Times,* January 6.

Jablonski, N. G. 2006. *Skin: A Natural History.* Berkeley: University of California Press.

Jablonski, N. G., and G. Chaplin, 2000. The Evolution of Human Skin Coloration. *Journal of Human Evolution* (39):57–106.

Jackson, J., and K. B. Warren 2005. Indigenous Movements in Latin America, 1992–2004: Controversies, Ironies, New Directions. *Annual Review of Anthropology* 34:549–573.

Jenks, C. 2005. *Culture,* 2nd ed. New York: Routledge.

Jiao, T. 2007. *The Neolithic of Southeast China: Cultural Transformation and Regional Interaction on the Coast.* Youngstown, NY: Cambria Press.

Johansen, B. E. 2008. *Global Warming 101.* Westport, CT: Greenwood.

Johanson, D. C., and T. D. White 1979. A Systematic Assessment of Early African Hominids. *Science* 203:321–330.

Johanson, D. C., and K. Wong 2010. *Lucy's Legacy: The Quest for Human Origins.* New York: Three Rivers Press.

Johnson, A. W. 1978. *Quantification in Cultural Anthropology: An Introduction to Research Design.* Stanford, CA: Stanford University Press.

Johnson, A. W., and T. K. Earle 2000. *The Evolution of Human Societies: From Foraging Group to Agrarian State,* 2nd ed. Stanford, CA: Stanford University Press.

Johnston, B. R. 2009. *Life and Death Matters: Human Rights, Environment, and Social Justice,* 2nd ed. Walnut Creek, CA: Left Coast Press.

Jolly, C. J., and R. White 1995. *Physical Anthropology and Archaeology,* 5th ed. New York: McGraw-Hill.

Jordan, A. 2003. *Business Anthropology.* Prospect Heights, IL: Waveland.

Jordan, A. T. 2013 *Business Anthropology,* 2nd ed. Long Grove, IL: Waveland.

Jordan, B., ed. 2013. *Advancing Ethnography in Corporate Environments: Challenges and Emerging Opportunities.* Walnut Creek, CA: Left Coast Press.

Jungers, William L. et al. 2008. Descriptions of the Lower Limb Skeleton of *Homo Floresiensis. Journal of Human Evolution* 57(5):538.

Jurafsky, D. 2014. *The Language of Food: A Linguist Reads the Menu.* New York: W.W. Norton.

Kamrava, M. 2011. *The Modern Middle East: A Political History since the First World War,* 2nd ed. Berkeley: University of California Press.

Kahn, J. 2011. Chimpanzees in Biomedical and Behavioral Research: Assessing the Necessity. Institute of Medicine (of the National Academies). December 15. http://iom.edu/Reports/2011/Chimpanzees-in-Biomedical-and-Behavioral-Research-Assessing-the-Necessity.aspx

Kan, S. 1986. The 19th-Century Tlingit Potlatch: A New Perspective. *American Ethnologist* 13:191–212.

———. 1989. *Symbolic Immortality: The Tlingit Potlatch of the Nineteenth Century.* Washington, DC: Smithsonian Institution Press.

Kaneshiro, N. K. 2009. Intersex. Medline Plus. National Institutes of Health, U.S. National Library of Medicine. http://www.nlm.nih.gov/medlineplus/ency/article/001669.htm.

Kaplan, H. R. 2014 *Understanding Conflict and Change in a Multicultural World*. Lanham, MD: Rowman & Littlefield.

Katzenberg, M. A., and S. R. Saunders 2007. *Biological Anthropology of the Human Skeleton*, 2nd ed. Hoboken, NJ: Wiley.

Kaufman, S. R., and L. M. Morgan 2005. The Anthropology of the Beginnings and Ends of Life. *Annual Review of Anthropology* 34:317–341.

Kearney, M. 1996. *Reconceptualizing the Peasantry: Anthropology in Global Perspective*. Boulder, CO: Westview Press.

Keim, B. 2014. An Orangutan Has (Some) Basic Human Rights, Argentine Court Rules. *Wired,* December 22. http://www.wired.com/2014/12/orangutan-personhood/.

Kellenberger, J. 2008. *Moral Relativism: A Dialogue*. Lanham, MA: Rowman & Littlefield.

Kelly, R. C. 1976. Witchcraft and Sexual Relations: An Exploration in the Social and Semantic Implications of the Structure of Belief. In *Man and Woman in the New Guinea Highlands*, P. Brown and G. Buchbinder, eds., pp. 36–53. Special Publication no. 8. Washington, DC: American Anthropological Association.

Kelly, R. L. 1995. *The Foraging Spectrum: Diversity in Hunter-Gatherer Lifeways*. Washington, DC: Smithsonian Institution Press.

Kenney, K. L. 2015. *Ancient Aztecs*. Minneapolis: Abdo.

Kent, S. 1992. The Current Forager Controversy: Real versus Ideal Views of Hunter-gatherers. *Man* 27:45–70.

———. 1996. *Cultural Diversity among Twentieth-Century Foragers: An African Perspective*. New York: Cambridge University Press.

———. ed. 2002. *Ethnicity, Hunter-Gatherers, and the "Other": Association or Assimilation in Africa*. Washington: Smithsonian Institution Press.

Kent, S., and H. Vierich 1989. The Myth of Ecological Determinism: Anticipated Mobility and Site Organization of Space. In *Farmers as Hunters: The Implications of Sedentism,* S. Kent, ed., pp. 96–130. New York: Cambridge University Press.

Keppel, K. G., J. N. Pearch, and D. K. Wagener 2002. Trends in Racial and Ethnic-Specific Rates for the Health Status Indicators: United States, 1990–98. *Healthy People Statistical Notes No. 23*. Hyattsville, MD: National Center for Health Statistics.

Kerbo, H. R. 2012 *Social Stratification and Inequality: Cass Conflict in Historical, Comparative, and Global Perspective*, 8th ed. New York: McGraw-Hill.

Kershaw, S. 2009. For Teenagers, Hello Means "How About a Hug?" *New York Times*, May 28.

Keynes, J. M. 1927. *The End of Laissez-Faire*. London: L. and Virginia Woolf.

———. 1936. *General Theory of Employment, Interest, and Money*. New York: Harcourt Brace.

Kimmel, M. S. 2007. *The Gendered Society,* 3rd ed. New York: Oxford University Press.

———. 2013. *The Gendered Society,* 5th ed. New York: Oxford University Press.

Kimmel, M. S., and M. A. Messner, eds. 2013. *Men's Lives*, 9th ed. Boston: Allyn & Bacon.

King, E. 2012. Stanford linguists seek to identify the elusive California accent. *Stanford Report*, August 6. http://news.stanford.edu/news/2012/august/california-dialect-linguistics-080612.html.

King, T. F., ed. 2011. *A Companion to Cultural Resource Management*. Malden, MA: Wiley-Blackwell.

Kinsey, A. C., W. B. Pomeroy, and C. E. Martin 1948. *Sexual Behavior in the Human Male*. Philadelphia: W. B. Saunders.

Kjaerulff, J. 2010. *Internet and Change: An Ethnography of Knowledge and Flexible Work*. Walnut Creek, CA: Left Coast Press.

Klass, M. 2003. *Mind over Mind: The Anthropology and Psychology of Spirit Possession*. Lanham, MA: Rowman & Littlefield.

Klein, N. 2000. *No Logo*. London: Flamingo.

Klein, R. G. 2013. Modern Human Origins. *General Anthropology* 20(1):1–4.

Kluckhohn, C. 1944. *Mirror for Man: A Survey of Human Behavior and Social Attitudes.* Greenwich, CT: Fawcett.

Kochhar, R., R. Fry, and P. Taylor 2011. *Wealth Gaps Rise to Record Highs between Whites, Blacks, Hispanics.* Pew Research Center. Pew Social and Economic Trends. http://www.pewsocialtrends.org/2011/07/26/wealth-gaps-rise-to-record-highs-between-whites-blacks-hispanics/.

Kochhar, R., and W. Fry 2014. Wealth Inequality Has Widened along Racial, Ethnic Lines since End of Great Recession. *Facttank, News in the Numbers,* December 12. Pew Research Center. http://www.pewresearch.org/fact-tank/2014/12/12/racial-wealth-gaps-great-recession/

Kolata, A. L. 2013. *Ancient Inca.* New York: Cambridge University Press.

Komar, D. A., and J. E. Buikstra 2008. *Forensic Anthropology: Contemporary Theory and Practice.* New York: Oxford University Press.

Kontopodis, M., C. Wulf, and B. Fichtner, eds. 2011. *Children, Development, and Education: Cultural, Historical, and Anthropological Perspectives.* New York: Springer.

Kottak, C. P. 1980. *The Past in the Present: History, Ecology, and Social Organization in Highland Madagascar.* Ann Arbor: University of Michigan Press.

———. 1990a. Culture and "Economic Development." *American Anthropologist* 93(3):723–731.

———. 1990b. *Prime-Time Society: An Anthropological Analysis of Television and Culture.* Belmont, CA: Wadsworth.

———. 1991. When People Don't Come First: Some Lessons from Completed Projects. In *Putting People First: Sociological Variables in Rural Development,* 2nd ed., M. Cernea, ed., pp. 429–464. New York: Oxford University Press.

———. 1999. The New Ecological Anthropology. *American Anthropologist* 101(1):23–35.

———. 2006. *Assault on Paradise: The Globalization of a Little Community in Brazil,* 4th ed. New York: McGraw-Hill.

———. 2007. Return to Madagascar: A Forty Year Retrospective. *General Anthropology: Bulletin of the General Anthropology Division of the American Anthropological Association* 14(2):1–10.

———. 2009. *Prime-Time Society: An Anthropological Analysis of Television and Culture,* updated ed. Walnut Creek, CA: Left Coast Press.

Kottak, C. P., and K. A. Kozaitis 2012. *On Being Different: Diversity and Multiculturalism in the North American Mainstream,* 4th ed. New York: McGraw-Hill.

Kottak, C. P., L. L. Gezon, and G. Green 1994. Deforestation and Biodiversity Preservation in Madagascar: The View from Above and Below. *CIESIN Human Dimensions Kiosk*—an electronic publication. http://www.ciesin.com.

Kottak, N. C. 2002. *Stealing the Neighbor's Chicken: Social Control in Northern Mozambique.* PhD dissertation. Department of Anthropology, Emory University, Atlanta, GA.

Kotz, D. M. 2015. *The Rise and Fall of Neoliberal Capitalism.* Cambridge, MA: Harvard University Press.

Kreider, R. M., and R. Ellis 2011. Number, Timing, and Duration of Marriages and Divorces: 2009. *Current Population Reports,* P70-125. http://www.census.gov/prod/2011pubs/p70-125.pdf.

Kretchmer, N. 1975 (orig. 1972). Lactose and Lactase. In *Biological Anthropology, Readings from Scientific American,* S. H. Katz, ed., pp. 310–318. San Francisco: W. H. Freeman.

Kuhn, S. L., M. C. Stiner, and D. S. Reese 2001. Ornaments of the Earliest Upper Paleolithic: New Insights from the Levant. *Proceedings of the National Academy of Sciences of the United States of America* 98(13):7641–7646.

Kulick, D. 1998. *Travesti: Sex, Gender, and Culture among Brazilian Transgendered Prostitutes.* Chicago: University of Chicago Press.

Kuper, L. 2006. *Race, Class, and Power: Ideology and Revolutionary Change in Plural Societies.* New Brunswick, NJ: Transaction Publishers.

Kurtz, D. V. 2001. *Political Anthropology: Power and Paradigms.* Boulder, CO: Westview Press.

Kutsche, P. 1998. *Field Ethnography: A Manual for Doing Cultural Anthropology.* Upper Saddle River, NJ: Prentice Hall.

Labov, W. 1972a. *Language in the Inner City: Studies in the Black English Vernacular.* Philadelphia: University of Pennsylvania Press.

————. 1972b. *Sociolinguistic Patterns.* Philadelphia: University of Pennsylvania Press.

————. 2006. *The Social Stratification of English in New York City.* New York: Cambridge University Press.

————. 2012. *Dialect Diversity in America: The Politics of Language Change.* Charlottesville: University of Virginia Press.

Lakoff, G. 2008. *The Political Mind: Why You Can't Understand 21st-century Politics with an 18th-century Brain.* New York: Viking.

Lakoff, G., and E. Wehling 2012. *The Little Blue Book: The Essential Guide to Thinking and Talking Democratic.* New York: Free Press.

Lakoff, R. T. 2004. *Language and Women's Place: Text and Commentaries,* rev. ed., M. Bucholtz, ed. New York: Oxford University Press.

Lambek, M., ed. 2008. *A Reader in the Anthropology of Religion.* Malden, MA: Blackwell.

Landes, D. 1999. *The Wealth and Poverty of Nations. Why Some Are So Rich and Some Are So Poor.* London: Abacus.

Lange, M. 2009. *Lineages of Despotism and Development: British Colonialism and State Power.* Chicago: University of Chicago Press.

Langergraber, K. E. et al. 2012. Generation Times in Wild Chimpanzees and Gorillas Suggest Earlier Divergence Times in Great Ape and Human Evolution. *Proceedings of the National Academy of Sciences* 109(39):15716–15721.

Largent, F. 2007a. Clovis Dethroned: A New Perspective on the First Americans, Part 1. *Mammoth Trumpet* 22(3):1–3, 20.

————. 2007b. Clovis Dethroned: A New Perspective on the First Americans, Part 2. *Mammoth Trumpet* 22(4):1–2, 13.

Larsen, C. S. 2000. *Skeletons in Our Closet: Revealing Our Past through Bioarchaeology.* Princeton, NJ: Princeton University Press.

————. 2015. *Bioarchaeology: Interpreting Behavior from the Human Skeleton,* 2nd ed. New York: Cambridge University Press.

Lassiter, L. E. 1998. *The Power of Kiowa Song: A Collaborative Ethnography.* Tucson: University of Arizona Press.

Laughlin, J. C. H. 2006. *Fifty Major Cities of the Bible.* New York: Routledge.

Leach, E. R. 1955. Polyandry, Inheritance and the Definition of Marriage. *Man* 55:182–186.

————. 1961. *Rethinking Anthropology.* London: Athlone Press.

Leadbeater, C. 1999. *Europe's New Economy.* London: Centre for European Reform.

Leakey, M. G., C. S. Feibel, I. McDougall, and A. Walker 1995. New Four-Million-Year-Old Hominid Species from Kanapoi and Allia Bay, Kenya. *Nature* 376:565–571.

Leakey, M. G., et al. 2012. New Fossils from Koobi Fora in Northern Kenya Confirm Taxonomic Diversity in Early *Homo. Nature* (August 9) 488:201–204.

Lee, R. B. 1979. *The !Kung San: Men, Women, and Work in a Foraging Society.* New York: Cambridge University Press.

————. 1984. *The Dobe !Kung.* New York: Harcourt Brace.

————. 2003. *The Dobe Ju/'hoansi,* 3rd ed. Belmont, CA: Wadsworth.

————. 2012. The !Kung and I: Reflections on My Life and Times with the Ju/Hoansi People. *General Anthropology* 19(1):1–4.

Lee, R. B., and R. H. Daly 1999. *The Cambridge Encyclopedia of Hunters and Gatherers.* New York: Cambridge University Press.

Lemonick, M. D., and A. Dorfman 1999. Up from the Apes: Remarkable New Evidence Is Filling in the Story of How We Became Human. *Time* 154(8):5–58.

Lenski, G. 1966. *Power and Privilege: A Theory of Social Stratification.* New York: McGraw-Hill.

Levine, N. E. 2008. Alternative Kinship, Marriage, and Reproduction. *Annual Review of Anthropology* 37:17–35.

Levinson, B. A. U., and M. Pollock, eds. 2011. *A Companion to the Anthropology of Education.* Malden, MA: Blackwell.

Lévi-Strauss, C. 1963. *Totemism.* R. Needham (trans.). Boston: Beacon Press.

―――. 1967. *Structural Anthropology.* New York: Doubleday.

Levy, F. 2010. The World's Happiest Countries. *Forbes,* July 14. http://www.forbes.com/2010/07/14/world-happiest-countries-lifestyle-realestate-gallup.html.

Levy, J. E., with B. Pepper 1992. *Orayvi Revisited: Social Stratification in an "Egalitarian" Society.* Santa Fe, NM: School of American Research Press, and Seattle: University of Washington Press.

Lewellen, T. C. 2003. *Political Anthropology: An Introduction,* 3rd ed. Westport, CT: Praeger.

―――. 2010. Groping toward Globalization: In Search of Anthropology without Boundaries. *Reviews in Anthropology* 31(1):73–89.

Lie, J. 2001. *Multiethnic Japan.* Cambridge, MA: Harvard University Press.

Lindenbaum, S. 1972. Sorcerers, Ghosts, and Polluting Women: An Analysis of Religious Belief and Population Control. *Ethnology* 11:241–253.

Lindquist, G., and D. Handelman, eds. 2013. *Religion, Politics, and Globalization: Anthropological Approaches.* New York: Berghahn Books.

Little, K. 1971. Some Aspects of African Urbanization South of the Sahara. Reading, MA: Addison-Wesley, McCaleb Modules in Anthropology.

Livingstone, F. B. 1969. Gene Frequency Clines of the b Hemoglobin Locus in Various Human Populations and Their Similarities by Models Involving Differential Selection. *Human Biology* 41:223–236.

Lloyd, A. B. 2015. *Ancient Egypt: State and Society.* New York: Oxford University Press.

Lockwood, W. G. 1975. *European Moslems: Economy and Ethnicity in Western Bosnia.* New York: Academic Press.

Loomis, W. F. 1967. Skin-Pigmented Regulation of Vitamin-D Biosynthesis in Man. *Science* 157:501–506.

López, A. A. 2011. New Questions in the Immigration Debate. *Anthropology Now* 3(1):47–53.

Lowie, R. H. 1961 (orig. 1920). *Primitive Society.* New York: Harper & Brothers.

Lu, H., et al. 2009. Earliest Domestication of Common Millet (*Panicum miliaceum*) in East Asia Extended to 10,000 Years Ago. *Proceedings of the National Academy of Sciences* 106(18):7367–7372.

Lucas, G. R. 2009. *Anthropologists in Arms: The Ethics of Military Anthropology.* Lanham, MD: Altamira.

Lugo, A. 1997. Reflections on Border Theory, Culture, and the Nation. *Border Theory: The Limits of Cultural Politics,* ed. Scott Michaelsen and David Johnson. Minneapolis: University of Minnesota Press, pp. 43–67.

Lugo, A., and B. Maurer 2000. *Gender Matters: Rereading Michelle Z. Rosaldo.* Ann Arbor, University of Michigan Press.

Lupton, D. 2012. *Medicine as Culture: Illness, Disease, and the Body.* Los Angeles: Sage.

Lyell, C. 1969 (orig. 1830–1837). *Principles of Geology.* New York: Johnson.

Lyons, A. P., and H. D. Lyons 2011. *Sexualities in Anthropology: A Reader.* Walden, MA: Wiley Blackwell.

Madra, Y. M. 2004. Karl Polanyi: Freedom in a Complex Society. *Econ-Atrocity Bulletin: In the History of Thought.*

Malinowski, B. 1927. *Sex and Repression in Savage Society.* London and New York: International Library of Psychology, Philosophy and Scientific Method.

―――. 1929. Practical Anthropology. *Africa* 2:23–38.

_____. 1961 (orig. 1922). *Argonauts of the Western Pacific*. New York: Dutton.

_____. 1978 (orig. 1931). The Role of Magic and Religion. In *Reader in Comparative Religion: An Anthropological Approach,* 4th ed., W. A. Lessa and E. Z. Vogt, eds., pp. 37–46. New York: Harper and Row.

_____. 2013. *Crime and Custom in Savage Society*. New Brunswick, NJ: Transaction.

Malkki, L. H. 1995. *Purity and Exile: Violence, Memory, and National Cosmology among Hutu Refugees in Tanzania*. Chicago: University of Chicago Press.

Mann, C. C. 2011. *1493: Uncovering the New World Columbus Created*. New York: Knopf.

Marcus, G. E., and D. Cushman. 1982. Ethnographies as Texts. *Annual Review of Anthropology* 11:25–69.

Marcus, G. E., and M. M. J. Fischer. 1986. *Anthropology as Cultural Critique: An Experimental Moment in the Human Sciences.* Chicago: University of Chicago Press.

_____. 1999. *Anthropology as Cultural Critique: An Experimental Moment in the Human Sciences,* 2nd ed. Chicago: University of Chicago Press.

Marcus, J. 1989. From Centralized Systems to City-States: Possible Models for the Epiclassic. In *Mesoamerica after the Decline of Teotihuacan: A.D. 700–900,* ed. R. A. Diehl and J. C. Berlo, pp. 201–208. Washington, DC: Dumbarton Oaks.

Marcus, J., and K. V. Flannery 1996. *Zapotec Civilization: How Urban Society Evolved in Mexico's Oaxaca Valley*. New York: Thames and Hudson.

Marcus, J., and P. R. Williams 2009. *Andean Civilization: A Tribute to Michael E. Moseley*. Los Angeles: Cotsen Institute of Archaeology.

Marger, M. 2015. *Race and Ethnic Relations: American and Global Perspectives*, 10th ed.. Stamford, CT: Cengage.

Margolis, M. L. 1984. *Mothers and Such: American Views of Women and How They Changed*. Berkeley: University of California Press.

_____. 2000. *True to Her Nature: Changing Advice to American Women*. Prospect Heights, IL: Waveland.

Marshall, R. C., ed. 2011. *Cooperation in Economy and Society*. Lanham, MD: Rowman & Littlefield.

Martin, D. 1990. *Tongues of Fire: The Explosion of Protestantism in Latin America*. Cambridge, MA: Blackwell.

Martin, D. L., R. P. Harrod, and V. R. Perez 2013. *Bioarcheology: An Integrated Approach to Working with Human Remains*. New York: Springer.

Martin, E. 1992. The End of the Body? *American Ethnologist* 19:121–140.

Martin, K., and B. Voorhies 1975. *Female of the Species*. New York: Columbia University Press.

Martin, S. M. 1988. *Palm Oil and Protest: An Economic History of the Ngwa Region, South-Eastern Nigeria, 1800–1980*. New York: Cambridge University Press.

Martinez, E., and A. Garcia 2000. What Is "Neo-Liberalism"? A Brief Definition. http://www.globalexchange.org/campaigns/econ101/neoliberalDefined.html.pdf.

Marx, K., and F. Engels 1976 (orig. 1848). *Communist Manifesto*. New York: Pantheon.

Mascia-Lees, F. 2010. *Gender & Difference in a Globalizing World: Twenty-First Century Anthropology*. Long Grove, IL: Waveland.

Mathews, G. 2000. *Global Culture/Individual Identity: Searching for Home in the Cultural Supermarket*. New York: Routledge.

Matsuzawa, T., ed. 2011. *The Chimpanzees of Bossou and Nimba*. New York: Springer.

Maugh, T. H., III 2007. One Language Disappears Every 14 Days; About Half of the World's Distinct Tongues Could Vanish This Century, Researchers Say. *Los Angeles Times,* September 19.

Maybury-Lewis, D. 2002. *Indigenous Peoples, Ethnic Groups, and the State,* 2nd ed. Boston: Allyn & Bacon.

Maybury-Lewis, D., T. Macdonald, and B. Maybury-Lewis, eds. 2009. *Manifest Destinies and Indigenous Peoples.* Cambridge, MA: David Rockefeller Center for Latin American Studies and Harvard University Press.

Mayell, H. 2003. Orangutans Show Signs of Culture, Study Says. *National Geographic News,* January 3. http://news.nationalgeographic. com/news/2002/12/1220_021226_orangutan. html.

———. 2004. Is Bead Find Proof Modern Thought Began in Africa? *National Geographic News,* March 31. http://news.nationalgeographic. com/news/2004/03/0331_040331_ostrichman. html.

Mayr, E. 2001. *What Evolution Is.* New York: Basic Books.

Mba, N. E. 1982. *Nigerian Women Mobilized: Women's Political Activity in Southern Nigeria, 1900–1965.* Berkeley: University of California Press.

McBrearty, S., and A. S. Brooks 2000. The Revolution That Wasn't: A New Interpretation of the Origin of Modern Human Behavior. *Journal of Human Evolution* 39:453–563.

McConnell-Ginet, S. 2010. *Gender, Sexuality, and Meaning: Linguistic Practice and Politics.* New York: Oxford University Press.

McDougall, I., F. H. Brown, and J. G. Fleagle 2005. Stratigraphic Placement and Age of Modern Humans from Kibish, Ethiopia. *Nature* 433:733–736.

McElroy, A., and P. K. Townsend 2009. *Medical Anthropology in Ecological Perspective,* 5th ed. Boulder, CO: Westview Press.

McKie, R. 2011. Wisdom of Grandparents Helped Rise of Prehistoric Man. *The Guardian,* July 23. http://www.theguardian.com/ science/2011/jul/24/prehistoric-man-helped-as-elderly-survived.

McKinnon, S. 2005. On Kinship and Marriage: A Critique of the Genetic and Gender Calculus of Evolutionary Psychology. In *Complexities: Beyond Nature and Nurture,* S. McKinnon and S. Silverman, eds., pp. 106–131. Chicago: The University of Chicago Press.

Mead, M. 1937. *Cooperation and Competition among Primitive Peoples.* New York: McGraw-Hill.

———. 1950 (orig. 1935). *Sex and Temperament in Three Primitive Societies.* New York: New American Library.

Meadow, R. H., and J. M. Kenoyer 2000. The Indus Valley Mystery: One of the World's First Great Civilizations Is Still a Puzzle. *Discovering Archaeology,* March/April 2000.

Meigs, A., and K. Barlow 2002. Beyond the Taboo: Imagining Incest. *American Anthropologist* 104(1):38–49.

Menez, B. H., and J. A. Ur 2012. Mapping Patterns of a Long-term Settlement in Northern Mesopotamia at a Large Scale. *Proceedings of the National Academy of Sciences* 109(14):E778–E787.

Menzies, C. R., ed. 2006. *Traditional Ecological Knowledge and Natural Resource Management.* Lincoln: University of Nebraska Press.

Mercader, J., M. Panger, and C. Boesch 2002. Excavation of a Chimpanzee Stone Tool Site in the African Rainforest. *Science* 296 (May 24):1452–1455.

Merry, S. E. 2006. Anthropology and International Law. *Annual Review of Anthropology* 35:99–116.

Mesthrie, R., ed. 2011 *The Cambridge Handbook of Sociolinguistics.* Cambridge, UK: Cambridge University Press.

Meyer, B. 1999. *Translating the Devil: Religion and Modernity among the Ewe in Ghana.* Trenton, NJ: Africa World Press.

Miles, H. L. 1983. Apes and Language: The Search for Communicative Competence. In *Language in Primates,* J. de Luce and H. T. Wilder, eds., pp. 43–62. New York: Springer Verlag.

Miles, W. F. S. 2014. *Scars of Partition: Postcolonial Legacies in French and British Borderlands.* Lincoln: University of Nebraska Press.

Millaire, J. F. 2012. Primary state formation in the Viru Valley, North Coast of Peru. 107(14): 6186–91 . *Proceedings of the National Academy of Sciences.*

Miller, N. F., M. A. Zeder, and S. R. Arter 2009. From Food and Fuel to Farms and Flocks: The Integration of Plant and Animal Remains in the Study of Ancient Agro-Pastoral Economies. *Current Anthropology* 50:915–924.

Mintz, S. 1985. *Sweetness and Power: The Place of Sugar in Modern History.* New York: Viking Penguin.

Mirrlees, T. 2013. *Global Entertainment Media: Between Cultural Imperialism and Cultural Globalization.* New York: Routledge.

Mitani, J. C., and D. P. Watts 1999. Demographic Influences on the Hunting Behavior of Chimpanzees. *American Journal of Physical Anthropology* 109:439–454.

Mitani, J. C., J. Call, P. M. Kappeler, R. A. Palombit, and J. B. Silk, eds. 2012. *The Evolution of Primate Societies.* Chicago: University of Chicago Press.

Molnar, S. 2006. *Human Variation: Races, Types, and Ethnic Groups,* 6th ed. Upper Saddle River, NJ: Prentice Hall.

Mooney, A. 2011. *Language, Society, and Power.* New York: Routledge.

Moore, S. F., ed. 2005. *Law and Anthropology: A Reader.* Malden, MA: Blackwell.

Moro, P. A. 2012. *Magic, Witchcraft, and Religion: A Reader in the Anthropology of Religion.* Dubuque, IA: McGraw-Hill.

Moro, P. A., and J. E. Myers 2012. *Magic, Witchcraft, and Religion: A Reader in the Anthropology of Religion,* 9th ed. New York: McGraw-Hill.

Morrill, C., D. A. Snow, and C. H. White, eds. 2005. *Together Alone: Personal Relationships in Public Places.* Berkeley: University of California Press.

Motseta, S. 2006. Botswana Gives Bushmen Tough Conditions. *Washington Post,* December 14. http://www.washingtonpost.com/wp-dyn/content/article/2006/12/14/.

Mounier, A., S. Condemi, and G. Manzi 2011. The Stem Species of Our Species: A Place for the Archaic Human Cranium from Ceprano, Italy. *PLoS ONE* 6(4): e18821. doi:10.1371/journal.pone.0018821.

Moyà-Solà, S., M. Köhler, D. M. Alba, I. Casanovas-Vilar, and J. Galindo 2004. *Pierolapithecus catalaunicus,* a New Middle Miocene Great Ape from Spain. *Science* 306 (November 19):1339–1344.

Mukhopadhyay, C. C., R. Henze, and Y. T. Moses 2007. *How Real Is Race? A Sourcebook on Race, Culture, and Biology.* Lanham, MD: AltaMira.

Mukhopadhyay, C. C., R. Henzie, and Y. T. Moses 2014 *How Real Is Race?: A Sourcebook on Race, Culture, and Biology,* 2nd ed.. Lanham, MD: Altamira.

Murdock, G. P. 1957. World Ethnographic Sample. *American Anthropologist* 59: 664–687.

Murdock, G. P., and C. Provost 1973. Factors in the Division of Labor by Sex: A Cross-Cultural Analysis. *Ethnology* 12(2):203–225.

Murray, S. O., and W. Roscoe, eds. 1998. *Boy-wives and Female Husbands: Studies in African Homosexualities.* New York: St. Martin's Press.

Mydans, S. 1992a. Criticism Grows over Aliens Seized during Riots. *New York Times,* May 29, p. A8.

———. 1992b. Judge Dismisses Case in Shooting by Officer. *New York Times,* June 4, p. A8.

Nadeem, S. 2011. *Dead Ringers: How Outsourcing Is Changing the Way Indians Understand Themselves.* Princeton, NJ: Princeton University Press.

Nader, L. 2007. *Law in Culture and Society.* New Brunswick, NJ: AldineTransaction.

Nagle, D. B. 2014. *The Ancient World: A Social and Cultural History,* 8th ed. Boston: Pearson.

Nagel, J. 1996. *American Indian Ethnic Renewal: Red Power and the Resurgence of Identity and Culture.* New York: Oxford University Press.

Nanda, S. 1996. Hijras: An Alternative Sex and Gender Role in India. In *Third Sex Third Gender: Beyond Sexual Dimorphism in Culture and History,* ed. G. Herdt, pp. 373–418. New York: Zone Books.

————. 1998. *Neither Man nor Woman: The Hijras of India*. Belmont, CA: Thomson/Wadsworth.

————. 2000. *Gender Diversity: Crosscultural Variations*. Prospect Heights, IL: Waveland.

National Academy of Sciences 2008. *Understanding and Responding to Climate Change: Highlights of National Academies Reports*. http://dels.nas.edu/dels/rpt_briefs/climate_change_2008_final.pdf.

National Research Council 2011. *America's Climate Choices*. http://nas-sites.org/americasclimatechoices/sample-page/panel-reports/americas-climate-choices-final-report/.

Nazarea, V. D. 2006. Local Knowledge and Memory in Biodiversity Conservation. *Annual Review of Anthropology* 35:317–335.

Ni, X., et al. 2013. The Oldest Known Primate Skeleton and Early Haplorhine Evolution. *Nature* 498, 60–64.

Nichols, D. L., and C. A. Pool 2012. *The Oxford Handbook of Mesoamerican Archaeology*. New York: Oxford University Press.

Nishida, T. 2012 *Chimpanzees at the Lakeshore: Natural History and Culture at Mahale*. New York: Cambridge University Press.

Nolan, R., ed. 2013. *The Handbook of Practicing Anthropology*. Malden, MA: Wiley-Blackwell.

Nolan, R. W. 2002. *Development Anthropology: Encounters in the Real World*. Boulder, CO: Westview Press.

Nononi, D. M, ed. 2014. *A Companion to Urban Anthropology*. Malden, MA: Wiley-Blackwell.

Nordstrom, C. 2004. *Shadows of War: Violence, Power, and International Profiteering in the Twenty-First Century*. Berkeley: University of California Press.

Nugent, D., and J. Vincent, eds. 2004. *A Companion to the Anthropology of Politics*. Malden, MA: Blackwell.

Nunn, N., and N. Qian 2010. The Colombian Exchange: A History of Disease, Food, and Ideas. *Journal of Economic Perspectives* 24(2):163–188.

Nystrom, P., and P. Ashmore 2008. *The Life of Primates*. Upper Saddle River, NJ: Pearson Prentice Hall.

Okely, J. 2012. *Anthropological Practice: Fieldwork and the Ethnographic Method*. New York: Berg.

Omohundro, J. T. 2001. *Careers in Anthropology*, 2nd ed. New York: McGraw-Hill.

Ong, A. 1987. *Spirits of Resistance and Capitalist Discipline: Factory Women in Malaysia*. Albany: State University of New York Press.

————. 1989. Center, Periphery, and Hierarchy: Gender in Southeast Asia. In *Gender and Anthropology: Critical Reviews for Research and Teaching*, S. Morgen, ed., pp. 294–312. Washington, DC: American Anthropological Association.

Ong, A., and S. J. Collier, eds. 2005. *Global Assemblages: Technology, Politics, and Ethics as Anthropological Problems*. Malden, MA: Blackwell.

————. 2010. *Spirits of Resistance and Capitalist Discipline: Factory Women in Malaysia*, 2nd ed. Albany: State University of New York Press.

Ontario Consultants on Religious Tolerance 2011. Religions of the World: Number of Adherents of Major Religions, Their Geographical Distribution, Date Founded, and Sacred Texts. http://www.religioustolerance.org/worldrel.htm.

Opie, C., et al. 2013. Male Infanticide Leads to Social Monogamy in Primates. *Proceedings of the National Academy of Sciences* 110(33): 13328–13332.

Oriji, J. N. 2000. Igbo Women from 1929–1960. *West Africa Review* 2:1.

Ortner, S. B. 1984. Theory in Anthropology since the Sixties. *Comparative Studies in Society and History* 126(1):126–166.

Ottenheimer, H. J. 2013. *The Anthropology of Language: An Introduction to Linguistic Anthropology*, 3rd ed. Belmont, CA: Wadsworth Cengage Learning.

Owen, J. 2006. "Lucy's Baby"—World's Oldest Child—Found by Fossil Hunters. *National Geographic News,* September 20. http://news.nationalgeographic.com/news/2006/09/060920-lucys-baby.html.

_____. 2012. "Lucy's Baby" a Born Climber, Hinting Human Ancestors Lingered in Trees. *National Geographic News,* October 26. http://news.nationalgeographic.com/news/2012/10/121026-australopithecus-afarensis-human-evolution-lucy-scapula-science/.

Oxford, University of 2013. Social Media: The Perils and Pleasures. http://www.ox.ac.uk/media/news_stories/2013/130411_1.html.

Özdoğan, M., N. Başgelen, and P. Kuniholm 2011. *The Neolithic in Turkey: New Excavations and New Research.* Galatasaray, Istanbul: Archaeology and Art Publications.

Paine, R. 2009. *Camps of the Tundra: Politics through Reindeer among Saami Pastoralists.* Oslo: Instituttet for sammenlignende kulturforskning.

Palmer, S. 2001. The Rael Deal. *Religion in the News* 4:2. Hartford, CT: Trinity College. The Leonard E. Greenberg Center for the Study of Religion in Public Life.

Pardo, I., and G. B. Prato, eds. 2012. *Anthropology in the City: Methodology and Theory.* Burlington, VT: Ashgate.

Parrillo, V. N. 2016. *Understanding Race and Ethnic Relations,* 5th ed. Boston: Pearson.

Parsons, J. R. 1974. The Development of a Prehistoric Complex Society: A Regional Perspective from the Valley of Mexico. *Journal of Field Archaeology* 1:81–108.

Parzinger, H., et al. 2006. Declaration (on the Bosnia pyramid hoax). *The European Archaeologist,* December 11. http://www.e-a-a.org/statement.pdf.

Patterson, F. 1978. Conversations with a Gorilla. *National Geographic,* October, pp. 438–465.

Paulson, T. E. 2005. Chimp, Human DNA Comparison Finds Vast Similarities, Key Differences. *Seattle Post-Intelligencer Reporter,* September 1. http://seattlepi.nwsource.com/local/238852_chimp01.html.

Peletz, M. 1988. *A Share of the Harvest: Kinship, Property, and Social History among the Malays of Rembau.* Berkeley: University of California Press.

Pelto, P. 1973. *The Snowmobile Revolution: Technology and Social Change in the Arctic.* Menlo Park, CA: Cummings.

Peregrine, P. N., C. R. Ember, and M. Ember 2007. Modeling State Origins Using Cross-Cultural Data. *Cross-Cultural Research* 41:75–86.

Perry, M. A., ed. 2012. *Bioarchaeology and Behavior: The People of the Ancient Near East.* Gainesville: University of Florida Press.

Petraglia-Bahri, D. 1996. *Introduction to Postcolonial Studies.* http://www.emory.edu/ENGLISH/Bahri/.

Pew Research Center 2011. *Global Christianity: A Report on the Size and Distribution of the World's Christian Population,* December. Washington, DC: The Pew Forum on Religion and Public Life.

_____. 2011. *The Pew Forum on Religion and Public Life.* http://www.pewforum.org/uploadedFiles/Topics/Religious_Affiliation/Christian/Evangelical_Protestant_Churches/Global%20Survey%20of%20Evan.%20Prot.%20Leaders.pdf.

_____. 2012a. *The Global Religious Landscape: A Report on the Size and Distribution of the World's Major Religious Groups as of 2010, Analysis,* December 18. http://www.pewforum.org/global-religious-landscape-exec.aspx#src=global-footer.

_____. 2012b. *"Nones" on the Rise, One-in-Five Adults Have No Religious Affiliation,* October 9. http://www.pewforum.org/unaffiliated/nones-on-the-rise.aspx.

Piperno, D. R. 2001. On Maize and the Sunflower. *Science* 292(5525):2260–2261.

Piperno, D. R., and D. M. Pearsall 1998. *The Origins of Agriculture in the Lowland Neotropics.* San Diego: Academic Press.

Piperno, D. R., and K. E. Stothert 2003. Phytolith Evidence for Early Holocene *Cucurbita* Domestication in Southwest Ecuador. *Science,* 299(5609):1054–1105.

Pirie, F. 2013. *The Anthropology of Law.* New York: Oxford University Press.

Podany, A. H. 2014. *The Ancient Near East: A Very Short Introduction.* New York: Oxford University Press.

Podolefsky, A., and P. J. Brown, eds. 1992. *Applying Anthropology: An Introductory Reader,* 2nd ed. Mountain View, CA: Mayfield.

Pohl, M. E. D., D. R. Piperno, K. O. Pope, and J. G. Jones 2007. Microfossil Evidence for Pre-Columbian Maize Dispersals in the Neotropics from San Andrés, Tabasco, Mexico. *Proceedings of the National Academy of Sciences of the United States of America* 104(29):11874–11881.

Polanyi, K. 1968. *Primitive, Archaic and Modern Economies: Essays of Karl Polanyi,* G. Dalton, ed. Garden City, NY: Anchor Books.

Pollock, S. 1999. *Ancient Mesopotamia: The Eden That Never Was.* Cambridge: Cambridge University Press.

Pospisil, L. 1963. *The Kapauku Papuans of West New Guinea.* New York: Holt, Rinehart & Winston.

Potash, B., ed. 1986. *Widows in African Societies: Choices and Constraints.* Stanford, CA: Stanford University Press.

Price, R., ed. 1973. *Maroon Societies.* New York: Anchor Press/Doubleday.

Price, T. D., ed. 2000. *Europe's First Farmers.* New York: Cambridge University Press.

Proquest 2013. *Statistical Abstract of the United States.* http://cisupa.proquest.com/ ws_display.asp?filter=Statistical%20Abstract.

Qian, Z. 2013. Divergent Paths of American Families. September 11. Brown University, US2010. http://www.s4.brown.edu/us2010/ Data/Report/report09112013.pdf.

Quitter, J. 2014. *The Ancient Central Andes.* New York: Routledge.

Radcliffe-Brown, A. R. 1952 (orig. 1924). The Mother's Brother in South Africa. In A. R. Radcliffe-Brown, *Structure and Function in Primitive Society,* pp. 15–31. London: Routledge & Kegan Paul.

Radcliffe-Brown, A. R. 1965 (orig. 1952). *Structure and Function in Primitive Society.* New York: Free Press.

Raffaele, P. 2010. *Among the Great Apes: Adventures on the Trail of Our Closest Relatives.* New York: Smithsonian, Harper.

Rak, Y. 1986. The Neandertal: A New Look at an Old Face. *Journal of Human Evolution* 15(3):151–164.

Ramos, A. R. 1995. *Sanumá Memories: Yanomami Ethnography in Times of Crisis.* Madison: University of Wisconsin Press.

Ranger, T. O. 1996. Postscript. In *Postcolonial Identities,* R. Werbner and T. O. Ranger, eds. London: Zed.

Rappaport, R. A. 1974. Obvious Aspects of Ritual. *Cambridge Anthropology* 2:2–60.

———. 1999. *Holiness and Humanity: Ritual in the Making of Religious Life.* New York: Cambridge University Press.

Rathje, W. L., and C. Murphy 2001. *Rubbish! The Archaeology of Garbage.* Tucson: University of Arizona Press.

Rathus, S. A., J. S. Nevid, and J. Fichner-Rathus 2014. *Human Sexuality in a World of Diversity,* 9th ed. Boston: Allyn & Bacon.

Redfield, R. 1941. *The Folk Culture of Yucatan.* Chicago: University of Chicago Press.

Redfield, R., R. Linton, and M. Herskovits 1936. Memorandum on the Study of Acculturation. *American Anthropologist* 38:149–152.

Reese, W. L. 1999. *Dictionary of Philosophy and Religion: Eastern and Western Thought.* Amherst, NY: Humanities Books.

Relethford, J. 2012. *Human Population Genetics.* Hoboken, NJ: Wiley-Blackwell.

Renfrew, C., ed. 2014 *The Cambridge World Prehistory.* New York: Cambridge University Press.

Renfrew, C., and P. Bahn 2010. *Archaeology: The Key Concepts.* New York: Routledge.

Reyhner, J., et al., eds. 2013. *Honoring our Children: Culturally Appropriate Approaches for Teaching Indigenous Students.* Flagstaff, AZ: Northern Arizona University.

Riach, J. 2013. Golf's Failure to Embrace Demographics across Society Is Hard to Stomach. *The Guardian,* May 22. http://www. theguardian.com/sport/blog/2013/may/22/ uk-golf-clubs-race-issues.

Rice, P. 2002. Paleoanthropology 2001— Part II. *General Anthropology* 8(2):11–14.

_____. 2012. Paleoanthropology 2012— Part II. *General Anthropology* 19(2):10–13.

Roach, J. 2007. "Hobbit" Human Was Unique Species, Wrist Bones Suggest. *National Geographic News,* September 20. http://news.nationalgeographic.com/news/pf/65255655.html.

Robbins, Jim 2012. The Ecology of Disease, *New York Times,* July 14. http://www.nytimes.com/2012/07/15/sunday-review/the-ecology-of-disease.html?pagewanted=all.

Robbins, Joel 2004. The Globalization of Pentecostal and Charismatic Christianity. *Annual Review of Anthropology* 33:17–143.

Robbins, R. H. 2011. *Global Problems and the Culture of Capitalism,* 5th ed. Boston: Pearson/Allyn & Bacon.

_____. 2014 *Global Problems and the Culture of Capitalism,* 6th ed. Boston: Pearson.

Roberts, S., A. Sabar, B. Goodman, and M. Balleza 2007. 51% of Women Are Now Living without Spouse. *New York Times,* January 16. http://www.nytimes.com.

Robson, D. 2013. There Really Are 50 Eskimo Words for Snow. *Washington Post,* January 14. http://articles.washingtonpost.com/2013-01-14/national/36344037_1_eskimo-words-snow-inuit.

Rodseth, L., R. W. Wrangham, A. M. Harrigan, and B. Smuts 1991. The Human Community as a Primate Society. *Current Anthropology* 32:221–254.

Romaine, S. 1999. *Communicating Gender.* Mahwah, NJ: Erlbaum.

_____. 2000. *Language in Society: An Introduction to Sociolinguistics,* 2nd ed. New York: Oxford University Press.

Romero, S. 2008. Rain Forest Tribe's Charge of Neglect Is Shrouded by Religion and Politics. *New York Times,* October 7, 2008.

Root, D. 1996. *Cannibal Culture: Art, Appropriation, and the Commodification of Difference.* Boulder, CO: Westview Press.

Rosaldo, M. Z. 1980a. *Knowledge and Passion: Notions of Self and Social Life.* Stanford, CA: Stanford University Press.

_____. 1980b. The Use and Abuse of Anthropology: Reflections on Feminism and Cross-Cultural Understanding. *Signs* 5(3):389–417.

Roscoe, W. 1991. *Zuni Man-Woman.* Albuquerque: University of New Mexico Press.

_____. 1998. *Changing Ones: Third and Fourth Genders in Native North America.* New York: St. Martin's Press.

Rothman, J. M., D. Raubenheimer, and C. A. Chapman 2011. Nutritional Geometry: Gorillas Prioritize Non-Protein Energy While Consuming Surplus Protein. *Biology Letters* 7:847–849. London: The Royal Society. sbi.royalsocietypublishing.org.

Rothstein, E. 2006. Protection for Indian Patrimony That Leads to a Paradox. *New York Times,* March 29.

Rouse, R. 1991. Mexican Migration and the Social Space of Postmodernism. *Diaspora* 1(1):8–23.

Royal Anthropological Institute 1951. *Notes and Queries on Anthropology,* 6th ed. London: Routledge and Kegan Paul.

Rugaber, C. S., and J. Boak 2014. Wealth Gap: A Guide to What It Is, Why It Matters. Associated Press, February 23. http://bigstory.ap.org/article/wealth-gap-guide-what-it-why-it-matters-0.

Ryan, S. 1990. *Ethnic Conflict and International Relations.* Brookfield, MA: Dartmouth.

Ryang, S., and J. Lie 2009. *Diaspora without Homeland: Being Korean in Japan.* Berkeley: University of California Press.

Rylko-Bauer, B., M. Singer, and J. Van Willigen 2006. Reclaiming Applied Anthropology: Its Past, Present, and Future. *American Anthropologist* 108(1):178–190.

Sabloff, J. A. 2008. *Archaeology Matters: Action Archaeology in the Modern World.* Walnut Creek, CA: Left Coast Press.

Sack, K. 2011. In Tough Times, a Boom in Cremations as a Way to Save Money. *New York Times,* December 8. http://www.nytimes.com/2011/12/09/us/in-economic-downturn-survivors-turning-to-cremations-over-burials.html?scp=1&sq=cremations&st=cse.

Sahlins, M. D. 1968. *Tribesmen.* Englewood Cliffs, NJ: Prentice Hall.

_____. 2004. *Stone Age Economics.* New York: Routledge.

_____. 2011 *Stone Age Economics.* New Brunswick, NJ: Transaction Books.

Salazar, C., and J. Bestard, eds. 2015. *Religion and Science as Forms of Life: Anthropological Insights into Reason and Unreason.* New York: Berghahn Books.

Saleh, A. 2013. *Ethnic Identity and the State in Iran.* New York: Palgrave Macmillan.

Salzman, P. C. 1974. Political Organization among Nomadic Peoples. In *Man in Adaptation: The Cultural Present,* 2nd ed., Y. A. Cohen, ed., pp. 267–284. Chicago: Aldine.

_____. 2004. *Pastoralists: Equality, Hierarchy, and the State.* Boulder, CO: Westview Press.

_____. 2008. *Culture and Conflict in the Middle East.* Amherst, NY: Humanity Books.

Salzmann, Z. 2012. *Linguistic Anthropology: A Short Introduction.* Prague, Czech Republic: Nezavisle centrum pro studium politiky.

Salzmann, Z., J. M. Stanlaw, and N. Adachi 2012. *Language, Culture, and Society: An Introduction to Linguistic Anthropology,* 5th ed. Boulder, CO: Westview Press.

Salzmann, Z., J. Stanlaw, and N. Adachi. 2014. *Language, Culture, and Society: An Introduction to Linguistic Anthropology,* 6th ed. New York: Westview.

Sample, I. 2012. "Red Deer Cave People" May Be New Species of Human. *The Guardian,* March 14. http://www.guardian.co.uk/science/2012/mar/14/red-deer-cave-people-species-human.

Sanday, P. R. 1974. Female Status in the Public Domain. In *Woman, Culture, and Society,* M. Z. Rosaldo and L. Lamphere, eds., pp. 189–206. Stanford, CA: Stanford University Press.

_____. 2002. *Women at the Center: Life in a Modern Matriarchy.* Ithaca, NY: Cornell University Press.

Santley, R. S. 1985. The Political Economy of the Aztec Empire. *Journal of Anthropological Research* 41(3):327–337.

Sapir, E. 1931. Conceptual Categories in Primitive Languages. *Science* 74:578–584.

_____. 1956 (orig 1928). The Meaning of Religion. In *Culture, Language and Personality: Selected Essays,* E. Sapir. Berkeley: University of California Press.

Saville, A., ed. 2012. *Flint and Stone in the Neolithic Period.* Oakville, CT: Oxbow Books.

Scheidel, W. 1997. Brother-Sister Marriage in Roman Egypt. *Journal of Biosocial Science* 29(3):361–371.

Schneider, D. M. 1967. Kinship and Culture: Descent and Filiation as Cultural Constructs. *Southwestern Journal of Anthropology* 23:65–73.

Schultz, S., C. Opie, and Q. D. Atkinson 2011. Stepwise Evolution of Stable Sociality in Primates. *Nature* 479:229–222, November 11. http://www.nature.com/nature/journal/v479/n7372/full/nature10601.html.

Schwartz, M. J., V. W. Turner, and A. Tuden, eds. 2006. *Political Anthropology.* New Brunswick, NJ: Aldine Transaction.

Scott, James C. 1985. *Weapons of the Weak.* New Haven, CT: Yale University Press.

_____. 1990. *Domination and the Arts of Resistance.* New Haven, CT: Yale University Press.

Scott, Janny. 2011. *A Singular Woman: The Untold Story of Barack Obama's Mother.* New York: Riverhead Books.

Scudder, T., and E. Colson 1980. *Secondary Education and the Formation of an Elite: The Impact of Education on Gwembe District, Zambia.* London: Academic Press.

Scupin, R. 2012. *Race and Ethnicity: An Anthropological Focus on the United States and the World,* 2nd ed. Upper Saddle River, NJ: Prentice Hall.

Sebeok, T. A., and J. Umiker-Sebeok, eds. 1980. *Speaking of Apes: A Critical Anthropology of Two-Way Communication with Man.* New York: Plenum.

Senut, B., M. Pickford, D. Gommery, P. Mein, K. Cheboi, and Y. Coppens 2001. First Hominid from the Miocene (Lukeino Formation, Kenya). *Comptes Rendus de l'Academie des Sciences, Series IIA—Earth and Planetary Science* 332. 2 (January 30):137–144.

Service, E. R. 1962. *Primitive Social Organization: An Evolutionary Perspective.* New York: McGraw-Hill.

———. 1966. *The Hunters.* Englewood Cliffs, NJ: Prentice Hall.

Shaffer, M. S., ed. 2008. *Public Culture: Diversity, Democracy, and Community in the United States.* Philadelphia: University of Pennsylvania Press.

Shannon, T. R. 1996. *An Introduction to the World-System Perspective,* 2nd ed. Boulder, CO: Westview Press.

Sharma, A., and A. Gupta, eds. 2006. *The Anthropology of the State: A Reader.* Malden, MA: Blackwell.

Sharpley, R., and D. J. Teller, eds. 2015. *Tourism and Development; Concepts and Issues.* Buffalo, NY: Channel View Publications.

Shermer, M. 2002. *In Darwin's Shadow: The Life and Science of Alfred Russel Wallace.* New York: Oxford University Press.

Sherwood, R. J., Ward, S. C, and A. Hill 2002. The Taxonomic Status of the Chemeron Temporal (KNM-BC1). *Science Direct,* February 27. http://www.sciencedirect.com.

Shivaram, C. 1996. Where Women Wore the Crown: Kerala's Dissolving Matriarchies Leave a Rich Legacy of Compassionate Family Culture. *Hinduism Today.* http://www.spirit-web.org/HinduismToday/96_02_Women_Wore_Crown.html.

Shore, C., S. Wright, and D. Però, eds. 2011. *Policy Worlds: Anthropology and the Analysis of Contemporary Power.* New York: Berghahn Books.

Shostak, M. 1981. *Nisa: The Life and Words of a !Kung Woman.* Cambridge, MA: Harvard University Press.

Shreeve, J. 1992. The Dating Game: How Old Is the Human Race? *Discover* 13(9):76–83.

Shryock, Andrew 1988. Autonomy, Entanglement, and the Feud: Prestige Structures and Gender Values in Highland Albania. *Anthropological Quarterly* 61(3):113–118.

Silberbauer, G. 1981. *Hunter and Habitat in the Central Kalahari Desert.* New York: Cambridge University Press.

Sillitoe, P., ed. 2007. *Local Science versus Global Science: Approaches to Indigenous Knowledge in International Development.* New York: Berghahn Books.

Simmons, A. H. 2007. *The Neolithic Revolution in the Near East: Transforming the Human Landscape.* Tucson: University of Arizona Press.

Simons, E. L., and P. C. Ettel 1970. Gigantopithecus. *Scientific American,* January, pp. 77–85.

Singer, M. 2008. *Drugging the Poor: Legal and Illegal Drugs and Social Inequality.* Long Grove, IL: Waveland.

———. 2012. *Introducing Medical Anthropology: A Discipline in Action,* 2nd ed. Lanham, MD: AltaMira.

———. 2015 *Anthropology of Infectious Disease.* Walnut Creek, CA: Left Coast Press.

Skoglund, P., H. Malmström, et al. 2012. Origins and Genetic Legacy of Neolithic Farmers and Hunter-Gatherers in Europe. *Science* 27 (April):336(466–469). DOI: 10.1126/ science.1216304. http://www.sciencemag.org/content/336/6080/466.

Smart, A., and J. Smart 2003. Urbanization and the Global Perspective. *Annual Review of Anthropology* 32:263–285.

Smith, A. T. 2003. *The Political Landscape: Constellations of Authority in Early Complex Polities.* Westport, CT: Praeger.

Smith, B. D. 1995. *The Emergence of Agriculture.* New York: Scientific American Library, W. H. Freeman.

Smith, C. S. 2006. Some See a "Pyramid" to Hone Bosnia's Image. Others See a Big Hill. *New York Times,* May 15.

Smith, M. E. 2009. V. Gordon Childe and the Urban Revolution: A Historical Perspective on a Revolution in Urban Studies. *Town Planning Review* 80(1). http://www.public.asu.edu/~mesmith9/1-CompleteSet/MES-09-Childe-TPR.pdf.

Smith, M. K., and M. E. Doyle 2002. Globalization. The Encyclopedia of Informal Education. http://www.infed.org/biblio/globalization.htm.

Solway, J., and R. Lee 1990. Foragers, Genuine and Spurious: Situating the Kalahari San in History (with CA Treatment). *Current Anthropology* 31(2):109–146.

Sotomayor, S. 2009 (orig. 2001). A Latina Judge's Voice. Judge Mario G. Olmos Memorial Lecture, University of California, Berkeley School of Law. Reprinted by the *New York Times,* http://www.nytimes.com/2009/05/15/us/politics/15judge.text.html.

Spencer, C. S. 2003. War and Early State Formation in Oaxaca, Mexico. *Proceedings of the National Academy of Sciences of the United States of America.* 100(20):11185–11187. http://www.pnas.org/cgi/doi/10.1073/pnas.2034992100.

Spencer, C. S., and E. M. Redmond 2004. Primary State Formation in Mesoamerica. *Annual Review of Anthropology* 33: 173–199.

Spencer, E. T. 2010. *Sociolinguistics.* Hauppauge, NY: Nova Science.

Spickard, P., ed. 2004. *Race and Nation: Ethnic Systems in the Modern World.* New York: Routledge.

———. 2012. *Race and Immigration in the United States: New Histories.* New York: Routledge.

Spindler, G. D., and L. Hammond, eds. 2006. *Innovations in Educational Ethnography: Theory, Methods, and Results.* Mahwah, NJ: Erlbaum.

Spindler, G., and J. E. Stockard 2007. *Globalization and Change in Fifteen Cultures: Born in One World, Living in Another.* Belmont, CA: Thomson/Wadsworth.

Spooner, B. 2015. *Globalization: The Crucial Phase.* Philadelphia: University of Pennsylvania Museum of Archaeology and Anthropology.

Spoor, F., M. G. Leakey, P. N. Gathongo, F. H. Brown, S. C. Anton, I. McDougall, C. Kiarie, F. K. Manthi, and L. N. Leakey 2007. Implications of New Early *Homo* Fossils from Ileret, East of Lake Turkana, Kenya. *Nature* 448 (7154):688–691.

Srivastava, J., N. J. H. Smith, and D. A. Forno 1999. *Integrating Biodiversity in Agricultural Intensification. Toward Sound Practices.* Washington, DC: World Bank.

Stack, C. B. 1975. *All Our Kin: Strategies for Survival in a Black Community.* New York: Harper Torchbooks.

Stanish, C., and A. Levine 2011. War and Early State Formation in the Northern Titicaca Basin, Peru. *Proceedings of the National Academy of Sciences* 108(34):13901–13906.

Statistics Canada 2001. *Census.* Nation Tables. http://www.statcan.ca/english/census96/nation.htm.

———. 2010. *Study: Projections of the Diversity of the Canadian Population.* http://www.statcan.gc.ca/daily-quotidien/100309/dq100309a-eng.htm.

Stavenhagen, R. 2013. *Pioneer on Indigenous Rights.* New York: Springer.

Stefoff, R. 2011. *Forensic Anthropology.* New York: Marshall Cavendish Benchmark.

Stein, G. 1994. Economy, Ritual, and Power in Ubaid Mesopotamia. In *Chiefdoms and Early States in the Near East: The Organizational Dynamics of Complexity,* G. Stein and M. S. Rothman, eds. Monographs in World Archaeology 18:35–46. Madison, WI: Prehistory Press.

Stein, R. L., and P. L. Stein, eds. 2011. *The Anthropology of Religion, Magic, and Witchcraft,* 3rd ed. Upper Saddle River, NJ: Pearson Prentice Hall.

Stern, A. 2000. Experts Say 138 World Primate Species Endangered. *Reuters.*

Stevens, W. K. 1992. Humanity Confronts Its Handiwork: An Altered Planet. *New York Times,* May 5, pp. B5–B7.

Stevenson, D. 2003. *Cities and Urban Cultures.* Philadelphia: Open University Press.

Stoler, A. L. 1977. Class Structure and Female Autonomy in Rural Java. *Signs* 3:74–89.

———. ed. 2013. *Imperial Debris: On Ruins and Ruination*: Durham, NC: Duke University Press.

Stoler, A. L., C. McGranahan, and P. C. Perdue, eds. 2007. *Imperial Formations.* Santa Fe, NM: School for Advanced Research Press.

Stone, L. S. 2004. Gay Marriage and Anthropology. *Anthropology News* 45(5).

———. 2010. *Kinship and Gender: An Introduction,* 4th ed. Boulder, CO: Westview Press.

Strathern, A., and P. J. Stewart 2010. *Kinship in Action: Self and Group.* Boston: Prentice Hall.

Strathern, M. 1988. *Dealing with Inequality: Analysing Gender Relations in Melanesia and Beyond: Essays by Members of the 1983/1984 Anthropological Research Group at the Research School of Pacific Studies, the Australian National University.* New York: Cambridge University Press.

Strier, K. B. 2011. *Primate Behavioral Ecology,* 4th ed. Upper Saddle River, NJ: Prentice Hall.

Stringer, C. 2012. *Lone Survivors: How We Came to Be the Only Humans on Earth.* New York: Henry Holt.

Sukarieh, M., and S. Tannock 2015. *Youth Rising? The Politics of Youth in the Global Economy.* New York: Routledge/Taylor and Francis.

Sullivan, M. 2012. Trouble in Paradise: UCLA Book Enumerates Challenges Faced by Middle-Class L.A. Families, June 19. http://newsroom.ucla.edu/portal/ucla/trouble-in-paradise-new-ucla-book.aspx.

Sunderland, P. L., and R. M. Denny 2007. *Doing Anthropology in Consumer Research.* Walnut Creek, CA: Left Coast Press.

Sunstein, B. S., and Chiseri-Strater, E. 2012. *Fieldworking: Reading and Writing Research,* 4th ed. Upper Saddle River, NJ: Prentice Hall.

Sutherland, A. 2014. Children Are Most Likely to Live with Two Parents in These Countries. Charlottesville, VA: Institute for Family Studies. June 10. http://family-studies.org/children-are-most-likely-to-live-with-two-parents-in-these-countries/.

Suttles, W. 1960. Affinal Ties, Subsistence, and Prestige among the Coast Salish. *American Anthropologist* 62:296–305.

Swift, M. 1963. Men and Women in Malay Society. In *Women in the New Asia,* B. Ward, ed., pp. 268–286. Paris: UNESCO.

Tague, R. G., and C. O. Lovejoy 1986. The Obstetric Pelvis of A. L. 288-1 (Lucy). *Journal of Human Evolution* 15:237–255.

Tanaka, J. 1980. *The San Hunter-Gatherers of the Kalahari.* Tokyo: University of Tokyo Press.

Tannen, D. 1990. *You Just Don't Understand: Women and Men in Conversation.* New York: Ballantine Books.

———. ed. 1993. *Gender and Conversational Interaction.* New York: Oxford University Press.

———. 2005. *Conversational Style: Analyzing Talk among Friends,* new ed. New York: Oxford University Press.

Tannen, D., S. Kendall, and C. Gordon., eds. 2007. *Family Talk: Discourse and Identity in Four American Families.* New York: Oxford University Press.

Tannen, D., and A. M. Trester, eds. 2012. *Discourse 2.0: Language and New Media.* Washington, DC: Georgetown University Press.

Tavernise, S. 2012. Whites Account for Under Half of Births in U.S. *New York Times,* May 17. http://www.nytimes.com/2012/05/17/us/whites-account-for-under-half-of-births-in-us.html?pagewanted=all&_r=0.

Taylor, C. 1987. Anthropologist-in-Residence. In *Applied Anthropology in America,* 2nd ed., E. M. Eddy and W. L. Partridge, eds. New York: Columbia University Press.

Taylor, P., M. H. Lopez, J. H. Martínez, and G. Velasco 2012. *When Labels Don't Fit: Hispanics and Their Views of Identity,* Pew Research Hispanic Center, April 4. http://www.pewhispanic.org/2012/04/04/when-labels-dont-fit-hispanics-and-their-views-of-identity/.

*Telegraph.* 2005. Third Sex Finds a Place on Indian Passport Forms. March 10, 2005. http://infochangeindia.org/human-rights/news/third-sex-finds-a-place-on-indian-passport-forms.html.

Terrace, H. S. 1979. *Nim.* New York: Knopf.

Tersigni-Tarrant, M. T. A., and N. R. Shirley, eds. 2012. *Forensic Anthropology: An Introduction.* Boca Raton, FL: CRC Press.

*The Week* 2013. Should Apes Have Legal Rights? August 3. http://theweek.com/articles/461480/should-apes-have-legal-rights

Thomas, L., and S. Wareing, eds. 2004. *Language, Society, and Power: An Introduction.* New York: Routledge.

Thomas, M., L. J. Butler, and B. Moore 2015. *Crises of Empire: Decolonization and Europe's Imperial States*. New York: Bloomsbury Academic Publishing.

Thompson, A. 2012. *Britain's Experience of Empire in the Twentieth Century*. New York: Oxford University Press.

Thompson, W. 1983. Introduction: World System with and without the Hyphen. In *Contending Approaches to World System Analysis*, W. Thompson, ed., pp. 7–26. Thousand Oaks, CA: Sage.

Tice, K. 1997. Reflections on Teaching Anthropology for Use in the Public and Private Sector. In *The Teaching of Anthropology: Problems, Issues, and Decisions*, C. P. Kottak, J. J. White, R. H. Furlow, and P. C. Rice, eds., pp. 273–284. Mountain View, CA: Mayfield.

Tishkoff, S. A. et al. 2007. Convergent Adaptation of Human Lactase Persistence in Africa and Europe. *Nature Genetics* 39(1):1–40.

Tishkov, V. A. 2004. *Chechnya: Life in a War-Torn Society*. Berkeley: University of California Press.

Titiev, M. 1992. *Old Oraibi: A Study of the Hopi Indians of Third Mesa*. Albuquerque: University of New Mexico Press.

Toner, R. 1992. Los Angeles Riots Are a Warning, Americans Fear. *New York Times*, May 11, pp. A1, A11.

Toth, N. 1985. The Oldowan Reassessed: A Close Look at Early Stone Artifacts. *Journal of Archaelogical Science* 2:101–120.

Totten, S., and R. Ubaldo, eds. 2011. *We Cannot Forget: Interviews with Survivors of the 1994 Genocide in Rwanda*. New Brunswick, NJ: Rutgers University Press.

Tougher, S. 2008. *The Eunuch in Byzantine History and Society*. New York: Routledge.

Trevathan, W. R., E. O. Smith, and J. McKenna 2008. *Evolutionary Medicine and Health*. New York: Oxford University Press.

Trigger, B. G. 2003. *Understanding Early Civilizations: A Comparative Study*. Cambridge: Cambridge University Press.

Trivedi, B. P. 2001. Scientists Identify a Language Gene. *National Geographic News*, October 4. http://news.nationalgeographic.com/news/2001/10/1004_Tvlanguagegene.html.

Trudgill, P. 2000. *Sociolinguistics: An Introduction to Language and Society*, 4th ed. New York: Penguin Books.

———. 2010. *Investigations in Sociohistorical Linguistics: Stories of Colonisation and Contact*. New York: Cambridge University Press.

Turnbull, C. 1965. *Wayward Servants: The Two Worlds of the African Pygmies*. Garden City, NY: Natural History Press.

Turner, V. W. 1974 (orig. 1967). *The Ritual Process*. Harmondsworth, England: Penguin Press.

———. 1995 (orig. 1969). *The Ritual Process*. Hawthorne, NY: Aldine de Gruyter.

Tylor, E. B. 1958 (orig. 1871). *Primitive Culture*. New York: Harper Torchbooks.

Ubelaker, D. H., ed. 2012. *Forensic Science: Current Issues, Future Directions*. Hoboken, NJ: Wiley.

Ulijaszek, S. J., and H. Lofink 2006. Obesity in Biocultural Perspective. *Annual Review of Anthropology* 35:337–360.

U.S. Bureau of Labor Statistics 2014. *Women in the Labor Force: A Databook*. BLS Reports 1052, December 2014. http://www.bls.gov/opub/reports/cps/women-in-the-labor-force-a-databook-2014.pdf.

U.S. Census Bureau 2010. http://quickfacts.census.gov/qfd/index.html.

U.S. Census Bureau 2012. *Statistical Abstract of the United States*. http://www.census.gov/prod/www/statistical-abstract.html.

U. S. Census Bureau 2014a. Facts for Features: Hispanic Heritage Month 2014: Sept. 15-Oct. 15. September 8. http://www.census.gov/newsroom/facts-for-features/2014/cb14-ff22.html 2014b.

———. 2014b. Gap Between Higher- and Lower-Wealth Households Widens, Census Bureau Reports. Report CB14-156. http://www.census.gov/newsroom/press-releases/2014/cb14-156.html.

Van Allen, J. 1971. *"Aba Riots" or "Women's War"? British Ideology and Eastern Nigerian Women's Political Activism*. Waltham, MA: African Studies Association.

Van Cantfort, T. E., and J. B. Rimpau 1982. Sign Language Studies with Children and Chimpanzees. *Sign Language Studies* 34:15–72.

van Schaik, C. 2004. *Among Orangutans: Red Apes and the Rise of Human Culture.* Tucson: University of Arizona Press.

Vayda, A. P. 1968 (orig. 1961). Economic Systems in Ecological Perspective: The Case of the Northwest Coast. In *Readings in Anthropology,* 2nd ed., volume 2, M. H. Fried, ed., pp. 172–178. New York: Crowell.

Veblen, T. 1934. *The Theory of the Leisure Class: An Economic Study of Institutions.* New York: The Modern Library.

Vekua, A., D. Lordkipanidze, and G. P. Rightmire. 2002. A Skull of Early *Homo* from Dmanisi, Georgia, *Science,* July 5, pp. 85–89.

Verdery, K. 1997. *What Was Socialism and What Comes Next?* Princeton, NJ: Princeton University Press.

_____. 2001. Socialist Societies: Anthropological Aspects. *International Encyclopedia of the Social & Behavioral Sciences,* pp. 14496–14500. New York: Elsevier.

Vidal, J. 2003. Every Third Person Will Be a Slum Dweller within 30 Years, UN Agency Warns: Biggest Study of World's Cities Finds 940 Million Already Living in Squalor. *The Guardian,* October 4. http://www.guardian.co.uk/international/story/0,3604,1055785,00.html.

Viegas, J. 2000. Planet of the Dying Apes: Conference Reveals Steep Decline in Primate Populations.

Vigil, J. D. 2010. *Gang Redux: A Balanced Anti-Gang Strategy.* Long Grove, IL: Waveland.

_____. 2012. *From Indians to Chicanos; The Dynamics of Mexican-American Culture,* 3rd ed. Boulder, CO: Westview Press.

Vigne, J-D., Briois, F. et al. 2012. First Wave of Cultivators Spread to Cyprus at Least 10,600 Years Ago. *Proceedings of the National Academy of Sciences* 109(22): 8445–8449.

Vinyeta, K. 2013. *Exploring the Role of Traditional Ecological Knowledge in Climate Change Initiatives.* Portland, OR: U. S. Department of Agriculture, Forest Service, Pacific Northwest Research Station.

Von Daniken, E. 1971. *Chariots of the Gods: Unsolved Mysteries of the Past.* New York: Bantam.

Wade, N. 2004. New Species Revealed: Tiny Cousins of Humans. *New York Times,* October 28, national edition, pp. Al, A6.

_____. 2005. For Gay Men, Different Scent of Attraction. *New York Times,* May 10, late ed.—final, p. A1.

_____. 2012. Earliest Americans Arrived in Waves, DNA Study Finds. *New York Times,* July 11. http://www.nytimes.com/2012/07/12/science/earliest-americans-arrived-in-3-waves-not-1-dna-study-finds.html.

Wade, P. 2002. *Race, Nature, and Culture: An Anthropological Perspective.* Sterling, VA: Pluto Press.

_____. 2010. *Race and Ethnicity in Latin America,* 2nd ed. New York: Pluto Press.

Walker, S. M., and D. W. Owsley 2012. *The Skeletons Speak: Kennewick Man and the Paleoamerican World.* Minneapolis: Carolrhoda Books.

Wallace, A. F. C. 1966. *Religion: An Anthropological View.* New York: McGraw-Hill.

Wallerstein, I. M. 1982. The Rise and Future Demise of the World Capitalist System: Concepts for Comparative Analysis. In *Introduction to the Sociology of "Developing Societies,"* H. Alavi and T. Shanin, eds., pp. 29–53. New York: Monthly Review Press.

_____. 2004. *World-Systems Analysis: An Introduction.* Durham, NC: Duke University Press.

Ward, C. V., W. H. Kimbel, and D. C. Johanson 2011. Complete Fourth Metatarsal and Arches in the Foot of *Australopithecus afarensis. Science* 331(6018):750–753.

Ward, M. C., and M. Edelstein 2009. *A World Full of Women,* 5th ed. Needham Heights, MA: Allyn & Bacon.

Ward, M. C., and M. Edelstein 2013. *A World Full of Women,* 6th ed. Upper Saddle River, NJ: Pearson.

Warms, R., J. Garber, and R. J. McGee, eds. 2009. *Sacred Realms: Readings in the Anthropology of Religion,* 2nd ed. New York: Oxford University Press.

Wasson, C., M. O. Butler, and J. Copeland-Carson, eds. 2012. *Applying Anthropology in the Global Village.* Walnut Creek, CA: Left Coast Press.

Waters, M. R., and T. W. Stafford, Jr. 2007. Redefining the Age of Clovis: Implications for the Peopling of the Americas. *Science* (February 23) 315:1122–1126.

Waters, M. R., et al. 2011 Pre-Clovis Mastodon Hunting 13,800 Years Ago at the Manis Site, Washington. *Science* 334(6054):351–353. doi:10.1126/science.1207663.

Waterston, A., and M. D. Vesperi, eds. 2009. *Anthropology off the Shelf: Anthropologists on Writing.* Malden, MA: Blackwell.

Watters, E. 2010. The Americanization of Mental Illness. *New York Times*, January 8. http://www.nytimes.com/2010/01/10/magazine/10psyche-t.html?pagewanted=all.

Watzman, H. 2006. The Echoes of Ancient Humans. *Chronicle of Higher Education,* January 27. http://chronicle.com/weekly/v52/i21/21a01601.htm.

Weber, M. 1958 (orig. 1904). *The Protestant Ethic and the Spirit of Capitalism.* New York: Scribner.

_____. 1968 (orig. 1922). *Economy and Society.* E. Fischoff et al. (trans.). New York: Bedminster Press.

*Webster's New World Encyclopedia* 1993. College Edition. Englewood Cliffs, NJ: Prentice Hall.

Weiner, M. 2009. *Japan's Minorities: The Illusion of Homogeneity,* 2nd ed. New York: Routledge.

Weiss, H. 2005. *Collapse.* New York: Routledge.

Wendorf, F., and R. Schild 2000. Late Neolithic Megalithic Structures at Nabta Playa (Sahara), Southwestern Egypt. http://www.comp-archaeology.org/WendorfSAA98.html.

Wenke, R. J., and D. I. Olszewski 2007. *Patterns in Prehistory: Mankind's First Three Million Years,* 5th ed. New York: Oxford University Press.

Weston, K. 1991. *Families We Choose: Lesbians, Gays, Kinship.* New York: Columbia University Press.

White, L. A. 1959. *The Evolution of Culture: The Development of Civilization to the Fall of Rome.* New York: McGraw-Hill.

_____. 2009. *Modern Capitalist Culture,* abridged ed. Walnut Creek, CA: Left Coast Press.

White, N. J. 2014. *Decolonisation: The British Experience since 1945,* 2nd ed. New York: Routledge, Taylor and Francis.

Whorf, B. L. 1956. A Linguistic Consideration of Thinking in Primitive Communities. In *Language, Thought, and Reality: Selected Writings of Benjamin Lee Whorf,* J. B. Carroll, ed., pp. 65–86. Cambridge, MA: MIT Press.

Whyte, M. F. 1978. Cross-Cultural Codes Dealing with the Relative Status of Women. *Ethnology* 12(2):203–225.

Wiley, A. S., and J. S. Allen 2012. *Medical Anthropology: A Biocultural Approach,* 2nd ed. New York: Oxford University Press.

Wilford, J. N. 2002. When Humans Became Human. *New York Times,* February 26, late ed.—final, sec. F, P. 1, col. 1. http://www.nytimes.com.

_____. 2006. Improved Science Puts Modern Humans in Europe Earlier. *New York Times,* February 23.

_____. 2007a. Fossils in Kenya Challenge Linear Evolution, *New York Times,* August 9, p. A6.

_____. 2007b. Fossils Reveal Clues on Human Ancestors. *New York Times,* September 20. www.nytimes.com.

_____. 2008. Genetic Study Bolsters Columbus Link to Syphilis. *New York Times,* January 15.

_____. 2009a. Feet Offer Clue about Tiny Hominid. *New York Times,* May 9. http://www.nytimes.com/2009/05/07/science/07hobbit.html?_r=1&scp=1&sq=feet%20offer%20clues%20about%20tiny%20hominid&st=cse.

_____. 2009b. Fossil Skeleton from Africa Predates Lucy. *New York Times,* October 2, pp. Al, A6.

_____. 2010. In Syria, a Prologue for Cities. *New York Times,* April 6. http://www.nytimes.com/2010/04/06/science/06archeo.html?_r=0&pagewanted=print.

_____. 2012a. Some Prehumans Feasted on Bark Instead of Grasses. *New York Times,* June 27. http://www.nytimes.com/2012/06/28/science/australopithecus-sediba-preferred-forest-foods-fossil-teeth-suggest.html?_r=0.

_____. 2012b. Artifacts Revive Debate on Transformation of Human Behavior. *New York Times,* July 30. http://www.nytimes.com/2012/07/31/science/cave-findings-revive-debate-on-human-behavior.html?_r=0.

Wilford, J. N. 2011a. Fossil Teeth Put Humans in Europe Earlier Than Thought. *New York Times,* November 3, p. A4.

_____. 2011b. In African Cave, Signs of an Ancient Paint Factory. *New York Times,* October 13, p. A14.

_____. 2013. Palm-Size Fossil Resets Primates' Clock, Scientists Say. *New York Times,* June 5. http://www.nytimes.com/2013/06/06/science/palm-size-fossil-resets-primates-clock-scientists-say.html?pagewanted=all&_r=0.

Wilk, R. R., and L. Cliggett 2007. *Economies and Cultures: Foundations of Economic Anthropology,* 2nd ed. Boulder, CO: Westview Press.

Williams, L. M., and D. Finkelhor 1995. Paternal Caregiving and Incest: Test of a Biosocial Model. *American Journal of Orthopsychiatry* 65(1):101–113.

Willie, C. V. 2003. *A New Look at Black Families.* Walnut Creek, CA: AltaMira.

Wilmsen, E. N. 1989. *Land Filled with Flies: A Political Economy of the Kalahari.* Chicago: University of Chicago Press.

Wilson, D. S. 2002. *Darwin's Cathedral: Evolution, Religion, and the Nature of Society.* Chicago: University of Chicago Press.

Wilson, M. L., and R. W. Wrangham 2003. Intergroup Relations in Chimpanzees. *Annual Review of Anthropology* 32:363–392.

Wilson, R., ed. 1996. *Human Rights: Culture and Context: Anthropological Perspectives.* Chicago: Pluto Press.

Winter, R. 2001. Religions of the World: Number of Adherents; Names of Houses of Worship; Names of Leaders; Rates of Growth. http://www.religioustolerance.org/worldrel.htm.

Winzeler, R. L. 2012 *Anthropology and Religion,* 2nd ed. Lanham, MD: Rowman & Littlefield.

Witt, J. 2011. *Soc,* 2nd ed. Boston: McGraw-Hill.

Wittfogel, K. A. 1957. *Oriental Despotism: A Comparative Study of Total Power.* New Haven, CT: Yale University Press.

Wolcott, H. F. 2008. *Ethnography: A Way of Seeing,* 2nd ed. Lanham, MD: AltaMira.

_____. 2010. *Ethnography Lessons: A Primer.* Walnut Creek, CA: Left Coast Press.

Wolf, E. R. 1966. *Peasants.* Englewood Cliffs, NJ: Prentice Hall.

_____. 1982. *Europe and the People without History.* Berkeley: University of California Press.

Wolf, E. R., with S. Silverman 2001. *Pathways of Power: Building an Anthropology of the Modern World.* Berkeley: University of California Press.

Wolf, M. 1992. *A Thrice-told Tale: Feminism, Postmodernism, and Ethnographic Responsibility.* Stanford, CA: Stanford University Press.

Wolpoff, M., B. Senut, M. Pickford, and J. Hawks 2002. Sahelanthropus or "Sahelpithecus"? *Nature* 419:581–582.

Wolpoff, M. H. 1980. *Paleoanthropology.* New York: McGraw-Hill.

_____. 1999. *Paleoanthropology,* 2nd ed. New York: McGraw-Hill.

Womack, M. 2010. *The Anthropology of Health and Healing.* Lanham, MD: AltaMira.

Wood, B. 2011. *Human Evolution.* New York: Sterling Books.

_____. ed. 2011. *Wiley-Blackwell Encyclopedia of Human Evolution.* Hoboken, NJ: Wiley-Blackwell.

World Health Organization 2014. Global Health Observatory Data. http://www.who.int/gho/urban_health/situation_trends/urban_population_growth_text/en/

Worsley, P. 1985 (orig. 1959). Cargo Cults. In *Readings in Anthropology* 85/86. Guilford, CT: Dushkin.

Wrangham, R., W. McGrew, F. de Waal, and P. Heltne, eds. 1994. *Chimpanzee Cultures.* Cambridge, MA: Harvard University Press.

Wright, H. T. 1977. Recent Research on the Origin of the State. *Annual Review of Anthropology* 6:379–397.

———. 1994. Prestate Political Formations. In *Chiefdoms and Early States in the Near East: The Organizational Dynamics of Complexity,* G. Stein and M. S. Rothman, eds., *Monographs in World Archaeology* 18:67–84. Madison, WI: Prehistory Press.

Yang, X., et al. 2012. Early Millet Use in Northern China. *Proceedings of the National Academy of Sciences* 109(10): 3726–3730.

York, A. 2009. Alaskan Village Stands on Leading Edge of Climate Change. *Mother Nature Network,* August 19. http://news21.jomc.unc.edu/index.php/stories/alaska.html.

Young, A. 2000. *Women Who Become Men: Albanian Sworn Virgins.* New York: Berg.

Yurchak, A. 2005. *Everything Was Forever until It Was No More: The Last Soviet Generation.* Princeton, NJ: Princeton University Press.

Zaborenko, D. 2012. In U.S., 2012 So Far Is Hottest Year on Record. *Yahoo News.* http://news.yahoo.com/u-2012-far-hottest-record-192659729.html.

Zeder, M. A. 2008. Domestication and Early Agriculture in the Mediterranean Basin: Origins, Diffusion, and Impact. *Proceedings of the National Academy of Science* 105(33):11597–11604, August 12. http://www.pnas.org/content/early/2008/08/11/0801317105.

Zimmer, C. 2010 Siberian Fossils Were Neanderthals' Eastern Cousins, DNA Reveals. *New York Times,* December 22. http://www.nytimes.com/2010/12/23/science/23ancestor.html.

Zimmer-Tamakoshi, L. 1997. The Last Big Man: Development and Men's Discontents in the Papua New Guinea Highlands. *Oceania* 68(2):107–122.

Zimring, C. A., ed. 2012. *Encyclopedia of Consumption and Waste: The Social Science of Garbage.* Thousand Oaks, CA: Sage.

Zukin, S., P. Kasinitz, and X. Chen, eds. 2015. *Global Cities, Local Streets: Everyday Diversity from New York to Shanghai.* New York: Routledge.

# Index

Note: Tables, figures, and illustrations are indicated by t, f, and i.